A SOCIAL AND RELIGIOUS HISTORY OF THE JEWS

High Middle Ages, 500–1200: Volumes III–VIII

VOLUME VII

HEBREW LANGUAGE AND LETTERS

A SOCIAL AND RELIGIOUS HISTORY OF THE JEWS

By SALO WITTMAYER BARON

Second Edition, Revised and Enlarged

High Middle Ages, 500–1200: Volumes III–VIII

VOLUME VII

HEBREW LANGUAGE AND LETTERS

COLUMBIA UNIVERSITY PRESS 1958

New York

LIBRARY OF CONGRESS CATALOG CARD NUMBER: 52-404

PUBLISHED IN GREAT BRITAIN, CANADA, INDIA, AND PAKISTAN
BY THE OXFORD UNIVERSITY PRESS
LONDON, TORONTO, BOMBAY, AND KARACHI

MANUFACTURED IN THE UNITED STATES OF AMERICA

CONTENTS

A SOCIAL AND RELIGIOUS HISTORY OF THE JEWS

Ancient Times

High Middle Ages

HEBREW LANGUAGE AND LETTERS

XXX

LINGUISTIC RENASCENCE

Hand in hand with the deepened and diversified interest in the Bible went the newly awakened scientific curiosity about the Hebrew language, its vocabulary and forms, and the rules governing its use in different contexts. This nexus was perfectly obvious to contemporaries. The distinguished Karaite grammarian and exegete, Abu'l Faraj Harun, voiced a commonplace sentiment among Jewish intellectuals when he wrote: "The need to gain an acquaintance with the Hebrew language brings with it the obligation of knowing the words of the Lawgiver in their true interpretation. No one can arrive at this whilst being ignorant of the language because he is liable to err and interpret falsely." In other words, knowledge of the Bible presupposed a good knowledge of the language and vice versa.[1]

Perhaps in no period of human history did preoccupation with the correctness and purity of the spoken and written language become such a deep concern of educated classes as during the Islamic Renaissance. The intelligentsia of the Graeco-Roman world had evinced deep interest in the elegance of the Greek or Latin style in letters or oratorical exhibitions. The talmudic sages, too, tirelessly reiterated that, even in ordinary speech, one must beware of profanities and employ only "clean language." They also insisted upon clarity and precision in speech and tried to support it wherever needed by mnemotechnic aids concerning literary usage, for they considered such clarity in formulation relevant to the proper grasp and preservation of substantive knowledge. "The inhabitants of Judaea," Rab declared, "who had been careful about their language, succeeded in preserving their Torah, while the population of Galilee, having become negligent in speech, did not preserve its Torah" ('Erubin 53a).

Not until the Muslim era, however, did fine points in grammar become the subject of passionate debate not only among specialists, but also among all other educated persons. From Ibn Janaḥ we learn that Spanish Jews, evidently following a widespread fashion among their Arab neighbors, heatedly debated philological minutiae in their social gatherings. Mental gymnastics on grammatical problems became such a popular pastime that poets like Abraham ibn Ezra composed many linguistic riddles, the solution of which taxed the ingenuity of generations of playful students. In all Arabic-speaking countries elegant speech was the hallmark of a gentleman. According to Baihaqi, the Meccans, who after a devastating flood in 823 received from the Caliph relief funds accompanied by a letter, evinced greater interest in the elegant diction of that letter than in the money. Accustomed as they were to discount such figures of speech, Baihaqi's readers believed that even a stricken population might be interested in stylistic niceties. Because of its intimate connection with sectarian interpretation of the respective Scriptures, grammar as such often became a matter of religious importance, and Hadassi was not alone in enjoining his readers to study the Hebrew language as a primary religious duty; in fact, as one of the ten cardinal duties of a Jew.[2]

DANGERS OF BILINGUALISM

In the case of Jews, however, their sacred language had to compete with their ordinary spoken dialects, especially Aramaic, Arabic, or both. True, their Muslim and Christian neighbors, too, were confronted by a sort of bilingualism of their own. The language of the Qur'an was often so remote from the language of the street that it required considerable intellectual effort to learn it. "Before the end of the first century of the Hejirah," observes Alfred Guillaume, "an Umayyad caliph was unable to convey his meaning to the pure-blooded Arabs of the desert." A similar gap existed between the "translation Greek" of the Septuagint and parts of the New Testament, or the canonical Syriac of the Peshiṭṭa and the local dialects. Yet Hebrew was not only more remote from these majority dialects, but its study required basically different linguistic approaches. To an Arab or Syriac student of language, the grammar and lexicography of the classical forms of their respective Scriptures completely overshadowed those of the spoken dialects, which were studied mainly for comparative purposes. In ninth-century Baghdad "people were surprised to find a man effortlessly speaking correct grammatical Arabic with case terminations." A Jewish philologist of necessity had to concern himself with the linguistic laws and vocabularies of both biblical and Mishnaic-rabbinic Hebrew, while never forgetting the grammatical rules of his daily Arabic speech and writing. A similar battle had also been fought by students of the Persian language. But once the victory had been won and, except for the adoption of the Arabic alphabet, Persian had reasserted its complete independence, Persian philology could freely develop along its own lines without constant regard to newer trends in Arabic linguistic studies. Jews, living as a permanent Arabic-speaking minority and using for literary purposes alone a language long in disuse as a spoken tongue, could never escape the impact of the Arabic world language and the superlative achievements of its grammarians and lexicographers.[3]

In the Jewish communities, moreover, this often became a three-cornered struggle. Especially in countries where Jews had for centuries spoken an Aramaic dialect and had created in it literary monuments of the grandiose sweep of Talmud, Targum, and Midrash, resistance against the conquerors' linguistic encroachments often was vigorous and protracted. In Babylonia, as we recall, Aramaic maintained its hold on both the masses and the intelligentsia down to the tenth century. During the first, almost inarticulate, two and a half centuries after the rise of Islam Jewish scholars were actually confronted with the serious complications of a genuine trilingualism.

In the long run, however, Aramaic was bound to lose and be replaced by Arabic, while Hebrew gained an ascendancy long unprecedented in Jewish life. Aramaic evidently went into total disuse most speedily in regions where it had never held uncontested sway over the Jewish community. Despite their age-old reverence for Onkelos, the Jews of Fez gradually abandoned its public recitation in the synagogue. Probably it was more than a mere claim that, as Yehudah ibn Quraish reports, they "did not need this translation," but in fact that translation had become quite meaningless to them, since they understood the Hebrew original much better than the Targum. If the old battle cry of Judah the Patriarch and the Babylonian R. Joseph for the use of either Greek or Persian, in lieu of Aramaic, as the Jewish majority's second language was not now replaced by the slogan of "either Hebrew or Arabic," this was doubtless owing as much to the rapid disintegration of Aramaic as to the Rabbanites' deep reverence for the Aramaic literary monuments of their classical tradition. Karaites, on their part, did not wish to invoke the watchwords of talmudic sages, although they meant the same thing when they accused their opponents of using "the language of Assyrians and Arameans, which is the shameful language of the men of the dispersion [Babylonia]. For its sake the Hebrews have neglected their own tongue and in it they laid down the fruits of their wisdom and thought in a jargon, which caused them to misunderstand Scripture, to weaken in its interpretation, and to abandon its ordinary meaning." [4]

Ultimately, Arabic won over the very leaders of the Babylonian academies, who, from Saadiah on, began using it even within the sacrosanct precincts of the Halakhah. Like the Karaite leaders, they yielded to the practical need of making themselves understood by the masses of the population which no longer spoke Aramaic and whose Hebrew equipment was likewise deficient. An increasing number of inquiries to the academies, even if written by experts in rabbinic law in various lands, were couched in Arabic terms, and the replies had to be given in the same language. Authors of works in the newer disciplines of Jewish and general learning found themselves under still greater pressure to use the ever more refined Arabic medium.

In his well-known apologia for the use of Arabic by the Eastern scholars, addressed to the communities in Christian lands, Yehudah ibn Tibbon explained that this had happened

> because all the people understood that language. Moreover, this is a rich and diversified language meeting the various requirements of speakers and authors. Its phraseology is precise, lucid, and presents the substance of each subject matter far more penetratingly than is possible in Hebrew. For all we possess of the Hebrew language is what we find in the Bible, which is not adequate for the needs of every speaking person. They [the Eastern scholars] also intended to benefit through their works the uneducated populace unfamiliar with the holy language.

Of course, these difficulties were not insuperable. Ibn Tibbon himself, and other members of his family, showed that where there was a will, or rather the inescapable need of the Jewish communities in Christian lands unfamiliar with Arabic, a way was found to translate these accumulated treasures of Arabic-speaking Jewry into Hebrew. For similar reasons Tobiah ben Moses, "the Translator" of Constantinople, had early in the eleventh century pioneered with his translation into Hebrew of Arabic works written by Palestinian Karaites for the benefit of his Byzantine coreligionists. If his, as well as the Tibbonide, Hebrew was marred by stylistic harshness and numerous conscious Arabicisms (some passages can actually be understood only by reference to the Arabic originals), this was entirely owing to the usual shortcomings of pioneers and the stubborn concentration of these men on precision and exactitude, rather than stylistic elegance. For this purpose the Tibbonide family developed a special Hebrew style, which might properly be called "translation Hebrew," reminiscent of the "translation Greek" cultivated, for analogous reasons, by the ancient authors of the Septuagint and the New Testament. More gifted littérateurs, such as Moses ibn Chiquitilla, Ibn Ezra, or Yehudah al-Ḥarizi, simultaneously working on the same materials, produced far more Hebraic and readable, if less exactingly accurate, versions.[5]

Clearly, had the original authors themselves made an effort from the outset to lend their philosophical and scientific ideas a Hebrew garb, they would undoubtedly have been far more successful, for they would not have had to operate within the straitjacket of someone else's thoughts. One need but compare Menaḥem ibn Saruq's pioneering *Maḥberet* (Dictionary) with Yehudah ibn Tibbon's translation of a similar work by Ibn Janaḥ to realize the advantages of such freedom. Similarly, as David H. Baneth has shown, Maimonides, reproducing in Hebrew some of his own writings, could freely adjust his style to the exigencies of a linguistic as well as a juristic or theological nature. However, lacking the compulsion of the Western unfamiliarity with Arabic, the Eastern authors preferred to use the already well-fashioned instrument of Arabic to express their ideas even within the traditional realms of law and biblical research.[6]

As a matter of fact the greatest of the Arabic-writing Jewish philosophers, Ibn Gabirol, Halevi, Maimonides, even Saadiah, had a much better command of the Hebrew than of the Arabic tongue. In their very Arabic writings they addressed themselves almost exclusively to the Jewish intelligentsia. That is why, as a rule, they wrote their Arabic books in the Hebrew alphabet and quoted all passages from Bible or Talmud in their originals, without adding an Arabic translation. The extant autograph fragments of Maimonides' writings are in this respect representative of the entire Arabic Jewish philosophic literature. At the same time, Samau'al ibn Yaḥya explained the failure of the Jewish masses to appreciate the beauty of the Qur'an by their deficient knowledge of Arabic. Ibn Janaḥ, too, scolded his Spanish-Jewish compatriots for their insufficient attention to the subtleties of the Arabic language. Indeed, Judeo-Arabic gradually developed many linguistic peculiarities which, coupled with obvious Hebraisms, must have been offensive to the ears of Arab purists. Some of these Hebraisms, as we remember from Saadiah's and Jephet's Bible translations, were not even unconscious, but represented a studied effort to render biblical phrases through like-sounding Arabic words, however far-fetched.[7]

Disregarding such deliberate affectations, the language of these medieval Jewish authors evidently reflected some of the divergent speech habits in the Jewish communities, which can only in part be accounted for by similar deviations in the local dialects of their Arab neighbors. After a careful examination of the Arabic employed by Maimonides, perhaps the best Arabic stylist among the medieval Jewish philosophers, Israel Friedlaender found that the Fusṭaṭ philosopher

> interchanges cases and modes, pays little heed to the rather complicated rules governing numbers, frequently removes sentences from the rigid control of the Arabic syntax, and uses a great many anacolutha. He makes use of a mass of new words, and still more frequently of old words in new meanings, rejected by the "classical" language.

True, irregularities of this kind can also be found among such contemporary Arab writers as the physician Ibn abi Uṣaibi'a, who hewed more closely to the popular, living language of his environment than to the artificially rigid "classical" patterns. However, there still remained a considerable residuum of Jewish peculiarities which can be explained only by some specific usages in the Jewish communities. These growing deviations, including a considerable number of Hebraisms, adumbrated the subsequent evolution of modern Judeo-Arabic dialects. That they never led to the development of an independent language similar to Yiddish or Ladino is fully understandable in the light of both the greater intimacy of social intercourse between Jews and Arabs and the absence of large and enduring settlements of Arabic-speaking Jews outside the Arab world. But, already in the Middle Ages, certain minor peculiarities in pronunciation and style and the use of loan words from Hebrew and talmudic Aramaic must have made the speech of the Jew on the street readily distinguishable from the respective dialects of his Muslim neighbors. Conversely, the medieval Hebrew language received many stimuli from Arabic as well as from other languages in vocabulary, syntax, and especially in pronunciation.[8]

It was indeed a high price that the Jewish people had to pay for its insistent bilingualism, occasionally even trilingualism (Hebrew and Arabic combined with Aramaic, Greek, Latin, or some other vernacular). Diaspora Jewry had long employed at least one language other than Hebrew in its intellectual as well as daily life, but not until the Arab period did the greatest creative minds of Jewry alternately use two media in their writings. In ancient times, Philo wrote only in Greek, a talmudic sage only in Hebrew or in the Talmud's peculiar blend of Aramaic and Hebrew. Even Josephus wrote Greek (with the aid of assistants) only after he had ceased writing Aramaic. Now, however, such great masters of Hebrew poetry as Ibn Gabirol or Halevi unhesitatingly turned to Arabic in their philosophic works. Moses ibn Ezra wrote his immortal lyrics in Hebrew, but used Arabic for instructing others in the art of writing Hebrew poetry.

Arabs, on their part, failed to recognize how much their linguistic studies had been promoted, especially in the formative years, by Greek, Hebrew, and Syriac prototypes. Far from believing, as Goethe was to express it centuries later, that one best learns the intricacies of one's native language by learning another, Arab philologists refrained, as a rule, from the study of foreign languages. There always were far fewer Muslim than Christian

Hebraists. More, backed by powerful public prejudices, Arab purists suspected every bilingual person, and still more every bilingual group, of unavoidable offenses against the purity and elegance of their Arabic speech. Al-Jaḥiẓ's comment on the feat of an eighth-century Iraqi orator is typical of the prevailing opinion. Musa al-Uswari, we are told, used to address an Arab crowd seated to his right and a mass of Persians placed at his left by impeccably using both languages. "This is one of the world's marvels," Al-Jaḥiẓ added, "for when the two languages meet on a single tongue, one usually hurts the other." The Arab public readily swallowed such assertions, since even without the knowledge of foreign languages many a Muslim writer suffered from a serious inferiority complex concerning his own ability to express himself in faultless Arabic—a complex steadily nurtured by the unceasing propaganda about the unparalleled mysteries of the Arabic language. It was indeed fortunate for Jewish literature that such a Jewish author as Baḥya ibn Paquda did not desist from composing his ethical treatise merely because he did "not possess an elegant style in Arabic." However, Arabic too had absorbed many ingredients of Hebrew and Aramaic, the very Qur'an being replete with loanwords from both these languages. Such an impact was even more constantly felt in Christian lands where "Hebrewisms" characteristic of all translations of the Old Testament deeply influenced the native languages, many of them in their formative stages. The continued preoccupation of many Christian Bible students with the Hebrew text injected further elements into these perennial, if often imperceptible, manifestations of Judeo-Gentile linguistic reciprocity.[9]

Bi- and trilingualism unavoidably had many serious effects on the Jews. On the one hand, sooner or later it necessarily led to some sort of "levantinization" of Jewish speech habits. Many Jews, and some Christians, doubtless developed in time certain traits of multilingual groups, speaking and writing in several languages sloppily, if not altogether incorrectly. In their early stages the Judeo-Arabic dialects, as spoken by the masses, must also have revealed certain typical characteristics of "jargons," until some of them became refined through literary usage into more disciplined "dialects."

On the other hand, Jews were induced to pioneer along the lines of comparative linguistics. The same factors which induced a Muslim like Ibn Ḥazm to become a pathfinder in the study of comparative religion, operated to make the North African Jew, Yehudah ibn Quraish, at least half a century before Ibn Ḥazm, a pioneer in the comparative study of languages. Islam, which had admittedly absorbed important ingredients from Judaism, Christianity, and Zoroastrianism, and whose entire career was permeated with sectarian strife, offered a clear challenge to inquiring minds to compare these faiths to one another and to derive certain generalizations, which ultimately proved valuable for the understanding of religion as such. Jews, who staunchly resisted the incursion of outside religious ideas and rituals (without necessarily succeeding in preventing gradual seepage), evinced only mild interest in other faiths. Many of them would have considered a calm comparison without any apologetic bias an outright blasphemy. At the same time, linguistic parallels of a sort necessarily evolved within their own Hebrew language in its development from biblical antiquity to their own days. Even before they learned the refined philological approaches of their Arab neighbors, they could not help noticing the differences as well as the similarities between the language of the Mishnah and that of Scripture, and they were prepared to elucidate one by the other.

From here it was but a step to the utilization of linguistic materials not only from other Semitic languages, primarily Aramaic and Arabic, but also from the unrelated Berber, Persian, and other Indo-European dialects. It probably was more than mere coincidence that Abu 'Ubaida Ma'mar ibn al-Muthanna (728–825), one of the founders of the great Arab philological school of Baṣra and the author of some two hundred philological treatises, allegedly was the grandson of a Persian Jew. He delighted in antagonizing Arab fellow students by pointing out the foreign origins of many words, institutions, and families cherished by proud Arab traditionalists. Harun ibn Musa al-Asdi (d. *ca.* 786), who was the first to compile a list of difficult words and passages in the Qur'an, seems to have been born a Jew. Ultimately, a sensitive student of Hebrew, Ibn Quraish, living in Tahort, Algeria, during the middle of the tenth century, evinced considerable interest in the dialects spoken by the Berber tribes in the vicinity and the linguistic residua of North Africa's Graeco-Roman heritage. He put them all to excellent use in explaining Hebrew words which, in his opinion, could not be adequately interpreted even with the aid of Aramaic and Arabic. He explained, for example, that the word *mesurah* (measure; Lev. 19:35) was identical with the Latin term, *mesura* (mensura), and found the equivalent of the Greek word, *kalós* in the Hebrew *le-qalles* (enhance; Ez. 16:31). An eleventh-century Cairo scholar (perhaps the liturgical poet Sahlal ben Abraham), finally, compiled a curious list of divine designations in fourteen languages. He was far surpassed by Sallam, the interpreter, who, as we recall, was allegedly able to speak in thirty languages.[10]

LEXICOGRAPHY

Comparative linguistics could the better be used for the elucidation of vocabulary, rather than of grammar or phonetics, as the meaning of words and phrases was generally the overriding concern of scholars and public alike. A proper understanding of the biblical, and to a lesser extent of the talmudic, terminology in all its shades of meaning became an indispensable prerequisite for both the new scholarly exegesis and the creative use of the resurrected Hebrew language in poetry and prose. At the same time the abundance of biblical homonyms and synonyms and the infinite variety of meanings which could be produced in words of the same roots by a slight change in vocalization alone challenged the ingenuity of students.

Concern for the significance, even spelling, of words was evident already among talmudic sages. On one occasion Rab suggested that in order to ascertain the correct spelling of two words in the Mishnah one should inquire among the inhabitants of Judaea, "who are punctilious in the use of language." On another occasion he (according to a variant reading it was Raba) speculated on the abridged form *ḥab* (guilty), instead of the more usual *ḥayyab,* in the Mishnah and concluded that the author of this phrase must have been a Jerusalemite. At times, of course, interpretation of a single word could have important legal implications. In a famous controversy over the meaning of the mishnaic term *mab'eh* (destroyer of crops) Rab and Samuel invoked two different biblical verses in support of their contentions that the Mishnah had in mind destruction caused by man or by the tooth of an animal. While the ensuing legal argumentation completely drifted away from the linguistic issue, these two founders of Babylonian Jewish learning evidently had two divergent grammatical theories in mind when they interpreted these biblical statements. Ibn Janaḥ was not too far off the mark when he supplied a good philological rationale for this controversy, adding in a self-congratulatory vein, "And I do not know of any student of the Talmud in this generation who realized the hidden meaning of these proofs which we have detected." Even more vital was such minute differentiation for the Masorites, whose decision in matters of spelling, punctuation, and statistical classification largely depended on the sense they attributed to each of two or three ostensibly similar words.[11]

The first, however, to compile a regular dictionary of terms was Ṣemaḥ bar Palṭoi Gaon (872–90). Curiously, his lexicon was entirely devoted to talmudic vocabulary, and it evidently pursued the practical pedagogic aim of facilitating the study of the Talmud. This had indeed become a necessity with the growing diffusion of talmudic studies outside the restricted halls of the academies. Certainly those countless private scholars who were now preparing at home for the semiannual *kallah* gatherings required some such written aids in the complex vocabulary of a language whose use was rapidly declining even in the cities of Babylonia. Such need was more strongly felt in the western Mediterranean communities, where Aramaic had never been a spoken language. Perhaps the gaon was prompted to compile his lexicon by an inquiry from Spain. According to the aforementioned report by Hezekiah ben Samuel of 953, his great-grandfather Ṣemaḥ Gaon had been asked by Spanish scholars for explanations of "difficult passages in the whole Talmud, so many that several donkeys could not carry that load." Since a donkey's load, a measure frequently used for manuscripts in contemporary Arabic letters, represented a considerable number of manuscript leaves, the grandson may indeed have alluded here to an extensive glossary of talmudic terms prepared by Ṣemaḥ Gaon.

One wonders, however, whether this work was not identical with those explanatory comments on the whole Talmud (*Pitron*) which, as we recall, the Spaniards had solicited from Ṣemaḥ's father, Palṭoi. The latter may have entrusted his son with the composition of the glossary, while ordering some scribe or scribes to copy the Talmud text itself for the benefit of his Spanish correspondents. If this be true, Ṣemaḥ's *'Arukh* probably followed the pattern of the early geonic commentaries, mainly devoted to the successive explanation of difficult terms, rather than that of regular alphabetic dictionaries, which came into vogue a century or two later. Such an intention to facilitate the reading of the accompanying text of the Talmud which, together with the glossary, certainly covered several donkeys' loads, may also explain the noteworthy inclusion in Ṣemaḥ's work of names of places and persons mentioned in the Talmud. For most readers these naturally required as much explanation as did some difficult or unusual terms. Moreover, such data may even occasionally have had a bearing on the *halakhah,* especially if they shed light on the chronology of a particular talmudic tractate. Was not even Yaqut's famous geographical dictionary written mainly "to enable the traditionalists to trace each transmitter of traditions to his home"? Unfortunately, Ṣemaḥ's dictionary, still known in the sixteenth century, has since been totally lost.[12]

Saadiah was somewhat more fortunate. At the age of twenty he made literary history by arranging a "Small Collection" (*Egron*) of Hebrew words in two alphabetic orders. One, giving the beginnings of words, was intended to facilitate the quest by poets of an appropriate vocabulary for acrostics, while the second listed words in the alphabetic sequence of their endings and was to serve as a regular rhyming dictionary. The explanations, always concise, often consisted only of references to pertinent passages in the Bible. All this was to promote the use of the Hebrew language, "which our God has chosen from the beginning and in which sing the angels of His holiness." In his Hebrew introduction, from which these words are taken, Saadiah also referred to the widely held chronology of the *Seder 'olam rabbah* that during the first 1,996 years after the creation of the world all mankind spoke Hebrew exclusively. Only since the Tower of Babel did men speak a variety of languages, and even the Hebrews themselves from the days of Nehemiah, some three years before the Seleucid era, began neglecting their holy tongue. In the dispersion, finally, the Jews learned the languages of their environment. To help stem this forgetfulness our youthful author prepared his dictionary, because "it is fitting for us and the whole people of God to study, comprehend and investigate it constantly, for us, our children, wives, and slaves, so that it not leave our lips. For by it we shall understand the laws of the Torah of our Creator, which are the core of our existence, our light and sanctuary from the beginning and unto eternity." [13]

Some years later, evidently after settling in Baghdad, Saadiah came under the spell of the then raging controversies between the Baṣran and the Kufan schools of Arabic philology, the headquarters of which had previously been removed to the imperial capital. He therefore reissued his lexicon in revised form by adding to it not only Arabic translations of the Hebrew terms, but also a new third section dealing specifically with the "burdens of poetry," that is with grammatical rules (including the then much-debated erratic performance of weak consonants), the use of metaphors, and other aids to poets. He also prefaced it by a less picturesque but more informative Arabic introduction. Quite appropriately he renamed this edition the "Book of Principles of Poetry," or more concisely, the "Book of Poetics." Later in life the gaon added, primarily for exegetical purposes, his brief lexicographical treatise on the *hapax legomena* of the Bible. He also compiled a "Dictionary of the Mishnah," probably in connection with his aforementioned *Commentary* on that basic code of rabbinic Judaism. In addition, he unhesitatingly enriched the Hebrew language by many new words and phrases, used to particularly good advantage in his poetic works.[14]

Like almost everything else written by this militant champion of Jewish learning, Saadiah's lexicographic contributions evoked a considerable debate. Apparently soon after the gaon's death, Mubashshir ha-Levi wrote his comprehensive critique of Saadiah's scholarly works, arguing against both interpretations of certain terms and some of the underlying grammatical rules. Without directly referring to the *Egron* or the gaon's other studies of the biblical vocabulary, Mubashshir objected to some identifications of biblical names which had already been featured in Saadiah's early work. According to Ibn Ezra, author and critic disagreed, for example, as to the location of the biblical Tarshish. While in his dictionary as well as in his translation of Genesis (10:4) Saadiah identified it with Tarsus, Mubashshir preferred to see therein a reference to Tunis, doubtless because he knew that an inland city like Tarsus could not be reached by ship. He may also have felt that the distance to the southeast coast of Asia Minor would not have warranted a three-year journey, as seemed indicated in the biblical story of Solomon's expeditions (I Kings 10:22). Hence he looked for a like-sounding but more distant location. None of Mubashshir's known comments revealed a sectarian bias, however, and although he occasionally accepted a Karaite interpretation, he definitely was a Rabbanite scholar. On the other hand, "the grammarian Abu Ya'qub [Joseph] al-Bakhtawi," mentioned by Salmon ben Yeruḥim, probably was a Karaite contemporary of Saadiah.[15]

We know too little about a lexicographic work by Abu Sahl Dunash (Adonim) ibn Tamim of Kairuwan, briefly referred to in later writings, to judge the extent to which it marked an advance over Saadiah. He, who in his *Commentary on Yeṣirah* boasted that at the age of twenty he had assisted Isaac Israeli (some time before 913) in replying to some of Saadiah's scientific inquiries and in correcting the Fayyumite's errors, certainly would not have hesitated to assert his views against the gaon also in philological matters. From a citation by Abraham ibn Ezra it appears that he tried to draw a parallel between the diminutive form in Arabic and such biblical words as *abiyonah* (Eccles. 12:5). Instead of the translation "And the *desire* shall fail," offered by Rashi, he suggested that the word was a diminutive of *ebyon* (poor) and referred to the poor soul which shall fail. Ibn Ezra repudiated both the interpretation and the underlying assumption, and pointed out that if ancient Hebrew had used diminutive forms, we "would find in the Bible hundreds and thousands" of illustrations and not only the three mentioned by Ibn Tamim. The latter seems also to have made some contributions to Hebrew phonetics going beyond anything suggested by his masoretic predecessors.[16]

Ibn Tamim was not alone in trying to relate Hebrew to Arabic grammatical forms. Another North African contemporary, Yehudah ibn Quraish (born in Tahort near Tlemçen, Algeria, about 900) went even farther afield. Apparently writing in Saadiah's lifetime, he took no cognizance of the gaon's pioneering work. He expressed concern not so much for the forgetting of Hebrew as for the growing oblivion into which the Aramaic Targum was falling among the Jews of Fez, and he addressed to them a comprehensive Epistle (*Risala*) pointing out not only the Targum's traditionally high standing, but also its usefulness for the proper understanding of Hebrew.

I, therefore, resolved [he informed his correspondents] to write this book for intelligent readers that they may know that Aramaic and Arabic words, nay foreign and even Berber expressions, are intermixed with the holy tongue, but Arabic in particular. For Arabic contains many words which we find to be pure Hebrew. . . . The cause for this resemblance and (consequent) interchange is to be found in the propinquity of habitations and consanguinity of races. . . . For this reason we find resemblances between Hebrew and Arabic apart from the natural kinship of the consonants used for structural purposes in the beginning, the middle, and ends of words. Hebrew, Aramaic, and Arabic are by nature fashioned on one form. . . . We will begin by giving an account of Aramaic elements in the Torah, then of such rare words as can only be explained from the language of the Mishnah and the Talmud, and finally of Arabic words. We will also explain those kindred consonants which in Hebrew, Aramaic, and Arabic stand in the beginning, in the middle and at the end of words, but in no other language than in these three. All these we will put down in alphabetical order, so that every letter wanted can easily be found in its place.

It may well be said that with this dictionary Ibn Quraish laid the foundation for a comparative study of grammar and etymology. Apart from this specialized work, our author seems also to have compiled a comprehensive general dictionary of the Hebrew language, which, apparently used to good advantage by Menaḥem ben Saruq and Dunash ben Labraṭ, is now totally lost. He may also have written a treatise in which he assembled some strange rabbinic *aggadot* and warned the reader against accepting them as literal truths.[17]

Fortunately, another major dictionary of the period has come down to us and is available in a fine critical edition. David ben Abraham, native of Fez but apparently a long-time resident of Palestine, was a Karaite. Although very likely but a convert to Karaism after his arrival in the Holy Land, he did not display the intolerance of many neophytes, but readily learned not only from Ibn Quraish and Saadiah (whom he mentions twice by name without the usual Karaite maledictions), but also from the Talmud and Rabbanite prayer books. In fact, he sometimes ascribed to the Mishnah words documented only from posttalmudic times. Like both his Rabbanite predecessors, he was also interested in comparative linguistics, except that, unlike Ibn Quraish, he quoted no Berber nor Graeco-Latin terms, but introduced much comparative material from the Persian with which he could have become familiar in both Fez and Jerusalem. Like Saadiah, he tried to identify many proper names. For example, he believed that the biblical Ophir was identical with Sarandib or Ceylon, and that Mount Ararat was located in Kurdistan. On the other hand, he wavered as to whether he should equate Ashkenaz with Khazars or Franks. He explained his method in a comprehensive introduction in which he also warned any would-be Bible commentator not to be "rash in his interpretations, but master first the grammatical rules, inflections, the causes for change of accents, and the syntax of the language, as well as its correct use in speech. This would stimulate thinking, enhance knowledge, do away with indolence, awaken the soul, and inspire one to the search of knowledge." [18]

All these authors, except Saadiah in the first edition of his dictionary, unhesitatingly used Arabic as a medium for explaining Hebrew terms and communicating their own observations to the public. Saadiah himself frankly referred to a story current among the Muslims about one of their leaders (Al-Aswad ad-Du'ali), who, allegedly saddened by the prevailing incorrect speech of his compatriots, composed for their guidance a brief grammatical tractate. One must bear in mind, however, that in Egypt, where Saadiah first composed his dictionary, philological studies had not been greatly cultivated in the ninth century. But there undoubtedly were Egyptian students of works produced in the two great centers of Arabic philology at Baṣra and Kufa. We know of an Egyptian contemporary of Saadiah, Aḥmad ibn Wallad, who, after prolonged study under the leading philologists of Baghdad, returned to Cairo, where he died in 943, one year after Saadiah. Very likely there also appeared in Fayyum some such learned eastern immigrants as the Armenian Al-Qali, who, after an apprenticeship of several years in Baghdad, arrived in 942 in Cordova, where he served as a highly popular teacher of language for the subsequent two decades. Nor was this an entirely one-sided influence. Certainly, in the formative stage of Arabic philology, the Arabs had learned a great deal from their Jewish and Christian neighbors, or from such men of Jewish origin as the aforementioned 'Ubaida and Harun ibn Musa. Saadiah seems to have been influenced particularly by his older contemporaries, Ta'alab (815–904) and Ibn Duraid (837–933), representatives of the schools of Kufa and Baṣra, respectively.[19]

SPANISH PHILOLOGISTS

Curiously, while Iraq held undisputed sway over Arabic philology for half a millennium after the rise of Islam, the Babylonian center of Jewish culture contributed but slightly to the evolution of the new linguistic studies in Hebrew. Even Saadiah and Qirqisani were newcomers from other lands. Dunash ben Labraṭ was perhaps the only Hebrew philologian of note to have studied in Babylonia. But, as we shall see, he produced his works only after settling in Spain. This reticence was not owing exclusively to the great Babylonian concentration on rabbinic learning, since some of the later geonim themselves dabbled in philology. Moreover, Palestine, too, the old center of masoretic and exegetical studies, brought forth only one real first-rate Hebrew philologist: the Karaite Abu'l Faraj Harun. In contrast thereto Ibn Tamim, Ibn Quraish, and David al-Fasi were all natives of northwest Africa—a region, undistinguished then and long after in the annals of Arabic linguistic studies.

Evidently these western Jews felt more acutely the prolonged struggle between the dying local cultures and languages and the overpowering influence of the conquerors. In the East there was more of a linguistic exchange. The Arabs themselves more readily learned there from the Syriac, Hebrew, Greek, and Persian philological achievements, though formally insisting on the absolute purity of their own linguistic heritage. In the western lands they uncompromisingly imposed upon themselves and their ever growing following the gradually evolving eastern patterns of speech and writing as the only legitimate forms; all resistance was driven underground. Jews, as often before and after, saw themselves placed between these conflicting groups. They reacted with redoubled energy, as they were simultaneously confronted, in their own midst, with the rapid disintegration of Aramaic and the renascence of Hebrew. Most profoundly sensitized on this score, naturally enough, were the Jews of Spain, that western outpost of the Islamic world, where the local Romance dialects and traditions were never fully suppressed by the Arab steamroller.

Even here, however, Arabic philological doctrines had to be accepted by the very men who rejected the use of the Arabic language in works on Hebrew lexicography. Another member of that highly gifted generation after Saadiah, Menaḥem ben Jacob ben Saruq of Tortosa, made a point of writing his dictionary in Hebrew and of giving it a purely Hebrew title, *Maḥberet* (literally: Set, following Lev. 26:4). A Hebrew lexicon of this kind must have been felt as a godsend by the Jewish intellectuals north of the Pyrenees, to whom Arabic works necessarily remained sealed books. Put to excellent use in Rashi's commentaries, it exercised a lasting influence on the philological thinking of many generations of European Jews. A protégé of Ḥisdai ibn Shapruṭ in Cordova, Menaḥem was undoubtedly familiar with the linguistic discussions evoked by Al-Qali and other grammarians among the Arabs of that city. He refused, however, to quote expressly Arabic words in explanation of biblical terms, though he not infrequently cited Aramaic words for this purpose.

Menaḥem's main strength lay in his attempt to understand each term out of its context in Scripture. This procedure, which he indicated clearly in his introduction, led him to an unprecedented stress on both omission and duplication of ideas in the Bible. His teachings of such elliptic and pleonastic usages became very influential in the subsequent philological and exegetical literature. He also stressed the importance of biblical parallelisms and stated that "one half of the verse instructs us in the meaning of the other half." On the other hand, he rejected some of Ibn Quraish's artificial explanations by the simple permutation of letters, and carefully scrutinized (sometimes in direct opposition to Saadiah) the nature of some of the weaker consonants. That his linguistic explanations had considerable bearing also on religious doctrine is self-evident. Sometimes he went out of his way to emphasize religious piety. Discussing the difficult term *ṭoṭafot* (usually translated "frontlets"; Deut. 6:8), he connected it with the verb *taṭṭifu* (preach; Micah 2:6, etc.), and explained it to mean that Moses enjoined Israel "My people! Place my words before thee and my laws before thine eyes." Menaḥem thus clearly alluded to the commandment of phylacteries derived by the rabbis from this biblical phrase. He also took occasion to explain away biblical anthropomorphisms and, apparently for the first time in the lexicographic literature, to attempt a full classification of the biblical commandments. In explanation of the divine designation *Ehyeh asher ehyeh* (Exod. 3:14), he denied that these words had any connection whatsoever with the Hebrew verb "to be" and the ensuing translation of "I am that I am." The conclusion of that verse, "*Ehyeh* hath sent me unto you," clearly showed, in his opinion, that this "holy, honored and awe-inspiring name" is like "one of those words which have no explanation, or like a name that has no derivation from any other word." [20]

Rarely in the annals of mankind has the publication of a simple dictionary created such a furor as did Menaḥem's *Maḥberet.* Hailed immediately and again in later generations as a masterpiece of Hebrew learning, it soon elicited the sharp opposition of a recent arrival from eastern lands. Dunash (Adonim) ben Labraṭ (about 920–80), for a time resident in Fez, had spent several years studying under Saadiah and other masters of language in his native Baghdad, the great center of philological learning. After his arrival in Cordova, where he looked down upon the local philological "upstarts," he felt doubly free to employ against Menaḥem's dictionary his sharp satirical pen, as he was soon thereafter to use it also against his celebrated master's treatise on the unique words in the Bible. In his polemical fervor Dunash not only used intemperate language (he did the same in his strictures on Saadiah), but he also placed at the top of the one hundred and sixty incriminated passages two which, in his opinion, best demonstrated Menaḥem's heterodox leanings. That the latter had denied the doctrine of free will seemed evident to Dunash from Menaḥem's interpretation of Lamentations 3:33–36, while he suspected serious legal deviations in Menaḥem's consistent literal acceptance of the spelling *lo* as a negative in several verses (Exod. 21:8, Lev. 11:21, 25:30, and Job 9:33). Menaḥem's explanation of Leviticus 1:15, which he, perhaps unwittingly, had shared with 'Anan the Karaite, was, of course, a perfect target for Dunash's shafts. Prefacing his attack with Hebrew poems in the Arabic meter, which became his most significant innovation in the history of Hebrew poetic forms, Dunash so persuasively repudiated many of Menaḥem's interpretations and grammatical assumptions that even Menaḥem's patron, Ḥisdai, lost his faith in his Spanish-born protégé. Apart from illustrating the constantly changing moods of a typical grandee at an Arab court, this sudden disgrace of a meritorious student mirrored to a great extent the prevailing feeling of inferiority of the Spanish scholars toward such newcomers from the East.[21]

It was a sign of Spain's rapidly growing maturity, therefore, that Menaḥem found three devoted disciples who took up the cudgels in his defense as well as in that of their country. Accusing Dunash of sheer envy and ignorance and harshly rejecting the application of Arabic meters to Hebrew poetry, these disciples (Isaac ibn Chiquitilla, Ephraim ibn Kafron, and Yehudah ben David) nevertheless had to prove to their readers that they, too, were capable of writing such rhythmic poetry. Apart from this stunt, however, they contributed some solid observations on fifty-five controversial entries in Menaḥem's dictionary. They defended, for example, Menaḥem's interpretation of the verses in the book of Lamentations as relating to the uncertainty of man's fate, rather than his lack of freedom. There was a considerable dose of demagoguery in some of their asides, too. For example, they imputed to Dunash the thought that, having disposed of Menaḥem, he had routed all Spanish scholars. They also rejected Dunash's equation of the word *pigru* (stayed behind; I Sam. 30:10) with "were destroyed" in analogy to an Aramaic term in the Targum, because the underlying assumption of all such linguistic comparisons is "that all languages are equal without discrimination." They also appealed to both the Spanish and the Jewish chauvinism of their readers. In reply, Yehudi ben Sheshet, one of Dunash's pupils, upheld his master's position. His answers are characterized by even greater venom. He not only pointed out that Menaḥem himself had not had the courage to answer Dunash's strictures, but that the pupils had dared to take issue with only fifty of the two hundred objections raised by Dunash (the ratio was more correctly 55:160). Moreover, Yehudi tried to show that, in at least thirty of their replies, they, and not Dunash, were wrong. This rejoinder he intended "to circulate in every city," so as to expose their foolishness, "and they become a laughing stock among all Spaniards." Whatever the merits of the two sides, this vitriolic controversy helped to stimulate broad public participation in the debate of philological minutiae and to refine the understanding by experts of the peculiarities of the Hebrew language.[22]

One of the debaters on Menaḥem's side, Yehudah ben David, was probably identical with the famous grammarian by that name known as Abu Zakariya Yaḥya ibn Daud Ḥayyuj (born in Fez about 940). Possibly stimulated by this discussion, Ḥayyuj soon made his great grammatical discoveries which will be discussed below. His theories became known also to the Jews of Christian Europe through Hebrew translations by Moses ibn Chiquitilla and Abraham ibn Ezra. Here, however, he refrained from polemics and but briefly intimated some of his new, revolutionary doctrines. Although not directly concerned with vocabulary (only in his *Kitab an-Nutaf* [Book of Glosses] on Prophets did he make a direct lexicographic contribution), his new theories naturally had considerable bearing also on Hebrew lexicography. Curiously, despite his use of the Arabic language and terminology, Ḥayyuj followed Menaḥem in abstaining from quoting any similarities between Hebrew and Arabic. Perhaps his previous commitment on this issue in the controversy with Dunash had made him doubly reticent.[23]

Such parochialism, completely out of keeping with the Jewish people's linguistic and social situation, was bound to fail. The comparative method reasserted itself fully in the *magnum opus* of Jonah (Abu'l Walid ibn Merwan) ibn Janaḥ, the great disciple of Ḥayyuj's colleague Isaac ibn Chiquitilla, the second part of which, entitled "Book of Roots" (*Kitab al-Uṣul*), was essentially a dictionary. In his earliest book, dedicated to corrections and additions to Ḥayyuj's lexicon (both these terms are included in the Arabic title *Kitab al-Mustalḥiq* and in the alternate Hebrew titles used by the author himself), Ibn Janaḥ expostulated:

> My observations [here] have not been stated by any of the Hebrews before me, and I hope that if any man of the humble ones will note what I have associated with Arabic usage as in [the explanation of] the present word, he will not condemn me. For I have not invoked the testimony of the Arabic language in order to confirm by it my personal opinion, nor because the Hebrew language requires the support of the Arabic tongue, but merely because I have stated views the like of which few Hebrews have been accustomed to hear, and I feared that they might hasten to repudiate me outright.

He repeated the same excuse a little more poignantly in the introduction to his main work, where he attacked "what I know of the evil conduct of the men of our time, their ignorance of the vicissitudes of authors and the difficulties of rhymsters, and their proneness to criticize the scholars, particularly as I have myself experienced their foolishness and have not escaped their evil designs." All his works, in fact, are studded with occasional digs at these unregenerate opponents. For one example, he tried to explain that the term, *shareṣu ha-mayim* (the waters brought forth abundantly; Gen. 1:21) could apply to an inanimate object like water. He combated here the views of a "devious" opponent (probably Samuel ha-Nagid) that *shareṣu* could be used only in connection with a living being "whose characteristic feature is its collective existence." Ibn Janaḥ added, "this is nothing new considering the general deviousness of the men of our generation." [24]

In his lexicon particularly, Ibn Janaḥ made a special effort to distinguish between the various shades of meaning appearing in the biblical use of words derived from the same root. In his introduction he pointed out that, for example, the word *paqad* had seven entirely different meanings in various contexts in Scripture, and he further illustrated this varied application in his entry under that root. Unfortunately he abandoned the effort of earlier Hebrew lexicographers to identify also the proper names in the Bible. Perhaps he realized that historical and ethnological research had made too little progress to enable him substantially to improve on the identifications by Saadiah or David ben Abraham. But Ibn Janaḥ came to grips with the no less complex designations of living or inanimate objects mentioned in the Bible. He recognized, for example, that the term *neṭifot* (often translated by "pendants" in Judges 8:26 and Isaiah 3:19) was only loosely connected with the root *naṭaf* (drop) of Canticles 5:5, Proverbs 5:3 and other verses. He suggested, therefore, that it might be related to the Arabic word *nuṭuf,* meaning pearls or earrings, and expressed preference for the latter meaning in the two biblical verses. One may readily see that such interpretations proved to be a boon to harassed Bible exegetes otherwise forced to rely on the limited biblical vocabulary.[25]

On the other hand, Ibn Janaḥ was not always fully explicit with respect to the reasons underlying his interpretations, but took for granted a good philological preparation on the part of his readers. In his introduction he warned them that he would presuppose their intimate familiarity with the two major works by Ḥayyuj, as well as with his own previous philological monographs. This was a tall order, indeed, and it is a testimonial to the great intellectual alertness of his Spanish contemporaries and successors and to their abiding interest in problems of Hebrew philology that they were not discouraged from continued, intensive study of these concentrated, stylistically unadorned works of scholarship. Although not only obscurantists but even such enlightened writers as the poet-statesman Samuel ibn Nagrela sharply protested against certain views and interpretations suggested by the great grammarian of Saragossa, his main contributions soon became the common property of the people. Like Ḥayyuj's work in grammar, that of Ibn Janaḥ in biblical lexicography, both based upon their authors' fine penetration of the profundities of the Hebrew language, remained unsurpassed achievements until the nineteenth century. If Ibn Parḥon's and later David Qimḥi's comparable works ultimately displaced that of Ibn Janaḥ in popular acceptance among both European Jews and Christian Hebraists, this was owing not so much to the relatively minor substantive advances made in the intervening century as to the literary smoothness of works originally written in Hebrew, while Ibn Janaḥ's compilation was accessible to Europeans only in the harsh Tibbonide translation. The shift in the centers of Jewish life alone prevented Ibn Janaḥ's lexicon from becoming that standard work for later Hebrew philology that Al-Jauhari's corresponding tenth-century compilation had become for Arabic lexicography.[26]

Ibn Janaḥ's lexicon completely eclipsed the works of his contemporaries in both the East and the West. Of the "twenty-two treatises" in philology by his opponent Samuel ha-Nagid (according to Ibn Ezra), only a few minor fragments have come down to us either directly or through citation in subsequent literature. The fragments of Samuel's *Kitab al-Istighna* (Book of Amplitude), published by Pavl Kokovtsov, show the great sweep and comprehensiveness of this lexicographic and exegetical work which, if fully preserved, might have established the author's reputation as a great philologist, as well as jurist, poet, and statesman. The distinguished Karaite "grammarian from Jerusalem," Abu'l Faraj Harun, wrote a *Kitab al-Mushtamil* (Comprehensive Book on the Roots and Branches of the Hebrew Language), the seventh part of which was wholly devoted to a dictionary, while the eighth represented a pioneering effort to come to grips with the philological problems of biblical Aramaic. Despite the ease of communications between Palestine and Spain, little of that work, completed in 1026, seems to have come to the notice of the circle around Ḥayyuj and Ibn Janaḥ. Ibn Ezra, who evidently knew more of this work than is extant today, was no longer familiar with its author's identity or Karaite biases. More astonishingly, notwithstanding the enormous prestige and popularity of Hai Gaon in the domain of law (contemporaries and successors, as we recall, unhesitatingly attributed to him countless responsa by other authors) his lexicographical *Kitab al-Ḥawi* (Book of Collection), arranged according to a contemporary Arabic fashion in the alphabetic order of the last letters of the Hebrew roots, is known to us mainly from a few brief quotations in Ibn Bal'am's commentaries.[27]

From then on western preeminence remained uncontested. Riding roughshod over all nationalistic objections, Isaac (Abu Ibrahim ben Joseph ibn Benveniste) ibn Baron (died before 1128) produced, some sixty years after Ibn Janaḥ, a notable treatise frankly entitled *Kitab al-Muwazana* (Concordance between the Hebrew and Arabic Languages). In this work, largely lexicographic in nature, the author ventured even to document his views by frequent quotations from Arabic poets and the Qur'an, as well as from Ḥalil's Arabic lexicon. Yehudah Halevi, a personal friend of Ibn Baron, finally supplied a characteristic historical rationale which must have appeased even the most ardently nationalistic opponents of comparative linguistics. Extolling the nobility of the original forms of the Hebrew language, his spokesman informed the king of the Khazars that

> according to tradition it is the language in which God spoke to Adam and Eve, and in which the latter conversed. . . . Abraham was an Aramaean of *Ur Kasdim,* because the language of the Chaldaeans was Aramaic. He employed Hebrew as a specially holy language and Aramaic for everyday use. For this reason Ishmael brought it to the Arabic speaking nations, and the consequence was that Aramaic, Arabic and Hebrew are similar to each other in their vocabulary, grammatical rules, and formations. The superiority of Hebrew is manifest, . . . [however].[28]

Equipped with this rationale, Solomon ibn Parḥon, a pupil of Halevi as well as of Ibn Ezra, succeeded in familiarizing the Jews of Christian lands with the main findings of Spanish Jewish philology and its comparative approaches. Settling in Salerno, Ibn Parḥon published (in 1160) a new dictionary, entitled *Maḥberet he-'Arukh,* based upon Ibn Janaḥ's masterpiece, but adding many data taken from other authors and a considerable number of new and acute observations. He contributed much especially to the understanding of biblical *realia* and gave an interesting sketch of the earlier developments in Hebrew philology, which effectively supplemented a similar survey by Ibn Ezra. The book's fluent and lucid presentation secured it almost instantaneous reception, and this dictionary, sometimes mistakenly considered an abridged translation of Ibn Janaḥ's work, enjoyed considerable popularity throughout the Middle Ages.[29]

TALMUDIC LANGUAGE

While biblical lexicography thus celebrated its greatest victories in the century and a half between Saadiah and Ibn Janaḥ, the far richer and more complicated vocabulary of Talmud and Midrash was not altogether neglected. Because of its very vastness and complexity, as well as the evident impact on it of a variety of Aramaic, Greek, Latin, and Persian dialects, rabbinic literature could not be subjected to such microscopic scrutiny as was the Bible. Sheer reverence for the revealed word of God had induced countless Masorites to go over with a fine comb every word in Scripture in order to ascertain its proper form and its relation to similar-sounding words elsewhere in the Canon. No such sanctity was attached to the talmudic text, which even today, after many more centuries of intensive study, is far from philologically dependable. Research in this field was aggravated from the outset by the variety of readings of talmudic texts current in different areas. It took, as we recollect, an enormous effort on the part of Gershom bar Yehudah, Rashi, and their schools to establish a uniform recension of the Babylonian Talmud for western Europe. But in the Eastern countries differences in readings continued to complicate the task of Talmud students for many generations thereafter. These differences, moreover, were based not only on occasional oversights by copyists, but also on deeply rooted regional variations in the pronunciation and even in the meaning of various talmudic terms. These variations have persisted until today in such outlying areas as Yemen, which generally preserved the Babylonian traditions in greater purity than Iraq itself. It is small wonder, then, that the preparation of a simple talmudic concordance—a task many times performed for the Hebrew Bible and almost performed by Ibn Janaḥ himself—still faces staggering difficulties. Only owing to Chaim J. Kasowski's extraordinary competence and industry have the first volumes of such a gigantic work seen the light of day. Supplementing that author's earlier concordances to the Mishnah, Tosefta, and Onkelos, this work, when completed, will lay foundations for new solid researches in the language of Talmud and Midrash.[30]

Yet students of the Talmud, too, required expert lexicographical guidance through the maze of the technical vocabulary used by their Palestinian or Babylonian predecessors. In fact, the very first recorded Hebrew dictionary, we recall, was entirely devoted to talmudic terms. Unfortunately, we know very little about the aforementioned pioneering works by Ṣemaḥ Gaon and Saadiah. From the few references by Abraham Zacuto, the distinguished scientist-chronicler of the early sixteenth century, we may judge that Ṣemaḥ's *Sefer he-'Arukh* (Lexicon) included identifications of many proper names—a task apparently performed also in Saadiah's dictionary of the Mishnah, but largely neglected by later students of talmudic letters. Building on these foundations, Nathan ben Yeḥiel of Rome (*ca.* 1030–1106) prepared an *'Arukh* (Lexicon) for the Babylonian Talmud (the Palestinian Talmud was little used even by most talmudic experts then and long after) which remained unsurpassed until the newly awakened philological curiosity of the nineteenth century. At that time Alexander Kohut found it advisable to reissue that lexicon in a revised and much enlarged edition.[31]

That Rome, rather than some Arabic-speaking city, should have become the place of origin of this major work of philological scholarship is not altogether surprising. Principally a direct offshoot of Palestinian traditions and learning, Italian Jewry must have found it particularly irksome to submit to the now uncontested hegemony of the Babylonian Talmud and Babylonia's geonic *halakhah*. Verbally, too, even its experts must have been less familiar with the eastern dialect of Aramaic prevalent in Babylonia than with its western, Palestinian idiom, just as conversely some Babylonian students of that period found an Arabic translation of the Palestinian Talmud helpful in penetrating the mysteries of that important, if to them secondary, compendium. Since Babylonian supremacy had now been definitely established, the Italian communities had to come to terms with Babylonian learning. For this purpose they, even more than any other Jewish group, needed assistance in comprehending words which had not been transmitted orally in their schools from generation to generation.

Nathan's dictionary is in its sphere as monumental an achievement as is that of Ibn Janaḥ in the area of biblical lexicography. In fact, having far fewer and philologically less well-trained predecessors as compared with the Masorites, Nathan ben Yeḥiel often had to cut his own path through the almost virginal forest of talmudic and midrashic letters. Like those Muslim scholars who traveled far and wide in search of authentic traditions, Nathan spent many years studying with R. Maṣliaḥ ben Elijah ibn al-Bazaq in Sicily, R. Moses Khalfo in Bari, and R. Moses ha-Darshan in Narbonne—all centers of Jewish learning where the relatively recent heritage of Arab rule was superimposed upon the more deeply ingrained memories of Graeco-Roman civilization. Nathan's journey to Babylonia is somewhat more dubious, but there is no question that his teacher Maṣliaḥ had spent some time there and had felt the impact of Hai Gaon's impressive personality. Hai's teachings are indeed quoted no less than 138 times in Nathan's dictionary, a figure exceeded only by the 142 quotations from Ḥananel ben Ḥushiel of neighboring Kairuwan. Although apparently unaware of Saadiah's philological works (of the two minor references to the gaon in the *'Arukh,* one expressly relates to a responsum), Nathan made a valiant effort to familiarize himself with the works of the eastern geonim as well as with those of such westerners as Samuel ha-Nagid, R. Gershom, and the "sages of Mayence." Gershom's brother, Makhir, may have served as a direct mentor through his lexicographical work, *Alpha Beta.* Nathan also gained access to a large number of rabbinic writings which, even in his day, must have been quite rare. Because of his conscientiousness in quoting illustrative passages verbatim from these sources, his work later became a treasure trove of lost midrashim and other ancient and early medieval writings. Apart from literary sources, however, Nathan utilized the fruits of his own and his friends' direct observations and reached many novel conclusions by independent reasoning. He was right, therefore, in informing his readers through an introductory poem that he wished to communicate to them the results of what "I have heard, seen, and thought about." [32]

So immediate and universal was the acceptance of Nathan's work by the Jewish scholars in both the West and the East that it discouraged further creative efforts along the same lines. Nathan's younger contemporary, Rashi, seems to have used the new dictionary for the revised edition of his commentaries on the Talmud. Quite independently, however, although doubtless using many of the sources at Nathan's disposal, Rashi suggested so many interpretations of talmudic words that a complete dictionary based upon these explanations would prove helpful to students of both talmudic and medieval lexicography. As we recall, to make his point clearer, Rashi often translated technical terms, names of plants and animals, and other not easily definable words into French. These foreign words (*la'azim*) in Rashi's commentaries, totaling some three thousand words, have long been recognized as a major source of information on the French spoken in eleventh-century Champagne and elsewhere. As a popular stylist, moreover, Rashi utilized much of the talmudic vocabulary in his own comments and thus helped to spread their knowledge among the masses. Subsequent generations followed Nathan's interpretations almost unquestioningly. Although some entries seem to have been lost in the process of constant copying, the lexicon reached the fifteenth century substantially in its original form and with undiminished popularity. It belonged indeed to the earliest printed Hebrew works (about 1480), and it has been frequently reprinted since.[33]

Later scholars concentrated largely on supplementing the *'Arukh,* rather than on writing new talmudic dictionaries of their own. One such early supplement, written by Tanḥum Yerushalmi, an Egyptian scholar of the latter part of the thirteenth century, is particularly interesting. As expressed in his introductory critique of Nathan's work, Tanḥum not only assumed an independent attitude toward various lexicographic problems, but he also pursued rather different aims. Within less than a century, the Maimonidean code had established itself in all eastern lands as the preeminent work of rabbinic scholarship and, as anticipated by the sage of Fusṭaṭ himself, had begun displacing there the very Talmud as the object of concentrated study. At the same time, familiarity with rabbinic Hebrew declined to such an extent that even the fairly simple and lucid vocabulary of the great codifier was no longer fully understood. In his *Kitab al-Murshid al-kafi* (Adequate Guide), Tanḥum supplied, therefore, a dictionary to Maimonidean and, incidentally, to mishnaic Hebrew which, he emphasized in his introduction, could easily be copied or acquired at low cost.[34]

GRAMMAR

Intimately connected with lexicography was the quest for basic rules of grammar which would explain the various forms under which a particular word or phrase appeared in Scripture. To the students of the Bible, and even of language as such, who were far fewer in number, the distinction between the two realms appeared decidedly secondary. Most of them searched for grammatical rules in order the better to understand the meaning of words, and, conversely, they often analyzed words as mere illustrations for the operation of diverse rules.

Once again we must go back to the largely anonymous students of the Masorah for the beginnings of a semisystematic exploration of laws governing the Hebrew language. To justify a specific spelling, vocalization, or accentuation, the masoretic schools early developed rationalizations which, however empirical in nature, established certain rules from which one could depart only in the case of avowed exceptions. Even the purely mnemotechnical rules included in Ben Asher's *Diqduqe ha-ṭe'amin* implied certain abstractions concerning the laws governing the Hebrew language which required but fuller formulation to become grammatical rules. The author of *Massekhet Soferim* had likewise stressed the distinction between the radical and the functional letters and stated that the latter, used for prefixes or suffixes, are frequently deleted. This distinction was greatly expanded by the Masorites. General political and cultural transformations aided in that transition. While contact with the Graeco-Roman civilization, as well as the rather sloppy speech habits of the Aramaic-speaking populations, tended to make many readers and writers slur over the so-called "weak" consonants, the new dominance of the Arabic speech in western Asia helped restore fuller appreciation for these important functional letters. Problems of the *sheva,* as we recall, and those of the *dagesh,* as well as of letters which could take no *dagesh,* likewise preoccupied the leading Masorites and constituted important ingredients of Ben Asher's major work. Ibn Janaḥ quoted a masoretic monograph in Arabic devoted wholly to phonetics, if we are to judge from its title, the *Kitab al-Musawatat* (in Hebrew *Sefer ha-Qolot*). It evidently dealt in particular with the pronunciation of the consonants *ḥet, 'ayin,* and *resh.* One is reminded, in this connection, of Aaron ben Asher's much-quoted statement that the differentiation between a *resh* with or without a *dagesh* was peculiar to Palestinians (or Tiberians) alone, "whether they read it in Scripture or use it in their conversation, in the mouths of men, women and children." The grammarian of Saragossa not only greatly admired the pronunciation of the "men of Tiberias, who in the clarity of their speech excel all other Hebrews," but also considered the Tiberian scholars' grammatical rules concerning these consonants as sufficiently inclusive not to require further elaboration on his part.[35]

Here, too, Saadiah's work marked an enormous step forward. Throughout his life the gaon was cognizant of Hebrew linguistic problems not only in his philological and exegetical treatises, but also in his poems and prayers. In vocalizing *ḥay* (not *ḥey*) *ha-'olamim* in the well-known exclamation "By Him that liveth for ever" (after Dan. 12:7), calling each of the Ten Commandments *dibber* rather than *dibbur,* or pronouncing the liturgical formula *le-'olam va'ed* (for ever and ever) with a *ṣere,* he deviated from what had already in his day become accepted linguistic practice. Far from being arbitrary in these decisions, however, he invoked in each case some well-established tradition, if necessary through some forced interpretation. Frequent exceptions of this kind must have stimulated his agile mind to search more deeply for the underlying reasons of these apparent irregularities.[36]

Noticing that many other Jews paid "no attention to our plain language, much less to its obscure forms," Saadiah decided to append to his dictionary in its revised Arabic edition a section dealing with the three "principles" of language which might prove useful to poets. The very quest for such principles reflects Saadiah's newly won preoccupation with fundamentals of grammar, undoubtedly the result of his acquaintance with similar quests of the Baṣran philologists from Sibawaihi (d. 794) to his own contemporary and possibly personal acquaintance Ibn Duraid (837–933). Although his own dogmatic aversion to the use of analogy (*qiyas*) in law and the limitations of the Hebrew language to the documentary records of past ages tended to make him sympathetic to the Kufan "anomalistic" approach, his general logical bent of mind drove him increasingly in the direction of the Baṣran "analogistic" search for comprehensive rules. The latter consisted in his opinion of "*first,* call, question, statement, command, and stipulation; *second,* descriptions, forming four classes defined according to either matter, form, action, or completion [aim], as I shall fully explain; *third,* classes of comparison, being similar to group two, with the difference that those refer to the object of comparison while the latter are taken from the result." Unfortunately, the subsequent parts of this work, in which he more fully explained the significance and objectives of this classification, are lost. But this very endeavor reveals a state of linguistic and stylistic sophistication which presupposed considerable familiarity with problems of language on the part of both author and readers. So do Saadiah's quite technical linguistic observations scattered through his commentaries on the Bible and the *Sefer Yeṣirah.* With reference to *Yeṣirah*'s mystically colored classification of letters, Saadiah recalled his suggestion that one must draw a distinction between the eleven letters of the Hebrew alphabet which remain unchanged, and the other eleven letters which undergo great changes and often even disappear completely in certain forms. He also identified *Yeṣirah*'s three "mothers" of all other letters with *alef, vav,* and *yod,* the very three consonants which were in the focus of the Baṣran-Kufan debate. Followed therein by Dunash ibn Tamim and 'Ali ben Yehudah 'Alan of Tiberias, Saadiah thus laid the foundation for further examination of the so-called weak consonants, out of which ultimately emerged Ḥayyuj's revolutionary discoveries.[37]

Apart from such more incidental suggestions, Saadiah prepared a major philological work in which he systematically developed his theories on the Hebrew language. His *Kutub al-Lughah* (Books of Language; or sometimes, more fully, "Books of the Elegance of the Hebrew Language") advisedly used the plural designation, because it consisted of twelve loosely connected philological monographs. It was indeed sometimes cited under the title of "The Twelve Parts." Because of its comprehensive nature and ensuing length, this pioneering venture suffered the fate of Saadiah's biblical commentaries and was allowed to sink into oblivion. It was no longer available to Ibn Janaḥ, who otherwise was the gaon's great admirer.[38]

In fact, only one incomplete later copy and small fragments of two others have survived to our day and have in recent years been gradually made available to scholarship by Solomon L. Skoss. The following passages from the third part will give the reader an inkling of Saadiah's remarkably advanced approach, as well as of his prolix, often repetitious, style, which helps to explain the work's speedy disappearance:

> It [this part] treats comprehensively of the aspects [of the language] of the Bible, called Inflection. The principles laid down in this part are not limited to Hebrew alone, but apply to all the languages with which we are familiar. . . . There are five premises which serve as bases for the study of Inflection: (1) Differentiation of expressions employed by rational beings, so as to classify them properly. On close study we have found them to fall into three groups: nouns, verbs and particles. . . . (2) We have separated the letters prefixed to nouns and found them to be eleven. . . . (3) The addition of affixed personal pronouns to nouns and verbs. On close study we found them to be ten, so we named them *the ten possessors*. . . . (4) Determining the tense; it is essentially divided into three parts: Past, Present and Future. . . . (5) Combining the four preceding premises together and the way it is done. We seek the aid of God, especially since our aim is that the students (hearers) be mindful of the language of His book, and state that while all four premises are fundamental for the present study, the first one, viz., the recognition of nouns, verbs, and particles, is like a pivot around which the remaining premises revolve.[39]

Saadiah then proceeds to analyze the various possible forms taken by Hebrew verbs with respect to functions. Commenting on *qal* and *hif'il* forms only, but referring to the various personal prefixes and suffixes, he enumerates, after leaving out the present tense, 48 simple and 368 more derivative forms. Including the present, he mentions elsewhere a total of 430 accepted formations of the inflection. With his penchant for careful statistics, Saadiah even figured out a theoretical total of formations of a typical verb like *shama'* (hear) to be 19,169. Dunash ben Labraṭ, to whom we owe this figure, not only claims that Saadiah was short of one formation, but also emphasizes that, by adding the *pi'el* forms, the gaon could have increased his total by several thousand. Of course, the number would have been further augmented if the other four conjugations were used. In a similarly detailed vein Saadiah analyzes the nature of the seven Hebrew vowels, examining in particular the position in the human mouth of the organs controlling the respective sounds, the laws governing the descent from *ḥolem* to *qamaṣ* and vice versa, and points out forty-nine possible combinations among these vowels. He does not include in this analysis the *sheva,* to which, because of its great importance, he devotes a separate (sixth) monograph.[40]

For reasons which cannot as yet be fully assessed, Saadiah's great philological work failed to exert its due influence on the subsequent development of grammatical studies. Undoubtedly, as in the case of his halakhic monographs, his excessive proclivity for classification into innumerable subdivisions proved discouraging. Although, unlike the legal domain where the talmudic sequences had long been familiar to all students, Hebrew philology had not yet developed accepted patterns of its own, the gaon's divisions, however logically impeccable, proved of little immediate assistance to either Bible exegetes or creative Hebrew writers. Only one early treatise dealing with various forms of the imperative and inflections quoted the gaon twice and in the selection of *shama'* as its example for the classification of its paradigms showed at least some superficial similarities with Saadiah's treatise on inflections. However, the author followed a substantially different arrangement and used the imperative as the verb's fundamental form, which seems to have early become typical of Karaite grammatical methodology.[41]

Nor did Qirqisani betray any outright indebtedness to the work of his geonic contemporary. To be sure, we know of the distinguished heresiologue's philological doctrines mainly through the debris of his thirty-seven exegetical propositions published by Hirschfeld. The selection of topics is here clearly determined by the primarily exegetical orientation of both author and readers. For this reason great emphasis is placed on such an apparently superfluous particle as *et,* which the author compares with, and differentiates from, the Arabic *iyya.* Qirqisani is likewise concerned with apparent irregularities in the logical succession of parts of sentences in the biblical syntax; the use of the future tense when the past is meant and vice versa; the *vav's* function in these and other matters; the use of singular nouns for collective and that of plurals for single entities; the carryover of negatives from one part of a sentence to another; the peculiarities of the *he interrogativum* and exceptions therefrom, and the irregular addition or omission of single letters. Qirqisani even gives a fairly clear adumbration of the theory concerning the elliptic and pleonastic mannerisms of biblical writers.[42]

Of course, in a less articulate form some such teachings are scattered through Saadiah's exegetical works and, probably, in part antedated both authors. Nor do even direct similarities found in later literature necessarily indicate borrowings from Qirqisani. Ibn Janaḥ, for example, reveals striking resemblances in approach and even in what might superficially appear as direct quotations, and yet he may not even have heard of the name Qirqisani. So many of these ideas were "in the air," and so much had become the common property of intellectuals, Jewish and non-Jewish, in the whole Muslim world, that we do not have to postulate any intervening literary links. If we possessed much more of the literary heritage of those vigorous and creative generations, we would probably find that many doctrines emerged from independent reasoning by men separated from one another in time and space, and sometimes among close neighbors who did not know of each other's discoveries.

Even more than their Rabbanite confreres, Karaite scholars, following in Qirqisani's footsteps, treated problems of Hebrew grammar as mere aids for their biblical exegesis. Salmon ben Yeruḥim mentioned in his *Commentary* on Lamentations 1:14 (written in 954) that he had written a treatise on the five Hebrew "letters of permutation." That this ardent defender of his faith, however, pursued here too principally exegetical and theological purposes is evident from the tenor of his other writings, and, particularly, from a sharp diatribe (included in his earlier *Commentary* on Psalms 102:5) against those of his coreligionists who engaged in the study of Arabic science and Arabic grammar. David ben Abraham al-Fasi likewise frequently inserted into his dictionary lengthy excursuses on grammatical problems. But, as we recall, he reiterated that he supplied such data chiefly "in order that anyone contemplating to write some commentary on the Books of the Scriptures should not be rash in his interpretations." That is why he, like Salmon, accorded special treatment to the problems of permutation or interchange and metathesis or transposition of letters. David discussed also at some length the various forms of the imperative. His overriding concern, however, remained the use of such data for the understanding of the Bible. Hence also came his more than passing attention to masoretic problems.[43]

The same holds true, to an even greater extent, of an outright exegete like Jephet ben 'Ali. This distinguished commentator often resorted to grammatical rules in his interpretations of biblical passages. Occasionally, as in his *Commentary* on Hosea, he added a special appendix in order to explain "difficult words in this book which I have translated and shown their derivations and grammatical forms so that the student may, if God so will it, dwell upon them." Jephet made, for example, an acute observation on the three different ways in which letters are redoubled in certain Hebrew words, dependent on whether such repetition affected only one letter or two letters of a biliteral or triliteral word. At times he even took a fling at Saadiah for some minor inaccuracy allegedly showing that the Rabbanite commentator had "no true insight into the rules of the language."[44]

The first Karaite author to compose a special grammatical work seems to have been Joseph ibn Nuḥ. Unfortunately, not even a fragment of his work has come down to us. From a brief reference by Abu'l Faraj Harun, however, we may judge that it was written in Hebrew and had the characteristic title of *Sefer ha-Diqduq* (Book of Grammar). Abu'l Faraj himself was among the most prolific grammarians of the Hebrew language. Reference has already been made to his *Kitab al-Mushtamil,* which in addition to its concluding two sections dealing with Hebrew lexicography and grammatical elements of biblical Aramaic contained six parts wholly devoted to an analysis of Hebrew grammatical problems. After a preliminary discussion of the "ten general principles about the forms of words, which can be applied to a great part of the Hebrew language," Abu'l Faraj concentrated the entire second section of eighteen chapters on a discussion of the Hebrew infinitive. He included here an analysis of the distinction between the infinitive and the verbal noun, which seems to have preoccupied his teacher, Joseph ibn Nuḥ. In subsequent sections this distinguished "grammarian from Jerusalem" made excellent use of Saadiah's division between the eleven radical and eleven functional or "servile" letters. But he failed to go beyond the gaon in generalizing from the particular use to which the radical letters were put in the Bible about the nature of the biliterality or triliterality of the Hebrew roots themselves. A similar color blindness seems to have characterized also his other philological works. One of these is described on its manuscript title page as "Pearl-Strings on the Grammatical Inflections of the Hebrew Language—may God make it useful"; another, bearing the title *Kitab al-Kafi* (Book of the Adequate), is said by its author to have embraced all sections of the Hebrew language "except the irregular ones." It was precisely through an intensive study of the irregular verbs, however, that a true insight could be gained into the function of the "weak" consonants, whose frequent baffling disappearance so greatly altered the shape of the same words in different grammatical forms.[45]

CREATIVE UPSURGE

Such a mental block to the understanding of the real nature of the Hebrew roots is doubly remarkable as the Arab grammarians had long reached the conclusion—far more obvious in the case of Arabic—concerning the basic triliterality of roots of both verbs and nouns. Everything deviating from this rule was relegated to the realm of exceptions. That students of Hebrew were so slow in adopting parallel assumptions was less the result of their nationalist pride, and their conviction that the two languages were as different as they were alike, than of their exclusive concentration on the Bible. So long as grammar was made but an ancillary science to be used exclusively for the interpretation of Scripture, the ensuing empirical approach proved to be a serious obstacle. It consisted mainly in the generalization of phenomena observed in the various formations of the limited remnants of ancient Hebrew which survived in the Bible.

Only when the Hebrew grammar became a vehicle for creative self-expression by philologically open-minded and well-trained poets and prose writers, as it had become among ancient Greeks or medieval Arabs, could it produce the necessary clarity about the operation of basic laws governing the use of that language to meet varying needs. That the composers of liturgical poetry from Yose ben Yose to Eleazar ha-Qalir had felt little of that need and compulsion is not surprising. Living in a Palestinian environment, where the heritage of ancient Hebrew dialects was still much alive and was influencing even the verbiage of the Palestinian Talmud and where, on the other hand, the masoretic schools operated as watch-dogs ever alert to the slightest deviation from the language of Scripture, these liturgical improvisers unconcernedly coined new terms and used unusual forms to convey their meaning. They paid little attention to any but the most obvious grammatical rules, by virtue of habit rather than conscious design. In other countries, however, especially where, as from Egypt to Spain, even the related Aramaic speech had no deep local roots, only a more conscious effort to uncover the intricacies of the Hebrew language as preserved in the extant literary documents could yield the appropriate linguistic tools for the more complex media of self-expression. Saadiah alone among these early grammarians was a creative writer who made use of his own philological discoveries for the expanded use of language in his sacred poetry.

Saadiah was well ahead of his time, however, which in part explains the neglect of his philological works by contemporaries and early successors. Even most other distinguished philologians of the period, down to Menaḥem and Abu'l Faraj Harun, were not poets, but mainly exegetes. In fact, the Karaites among them largely followed 'Anan in his sharp condemnation of the Rabbanite liturgical "innovations" and demanded that all prayers be selected from the Psalms and other ready-made biblical sections. Qirqisani, outstanding grammarian though he was, blocked his own and his contemporaries' self-rejuvenating interpenetration of linguistic theory and practice when he assailed the Rabbanites because "for prayers (consisting of citations) from the book of Psalms they substitute some composed by themselves, contrary to what is exjoined in the Scripture [Ezra 3:10]: 'To praise the Lord by the words of His servant David.' "[46]

Not surprisingly, therefore, the first man to stumble on the principle of triliterality was Dunash ben Labraṭ, who also was the first to introduce Arabic rhythm into Hebrew poetry. Characteristically, the very term he used for the rhythmic "weight" of syllables, *mishqal* (borrowed from the Arabic *wazm*), was employed by him also for the designation of the basic form of a word in contradistinction to its variable suffixes or prefixes. If it be true that he made a living as a synagogue reader (*ḥazzan*), he must frequently have improvised liturgical poems and hence doubly resented the shackles imposed upon the poet by the Bible's limited vocabulary and grammatical forms. He allowed himself, therefore, to use, "because of rhythmic exigency," new turns in analogy to some rare, even unique phrases in Scripture.

Dunash himself still had little feeling for the new distinctions, and in his major attack on Menaḥem's dictionary he still adhered to his opponent's belief that Hebrew roots ranged from one to five letters. But the bitter attack of Ben Saruq's disciples on his poetic *mishqal* seems to have set him thinking about the latter's practical aspects as pertaining to basic grammatical forms as well. In his rather incomplete notes, reproducing a number of strictures on his master Saadiah's grammatical views and apparently composed toward the end of his life, he claimed that "it is a matter of common knowledge that neither Saadiah nor the other eastern students had an understanding for the nature of the rhyme and the rhythm in poetry." But he sensed the importance of weak or, as in emulation of an Arabic term he called them "dangerously sick," consonants, which frequently vanish in the first, second, or third letter of the root. These letters were soon standardized as *pe, 'ayin,* or *lamed,* the components of the term *p'al* (verb). Dunash thus adumbrated the new emphasis on the triliterality of all roots, which was to revolutionize the whole approach to Hebrew grammar. In "awakening from the slumber" of ages, as Moses ibn Ezra graphically described his significant though as yet rather inarticulate discoveries, he did not hesitate to defy long accepted teachings and practices. For example, he rejected even Saadiah's then almost universally accepted division into eleven radical and eleven servile letters by adding to the latter the *dalet* and *ṭet,* merely because of their phonetically determined usage after sibilants in the *hitpa'el* form. With a typical dash of brilliance and vanity, he gave students a mnemotechnic formula for these thirteen servile letters, *Dunash ha-levi emet ke-tob* (Dunash the Levite as true as good).[47]

Possibly stimulated by Dunash's intimations, Yehudah Ḥayyuj established once and for all the theory of triliterality in his memorable *K. al-Af'al dhawat ḥuruf al-lin* (Book of Verbs Containing Weak Letters), followed by a detailed study of "Verbs Containing Geminative Letters." Unlike most of his predecessors, other than Dunash, Ḥayyuj did not pursue principally exegetical purposes. In fact, his quotations from the Bible often revealed glaring inaccuracies, explainable only by their citation from memory, the author's apparent haste in writing his works, and his failure to revise them. On the other hand, he was distressed by the improper use of verbs by many persons "in their sayings and verses" and decidedly considered the growing needs of the contemporary writers. He tried to utilize for this purpose all linguistic materials in the Bible so as to fashion from them workable linguistic tools. In his programmatic introduction, he explained how he was led to compose his book on the weak letters:

> When I saw the confusion occurring in these letters, with the help of the Lord I composed this book, in which I have explained all their secrets, and mentioned the occasions when they fall out, are changed, or hardened by daghesh, after stating why they are called latent or lengthening letters and also everything else bearing on the subject. In all this my purpose is to argue from what is contained in Scripture to what is not contained therein. . . . It is moreover the duty of us who desire to write in the holy tongue and to know its ways, to acquire it from the ways of the early Hebrews, who were born in it, grew up in its ways, and established its boundaries: especially should we imitate the language of vision and prophecy.

In other words, he wished to study the Bible, in order the better to comprehend the laws of the Hebrew language, rather than to study Hebrew grammar and vocabulary, in order the better to comprehend the Bible! [48]

For this purpose Ḥayyuj went over in considerable detail the whole range of weak verbs and showed what happened to them when the first, second, or third letter of their roots was an *alef, vav,* or *yod.* His characteristic omission of the letter *he* in this context, however, shows that even this radical innovator still bowed to the tradition, initiated by the author of *Yeṣirah* in Saadiah's and Ibn Tamim's interpretation and reinforced by the fact that these three weak consonants had also become commonplace in Arabic grammar. Ḥayyuj supplemented this theory by others dealing with verbs, whose middle and third radicals were identical or "geminative." Here, too, he consistently followed his logical rather than empirical method, and included postulated triliteral verbal forms even where the biblical text had preserved only such abbreviated nominal forms as *har* (mountain) or *tokh* (inside). These treatises were preceded by an essay on Hebrew vocalization and followed by his *Kitab an-Nutaf* (Book of Glosses), consisting of disjointed philological notes on Prophets. Although very little of the latter works has survived, the available samples reveal not only their author's consistency but also his concern for philology as a practical and not purely an exegetical instrument. Even the limitation of his exegetical work to the books of Prophets, which has long puzzled scholars, is understandable in the light of his advice to readers to "imitate the language of vision and prophecy." His selectivity, too, and his admission, "I have omitted from the sections [of the book] those passages the meaning of which is hidden on the whole even from experts, also those the meaning of which I could not grasp," clearly indicate that his chief aim was to marshal the available linguistic resources, rather than to elucidate difficult passages in Scripture.[49]

Ḥayyuj's new theories, buttressed by tremendous illustrative material and ingenious interpretation of apparent contradictions, were bound sooner or later to create a deep impression. While apparently ignored in his lifetime and even for a time thereafter unable to silence opposing voices, his views and, particularly, his insistence on the principle of triliterality, before long dominated all grammatical discussions. Unilateral roots disappeared forever from the Hebrew grammars of the following generations, and even biliteral roots made only sporadic bows until they found some new advocates in modern philology. Ben Zion Halper is not altogether wrong in his contention that Hebrew grammar of our own days has advanced little beyond the vital discoveries of this eleventh-century Spanish immigrant from Fez.[50]

Whatever doubts might still have been entertained concerning the acceptability of Ḥayyuj's theories were dispelled by a succession of monumental philological works of Jonah ibn Janaḥ, in whom Ḥayyuj found a faithful and eloquent, if frequently independently creative, successor. From his early *Kitab al-Mustalḥaq,* entirely devoted to the supplementation of "the lacunae which the illustrious teacher and perfect chief, Abu Zakariya Ḥayyuj (may the Lord be merciful to him and make shine his face) has left in his list of weak letters and geminative verbs," to the crowning achievement of his bipartite *Kitab at-Tanqiḥ* (Book of the Detailed Investigation), Ibn Janaḥ elaborated the grammatical rules and reinterpreted the entire body of the Hebrew linguistic heritage in the light of Ḥayyuj's new findings. Ibn Daud was right in stating in his Chronicle that, after Ḥayyuj had "placed on solid foundations the Hebrew language which had been forgotten throughout the dispersion," came R. Marinus (Jonah) ibn Janaḥ "and completed what R. Yehudah ben David had begun" (*MJC,* I, 81).

Although, like his master, writing in Arabic and using to good advantage the precise philological terminology of Arab grammarians (he once referred to Sibawaihi by name) Ibn Janaḥ, too, was primarily concerned with the improvement of the quality of the Hebrew writing of his generation. Through the maze of his philological verbiage one may still sense the impression made upon him by his teacher, the poet Isaac ben Saul. When the sensitive youth recited before the master one of the latter's poems, he followed several manuscripts in which a crucial word, *qerab,* had been corrected by outsiders into *segor* (both meaning "innermost" heart), the better to conform with the accepted grammar. Isaac insisted, however, upon the original version. True, constantly on the defensive against obscurantist attacks on philological studies, Ibn Janaḥ often reiterated that without some such precise knowledge neither Bible nor Talmud could be properly understood. But his main interest evidently lay in the much deplored neglect of the Hebrew language, which he contrasted with the high degree of cultivation of the Arabic speech "among the people in whose midst we live." He deeply deplored the view of some learned talmudists, running counter to that of most cultivated Arabs, that "the science of proper grammatical usage [or more specifically of declension and conjugation] and speech is mere guesswork; in fact, almost borders on heresy." In his detailed grammar (*luma'*) of forty-six chapters and his equally comprehensive dictionary of "roots" (*uṣul*) he wished to place in the hands of the public manuals with the aid of which intelligent readers and writers might tackle even the most intricate problems of the Hebrew language. More than any of his predecessors, he also paid special attention to stylistic problems and, not unjustly, he has been called the "father of Hebrew syntax." [51]

Understandably, Ibn Janaḥ's theories did not remain unchallenged. Not only conservatives, who had little use for the "newfangled" philological approaches, but even trained grammarians found many of Ibn Janaḥ's theories unacceptable. Among Abu'l Walid's powerful opponents was no less a master than Samuel ibn Nagrela, who, although likewise a pupil of Ḥayyuj, believed that he could still uphold the existence of certain biliteral roots. Only small parts of the Nagid's *Kitab al-Istighna* (in Hebrew: *Sefer ha-'Osher;* Book of Amplitude) have thus far been recovered; we cannot even tell for certain whether the twenty-two grammatical treatises alluded to by Abraham ibn Ezra were indeed but chapters of a comprehensive work, like the twelve monographs of Saadiah's *Kutub al-Lughah.* If we may draw a parallel from the recently recovered portions of the Nagid's juristic *magnum opus,* he probably made an effort here, too, to quote his predecessors at great length. Of course, the philological materials coming from the East were far sparser and less authoritative than the decisions rendered by the geonim in the juridical domain. But, for an assiduous collector like Samuel, who had made it his business to employ numerous copyists to reproduce older books for the use of scholars in many lands, the accumulation of works by older authorities and ample citations therefrom must have appeared a meritorious deed, quite apart from his own conclusions. Possibly this very involvement in the older literature prevented the great poet-statesman from fully subscribing to the teachings of his revered master, Ḥayyuj. In any case, he found Ibn Janaḥ's position too radical; it was perhaps made doubly distasteful to him by the Saragossan grammarian's almost provocatively self-assertive tone. Curiously, the controversy soon assumed the character of a grand debate, in which large groups of intellectuals were arrayed on both sides. Because of the intensive preoccupation of the Spanish-Jewish intelligentsia with all problems affecting the Hebrew language, it was easy for the Nagid's messenger in Saragossa to convert a purely social gathering in his honor into a forum in which he challenged Ibn Janaḥ, an unwary guest, to a progressively complicated and technical debate. Only a few of the pamphlets exchanged on this and other occasions have come down to us. But whatever one thinks of the tone of the debate, which often degenerated into personal recriminations and outright vilification, it did contribute much to the clarification of many issues in the minds of the main protagonists. It also helped dramatize even the more esoteric philological minutiae before a broad public, which for generations thereafter continued to discuss the relative merits of the respective arguments.[52]

GRADUAL ACCEPTANCE

Curiously, the discoveries of Ḥayyuj and Ibn Janaḥ, though quick to reach Christian Europe as well as the Arabic-speaking East, long remained without any noticeable influence on the philological thinking of both these regions. True, some Eastern scholars, possibly including Hai Gaon, friend and correspondent of Samuel ibn Nagrela, paid grudging recognition to Ḥayyuj's work. According to Ibn Parḥon they exclaimed, "We have not yet received anything worth while from the West except this book, which surpasses in excellence anything written on this subject." Nevertheless, a long time thereafter, Abraham the Babylonian and other Eastern grammarians still seriously discussed uniliteral roots as if Ḥayyuj had never said anything about the disappearance of letters in weak and geminative verbs. A fragment of a grammatical work, written by one Nathanael of Yemen and published by Kokovtsov, betrays utter unfamiliarity with the achievements of the Spaniards, although the author seems to have been of Egyptian origin and was clearly imbued with the spirit of independent philosophic inquiry. In the West, too, Rashi and his school never went much beyond Menaḥem. Not even Rashi's acute observations on the peculiar formation of verbs beginning with *nun,* or whose middle letter is *'ayin,* and his use of the term "fallen root" (*yesod nofel*), marked any real advance over Menaḥem's views or terminology. Rashi's grandson, Jacob Tam, as we recall, still labored over deciding the merits of the controversy between Dunash ben Labraṭ and Menaḥem's disciples. A later German exegete (whose biblical glosses seem not to antedate much the only copy now extant, written in 1337) knew of Ibn Parḥon, but never cited Ḥayyuj, Ibn Janaḥ, or Ibn Ezra. For him Menaḥem's dictionary still represented the acme of philological achievement.[53]

Undoubtedly, general conservatism and bowing to long-accepted authority account for much of that neglect of the new philological discoveries in both East and West. One wonders, however, whether the absence of a widely felt need did not contribute its share to this consistent disregard of the masters' persuasive teachings, soon available also in the Hebrew translations by Moses ibn Chiquitilla and Ibn Ezra of Ḥayyuj's works, and by Yehudah ibn Tibbon of Ibn Janaḥ's *magnum opus.* These had been further popularized with great ingenuity by Ibn Ezra in his original writings. In the East, Hebrew poetry and prose declined constantly and gave way to almost exclusive productivity in the Arabic language. This was true even in the Palestinian communities after their destruction by the Crusaders. As late as the tenth century Dunash ibn Tamim still believed that "the inhabitants of Palestine and [especially] the men of Tiberias are the guardians of the Hebrew language and its natural heirs, while the rest of the people, that is our folk, know the language only from literary rather than natural usage." Now the opposite became true. In Spain, under the impact of the great poetic creativity, linguistic flexibility evolved naturally from the daily use of Hebrew in writing, if not in speech. On the other hand, in Christian Europe Jews wrote Hebrew, but it was a rather poor language, rich in neither vocabulary nor grammatical forms and hence able to get along entirely with the traditional patterns. Menaḥem ben Saruq's dictionary was about all the Franco-German authors needed for their practical purposes, while their Bible exegesis was altogether dominated by the superlatively appealing commentaries of Rashi. Even in Rome, which soon was to produce a poet of the rank of Immanuel, an effort was made to uphold Menaḥem's authority. Several years after Ibn Ezra's visit to Rome, Menaḥem ben Solomon produced there an encyclopedic philological-exegetical work, *Eben boḥan* (Touchstone), which still was entirely based on Menaḥem ben Saruq's, and not Ibn Janaḥ's, dictionary.[54]

On the other hand, it was a young Frenchman who, perhaps on a visit to Spain not long after 1050, induced Moses ibn Chiquitilla to translate into Hebrew Ḥayyuj's two main treatises. This translation was in itself a great pioneering venture. Next to the more or less synchronous translations of Karaite Bible commentaries by Tobiah ben Moses of Constantinople, Moses' work ranks as the first major work of translation from Arabic into Hebrew. Remarkably, it showed none of the signs of the strains and stresses of the later Tibbonide versions. Its smooth and idiomatic Hebrew is often superior to the Hebrew originals of Menaḥem and the writers involved in the ensuing controversy around him. That he had to pay a price for this felicity of expression and often admittedly reproduced the author's ideas a little too freely was of minor concern to Ibn Chiquitilla, since he did not even hesitate to amplify the translation by numerous observations of his own, which unwary readers often confused with Ḥayyuj's views.[55]

Nor was Ibn Chiquitilla an uncritical follower of the great masters. He himself wrote an independent monograph on the grammatical aspects of the masculine and feminine genders, in which he took up a number of related issues. He pointed out, for example, the exclusively singular use of the names of six metals recorded in the Bible. Even on the vital problem of triliterality, he offered a new "definitive proof" by arguing that, if there had existed biliteral roots, verbs originally composed of two constantly disappearing "weak" letters might, under circumstances, evaporate into thin air. In this argument he made excellent use of his independent study of Scripture, as well as of the teachings of Arab grammarians. On one occasion he went so far as to postulate the existence in Hebrew of seven, rather than the accepted six, forms of transitive verbs. He believed that, as in Arabic, one might construe a sentence in which the verb would have a threefold transitive meaning. But his example, "The Lord taught Israel the right way," merely showed that the verb could govern three words, but not three objects. Ibn Baron, to whom we owe this citation, rightly countered that, by increasing the number of adjectives (for instance, the "good, proper and straight" way), one could multiply the transitive functions of a verb indefinitely.[56]

Although far from deserving the praise showered upon him by Abraham ibn Ezra, who once called him "the greatest of grammarians," Ibn Chiquitilla had not only the merit of opening up the treasures of Spanish Jewish learning to Hebrew-reading Europeans, but also, together with Samuel, Ibn Janaḥ's princely opponent, and other contemporaries, that of maintaining the continuity of independent philological research and preventing Spanish-Jewish scholarship from smugly resting on the laurels of Ḥayyuj and Ibn Janaḥ. Moses' enemy, Ibn Bal'am, too, entered the debate by contributing monographs on homonyms, particles, and denominative verbs (verbs derived from nouns), and by writing a more introductory "Guide for Bible Readers." Here he seems to have refrained from his customary attacks on Ibn Chiquitilla, probably because grammatical views were less dependent on differing theological preconceptions. For the same reason, Ibn Yashush's monograph on inflections seems to have evoked less controversy than his Bible commentaries, but apparently it also attracted less attention.[57]

A remarkable inversion of the use of poetry for the teaching of grammar, rather than the usual utilization of grammatical rules for the composition of verses, is offered by Ibn Gabirol's poem *'Anaq* (The Necklace). In this poem of 400 double verses (only 98 are extant today), the author, then only nineteen years old, undertook to summarize for the benefit of the uninitiated some major grammatical rules. From his own description and a few subsequent quotations we may deduce that in the poem's four sections he described the respective functions of the radical and servile letters (eleven each as in Saadiah, but with a new anagram for each, which may best be translated as "I Solomon the Writer," and "The Spanish race alone is irreproachable") and the usual tripartite division of the parts of speech into nouns, verbs, and "words" of the "third" type (particles). This pedagogic purpose was inspired by his doleful observation of the great neglect into which Hebrew had fallen among his people, "half of whom speak Edomite [Romance languages], and the other half talks in the dark language of the children of Qedar [Arabic]." He hoped thereby to "open up mouths hitherto locked in muteness." [58]

Pedagogic aims of this kind inspired Abraham ibn Ezra to compose a series of grammatical treatises, which in popular acceptance and historical influence far exceeded those of the more original and laborious works of his predecessors. Beginning with his early *Sefer Mo'znayim* (Book of Scale), which he prefaced with an interesting historical introduction reviewing the previous achievements of Hebrew philology, he continued with a treatise in defense of Saadiah against Dunash ben Labraṭ's criticisms, and finally published his main philological works the *Yesod diqduq* (Foundations of Grammar, hitherto unpublished), *Sefer Ṣaḥot* (Book of Clarity) and *Safah berurah* (Pure Language; reference to Zeph. 3:9). The latter two titles indicated his quest for "correct speech." Throughout these works courses the author's intention to communicate especially to his coreligionists north and east of Spain the results of the great philological learning of his Spanish predecessors. At the same time he sought to "purify" the Hebrew style in use everywhere.

Unflinchingly condemning every deviation from the grammar as it had become standardized in the Spanish schools, Ibn Ezra tried to make all students of Bible, rabbinics, philosophy, and science conscious of the rigid requirements for the correctness of their speech and writing. In a characteristic fashion he also liked to supply philosophic, even astrological, rationales for some of his linguistic concepts. Typical of his general approach is the opening statement in his *Yesod,* starting with the praise of the Lord according to a custom long prevalent in Arabic letters.

At the beginning of every thought, at the outset of all speech, let me give praise to Him who teaches man knowledge so that he may think; who "createth the fruit of the lips" so that he may speak correctly; and who gives the being endowed with reason the power to bring forth from his mouth words which resemble bodies, while their meaning resembles souls. Just as the activity of the soul becomes visible only through the body prepared to serve as its abode, and just as the soul receives its strength only in consonance with its body's natural composition, so do meanings achieve reality only through words. Therefore, no matter with how much understanding he listens, he who tries to explain Scripture without penetrating the mysteries of Hebrew grammar gropes along the walls like a blind man and does not know on what he stumbles.

Ibn Ezra objected, in particular, to the assumption that a verse may have ten different meanings or, as Menaḥem had taught, that a word may signify something in one context and the exact opposite in another. For this reason he also stressed, more than any other Bible commentator, the grammatical aspects of each word or phrase commented on by him, often prefacing his exposition of a chapter by a discussion of grammatical problems related to that chapter. He inserted extensive grammatical excursuses also into such semiphilosophic tractates as the one on the divine names (*Sefer ha-Shem*) or the principles of Judaism (*Yesod mora,* or Principles of the Fear of the Lord) and such semimathematical analyses as his *Yesod mispar* (Principles of Numbers).[59]

Ibn Ezra evinced also great concern and understanding for the problems of philological terminology. Going beyond all his predecessors, he compiled lengthy lists of gramatical terms and analyzed their meaning. At the same time he did not hesitate to condemn a particular grammatical or lexicographic interpretation as heretical. He aimed his shafts not only at Karaites who, disregarding tradition, interpreted, for example, the *he* of *ha-yitab* (would it have been well-pleasing? Lev. 10:19) as an article rather than as an interrogation, but also at such Rabbanites as Dunash ben Labraṭ and Ibn Yashush. In his defense of Saadiah against Dunash, bearing the characteristic title *Sefat Yeter* (Overbearing Speech; namely, by Dunash, a reference to Prov. 17:7), he accused Dunash of outright blasphemy because the latter misinterpreted the word *re'ekha* (which Saadiah had translated "how weighty also are *Thy thoughts* unto me, O God!"; Ps. 139:17) to mean "Thy friends and companions." In his wrath over this anthropomorphism, incidentally also shared by Rashi, Ibn Ezra exclaimed: "His [Dunash's] book is worthy to be burned!" He used the same phrase also with respect to ultracritical utterances by Ibn Yashush. All of this sound and fury did not prevent him, however, from frequently accepting Dunash's views, rather than Saadiah's, in his own Bible commentary.[60]

His breadth of vision and wide practical experience prevented Ibn Ezra from overstressing the merely exegetical importance of grammatical studies. While he often reiterated that "we the grammarians always run after Scripture," and pointedly warned students always to follow the biblical accents, for "any interpretation which does not do justice to the accents thou must not accept or listen to it" (*Sefer Mo'znayim,* fol. 4b; aimed at Saadiah), he nevertheless advocated with equal insistence that linguistic rules could also be derived from analogy and through other forms of reasoning. In fact, in his philosophic-ethical treatise, *Yesod mora,* he discoursed at great length on grammatical problems because of their equal importance to letter and verse writers and students of Scripture.

Practical considerations of this kind evidently animated two other Spaniards who settled in Christian lands. Ibn Parḥon, as we recall, was under Ibn Ezra's strong influence when he compiled his readable and stimulating dictionary for the benefit of Jews in his adopted Italian fatherland. Less obvious but quite noticeable also is Ibn Ezra's influence on Joseph ben Isaac Qimḥi, a Spanish settler in Narbonne. Even in this formerly Arab-occupied city the knowledge of the great works of Spanish philology was very limited. As in the north, Frenchmen still consulted Menaḥem ben Saruq's dictionary. For this reason Joseph composed both a new grammatical work in a more popular vein, entitled *Sefer Zikkaron* (Book of Remembrance; reference to Mal. 3:16), and a book in two parts mainly devoted to a critique of Menaḥem's views, which he called *Sefer ha-Galui* (Open Book; reference to Jer. 32:14). In the former he expatiated on his significant discovery of a tenfold division of Hebrew vowels (five long and five short, including the *qamaṣ qaṭan* as an offshoot of the *ḥolem,* rather than of the *qamaṣ gadol*), which greatly simplified the use of Hebrew words and before long won universal acceptance, although it has encountered some serious objections in recent decades from the standpoint of comparative Semitic philology. It speedily replaced the system of seven vowels (or "kings," as the Masorites had designated them because of their controlling role in the formation of words), to which the original Semitic *A, I, O* sounds had long been expanded.

In his second work Joseph had to contend against the enormous popularity of Menaḥem's work buttressed by the great prestige of Rashi and Jacob Tam. He therefore had not only to criticize Menaḥem's own views, but also to enter the ranks against the revered rabbinic master of Rameru by frequently giving preference to Dunash ben Labraṭ's views against the latter's "Decisions," or by voicing opinions at variance with them all. Qimḥi realized, of course, that opposing Jacob Tam in his own country was an act of great daring. Anticipating objections by readers, "Who art thou that criest to the king?" (I Sam. 26:14), he argued that, despite R. Jacob's incontestable authority in talmudic learning, the latter had never made a real effort to penetrate the profundities of Hebrew grammatical literature—in fact had never considered the science of speech a full-fledged discipline. "I, on the contrary, have grown to be sixty years old, working constantly, day and night, in this field." Qimḥi also explained the widespread public prejudice against the scientific character of grammatical studies by the proverb that "he who does not know a craft, despises it." [61]

Joseph Qimḥi found excellent collaborators in his two sons, Moses and David, ranking philologists in their own right. David's fame soon eclipsed that of his father and brother, indeed of almost all his predecessors, and, during the Renaissance, his work served as the fountainhead of most Hebraic studies among the Christians. In his *Mahalakh shebile ha-da'at* (The Course of the Road to Knowledge), the first Hebrew grammar to appear in print, Moses Qimḥi made a definitive contribution to Hebrew grammar by systematically developing the doctrine of the seven paradigms of the Hebrew verb from *qal* to *hitpa'el,* for which Saadiah's discussion of the various forms of *qal* and *hif'il* of the verb *shama'* had laid the foundations. For obvious reasons Moses preferred the use of a verb like *paqad,* which did not have to contend with the presence of the weak consonant, *'ayin.* In a trilogy, *Mikhlol* (Perfection; a Hebrew grammar), *Sefer ha-Shorashim* (Book of Roots;

a lexicon), and *'Et ha-sofer* (The Scribe's Pen; on the Masorah), David summarized the results of the preceding two centuries of philological research for the benefit of scholars and the general public alike. Although to our taste not always systematic, often both verbose and repetitious, the former two works speedily gained widespread acceptance. In his modesty, David disclaimed all originality and called himself but "a gleaner after the reapers." However, it took much ingenuity and independence of judgment for any author to find his way through the perplexing maze of sharply conflicting opinions advanced by the earlier scholars and to make decisions in innumerable minutiae which would not be wholly inconsistent in themselves. These works thus mark a worthy conclusion to the most creative epoch in the history of Hebrew philology.[62]

The missionary zeal with which Ibn Ezra, Ibn Parḥon, and the Qimḥis embarked upon the propagation in Christian lands of the new grammatical rules and usages established in Spain is understandable only because of their conscious or instinctive feeling that the future of Jewish learning lay now in the Jewish communities of the former Frankish Empire and Italy. This expectation was clearly voiced in those very years by the great sage of Fusṭaṭ in his famous correspondence with the scholars of Lunel. Although frequently repeating the pious cliché that one could not properly understand the Bible without a clear comprehension of the laws of Hebrew grammar, their interest evidently went much further. They wished to purify the Hebrew style generally used in Christian lands from what they considered barbarous accretions and to enrich it by the new vocabulary and grammatical forms developed by the great Spanish littérateurs.

Not unexpectedly, they encountered considerable resistance. Their new approach certainly failed to satisfy those conservatives who wished to maintain philology in its former purely ancillary position to biblical exegesis. Doubtless typical of such reactionary trends was the protest voiced by the author of an anonymous thirteenth-century grammatical work published by Poznanski. This writer, possibly though not likely a resident of Byzantium, fulminated against the use of any words and forms unrecorded in Scripture:

The person [he declared] who ventures highhandedly to invent from his own mind [new forms] and says, "I may do so even though I have not found [them] in the Bible," breaks the commandment of "Thou shalt not add thereto, nor diminish from it" [Deut. 13:1]. For we are not entitled to use any language other than that spoken by the prophets and early sages. If one alters their language and uses a speech of his own "all that hear will laugh" at him [Gen. 21:6]. The poets of our generation are mistaken in this matter, as when they use in their poems words like *yiqru* or *idru* [in the *pi'el* form, unrecorded in the Bible]. We need not expatiate on this matter, for the error is widespread and the language has been ruined.

Ultimately, however, the needs of northern writers, aided and abetted by the popularity of the Hebrew-writing grammarians from Ibn Ezra to David Qimḥi, caused the new grammar to prevail over the old in the Franco-German and Italian schools as well.[63]

HISTORICAL SHORTCOMINGS

Ironically, these fulminations of the Ashkenazi author were written at the very end of a period of greatest revival of the Hebrew language and of the "golden age" of the postbiblical Hebrew literature. The immortal lyrics of Ibn Gabirol, Halevi, or Moses ibn Ezra had been made possible precisely because these great poets, and a host of lesser ones, had been constantly enriching their linguistic heritage by new words and forms not found in the Bible. In their persistent quest for self-expression on an endless variety of religious and secular subjects they were greatly helped by the creative work of the great philologists of the age, who supplied rationales and refined the instrumentalities of such linguistic expansion.

Of course, these poets and philologists were not altogether conscious of their revolutionary role. They viewed themselves rather as mere restorers of the ancient Hebrew language, of which only very small fragments had survived the ravages of time. In their historic naïveté they were prepared, with Abraham ibn Ezra, to assert that at the dawn of history "the holy language was the richest of all the languages spoken by the nations, because it was prior to them all." They believed that the Hebrew language had sprung ready-fashioned from the hands of the Creator in the days of Adam, and that the first man knew it all as well as, or better than, any of his successors among the Hebrew prophets or psalmists. With their general "devolutionary" view of the world, they could see only constant deterioration in the linguistic as in all other areas of history, and thought it incumbent upon themselves to recapture some of that ancient glory.[64]

We may understand, therefore, their ambivalent attitude toward the language of Mishnah and Talmud. Our Byzantine author was not alone in postulating the permissibility of borrowings from the language of "the early sages," although theirs, too, evidently was an obvious "addition" to the biblical speech and as such should have been equally outlawed. Even the majority of Karaites, despite their general rejection of the Oral Law and their occasional animadversions on the "shameful" use by the Rabbanites of the "language of the Assyrians and Aramaeans" (Nissi ben Nuḥ), made good use, as we recall, of the linguistic materials accumulated in the rabbinic literature.

Nevertheless, most scholars drew a sharp distinction between the "language of the sages" and the "language of Scripture." This was no longer, as it had been in talmudic times when it first appeared, a mere empirical observation of existing differences, but was now elevated into a major linguistic criterion. In fact, from Ibn Quraish on the rabbinic dialect was treated as an independent language almost on a par with Aramaic and Arabic and, like the latter, viewed merely as a more or less fit source of comparative materials for the language of the Bible. It never occurred to these penetrating minds to consider mishnaic Hebrew as a newly developed form of the same language, and to inquire about the individual stages which had led up to that development. Of course, to assume that the biblical language itself had undergone some major changes in the course of its historic evolution would have sounded like outright heresy even to most of these rationalist grammarians. Ibn Ezra was reluctant to admit that the square characters had been introduced at a later date. He explained their designation, *ashshurit,* as referring not to the script being of Assyrian origin, but rather to its being even and correct. Rather inconsistently, however, he rejected the explanation by some exegetes of the term *Ashshurim* (Gen. 25:3) as relating not to a proper name but to men familiar with roads. In short, there was not even a remote adumbration of an historical grammar of the Hebrew language. This discipline, which even in our overwhelmingly history-conscious age still is in the early stages of development, was not as much as thought of in that era of greatest flowering of Hebrew philology.[65]

Perfectly understandable in the mental climate of the age, this historical unawareness also had serious practical implications. When Saadiah prepared his first manual for the use of aspiring Hebrew poets, he did not hesitate to draw some of his illustrative materials from the largely posttalmudic *piyyuṭim*. Historically uninformed as he often was, he considered not only Yose ben Yose, but also Yannai, Eleazar ha-Qalir, and the less well-known Joshua and Phineas as "ancient poets," more or less contemporary with the talmudic rabbis (Harkavy, *Zikhron,* V, 50 f., 105 ff.). He was even prepared to quote more recent poets, provided he approved of their use of the Hebrew language. Linguistically always an empiricist, he took his examples indiscriminately from any Hebrew source down to his own age, without realizing that the underlying grammatical rules differed from, and at times even controverted, one another.

As time went on, however, it dawned upon the grammarians that the use of language by the *payyeṭanim* was not quite reconcilable with the grammatical laws they had themselves evolved from their biblical studies. The more systematic Hebrew philology became from Ḥayyuj on, the more evident became the disparity between the biblical and the *payyeṭanic* grammar. But, rather than acknowledge the difference in time and the different evolutionary stages of the Hebrew language, the twelfth-century philologists simply treated the *payyeṭanic* "deviations" as illegitimate departures from the established patterns of the biblical language. Moses and Abraham ibn Ezra were the most outspoken and the most influential among these purists. Moses ibn Ezra, himself equally distinguished as practitioner and theorist of the Hebrew poetic arts, wrote:

> You may use what is found in Scripture [of words and linguistic forms], but what is not found there you must not employ in your poems by way of analogy. The way the [biblical] language goes you go, where it rests, you rest. You must imitate it, not create anything new; follow

it, not run ahead of it. As one of the wise men has said: "Thou shalt walk with the mass, for a wolf will seize the sheep straying by itself." This simile applies also to religious and worldly matters. There is another adage: "The public's dirty waters are better than the clean waters of an individual." Indeed, one of the most incontestable proofs [for truth] is the general agreement of the people, or of their majority together with their sages.

So our poet argued in favor of "common consent" (*idjma'*), against individual analogy (*qiyas*), and thus indirectly combated the fundamental method of linguistic evolution defended in Arabic philology by the school of Baṣra. At the same time he also rejected the Kufic school's latitude in using linguistic materials other than those sanctioned by the Qur'an and pre-Islamic Arabic poetry. In Hebrew letters this meant primarily the rejection of the *payyeṭanic* language with its underground survivals of the ancient Palestinian popular idiom. By thus repudiating both the anomalistic and the analogistic approaches, Moses ibn Ezra advocated an unheard-of crystallization of language, to which no creative poet, including himself, could ever fully adhere. His kinsman, Abraham, likewise declared that "in the hands of R. Eliezer [ha-Qalir] the language became like a wide-open unwalled city, for he turned masculine into feminine forms and vice versa." [66]

True, neither poet could entirely refrain from using many long accepted poetic and linguistic patterns developed by these predecessors. Nevertheless, under the impact of their insistent denunciations, generations of Hebrew grammarians and poets derided the Hebrew of Qalir and his associates as a degradation of the Hebrew language, from the emulation of which any self-respecting Hebrew writer must absolutely steer clear. Puristic preconceptions may also have colored Yehudah al-Ḥarizi's censure of the lack of Hebrew knowledge of the eastern synagogue readers. Even in the thirteenth century these *ḥazzanim* in the Near East doubtless pursued their old calling of not only reciting the accepted prayers with traditional or newly invented tunes, but also of enriching the services by liturgical compositions of their own. Probably these new poems, written in the long-dominant *payyeṭanic* style, greatly aroused the purist in Al-Ḥarizi and elicited his irate observations. Such anti-*payyeṭanic* prejudices, further nurtured by reformist trends in the Jewish liturgy of the nineteenth century, persevered down to our own age. Only in recent years has there emerged a new understanding for the autonomous legitimacy of the Hebrew used by the writers of the early posttalmudic period.[67]

CONTINUED DEFIANCE

Historical unawareness of this kind, here and in the area of biblical criticism, seemed aggravated by the people's apparent loss of all interest in recapturing their ancient and more recent past. The people of history appeared to have forgotten its own history. Moreover, the forces of nature, now represented by the overwhelmingly assimilatory trends in Muslin society, reasserted themselves with renewed vigor. The new civilization, emerging from a synthesis of all previous Near Eastern cultures, had absorbed so many elements from Judaism that transition from the one to the other community seemed but a minor step. The drive toward "normalcy," which gradually leveled most ancient differences, also exerted great, almost irresistible pressures. This desire was spearheaded by the Arabic language, which in its contact with the world languages of Aramaic, Hebrew, Greek, and Persian and through the absorption of some of their most gifted exponents (not by accident did Baṣra, Kufa, and later Baghdad, all outside the original Arab habitat, become the main seats of Arab philology) had developed into a refined instrument for the expression of thoughts and emotions from the most vulgar to the most sublime. No wonder that the new Arab world culture penetrated even the innermost precincts of Jewish law and religion.

Yet Judaism had by that time become such a well-rounded and well-rooted entity that, rather than surrender its identity to the new amalgam of races and cultures, it emerged from this tempting experience with new and deepened self-realization. It absorbed a great deal from its neighbors, just as it furnished them a great deal in return, but it incorporated all such borrowings into its own millennial tradition and reinterpreted them, even twisted them, into something new and peculiar to itself. When it accepted the Arabic speech and wrote its literature in Arabic, it permeated them so deeply with its Hebraic spirit that only the continuity of sojourn in an Arabic-speaking environment prevented this blend from becoming an independent new language and literature. Judeo-Arabic, as spoken by the masses and even as written by some of the most educated Jews, was distinguishable enough from both the local dialects and the classical Arabic. As a matter of supererogation, many authors wrote their works in the Hebrew alphabet and buttressed their views by quotations from Bible and Talmud without bothering to translate them.

All Jews were convinced, moreover, that their Hebrew language was older than and essentially superior to, all other languages. Arabic, if not altogether a corruption, was but a derivation from the divinely ordained speech of Adam and Eve, whose Hebrew had come into the world in its fullest richness and flawless perfection. Artificial as this historical reconstruction evidently was, it helped furnish a rationale for the rebirth of the Hebrew language after the centuries of its slumber under the veneer of the peculiar blend of Hebrew and Aramaic in the dialect of the Talmud. It also stimulated Jews in their pioneering efforts to compare their biblical Hebrew with its Arabic and Aramaic and even more remote "derivatives," and thus to lay foundations for the science of comparative linguistics. Most of all, it helped the Jewish people to view its own destiny in the broad historic perspectives of world history. For this reason Jewish intellectual leaders regarded every minutia of the Hebrew language as a sacred relic from that earliest, "golden" age of mankind. Typical of prevailing opinion was a thirteenth-century author's extreme postulate of remote antiquity even for the Hebrew vowels. "It is true," he contended, "that punctuation was given on Sinai, but it was forgotten until Ezra came and made it public. . . . It could not be recorded in writing, because legally it had to be treated on a par with the Oral Law" (cited by John W. Nutt in his edition of Ḥayyuj's *Two Treatises,* p. xii). Did not even hypercritical Ibn Ezra insist that the Bible could properly be understood only when read in the light of the masoretic vowels and accents?

History-mindedness of this type was not backward-looking, of course. Perhaps more than in any other generation before the Emancipation era the Jewish literature during the Renaissance of Islam was concerned with all aspects of contemporary life—ethical, legal, ritualistic, even private. At the same time it never ceased to look forward, especially to the ultimate end of days. We have seen how deeply permeated with the messianic ideal was the thinking of medieval Jewry, whether under Christendom or under Islam. This combination of biblical-talmudic traditionalism with deep concerns for the ever changing contemporary trends in the Jewish position in the world and undaunted faith in the ultimate outcome of these historic struggles was, indeed, also the keynote of the immortal Jewish poetry and philosophy of the period.

XXXI

WORSHIP: UNITY AMIDST DIVERSITY

Revival of Hebrew and biblical research deeply affected the synagogue ritual. "No religion in the world," rightly observes Frederick C. Grant, "can be thoroughly understood if its normal daily worship of God is left out of account: for here is where the real pulse-beat of every genuine religion is to be felt" (*ZAW*, LXV, 73). This is doubly true of the Judaism of the post-talmudic period, when, perhaps ironically, the synagogue was constantly gaining in importance while the number and status of the Jewish people declined. An autochthonous growth of the Diaspora community, the synagogue had long been overshadowed by the Temple, not only while the latter existed, but also while there was still a spark of reasonable hope for its early restoration. Merely tolerated by the Temple hierarchy, it was allowed to grow anarchically and largely without regulation by the central authorities before 70 C.E. and, to some extent, even throughout the tannaitic age. The third-century Amoraim, especially R. Johanan and Simon ben Laqish in Palestine and Abba Arikha in Babylonia, tried to strengthen it and to lend it greater dignity by fostering synagogue attendance and composing new prayers for its services. But even they did not hesitate to stress the academy above the house of worship. With the decline of the central academies in the sixth and seventh centuries, however, the synagogue emerged as the mainstay of Jewish life. The diminution of Jewish population, too, combined with a continued enlargement of the area of dispersion, resulted in the thinning out of the Jewish communities, most of which were now too small to maintain more than one major institution. All public life began clustering around the local house of worship, which, as a rule, also accommodated the school, the charities, and the court of justice.

Developments in the outside world added force to the new

appreciation of synagogue worship. No longer were the Jewish communities under Byzantine and, later, under Arab domination surrounded by pagan temples offering sacrifices which dolefully reminded them of the lost glories of their own sacrificial system. On the contrary, stimulated by the general acceptance in the Christian and Muslim worlds of corporate worship, along precisely those lines pioneered by the synagogue, prayerful assemblies now became the very core of Jewish public life. We no longer hear of distinguished rabbis and leaders abstaining from synagogue attendance and preferring private devotions in the "four ells" of their studies—a fairly common phenomenon in the talmudic age. To the masses of uneducated and communally rather inactive Jews, daily participation in public worship was the main expression of their communal allegiance. Here they also found their opportunity for cooperation with fellow members in matters of general concern, since the synagogue, as in its emulation the mosque, continued to serve as the "house of the people" in areas transcending the narrow confines of "religion." Under these circumstances the existing anarchical diversity of rituals from community to community, or even from congregation to congregation in the same locality, might have undermined the entire, basically unitarian, structure of Jewish group life.

Perhaps even more, therefore, than in other spheres of Jewish intellectual endeavor, the saboraic and early geonic periods (500–800 C.E.) were marked by efforts to assemble and solidify the accumulated liturgical treasures. They were followed by a period of memorable literary creativity, reaching its apogee in the sacred poetry of the Spanish immortals. However, neither was the earlier period devoid of noteworthy creative achievements in the specific forms of liturgical poetry, known as the *piyyuṭ,* nor was the work of consolidation completed before 800 C.E. In fact, only the subsequent four centuries witnessed the compilation of the great Jewish liturgical classics, in the form of both prayer books and liturgical codes written by, or attributed to, Amram, Saadiah, Rashi, Simḥah of Vitry, and Maimonides.

LITURGICAL CONSOLIDATION

Heretical trends, so powerful in the early Muslim period, sharply underscored the menace of liturgical disunity. Most sectarian movements sooner or later found their counterparts in important ceremonial deviations, if they did not altogether originate from ritualistic controversies. It was not only the larger Samaritan and Karaite sects which developed early liturgies of their own; the various splinter groups also, including those belonging to the "lunatic fringe," had prayers, even orders of prayers, peculiar to themselves. Unfortunately, no texts of the latter are extant. We possess a considerable body of Samaritan liturgy, in part going back to ancient times, especially to the fourth-century poet Marqa. The Karaites, too, beginning with 'Anan himself, left behind a mass of prayers and liturgical regulations ultimately reflected in a more or less standardized prayer book, but the services held by the lesser sectarians are nowhere recorded. At best we know that Abu 'Isa al-Isfahani instituted seven daily services, outdoing therein the orthodox Jews and Muslims. But we are utterly uninformed about the form and content of these ritualistic performances, or whether they were designed primarily for public or for private devotion.[1]

Some of the new religious reformers undoubtedly represented borderline cases between outright heresy and a somewhat irregular type of piety. Their variations of old and introduction of new liturgical pieces reflected their feeling of closeness to the Creator and his angelic entourage. Such informality may have sounded blasphemous to some "enlightened" leaders, but it appealed, through inwardness and picturesqueness, to the masses and ultimately secured the sanction of the scholars as well. This was particularly true, as we shall see, in the case of prayers imbued with the mysteries of the contemporary "secret lore."

Obviously, the leaders' ingenuity was often severely taxed in distinguishing between heretical and permissible innovations. Prompted by the necessity of erecting anti-heretical ramparts, the Babylonian academies betrayed an ever growing intolerance toward ritualistic diversity. Reflecting their stiffened attitude,

Amram Gaon declared sweepingly: "We must not deviate in anything from what the sages had said in the Talmud [about either holiday or Sabbath prayers]. . . . When we come to a place where the reader recites a prayer at variance with the mold formed by the sages, we depose him." Needless to say, the gaon had the Babylonian Talmud alone in mind. Even the recognition of Palestine's ritualistic autonomy, which characterized the outlook of the Amoraim in both lands, now gave way to an attempt to impose Babylonian patterns on the communities of the Holy Land. Pirqoi ben Baboi, a native Palestinian turned pan-Babylonian, attacked with particular relish some of Palestine's liturgical "deviations," for which he offered his stereotype explanation of their origin from real or alleged anti-Jewish persecutions. Even Naṭronai bar Hilai Gaon, generally far more responsible and cautious, once sharply denounced a Palestinian law: "They err and have gone astray." Ultimately, Babylonian immigrants into Palestine herself began battling the established modes of worship. After bitter communal strife, some Babylonian settlers in Jerusalem and other communities succeeded in forcing the local congregations to recite daily the ancient *qedushah* (sanctification of the divine name, similar in tone to its Christian derivative, the *Sanctus*), whereas in other communities which did not submit to Babylonian pressure that prayer continued to be recited only on the Sabbath and holidays.[2]

Forcible unification of this kind, however, though buttressed by interterritorial Jewish migrations, growing ease of communications, and, for a time, effective central controls, also encountered some formidable, indeed insurmountable obstacles. Staunch adherence to accepted ceremonies is one of the most widespread and deepest manifestations of religious conservatism. That is why, for example, the liturgy of St. Basil the Great in the Greek Orthodox Church, and that of St. James in the Syrian Church, could remain so substantially unaltered for fifteen centuries. Similarly, some of the basic Jewish prayers (German scholars like to call them *Stammgebete*) indubitably go back to remote antiquity, in part even to the pre-Maccabean age. Since, next to Scriptural readings, prayers always characterized services in the synagogue, R. Johanan's tradition that "the Men of the Great Synagogue introduced for Israel benedictions and prayers, formulas of sanctification and separation [between holy and profane; *habdalot*]" (Berakhot 33a), is not so unhistorical as it appears. For example, the first three and the last three benedictions of the silent prayer *'Amidah,* which are common to all Jewish services throughout the year, may well have been recited in substantially the same form by all Jewish communities for more than two thousand years.

So convinced were the Jews of the immemorial antiquity of the first three benedictions (often styled, because of their content, the "Fathers," divine "Power," and "Holiness") that they attributed their composition to Abraham, Isaac, and Jacob. This view, possibly intimated already by Sirach, is quietly taken for granted by the authors of *Pirqe de-R. Eliezer* and of several *qerobot* (liturgical poems woven around these benedictions). A geonic tradition had it that as early as the First Commonwealth Jews had recited daily these three as well as two other benedictions of the *'Amidah,* the Ten Commandments, *Shema'* and its adjoining prayer, *Emet veyaṣib* (True and Firm). Such staunch adherence must also have characterized the regional rites. We recall how the ancient Palestinian sages had already been forced to compromise with respect to certain ritualistic customs developed in the city of Jericho. In the course of time, and particularly during the period of weakened central controls from the fifth to the eighth centuries, these regional diversities must have increased in both number and intensity. They now became a major stumbling block to all unifying efforts.[3]

Linguistic difficulties were no less serious. Realizing from the outset that Hebrew prayers alone could not satisfy the spiritual cravings of the Aramaic and Greek-speaking majority of world Jewry, indeed of the very populace inhabiting the Palestino-Babylonian heartland of Jewish life, the ancient sages permitted the recitation of prayers in any language. To be sure, in their effort to stem neglect of Hebrew, R. Johanan and R. Judah warned worshipers not to employ Aramaic in their prayers for divine intervention in the satisfaction of their wants, because the ministering angels would not understand them. But these warnings often went unheeded. Sherira Gaon, citing many talmudic illustrations in theory and practice, asserted that "since the ancients paid no attention to them, neither do we." In this respect some segments of Palestinian Jewry need not have differed greatly from the Samaritan sectarians, whose ancient liturgy is almost exclusively Aramaic. At times, the Jewish teachers themselves composed Aramaic prayers, such as the well-known prayer for mourners, the *Qaddish,* which had evident affinities with the Lord's Prayer among the early Christians. Even much later (in the fourteenth century?) a Yemenite author produced a regular *targum* of the *'Amidah.* According to the uncontroverted inquiry of 992 C.E., which gave rise to Sherira's aforementioned ruling, "all the prayers of petition and request which came to our ancestors blessed be their memory, from the holy academy, are in the Aramaic language. . . . Also most benedictions, composed by the geonim for both private and public use, are written in that language." Even the newcomer, Saadiah, adopted the Babylonian custom of counting the days and weeks between Passover and the Festival of Weeks (the so-called *Sefirah* season) in Aramaic—a custom which, because of his authority, spread also to Yemen. In addition to these more sophisticated liturgical pieces, sophisticated in content as well as through the use of the more refined literary style developed in the academies, there must have been in circulation many compositions in local dialects, enjoying at least a temporary vogue, local or regional.[4]

Gradual replacement of Aramaic by Arabic in the speech of the masses, combined with the revival of Hebrew linguistic studies among the intelligentsia, now complicated the task of unifiers. Reluctant consistently to apply the old principle and to permit any widespread liturgical use of Arabic, the intellectual leaders encouraged the communities to enrich their rituals by selections from the constantly growing treasury of Hebrew sacred poetry, although, as we shall see, such encouragement ran counter to their deep-seated suspicions of the existing *piyyuṭim.* Because of this ambivalence, communities were allowed much leeway in making their own selections. On the other hand, the Hebrew renaissance, with its classicist and puristic predilections, led to occasional questionings, even abandonment, of long accepted liturgical formulas. Some local readers hesitated to use the word *qalles* in the *Qaddish,* because, while reflecting the talmudic connotation of praise, it had in biblical Hebrew the opposite meaning of blame. Hai Gaon had to intervene and point out, on the basis of Arabic examples, that the meaning of a word is often determined only by its context. Finally, rabbinic opinion veered away entirely from the early latitudinarian attitude, still adhered to by Aḥai of Shabḥa, Simon Qayyara, and even Amram Gaon, and insisted that one must recite both the *Shema'* and the *'Amidah* in Hebrew, even if one does not understand their meaning. At the same time, the Arabic-Hebrew linguistic revolution undoubtedly weakened the resistance of local liturgical traditionalists and made the work of unification doubly imperative.[5]

The linguistic vicissitudes of the Christian churches in both East and West must also have served as a warning to those Jewish leaders who had even remote familiarity with what was happening in neighboring Christian quarters. At first the Church followed Judaism in its permission for worshipers to use "any language one understands." John Chrysostom, though a native of Antioch, may have known no Syriac at all; yet, he did not dream of forbidding the use of that language by neighboring farmers. Ultimately, by a curious historical revenge, Syriac liturgical patterns conquered the very citadel of Greek worship, the Byzantine Church. On principle, the Eastern Churches maintained linguistic freedom in the older countries, and they even succeeded in introducing novel liturgies into such newly converted areas as eastern Europe. Yet, in time, these native liturgies, which because of their inherent conservatism could not participate in the general linguistic evolution, became as meaningless to the masses as if they were couched in some foreign dialect. To the majority of Arabic-speaking Syriac and Egyptian Christians, as well as to the Slavs and even the Greeks, their ecclesiastical jargons were no more comprehensible than was, for example, the consistently Latin liturgy of western Christianity. However little cognizance Jewish leadership overtly took of such outside developments, it could not fail to redouble its efforts to establish a single universal Hebrew liturgy, with whatever concessions could safely be made to local Hebrew variations. Although some of the newer *piyyuṭim* may likewise have become progressively incomprehensible to ordinary worshipers, the Hebrew literary language maintained its living continuity and, hence also, its general intelligibility to the large and influential segment of well-educated men.

Economic transformations and growing literacy likewise served as a double-edged sword, both stimulating and complicating the task of consolidation. Increasing urbanization led to the formation of a fairly large leisure class, and even many merchants and artisans were now able to devote proportionately more time to the daily services. As a consequence, the latter grew longer and longer, meeting a growingly powerful trend toward a combination of conservative adherence to traditional orders of prayer with numerous, more recent innovations. Gone were the restraints of the ancient rabbis who, to relieve the tired and hungry farmers returning from a hard day's work, shortened the evening services by declaring the recitation of the evening *'Amidah* as merely permissive and substituting for it a prayer (*Barukh Adonai le-'olam amen ve-amen;* Blessed be the Lord forever more, amen and amen) originally containing but eighteen verses, rather than benedictions. Now both prayers became obligatory.[6]

Similarly, a prayer recited by the relatively few members who after the completion of the morning services could indulge in study was amplified by a skillful selection of biblical verses at the beginning and the end, and ultimately made part of the standard liturgy for all (the prayer beginning *U-ba le-Ṣiyyon Goel;* And a Redeemer Shall Come to Zion). The morning services were further expanded by the addition of lengthy selections from both the Psalms and the Talmud. Psalms had always been an integral part of Jewish worship, but in the talmudic age their daily recitation was left entirely to the discretion of the individual worshiper. While R. Jose prayed that he be given the opportunity of completing the so-called Egyptian *Hallel* (Ps. 113–18) every day, a later sage actually declared that "he who recites *Hallel* every day is a blasphemer." The late Amora R. Abina encouraged only the daily recitation of a single psalm (145), distinguished, as was later explained in Amram's prayer book, by its alphabetical arrangement and its reference (in verse 16) to God's furnishing sustenance to all living beings. Even Saadiah still argued against the wholesale use of chapters from Scripture, though of course not of biblical phrases, or detached verses, the very mainstay of Jewish liturgy.

His reasoning, however, had already lost sight of the initial social motive. "Every chapter in the Bible," the gaon contended on purely formal grounds, "is mixed with commandments and prohibitions, promises and warnings, and reason rebels against the inclusion of such matters in prayer." That is why his own prayer book began directly with the ancient prayers preceding the *Shema'* in private devotions and added but two brief benedictions, a selection of pertinent biblical phrases, and Psalms 145 and 147–50 for volunteers.[7]

Saadiah was sharply attacked for these views by the Karaites Qirqisani and Salmon ben Yeruḥim for, ever since 'Anan, these sectarians had assigned to the psalms and other biblical chapters the lion's share in their liturgy. Qirqisani pointed out that, according to their own ritual (not recorded by either Amram or Saadiah), the very Rabbanites opened their prayers with a formula, "He who chose His servant David, and graciously accepted the sacred hymns." In practice, however, the majority of Rabbanites had likewise by that time incorporated a number of stated psalms (the so-called *pesuqe de-zimra*) in their daily liturgy. This is attested by Saadiah's predecessor, Amram, whose introductory announcement that his work was "in accordance with the tradition which is in our possession, in conformity with the institution of the Tannaim and the Amoraim," clearly betrayed his anti-Karaite bias.[8]

Out of opposition to the Karaite overemphasis, however, the later geonim displayed a curious hostility to any worshiper reciting these psalmodic selections after the *'Amidah*. Generally speaking, the prayers said after the completion of these more formal services still were far from standardized. In fact, worshipers were encouraged to add any number of prayers of petition (*taḥanunim*) of their own. Amram, Saadiah, and Maimonides merely offered suggestions as to what texts might be used for such devotions, since many individuals, even congregations, doubtless were at a loss in formulating appropriate petitions. There certainly seemed to be no reason for any Jew to refrain from using psalms in this or any other connection. Understandably, therefore, neither the questioners of R. Yehudai Gaon, nor the gaon himself, saw any objection to anyone reciting the *pesuqe de-zimra* after the services rather than at their beginning. Yehudai merely decided that in such a case no preliminary blessing be required. But, not long thereafter, the controversy with the Karaite schismatics began assuming serious proportions. Hence the geonim Moses and Naṭronai decided that a worshiper arriving late at the synagogue ought to shorten these selections from the psalms, or even eliminate them entirely, so as to catch up with the congregational recitation of *Shema'* and *'Amidah*. In no case must he recite the psalms after the silent prayer. Naṭronai's explanation that "there is disrespect in reciting [God's] praise after the prayer," is evidently forced. Very likely the unspoken motivation of these geonic leaders was to emphasize the essential superiority of the post-biblical *'Amidah* as the liturgical *pièce de resistance*. They may also have wished to prevent those Karaites who, living in smaller communities, were forced to attend Rabbanite services from perfunctory participation in the other parts of the ritual and concentration of their own worship on the generally accepted psalms. That is perhaps also why neither Amram nor Saadiah included any psalms in their suggestions for the concluding recitations, whereas the Spanish and Franco-German communities, unaware of the original schismatic threat, glibly inserted at least one psalm each (6 or 25) into this part of the service, now become more and more standardized for congregational rather than private devotions.[9]

Extremists went further. In a case referred to an unnamed gaon, an overzealous elder tried to stop members of his congregation who were wont to arrive at the synagogue before the sunrise of Sabbaths and holidays and recite their psalms until the beginning of services. He endeavored to force these pious Jews to spend their waiting time on the study of Mishnah, Talmud, or halakhic writings, despite the fact that some of them were not learned enough to engage in such studies (*Teshubot ha-geonim*, ed. by Assaf, 1942, pp. 107 f.). Incidentally, however, this and several related inquiries show that the immortal lyrics of the book of Psalms continued irresistibly to attract pious souls, notwithstanding the cloud cast on their recitation by the sectarian discord.

Precisely this opposition to Karaism may also have inspired the inclusion of talmudic passages relating to talmudic methodology, the kindling of Sabbath lights, and the sacrificial services at the Temple. Only the latter could be rationalized as reflections of the basic idea that prayers served as a substitute for sacrifices. Amram and his school, however, explained all these talmudic accretions as a mere compliance with the talmudic injunction that every Jew should divide his time equally between the study of the Bible, Mishnah, and Talmud. At the same time, the particular selections and their inclusion among the obligatory prayers clearly reflected the antisectarian animus. In any case, such vast extension—indeed more than doubling in size—of the required recitations was possible only because so many more Jews could now afford to spend almost half an hour in private prayer, or an hour in synagogue attendance, each morning before embarking on their daily chores. Ultimately, despite protests by Hai Gaon and others, congregational services, particularly during the High Holidays season, expanded to such an extent that the *Shema'* was often recited outside the permissible limit of three hours after sunrise.[10]

On the other hand, the geonim refused to budge from the talmudic practice of reciting on Saturdays alone the full weekly lessons from the Pentateuch. Originally prompted by considerations for the hard-presssed workingman and farmer, the ancient sages had restricted such weekday recitation to a small initial section, and to Mondays and Thursdays only. This practice was consistently maintained also on Purim, Ḥanukkah, and fastdays—workdays all—as well as on Sabbath afternoons. More significantly, Saadiah voiced a long-accepted opinion when he forbade on all these days the calling of more than three men (four men on new moons and the half holidays of Passover and the Feast of Tabernacles) to the Torah, whereas on all other holidays and Sabbaths requiring summons to five or more members the congregations enjoyed full discretion in adding as many more as they wished. On all these festive days, of course, abstention from work was obligatory, hence congregations could freely extend the duration of their services. If 'Anan suddenly introduced two daily recitations of Numbers 1–8 from the Scroll of Law, he was guided therein not only by his strict formalism and his general disregard of economic interests, but also by the class outlook of the urban intelligentsia to which he primarily appealed.[11]

With utter abandon, 'Anan demanded additional scriptural readings not only on Sabbaths and holidays, but also on fast days. We recall that these included a Ramadan-like stretch of seventy days from Nisan 13 to Sivan 23. On each of these days the congregation had to listen to the reading of pertinent passages from the Pentateuch and of a section from the scroll of Esther (3:8–4:17). It stands to reason, although it is not specifically mentioned in the extant fragments, that 'Anan also required two recitations each during New Moon services falling on weekdays, just as he insisted upon three readings at Sabbath New Moons. In his complete disregard for tradition, as well as the worshiper's convenience, the heresiarch also insisted that they read such scattered passages from the Pentateuch from the same scroll. He knew that the talmudic sages had already introduced readings from different scrolls so as to enable synagogue officials to prepare the scrolls ahead of time and to spare the congregants the annoyance of waiting until the single scroll was unrolled from one section to another. During the seventy-day fast, for example, the Karaite congregations had to wait until their scrolls were rolled back from Numbers 28 all the way to Exodus 17. Like many other of 'Anan's doctrinaire postulates, this procedure was abandoned by later Karaites, who allowed the daily readings from ordinary Bibles or prayer books (see Hadassi, *Eshkol,* fol. 15bc).

INWARDNESS AND STANDARDIZATION

Rabbanite adoption of intellectually significant, but devotionally totally uninspiring, talmudic excerpts as part of the daily ritual reveals from another angle how much the medieval rabbis were true heirs of the talmudic sages in their general appreciation of the synagogue as an educational as much as a devotional institution. Popular opinion seems to have shared this view. As in all other matters echoing widespread folklore, the medieval Hebrew paraphrast of Josephus stated, "He who prays talks to God, he who studies the Torah is spoken to by God." Saadiah, whether or not he knew Yosephon or the latter's source, expressed a similar idea in one of his beautiful prayers of petition, when he asked the Lord, "Turn my heart to Thy message and Thy counsels," that is, to the study of Torah.[12]

At the same time, the geonim and other jurists realized that prayer differed from most other ceremonial laws by its utter dependence on the worshiper's comprehension of its meaning. Ancient and medieval sages untiringly expatiated on the importance of *kavvanah* (intention), or rather, of the worshiper's complete absorption in the meaning of each prayer. In his philosophic work, Saadiah counted lack of concentration among the behavior patterns which invalidated the ceremonial value of prayers. Citing the psalmist (78:35–37) rather than any talmudic authority, Saadiah failed to consider the grave danger of saddling large masses of conscientious citizens with a guilt complex for every set of prayers recited without due concentration. Apprehensions of this kind doubtless prompted many other sages, ancient and medieval (for instance, R. Ḥananel), to declare sweepingly that "fulfillment of commandments is not contingent on [the performer's] intention." But no one denied that a Jew ought to pay undivided attention to his prayers, since "our main purpose in praying is the soul's yearning to God and its submission to Him." Such a restrained jurist as Maimonides waxed eloquent when he wrote: "Intention consists in freeing oneself completely from all other thoughts and considering oneself as standing before the Lord's presence [*shekhinah*]." All scholars agreed that if a member was silently reciting the *'Amidah* he must not interrupt it in order to join in the communal response to the reader's recitation of the *qedushah*. Nor should he remain silent while the others responded; rather he ought unperturbedly to continue being engrossed in the meaning of his own prayer.[13]

To encourage concentration, the geonim and their successors sanctioned the widespread custom of bowing, even prostrating oneself, before God during certain prayers, and of praying aloud, except for the silent *'Amidah*. Going beyond the example set by R. 'Aqiba, who in the privacy of his home used to pray with such fervor and with so much physical commotion that he usually wound up at an opposite corner, medieval Jews prayed noisily and with frequent disregard of decorum. In the case of the *Shema'*, loud prayer was specifically enjoined in both the Talmud and medieval law. Curiously, Amram as well as Saadiah, insisted that the more customary way of reciting it was in a sitting position, in contrast to the *'Amidah* which, everyone agreed, had to be read standing up. In a characteristic response to an inquiry addressed to him from a Christian country, Maimonides advised against the local observance of having the reader recite the *'Amidah* aloud twice, the first time in order to assist ignorant members. Such repetition could, in his opinion, lead only to annoyance and ensuing unruly behavior of the congregation and the "desecration of the name of the Lord among the Gentiles." [14]

Deep inwardness was easily jeopardized by excessive standardization. Even the most rigid exponents of communal controls could not remain unmindful of R. Simon's ancient injunction, "When thou prayest make not thy prayer into a fixed form." They also remembered the significant debate between R. Gamaliel, R. Joshua, R. 'Aqiba, and R. Eliezer, in which the latter, arch-conservative upholder of rooted tradition, opposed altogether the recitation of prescribed prayers. A fairly common opinion among later sages held that the worshiper "shall add something new every day" to the meaning of his accustomed prayers. That is why then and later Jews were encouraged to add any number of private prayers of petition (*taḥanunim*), especially after the completion of the morning *'Amidah.* An early homilist observed that from generation to generation "Israel recites a new poem every hour, just as a well pours out fresh waters every hour." Even at the end of the tenth century, the Spanish poet-wanderer, Joseph ibn Abitur, sang,

Each day I compose a new blessing
  On God's works and feats,
He who renews Creation daily
  With His mighty deeds.[15]

Many such private prayers ultimately found their way into congregational services. The brief petition, *Elohai neṣor* (Oh My God! Guard My Tongue from Evil), first composed by "Mar" bar Rabina in the fifth century, was soon recited by each individual at the conclusion of his silent prayer. The much-embattled *'Alenu le-shabbeaḥ* (It is Our Duty to Praise the Lord of All Things), which combined exaltation of the one God of Israel with a sharp disparagement of unbelieving nations, seems to have been compiled by Rab from liturgical phrases dating from various periods (some undoubtedly even then of immemorial antiquity and hence attributed by medieval rabbis such as Eleazar Roqeaḥ of Worms to Joshua son of Nun) and inserted into the prayers to precede the blowing of the horn on New Year's day. In medieval Europe, howdever, the Jewish leaders (beginning with Eleazar of Worms?) decided to recite it at the end of every service, and adhered to it in defiance of increasingly bitter attacks by Jew-baiters from the fourteenth century on.[16]

Rationalists doubtless heartily disliked some newer prayers which presupposed the intervention of heavenly intermediaries, be they deceased prophets or angels. They certainly had no use for the Jewish *weli* worship, which, in imitation of a widespread Arab custom, was rapidly gaining ground among the masses. But there is no record of any official action against the recitation of such prayers as were read by pilgrims at the alleged tomb of Samuel the Seer: "Let my soul and the souls of thy servants who believe in thy prophecy and come to prostrate themselves on thy grave find favor in thine eyes. Beseech, please, the Lord, thy great and awe-inspiring God, for the remaining remnant" of the Jewish people. Especially the belief that the angelic hosts in Heaven praise the Lord on a par with man, was too deeply rooted to be eradicated even by the most determined rationalist leaders. They could stem certain excesses, as did for instance Naṭronai Gaon, when he learned that some overzealous worshipers insisted on holding the showfringes during the entire recitation of *Shema'*. The gaon condemned these proceedings as sheer ostentation. But neither he nor any of his successors ever seriously attempted completely to sever the nexus which allegedly tied earthly prayers to some such supernatural mediation.[17]

Conversely, human prayers were supposed also to influence the behavior and fate of celestial hosts. An ancient prayer, recited by R. Safra at the conclusion of his morning devotions, was frequently repeated thereafter by pious individuals: "May it be Thy will, O Lord, our God, to establish peace among the family above and the family below, and among the pupils studying Thy Torah, whether they study it for its own sake or for some external reasons; as to those who study it for external reasons, may it be Thy will that they shall study it for its own sake." True, many rabbis, including some mystics, emphasized the superiority of Israel's prayers over those of the divine hosts. The very author of *Hekhalot* (Book of Sanctuaries), an early classic of mystical literature, wrote in the name of R. Ishmael:

When the ministering angels wish to sing praises before the Supreme Being, they first foregather around the throne of glory like mountains of fire and hills of flame. The Holy One, blessed be He, tells them: Remain silent before me, every angel and [heavenly] creature, every wheel [*ofan*] and seraph whom I have created, until I shall first hear and listen to the songs and praises of My son, Israel. It is written: "When the morning stars sang together [Job 38:7]"; that is Israel; "And all the sons of God shouted for joy [*ibid.*]"; that is the family of angels.

For similar reasons a talmudic sage had contended that the angels sing only at night, leaving the day entirely to the earthly devotions of pious Jews. Even the medieval midrash which reversed that order admitted that angels observed silence at night, while Jews could freely indulge in prayers at any time.[18]

And yet the conviction grew that in their prayers the Jews should take increasing cognizance of the heavenly "family." The *Qedushah,* especially, which even in Saadiah's formulation still merely alluded to some such dialogue with the supernatural world, now began, "We will sanctify Thy name in the world even as they sanctify it in the highest heavens." More pronouncedly, according to Amram, the reader, while repeating the *'Amidah,* introduced the Hebrew *Sanctus* by referring to the multitudes above which, together with the gatherings below, give the mystical "crown" to the Lord. But Saadiah himself saw no harm in suggesting that at the conclusion of the *'Amidah* every worshiper should take three steps backward, "just as slaves step backwards when they leave the royal chamber," and then silently bow to the left and to the right "in tribute to the angels, after he had fulfilled his duty to the Lord, as it is written, 'And all the host of heaven standing by Him on His right hand and on His left' [I Kings 22:19]." Another gaon, Ḥanokh, elaborated on an Amora's counsel that men wishing to become wise turn in their prayers in a southerly direction, while those seeking riches pray northward, by relating such orientation to the position of various implements in the ancient Temple. The candelabrum, symbol of wisdom, had been located in the sanctuary's southern end, while the showbreads, symbolic of wealth, had stood in the northern section.[19]

Minor concessions of this kind, however, did not satisfy the craving for the supernatural of the ever more numerous students of secret lore, and this desire is reflected in the *hekhalot* and *merkabah* literatures. We shall see how greatly Ṣufism and other trends in Islamic mysticism now stimulated parallel expressions among the Jewish minority. The so-called "descenders into the Chariot," who often prayed with their heads between their knees and indulged in other gestures conducive to ecstatic self-forgetfulness, laid particular stress upon the *Qedushah,* whose glorification of the mystic "crown" they doubtless helped to formulate. According to one of their writers, whenever God listens to Israel reciting this trishagion (three times "holy") He embraces the image of Jacob and contemplates the speedy redemption of the Jewish people. Many indeed were the liturgical innovations which, stemming from these mystic conventicles, sooner or later were adopted by large segments of the people. At times geonic leadership, yielding to popular pressure, accepted such innovations willingly; on other occasions it yielded only after a hard struggle. The geonim of Sura, for example, condemned the recitation of the *Kol nidre* prayer, with its magic fear of the vows unwittingly broken, as a "foolish custom" (Naṭronai) long after those of Pumbedita had submitted to popular clamor for it. Before long, however, Saadiah (despite his silence on this score in his prayer book) accepted the Pumbedita custom. Doubtless on Saadiah's authority Yemenite Jewry adopted it and continued its recitation in defiance of Maimonides' tacit rejection. No such difference of opinion among the geonim is recorded concerning the *kapparot* ceremony on the eve of the Day of Atonement, which, first mentioned in the ninth century, brought back to the surface of Jewish life long-buried memories of the sacrificial substitution of a condemned animal for the sinner himself. This ceremony, indulged in by some overzealous or overanxious persons on the eve of the New Year as well (some rich people slaughtered deer, sheep, or lambs and distributed the meat among the poor), was reluctantly tolerated by the geonim, although it was still condemned by Ibn Adret and Karo (in the first edition of his *Code*). Evidently, popular persistence could not be denied.[20]

Despite the incursion of such "animistic and demoniac" elements into Jewish liturgy, its predominantly rational tone remained uncontested. The largely uncontrollable infusion of such folkloristic ingredients sufficed, however, to underscore the existing liturgical diversity. Through the partial acceptance or rejection of various groups in Jewry it created another stumbling block to complete unification.[21]

READER'S DISCRETION

The original, fairly brief, and simple services required little professional mediation, since basic prayers were easily learned by heart through constant repetition and each individual was encouraged to formulate additional prayers in his own language. Tertullian's description, "We pray from the heart without a monitor," applied to the second-century synagogue as well as to the church. In time, however, the constant additions to the required liturgy and the growing insistence upon Hebrew prayers made it impossible for many unlearned Jews to memorize them adequately. On the High Holidays, especially, the services became so lengthy and the assembled congregation, often reinforced by arrivals from the neighboring villages, so unfamiliar with the very sequence of prayers that, as we learn from an interesting geonic responsum, the reader had to take time out to instruct the congregation in the general liturgy of the Day of Atonement.[22]

The gradual growth of liturgical formulas through progressive accretions is best illustrated by the development of the confession (*viddui*). Emphasized from time immemorial as a part of the much-stressed repentance of the individual sinner, it was elevated into a major liturgical performance in the high-priest's annual confession in behalf of the whole people at the Temple of Jerusalem. From there it spread to both homes and synagogues. R. Joshua ben Levi promised this-worldly, as well as well as other-worldly, rewards to him who "sacrifices his evil spirit and confesses his sins." However, precisely because they wished to retain the spontaneity of such confessions, the rabbis refrained from introducing obligatory formulas, several of them suggesting different models for individual worshipers. In time, many of these formulas began to be combined in alphabetic order, and they were constantly amplified by additional sins to be confessed. In the present-day Ashkenazic ritual it embraces fifty-four sentences.[23]

Quite early, therefore, more learned or specially trained members played a preponderant role in the congregational services. Although believing, as did later the Quakers, in "the priesthood of all believers," Pharisaic Judaism, as attested by Philo of Alexandria, encouraged better informed members to lead the congregation. As the divine services grew longer in the talmudic period, the "messenger of the people" was given considerable leeway in the selection of new prayers and served as guardian of their correct textual transmission. Before long, this task became so arduous that at least the larger congregations began entrusting it to full-time professionals. The *ḥazzan,* in ancient times primarily a sexton, elementary schoolteacher, and general communal factotum, now became principally the congregational precentor during services. Such an official is casually mentioned in the Palestinian *Sefer ha-Ma'asim,* whose phrasing reflects a long-established institution. True, the old title "messenger of the people" still persisted, and it continued to apply to nonprofessional readers as well. But, characteristically, Naṭronai Gaon had already begun to distinguish between the "messenger" and the ordinary layman who "descended to the pulpit." Without altering the law which recognized the right of any thirteen-year-old to lead in services, Amram Gaon insisted that, except for emergencies, the congregations be led by qualified adults. Other geonim emphasized the need of fully understanding the meaning of prayers, which likewise tended toward professionalization of congregational leadership. At that time, indeed, official "readers" seem to have officiated in most large communities. A century later we even hear of a "chief *ḥazzan*" in Baghdad who served as the officer in charge of all Babylonian *ḥazzanim.*[24]

Lay or professional, the "messenger of the people" read aloud the prescribed prayers as a substitute for members unable to recite them by themselves. This primary function was never completely abandoned, not even after the printed prayer book had reduced the number of such male congregants to a minimum. Probably with this idea in mind some congregations made the reader recite the entire set of a hundred prayers enumerated by Amram at the beginning of his prayer book, including several benedictions over food and drink and after meals, so as to anticipate later occasions during the day when a particular member might be unable to recite them. Of course, the "messenger" himself, as well as many other members, had no occasion to partake of all those meals during the following twenty-four hours. This practice, understandably, evoked the sharp censure of Maimonides, who strictly forbade the recitation of any benediction in anticipation of possible future needs.[25]

Independently some leader was expected to explain to the congregation the meaning of the scriptural lessons. In larger communities, there undoubtedly existed enough scholarly members to alternate as preachers and "messengers." Elucidation through appropriate homilies rested there with revered masters of Jewish lore, especially the heads of leading academies. In the smaller communities, however, such division of labor must often have proved impossible. A congregation which had but one outstanding scholar would naturally entrust to such a "messenger" the double task of leading in prayer and delivering the sermon. The combination of offices, recorded already in the ancient community of Simonias, continued throughout the Middle Ages and modern times, except that now the *ḥazzan,* instead of being primarily the sexton, became first of all a "messenger of the people." The medieval compiler of the Midrash on the Song of Songs doubtless had his own, as well as ancient, times in mind when he described Eleazar, son of R. Simon ben Yoḥai, as "Bible reader, memorizer, poet, and preacher." On his visit to Mosul, Yehudah al-Ḥarizi heard the community boast of its distinguished "cantor-preacher . . . who explains the Prophets with many interpretations, knows precious poems, and sings songs." This factor may indeed have contributed greatly toward the forging of those intimate links between the early medieval liturgical and homiletical creativity which struck so many keen students of both literatures. Nor was this phenomenon limited to Jews. The great ecclesiastical poet of Jewish descent, Romanos, brought with him from his Syrian homeland the "poetic sermon," called *Kontakion*. After settling in the imperial capital (about 500 C.E.) he is said to have composed no less than a thousand *kontakia,* including a famous Christmas hymn and, not surprisingly, a diatribe against the treacherous act of Judas.[26]

It is generally assumed that the liturgical author took over concepts and legends previously developed in the Midrashim and invested them with some poetic imagery. This assumption underestimates, however, the creative spark in the liturgical poet, which often equaled or surpassed that of the homilist. Maimonides was not altogether wrong in speaking interchangeably of "compositions of the singers, preachers, and others who imagine themselves to be able to compose a poem." In his explanation of the origin of the *piyyuṭ* (which he calls *ḥizana*), Samau'al ibn Yaḥya describes the role of the precentor as that of leader in ordinary prayers, but, while reciting these additional poems, "he is accompanied by the public with shouts and songs." This well-informed convert thus unwittingly testifies to both the informality of the new poetry and its origin from the precentors' creative improvisations. Even the Palestinian Targum contained, according to Samuel ibn Nagrela, "many aggadic accretions, inserted by synagogue readers on their own." Certainly, what was said of Ephraem the Syrian, that he had "conceived the great idea of utilizing the scriptural lesson as a basis for a festival sermon in hymnal form, that is in artistic fashion," applied also to the Jewish masters of liturgical poetry. In some cases a preacher's indebtedness to the poet can actually be documented. For example, a lengthy passage in Tobiah ben Eliezer's *Leqaḥ tob* is but a midrashic commentary on an old *qerobah* (probably an Aramaic derivative of the messenger "approaching" the Lord) by Eleazar Qalir. At times, the *proem* introducing the sermon was couched in poetic-liturgical form. The old lamentation for the Ninth of Ab published by Zulay was not, as is usually assumed, derived from existing introductory homilies to the Midrash on the book of Lamentations, but, in part, their fountainhead. Although otherwise known only from such relatively later midrashim as fragments published by Ginzberg and, particularly, the Yemenite *Midrash Haggadol,* there is no reason to doubt the extensive interplay between reader and preacher in the earlier periods as well.[27]

Few sermons began with such outright quotations from liturgical poems, but many more seem to have borrowed from them leading ideas, felicitous phrases, or apt hermeneutic interpretations of scriptural passages. Certainly the prolific mind of a liturgical author, himself often a religiously dedicated person rather than poet by grace divine, would often detect an apparently hidden meaning in Scripture or elaborate on a long-accepted theological or ethical doctrine with no less enthusiasm than any preacher. This was particularly true when the same person served as both reader and preacher in some smaller community. In both capacities he frequently alluded to existing rabbinic interpretations and legends, more or less familiar to his audience. But he also often improvised new similes and stories and, with the aid of words, created new images derived from a biblical phrase, which greatly enriched the ever growing domain of Aggadah. That is why the eternal quest for the "lost" midrashic sources of the liturgical poems may, to a large extent, be doomed to utter futility.

Outside pressures, too, undoubtedly helped shape the performance of either task. Ever since Yehudah bar Barzillai, scholars have connected the spurt in liturgical creativity during the early post-talmudic age with anti-Jewish persecutions. Although in many ways a cliché, often merely serving to rationalize historic phenomena whose origins had become obscure or unwelcome, this explanation is indubitably true with respect to Justinian's *Novella* 146. Clearly, a prohibition to expound the Oral Law (*deuterosis*) in any formal instruction easily shifted the burden from the aggadic sermon, now prohibited, to the equally aggadic poem imbedded in the accepted liturgy and hence not outlawed. Of course, Christian antagonism to the Oral Law did not begin in the sixth century. In the growingly intolerant clime of the Eastern Roman Empire, which protected the synagogue while persecuting Jews, there existed many incentives to exploit to the full the educational as well as devotional features of the synagogue liturgy, the fundamentals of which admittedly antedated Christianity. Justinian's *Novella* of 553, however, never formally revoked, added strength to these internal transformations within Byzantine Jewry before and after the rise of Islam. If we are to believe a tradition, recorded by biased Pirqoi ben Baboi though unattested elsewhere, that the Byzantine rulers also at one time forbade the recitation of the *'Amidah* and the *Shema'*, such a prohibition must have added great impetus to the quest for liturgical substitutes of approximately the same content.[28]

Nor may we neglect the impact of daily contacts with Israel's neighbors. Although the personal relations between Jewish and Christian leaders were far from intimate and even the consultation of Jewish experts was far less frequent in the liturgical area than in that of Old Testament translations, there were enough Christian visitors in the contemporary synagogues to loom as a major threat to Christian orthodoxy in the eyes of St. John Chrysostom, Agobard, and other churchmen. The tireless efforts of Christian missionaries could not fail to acquaint some Jews with the tenets and the external forms of Christian worship. Nor did full-fledged Christian proselytes, whose presence seems confirmed by two poems of Yannai, wipe out all traces of their previous observances as was demanded by Jewish law. Even Jews who never stepped over the threshhold of a church must often have learned from such newcomers or visitors something about Christian modes of worship. Nor was surreptitious listening to church music by Jewish cantors in quest of thematic enrichment of their own services, such as is mentioned by a nineteenth-century rabbi of Smyrna, Israel Moses Ḥazzan, quite so impossible as it appears from the official antagonism on the part of both rabbis and churchmen.[29]

In Palestine, Christians and Jews alike recited many prayers in the same Syriac-Aramaic dialect, and probably no fulminations of their own extremist leaders wholly deterred inquisitive Jews from examining the form and content of some beautiful poems by Ephraem Syrus. Since the Greek churches, too, were increasingly imbued with the spirit of the Syriac Christian liturgy, the services in neighboring churches may have been far less of a mystery to some Greek-speaking Jews surviving in the former Hellenistic Diaspora than they were to become to their medieval descendants.

And the three centuries between Constantine and Mohammed marked the period of highest achievement in the evolution of both the Greek and the Syriac liturgies!

The subject matter of some Christian liturgical poems, too, must have whetted the curiosity of Jews. Apart from the frequent treatment in an entirely aggadic vein of such Old Testament subjects as the sacrifice of Isaac, these poems often described contemporary events, especially the catastrophic effects of earthquakes or conflagrations, from which the local Jewish inhabitants had suffered equally. Even poems filled with anti-Jewish polemics were not devoid of interest to Jewish audiences, or at least to their leaders, who often had to learn how to forestall threatening anti-Jewish reactions among the masses. For instance, one of Ephraem's very popular *memre* (didactic poems) was best known under the stereotype title "Against the Jews," although it merely tried to describe in poetic form Jesus' entry into Jerusalem.

Needless to say, these influences were reciprocal. In fact, Jews refusing to recognize the revealed character of the New Testament could more readily ignore Christian teachings than the Christians could disregard Jewish concepts and liturgical forms associated with the Old Testament. We recall how all-pervading the Jewish influences had been on the Christian liturgy in its formative stages. Another illustration may be adduced from a liturgical formula recorded in a fifth-century inscription. Beginning *Heis Theos* (God Is One), it was clearly but a variant of the Jewish *Shema'*. Curiously, the main variant, namely the addition of "and His Christ is one," may in some indirect way have contributed to the well-known Muslim credo. Such Jewish influences continued to operate also in the subsequent centuries, and they helped to shape the form as well as the content of the liturgies of the eastern churches.[30]

FAITHFUL RECORDING

In many respects, however, Jewish congregations differed from their Christian counterparts, especially in their having no written prayer books before that of Amram. Jewish liturgy shared therein the destinies of the other realms of Oral Law. Whether we ascribe this phenomenon to the sheer force of tradition, to the rabbis' fear that circulation of differing records in the far-flung Diaspora might lead to sectarian divergences (their observation of the sectarian strife among their Christian neighbors over liturgical minutiae must have reinforced such fears), or to their apprehensions that possession of books other than the Bible might make their followers vulnerable to special persecution—just as the possession of Bibles had endangered the lives of their Maccabean ancestors (I Macc. 1:56–57)—the effect was that the Jewish communities long possessed no written records of their prescribed or voluntary prayers.

Such absence of liturgical writings was none too serious so long as the Jewish communities possessed but brief weekday, Sabbath, and holiday rituals. These could be memorized by a sufficiently large number of worshipers, and in particular by their "messengers." Additional prayers could readily be improvised by each individual, as well as by the congregational leaders. Improvisation remained indeed a characteristic feature of synagogue services throughout the talmudic and early posttalmudic periods, when it actually served as a vehicle for imparting to broad audiences some information on Oral Law. The reader himself did not always remember his improvisation after a lapse of time. Before a year rolled around, he often forgot his own *ḥazzanut* on the theme of a particular holiday *'Amidah,* and he improvised another piece for the same prayer on each subsequent occasion. That is probably why we find so many parallel *qerobot* on the same benediction from the prolific mind of Eleazar Qalir.[31]

Sensing the great responsibility of serving as their congregations' spokesmen before the Lord, many "messengers" prefaced their prayers with poetic appeals for divine forbearance toward their shortcomings and assistance in finding the proper words to express the people's deep yearnings. Some of these moving petitions have become part and parcel of the accepted liturgy. For instance, "I look to the Lord [*oḥilah la-El*] and beseech His presence, I beg from Him the fluency of my tongue," included in the *Musaf* prayer of the Day of Atonement, was originally but such a personal outcry for divine help. Of course, these improvisations were but variations on the theme of the long-standardized, introductory petitions recited by every Jew before and after the silent prayer. They began "O Lord, open Thou my lips," and ended with "May the words of my mouth and the meditation of my heart be acceptable unto Thee." Less well known is Saadiah's Hebrew quatrain, included in his Pentecostal poems:

> To Thee, uplifter from the deepest mire,
> I look for guidance to freedom's lot,
> May my heart harbor no foolish desire
> My innermost self be free from rot.
> Glory unto Thee for cleansing the grime
> Of those pacing Thy mosaic floors.
> Let me but rejoice in Law's peaceful clime,
> And restore my soul through wisdom's doors.

To realize the fear and trepidation with which most readers approached their improvisations, one must bear in mind the power of the word which, ever since ancient times, had loomed large in the minds of all Near Eastern peoples. A wrong word, or even a right word uttered, however unwittingly, at the wrong time, might, it was generally believed, cause incalculable harm not only to the speaker, but also to his community.[32]

Nor must we overlook the basic difference between the oral transmission of liturgical passages and that of the main halakhic and aggadic traditions. The latter depended entirely on professional memorizers at the central academies who, after arduous training for this particular task, could transmit verbatim thousands of sayings with a fidelity which far transcended that of most copyists of manuscripts. The synagogue ritual, however, was the common possession of the whole people. Jews everywhere wished, indeed were obliged, to commune directly with their Creator. Even the expedient of qualified "messengers" leading in prayers proved insufficient when the liturgy expanded and the local messengers themselves could no longer trust their memory. After all, persons like the Muslim scholar Abu'l Fadl (d. 1067), who achieved great fame because he was able after once hearing a poem of fifty verses to repeat it accurately, must have been very rare among the Jews, too. Even the best men in the thousands of small and scattered communities might prove unreliable recorders.

We can understand, therefore, not only the extraordinary forbearance toward the diversity of detailed formulations evinced by the otherwise quite authoritarian talmudic and early posttalmudic sages, but also their evident quest for mnemotechnic aids which could help impress new prayers upon the minds of listeners and precentors. One such time-honored aid was the alphabetic acrostic. Perhaps the Old Testament poets themselves had already used that expedient to secure their poems against partial oblivion during the long periods of their oral transmission. Following the psalmists' example (especially that of the long Psalm 119), many medieval authors facilitated the memorization of their poems by such alphabetic sequences, which made any omission easily noticeable. Later on they added verses beginning with the letters of their own names, thereby safeguarding also the memory of their authorship. Another aid consisted in the use of certain crucial catchwords, taken from either the content of the poem, the liturgical passage to which it was appended, or a pertinent biblical phrase. Placed at decisive points in the poem, such catchwords helped both in confiding that sequence to memory and in faithfully preserving it for posterity.[33]

Finally, a decisive step was taken by those unknown inventors of rhymed poetry whose influence on the destinies of all Western letters can hardly be overestimated. Possibly stimulated by the example set by the ancient authors of the focal *'Amidah,* the probably unintentional rhymes of which resembled those found in a Philistine war song against Samson, a prophecy of Isaiah, or Homer, these poets began using the rhyme as the most effective vehicle for both memorization and faithful transmission. At first the rhyme was rather simple, and for the most part consisted of words ending in the same grammatical form, such as the plural or the second person masculine or feminine. Nor did the same poet necessarily apply the new technique to all his poems, or even to entire poems. Just as Yose ben Yose used the acrostic only in some of his liturgical pieces, so did the new rhymsters also produce much unrhymed poetry. In time, however, the rhymes became more sophisticated. Coming in contact with the Arabs, who in pre-Islamic times had faced the same problem of fidelity in oral transmission and had, perhaps in complete independence, developed the same rhyming technique, the Jewish authors kept on refining their own methods. We shall see what degree of sophistication, even artificiality, rhyming and other modes of versification had reached already in the days of Saadiah Gaon. Not surprisingly, the gaon had begun his literary career with a rhyming dictionary intended for the use of aspiring poets. Moreover, these various techniques could easily be combined. Thus many a liturgical creation, protected at its verse beginnings by an acrostic, single or multiple, its ends safeguarded by a rhyme, however crude, and all of it often further sheltered behind an umbrella of recurring catchwords, had a chance to weather, more or less successfully, the debilitating influences of uncontrolled transmission.[34]

PIYYUṬ

Out of these conflicts between creative inwardness and adherence to tradition was born that peculiar type of liturgical poetry known as *piyyuṭ*. Clearly derived from the Greek term *poietes* (poet; the Byzantine Tobiah ben Eliezer consistently used the more correct derivative form, *poyyeṭan,* in lieu of the usual Aramaic term, *payyeṭan*), this designation was not quite as descriptive of the peculiar nature of this poetry as its less frequently used synonym, *ḥazzanut;* that is, compositions of synagogue readers. In Arabic writings we frequently find the Hebrew loan word *ḥizanah*. Even in its most advanced and complex forms, this poetry still betrays its origin from improvisations during synagogue services.[35]

For a long time there was little to distinguish the new creations from other prayers introduced by some such outstanding rabbinic leader as Rab. Endowed with a beautiful voice, this third-century founder of the academy of Sura is said to have been "accustomed to descend to the pulpit" and improvise new prayers. A number of important prayers, still recited in Jewish houses of worship today, such as the aforementioned *'Alenu,* owe their origin or final formulation to Rab's poetic and musical talents. A century later, one Bar Abin greeted Raba, on the latter's visit to his city, with a brief poem which, apart from a clever allusion to the visitor, included hints to biblical events, the sins of the generation, and an appeal for divine mercy—all of them popular themes in the later sacred poetry. It appears that this art was cultivated with particular devotion in priestly circles. Remembering their ancient glory, descendants of priests, still living in Palestine in closed settlements centuries after the Temple's destruction, seem to have preserved many memories of their ritualistic performances at the ancient sanctuary, and long continued to bask in their reflected glory. Some of them seem to have composed poems on the theme of the ancient "watches," reflecting their extraordinary readiness to spring into immediate action upon the advent of the Messiah, and without delay to restore the ancient rituals into full operation.[36]

Prominent among these priestly poets is one Haduta or Ḥaduta, who lived, according to M. Zulay, "among groups of priests, each of which knew and recognized its particular watch and looked forward every day to the restoration of the Temple and its own return to its pristine function." Haduta composed twenty-four poems commemorating the twenty-four "orderings" as recorded by the chronicler (I Chron. 24:7–19). Evidently intended for recitation on the twenty-four Sabbaths, when these groups had traditionally served at the Temple, these poems are among the earliest *piyyuṭim* devoted to Sabbath rather than holiday services. This circumstance alone need not militate against their antiquity. While their origin is altogether uncertain, they almost surely antedate the rise of Islam and may belong to the very oldest recorded writings of this genre.[37]

Much better known is another priestly poet, Yose ben Yose, often called the Orphan, possibly for no other reason than his patronymic. But in many medieval communities, including those in Spain, Jews did not hesitate to call a child by the name of his living father. Although not, as another legend had it, a high priest at the Temple, Yose was a Palestinian priest profoundly cherishing the ancient distinction of his class. His greatest contribution to Jewish liturgy consisted, appropriately enough, of a poetic description of the Temple services on the Day of Atonement, the climactic point in the career of the ancient priesthood. This service, briefly called *'Abodah* (worship), had already been dramatized in the epic description of the Mishnah. Using the mishnaic text, in fact quoting parts of it verbatim, Yose composed three lengthy poems on this subject.

It is often assumed that the three texts were intended for recitation at the morning, the *Musaf* (supplementary morning prayers), and the afternoon services of the Day of Atonement. One of them is, indeed, specifically inscribed by a later copyist "for *Minḥah.*" But it appears more likely that the poet had originally improvised them on three different annual occasions, and only later communities, confronted by a choice between three equally distinguished texts, decided to use them all during the lengthy devotions of that supreme annual fast. According to Hai Gaon, neither academy had originally approved the recitation of the *'Abodah* at any time except during the *Musaf* services. Only from the days of Hai ben David, the first academy head to reside permanently in Baghdad, was the local custom of reciting it also during morning services quietly tolerated. Later Saadiah, another Baghdad resident, quoted two of the three poems by Yose, together with a poem of his own. He suggested the use of one at the morning services, and the second or his own for *Musaf,* pointedly omitting any reference to the afternoon recitation.[38]

Stylistically and technically Yose used simple means to convey his ideas to his fellow worshipers. A later Arabic-Jewish literary historian was not unjustified in calling his style of writing *khuṭab,* or rhetorical discourse. The long poem *Azkir geburot Eloah* (I Shall Record God's Mighty Exploits) consists of two hundred and twenty-eight verses arranged according to an alphabetic acrostic (ten verses for each letter of the Hebrew alphabet, except the last, which is used in eighteen verses). Adumbrating a division which became important in the later liturgical creativity, Yose devoted the first twelve letters (or one hundred and twenty verses) to a poetic paraphrase of the events described in the Bible from the Creation to the first "high priest" Aaron. The remaining ten letters (one hundred and eight verses) gave a detailed description of the Temple services on the Day of Atonement, interrupting the narrative at three crucial points by telling quotations from the Mishnah. Essentially the same technique is used in the shorter poem of sixty-six verses beginning *Attah konanta* (Thou Hast

Set Up the World). Here the historical introduction is limited to the first fifteen verses. The acrostic covers twenty-two verses running forward from A to T, then twenty-two verses going back from T to A, and finally twenty-two verses resuming the usual sequence. The quotations from the Mishnah are even more numerous.[39]

Curiously, one may mention in passing, the *Attah konanta* was long recited in some French communities together with a brief introductory poem beginning *Etten tehillah* (I Shall Give Praise), ascribed to no less an author than the apostle Peter. In this case Simon Peter was definitely confused with an early *payyeṭan,* probably Simon ben Megas the Priest, a near contemporary of Yannai. A medieval homilist doubtless had this poet in mind when he spoke of the author of all sorts of liturgical poems for use "during the entire year, like Qalir." [40]

Simplicity also reigns supreme in Yose's "confession" (*Omnam ashamnu;* Indeed We Have Sinned), still recited in Ashkenazic congregations on the evening of the Day of Atonement. Written in a double acrostic, with two verses for each letter, this poem is distinguished by a refrain, doubtless reflecting the responsive reading in the synagogue, and pithily expressing one of the major themes in the older Jewish liturgy. The author fervently stressed here God's great forbearance toward the evil as well as the good, and prayed for His forgiveness of Israel's sins for His sake rather than theirs. Neither Yose nor any of his successors, however, would have dared to go the whole length of Yose's Syriac compeer, Cyrillonas (*ca.* 400). In his poem on the locust plague and the Hun invasions of 395–96 this Syriac churchman prayed: "Desist of Thy punishment for I am united with Thee; when Thou chastiseth me Thou aimest at Thyself. For Thy body is in mine, let it not be affronted; Thy secrets have entered into me, let them not be derided." More remarkably, in a recently published brief introductory poem requesting the Lord's permission (*reshut*) for the presentation of the congregation's case, Yose used both the acrostic and the rhyme. This poem, beginning *Erasheh liftoaḥ* (May I be Permitted to Open with Songs), has the same rather primitive rhyme *mot* in all its twenty-two half-verses.[41]

One wishes that one might speak with greater assurance about the period of Yose's activity. Apart from the certainty that he flourished some time after the compilation of the Mishnah, we may perhaps assume that he lived before Justinian, most probably in the fifth century. The fact that he composed poetry primarily for use during the High Holidays, and that he made but occasional, often evidently unconscious, use of aggadic themes, clearly indicates that he was not yet concerned with replacing through his poems the forbidden teaching of Oral Law. His simple style, his uncomplicated technique, his fervent piety, and his combination of epic reworking of biblical history with graphic descriptions of major rituals and inward appeals for God's forgiveness—all these remind us of Ephraem the Syrian. But there is no evidence of any personal or literary relations between the two poets, or even of their familiarity with each other's works. They seem merely to reflect the same general intellectual and religious atmosphere in that period of transition from the ancient to the medieval period.

YANNAI AND QALIR

No less obscure is the background of Yose's contemporaries and early successors. Only two names emerge distinctly from the mist of ages: Yannai and his alleged pupil, Eleazar (not Eliezer) Qalir (also called ben Qallir or ha-Qalliri). A century ago hardly more than a name, called to the attention of scholars by Rapoport's fine detective sense, Yannai belongs among the shining stars in the firmament of medieval Hebrew letters. No less than 138 of his certain and 38 of his doubtful *qerobot* (including more than eight hundred individual poems) were assembled from 173 scattered manuscripts (157 from the Genizah) by M. Zulay in the edition of Yannai's collected poems published in 1938. Several more poems have since come to light. Apart from their impressive number, the form and quality of most of these poems have attracted considerable attention from specialists in medieval Hebrew poetry.[42]

Almost all of Yannai's *qerobot* are attached either to scriptural lessons according to the triennial cycle used in Palestine or to the silent prayers recited on holidays. Only a few are connected with the *'Amidah* of one or another "distinguished" Sabbath. None seem to relate to other parts of the synagogue services. Certainly a poet-reader who could improvise a poem for each of 150 weekly lessons of a single cycle—he may of course have originally composed a poem or poems on the same lesson every three years—did not lack the creative power to provide other sections of the liturgy with his poetic comments. The content of his poems is likewise startling: they are often halakhic rather than homiletical in nature. For this reason they may indeed have served as a source of legal information to 'Anan the Karaite—a fact allegedly discovered by the gaon Hai ben David. Most startlingly, in contrast to Yose's and all earlier practices, Yannai's poems often served not to supplement existing prayers, but rather to interrupt them by lengthy additions, if not altogether to replace them. From time immemorial, congregations recited his *qerobot* in the middle of the messenger's loud repetition of the *'Amidah.* They thus ran counter to clear and reiterated prohibitions in both Talmudim. The whole tenor of Yannai's poems likewise suggests that from the outset they were designed for such reading during, or in lieu of, the *'Amidah.*[43]

These extraordinary features of Yannai's poetry may best be explained by external pressures. Justinian's prohibition of instruction in the Oral Law undoubtedly stimulated our author to communicate to synagogue audiences, as part of their still permissible liturgy, a variety of legal regulations, especially those governing the observance of major holidays. That many of these poems should be attached to the weekly recitations from Scripture is less surprising, as Justinian's *Novella* of 553 had tried to influence the Jews to read their Scriptures together with the Septuagint or another "accurate" version. Justinian's ill-concealed missionary objectives seem to have influenced the Palestinian Jews not only to elaborate their *Targum* by inserting into it much aggadic material, but also to expatiate on the meaning of each weekly Pentateuchal lesson and its prophetic supplement in didactic poems of halakhic, as well as aggadic, content. This was the Palestinian community's effective answer to the imperial challenge expressed in the following paragraph of the *Novella:*

We pray that when they [the Jews] hear the reading of the books in one or the other language, they may guard themselves against the depravity of the interpreters, and, not clinging to the literal words, come to the point of the matter, and perceive their divine meaning, so that they may start afresh to learn the better way, and may cease to stray vainly, and to err in that which is most essential, we mean hope in God. For this reason we have opened for them the door to the understanding of Scriptures.[44]

Of unknown provenance is another governmental infringement of Jewish ritualistic autonomy, recorded in Pirqoi ben Baboi's rather confused account. Some five hundred years earlier, we are told, that is about the fourth century, the Romans had forbidden the Jews to study the Torah. In another context we are informed that the administration had "instituted a severe persecution [*shemad;* literally, extinction] against the inhabitants of Palestine by prohibiting them from reciting the *Shema'* and praying [the *'Amidah*], but it allowed them to congregate on Sabbath mornings and to recite and chant prayers of petition [*ma'amadot*]." To be sure, no such prohibitions are recorded in any of the extant Christian-Roman sources, which are otherwise quite explicit with respect to the anti-Jewish regulations. Certainly the date of five hundred years cannot be taken literally, for it would take us back to Constantine's incipient and rather restrained anti-Jewish legislation. Quite possibly Pirqoi confused here some dim recollections of the Hadrianic prohibition of the study of the Torah with the general hostility of the Christian regime after Constantine. Nor was there any reason for Christians to outlaw not only the *'Amidah,* whose anti-heretical benediction they doubtless resented, but also the *Shema',* taken in its entirety from the book of Deuteronomy. Very likely Pirqoi, or his Babylonian teacher, Yehudai, confounded here some recollection of a local Palestinian prohibition of the *'Amidah,* which because of its local limitations never penetrated the imperial codes of Theodosius or Justinian, with one relating to Persian legislation against the recitation of *Shema'.* Clearly the recitation twice or thrice daily of this Jewish credo in the unity of God literally shouted defiance at Zoroastrian dualism. That Persian prohibition may then have been extended to Palestine during the brief occupation of 614–28.[45]

Against this background we may understand the newer developments in the Hebrew liturgical poetry. Reacting to the local outlawry of the *'Amidah,* as well as to Justinian's prohibition of the exposition of Oral Law, Yannai composed numerous *qerobot* around themes suggested by the silent prayer, especially its fairly immutable first three benedictions. By reciting these poems, congregations could replace in some way the entire silent prayer. Even if some communities succeeded in evading the prohibition and in stealthily reciting the traditional prayers, they doubtless found it convenient not to have the reader repeat it aloud publicly, but to substitute the new compositions for the second recitation. This is probably what Samau'al al-Maghribi had in mind when he described the *piyyuṭ* as a sort of dialogue between the reader and the audience, in lieu of the former's solo recitation of the *'Amidah*. In fact, Yannai himself probably started this custom by improvising these new liturgical pieces when called upon to recite the *'Amidah* aloud. Before long, when the prohibition was relaxed, and certainly after the Muslim conquest of Palestine, it became customary to combine both recitations. As before, most congregations prayed the *'Amidah* silently, although some Byzantine groups, perhaps bent on demonstrating their regained freedom of worship, recited it aloud but, during the repetition by the "messenger," inserted the new poems between the respective benedictions.[46]

Qalir (whose name possibly originated from an inversion of Kyrill or Cyrill), according to a medieval legend pupil of Yannai and victim of his master's jealousy, went further. Possibly living in Palestine during the Persian occupation, he felt induced not only to compose ever new *qerobot* for the *'Amidah* of various holidays, fasts, and even some extraordinary Sabbaths, but also occasionally to surround the *Shema'* with a garland of poems relating especially to the themes of the antecedent and subsequent benedictions. This doubtless was one of the subterfuges which enabled the Jews, in Pirqoi's words, "on Sabbath mornings stealthily to recite the *Qedushah* and *Shema'*." Evidently the intermingling of three prayers made detection much more difficult. Since the first blessing of the daily *Shema'* cycle concluded with the benediction "Blessed art Thou, O Lord, Creator [*yoṣer*] of the luminaries," these compositions came to be known as *yoṣerot*. Qalir's prolific mind also was constantly at work in reshaping with ever new formulations the services on evenings and afternoons of holidays, and in thus providing the traditional liturgies with a sort of running poetic commentary. He apparently desisted only from amplifying the weekday services, perhaps in recognition of the necessary time limits on the ritual of a working population.[47]

Living in the period of great tension between the Jews and their Byzantine overlords, Yannai and Qalir often inserted into their liturgical poetry allusions to the existing hostile regime and the hope for its speedy downfall. True, an overt statement like "May Rome fall," in one of Yannai's *qerobot,* was early replaced by a more innocuous phrase, either because of fear of reprisals or because, with the passing of the Byzantine regime over Palestine, such sharp attacks had lost their point. But there remained many allusions to the kingdom of *Dumah* (this biblical term for silence was used as a synonym for death in Ps. 115:17 and could be used as a transparent veil for *Romah*), pork and reptile eaters, despisers of circumcision, and even worshipers of idols (icons). The prayer for "ousting the pig from His dwelling, / And giving the holy abode to His community" combined anti-Byzantinism with the hope for restoration to Zion, where Jews had been barred since the days of Hadrian.[48]

Qalir, however, seems to have lived to see not only the temporary liberation of the Holy Land by the Persians, but also its conquest by the Arabs. This world-shaking event inspired him to the composition of an apocalyptic poem, showing this most versatile of the *payyeṭanim* in a novel, semi-messianic mood. Sharing the exaltation of many contemporaries who, under the impact of the unexpected upheaval, rediscovered the long-forgotten apocalyptic overtones of the visionaries during the Second Commonwealth—we recall in particular the apocryphal midrash entitled the "Mysteries of R. Simon ben Yoḥai"—Qalir improvised, perhaps while performing at the pulpit, a poetic vision of "that day [*oto ha-yom*]" when "the Messiah, son of David will come." In the ensuing struggle between Gog and Magog, or the kings of West and East, the whole world would be frightened, even the sun and the moon would be smitten, but "Israel will be cleansed of their sins, and no longer be alienated from their sanctuary." This rhymed, but otherwise artistically unpolished poem, reveals the state of ecstasy permeating the Palestinian community at the arrival of the Arabian horsemen.[49]

Political, military, and legislative challenges offered, however, but the external stimuli to the extraordinary flowering of the new Jewish liturgy. The same creative *élan* which accounted for the rise and development of the magnificent Church poetry in Syriac and Greek, operated also to loosen the tongues of the Jewish "messengers" and to urge them to improvise ever new poems to enhance the richness and beauty of their divine services. Moreover, once some pioneering precentor discovered a new form, or a congregation developed a new taste for such poetry, a host of imitators joined the ranks. Certainly a poem like Qalir's *Ṭal ten* (Give Dew), still recited in many congregations in connection with the prayer for dew on the first day of Passover, caught the spirit of the ancient Jewish peasantry reveling in the blessings of the Palestinian soil. Reflecting the *joi de vivre* of a still predominantly agricultural population, rather than a purely antiquarian reminiscence, the poet sang:

Dew, precious dew, unto Thy land forlorn!
Pour out our blessing in Thy exultation,
To strengthen us with ample wine and corn
And give Thy chosen city safe foundation
  In dew.

. . . .

Dew, precious dew, that we our harvest reap,
And guard our fatted flocks and herds from leanness!
Behold our people follows Thee like sheep,
And looks to Thee to give it back its greenness
  With dew.[50]

Nor was the field of these endeavors limited to sacred poetry in the stricter sense. With religion permeating all aspects of Jewish private and public life, the distinction between sacred and secular poetry was often artificial, as we shall learn even with respect to the Spanish poetry of the Golden Age. For example, an elegy on the death of a friend, although entirely private in nature, lent itself to public recitation in the synagogue on a par with an homiletical eulogy, which it seems at times to have displaced. The Cairo Genizah has, indeed, yielded a copy of an old Aramaic

Afṭarta (Leave Taking), which seems to date back to the time when Palestinian Jewry indulged many Aramaic prayers. A beautiful poetic eulogy by Qalir has likewise been found. Weaving with consummate skill a word each from the appropriate verses in Zechariah 12:12 and Isaiah 57:1 before the first and third half-verse; inserting into the latter a clear acrostic of his own name, Eleazar berabbi Qilir; and yet maintaining throughout the poem the rhyme of each strophe of four half-verses, the *payyeṭan* succeeded in offering an eloquent tribute to a deceased leader distinguished by both piety and learning.[51]

Unfortunately, only few of such semiprivate poems have come down to us from the early period of medieval Hebrew poetry. When compared with the vast output of Syriac Church poetry related to current events, extant *piyyuṭim* of even more general contemporary interest are extremely scarce. However, many more seem to have been written than appears in the record. Being of a personal or, at best, local interest, these poems did not have a wide enough appeal to be frequently copied or incorporated into rituals of major scope. In fact, if they happened not to be of special interest to the community of Fusṭaṭ they never found their way into the Cairo Genizah, and such accidental failure alone often sufficed to commit them to total oblivion. This regrettable communal forgetfulness is made doubly poignant by a comparison with the later *seliḥot,* which, especially when relating to contemporary massacres in western Europe, were recited at memorial services for many generations, often copied by zealous scribes, and even included in major liturgical handbooks.

With Qalir the *piyyuṭ* reached the acme of its popularity, and none of his numerous successors enjoyed equally widespread and responsive audiences. In his handbook for Hebrew poetry Saadiah mentioned Joshua and Pinḥas (Phineas) alongside Yose, Yannai, and Qalir as the classics of *piyyuṭ,* yet little of their work was permanently incorporated in the liturgy of any group, and only a few remnants could be laboriously restored from the Genizah materials with the aid of identifying acrostics and rhymes. In this way Zulay reconstructed, for example, one of Joshua's poems from three fragments now located in New York, Oxford, and Cambridge. In the days after Saadiah, too, only a few *payyeṭanim* enjoyed more than a local and temporary vogue. Even so prolific an author as Solomon-Sulaiman, a native of Sanjar near Mosul some time between the ninth and the eleventh centuries—nearly a thousand of his poems are still extant in some three hundred manuscripts—is now known chiefly through careful examination of the surviving medieval fragments, rather than through a living tradition and continued use in synagogues of any rite. The same holds true for another prolific liturgical poet, Samuel "the Third." And yet, the cumulative impact of these lesser lights exceeded greatly that of the founders. In many congregations the very works of Qalir underwent numerous transformations or modifications by the intermingling of poems of later vintage, written in the same vein, if not altogether in direct imitation of the master's form and style.[52]

WEAK OPPOSITION

Varying needs of respective generations helped determine their choices. There had been no room for *piyyuṭ* in the technical sense in the days before the standardization of the main prayers, when any worshiper, not only his "messenger," was entitled to add as many prayers as he wished. Similarly, after the rise of Islam, the growing distinction between the universally accepted liturgy, which already included some previously incorporated *piyyuṭim*, and the purely elective accretions militated against the latter's universal acceptance. Generation after generation still added new selections to its diversified liturgical treasures, but few of these new poems, whether improvised by cantors or written by poets in the privacy of their homes, became part and parcel of the recognized liturgical practice.

Nor was opposition on principle completely absent. Since the *piyyuṭ* not only originated in Palestine but in all its decisive evolutionary stages reflected the needs and conditions of that country, it encountered mounting resistance in Babylonian circles. From the eighth century on, in particular, the Babylonian leaders' growingly intensive drive for power and control of world Jewry made such liturgical creativity suspect, because it was both uncontrollable and Palestinian. True, even the more law-centered Babylonian community indulged in the recitation of new prayers. Yet Saadiah apparently exaggerated when, after offering in his prayer book a poem for each day of the Feast of Tabernacles to be recited in connection with the *Hosha'anot* cycle, he added, "The Palestinians have additional recitations for the day of the *'Arabah* [the willow-branch, that is the seventh day of the Feast of Tabernacles], while the Babylonians and others also have unbelievably many." Moreover, whatever new prayers were composed in the Euphrates valley during the late talmudic and posttalmudic age were, as we recall, read almost exclusively in Aramaic. Now, under Arab domination, these prayers shared the fate of all noncanonical Aramaic letters; they were eclipsed by Arabic in daily use, and by Hebrew in the synagogue. And Hebrew liturgy could more readily be imported from Palestine than created on the spot.[53]

Whatever its ultimate motivations, the opposition, understandably enough, advanced mainly legalistic objections to the spread of the *piyyuṭim*. Such objections were readily available in talmudic law, which had long tried to protect the basic prayers against adulteration by inappropriate additions. To be sure, even in the geonic period Jewish liturgy was still in a state of flux, and no gaon dared to assert, as Eleazar of Worms did later, that "the mystery of prayers had been transmitted to us by teacher after teacher all the way back to the prophets, the elders, *ḥasidim,* and Men of the Great Synagogue who had introduced them. Hence woe unto him who adds to, or subtracts from, them a single letter or word, woe in this world as well as in the world to come." According to formal law, additions even to the *'Amidah* could not be outlawed so long as they dealt with the theme of the concluding blessing of each benediction. Even opponents, therefore, merely tried to lower the dignity of these additional poems by claiming that they had been intended only for the unlearned, and still appealed only to the illiterate masses. Typical of such denunciations is a responsum attributed to R. Naḥshon of Sura, which states:

> At the academy or any other location where there are scholars we never deviate from the prayers instituted by the sages, [and recite no] *piyyuṭ*. Neither do we allow a reader familiar with *piyyuṭ* to officiate in the synagogue. Every congregation reciting a *piyyuṭ* testifies thereby that they are no scholars.

While Amram still demanded only that no one change the pattern of existing prayers, his assistant, Ṣemaḥ, "judge of the court" (this seems to have been his title, rather than the great judge), declared succinctly, "A messenger of the public who adds to the pattern set by the sages for prayer, and heaps words upon words, is liable to excommunication and ought to be discharged." Ultimately, Yehudah bar Barzillai (who may have quoted these three geonic authorities) summarized the prevailing rabbinic view that *piyyuṭim* had originated from a reaction to anti-Jewish persecutions and were intended only "to remind and warn the illiterate of the laws and regulations governing holidays and Sabbaths and the minutiae of law." After the cessation of persecutions, he declared, these "foolish and ignorant matters" had no place in Jewish services.[54]

With less acidity, but no less determination, the *piyyuṭim* were also rejected by Maimonides and other rabbis. Maimonides' own inclination was to dispense with them altogether. Only if the populace was very insistent, he declared, one might recite them before the benedictions of the *Shema'* cycle. But "one must add nothing whatever in the midst of these benedictions, nor cause any interruption between them and the recitation of *Shema'*." The philosopher of Fusṭaṭ censured, in particular, their objectionable content, and in his philosophic *magnum opus* he waxed eloquent on this score:

> We cannot approve [he wrote] of what those foolish persons do who are extravagant in praise, fluent and prolix in the prayers they compose and in the hymns they make in the desire to approach the Creator. They describe God in attributes which would be an offense if applied to a human being; for those persons have no knowledge of these great and important principles, which are not accessible to the ordinary intelligence of man. Treating the Creator as a familiar object, they describe Him and speak of Him in any expressions they think proper; they eloquently continue to praise Him in that manner, and believe that they can thereby influence Him and produce an effect on Him. . . . This license is frequently met with in the compositions of the singers, preachers, and others who imagine themselves to be able to compose a poem. Such authors write things which partly are real heresy, partly contain such folly and absurdity that they naturally cause those who hear them to laugh, but also to feel grieved at the thought that such things can be uttered in reference to God.

It is only to be regretted that out of "pity" for those authors Maimonides refrained from citing telling examples. So impressed by these arguments was his son Abraham that, although generally far more pietistic than the father and inclined to increase individual devotions far beyond the prescribed ritual, he sharply combated the *piyyuṭim*. "As soon as I assumed office [as *nagid*]," he later reminisced, "I eradicated this error from Egypt, and restored the ritual to the forms required by law." [55]

The originator of the "persecution theory" concerning the rise of the *piyyuṭ* was, as we recall, Pirqoi ben Baboi. This Babylonian patriot was not so much concerned with the "nonsense" in the new liturgical output as with the underlying legal deviations. As was noted later by Simḥah of Vitry, Qalir's poems often reflected laws recorded only in the Palestinian Talmud. That is probably why his *Maḥzor,* even in its enlarged versions, contained only one Qalirian poem, the true authorship of which, still rather dubious, was surely unknown to the compiler. Dependence upon the Palestinian Talmud and, more generally, Palestinian law is even more pronounced in Yannai's poetry, with its greater emphasis on legal teachings. It appears that not his excessive concentration on legal complexities, but rather his emphasis on the wrong kind of law later militated against Yannai's popularity in the Western countries which had come entirely under the sway of the Babylonian Talmud. In the ninth century this struggle for supremacy was far from decided, however. Fearing the impact of the popular Palestinian *piyyuṭim* on the mass of uninformed congregants and the ensuing widespread acceptance of the Holy Land's legal "deviations," Pirqoi, a radical champion of Babylonian hegemony, condemned all these "departures" from Babylonian observance as the unwelcome result of external pressures alone.[56]

Much later came objections on linguistic grounds. Living in Palestine, where the Hebrew language, although no longer widely spoken, had maintained an unbroken continuity from the days of the Bible, these early medieval poets were able to marshal linguistic resources entirely unknown to Jews of other lands. They had at their disposal a far richer vocabulary, which is partly reflected also in the Palestinian Talmud. Nor did they hesitate to expand it by adjusting existing roots to new forms, or even by coining new terms. Forced by their increasingly rigid requirements with respect to meter, rhyme, acrostic, and strophe to resort to much poetic license, these poets often unwittingly enriched the Hebrew language with new words and turns.

Of course, not all the new terms and phrases were felicitous; still fewer appealed to the changing tastes of later generations. Hebrew philological studies, still in their infancy in the days of Yannai and Qalir, allowed for a more instinctive use of grammatical forms which were subsequently repudiated by the more rigorous and consistent grammarians of the school of Ḥayyuj and Ibn Janaḥ. Many word formations, in particular, based upon biliteral roots, appeared malformed to the Spanish classicists. Although themselves indebted to their *payyeṭanic* predecessors, Moses and Abraham ibn Ezra haughtily dismissed their works on such formal grounds. While praising to the sky the two prayers of petition by Saadiah, apparently the only poems by the gaon known to him, Abraham declared: "In the hands of R. Eliezer [more correctly Eleazar Qalir], may his soul rest in Eden, [the language] became like a wide-open unwalled city. . . . I shall not be able to describe one-thousandth of the *payyeṭanim's* errors. Hence I believe that one should not use them [the *piyyuṭim*] for prayer, but limit oneself to the accepted liturgy. Let our words be few, and we shall not be found wanting at the time of judgment." [57]

Defying all such objections, ever new synagogue readers improvised new poems, and more and more congregations incorporated them in their regular services. Each region, sometimes each congregation, followed the dictates of its own conscience as to how many and which poems it wished to use. At times, following changing tastes or fashions of the age, a congregation replaced a long-accepted poem by another, or even combined both by partially supplanting a section of an older work by a newer creation. Outright imitations, too, crept into the existing handbooks, and it was not always easy to distinguish between a master's genuine work and some effective mimicry. Poets bearing like-sounding names were the more likely to be confused, since the acrostics themselves were often identical or otherwise misleading, as happened in the case of the two Eleazars (Qalir and Ben Abbun).

Finally, the geonim themselves compromised with reality. Saadiah, although still reluctant to assign to *ḥizanah* much space in his prayer book, did not hesitate to compose *piyyuṭim* of his own, or to reproduce liturgical variants for such prayers as those recited during the *Shema'* cycle on the Sabbath eve. "Although not required by law," he declared, "it is permitted to recite these formulas." He thus controverted a view long held at his own academy of Sura. Not long thereafter Hai, head of the academy of Pumbedita, likewise joined the ranks of the liturgical poets. Even Maimonides, by temperament and reasoning anything but a friend of poetic arts, not only dolefully admitted his own youthful indiscretions in composing poetry in the fashion of his Spanish homeland, but also accompanied each major work with a prefatory or concluding poem. Unhesitatingly he provided his Arabic *Commentary* on the Mishnah with a lengthy, rhymed Hebrew introduction. None of the latter compositions, however, were ever intended for liturgical use. On the other hand, in Ashkenazic countries the *piyyuṭim* secured a responsive echo. The few which found their way into prayer books became the subject of intensive study and models for imitation. Some of the *Geshem* compositions by Qalir, for example, even found eager commentators in the school of Rashi.[58]

PRAYER BOOKS

When in the eighth and ninth centuries the Jewish people finally regained its voice after the long nightmare of Christian and Zoroastrian persecutions and the traumatic experience of the rise of Islam, Jewish liturgy thus consisted of a number of basic prayers more or less universally accepted, and much supplementary material which enjoyed only local or regional circulation. On the fringe loomed an ever vaster accumulation of liturgical compositions, whose use by congregations and their readers was definitely elective, although some of them acquired an enduring reputation for the piety and depth of their sentiments or the beauty of their expression.

Even the long-accepted basic prayers still offered considerable textual variations. With respect to the *'Amidah,* we possess the testimony of the fourteenth-century liturgical expert David Abudarham that he had tried in vain to count the words of that prayer, for no two places in the world had precisely the same text. Four centuries earlier the situation was in even greater flux, and

Saadiah Gaon complained that, on his extended journeys, he had noticed that

> with respect to our people's traditions concerning prayers and benedictions there are matters whose practice had been so neglected that they were completely forgotten except by a few select individuals; others were either so amplified or so truncated that they were completely altered and lost their original meaning and purpose; still others suffered amplification or deletion, without alteration, however, of the purposes for which they had been instituted.

The gaon did not really object here to the practice of adding new prayers to the traditional liturgy. Despite his serious reservations concerning the work of *payyeṭanim,* he himself composed several supplementary prayers of sublime beauty and inwardness, and others revealing an astounding technical skill, all of which he wished to see employed at least in private devotions. His main concern, however, was for the preservation of the traditional liturgy according to rabbinic law. He feared that, if the existing conditions were allowed to persist, the world Jewish community might be plunged into total liturgical anarchy, which would seriously undermine its cohesiveness and weaken its powers of survival.[59]

Out of this perennial conflict between communal control and individual freedom, made doubly poignant by the need of reconciling adherence to established tradition with personal inwardness and the worshiper's direct communion with the Deity, arose those manifold attempts at liturgical standardization which occupied the minds of some outstanding Jewish leaders between the ninth and twelfth centuries. These efforts encountered, however, an equally powerful, if less articulate, resistance on the part of the defenders of local autonomy, recruited from adherents of local customs and traditions, as well as from pious groups or individuals bent on finding ever new ways of voicing their innermost religious yearnings. The ensuing compromises found their expression in several successive prayer books and legal summaries.

Babylonian leaders were long concerned with the *order* of prayers prescribed for particular services rather than with the formulation of these prayers as such. From talmudic times they were prepared to leave the decision about particular readings to the local "messengers of the public." They long harbored suspicions about committing to writing any liturgical matters. A talmudic sage coined the irate phrase, "Those who write down benedictions are like those who burn the Torah." Such utterances were to vex greatly the medieval rabbis who had become inured to written liturgical texts. In the thirteenth century Zedekiah Anav degli Mansi still debated the legality of such texts, defending them merely on the ground that Jewish leadership was always entitled to adjust the law to emergency situations. He concluded lamely, "These are the facts of everyday life and a widespread observance in Israel, and we have seen no one objecting to that practice." [60]

Zedekiah was not the only Westerner to express bewilderment over the conflict between the existing liturgical practices and the talmudic views. The farther away Jews lived from the centers of Jewish life, the greater became the divergence of their local observances, gradually evolving over a period of countless generations, from the formal Babylonian laws. When the Great Caliphate suddenly reunited the Jewries of the Mediterranean world, the communities in the successor states of the Western Roman Empire were doubly puzzled by the discrepancies between their own and the Babylonian rituals.

On the other hand, the Eastern leaders, accustomed though they were to the differences between Palestine and Babylonia, were quite impatient with rituals developed in the periphery of Jewish life. In a characteristic responsum attributed to Hai Gaon, certain practices concerning the blowing of the horn on New Year's day were condemned as part and parcel of those "errors with which the scholars coming from Rome have infected you." On the other hand, the Westerners were, on the whole, ready to submit to Babylonia's superior wisdom and traditions. The Spanish Naḥmanides declined to follow a decision by the revered Isaac ibn Gayyat concerning the uniform recitation of nine blessings in the *Musaf 'Amidah* of the New Year by both public and precentor, although Ibn Gayyat had invoked the testimony of "great sages, teachers of law, and communal leaders" in Spain, including Samuel ibn Nagrela and the very founder of the Spanish school of Jewish jurisprudence, R. Ḥanokh.

It is true [Naḥmanides contended] that the master's arguments are very plausible. Yet, the geonim testify that such had never been the practice at the academy, but that the individual congregants read only seven blessings, the reader alone reciting nine blessings, and that this was their practice at all times. We must perforce accept their testimony. For the geonim have received their traditions from the Saboraim, and the Saboraim from the Amoraim, and they themselves still occupy R. Ashi's chair and pray at his synagogue. Moreover, their observance had been adopted by the majority of Jews, until R. Isaac Gayyat persuaded parts of the West to adopt our present customs.

Naḥmanides may indeed have had in mind here the synagogue originally founded by Rab, and later rebuilt by R. Ashi in Sura, whose ancient ritual had often been invoked by various Sura geonim as the authoritative practice of "the house of our teacher in Babylonia." [61]

Growing literacy and the spread of talmudic literature throughout the Jewish world added to the frequency and intensity of such questions. Gone was the traditional reliance of congregations on their local readers, who for a long time had more or less freely determined the form and content of individual prayers within the generally accepted framework of traditional liturgy. Even Maimonides still restated the older law when he allowed any totally ignorant person to disregard the required liturgy and to pray in his own way and at his own time (*M.T.* Tefillah 1.3).

Now, however, worshipers in increasing numbers were able to recite the required prayers by themselves and to ponder over their liturgical and legal implications. With the growing availability of talmudic texts and their subsequent rabbinic interpretations, the local diversities became far more startling. The Talmud, to be sure, as a rule did not cite detailed formulas, discussing mainly the general framework and sequence of prayers, as well as the laws governing their recitation. Its redactors evidently took most of the stylistic details for granted because they had been the common possession of all informed groups. Here, too, the peculiar genius of the Jewish religion manifested itself. The main emphasis lay on the exact performance of prescribed rituals at stated times and on the underlying *general* intentions, but the specific formulas were left to individual or group discretion. Certainly there existed in talmudic Judaism no counterpart to the heated dogmatic controversies over liturgical phrases such as came to the fore in the struggle over *filioque* among the contemporary Christian groups. We shall see presently how a small liturgical change, postulated on dogmatic grounds by Saadiah, failed to gain acceptance even at his own academy. Nonetheless, there was enough material in the recorded amoraic arguments to raise questions in inquiring minds as to whether the existing practices did not too seriously deviate from the demands of the Talmud.

Questions of this kind were aggravated by the occasional discord in the ancient sources themselves. Such differences appeared, for example, in the case of the very first benedictions with which a pious Jew ushered in his morning devotions. Originally Palestinian Jewry, evidently adopting a formula which enjoyed wide circulation in both the Hellenistic and Zoroastrian Near East, made every male Jew express daily thanks for not having been made a Gentile (or, more affirmatively, having been made an Israelite), a woman, or a slave. It doubtless was this formula which Paul had in mind when he asserted to the Galatians that "there is neither Jew nor Greek—there is neither bond nor free, there is neither male nor female; for ye are all one in Christ Jesus." Later on, perhaps prompted by the observation of the actual paucity of Jewish slaves and the desire to emphasize that no Jew be made a slave, the rabbis substituted for the third benediction one of thanksgiving for not having been made an ignoramus (*bor*). Some texts still contain the indubitably original form *'am ha-areṣ,* clearly betraying the old rabbinic animosities toward the "people of the land" which so greatly colored Palestinian life before, and shortly after, the fall of Jerusalem. In time, however, these animosities receded, and in the fourth century R. Aḥa bar Jacob reintroduced the older and more standardized form of thanksgiving for the enjoyment of freedom.[62]

The intervening formula, however, never died out. Rationalized by reference to Hillel's observation that "there is no ignoramus [*bor*] who fears sin," thanksgiving for a measure of education persisted to such an extent that Amram Gaon felt the need of combating it as contrary to law. Saadiah, on his part, took for granted the formula of not being made a slave. Clearly, at a time when more and more Jews were expected to recite their own prayers rather than rely on the mediation by congregational readers, a benediction for not having been made an ignoramus became less and less meaningful. In any case, no substitute had been devised to be recited by an illiterate person similar to the one introduced for the woman ("who hast made me in accordance with Thy will").[63]

This bewilderment, particularly of the Western scholars, gave rise to their growing preoccupation with liturgical problems. It began already in the middle of the ninth century, when the relatively large and intellectually alert community of Lucena in Spain addressed to Naṭronai bar Hilai Gaon of Sura an inquiry as to the nature and precise sequence of the hundred benedictions which, according to an old maxim of R. Meir, God required daily from every Israelite. This number, perhaps used merely as a round figure by R. Meir himself, was never elaborated in the Talmud. Nor is there any evidence that R. Meir's homily based on his predilection for puns—here the similarity in sound of *mah* (what) and *meah* (a hundred; in Deut. 10:12)—was ever taken literally in the Eastern communities of the talmudic and early posttalmudic age.[64]

Under the challenge of the Lucena inquiry, however, Naṭronai and his associates now proceeded to enumerate the required daily blessings, and with some difficulty they reconstructed the total of one hundred. Without going into precise details, and for the most part giving only the beginnings and a few phrases to identify the specific benedictions, Naṭronai's responsum thus became the nucleus of the Jewish prayer book.[65]

Externally, Naṭronai's responsum was a juridical rather than a liturgical composition, and there was nothing to distinguish it from similar geonic replies on other points of Jewish law. In fact, it had long been customary among both Rabbanite and Karaite leaders to discuss liturgical problems in connection with other halakhic deliberations. Aḥai of Shabḥa's and Simon Qayyara's codes had included lengthy sections on prayers, benedictions, the recitation of weekly lessons or the scroll of Esther, and other aspects of divine service at home or in the synagogue. 'Anan, too, despite the revolutionary nature of his liturgical reforms, was satisfied with presenting them as part and parcel of his total revamping of the existing Jewish legal system. But his innovations forced him to spell out his newly introduced prayers much more fully than did his Rabbanite counterparts, who could presuppose widespread knowledge of the accepted rituals. That is why the pertinent sections of 'Anan's *Book of Commandments* reveal so many characteristics of the later Rabbanite prayer books. To a lesser extent the same holds true of the numerous *Books of Commandments* produced by 'Anan's Karaite successors. Although, being incorporated in larger juridical manuals, such liturgical sections were devoid of a peculiar identity of their own, the Karaite challenge may have been provocative enough to stimulate reconsideration and final reformulation of the liturgical heritage on the part of Rabbanite leaders as well. Perhaps it was more than accidental that Naṭronai took up the gauntlet here, as he did in other areas under Karaite attack. Without taking direct cognizance of the Karaite opposition, he may indeed have welcomed the Spanish inquiry as an opportunity to restate the official position of Rabbanite Jewry in a phase of Jewish observance which cut so deeply into the daily life of the people.[66]

AMRAM AND SAADIAH

Within two decades after this exchange, another Spanish inquiry, accompanied we are told by a handsome gift of twenty gold pieces (five for the gaon and fifteen for the academy), stimulated Naṭronai's successor, Amram, to take up the liturgical problems in greater detail (about 870). While leaning heavily on Naṭronai's reply, Amram, together with his principal associate Ṣemaḥ bar Solomon, prepared "an order [*seder*] of prayers and benedictions for the entire year." Evidently the term *seder* did not yet possess the technical connotation of a regular prayer book, but simply referred to some systematic review of the prescribed rituals. This is, indeed, what the gaon offered to his Spanish correspondents. Unfortunately, we cannot fully reconstruct the original form of Amram's responsum. Apart from a few minor and far from illuminating fragments found in the Cairo Genizah, we possess only three more or less complete manuscripts from the late Middle Ages (the two better ones were completed in 1426 and 1516, respectively). Even these differ greatly among themselves, and they were hardly based on a single authentic tradition. Generally faithful in preserving the legal requirements summarized by the gaon and his associates, the medieval copyists freely expanded and modified the prayers themselves to conform with the texts used in their communities. Such alterations may have been perfectly unconscious, as many a writer filled in readings with which he had become familiar through a lifetime of recitation. Partly, however, they may have sprung from the fear of offending readers inured to particular versions. It is small wonder, then, that Amram's prayer book offers many challenging, indeed often unanswerable, problems, and that it has given rise to many irreconcilable theories.[67]

On the whole, the basic prayers weathered spoliation by time and overzealous copyists much better than more recently adopted liturgical pieces. The *Shema'* cycles and the *'Amidah,* long the universal heritage of the people, were carried down through the ages with astounding accuracy, not only by the few professional "memorizers," but also by the masses of worshipers. The more recent prayers, however, enjoying far less canonical sanctity, were often infringed upon by local readers and showed great variations. Very likely neither Amram nor his vice-chairman Ṣemaḥ bar Solomon cared to lay down the law for the textual correctness of such relatively late accretions.[68]

Despite the authoritarian tone characteristic of this and most other geonic replies, the leaders of the Suranic academy were evidently bent on supplying the Spanish communities with a handy reference book to the liturgical laws and regulations, rather than on spelling out for them specific readings. They knew that such readings varied widely even in Sura's immediate environment. Very frequently they pointed up certain observances at their academy or earlier decisions by their predecessors as profitable examples to be followed. They doubtless indicated the various liturgical pieces only by headings or other identifying words, supplying the full texts only when they doubted the recipients' familiarity with them or wished to prevent likely errors. When they referred, for example, to a previous discussion concerning the required insertion after the early morning benedictions of certain excerpts from Bible and rabbinic letters, they never cited the texts of these excerpts. They merely stressed their importance for daily compliance with the advice of ancient sages that every Jew should divide his time equally between Bible, Mishnah, and Talmud. This liturgical practice, they emphasized, "is thus found in the responsa, and this is the usage of all Israel," to which a patriotic Spanish scribe added "in Spain." Other scribes went further, and altered or amplified the prayers themselves. Hence, Louis Ginzberg's pessimistic observation is as valid today as it was some four decades ago: "We shall probably never know its [Amram's prayer book's] true, original form. It was used until it was used up." [69]

Curiously, Amram's compilation came into general use only in the Western countries, where it was constantly copied and recopied. In the East it long remained slumbering in the archives of the academy of Sura, exercising little influence on the subsequent liturgical evolution. Saadiah made no use of it in the compilation of his own prayer book half a century later, although from the acrostic to one of his poems of warning (*azharot*), misnamed by the first editor the poem of "six hundred and thirteen commandments," we may conclude that Saadiah served at that time as a high official (*alluf*) of Amram's own academy. The only other geonim who evinced interest in similar liturgical compilations, Sherira and Hai, both of Pumbedita, had no access to Sura's archival records. From Hai's reply to an inquiry quoting Amram's work, it is evident that he had not consulted it himself.[70]

Saadiah's prayer book is, therefore, not only completely independent, but also differs fundamentally from Amram's work in approach and motivation. It owed its origin not to outside prompting (the frequent assertion that the gaon prepared it at the request of Egyptian communities is unsupported by any evidence whatsoever), but to the author's inner urge. The more concerned Saadiah had become about the growing signs of Jewish communal disintegration in the decaying Caliphate, and the more passionately he dedicated himself to the task of reunification of world Jewry, the more dangerous appeared to him the existing liturgical anarchy. In his numerous travels he had observed widespread liturgical "neglect, addition, and omission." He became increasingly apprehensive lest such anarchy result in both "forgetfulness and permanence of deviation." For this reason, he added,

I have decided to assemble in this book the authoritative prayers, hymns, and benedictions in their original form as they existed before the Exile and after, and place them in their proper order. I shall also mention what I have learned about additions or omissions according to the arbitrary opinions of individual groups residing in a village or city, a district or country. Whatever runs counter to the fundamental objective, I have forbidden to recite; even with respect to prayers which do not nullify it. I have pointed out that they were unsupported by tradition. I shall further append a description of how one is to fulfill the commandments prescribed for every season of the year, after having first analyzed the commandments which are to be observed daily. I am indeed dividing [the whole work] into two parts: the general duties for every day, and the peculiar matters pertaining to specific periods of the year. In conclusion, I shall cite some beautiful prayers and appropriate hymns for the use of the servant who, someday, may wish thus to approach his Master. These are elective, and I shall not require their recitation, as I do that of the essential portions of the book.[71]

From the outset Saadiah wished to make this work as popular as possible. That is why he avoided all technical discussions of the law and even refrained from quoting his talmudic sources. He generally referred the reader to his earlier, elaborate *Commentary* on the Pentateuch. On the other hand, he included a brief treatise "On the Obligation of Prayer," which he seems to have distributed independently before his major compilation. Here he emphasized the greater frequency and variety of prayers of petition as compared with those devoted to thanksgiving or praise of the Lord. He also tried to explain the meaning and logical sequence of the *'Amidah,* adducing no less than twelve arguments (only three are preserved in our manuscript) for the specific number of its eighteen benedictions.[72]

No less individualistic was Saddiah's arrangement of the different sections. In contrast to Amram's purely pragmatic approach, Saadiah sought to introduce a systematic order based on certain logical, even philosophic, assumptions. Amram had arranged his compilation so as to give a handy guide to the worshiper, or rather to the congregational leader. That is why he began with the sequence of a typical day and, after describing the devotions during the morning prayers, discussed in detail the blessings required before, during, and after meals. Only then did he resume the description of the afternoon and evening services. To Saadiah such an interruption through prayers of a different category seemed highly illogical. He therefore relegated the analysis of the prayers connected with meals to a section dealing with benedictions arising from specific occasions. This section followed his extensive analysis of all regular daily services, both private and congregational, as well as of some of those additional voluntary prayers of petition which he had himself composed for the use of ultrapious worshipers.[73]

Dogmatic preconceptions likewise colored Saadiah's formulations far more than those of his predecessor. Discussing, for example, the required blessings before and after *Shema'*, Saadiah was prepared to accept many variants, but he strenuously objected to two phrases which, in his opinion, "nullified the fundamental objective." He condemned the insertion of the phrase "O cause a new light to shine upon Zion" before the conclusion of the first of these benedictions, because he felt that "the light for which we give thanks to God every day is the light of the sun itself, and nothing else." He disregarded here the pietistic yearnings to imbue even such simple thanksgiving with a messianic significance. Similarly, he denounced the replacement of the final sentence before the *'Amidah*, "Blessed art thou, O Lord, who hast redeemed Israel," by the more futuristic "Blessed art thou, O Lord, king of Israel and his redeemer." The gaon made it clear that the past tense was necessary, because the blessing related only to the redemption from Egypt, whereas the future redemption was left to the benedictions included in the silent prayer. Apart from these formalistic considerations, however, Saadiah's decisions running counter, at least in the former case, to a practice well accepted in the two academies (Sherira), may have been dictated by his pro-Babylonian bias, which had reached a high pitch in those very years of his service as *alluf* and Babylonia's chief spokesman in its controversy with Palestine's Ben Meir.[74]

Saadiah's prayer book enjoyed wide circulation in the Eastern lands to which it addressed itself—particularly its legalistic sections, written in Arabic and never translated into Hebrew. The fragments at the disposal of modern editors are remnants of at least thirty-five copies made by various scribes. Further copies are likely to come to light, especially when the treasures assembled in the Soviet libraries have become fully accessible to specialists in this field. Regrettably, the liturgical compilations of his geonic successors Sherira and Hai are totally lost, hence we cannot trace their detailed indebtedness to Saadiah's work. However, in at least one case Sherira expressly quotes it with approval. Sherira upholds the "new light on Zion" with obvious reluctance and only because "they have always recited it at both academies." But he adds on his own, "He who fails to recite it, will not be hurt." In answering a Kairuwan inquiry quoting Saadiah's work, Hai pointed out that some Babylonian rabbis, too, had deduced from Saadiah's *Siddur* that one had better refrain from drinking a fifth cup of wine during the Passover ceremony. But he viewed with alarm the numerous corruptions which, already at that time, had crept into the existing copies. We must remember, however, that such scribal abuses were perhaps the highest compliment unwittingly proffered to any medieval author. In the West, on the other hand, Saadiah's work remained largely unknown. Although the gaon's posthumous son, Dosa, doubtless sent a copy of the *Siddur* along with other works by, and his own biography of, his father to Ḥisdai ibn Shapruṭ in Cordova, the only Spanish scholars who seem to have had first-hand acquaintance with this great liturgical work were the tireless collectors of all geonic writings, Samuel ibn Nagrela of Granada, Isaac ibn Gayyat of Lucena, and Yehudah bar Barzillai of Barcelona. After the eleventh century most Western scholars, including Saadiah's great admirers Naḥmanides and Abraham ben Nathan of Lunel, apparently learned about his decisions only from second hand.[75]

In Kairuwan, too, that intermediary link between East and West, the impact of Saadiah's prayer book was hardly noticeable. True, we cannot confidently speak of this subject until we recover at least some significant fragments of the liturgical compilations or codes allegedly prepared there by Ḥananel, Nissim, and Shemariah ben Ephraim, as well as by Solomon ben Nathan of neighboring Segelmessa. Nissim's pupil Ibn al-Jasus (or al-Gasum), doubtless had Saadiah's work in mind when he wrote of a prayer book which was "second to none in brevity and thoughtfulness. We rely on it, it is a model for us, and one ought to cleanse it from the copyists' mistakes." Yet the fact that Alfasi, a devoted pupil of the Kairuwan sages, betrayed so little familiarity with Saadiah's compilation makes one wonder whether the book was not rejected there on practical, even more than on dogmatic or legalistic, grounds. It thus shared the fate of the great gaon's equally learned but impractical halakhic monographs, of which in a sense it was the most illustrious example.[76]

Even in the East Saadiah's ritual evidently was nowhere accepted in exactly the form suggested by the gaon. Trying to use it as an instrument for the unification of world Jewry, Saadiah had obviously sought to reduce the practices prevailing in Babylonia, Palestine, and Egypt to a common denominator. Such eclecticism necessarily ran counter to some existing observances in each particular congregation. As usual, the rank and file of congregational members, even more than the leaders, resented the smallest deviation from their accepted ritualistic norms, while merely taking in their stride the gaon's approval of their other practices. Saadiah's acerbity in dismissing objectionable phrases or motions likewise antagonized many worshipers accustomed to them for many years. Apart from disliking Saadiah's tone, many doubtless viewed some of his critical remarks as direct slurs on their revered ancestors. Moreover, Saadiah's book was much too sophisticated. Ironically, Amram's responsum was addressed to informed correspondents and was, therefore, studded with quotations from talmudic and earlier geonic sources, a rather unusual feature in geonic responsa. Nevertheless, it made much simpler reading than Saadiah's more penetrating and theologically more closely reasoned observations, unburdened though these were by supporting source material. Saadiah's systematic arrangement, too, highly satisfactory to the serious student, must have proved difficult for anyone who without acquiring full familiarity with the whole work wished to locate therein a particular prayer or regulation. The medieval reader certainly did not have at his disposal the fine indexes provided for the book by its modern editors.[77]

For these reasons Saadiah found more students and copyists

than direct imitators, even in the Eastern communities. Secure in the possession of their ancestral customs, their leaders studied with great interest the decisions of Saadiah as compared with many rendered by his geonic predecessors and successors. But they unperturbedly continued to adhere to their own local or regional peculiarities.

MAIMONIDES' SUMMARY

Spanish Jewry, though entering at that time the period of its greatest intellectual creativity, contributed relatively little to the unification and standardization of Jewish liturgy. Perhaps its very creative *élan* militated against concentration on rigid requirements in this domain, while its great poets unstintingly devoted their creative energies to the enlargement and embellishment of the inherited liturgical treasures. We shall see that their new compositions penetrated the synagogue services in many lands. While Spanish jurists continued to make significant contributions to this field as well, the only lasting monograph entirely devoted to liturgy seems to have been written by that distinguished student of geonic lore, Yehudah bar Barzillai of Christian Barcelona. In his *Sefer ha-'Ittim* (Book of Seasons), later epitomized by the French Abraham ben Isaac of Narbonne in his *Sefer ha-Eshkol* (Cluster of Grapes), Spanish Jewry produced a ritualistic classic of the first order. The excessive length of this work, however, militated against its popularity even among the Spanish Jews, and only some relatively small segments could be recovered by its modern editors from the few extant manuscripts. Another liturgical work, perhaps combined with a more regular prayer book prepared about the same time by Ibn al-Jasus (or Al-Gasum), a pupil of R. Nissim, fared worse; only a small fragment seems to have survived in the world's libraries.[78]

The only scholar after Saadiah to exercise a lasting influence on the liturgical evolution of the Jewish communities in the Muslim world was Maimonides. But he achieved this effect precisely because he did not produce an independent prayer book. A comprehensive liturgical volume from even his pen would probably have remained but a flash illumining the momentary state of

Jewish liturgical practice. Only because the sage of Fusṭaṭ included the liturgical regulations in his own superlative legal code, and with them a brief enumeration of the required prayers and benedictions, was he successful in deeply influencing the liturgical evolution as well.

Accepting many (but also rejecting some) of Saadiah's rules and reasons, showing familiarity with a wide range of rituals extending from Spain and Morocco to Egypt and Palestine, and utilizing the diversified experiences of the Egyptian communities themselves, Maimonides was able to produce another composite summary. On the whole, he tried to revert to the bare essentials laid down in the Talmud, but since the Talmud was far from explicit in regard to most controversial problems, the codifier had to pave his own way, generally adhering to his much cherished "golden mean" and seeking a compromise between some universally acceptable rituals and the chaotic variety of local observances. Because it was far less revolutionary in content, his eclecticism was evidently found less objectionable. During the century and a half since Saadiah, moreover, the continuing symbiosis of congregations of different rites in such cosmopolitan centers as Fusṭaṭ-Cairo and the increasingly vigorous cultural exchanges between the Jewries of various lands had produced a certain growing mutual toleration, as well as a leveling down of existing differences. Without completely smoothing over the ritualistic disparities, the deepening social and cultural homogeneity of the Eastern communities, sharpened by the incipient intellectual lassitude and opposition of independent creativity, bred a more general receptivity for final and authoritative regulation of both domestic and synagogue rituals.[79]

Maimonides and his son Abraham doubtless dreamed of completely unifying the liturgy of Egyptian Jewry under the aegis of the new *Code,* although progress in this direction must have appeared to them disappointingly slow. Only after several generations of living under the communal control of "princes" of the house of Maimon did Egyptian Jewry gradually slough off its ritualistic divergences. At the end of the Middle Ages, indeed, we no longer hear of congregations in Cairo or Alexandria adhering strictly to their inherited Babylonian or Palestinian rites. To foreign visitors like Obadiah Bartenora, all Egyptian Rabbanites appeared as a ritualistic unit, opposed only by such sectarians as Samaritans and Karaites. In far-off Yemen, too, the combined influence of Saadiah and Maimonides, revered there above all other masters of Jewish lore, produced a liturgical synthesis which was authoritatively summarized in the comprehensive native product called *Takhalil* and outlasted all subsequent political storms and individualistic innovations. It still forms the foundation of the Yemenite liturgy of today.[80]

Curiously, even Maimonides and his son did not always see eye to eye in liturgical matters. This area, so closely related to the worshiper's communion with God, necessarily reflected the temperamental disparity between the rationalistic father and the mystically minded son. Moses Maimuni considered himself the watchdog of the universal tradition of his people, and he sought to discourage individual departures, even when dictated by excessive piety. With particular reference to the cycle of benedictions accompanying the recitation of *Shema'*, he insisted that "these blessings, together with the other blessings recited by all Israel, were instituted by Ezra and his court, and no one is entitled to subtract from, or to add anything to, them." He therefore opposed not only the addition of *piyyuṭim*—he shared this hostility with many illustrious predecessors—but also the inclusion of any personal petitions within the stated liturgy or even its interruption for the purpose of reciting an individually required benediction. In reply to an inquiry, he wrote tersely: "It is not appropriate to interrupt them [congregational prayers] for anything, not even for benedictions, for he [the worshiper] is engaged in the fulfillment of a commandment; why, then, should he interrupt it for the sake of another commandment?" Maimonides also objected strenuously to the wholesale recitation of the numerous morning benedictions enumerated in Amram's prayer book and widely adopted in the contemporary communities. "This is a mistake," he exclaimed, "one must not do so; one should recite a blessing only if one is personally obliged to recite it" because of particular circumstances. Abraham Maimuni concurred with this view and even tried to enforce it by administrative orders. Yet, at variance with the entire tenor of his father's decisions if not with their clear formulation, he wished to encourage private devotions going far beyond the accepted limits. With some evident embarrassment, he replied affirmatively to an inquiry concerning the permissibility of constant prostrations: "As to a voluntary fast, voluntary prayer, or [other] acts of piety, may they multiply and spread widely. There is not the slightest suspicion of their being prohibited, but it is rather forbidden to place any obstacles in the way of Israel's worship, devotion, and immersion in prayer." [81]

WESTERN COMPILATIONS

In the West the output of new liturgical handbooks may have been slowed down by the publication of the Maimonidean Code, but it did not stop. In the increasingly feudalistic environment of Christian Europe the Jews shared with their neighbors an extreme reverence for local custom. Since no domain of Jewish private or communal life was dominated by custom to a greater extent than that of liturgy, European Jewry evinced an insatiable curiosity about every minutia of liturgical practice. It unceasingly contrasted the formal law, grown familiar through ever more intensive study of the Talmud and geonic letters, with its daily ritualistic practice, the heritage of those "dark" and inarticulate ages which had preceded the rise of the Franco-German schools in the Provence, Champagne, and the Rhine lands.

Beginning with Joseph Tob 'Elem (Bonfils), therefore, French rabbis, particularly of Rashi's school in Troyes, produced many liturgical treatises. Rashi's pupils adopted the custom, which was soon to prevail in the Christian universities as well, of taking copious notes. Since the master undoubtedly repeated his lectures every few years, there arose numerous divergences in the notes compiled by different pupils at different times. The disciples often included observations on the master's personal conduct on certain ritualistically significant occasions. In contrast, therefore, to Rashi's *Commentaries* on Bible and Talmud, which were either originally written or at least carefully revised by him and bear the full imprint of his personality and editorial care, the juristic-liturgical treatises attributed to him were never seen by him in their present form. Hence come, as we recall, their constant repetitions and frequent contradictions. Nevertheless, they often complement one another significantly. Between them the aforementioned juridical miscellanies entitled *Sefer ha-Pardes* (Orchard), *Ha-Orah* (Light) or *Oreh* (Plucker), and *Siddur* (Prayer Book), attributed to Rashi himself, the *Maḥzor Vitry* compiled by his pupil, Simḥah bar Samuel, as well as two as yet unpublished works, entitled *Sefer ha-Sedarim* (Book of Liturgical Orders), and *Sefer Issur ve-hetter* (Book of Forbidden and Permissible Matters) have given us deep insights into the entire realm of legal practice and ritualistic thinking of the founders of Jewish learning in western Europe. They have also served as an inexhaustible mine of information on the preceding liturgical evolution in all of Jewry.[82]

With the exception of Simḥah of Vitry's work, none of these collections of notes deserve the name prayer book. Though largely concerned with liturgical problems, they also included many other legal materials. Both the *Pardes* and the *Orah* actually begin with semilegal and semimoralistic discourses on certain aspects of family relations. Even the *Siddur,* which generally hews somewhat more closely to the line of ritual, has many admixtures from other domains of law. While discussing, for example, the services for the Day of Atonement, the compiler also treats of the required forms of self-mortification during that supreme fast. The whole work concludes with an analysis of the laws of mourning and a variety of dietary regulations, but it interrupts them with a brief discourse on the scriptural lessons prescribed for holidays. Similar haphazard notes thrown together in the *Pardes* became so irksome to readers that, before long, an Italian disciple felt prompted to summarize and rearrange them in a more systematic collection, called *Liqquṭe Pardes* (Pluckings of the Orchard). The original confusion became even more confounded as a result of ruthless handling by copyists, who unperturbedly omitted passages and, more frequently, added pertinent (and not so pertinent) decisions by later authorities or marginal notes by assiduous readers. If the original compilers had few compunctions about lifting passages from the notebooks of fellow students, the later copyists with even greater abandon inserted into their own texts borrowings from other compilations.[83]

By far the most important liturgical work from the school of Rashi is, therefore, the *Maḥzor Vitry,* for which Rashi's authorship was never claimed. Although likewise suffering from lack of careful planning and organization (the usual concomitant of the dynamic approach of the Ashkenazim) and subjected to equal tampering by undisciplined copyists and interpolators, it bears the earmarks of greater fidelity to the author's original intentions. More significantly, it is the first real prayer book compiled by a Western rabbi to combine ritualistic regulations with verbatim texts of prayers.

R. Simḥah made extensive use, both overt and tacit, of Amram's prayer book, which he sometimes called *Maḥzor,* a term borrowed from the astronomic "cycle." He also was familiar with other "ancient prayer books [*maḥzorin*]." However, despite his occasional references to Saadiah, his direct acquaintance with the gaon's liturgical work is very doubtful. He nevertheless followed Saadiah's example in supplying full texts of many long-accepted prayers, as well as inserting numerous more recent *piyyuṭim* for the free choice of synagogue readers. It is small wonder, then, that his own *Maḥzor* vastly exceeded in size Amram's popular responsum and the ritualistic works compiled by his fellow students of Troyes. Despite its great bulk, R. Simḥah's book seems to have immediately captured the imagination of his ritualistically minded contemporaries. By offering the synagogue readers an authoritative text, buttressed by extensive halakhic discourses and quotations from older sources, including Rashi himself (frequently referred to by name), it also met an important communal need. That is why many communities secured copies, laboriously transcribed and partly vocalized by more or less competent scribes. If we are to believe R. Jacob Tam, within a few decades after R. Simḥah's death the *Maḥzor* was to be "found in most places." [84]

Clearly, R. Jacob did not mean to imply that R. Simḥah's voluminous work was available in many copies throughout western Europe. Its size alone, even without the numerous subsequent interpolations, must have made its price prohibitive to all but a few wealthy booklovers or synagogue treasuries. Its use was further aggravated by its mixture of prayers with extensive and often complicated regulations for their recitation, constantly interspersed with halakhic discussions on other ritualistic matters. In this respect, the *Maḥzor Vitry* was even less handy as a prayer book in the modern sense than was Amram's *Seder* in its original form. Although more practical than Saadiah's systematic compilation, both these works were likewise designed principally to offer guidance to the intellectual élite, particularly the men in charge of congregational worship. Ordinary members, even if perfectly literate, did not have a regular prayer book at their disposal until after the invention of printing. Smaller congregations, such as were the rule in western Europe and the Near Eastern countryside, doubtless possessed only one or two copies of these ambitious handbooks. Kept in the local synagogues, these were always available for consultation by interested persons, especially synagogue readers.

Against this background of great scarcity and high prices, we may also understand the continued insistence of the medieval rabbis upon recitation of prayers from memory. Even the best informed worshipers as a rule did not own texts containing all the prayers likely to be used. This was doubly true in the case of holiday prayers. More extensive and complicated, a holiday *maḥzor* always commanded a far higher price. At the same time it was of direct use only during a few days each year, parts of it only once a year. Clearly, most congregants could learn only certain prayers by heart and had to rely on the precentor and his authoritative copy for reading aloud all the less familiar liturgical pieces. In the days of Yehudai Gaon, even the readers were not allowed to use written texts, except in the case of the lengthy and complicated prayers recited on the Day of Atonement or other fasts. Saadiah observed that many contemporaries preferred to omit verses rarely used in holiday services rather than commit errors in quotation. He felt prompted, therefore, to warn worshipers against excessive caution on such stated occasions as the holiday *Musaf*. Rashi, still echoed by Abudarham, however, forbade the recitation, except on Sabbaths and New Moons, of verses whose frequency alone offered a sufficient safeguard for correct memorization.[85]

SYNAGOGUE CHANT

Memory was at times aided by a uniformly accepted tune. Once a melody became associated with a particular prayer, most changes in phrasing, willful or erroneous, caused a noticeable alteration also in the melody. Such a deviation was less likely to escape the attention of the audience than was the textual variant itself. The distinguished sixteenth-century rabbi Mordecai Jaffe complained that his efforts to correct certain errors in the text of the *Kol Nidre* prayer proved unavailing because the cantors "were unable to change [the text] during the services on account of the tune to which they had become accustomed." To make doubly sure that the "messenger" would make no mistakes, ancient congregations often associated with him one or two assistants (so-called "supporters" or "helpers"), who served primarily as prompters. Later, when written prayers were available, it became their principal duty to assist the precentor in his musical performance. Occasionally, especially for some major celebrations such as the installation of a new exilarch, these helpers, who were usually young boys, formed regular choirs.[86]

Otherwise, synagogue chanting was either a solo performance on the part of the precentor, only occasionally interrupted by brief congregational responsoria and exclamations like *amen* or *halleluyah,* or congregational singing in unison. Despite the impression created by Philo's description, Jewish congregations were never as passive as many Christian church assemblies were to become in the days of the Graeco-Syrian *Testamentum Domini* (about 400). The fundamental Jewish belief in the "priesthood of all believers" necessarily placed the emphasis on the congregation rather than on its "messenger." Later, Pirqoi observed that, despite governmental persecutions, Jews were allowed "to foregather on Sabbath mornings to read and sing" *piyyuṭim.* Samau'al ibn Yaḥya likewise observed that the authors of these new poems

composed for them numerous melodies. The Jews used to assemble during their services to sing and to read them. The difference between the new poetry [*ḥizanah*] and the obligatory prayer [*ṣalat*] is that the latter is recited without a melody. Only the precentor reads it, and no one shouts it together with him. At the *ḥizanah,* however, he is assisted by many members of the audience with shouts and songs as an accompaniment to his melodies.

Samau'al did not mean that the obligatory prayers were recited in a complete monotone. On the contrary, even the scriptural lessons were from very early times read with a particular cantillation, for which the masoretic schools introduced specific symbols. In contrast to modern notation, however, which has developed slowly and painfully over the last millennium, the masoretic *ṭe'amim* (accents), like their Byzantine and Syriac counterparts, indicated musical phrases rather than individual sounds. While less precise than modern musical notes, these accents offered sufficient guidance to establish a certain basic uniformity, which has outlasted many social and environmental changes. To this very day Bible reading in the world's synagogues sounds very much alike.[87]

Because of a certain vagueness of the exact musical equivalents of each symbol, it was possible to use the same thirty (in Ben Asher's time only nineteen) symbols for the entire Bible, except for the books of Psalms, Proverbs, and Job, which were equipped with an independent system. Evidently responding to the need for distinguishing the cantillation of psalms from the ordinary scriptural lessons, the Masorites introduced twelve different symbols. Even with the same accents, however, it was possible to vary greatly the cantillation between the Pentateuchal lesson and the prophetic selection, as well as between the readings on Sabbaths and on holidays. Different tunes were used for the Five Scrolls, especially for the mournful recitation of Lamentations on the Ninth of Ab. Equal latitude was given to regional and individual preferences. The fourteenth-century Yemenite author of the *Manuel de lecteur* declared that "every main and subsidiary accent has tone and melody of its own. They do not resemble one another, except perhaps in regard to one or two turns." The psalmodic tunes, on the other hand, were often neglected, and the morning selections from the psalms were almost universally recited without the prescribed cantillation. Only in Baghdad, we learn from Petaḥiah, did they have several tunes for each psalm, Psalm 6 being recited in eight and Psalm 92 in ten modes. As late as the thirteenth century some congregations in western Europe likewise recited Psalm 91 in a particular cadence.[88]

Most of these accents seem to be derived from hand signals which the precentors used to give to their audiences, especially with regard to the raising or lowering of their voices or of maintaining a tune on an even pitch. As has been pointed out, many symbols transcended linguistic or national boundaries and there were resemblances between the Byzantine, Syriac, and Jewish modes of cantillation. For example, the ascending *qadmah,* the descending *ṭipḥah,* and the constant *etnaḥ* look very much like their Romance counterparts, the acute, grave, and circumflex accents. Such visual conducting of the congregational chant seems to have continued at least to the eleventh century. According to Rashi, cantors from Palestine visiting western Europe still lifted or lowered the second finger to warn the audience of an ascending or descending tone to follow.[89]

No such system of cantillation was employed for prayers, yet there developed in the course of time certain basic tunes for a few major daily recitations (even more for holiday prayers) which successfully weathered changes of habitat and the corrosive forces of time. For example, the magnificent tune of the beautiful *Musaf 'Amidah* of New Year's day shows fewer and less far-reaching local or regional variations than one would normally expect. Most prayers, however, were not recited in such uniform fashion. Newly inserted supplications or laudations usually were set to music by the authors themselves while they improvised the prayers. Jewish authors probably differed little in this respect from their Christian counterparts such as the great *melodos,* Romanos. Whatever accompaniment was offered by the assistants and the public evidently was unrehearsed. Nor was Hai Gaon alone in permitting a congregation to silence its "messenger" if the latter committed some serious error. Such accompaniment must long have been limited largely to the congregational responsoria. Many *piyyuṭim,* indeed, made a point of having refrains, often consisting of passages from the Bible, or the particular prayer to which they were appended. These refrains were doubtless recited by the congregation in some kind of singsong. Probably at first completely untrammeled, responses were later regulated as to timing and tune and became standard prayers of the liturgy. However, if we are to believe Samau'al even in his day there was still a great deal of freedom for individual and mass improvisation. Certainly, the medieval Jewish congregations evinced far greater interest in inwardness and intensity of prayer than in outward decorum, evoking, as we recall, a sharp censure from Maimonides.[90]

Chanting was nevertheless considered but a secondary aspect of worship. From its inception, the synagogue made a studied effort to avoid too close emulation of the Temple services. Circumstances, too, as we remember, had forced the ancient congregations in the dispersion to follow increasingly austere lines. Moreover, because of their association with both Graeco-Roman worship and licentiousness in public and private festivities, musical performances as such fell into disrepute among the more ascetically minded Jews as well as among Christians. We shall see how deeply this antagonism affected the attitude toward secular music of most ancient and medieval Jewish communities. It is small wonder, then, that liturgical music, which had played such a great role in the Christian heresies from the days of Bardeisan and Arius, never became a major subject of controversy between orthodox and sectarian Jews. There is hardly any reference to it in the vast Karaite and anti-Karaite literature of the tenth and eleventh centuries. Nor do we hear of any outright opposition to the chanting of new musical creations, such as was attempted for a time by the Council of Laodicaea (about 370). Hostility was directed against the content of the *piyyuṭim* rather than against their melodies.

Drawing a sharp line of demarcation between sacred and secular music, the Jewish leaders permitted the former, provided that it was clearly imbued with the spirit of worship and shunned purely external aesthetic and emotional appeals. True, they realized that synagogue music, along with the sermon, often attracted even Gentile worshipers. It has been suggested that a Pahlavi inscription recovered from the ruins of the Dura-Europos synagogue commemorated such a Gentile who "looked there where the Jewish chant was, he destroyed the other god, came and listened," and it is reminiscent of R. Judan's aforementioned homily about the preacher whose sermons brought Gentiles to the synagogue.

Nevertheless, music was not considered of focal importance in the Jewish liturgy. Instrumental music, in particular, was considered objectionable even on weekdays, and doubly so when it violated the Sabbath or holiday rest. The Baghdad custom, observed by Petaḥiah of Ratisbon, of reciting psalms with the accompaniment of instruments during the half holidays was quite exceptional. Even singing was to be limited to sacred themes and to male voices. "An ear listening to [secular] music shall be torn out," said none other than Rab, himself a distinguished liturgical writer and leader in prayers. Endowment with a beautiful voice, the rabbis agreed, was only one of many prerequisites for a precentor. Defining the qualifications of the elder and experienced person demanded by the Mishnah, R. Judah taught that it ought to be

> a man burdened with a family and unable to provide for it, working hard in the field and yet having an empty house, a man of attractive appearance, humble and popular with the community, who has musical understanding and a pleasing voice, is competent to read the Torah, Prophets, and Hagiographa, knows how to study halakhic and aggadic hermeneutics, and is perfectly familiar with all the benedictions.

To be sure, the requirement of poverty, intended to make his supplication for the welfare of the entire community the more deeply felt, was often overlooked. When it came to a test, R. Ḥisda interpreted away that requirement by declaring that the "empty house" really meant a house devoid of sin. Wealth thus ceased to be a deterrent, but it never attained the importance of piety, learning, or a good singing voice. In the words of Maimonides, "We appoint as messenger of the community only its most distinguished member by learning and good deeds. An old man is most eligible. We also try to choose a man possessing a pleasant voice and experience in reading." If we must choose, decided Yehudai Gaon, we should rather select a scholar without a voice, than a singer without learning.[91]

Ultimately, however, vocal endowment, training, and good musicianship outweighed all other qualifications. With the progressive lifting of the ban on secular music, indeed with the growing appreciation of beautiful songs for their own sake, the cantorial performances in the synagogues likewise became artistic, as much as devotional, feats. The old austerity, still maintained in the poverty-stricken, insecure communities north of the Alps or in Yemen, gave way to an increasing *joie de vivre* in most Mediterranean lands. With it came also a greater appreciation of the aesthetic and emotional values of sacred music. The medieval compiler of *Pesiqta rabbati* had already impressed on the minds of his readers the story of an ancient cantor named Nabot, who, on his pilgrimage to Jerusalem, attracted "all Israel" to listen to his performances. Because he once failed to come to the Holy City, he died before his time. Late in the thirteenth century, Immanuel of Rome depicted a cantor boasting,

> When I recite the great *Qedushah,* a *yoṣer,* or a *qerobah,* all the wells of the great abyss break lose [that is, even the most hardened members are swept off their feet]; when I pray on the Day of Atonement, read the scroll of Esther on Purim, recite the *En kamokha* [There is None like unto Thee] on the three pilgrims' festivals [Passover, Festivals of Weeks, and Tabernacles, before the Reading of the Law], or chant a psalm, the mighty ones tremble before my voice; and when I read "the Vision of Isaiah," intone the Lamentations, or recite the evil forebodings of Jeremiah, all tongues remain silent, and no eye is free of tears.

Immanuel also emphasized the high social standing of the cantors of his day, a fact which had incidentally found expression in the early inclusion of the *ḥazzan* among the communal dignitaries, for whom a special blessing was recited. Our poet clearly sensed that some of the tunes heard in the Italian synagogues were of non-Jewish origin, a practice frowned upon by medieval rabbis such as Alfasi. But Immanuel comforted himself with the old rationale that "the whole science of music among Christians was certainly pilfered from the land of the Hebrews." This reputed friend of Dante could, indeed, cite ample patristic testimony for the Church's early borrowings from synagogue chants.[92]

At times these artistic exhibitions distorted the relation between the established prayers. In some congregations the elective new poems, lending themselves to fine musical interpretation, overshadowed some of the basic prayers whose musical interpretation followed long-accepted patterns and left little scope for individual artistry. A gifted cantor might spend a whole hour on the recitation of the psalms, or even on a single liturgical piece. Although generally annoyed with such undue lengthening of services, the rabbis encouraged it where it enabled latecomers to catch up with the congregation. Especially on Friday evening such lengthy chants became customary. The *Kol Nidre* recitation, which had to begin long before sunset, was usually repeated three times in a constant crescendo. On the other hand, some cantors, invoking an ancient tradition, permitted themselves to cut down the very *'Amidah* of the Sabbath and holiday eves to but three brief benedictions. They were evidently trying to facilitate the congregants' homeward trek while there still was some twilight. Mystically-minded precentors were encouraged to imbue certain laudations with mystic meanings by the spreading belief that earthly services were but a direct emulation of the homage rendered the Almighty by the heavenly hosts. Did not the Talmud depict the Lord himself in the role of a precentor instructing Moses in the fundamentals of Jewish liturgy? Such passages may have caused much grief to Saadiah and other philosophic expounders of God's incorporeality, but they did not fail to stimulate popular cantors, and their enthusiastic followers, to musical ecstasies in their adoration. For this reason the German pietists soon urged every precentor to look for a suitable tune for each piece. In short, overriding reiterated protests by intellectuals on philosophic as well as legalistic grounds, musical performances, in constant interplay with the rising tide of *piyyuṭim,* assumed a focal position in congregational life.[93]

RITUALISTIC DYNAMISM

In the end a balance was struck between the old and the new. Rigid adherence to tradition was mitigated by the creative reshaping of old forms to adjust them to newly awakened needs and desires. The original nucleus of universally accepted prayers and benedictions, supplemented by an anarchical variety of personal devotions, now gave way to a comprehensive communal liturgy incorporating the original prayers together with a vast array of elective liturgical pieces. Congregations, and particularly their professional or lay "messengers," could decide whether and how many of these voluntary additions they wished to incorporate into their services, both regular and extraordinary.

Musical recitation was even less regimented. Apart from the

biblical accents, which served as more or less definite guides in reading scriptural lessons, there was considerable freedom in the selection of new tunes, or variations of older ones. Of course, here too tradition played a great role. Before long certain prayers came to be chanted in approximately the same way in each congregation, region, or even throughout the entire Jewish world. However, even in the biblical cantillation, and still more in such traditional chants, much room was left to individual variation. Precisely because the biblical accents did not resemble modern notes indicating specific sounds, the reader could express the same general theme in a more personal fashion than is possible even for a creative modern virtuoso who is necessarily restricted by the particular score.

In this way Judaism succeeded in dynamically developing its system of worship, which reconciled personal inwardness and the individual's communion with his Deity with a modicum of communal control and an all-pervasive unity. During the geonic period, to be sure, at the height of Jewish communal centralization an attempt was made to standardize Jewish liturgy too. Some leaders objected, in particular, to many popular *piyyuṭim,* whose content, attuned to the mass mind, no longer agreed with their own more refined legal or theological concepts. They also viewed with disfavor the improvisation of ever new tunes, some undoubtedly borrowed, however unconsciously, from non-Jewish folksongs or ecclesiastical music, which made listening to the new poems often more attractive to the masses than hearing the relative monotone of the old prayers. Their general sense of propriety and orderliness, enhanced by their legal training and unbounded reverence for tradition, was likewise offended by the anarchical nature of this entire output. As long as the *piyyuṭ* consisted merely of oral improvisations by gifted cantors enjoying local reputation, the harm did not appear to be great. But when more and more of these poems began circulating in writing and capturing the imagination of audiences in many lands, the danger to Jewish unity loomed large. Nevertheless, even the most authoritarian of the geonim, Saadiah, himself a genuinely dedicated person and liturgical poet by grace divine, did not try to outlaw these new creations completely, but merely to subsume them under some such authoritative order as that summarized in his prayer book.

After Saadiah the communal control declined, while the original fears of the disintegrating influence of the *piyyuṭ* and its musical exercises were greatly mitigated. Some of the geonim themselves became friendly to the new poetry which, following Saadiah's lead, they themselves were helping to expand. If the equally rationalistic and authoritarian codifier Maimonides still remained unreconciled, he never really ventured to suppress completely what had in the interim become a hallowed tradition. Moreover, he was himself too religious a person to wish to see the liturgy entirely crystallized. In his codification of the laws governing prayer he, therefore, not only reminisced romantically about the lost glories of the complete liturgical freedom during the First Commonwealth, but he actually allowed variations within the text of the *'Amidah* (except for the first three and the last three benedictions).

These prayers [he declared] must not be reduced, but they may be increased. If a man wishes to pray the whole day, he is entitled to do so, and all his additional prayers will be considered as if he brought a free-will offering. In fact, when reciting any of the middle benedictions he ought to add something new. Once he adds some new turn to a single benediction, he has done his duty, for he has shown that he made a free-will offering, and not merely fulfilled an obligation [*M.T.* Tefillah 1.9].

Such reconciliation of the general interests of the community with the individual's quest for religious self-expression was facilitated by the entire tenor of Jewish liturgy. Here individual and national wants merged so imperceptibly and naturally that the worshiper could hardly draw a line where his own supplication ended and that of the nation began. In fact, under the combined impact of tradition and existing circumstances, the Jew viewed his individual salvation as intimately linked with the salvation of the whole people. Eleazar Qalir and other poets often started their poetry in a purely individualistic vein. Their personally colored laudation of the Creator and His works was often followed by a purely personal supplication. But in most cases their prayer ended on the theme of national redemption as a cosmic event superseding all else. Most of these poets, moreover, invoked the testimony of history. They quoted the sacred history of their people and of the world at large, as it was mirrored in the ancient stories of the Bible and recreated and expanded in the Aggadah, which many of them constantly helped to enrich. With such an underlying unity in outlook, the individual and regional divergences were minor indeed. Despite the proliferation of local and regional rites, the Jewish people pursued its historic career with an essentially uniform liturgy in an overwhelmingly unitarian, though basically free, synagogue.

XXXII

POETRY AND BELLES-LETTRES

LEGAL and homiletical compilations, Bible commentaries, grammars, and prayer books became the major, but far from exclusive, branches of a rich and variegated literature in both prose and poetry. Long called by their Arab neighbors the "people of the book," namely of Scripture, the Jews became under Arab domination a people of many books. Previously their leaders had often harbored serious misgivings about committing to writing any of their countless oral traditions. Nor did the Jewries of Palestine and Babylonia ever evince any serious interest in the works of their Greek-writing coreligionists, including Philo and Josephus. Since their own literary output in Aramaic, outside the realm of Oral Law which long continued to be transmitted only in oral form, was extremely limited, the libraries in the possession of individual scholars and synagogues, and even of the central academies, must have been very small indeed.

BOOKS AND LIBRARIES

A tannaitic law provided only that "members of a community shall force one another to acquire the Torah and Prophets" at public expense. These biblical books (not the Hagiographa) were, of course, required for public recitation in the synagogue, and no obstreperous congregational minorities could be allowed to interfere with their acquisition. It was also exclusively with the view to propagating the production and distribution of biblical writings that tannaitic law exempted scribes and booksellers from the required recitation of prayers at stated times or the wearing of phylacteries, "for he who is engrossed in the performance of one commandment is free from performing another commandment." Whatever homilies or liturgical works may have circulated in the Jewish communities, apart from the still popular magic scrolls or codices, there certainly was no Jewish writer of the fourth or fifth century who could rival the literary output of such Syriac contemporaries as St. Ephraem or Theodore of Mopsuestia. The reputed three million lines of text produced by the great Syriac poet-homilist and the forty-one works attributed to the distinguished Christian Bible scholar (Theodore's contemporary Ma'na allegedly wrote sixty or even eighty works) easily exceeded in size anything produced in written form by entire generations of talmudic rabbis.[1]

Under Muslim domination the roles were reversed. While Syriac and Greek letters, even in areas still under Byzantine sovereignty, deteriorated in quality and gradually diminished in quantity, the Jewish literary output increased by leaps and bounds. We have already noted the great flowering of Jewish legal, homiletical, and polemical literatures, as well as of Bible exegesis and philology during the three centuries from 900 to 1200. The same prodigious effort also characterized the creativity in the fields of sacred and profane poetry, of philosophy and science. This veritable literary revolution, reaching its apogee in Islam's western outpost, Spain, not unjustifiedly earned for that period the designation of the "Golden Age" of Jewish literature.

Apart from the great intellectual stimulus generated by the rise and spread of the new expansive civilization, the Jews owed their new masters the reunification, under one regime, of the overwhelming majority of their people, including their two chief intellectual centers of Palestine and Babylonia. The growing ease of communications and the large-scale entry of Jews into world trade tied together that far-flung dispersion and produced a vast and responsive audience for the creative efforts of leaders. The Jewish, as well as the non-Jewish, output of books was affected even more directly by the new facilities for production and distribution. Expensive ancient materials, such as parchment and papyrus, now gave way, to relatively inexpensive paper, which was within the reach of even impecunious authors and readers. Conditions remained far less propitious in Christian Europe. Throughout the Middle Ages, Western Jewish leaders were forced to issue public warnings against the mutilation of existing manuscripts by cutting out margins for use as notes of indebtedness, talismans, and the like.[2]

Every book still had to be copied by hand, however. This required the training of a class of skilled and informed scribes, who would not only cultivate their calligraphy, but also familiarize themselves with a great variety of subjects. Many of these scribes, being scholars in their own right, were frequently tempted to eliminate "errors," both formal and substantive, from the texts before them. While some were careful to suggest such alterations on the margin, others changed the text with complete insouciance. The greatest culprits were those who for dogmatic rather than scholarly reasons tampered with existing versions and considered such "improvements" the fulfillment of their religious duty. Others abbreviated given texts when they regarded certain portions as unnecessary ballast. For example, the prayers cited in the Maimonidean *Code* are so truncated by both author and copyists that the reconstruction of the underlying prayer book is very arduous. These willful, as well as unconscious, mistakes in transmission generally escaped the attention of all but the most critical readers. As the latter group increased in number and influence, there also arose a growing demand for old and reliable manuscripts, not only of Scriptures considered sacred by the respective faiths, but also of works of secular scholarship. One can envisage, therefore, the joy of Maimonides when he was able to consult the masoretically impeccable copy of the Bible in the possession of the Rabbanite community of Cairo and a copy of the Talmud allegedly five hundred years old.[3]

Understandably, the cost of labor still was very high. Despite the reduction in the price of raw materials, many students could not satisfy their craving for books. On the other hand, apart from appealing to the intellectual curiosity of readers, possession of books was considered both meritorious and fashionable among the educated classes. Many intellectuals echoed Hai Gaon's epigrammatic advice that everyone do three things of merit and beauty: "Acquire land, friend, and book." Some patrons of Jewish learning, like Samuel ibn Nagrela, gave away books free of charge to impecunious students in Spain and other lands. This poet-statesman had no use, however, for those wealthy illiterates who purchased books only for display. In his widely read collection of epigrams he wrote:

> He who buys books at great expense,
> But leaves his heart empty and bland,
> Is like the lame who on a wall
> Paints a leg, and yet cannot stand.

At the same time he admonished his readers that

> A wise man will give up the life of pleasure
> So that in reading he may find his leisure.

Quoting both these passages, Yehudah ibn Tibbon, the famous translator, extolled the merits of the large library he had assembled, which included even some duplicates and triplicates. This collection, he assured his son Samuel in his "ethical will," would make it unnecessary for Samuel to borrow works of scholarship, while other less fortunate students "must bustle about to seek books, often without finding them." [4]

Private collections doubtless were overshadowed by some school and congregational libraries. Throughout the Muslim world many libraries were attached to mosques or academies (often housed in the same buildings), beginning with Al-Ma'mun (813–33) who had founded the first of three famous libraries which were destined permanently to enrich the intellectual life of Baghdad. Although we possess no specific information, Jewish congregations and colleges doubtless followed suit. Of course, none of the Jewish libraries could compare in size with such famous collections as those of the Fadhiliya mosque in Cairo which, according to Maqrizi, embraced a hundred thousand volumes, or that of Cordova, which already in the days of Al-Ḥakam II (961–76) allegedly owned four hundred thousand volumes (Ibn Khaldun). Even the size of some private Muslim libraries was often staggering. We are informed by Yaqut that Waqidi's library, when he moved from the western to the eastern section of Baghdad, consisted of one hundred and twenty camel loads.[5]

No such collections, it appears, were ever assembled by medieval Jews. Even with their growing articulateness during the period of the Islamic Renaissance, Jewish authors, with rare exceptions like Saadiah, produced fewer books than their Muslim confreres. Moreover, not many of their works were considered by even wealthy bibliophiles to be worthy of reproduction and inclusion in a private collection. The difficulties confronting Jewish students in securing necessary books are well illustrated by the conditions in medieval Narbonne, which, situated at the crossroads between Muslim Spain and Christian France and Italy, was a major center of Jewish intellectual activity. And yet a distinguished scholar like Abraham ben Isaac, author of the important halakhic treatise *Eshkol,* could not locate in the city a copy of the Palestinian Talmud or even of the first section of the Mishnah. Two centuries later Immanuel of Rome and his friends in Perugia were overjoyed when they secured a list of one hundred and eighty titles from a visiting bookseller, Aaron of Toledo. No sooner did Aaron depart from Perugia when, despite his insistent warnings, Immanuel and his friends opened the boxes he had left behind and copied ten of the most precious works. Even in the more populous and literary-minded Eastern communities the libraries evidently were very small. One need but study the few extant book lists of that period to realize how comparatively small were the Jewish collections, indeed the whole Jewish literary output.[6]

Communities and individual booklovers often tried to make up for this quantitative paucity by the great care they lavished on the preservation of even the smallest fragments. Reverence for the book, especially one that might contain the divine name, was so great that synagogues as a rule set aside boxes in which members deposited torn books, or sections thereof, which had outlived their usefulness. In time such boxes were filled with fragments, often single torn leaves, given the characteristic name of *shemot* (names). Ultimately, these receptacles were either formally buried in cemeteries or else preserved in synagogue attics. It is to this practice that we owe the preservation of the Cairo and other genizahs, which have so immeasurably enriched our knowledge of medieval Hebrew letters. Yehudah ibn Tibbon, who in his will enjoined his son to "make thy books thy companions, let thy cases and shelves be thy pleasure-grounds and gardens," also gave him good practical advice as to how to take care of the precious library he was bequeathing him:

Examine thy Hebrew books at every new moon, the Arabic volumes once in two months, and the bound codices once every quarter. Arrange thy library in fair order, so as to avoid wearying thyself in searching for the book thou needest. . . . A good plan would be to set in each compartment a written list of the books therein contained. . . . Examine the loose leaves in the volumes and bundles, and preserve them. These fragments contain very important matters which I collected and copied out. Do not destroy any writing or letter of all that I have left. And cast thine eye frequently over the Catalogue so as to remember what books are in thy library. . . . Cover the book-cases with rugs of fine quality; and preserve them from damp and mice and from all manner of injury, for thy books are thy good treasure. If thou lendest a volume make a memorandum before it leaves thy house, and when it is returned, draw thy pen over the entry. Every Passover and Tabernacles call in all books out on loan.

In view of the general scarcity and high cost of manuscripts, book-lending to needy students was considered a high moral obligation. Especially in the small and struggling communities of medieval Europe, public opinion often forced the hands of reluctant lenders.[7]

While high prices and the limited Jewish book market impeded commercialization of learning and the spread of much "lowbrow" literature catering to mass appetites, they also greatly increased the dependence of Hebrew authors on the good will and financial support of wealthy patrons. Even more than the contemporary Arabic letters, therefore, medieval Hebrew poetry, particularly that of the "Golden Age" in Spain, has the aspect of a typical "court poetry." [8]

POETIC SOPHISTICATION

The dichotomy between the fairly simple technique of synagogue poetry addressed to the masses of worshipers and the far more complex structure of poems written for the benefit of the intellectual élite is noticeable as early as the writings of Saadiah Gaon. The two prayers of petition which he inserted in his prayer book are models of simplicity. Written for the benefit of the perplexed worshiper, who "instead of coming closer to his Master might alienate Him by mistaken utterances," these prayers (*baqqashot*) were written in simple biblical language understandable to all. They elicited the highest words of praise from Abraham ibn Ezra, generally an unrelenting critic of the older liturgical poetry. They were intended to convey the simplest ideas of "praise and adoration for the Lord, and humility on the part of man; a confession of sins, and the request for forgiveness and success in matters of this world as well as one for the comfort and salvation of the Jewish people." To facilitate further the understanding of the second, somewhat longer, and more complicated prayer intended for recitation on fast days, the gaon himself supplied an Arabic translation. Before long the first prayer, too, was translated into Arabic (by one Ṣemaḥ ben Joshua), and both were recited widely and with great veneration. In fact, several generations later Maimonides was asked "whether one was required to stand up while reciting Saadiah's prayer." [9]

At the same time the gaon composed a great many liturgical poems in the style of Yannai and Qalir, but he included only a few of these among the elective recitations of his own prayer book. In some cases he so clearly composed a liturgical piece only for a special occasion that, rather than sign his own name in the acrostic, he arranged the concluding letters to read "Solomon," doubtless the name of the precentor who was to recite them in the synagogue. Such devious designation was to be emulated later by Hai Gaon and others, greatly complicating the task of modern investigators, who usually rely on the acrostics for the identification of the poet himself.[10]

Some of these poems were clearly intended only for the Hebrew intellectual élite. Saadiah's variation on the theme of the Ten Commandments, for example, ending with a single rhyme *lar,* used almost exclusively Graeco-Roman and Persian loan words scattered through the remote recesses of the Babylonian Talmud or the Aramaic versions. Only linguistically well-trained students of the Talmud and the Targumim could penetrate the meaning of this poem and its hidden allusions.

In such linguistic artifices the gaon merely followed the fashion of the age. Just as among the Jews the provocatively complicated structure and verbiage of Qalir's *piyyuṭim* had overshadowed for a long time the less sophisticated creations of his predecessors, the Greek-speaking churches now neglected the memorable *kontakia* of Romanos for the sake of the difficult and intentionally obscure poems of John of Damascus and Cosmas of Jerusalem. These Christian writers lived in Qalir's region a century after Qalir. Saadiah, who wrote some of his poetic works during the years of his stay in the Holy Land, also shared with the Arab poets of that age the quest for innovation (*bid'a*) which had inspired the outstanding poet and theorist of poetic arts, Abu'l 'Abbas 'Abdullah ibn al-Mu'tazz, to compile an anthology of difficult poems for the guidance of both readers and aspiring poets to which he gave the title *Kitab al-Badi'*.[11]

Saadiah went even further in his nonliturgical poetry. Particularly his polemical pamphlets, usually written in single-rhymed strophes, taxed the ingenuity of readers. They were clearly intended for assiduous study rather than quick perusal. Occasionally the gaon himself felt impelled to add an Arabic commentary. His *Essa meshali* (I Shall Take Up My Parable), of which about a third has been recovered from various manuscripts, is filled with so many obscure allusions to talmudic sayings, both halakhic and aggadic, that only a fine student of the Talmud, reading and rereading it with attention to every detail, could derive from it any meaning whatsoever. An entire section is devoted to biographical details concerning certain Tannaim—true to form, Saadiah did not fail to mention in this connection "my grandfather Dosa who has turned me to my Creator and carved out for me my niche"—which only a fully informed talmudic scholar could comprehend. It required further concentrated thought to place this section in the general anti-Karaite framework of this lengthy poetic treatise which embraced some five hundred and seventy-five strophes, each provided with a single rhyme in alphabetic order. Whether or not specifically aimed at the great Masorite Aaron ben Asher, who certainly was not a militant exponent of the sectarian viewpoint, this difficult exercise was no more intended for mass circulation than was Saadiah's even more complicated poem on the alphabet.[12]

We may indeed believe the Karaite assertion that none of the gaon's antiheretical writings were "published," that is, widely distributed, in his own lifetime. Nor do they seem to have been much in vogue in subsequent generations. Not only the *Essa meshali* and his rhymed reply to Ḥivi's antibiblical strictures, but even his *Sefer ha-Galui,* provided with an Arabic translation and hence clearly intended for mass distribution during his life-and-death struggle with the exilarch, apparently were neither copied nor quoted frequently by later generations of scholars.

Did all this creativity belong in the realm of sacred or of secular poetry? If asked, Saadiah himself would doubtless have refused to draw any such distinction. Clearly such controversial poems were not meant to be recited in the synagogue, but they might conceivably find a place in one's private devotions. The line between study and prayer being quite tenuous, especially in private worship, many an admiring student might have considered immersion in the fine points of *Essa meshali* as the equivalent of the recitation of any *piyyuṭ*. Certainly the introductory strophe, stating the poet's intention to "ascribe unity to my Maker" and exhorting all creatures to "praise and exalt Him," could have served as an opening for any liturgical poem as well. Similarly, Saadiah's "Hymn for the Bridegroom" had a "sacred" character in so far as it was evidently intended for recitation during a religious wedding ceremony.[13]

More significant was the distinction that, while the ancient *piyyuṭim* largely consisted of on-the-spot improvisations by precentors during services, the new sacred poetry, liturgical as well as academic, was but a literary product by authors writing in the seclusion of their studies. True, this distinction cannot always be documented, and indeed it may never have existed in such clearcut fashion. Qalir's enormous and technically often very complex output, in particular, cannot readily be envisaged as the exclusive result of momentary inspiration at the pulpit. Certainly the twenty-one different poems composed by him for the Ninth of Ab, quite possibly in twenty-one successive years, show in their rich variations on the same theme signs of premeditation and conscious differentiation. Very likely many other early cantorial "improvisations" were also born with no less travail than were the "inspired" sermons of many medieval and modern homilists, memorized to the last letter several days in advance of their delivery. Yet only in the increasingly literate era of the Islamic Renaissance could Saadiah and his confreres consciously produce liturgical poems with no intention whatsoever of reciting them in person before an assembled congregation. By substituting the name Solomon or David for his own (Sa'id) in the acrostic of some poems and thus intimating that it was to be recited by the one or other precentor, the gaon clearly underscored the literary nature of his liturgical works, although they differed in no way from his other poetic or prose writings, always produced with some "sacred" objective in mind. Saadiah's older contemporary, Nissi al-Nahrawani, who had allegedly warned the exilarch against the appointment of the self-assertive gaon, could not recite any prayers from the pulpit, since his blindness disqualified him from leading the congregation. Yet some moving liturgical pieces by the blind bard, evidently written for recitation by others, have come to light in recent years.[14]

Not that cantorial creativity completely died out. Apart from supplying appropriate tunes for poems written by others, many precentors continued to write their own liturgical poetry. Now, however, they too became primarily *littérateurs*. The family Al-Baradani, especially, whose members long occupied leading cantorial positions in Baghdad, also produced significant poets in Joseph and his son Nahum. In the West, the foundations of liturgical poetry were laid by such cantors as Simon bar Isaac "the Great" of Mayence (*ca.* 1000), or Meir bar Isaac "the Messenger of the People" of Worms (*ca.* 1050). However, the cantorial monopoly was definitely broken. Some of the most prolific liturgical poets, such as Sulaiman of Cairo, seem no longer to have officiated as synagogue readers.[15]

This new literary character and speedy distribution of liturgical poems through many countries of the dispersion counteracted the forces of regional or parochial separation. The fact that the Cairo Genizah preserved two fragments of poems by Simon bar Isaac need not indicate the presence in the Egyptian capital of a congregation of German rite, as suggested by Habermann, but rather that poems traveled from community to community and were incorporated into local liturgies whenever they struck the fancy of worshipers or cantors. For this reason, too, we may understand the relative paucity of Franco-German liturgical poetry included in Simḥah bar Samuel's *Maḥzor Vitry*. While in matters of law and observance R. Simḥah followed primarily Ashkenazic authorities, he was far more cosmopolitan in the selection of liturgical poems. Among the authors quoted, most of the Franco-German poets are represented only by one piece each, while no less than eight poems by Ibn Gabirol, twelve by Abraham ibn Ezra, and twenty-six by Yehudah Halevi are included. The latter number amounts to about one fourth of the entire collection.[16]

Poetry had acquired so great a prestige among both Arabs and Jews throughout the Caliphate that spiritual leaders of the people, whether or not endowed with poetic gifts, often felt it incumbent upon themselves to versify in honor of the Lord. We possess penitential poems composed by an Exilarch David, who may well have considered such recitations on a par with homiletical performances. Hai Gaon himself, although head of the academy of Pumbedita which had long opposed the proliferation of *piyyuṭim,* joined the ranks of liturgical poets. His poetry, to be sure, reveals his deep preoccupation with public affairs. Even in his most elegiac outpourings he is less concerned with the trials and tribulations of the individual soul than with the sufferings of the people. Israel's degradation, contrasted with the power and affluence of the other nations, is the constant refrain of his lamentations. "Be jealous," he appealed to God, "for the sake of our humiliation. Or else, be jealous for the sake of Thy name!" In one poem Hai contrasted the beautiful attire of the ancient priests sacrificing the daily offering with the discriminatory garment reimposed by an imperial decree of 1031 upon the "protected subjects" throughout the Empire. He also turned to good advantage the like-sounding Hebrew words, *'ebed* and *'obed,* when he echoed the stereotype complaint of Jewish homilists and poets under Islam: "We the sons of the mother [Sarah] have become slaves to the sons of the slave-girl [Hagar], and the servants of God are in bondage to worshipers of idols," that is to Christians—a distinct echo of the iconoclastic controversy. Written in simple biblical style, these elegies lent themselves very well to public recitation. They were dedicated to individual readers (especially one Abraham ben Isaac), whose names in the acrostic long obscured the authorship of the last of the great geonim.[17]

Despite Hai's great prestige, however, which extended into the Western countries as well, his liturgical poems seem never to have enjoyed wide acceptance. Except for a Day of Atonement prayer, *Shema' qoli* (Hearken to My Voice), and to a lesser extent a penitential prayer of questionable authorship, *Et mi zanaḥta* (Whom Didst Thou Forsake), they were never incorporated into any permanent ritual. They had to be laboriously pieced together by their modern editor from a few scattered Genizah fragments. Curiously, Hai's more secular, didactic work, *Shire musar haskel* (Poems of Wise Conduct), was far more avidly read. It belongs among the early classics of the ever growing ethical literature of medieval Jewry. Evidently public and cantorial tastes, even whims, were often more decisive than uncontested reputations gained in other fields of learning or communal leadership. Neither were Hai's compeers, such as David (probably ben Zakkai) the Exilarch, the Palestinian gaon Solomon ben Yehudah, or even the Western "Light of the Exile," R. Gershom of Mayence, more successful. More or less gifted liturgical poets though they all were, little of their poetic output found its way into the prayer books of any rite.[18]

SPANISH COURTS

If in the Near East the choice of subjects and techniques was often determined by the growingly sophisticated tastes of the small intellectual minority, the poets of Spain and neighboring Provence frequently had to cater to the wishes of a few powerful individuals and their court camarillas. Moses ibn Ezra may have been right when, in his classical survey of Spanish Hebrew poetry, he referred to Isaac ibn Ḥalfon (early 11th cent.) as the first "professional" poet. Before him Dunash ben Labraṭ, for instance, seems to have derived his livelihood from the occupation of synagogue reader. Yet even Dunash, in addressing a poem, *De'eh libbi ḥokhmah* (My Heart, Know Wisdom), to Ḥisdai ibn Shapruṭ (some time after 958) could not refrain from extolling the scholar-statesman's great generosity, extending all the way to the academy of Sura. Calling himself Ḥisdai's "servant, the youngest of teachers," he referred to this patron with such unmistakable allusions as

He is to the destitute
Like to children a father,

From his rain-pouring hands much
Bounty verse makers gather.

Much of the heat which developed in his controversy with Menaḥem ben Saruq evidently stemmed from the then customary rivalries among protégés of the same grandee.[19]

The dissolution of the 'Umayyad Caliphate and the subsequent internecine struggles among the petty rulers throughout the Peninsula during the eleventh century further stimulated the evolution of court florid poetry among both Jews and Arabs. The more complicated the game of petty power politics became, the more room was there for domestic intrigues, the meteoric rise and decline of momentary favorites, and the desire of the ever embattled princes and their chief counselors for inner reassurance by poetic flattery. Laudatory or satirical poetry, morever, played at that time a major political role as the most effective press agentry in support of, or in opposition to, certain personalities or ideas. Influencing public opinion among one's own subjects, as well as among the subjects of one's friendly or hostile neighbors, certainly was worth a considerable investment in the patronage of talented poetic propagandists. Todros Abulafia's characterization of genuine magnate as a gentleman "who disperses his fortune to accumulate laudations" held largely true for the entire Golden Age. Apart from the immediate advantage of a good press, many a grandee sought in this way to influence the judgment of posterity as well, and to secure for himself a bit of immortality. Many believed, with Moses ibn Ezra, that "a statement in prose vanishes like the flight of cinders, while a poem remains like an inscription engraved in stone. Through poems are eternally recorded the virtues of generous men and the faults of misers." The patrons therefore treated their gifted protégés with a mixture of awe and condescension and assigned to them positions ranging all the way from glorified domestics to close confidants.[20]

Such quest for immortality through the medium of poetic laudations was itself a novel feature in Jewish life. In the talmudic age and after, great leaders of the academies were remembered for their sayings and exemplary conduct, but their memory was preserved by posterity essentially as a lesson to subsequent generations. Their halakhic decisions, moreover, had to be recorded in their names, for, according to certain long-accepted rules, majority opinion followed some sages in certain legal areas and others in their particular specialties. During the geonic age, too, decisions rendered by academic leaders were recorded in their names, not for the purpose of their authors' glorification, but rather in order to lend them greater canonical validity and to enable students to trace them back to the sources in case of conflicting transmission. The rank and file of academic teachers, on the other hand, like the innumerable homilists and synagogue readers, were largely satisfied with the recognition by colleagues and informed contemporaries, and rarely shed the cloak of anonymity which enveloped their contributions. Nor had communal leaders done much about perpetuating their own memory. Not even exilarchs are known to have employed court historiographers or poets to hand down the record of their achievements to posterity. However, once Spanish Jewry had caught the bug of literary immortality from its Arab neighbors, the fashion rapidly spread to the Eastern lands and gradually made its way into Christian Europe as well.

One must not overlook the basic difference between the power of Jewish and Arab patrons. The latter were as a rule kings or viziers who, however impotent in relation to their neighbors, reigned despotically and often quite arbitrarily in their own domains. Samuel ibn Nagrela himself wrote from personal observation,

> Kings frequently forgive some grievous sins,
> But make heads roll for minor digressions.
> At times they gladly hearken to lies
> But shut their ears to honest confessions.

Nor can one miss the tone of personal anxiety in Samuel's query,

> Is there a joy which equals that . . .
> Of lifting friends and humbling foes,
> Or sleeping without the fear of kings?

or in his remarkable simile,

> A royal favorite
> Is like a lion rider
> Feared by all who see him,
> He trembles at his bearer.

In contrast thereto, Jewish grandees, even Samuel himself, could punish a recalcitrant poet by withdrawing his pension or even forcing him to leave the community. But they could never seriously endanger the life of a protégé. Even the excommunication and self-imposed exile of the jurist-poet Joseph ibn Abitur was an exceptionally drastic penalty inflicted on a leader who had antagonized both a community and its commanding personality.[21]

Long before Pietro Aretino, on the other hand, Arab and Jewish poets had discovered the great power of character assassination inherent in satirical poems, and their enormous blackmailing potential. Already Menaḥem ben Saruq, countering the disgrace into which he had fallen with Ḥisdai ibn Shapruṭ, pointed out to the statesman the power of his pen in combating Ḥisdai's enemies, but he also unmistakably warned his former patron that the direction of these shafts could easily be changed. In the hands of unscrupulous poets this could indeed become a dangerous weapon, and moralists like Baḥya and Maimonides strongly objected to its indiscriminate use. Ultimately, the thirteenth-century ethical philosopher, Israel al-Naqawa, characterized the abuse heaped by poets on their personal enemies as "the worst kind of an evil tongue." Such unsavory practices could but accentuate the antipathy of many jurists, both Arab and Jewish, toward poetry, as we have noted already in the case of *piyyuṭim*.[22]

It is difficult today to gauge the extent of the political and social influence wielded by gifted versifiers in eleventh- and twelfth-century Spain. Literary talent often became a prerequisite for a political career, inasmuch as official and especially diplomatic correspondence, following the fashion of the age, had to be couched in literary, often outright poetic, forms. That is why so many rulers and statesmen themselves joined the ranks of poets and writers. According to a wholly credible story recorded by Ibn Daud, Samuel ibn Nagrela owed his sudden rise to power in Granada to his scribal elegance in the composition of letters for one of the vizier's slave girls. Of course, this was only an entering wedge for the Jewish shopkeeper to become acquainted with the royal counselor, who soon appreciated Samuel's extraordinary versatility and sound talents. However, even at the acme of his power as chief diplomatic and financial adviser and on occasion, military commander for the Crown, the Nagid's literary abilities helped him to stave off many an attack by rivals and Muslim bigots. He thus maintained himself in his exalted position to the end of his days, and even transmitted it as an inheritance to his less able son. It is small wonder, then, that time and again he extolled in his poems the power of his pen:

A man's wisdom rests in his writing,
Through the pen his reasoning is shown,
By his pen he may wind his way up
To the splendor of the royal throne.

Although for this purpose full command of the Arabic poetic arts was a major requirement, the knowledge of other languages spoken in the multinational Peninsula proved of great utility to any negotiator and statesman. Samuel himself trained his sons in the Arabic language and poetry from their early childhood. But such preference indirectly accrued to the benefit of Hebrew poetry as well. In fact, the Nagid taught his son Eliasaf, then aged six, to transcribe his Hebrew poems, and he aided his other son and successor, Joseph, in composing a poem at the age of nine.[23]

Such impact on public opinion can be explained only by the presence throughout Spain of a relatively large and influential intelligentsia to whom poetry, even more than grammar, was of vital personal concern. Not only were poems widely read and frequently copied, but oral improvisations were often quickly memorized and more or less accurately transmitted to other groups. In his *Kitab al-Luma'* (XVIII, pp. 207 f.; *Sefer ha-Riqmah,* pp. 226 f.), Ibn Janaḥ reminisced that he himself had incorrectly recited a verse by his teacher, Isaac ben Saul, because the copyists of "most books" had replaced there a difficult word by a simpler one. Like many of his contemporaries, Isaac evidently delighted in using here an extraordinary grammatical form which could be understood only through a clever application of a rare biblical parallel.

Frequent parlor games tested the guests' powers of improvisation. Some poets developed an astonishing technical mastery, and produced verses of complicated rhythm and rhyme according to a pattern set by an opposing player, or else in emulation of some celebrated poem. In one of his letters, Yehudah Halevi described such an exhibition of skills in imitation of a poem by Moses ibn Ezra. For the amusement of sophisticated audiences some poets produced poems making sense when read both forward and backward. Al-Ḥarizi, for example, dedicated a poem to a well-known miserly patron. When read straightforwardly it consisted of a series of blessings, but in reverse it contained as many curses. At times poets improvised on street corners, vying there for popular favor with the storytellers and itinerant preachers. When they overstayed their welcome at one court or lost their popularity with the public of one city, they often moved to another. Thus arose in Spain and neighboring Provence the traveling troubadour, Arab, Jewish, or Christian, who apparently paved the way for his more renowned medieval French successor. Isaac Gorni, in particular, wandered for years through southern France, half tramp, half revered poet.[24]

While increasing the temptation to pure virtuosity and even meaningless poetic acrobatics, this widespread popular acclaim lent the poet a social standing and influence such as he has enjoyed in few historical periods. Among Spanish Jews, too, the poet ranked with the jurist and the philosopher as the main intellectual spokesman of the people. In fact, some of the greatest poets were themselves either famous jurists (Joseph ibn Abitur, Isaac ibn Gayyat, Samuel ibn Nagrela) or keen philosophers (Ibn Gabirol, Halevi). To secure complete popular acceptance, however, as well as a measure of immortality among the masses, poets depended on the inclusion of some of their sacred lyrics in one or another recognized prayer book. At times even great poets like Ibn Gabirol composed old-style *piyyuṭim* after the manner of Yannai and Qalir, side by side with philosophically more refined prayers of adoration of the type of Ibn Gabirol's masterpiece, the "Royal Crown."

STELLAR ACHIEVEMENTS

Out of this spiritual and intellectual ferment arose a gallaxy of great poets and grandmasters of Hebrew style such as the world had not seen since the days of the Old Testament prophets. Samuel ben Joseph ha-Levi ibn Nagrela (993–1056), Solomon ben Yehudah ibn Gabirol (*ca.* 1022–51 or 1022–70), Moses ben Jacob ibn Ezra (*ca.* 1060–1138), and Yehudah ben Samuel Halevi (*ca.* 1075–1141) were but the greatest of these immortals. Even Samuel's star was long obscured by the shining brightness of his three successors, whom Al-Ḥarizi had already glorified as the supreme and unsurpassable triad. Only in recent decades have scholars become acquainted with most of the poems of the statesman of Granada, whose claim to immortality had theretofore rested chiefly with his political successes and his significant halakhic contributions. But, since the recent discovery and publication of his *Diwan,* he has emerged as a poet of prime magnitude, one who introduced into Hebrew letters themes and poetic moods unheard of since the loss of Jewish independence.[25]

Ibn Gabirol of Malaga ultimately joined the ranks of Samuel's pensioners. For a number of years, however, he had lived in Saragossa on the payroll of another Jewish grandee, Yequtiel ibn Ḥassan, whom he immortalized in several poems. Extraordinarily precocious, Solomon composed some of his most beautiful and thought-provoking poems, including a lengthy poetic discourse on the six hundred and thirteen commandments, at the age of sixteen. At nineteen he added his aforementioned poem on grammatical rules (*'Anaq*). He was orphaned in his childhood, and he never married, although later legend supplied him with a woman created by magic. The celibatarian poet-philosopher considered himself fortunate for being "consumed with the quest for wisdom, while others allow love to devour their substance." He spent his span of life (less than thirty years, according to Al-Ḥarizi, though he seems to have lived much longer) on writing several philosophic and ethical treatises and creating, in an almost endless flow, poems on a vast variety of subjects.[26]

Although more than three hundred of these poems have already been included in the major collection of Ibn Gabirol's poetic works, additional poems are still emerging from the obscurity of medieval manuscripts and rare early prints. Besides religious themes, they include the usual encomia on benefactors, bitter attacks on private enemies, poems of self-glorification, and other secular topics. Embittered by the constant chicaneries of his rivals,

Ibn Gabirol combined utter contempt for them with new heights of self-laudation. Typical of many others is his sneer:

Crooked as a camel, trivial as an ant,
  Devious as a fox, as a steer unyielding
They are wholly clad in pettiness and shame,
  Utter folly being sown unto their frame.

In contrast thereto he claimed for himself that "I am the boy endowed even before my birth / With the understanding of a sage of eighty." Most of the Saragossan poet's creativity, however, is permeated with a deep quest for new religious truths. At the same time, as noted by Moses ibn Ezra, "he emphasized in his poems ideas based on the laws of the Torah in consonance with tradition." His religious poetry, culminating in the "Royal Crown" recited by countless thousands on the evening of the Day of Atonement, elicited universal admiration, "and even the jealous praised him." He thus fulfilled the vow so beautifully expressed in his poem:

Thy name I remember and whisper
  As waters whisper in constant flow
My mind refuses to abandon
  Thy keen remembrance stamped on my brow
As Thou hast never withheld Thy grace
  I shall forever strive Thee to praise.[27]

Moses ibn Ezra was born in the last years of Ibn Gabirol's life, or perhaps even after his demise. Recognizing in his predecessor a "knight of style and master of poetry," Moses modeled himself after the sage of Saragossa in many ways, but he refrained from venomous attacks on personal enemies. He regretted, as we recall, even the few satirical poems he had written in his youth. If his poems are permeated with pessimism, and even more frequently filled with complaints about personal misfortunes, this was owing to his truly unhappy career. Although, like Ibn Gabirol and Halevi, he was envied by the mercenary Al-Ḥarizi for the patronage extended to him by wealthy benefactors, he was really an unlucky wanderer, who, leaving his native Granada some time after the city had fallen into the hands of the intolerant Almoravids in 1090, moved from place to place in Christian Castile and Aragon.

The difference in the general level of civilization between the northern and the southern regions still was so great that, as we recollect, our poet could never reconcile himself to the life of an exile in the new, backward environment. He did not, however, allow his personal unhappiness to overwhelm him. Apart from his complaints and his constant reassertions of his superiority (he felt "like a plucked rose among thorns"), his writings, both in verse and in prose, bear testimony to a gentle, deeply ethical, and, in the ultimate sense, even serene soul.[28]

Ibn Ezra's younger friend Halevi tried to comfort him. In a moving poem on parting, Halevi wrote to the ever disconsolate master:

> We have known thee to roam from thy days of youth
>   Shed of tears a river flowing in a torrent.
> But shall we spar with time which has never sinned,
>   And with days that harbor no design abhorrent? . . .
> For man was united, only to divide,
>   That a people bring forth diverse populations,
> Had the sons of man not parted from of old,
>   Our earth would not be settled now with many nations.

Not that Halevi himself was altogether reconciled to the existing realities. Of a far sunnier disposition than either Solomon or Moses, Yehudah might have felt perfectly happy with his medical career, his loving family, and his host of devoted friends. Even in his mature years, when he turned to philosophy, for "if wisdom is like the sea's expanse, poetic rhymes are like its foam," he could no more help versifying than could young Ovid in his well-known *iam iam*. But, living on an erupting volcano, on the very frontier between the retreating world of Islam and advancing Christendom, then permeated with an ardent crusading spirit, he felt more keenly than his predecessors the untenability of the Jewish position in that divided world. Creatively responding to the great world crisis of his time, he sought not only personal salvation by leaving his country for the land of his forefathers, but he also began singing his immortal odes to Zion. He soon became the national bard, as he was also to become the philosopher of the Jewish national heritage for medieval Jewry.[29]

Apart from these four shining luminaries, eleventh- and twelfth-century Spain brought forth an array of other outstanding poets. Moses ibn Ezra, as unerring in his critical evaluation of the poetic achievements of others as he was severe in the standards he had set for himself, enumerated in a lengthy sketch the great poets of the preceding generations on the Iberian Peninsula. Of many poets whom he extolled, not a single poem has come down to us. Only a few proved to have had an enduring influence. Among these one need mention only the distinguished jurists Joseph ibn Abitur and Isaac ibn Gayyat, the great Bible commentators Moses ibn Chiquitilla and Abraham ibn Ezra, and, like the latter, the world wanderer Yehudah al-Ḥarizi, whom Heinrich Heine once called a "Voltairian six hundred years before Voltaire." With Al-Ḥarizi, the "Golden Age" of Spanish-Jewish poetry drew to its close, although a number of significant poetic creations continued to emanate from the Iberian Peninsula to the very era of expulsions. The poetic works of Abraham's son, Isaac ibn Ezra, are more important from the standpoint of social than of literary history, because they shed a weird light on the thought processes of the scion of a distinguished Jewish family, first converted to Islam, probably out of love for a Muslim woman, then repenting and returning to the fold. Similarly, Yehudah ibn 'Abbas (d. 1177), is known not only as a poet of distinction, but also as the father of the convert Samau'al al-Maghribi, to whose anti-Jewish work we owe so much information on the Judeo-Muslim religious controversies, as well as on some forgotten phases of Jewish history, including the evolution of early medieval liturgy.[30]

SECULAR THEMES

The upsurge in Spanish-Jewish creativity found expression not only in the growing quantity and ever more refined quality of the new output, but also in a great thematic revolution. Theretofore Hebrew poetry was mainly concerned with religious topics, and, to all intents and purposes, it had served as a handmaiden of liturgy. Even poems never intended for recitation in the synagogue, such as wedding songs, dirges, or poems for circumcision, had a more or less direct connection with religious ceremonies. In medieval Spain, however, the progressive secularization of Hebrew poetry led to a thematic diversification which ultimately covered a wide range of human relations. After timid beginnings concerned chiefly with friendship poems, versified polemics, and poetic exaltation of patrons, with which the Golden Age was ushered in in the days of Ḥisdai ibn Shapruṭ, topical diversity reached a sudden climax in the work of Samuel ibn Nagrela.

As a poet Samuel responded to the inner urge of an egocentric memorialist, recording all significant happenings in a sort of running poetic diary, as much as to fashions prevailing at the Arab court, where he lived constantly on the alert against the fluctuating friendly and inimical forces. A long series of his poems describes in graphic detail his military and political exploits. Since he often accompanied the armies, and on more than one occasion faced death on the battlefield, his vivid descriptions of battle scenes have no peer in Hebrew letters. Hardly any other Hebrew poet of the pre-Emancipation era could have written a description of such colorful immediacy as the following:

> The two armies confronted one another
> Host deployed against host standing at bay,
> Men felt like first-born, proud of partaking
> Of a day of wrath, jealous in the fray,
> Each striving to gain glory and fame—
> While life's strength was ebbing away.
>
> The earth was stirred up from its foundations,
> Plunged in turmoil as at Gomorrah's quakes,
> Faces which had shone with strength and beauty
> Were darkened now like stove-blackened rakes.
>
> The day was clouded in mist and darkness,
> The sun, like my heart, covered by a veil,
> The crowd's shouts resembled thunder and sea roar
> With waves whipped high by a powerful gale.
>
> At sunrise the ground seemed to heave and tremble,
> Shaking like a drunkard to walk unfit,
> Horses running wild darted back and forth,
> Like startled reptiles thrown out of their pit.
>
> Untold numbers of lances, like lightning,
> Filled the air with sparks of illumination,
> Arrows pouring out, like raindrops, in sheets
> Gave men's backs a sieve-like perforation.

Bows in archers' hands resembled irate snakes,
  Spitting out swarms of vicious stinging bees,
The riders' swords aflame high over their heads,
  Suddenly turned dull when below their knees.

Men's blood began flowing, drenching the ground,
  Like the blood of cattle beside an altar,
Mighty men of valor lost their will to live,
  Preferring the choice of victory or slaughter,

Young lions gloried in a festering wound
  In their heads, as if it were a crown.
Slaying a neighbor became a good deed,
  Letting live the cause of a serious frown.

Even in the description of this battle with the enemy forces of the prince of Almeria, which in 1037 saved the Jewish vizier from the intrigues of his inveterate enemy Ibn 'Abbas, Samuel could not quite refrain from such ethical asides as the last-quoted verses. If on other occasions he did not hesitate to fill pages with invective and bloodthirsty gloating over the downfall of his enemies, these passages often sound more like a reprise of phrases long common in Arabic letters than an expression of the author's innermost feelings.[31]

Equally stereotyped are most of the love poems of the period. Even Yehudah Halevi, who came closer than any of his compeers to resuscitating the ardor of the Song of Songs in Hebrew letters, frequently adhered to widely accepted erotic themes and imagery which tended to obscure the personality of both lover and beloved. For example, his complaint of total enslavement to his self-assertive 'Ophrah (synonym for sweetheart) could have been voiced in exactly the same words by any other poet:

'Ophrah launders her clothes in buckets of my tears,
  And spreads them out to dry in her beauty's sunlight,
She needs no spring water, since she controls my eyes,
  Nor looks for the sun, since radiance is her birthright.

Even more stilted are many comparisons adduced by Samuel ibn Nagrela to extol the charms of his beloved. In one of his fifteen poetic variations on the old Arabic theme that the apple was meant to be admired because of its smell, looks, and touch but not to be bitten into, the Nagid praised his sweetheart's likeness to the apple and characterized her as being "as smooth as its texture, as sweet as its taste, and as red-cheeked as its skin." [32]

Ibn Gabirol wrote no erotic poetry at all. Many of his poems attest to his conscious abnegation of worldly rewards, which may have been but the result of the apparently permanent physical ailments of which he allegedly died at the early age of twenty-nine, at least according to a persistent tradition. The following brief stanzas may serve as a telling illustration:

If you desire to live with men of eternity,
  Your soul trembles before the underworld's flame,
Make light of worldly values, and be not misguided
  By riches, honors, an heir to your name.

You must cherish highly poverty and debasement,
  And die, as Seled did, without a kin.
Try to know intimately your soul, for it alone
  Will endure beyond all your flesh and skin.

Childless Seled (I Chron. 2:30) had long engaged the attention of homilists, but he had rarely been invoked as an example to be followed. Like most of his colleagues, Solomon spiritualized earthly love into an *amor Dei intellectualis,* so fully developed already by the ancient allegorizers of the biblical Song of Songs. At times such Platonic love was transferred to the poet's men friends, but without smacking of quite the outright homosexuality that characterized much of contemporary Arabic poetry. Most of the wine ditties, too, very widespread in Spanish-Hebrew poetry, betray little originality. Devoid of the added sweetness of "stolen waters" —neither Jewish law nor society frowned on moderate consumption of alcoholic beverages—many of these creations followed accepted patterns and, for the most part, could readily be interchanged among their authors. And yet, the very fact that so many lyrics could be dedicated to the praise of worldly enjoyments was a startling innovation in Hebrew literature. At the same time, this extreme imitation of Arabic patterns, in themselves often strongly influenced by ancient Greek prototypes, at times had a distinctly nationalistic motivation. Proud not only of the antiquity but also of the richness and pliability of their ancient Hebrew language, these Jewish poets often tried to show that their ancestral tongue lent itself to the exercise of sophisticated poetic techniques, even stunts, on an infinite variety of subjects.[33]

Friendship poems, on the contrary, and those relating to personal joys and sorrows, have for the most part an authentic ring. Discounting obvious exaggerations, even the glorification of patrons often lends expression to genuine feelings of gratitude and admiration. For example, Ibn Gabirol's several poems exalting his Saragossan benefactor, Yequtiel ibn Ḥassan, have all the earmarks of a sincere personal attachment which did not cease even at moments of temporary misunderstanding. When such unavoidable differences arose among the friends, the poet may have felt deserted by his old benefactor, whom he then styled "father of abandonment," but he still claimed that there was not enough water in the world to extinguish the ardor of his love for Yequtiel, since, after the days of Noah, God had forsworn the use of another deluge. Upon the tragic death of his patron, Ibn Gabirol composed a long, moving dirge, beginning *Bi-Yeme Yequtiel* (In Yequtiel's Days), in which he erected for his departed friend a monument far more enduring than any stone placed on the latter's grave. Ibn Gabirol's several poems addressed to Samuel ibn Nagrela, on the other hand, combined acknowledgment of benefactions with genuine reverence for the intellectual accomplishments of the great Nagid, whom he once extolled as "my father, my rider, and my chariot," terms borrowed from the ancient prophetic exaltation of the Divine power. His versatile pen could, on the other hand, be as sharp in adverse criticism as it was warm in praise. In fact, his attacks on enemies, real and imaginary, were more widely quoted than his poems of friendship. Moses ibn Ezra was not altogether wrong in writing that "although he [Ibn Gabirol] by nature and training belonged to the philosophers, his excitable temper dominated his reason. He never could suppress his anger nor overcome his inner Satan. It was easy for him to make fun of distinguished men, and write about them in derisive and debasing terms." [34]

Samuel ibn Nagrela, on his part, devoted much of his poetry to his own family, recording as if in a poetic memoir his immediate reactions to such family events as the illness of a child. The following dirge on the death of his brother Isaac may serve as a telling illustration of the poet's uncontrolled grief and his unwillingness later to expunge passages which, upon calmer reflection, he might have left unwritten:

I journeyed to visit my brother on hearing
  Some men talk about his lying broken and ill.
A harbinger of evil met me in silence,
  I inquired, "Is Isaac among the living still?"
The messenger said bluntly, "He has passed away!"
  "Keep quiet!" I cursed him, "and control your tongue wild,
May your ears be filled with all sorts of misfortunes,
  Your father and mother be bereaved of their child!
I have brought here with me a famous physician,
  Who's healed many patients as helpless as my kin.
Why, then, should a leader, by his brethren beloved,
  Be allowed to perish to his nation's chagrin?"
He answered me curtly, "No one managed to wince,
  After a fatal illness, be he pauper or prince."

Some time later our poet, still disconsolate, added a stanza:

My heart has despaired of his coming back to life
  And of my ever seeing his image again,
I must live on in sorrow, or else seek respite,
  By following him in death, from my mourning's strain.

Even more eloquent was Abraham ibn Ezra's famous dirge over the loss of his son Isaac. This dirge may be taken literally as the outcry of a bereaved father weeping over his son's death in a strange land three years previously, although it could have referred to the latter's spiritual "death" through conversion to Islam. The blow occasioned by the son's voluntary act may have proved even more lastingly painful than would have been his natural death, and the wound might well have refused to heal even after the passage of three years. In any case, the son's ultimate repentance and return to the ancestral faith, became, in turn, the source of many memorable poetic confessions from Isaac's pen.[35]

None of the Spanish poets, however, could rival Yehudah Halevi in the number and eloquence of his poems, relating to friendship of a dedicated type toward a host of individuals. Endowed with a real genius for friendship, this warm-hearted poet seems to have attracted devoted companions wherever he chanced to come during his numerous wanderings. Moses ibn Ezra, whom he always cherished as his mentor, inspired him to compose no less than fifteen poems of glowing praise and devotion. Halevi could never reconcile himself to parting from this beloved friend or to the latter's settling among the relatively uncouth coreligionists of Christian Spain. Time and again he punned on this "western light" (*ma'arabi*) returning to his original habitat (*ma'arabkha*). Leave taking of beloved companions was generally very serious, in so far as the political divisions and mutual hostility prevailing among the states of the Iberian Peninsula greatly diminished the chances for parting friends ever to see each other again. On the other hand, upon his arrival in Egypt Halevi quickly acquired a great host of admirers who made his stay so pleasurable that he constantly put off his departure for the inhospitable shores of the Holy Land, the ultimate and unwavering goal of his life's journey. Since many of these friends in both Egypt and Spain were gifted poets in their own right and several answered Halevi in kind, only the overshadowing beauty of expression and the good taste of these authors prevented the Halevi circle from degenerating into one of the then not uncommon mutual admiration societies.[36]

Among those quick to respond was Moses ibn Ezra. But, unlike his younger friend, Moses filled his own poems with unending complaints about the cruel treatment he had received from life. One need but compare his plaintive *Eyne sela'im dam'u damo'a* (The Rocks' Eyes Were Filled with Tears) with Halevi's briefer lyric, *Ekh akhrekha emṣa margo'a* (How Shall I Find Peace after Thy Departure?), to which it was a direct reply. This exclusive preoccupation with his own fate, however, was not owing to Ibn Ezra's pronounced egocentricity alone, but also to his inability to make new friends in his places of exile. He was eternally starved for some deep personal attachments such as those he had known in his youth in Granada. We may, indeed, believe his assertion that

> If in mine exile I might meet but one,
> With whom to hold sweet converse of the mind,
> Then I would willingly forgive Fate's spite,
> That sent me forth, so dear a friend to find.

Moses ibn Chiquitilla, finally, complained of unreciprocated friendship. Perhaps referring to olive branches he had extended to his unrelenting critic Yehudah ibn Bal'am, he lamented, "I love and they hate, / I make peace, they war, / I even kiss their hand, / But they slap my face." [37]

Poetry now branched out into all fields of human endeavor. We recall that the struggle over grammatical rules was conducted by the disciples of Dunash ben Labraṭ and Menaḥem ben Saruq under the guise of polemical rhymes, and that even Menaḥem's pupils found themselves forced to employ the Arabic meter so as to demonstrate their equal linguistic mastery. Such superficial rivalries may appear rather childish to us, but they made good sense to a generation accustomed to the linguistic acrobatics of minority groups bent upon proving that their own languages were no less pliable than Arabic. Did not Ibn Gabirol himself poetically expound his philological concepts in his famous "Necklace"? The extant fragment of this poem demonstrates that in the hands of a master even such a technical exposition could combine exactitude in philological detail with lyrical beauty. Didactic poems soon spread to other branches of human knowledge, and finally penetrated also the realm of science. It was particularly Abraham ibn Ezra who devoted (in his philosophical *Hai ben Meqiṣ*) a number of distinguished lyrics to a variety of astrological topics, which had become, next to the study of the Bible, the overriding passion of his life. From the days of Dunash ben Labraṭ, moreover, gifted Spanish-Jewish poets, like their Muslim confreres, spent much of their energy in formulating clever riddles taxing the ingenuity of readers. They covered a multitude of subjects, all designed to test the listener's erudition as well as his quick wits with respect to some linguistic or juridical problem. Many a reputation was established through such contributions to parlor games, often improvised on the spot. While the early riddles by Dunash still reveal technical inadequacies and sound belabored, those of Halevi combine ingenuity with grace. For example, his quatrain

> An object embracing the infinite,
>   So tiny your hand can conceal,
> Too far from your reach its contents to seize,
>   And yet near enough to reveal,

was often quoted to indicate a mirror. This importation from the East became contagious in Spain, and from there was reexported to others lands of Jewish settlement.[38]

ETHICS AND HISTORY

Medieval Hebrew poetry would not have been true to the entire Jewish tradition had it not dealt at great length also with ethical teachings and historical narratives, particularly those related to biblical events. Clearly, both of these subjects closely bordered on religious interests, and sometimes their treatment may be subsumed under the general term of sacred poetry. However, most ethical teachings were concerned with purely worldly wisdom, even more secular in nature than the biblical Proverbs from which many authors drew their main inspiration. The historical poems, too, often assumed a new, secular coloring. Not only were many contemporary events recorded by their poetic chroniclers, with little if any reference to the general divine guidance of history, but almost all descriptions were now permeated with a new, semimodern spirit of nationalism. Although ancient Hebrew poetry too had always been infused with the idea of national self-realization, there was a basic difference between the nationalism of tribes living on their own soil and the national aspirations of a scattered people in exile, which, despite all odds, yearned deeply for its ultimate redemption in the land of promise.

Even physical manifestations in nature were often imbued with some ethical or historical meaning. These artists had an eye for lovely landscapes and turbulent seas, but they made nature itself subservient to their own emotion by depicting it either as but a blind instrument of the divine will, or else as an unwitting reflection of their own momentary feelings. For example, without the conclusion, Ibn Gabirol's beautiful description of a sunset would have been but another impressive word painting of a recurrent natural phenomenon. But the last verse turned it into a moving dirge on Yequtiel's assassination:

See the sun redden on evening's approach,
  As if it were clad in a crimon spread,
It disrobes the corners of north and south,
  And covers the sea with a purply red.
It leaves the earth behind, naked and bare,
  Hovering calmly in the shadow of night.

Of a sudden the sky grows dark, as if
It donned a sack on Yequtiel's blight.

Similarly, Halevi's renowned cycle composed during his stormy sea journey to Egypt includes precious gems of descriptive power. But it invariably turns to the poet's feelings of loneliness away from his accustomed environment, his helplessness in the face of danger, where "glory comes not to wise and knowledgable men, but to those who know how to swim," and his ultimate reliance on the saving grace divine. The same holds true for the graphic artistry of Moses ibn Ezra and the other poets. In fact, as in contemporary Arabic letters, the sun and the stars, clouds and snow often became stereotype symbols of human actions and reactions. Only occasionally were they to be taken literally, as in the witty complaint of the distinguished jurist-poet R. Meir ha-Levi Abulafia (*ca.*1170–1244) about the combination of heat and rain which bedeviled his journey:

The burning heat of wandering has consumed my heart and soul,
While streams from the sky came down on my head, and engulfed my knees,
I said, "O Lord, Thou causest fire to run of water afoul,
Please choose one, and don't chastise me with both fire and dripping seas.[39]

The progressive rediscovery of the works of Samuel ibn Nagrela also brought to light his large collection of aphorisms, entitled *Ben Mishle* (Offshoots of Proverbs)—a clear indication of the author's indebtedness to the biblical book. The fairly complete text now embraces a total of 1199 epigrams, for the most part consisting of four-verse stanzas, although many extend to a dozen lines and more. Apparently arranged by the Nagid's young son Eliasaf under his supervision and according to a formal scheme of its own, the collection included observations on a wide range of human activities, partly borrowed from literature, but largely derived from the author's own rich experience. That he would not indicate his sources lay not only in the nature of this type of literature, but also in the then fairly general custom of disregarding literary property in the exposition of what one believed to be true. It is generally agreed that the compiler of the biblical Proverbs need not have been familiar with similar ancient Near Eastern collections even where his formulation bears close resemblance to theirs; only the sequence of Amenope's book of wisdom indicates some direct indebtedness. In the same manner, even great verbal similitude in medieval words of wisdom, if not altogether accidental, proves little more than that two authors apparently drew their inspiration from the same apothegms freely circulating from mouth to mouth through many lands. The topics were as a rule of such wide interest that they lent themselves to constant repetition, as well as unconscious rediscovery, by writers completely unbeknown to one another. A stanza like the following from the Nagid's pen could have been written by any number of keen observers of human life:

> Three persons answer softly,
>   Even when they rant and rail,
> Your reigning king, a patient
>   In great pain, and—a female.

We surely should not be astonished to find a disproportionately large number of Samuel's aphorisms dealing with court life and the behavior of rulers. In these matters he spoke indeed with great authority.[40]

Samuel's great personal popularity added to the influence of his ethical teachings. As a distinguished jurist and leader of the Jewish community in his own country he maintained an extensive correspondence with Jewish leaders in other lands, including Ḥushiel and Nissim of Kairuwan (the latter's daughter became his son Joseph's wife), Exilarch Hezekiah, and Hai Gaon in Babylonia. According to fashion, such correspondence was sometimes couched in poetic terms, and often included gifts of excerpts from one's poetic works. Supported by the Nagid's growing reputation as statesman and philanthropist, his works became known "to the ends of East and West." Moses ibn Ezra, extolling this worldwide popularity, admits that after the Nagid's death there arose many carping critics who found fault with Samuel's grammar. In this formative period of Hebrew philology, we recall, controversies over minutiae of language often raged with the fervor of political or religious conflicts. However, the wisdom of his epigrams remained uncontested. "They are more renowned and accepted by all," Ibn Ezra added hyperbolically, "than the miracle in Gibeah, and more sparkling than the very sun in the midst of the skies." [41]

Samuel's example could not fail to stimulate the interest of authors and public in ethical poetry. Ibn Ezra spoke of numerous imitators, even plagiarists, conscious and involuntary. Among the authors distinguished in their own right who enriched the Jewish ethical literature by a considerable number of new, or newly reformulated, pearls of wisdom were Hai Gaon and Ibn Gabirol. Although of somewhat uncertain authorship, the lengthy didactic poems *Shire Musar haskel* (Wise Conduct) were early attributed to the great gaon of Pumbedita. Because of Hai's great fame, this collection enjoyed considerable reputation throughout the Middle Ages, and ultimately it was twice translated into Latin.[42]

Ibn Gabirol, too, always deeply interested in ethics and the author of a fine Arabic treatise "On the Improvement of the Moral Qualities of the Soul," wrote a collection of moral apothegms known only in the Hebrew text under the title *Mibḥar ha-peninim* (Choice of Pearls). It seems that the original, since lost, was written in Arabic, and that the highly popular Hebrew text came only from a translation by Yehudah ibn Tibbon. If so, Ibn Gabirol probably wrote it in Arabic prose. However, before a century passed it was recast in poetic form by Joseph Qimḥi and republished under the title *Sheqel ha-qodesh* (Sacred Shekel). It too was also later published in a Latin translation. Poetic and prose epigrams were also composed by most other famous Spanish poets, some being widely quoted in such prose works as ethical wills. We recall the extensive and reverent use to which Samuel's *Ben Mishle* was put by Yehudah ibn Tibbon in his "Will." [43]

Contemporary historical events, on the other hand, were far less frequently the subject of poetic description in Muslim lands, although, as we shall see, they were to become a primary subject for the penitential prayers composed in the Franco-German communities. In the south we must often be satisfied with such generalities as Moses ibn Chiquitilla's telling distinction between the "wounds" inflicted by Edom's knights and the "yoke of taxes" imposed by the valorous sons of Qedar. Undoubtedly many more poems of contemporary relevance were written in Spain and elsewhere than are now extant. For the most part of interest only to a particular region, locality, or even family, such poems carried little appeal outside the immediate range of interested groups, and hence they were rarely copied. That is why even the historically and autobiographically significant poems by Samuel ha-Nagid have been preserved in few manuscripts. The Cairo Genizah itself, a rich treasure trove for all other branches of literature, has yielded only a few relatively minor epics or litanies relating to contemporary historical developments. Those hitherto uncovered are often far from specific, and pass over concrete details in favor of pious sentiments which could relate to almost any similar situation. A poem describing a Palestinian earthquake, for example, is uncertain as to both date and authorship, although it seems to refer to events of 1033 and was possibly written by one Samuel bar Shalom. Of greater interest is a poem relating to anti-Jewish riots in Egypt (in 1011–12), written by the prolific poet Samuel ben Hosha'nah (the Third), while the personal lamentation by one Yeshu'a ben Nathan on the death of his son in 1025 belongs to the class of friendship poems and dirges, of which a large number is extant from Spain and other countries. However, the Spanish and other Mediterranean communities did not have the good fortune to preserve their genizahs.[44]

Of a different kind were poems describing episodes from biblical history which were of universal interest and had long been embellished by the fertile imagination of homilists and liturgical writers. To be sure, Muslim leaders frowned upon the retelling of the Qur'anic stories in any form other than that contained in the sacred book itself. This negative attitude may have put a damper on the zeal of Jewish poets, too, accounting for the relative paucity of epics on biblical themes, such as had been written by Philo the Elder. However, the tradition of talmudic homilists and *payyeṭanim* offered strong encouragement, with added incentive arising from the new general preoccupation with scriptural studies. From ancient times, moreover, biblical stories lent themselves to allegorical reinterpretation, which lifted them from the realm of historical accident into that of timeless metaphysical and ethical doctrines. In a recently recovered liturgical poem by Ibn Gabirol, for instance, the entire sacred history from the Creation to the building of the First Temple is reviewed in symbolic terms of sin and its forgiveness through repentance. Such allegorization of biblical history is characteristic in fact of much of Ibn Gabirol's poetic as well as philosophic creativity. Other philosophizing poets, like Yehudah Halevi, used such biblical materials with less overt allegory, but essentially also with the aim of conveying some moral. Only occasionally did Halevi follow the usual theme of earlier liturgical poets, as in his poem on "Elijah and Elisha" for recitation at the *Habdalah* ceremony on Saturday night. This poem is prefaced by the characteristic messianic exclamation "Our signs have been delayed, / Where is the God of Elijah?" [45]

As in the case here mentioned, most such historical poems belonged to the domain of sacred, rather than secular poetry. Even contemporary historical events in both the Mediterranean and the northern countries were largely recorded in poems designed for synagogue recitation at memorial services or ritualistic occasions. Of course, some of these lyrics may have originated from personal utterances of pious souls in their private communion with God. Only later one or another congregation, impressed by their content, may have decided to include them in its worship on special occasions. Such undoubtedly was the origin of the famous Zionide elegies by Yehudah Halevi—that purest and loftiest expression of medieval Jewish nationalism. When he composed the moving poem *Ṣiyyon ha-lo tish'ali* (Zion, Dost Thou Not Ask for the Peace of Thy Captives?), Halevi conceived it as a personal confession of himself as the "captive of hope," longing to shed his tears on the desolate hills of Judaea. Little did he dream that before very long almost all Jewish congregations in the world would incorporate this elegy, alongside the biblical Lamentations, in their rituals for the Ninth of Ab. Nor could he anticipate that the cries of anguish of his perceptive soul responding to the Jewish and universal crisis in a deeply divided world would evoke their greatest emotional response in the era of a resuscitated modern Jewish nationalism, long after that particular separation between the Christian West and Islamic East had given way to other imperial and ideological divisions. For more than eight centuries Halevi's exclamation,

My heart is in the East, and I in the far West,
  How can I savor food, and find in it delight?
How shall I pay my vows and self-denying oaths,
  When Zion bows to Edom, and I to Arab might?
I find it easy to leave all the bounty of Spain,
  And to cherish instead the dust on the Temple's site,

inspired many would-be pilgrims to the Holy Land, and gave an emotional uplift to the entire people in its darkest hours.[46]

SACRED POETRY

Messianic, nationalist, and historical themes naturally occupied a prominent role also in these writers' liturgical poetry, which, in fact, can rarely be distinguished from poems originally composed for private circulation. Our scanty biographical data, often laboriously reconstructed from the contents of poems themselves, will hardly ever allow for a definite assessment of the authors' intentions or of the earliest use to which their lyrics were put. It appears, however, that when conscious of writing for congregational use even the greatest of these poets were forced to make concessions to popular taste and the old traditions of liturgical poetry.

Although far less pronounced than in the works of the tenth-century Baghdad poet Abu'l 'Ataluj, whose erotic court poetry differed radically from his pious outpourings for mass use, there exists a line of demarcation even between the religious poetry written by Ibn Gabirol for self-edification and the religious contemplation of a few friends and his regular *piyyuṭim*. The former are sophisticated in both form and substance. There is little to distinguish, for example, his beautiful poem *Sha'ali yefeh-fiah* (Ask of Me, Beautiful) from similar historical-messianic poems by Yehudah Halevi. Alluding to Daniel's vision of the four beasts, the poet bewails the historic fact that hardly had the Lion and the Leopard (Babylonia and the Hellenistic empires) ceased their depredations of Judah when the Wild Ass (the Arabs) appeared "out of midnight . . . to trample and dwell on our soil." The poem concludes with the prayer that Ishmael's offspring be commanded back to Arabia, as his mother had been sent off by Sarah.

Although perfectly lucid, this poem is written with Ibn Gabirol's usual sophistication in both form and content. In contrast thereto another *reshut* (prayer of authorization), which appears in much expanded form in one of the Sephardic collections of penitential poems, renders long-accepted ideas in language so simple that it might have stemmed from the pen of any average penitent. Here simplicity borders on cliché, as may be noticed even through the protective screen of the following translation:

When I knock at Thy gates, O Lord, please unlock them,
  Stretch out Thy pitying hand, when to Thee I weep.
Let my prayer and wailing rise up before Thee,
  And take the honored place of former tithes and sheep.
Light of my eyes! please guard from evil words my tongue,
  And forgive if I err, and utter something wrong.
I have lifted up to Thee my eyes and my heart,
  Lend me Thy willing ear, and throw a friendly gaze;
Recognize my spirit humiliated to its depths,
  My overbearing fat become so lean and base.

In fact, some of these *piyyuṭim* so consciously followed long-accepted patterns that Ibn Gabirol was prepared to sacrifice for them his otherwise scrupulously observed rules of language and poetic arts. For exactly the same deviations Abraham ibn Ezra was soon sharply to censure the chief *payyeṭan,* Qalir.[47]

Among the outstanding liturgical poets in Spain were, not by mere accident, the distinguished talmudic scholars Samuel ibn Nagrela, Ibn Abitur, Ibn Gayyat, and, later, Meir ha-Levi Abulafia. Samuel's poems hark back to the early origins of the *piyyuṭ,* and they have the perfect simplicity of a Yose ben Yose or the talmudic sages. For example, his poem for the eighth day of the Feast of Tabernacles (*Shemini ḥag aṣeret*) uses neither the artifices of the later Qalirian school nor the advanced Spanish techniques, including his own. It merely harps on the themes of divine greatness and forgiveness and the love of the Law, appropriate for a Festival of Rejoicing in the Torah. Perhaps that very simplicity accounts for the lack of appeal of such poems to the more sophisticated Spanish congregations, which did not include them in their congregational recitations. Ibn Abitur, taking seriously the earlier talmudic urging to constant liturgical innovation, clung more closely to the forms of the schools of Qalir and Saadiah. But his language aimed at greater simplicity of expression than was customary among poets of these schools, other than the gaon himself in his memorable prayers of petition. The Cordovan exile's allusions to talmudic and midrashic teachings, though presupposing a considerable amount of talmudic learning on the part of readers, were less obscure than those of his Eastern predecessors, with whose works he must have become fully familiar after his departure from Spain. To judge from his extant poems, Ibn Abitur evinced particular interest in the eternal dialogue between Israel and the celestial powers, and the praises of the Lord sung in unison by the Jews on earth and the angels on high.[48]

In external techniques very similar, the sacred poetry of Ibn Gayyat was distinguished by its novel content. Deeply interested in the new philosophic and scientific discoveries, this great rabbi included some of the newly evolving doctrines and concepts in his poems relating to cosmogony and manifestations in nature. Many readers must have found these poems "difficult to understand," as was observed by Al-Ḥarizi. Nevertheless, already in the days of Moses ibn Ezra they circulated widely in Spain, and before long they were incorporated in the liturgical collections of the Jewish communities throughout the Mediterranean world. More than three hundred of his poems, largely of liturgical character, have been preserved in manuscripts and early editions, and many more are still likely to emerge from the recesses of the world's libraries.[49]

Philosophic concepts, particularly as derived from the new and intensive preoccupation with Platonic and Aristotelian teachings and their application to Jewish religious problems, now colored more and more the poetic writings of Spanish Jewry. The distinguished poet-philosophers, Ibn Gabirol and Halevi, frequently expressed in concise poetic form thoughts on which they expatiated at length in their major philosophic prose works. In fact, the full import of many a poem can be understood only by reference to some such more extended discussions in their own or their contemporaries' philosophic treatises.

One of the most celebrated philosophic poems is Ibn Gabirol's "Royal Crown," long since adopted by many Jewish congregations for recitation at the height of their religious ecstasy on the evening of the Day of Atonement. Setting out to aid the worshipers in the understanding of the mysteries of the universe, the suffering poet of Saragossa composed this lengthy poem of 640 verses, in which "The living God's wondrous ways / Are briefly told in songs of praise." He tried to explain, for example, the unity of God, by pointing out that it is not like any other oneness, but that its mystery escapes the understanding of the wise. "Thou art One, but not like a unit to be grasped and counted, / For neither number nor change, neither attribute nor surname can reach Thee. / Thou art One, but my mind has failed to set Thee within bounds, / Therefore I have decided to guard my ways from sinning with my tongue." Or, in another context, "Thou art God, and there is no difference between Thy Godhead and Thy Oneness, Thy preexistence and existence—For all is one mystery." In this vein the poet reviewed the divine government of the universe, discussing the superlunary world in terms of the contemporary astronomic views of the spheres permeated with the divine spirit, and then turning to the fate of the departed souls and the actions of man on earth. The poem concludes with a traditional prayer for forgiveness and mercy, and a reminder that it is the duty of all to praise the Lord. On closer examination, even Ibn Gabirol's views on immortality and his ethical teachings reveal certain individual nuances which set him aside, in content as well as in form, from the general run of worshipers. If this poem, and still more his *piyyuṭ Shokhen 'ad* (He who Dwelleth Forever), recited by Sephardic congregations during the *Musaf* services of New Year's day, reveal the impact of certain doctrines of *Yeṣirah*, another lengthy liturgical piece of 512 verses, devoted to so-called *Azharot* (Warnings), follows rather closely the then widely accepted enumeration of the six hundred and thirteen commandments given in Simon Qayyara's law book. Curiously this poem, widely accepted by Jewish communities for recitation on the Festival of Weeks and provided with exegetical notes by several commentators, betrays in neither form nor content any indebtedness to Saadiah's similar work, with which Ibn Gabirol may indeed not have been familiar.[50]

Less philosophically creative, pessimistic Moses ibn Ezra constantly emphasized the inadequacy of the human mind to grasp the mysteries of existence. In one of his penitential prayers Moses especially enjoined the worshiper, "Who is to dare partake of the Lord's secrets and mysteries, / And how shall a mere mortal gauge the majesty of the living God?" His religious fervor reached its greatest heights during his ecstatic contemplation of God's grandeur, which he time and again contrasted with man's total unworthiness. One of his major religious poems, *Be-shem El asher amar* (In the Name of God Who Said), in particular, expatiated on the theme of God's inaccessibility to human cognition except indirectly through the contemplation of His works. This poem so impressed Meir ha-Levi Abulafia that the latter composed a poem on this very subject, closely imitating Ibn Ezra's rhyme and rhythm. The acme of Moses' religious poetry was attained in such penitential prayers as his *Be-leb ḥared,* whose remarkable rhythm and spirit, though not rhyme, are caught in Solis-Cohen's apt translation:

> With trembling heart, in fear profound,
> I ask of God forgiveness.
> For secret sins in days of youth,
> Prostrate I fall before Him.
> May fitting words come to my lips—
> And thus I make beginning:
> "Upon the Lord my soul doth wait,
> His saving word I hope for."

Notwithstanding the relative paucity of Ibn Ezra's liturgical output, a grateful posterity nicknamed him *sallaḥ* (penitential poet) and included several of his poems in its liturgy. His influence soon transcended all national boundaries, and before long some of his liturgical poems became part and parcel of the synagogue worship north of the Pyrenees.[51]

World-wide influence was achieved to an even greater extent by Moses' namesake Abraham ibn Ezra and his close friend Yehudah Halevi. Through his extended journeys and protracted residence in Christian lands, Abraham became the great historic mediator between the two worlds, transmitting to the growing communities under Christendom not only the results and methods of Spanish philology, Bible exegesis, and science, but also the new approaches of Spanish poetry. Abraham himself composed numerous short liturgical pieces. More notable for their technical perfection than for contagious religious enthusiasm, they were nevertheless much admired, and often put to liturgical use.[52]

Surpassing all others in variety, as well as in depth and vigor, Halevi's religious poetry extended into every traditional nook of Jewish liturgy and refashioned into memorable personal confessions ideas and images long since become commonplace. For example, in a poem called *Yah anah emṣa'akha,* filled with pithy paradoxes, he inquired, "O Lord, where shall I find Thee / Hid in Thy lofty place? / And where shall I not find Thee, / Whose glory fills all space?" Combining a general epistemological skepticism in metaphysical speculation with national-historical positivism, Halevi constantly harped on the theme that the divine regimen of the world cannot be grasped by the mind but only by the heart. Time and again the poet begged for divine grace and aid in this emotional comprehension. Skillfully climaxing his own meditations with pertinent biblical passages, he wrote:

The Creator who's fashioned all from naught
Stands revealed in the heart, not to the eye.
Hence do not ask about how, where and why,
For it's He who "filleth heaven and earth" [Jer. 23:24].

When thou removest thy innermost lust
Thou shalt find thy Master live in thy heart,
Gently pervading each and ev'ry part—
"He bringeth low, He also lifteth up" [I Sam. 2:7].

Contemplate well the mystery of soul,
Search, and thou wilt find in it restful glee,
Then He will make thee wise, and set thee free,
Who art prisoner now, in the world's gaol.

Make knowledge mediate between thee and Him,
Suppress thy will before the will divine,
Know that His eye roams over all secrets thine
And that "there is nothing too hard for Him" [Jer. 32:17].

Knowledge as postulated here by Halevi was neither the gnostic kind, although he like Baḥya seems to have been quite familiar with some surviving Hermetic writings, nor even that of a metaphysical kind. As we shall see, Halevi did not share the view, held by some Karaites, Baḥya, Abraham ibn Ezra, and other thinkers, that David's injunction to Solomon, "Know thou the God of thy father" (I Chron. 28:9), was tantamount to a commandment to study religious philosophy. He rather referred here, as elsewhere, to the traditional lore which, as he sang in another poem, "I have heard and believed, without questioning and testing." [53]

Nor could even the more rigid rationalists entirely escape the powerful trend toward poetic self-expression. Not only is the semimystic Baḥya ibn Paquda known as the author of two fine prayers of petition and exhortation, but also Joseph ibn Ṣaddiq, author of the rationalistic "Microcosm," composed a series of poems. One of these actually served as a model for his friend, Halevi, who answered him in a poem of exactly the same rhythm and rhyme. Maimonides himself, at least in his younger years, paid homage to the prevailing fashion and wrote a number of liturgical poems. However, the well-known *Yigdal* prayer, recited by many Ashkenazic and Sephardic (though not Italian) congregations at the beginning of their morning services, is most definitely not of his pen, although it is a fairly correct poetic restatement of his Thirteen Principles. It begins with a typically Maimonidean emphasis:

The living God be magnified and praised,
He who exists outside time's eternal drone;
The One and Only, with none like Him alone,
In mystery veiled, of oneness infinite.

There were other poets, however, especially during the heated anti-Maimonidean controversy (for instance, Meshullam da Piera), who wrote verses attacking one or another doctrine of the sage of Fusṭaṭ.[54]

ITALO-GERMAN PIETISM

Compared with the extraordinary richness and variety of Spanish poetry, that of the other European countries appears narrow and confined. S. J. L. Rapoport, one of the earliest scholarly students of medieval Hebrew letters, noted that "in the poetry of the Spaniards it is man's soul which converses with its Creator, in that of the Ashkenazim—the people of Israel converses with its God." This difference clearly mirrors the divergences in social structure and world outlook among the Jews of those countries.

Muslim Spain had received from the Great Caliphate all those vital impulses of a competitive, individualistic society, which had so vitally contributed to the multicolored patterns of the new civilization during the Renaissance of Islam. It added to them further intellectual stimuli, through its frontier life facing the challenges of neighboring Christian states and the fermentation of mutual adjustments by its various ethnic and cultural groups. Western Europe, on the other hand, increasingly felt the impact of the feudal order with its ever stricter social controls and its closed Catholic *weltanschauung*. There was little room within its struggling and segregated Jewish communities for indulgent heralding of purely private sentiments of friendship, love, or the ordinary pleasures of life—indeed for any kind of secular poetry. Even in the relatively friendlier climate of southern Italy, the ninth-century poet Amittai ben Shefaṭiah knew of no better way of celebrating the wedding of his sister Kassia than by a liturgical poem (*yoṣer*), extolling the wisdom of the divine order which includes the commandment of procreation and concluding with a prayer for ultimate messianic redemption. Only in the twelfth century did the new, Spanish-oriented, secular poetry, like Spanish science and philosophy, find devotees in southern Italy and later also in Rome. The new poetry of the Sicilian judge Anatoli ben Joseph and his associates finally led up to the wholly secular, erotic poetry of Immanuel of Rome, which, though quite in line with the prevailing tastes of the rising Italian Renaissance, were to shock many generations of northern pietists.[55]

Religious poetry reigned supreme also because of the overshadowing role of religion in all walks of life and particularly in all Judeo-Christian relations. Compared with the breadth of human concerns reflected in the Jewish literature, as in non-Jewish literature under Islam, Franco-German and even Italian and Byzantine Jewish letters were dominated by religiously dedicated persons who hardly deigned to look at ordinary human problems and daily preoccupations unrelated to law, ethics, or religious doctrine. Cultivating the subject matter as well as the forms developed in Palestine during the Byzantine period, the Western poets, too, were but gifted disciples of the pre-Islamic Palestinian *payyeṭanim* and homilists. Had not even some southern Italian Christian poets written Greek poetry after Byzantine models?

Western Jewry's relations with its Christian neighbors had become ever more tense. When Christian missionary undertakings were coupled with the use of force, and when popular and governmental persecutions became a recurrent phenomenon, Jewish poets often reacted vehemently. Their bitterness, far exceeding any sentiment displayed by Yannai and other sufferers from Byzantine implacability, was often sharpened by personal experiences. When R. Gershom bar Yehudah, deviating from the established law, mourned for two weeks the apostasy of his son (a week each for his soul and his body), he must have loved the boy dearly. How much must such paternal grief have deepened his hatred of the Church, the source of his personal misfortune, as well as of the misfortunes of his people! The same was true of his elder contemporary, R. Simon bar Isaac, the poet and leader whose converted son Elḥanan was invested by later Jewish legends with the Roman pontificate. R. Simon's sense of loss, we are told, was ultimately mitigated when, on a mission to Rome in behalf of his persecuted people, he was led by peculiar moves on the chess board to recognize his son in the reigning pope, and to secure from him the requested pro-Jewish decree. Needless to say, any enforced mass conversion of Jews, such as seems to be reflected in a liturgical piece by Amittai ben Shefaṭiah, left an even more indelible imprint on the minds of Hebrew poets who went through that tragic experience.[56]

It is small wonder, then, that controversial topics in the Judeo-Christian debate occupied a prominent place in all northern poetry. Ever since ancient times, we recall, the problem of Jewish exile and powerlessness had engaged the attention of polemical writers of both faiths, the Christian apologists frequently quoting it as positive proof of God's anger at the Jews for their repudiation of Christ. "Why are you put to shame?" Christian missionaries are quoted by Simon bar Isaac as saying to the Jews, "On account of the sin of the cross / You, like the dead, are totally forgotten." Medieval controversialists belabored this point in a way reminiscent of the ancient pagan argument that a victorious nation had *ipso facto* proved also the superiority of its deities over those of the vanquished people. For this reason Jewish poets in the Christian orbit dwelled at great length on the theme of their divinely willed political inferiority. "They glory in chariots and horses," declaimed Simon bar Isaac in another lengthy penitential prayer, "but we remember the name of the Lord, our God." At the same time these poets stressed their yearning for the speedy restoration of Jews to their own country, and for divine vengeance on their ruthless enemies. The following *piyyuṭ* on the Thirteen Attributes of God (which serve as a refrain) from the pen of Amittai may be cited here as a fairly typical, though rather tame, example:

I remember the Lord, and am keenly distraught,
  When I see each town built on its foundation,
  But God's city doomed to utter humiliation.
Yet we belong to God, and to Him goes our striving.

O Attribute of Mercy, intercede for us!
  Before Thy Master kindly place our entreaty
  In behalf of Thy people invoke divine pity,
Because "the whole head is sick, and the whole heart faint" [Isa. 1:5].

Unto these thirteen words I have anchored my stand,
  And to the gates of tears which never come to rest,
  My speech flows forth to Him who submits hearts to test.
I rely on these and the merit of fathers.

Let it be Thy will, O God, listener to wailings,
  To receive our tears and preserve them in Thy bowl,
  So that we may be spared decrees, cruel and foul,
For it's to Thee alone that our eyes are clinging.

Apart from the acrostic Amittai, there is little in this poem, *Ezkerah Elohim,* to distinguish it from any of the early *piyyuṭim.* Through the very simplicity of its technique it carries great appeal, and it is still fervently recited today by Polish congregations on the Day of Atonement. On the other hand, the equally melancholy poems by Solomon ben Yehudah, "the Babylonian," resident of Rome (tenth century), were very complicated. Perhaps for this reason they failed to attract a large following among the European communities.[57]

Of course, the advent of the Messiah, that focal point in the Judeo-Christian controversy, likewise left its distinct traces. Because of its intimate connection with Christian Trinitarianism, it was often treated within the poetic cycle *zulat,* recited immediately after the passage in the morning prayer proclaiming that "there is no God beside Thee" (*zulatekha*). In one such poem Amittai bitterly complained of those "sinners against God" who loved to start a religious disputation by exclaiming, "Where is your Messiah, and where the place of your Redeemer? Ye have been sold forever." With equal acrimony Gershom bar Yehudah complained of the ruthless foes who were "forcing Thy chosen people to exchange its [messianic] hope for a man earth-born and hanged." Both these poets and their confreres naturally wound up with a prayer to the Lord finally to usher in the true messianic era.[58]

Bitterness mounted in the course of the eleventh century, and it reached its highest pitch after the massacres of the First Crusade. Even the scholars gathered around the gentle and humane Solomon Yiṣḥaqi, who like his immediate rabbinic predecessors had also joined the ranks of liturgical poets, now spoke in a voice of wrath reminiscent of ancient Israelitic prophets. Emulating the Deuteronomic litany of curses (28:15–68), one of Rashi's disciples, in the poem *Titnem le-ḥerpah* (Put Them to Shame, Curse and Desolation), made fully known only in recent years, prayed that God should bring all these plagues "on Edom, Ishmael, and the entire host of Rome, together with the rest of Thine enemies from every nation." Compared with this recital of maledictions, the lamentations of Baruch bar Samuel of Mayence on various tragic events including the ritual murder libel of Blois (1171), and even of Ephraim bar Jacob of Bonn, the graphic chronicler of the massacres during the Second and Third Crusades, pale into mild stereotypes.[59]

Apart from such polemical outbursts, the liturgical poetry of the Italian, French, and German writers contained many expressions of inward piety and of the striving of tormented souls toward communion with their Deity. For example, in a moving penitential poem, *Gadol 'avoni* (My Transgression is Great), Gershom bar Yehudah used the technique of a chain verse (here the last word of each of the forty-seven lines also starts the following verse) to convey the sinner's agonizing feeling of inadequacy while standing before his Creator. The first and the last strophes may serve here as an illustration of both the technique and, despite its obvious artificiality, its basic effectiveness:

> My transgression is great, in sin persevering,
> Persevering in guilt, how grave is my offense!
> My offense is serious, to flogging convicted,
> Convicted to exile, My abode I forgot.
>
> Let forgiveness be granted today before Thee!
> Before Thee plead the Thirteen, signed to Thy faithful.
> Thy faithful remember, and forgive Thy children,
> Thy children, sons of martyrs, do not repudiate.

The main themes of the respective holidays lent themselves to most frequent versification, as many of these poets were synagogue readers trying to supplement the accepted Palestinian ritual. This need was greatest during the second days of holidays, which, never having been observed in the Holy Land, often required complete new sets of *piyyuṭim*.[60]

Ethical-didactic poems, on the other hand, were rather neglected here. Their paucity, however, was not owing to any basic lack of interest, as is evident from the large and ever growing ethical prose literature in the Ashkenazic communities, but essentially to the character of these liturgical poems. Addressed to God, rather than to the reading public, they emphasized the weaknesses and sinfulness of human nature much more than ethical postulates. Only occasionally could a poet like Amittai, in verses dedicated to the sanctification of the marriage ceremony, glorify Jewish sexual ethics and the basic virtues of Jewish marital unions. He contrasted especially "the nations' proclivity to fornication and their revelry in sin and obscene language" with the attitude of Jewish bridal couples who "in their very festivities rejoice only in their God." [61]

Partly for the same reason history played a relatively greater role in the poetry of Christian lands. Holiday liturgy lent itself admirably to the retelling of biblical narratives connected with each festival, as amplified by ancient and early medieval homilists. Whatever unconscious restraints may have hampered Jews in Muslim lands, because of excessive Arab fears of despoiling the Qur'an's matchless beauty by any purely human reformulation, were totally absent in the lands of Christendom which had long accepted the artistic rewriting of biblical stories as an integral part of Christian liturgy and homiletics.

Passover especially, with its underlying drama of liberation from Egyptian bondage, inspired many Jewish poets to compose new narratives. To a Franco-German Jew, even before the Crusades, the unrelenting political and religious pressures of the Christian majority often appeared as a direct parallel to the regime of the ancient Pharaohs. Hence the story of the miraculous liberation of his ancestors carried a message of ultimate salvation for himself and his generation as well. This is indeed the theme of practically all the extant poems by the earliest German poet, Moses bar Kalonymos, who had apparently emigrated from Italy to Mayence in the early part of the tenth century. Similar contemporary overtones are audible in the poetic elaborations of the Passover story by Simon bar Isaac, Gershom bar Yehudah, and other northerners.[62]

At the same time there began a new, perfectly articulate poetic martyrology describing the actual suffering of Franco-German Jewry. During the period of the Crusades these voices swelled into a powerful chorus. Despite their natural vagueness and frequently stereotyped phrasing, some of these successive lamentations from Kalonymos bar Yehudah, father of the famous mystic Eleazar of Worms, to Ephraim bar Jacob of Bonn possess great documentary value. They bear witness to their author's preoccupation with at least the more gory facets of current history.

Nor were these poets indifferent toward the basic riddles of the universe and of human existence. However, their philosophy, like that of their prose-writing contemporaries, was long but a continuation of the mystical speculations of their Palestinian predecessors. The mysteries of the *Hekhalot* literature, which as we shall see brought into the open some underground traditions of ancient gnosticism, deeply influenced Italians like Amittai and received memorable reformulation from Eleazar of Worms and his school of German pietists. Especially the so-called *ofanim,* prayers describing the participation of celestial hosts in the recitation of the morning *qedushah,* served as admirable vehicles of such mystic speculation. In his poem *Er'elim u-mal'akhim* (Divine Spirits and Angels), for example, Amittai described in graphic detail the actions and utterances not only of such long accepted angelic figures as Michael and Gabriel, but also of the more obscure divine "messengers" like Hadarniel, Sandalfon, or Galiṣur. Underlying this description, or the related one concerning the reception given Moses by the heavenly hosts on his arrival to receive the Torah, were such older Aggadot as had found their way into the *Pesiqta rabbati.* But they also contained novel elements, represented only in later mystery books. Similarly, the poem *Ve-'attah banim* (And Now My Sons, Sing to the Lord) by Simon bar Isaac is correctly characterized by its later heading, "An *ofan* based on the book of *Hekhalot.*"[63]

A peculiar branch of this mystic poetry, cultivated especially by the German pietists, came to be known under the name of *Shire ha-yiḥud* (Poems of Unity). Briefer versions were often styled the *Shire ha-kabod* (Poems of Grandeur). Although akin to Saadiah's philosophically oriented poems of petition and Ibn Gabirol's "Royal Crown," they were keyed to less complex professions of faith in God's unity and omnipotence. One of the earliest of these poems, *Ashirah ve-azamrah* (I Shall Sing and Chant), is sometimes ascribed to Samuel, father of Yehudah the Pious, and sometimes to Yehudah himself, as well as to other writers. In view of its considerable length, it was subdivided for recitation on the six weekdays and the Sabbath. Like its thoughts, its technique is perfectly simple; the author is neither bound by the rigid exigencies of rhyme and meter of the Spanish schools, nor does he indulge in the linguistic gymnastics of the school of Qalir. If, nevertheless, some later students felt impelled to provide this "sacred" poem with extensive commentaries, their main purpose was further elaboration, rather than explanation, of the ideas expressed by its author—a fairly common phenomenon among medieval exegetes. We need but compare with it a similar effusion by the fourteenth-century Spanish kabbalist, Joseph ibn Waqar, to note its essential lack of sophistication. Ibn Waqar's poem *Adonai eḥad* (God Is One) is so deeply permeated with kabbalistic allusions, obscure to all but the fully initiated, that the author himself felt obliged to supply a detailed commentary.[64]

Of course, even the simplest poetic refinements of such theological ideas as unity and omnipotence taxed the understanding of the rank and file of Jewish worshipers. For this reason there developed at times a strong opposition to their recitation as integral parts of daily or Sabbath services. Some uncontrolled rumors, moreover, attributed the composition of *Ashirah ve-azamrah* to a Christian monk, Michael Basilius. For these reasons, the distinguished eighteenth-century rabbinic leader, Elijah Gaon of Vilna, for many years engaged in a losing battle against the rise of the new popular mystic movement of Ḥasidism, tried to eliminate that poem from the synagogue liturgy. Two centuries earlier Solomon Luria had endeavored to suspend at least its daily recitation, because constant repetition of such lofty professions tended, in his opinion, to weaken their impact on the worshiper. Nonetheless, most congregations of the Ashkenazic rite have continued reciting its final section, *An'im zemirot* (I Shall Intone Sweet Chants), at the conclusion of the Sabbath morning services.[65]

ROMANCES AND PARABLES

Wide popular interest in Hebrew poetry also stimulated the rise of a new genre: fictional narratives (*sadj*) with sections ending in rhymes and interspersed with poems. Jewish interest in such novelistic accounts was very old. It went back to the ancient Aramaic translation of the Aḥiqar story and the biblical or apocryphal elaborations of the stories of Esther, Tobit, or Judith. As we recall, subsequently ancient and medieval homilists often indulged in the recitation of tales and parables, and, particularly in the Arab world, Jewish preachers had their field day in including regular storiettes in their sermons, oral or written. Nissim of Kairuwan's comprehensive folkloristic collection in Arabic became, at least in its later Hebrew garb, a regular "best seller."

Growing secularization of Hebrew life and letters, as well as the widening of geographic horizons, caused travelogues, real and fictitious, to kindle popular imagination with respect to adventures in distant lands. Following the fashion set by such popular Arab writers as Hamadani and Hariri, there began growing also among the Jews of Spain and the Near East a branch of literature known under the Arabic name *maqamas*. Neither this designation, originally derived from the "place" and the assembly where these stories were told, nor its Hebrew counterpart, *Maḥbarot* (Notebooks; apparently coined by Al-Ḥarizi), comes anywhere near describing the multicolored pattern of these poetic miscellanies. Loosely connected by some imaginary hero traveling from one town and country to another, meeting all sorts of people and finding himself in many unexpected and even dangerous situations, these narratives gave free reign to the poetic imagination and allowed for the treatment of almost any subject, ethical, psychological, literary, or linguistic. Unbound by rhythmical exigencies and, by the nature of Hebrew and Arabic suffixes, given great leeway in the selection of rhymes, some of these authors could devote their talents to the exploration of the hidden possibilities inherent in their linguistic medium.

Linguistic acrobatics came to the fore in Yehudah ben Solomon al-Ḥarizi's translation, or rather Hebrew paraphrase, of Hariri's *Maqamas,* entitled *Maḥbarot Ithiel* (the biblical hero of Prov. 30:1 replacing Hariri's narrator, Harith ibn Hamman). Prepared at the instance of some Spanish patrons, some time before Al-Ḥarizi's departure for the Orient about 1211, this work has come down to us in a single manuscript, which fails to supply information concerning the author's avowed objectives and methods. We are doubly grateful, therefore, for the brief, but illuminating excursuses included in the introduction to his own similar work in Hebrew, the *Taḥkemoni.*

The consideration [he wrote] which gave me the impetus to the composition of the present work was that a man from among the Ishmaelite sages, one of their superior intellects, whose tongue overflowed with Arabic phrases and through whom the art of poetry stood widely revealed, had written a book in Arabic, dispensing words of great beauty. He is known under the name of Al-Hariri, and compared with him every other father of parables appears barren. To be sure, all his topics are derived from Hebrew, and all his precious parables are borrowed from our books. Should anyone ask any of these phrases, "Who had brought thee into the language of the descendants of Hagar?" it would reply, "For indeed I was stolen away out of the land of the Hebrews" [Gen. 40:15]. When I saw that work, the skies of my rejoicing rolled up like a scroll, and the streams of my sorrow flowed forth. For every people carefully expresses its thoughts and guards itself against sinning with its speech, but our language, which had been the delight for every onlooker, . . . has now been deprived of pride and beauty. Our people's children have cast aspersion on it, and aimed at it the shafts of their ridicule. They contend that our speech is inadequate and short of phrases, not knowing that that shortcoming lies with themselves, because they fail to understand its vocabulary, and to recognize its delights.

Just as Hariri used with extraordinary skill the rich resources of the Arabic style and lexicography, Al-Ḥarizi exploited to the full the Hebrew linguistic refinements of his Spanish predecessors. His task was even more arduous in so far as he tried to reproduce in some corresponding Hebrew form all the extraordinary turns and unusual poetic forms of the Arabic original. At times this undertaking proved impossible of attainment. Al-Ḥarizi himself twice had to admit that he had been unable adequately to render Hariri's sixth *maqama,* which had purposely been so arranged that each word was composed alternately of consonants written with and without diacritical marks, while in the twenty-sixth *maqama* each letter alternated between marked and unmarked forms. Since the Hebrew alphabet had no equivalent to the Arabic division into fourteen diacritically distinguished and fourteen simple letters, the Hebrew poet had to limit his rendition of these *maqamas* to their content and structure. Neither was Al-Ḥarizi able to reproduce Hariri's five-verse poem of six words each, all of which made good sense whether the letters were read forward or backward. On the other hand, he outdid his model when, in another context, he replaced a sentence of seven such words by four Hebrew sentences using the same artifice. Al-Ḥarizi proved an even more consummate craftsman when he had to find biblical and Jewish equivalents for Qur'anic and other Muslim allusions.[66]

In his own original Hebrew work, *Taḥkemoni* (Poetic Miscellany; the title is borrowed from II Sam. 23:8), Al-Ḥarizi produced a truly classical work of the same genre. Having had on his numerous journeys in Spain, North Africa, and western Asia the opportunity to observe human behavior under different social conditions, Yehudah ben Solomon combined the fruits of this direct experience with ample erudition in contemporary letters, both Hebrew and Arabic. On the order of the Roman Jewish elders, he had produced an elegant, if not precise, Hebrew version of a part of Maimonides' *Commentary* on the Mishnah. He later translated that author's philosophic *magnum opus* into readable Hebrew and, on his own, wrote a commentary on Job and other works. Yehudah evidently combined expertness in biblical, talmudic, and philosophic problems with excellent familiarity with the earlier Hebrew poetic literature, a keen sense of humor, and an almost uncanny mastery of the Hebrew language. Two of the fifty chapters in his work (III and XVIII) are entirely devoted to literary criticism and a brief survey of the Hebrew poetic achievements in East and West, and these have long served as guides for the rediscovery of many artistic treasures.

True, in dispensing praise or blame, Al-Ḥarizi was far from objective. He shared with many of his contemporaries an ardent Jewish patriotism which made him believe in the ultimate superiority of Hebrew over all other languages. Would otherwise, he asked, the Creator of all languages have chosen it as the instrument of His creation in lieu of another more perfect tongue? He was also a staunch Spanish patriot, convinced that whatever achievements the various centers of Jewish learning may have had in other fields of literary creativity, they fell far short of the high standards of Spanish poetry. In fact, by establishing seven major negative criteria which seriously vitiated poetic quality, he tried to prove that Spain rather than Arabia had been the fountainhead of all great poetry. With his penchant for generalization, he illustrated these faulty techniques by attributing each of them to poets of particular countries. Al-Ḥarizi also evinced strong personal likes and dislikes. Quite avowedly mercenary, he heaped unmeasured abuse on those who failed to support him financially, while he praised to the sky each of his generous patrons. The unresponsiveness and lack of generosity of his generation became one of the recurrent themes in his writings—a *leitmotif,* incidentally, also for the chorus of Spanish-Arabic writers ever since the Almoravid regime. Al-Ḥarizi contrasted this miserliness of his contemporaries with the liberality of the Jewish grandees in the days of Solomon ibn Gabirol, Moses ibn Ezra, and Yehudah Halevi. In one of the poetic miscellanies appended to the last chapter of his main work he complained:

When the suns of Solomon, Yehudah, and Moses,
Fathers of our poetry, had risen in the West,

They were fortunate in finding patrons of learning,
  To whom they could sell their pearls for a silver-filled chest.
But soon after my birth generosity had vanished,
  The patrons' sun had set, followed by a pitch-dark night.
While the great masters had bathed in refreshing rivers,
  Whichever way I turned, I found only drought and blight.

Very likely, however, his arrogance antagonized a great many would-be patrons accustomed to insistent demands of literary carpetbaggers. Nor was Al-Ḥarizi's personal life above all reproach. Not only is his book filled with outspokenly erotic, sometimes obscene passages—he followed therein the prevailing fashion among the Arab authors of *maqamas,* including Hariri himself—but he seems to have at times rather too readily yielded to the numerous temptations encountered on his extended journeys. In a poem on the subject of sexual "desire" (*ḥesheq*) he himself alluded to "opponents who quarrel with me on account of my desire." [67]

Such smiling acceptance of human weaknesses must have aroused the ire of a large segment of the reading public, as condemnation of erotic and other physical appetites had become a commonplace in the moralistic and even in the romanticizing letters of the period. Joseph ben Meir ibn Zabara, for example, whom Al-Ḥarizi himself counted among the greatest Spanish poets, frequently spoke of them derogatorily. He voiced the generally accepted ethical views, whether or not complied with in practice, when he wrote, "Asked as to which was the best and most honored companion, a wise man replied, 'The good deed and fear of the Lord.' And as to which [companion] was evil and despised, he answered, 'The covetous soul.' " Ibn Zabara also cited Diogenes' saying that "A man's virtue is measured by the supremacy of his reason over his desire, and his shortcoming by his desire's control over his reason." Otherwise he had much in common with Al-Ḥarizi. Born in Barcelona (about 1140), he apparently traveled extensively, although he seems never to have gone beyond the confines of the Iberian Peninsula and the Provence. Even this lesser area, however, then broken up into innumerable small principalities and feudal lordships, both Muslim and Christian, offered to this keen observer of human nature a considerable variety of mores and folklore which he depicted for his readers in a series of charming anecdotes, ethical sayings, and parables. Some of these were original with him, while many others he quoted from Jewish and Arabic sources. His *Sefer Sha'ashu'im* (Book of Delight) speedily became a classic of that peculiar literature of adventure, and doubtless influenced Al-Ḥarizi and other writers. Also largely composed in rhymed prose, it was prefaced by one long and three short poems and contained twenty-two additional poems interspersed throughout the text. Many of the latter, however, were borrowed from other authors, such as Halevi.[68]

Ibn Zabara's contemporary, Yehudah ben Isaac Shabbetai, likewise practicing medicine in Christian Barcelona during the twelfth century, addressed himself principally to the then widely debated status of women, and to the merits and demerits of married life. In his delightful *Soneh nashim* (Misogynist) he described in graphic detail the vicissitudes of his young hero, who together with three youthful companions pledged himself to combat matrimony. Ultimately, the would-be celibatarian fell victim to a successful feminine cabale and not only succumbed to the charms of a beautiful "gazelle," but married an ugly, quarrelsome hag, whom the women substituted for his intended bride. This substitution theme was generally quite popular in contemporary letters. Going all the way back to the biblical story of Leah and Rachel, it was retold many times by various authors. One of the earliest Jewish *maqama* writers, Solomon ibn Ṣiqbal, made it a major topic of his poetic miscellany *Ne'um Asher ben Yehudah* (Thus Spake Asher ben Yehudah). A century later Al-Ḥarizi was so impressed by Solomon's tale that he reshaped it in a story of "seven virgins" and incorporated it as a special chapter (xx) of his work. However, the moral of Yehudah ben Isaac Shabbetai's story was evidently pro-feminist, and in his conclusion the author himself professed to love his wife and child "more than anyone who lived before me." Nevertheless, the provocative title of his book elicited many a defense of womanhood. One need but mention an interesting poem, written in 1298 by the then eighteen-year-old philosopher Yedaiah ben Abraham ha-Penini or ha-Bedershi (of Béziers, Provence), and pointedly entitled *Oheb nashim* (Philogynist).[69]

Other classics of that literature included the story of the "Prince and Dervish" (*Ben ha-melekh ve-ha-nazir*) by another member of the Barcelona community, Abraham ben Samuel ibn Ḥisdai. The antecedents of this epic yarn on the conflict between a hedonist king and his ascetic son, aided and abetted by a "subversive" dervish, went back to an old Indian tale frequently modified in its subsequent migrations through the Christian and Muslim Near East. Among the numerous poetic gems of worldly wisdom, one is not altogether surprised to find also a religious, almost liturgical poem. Jacob ben (or rather, ibn) Eleazar (Abenalazar), another occasional Spanish liturgical poet of that period, achieved considerable popularity through his Hebrew translation of the Near Eastern classic *Kalilah ve-Dimnah,* a book which in the Latin translation by the converted Jew, John of Capua, became very popular in the Christian West as well. Ibn Eleazar's own *Sefer Meshalim* (Book of Parables), a collection of *maqamas,* and his related ethical-philosophic speculations, partly in rhymed prose, under the picturesque title *Sefer Pardes rimmone ha-ḥokhmah* (Orchard of Pomegranates of Wisdom), seem to have been far less widely read. Only the second half of the latter work and the "love stories" included in four chapters of the "Book of Parables" have thus far appeared in print.[70]

Closely akin was another branch of popular Hebrew letters consisting of extensive collections of fables. Such were compiled especially in the thirteenth century by Isaac ibn Sahula and Berakhiah ben Naṭronai ha-Naqdan (the Punctuator). The former's *Mashal ha-qadmoni* (Ancient Parable) reproduced in an original and attractive form the thrice-told tale of the ultimate failure of an ingenious scheme by a dishonest depositary to embezzle a precious purse entrusted to him. Berakhiah the Punctuator of northern France (and possibly England), well-known also for his exegetical work on the Bible and his ethical treatises, presented in his *Mishle shu'alim* (Fox Parables) one hundred and nineteen graphic animal tales, which in part went back to Aesopian traditions. The French author borrowed also much from the *Kalilah ve-dimnah,* the related *Mishle Sindbad* or *Sendebar* (Parables of Sindbad), and other current folktales, particularly those of Maria de France, as well as from rabbinic legends.[71]

Berakhiah went further than any of his predecessors in spelling out the moralistic purpose of his collection. Apart from generally safeguarding himself in the introduction against the imputation that he had merely furnished "a parable in the mouths of fools, filled with dreams and vanities," he concluded each story with a forthright explanation of its intended lesson. Though less articulate, the Jewish authors of *maqamas* likewise pursued principally moralistic aims. Despite differences in form and their greater appeal to popular imagination, they therefore belonged essentially to the class of ancient homilists and more recent writers of ethical treatises and apothegms. In fact, it is not easy to draw a sharp line of demarcation between the sententious observations on human behavior included, for example, in Samuel ibn Nagrela's *Ben Mishle* and Ibn Gabirol's *Choice of Pearls* (especially in its rhymed paraphrase by Joseph Qimḥi) and the moralistic epigrams of Ibn Zabara and Al-Ḥarizi, or between the two aforementioned works by Jacob ibn Eleazar.

NON-HEBRAIC POETRY

Remarkably, despite these close interrelations with Arabic poetry, Jews themselves wrote relatively little poetry in any language other than Hebrew. Many of them undoubtedly had sufficient command of the Arabic language and meter to compose any number of poems in that language. Yet there was a sort of conspiracy of silence which discouraged all but the hardiest souls to defy tradition.

Probably the problem of the Arabic script had something to do with this extraordinary restraint. We recall that the Muslims had long viewed with disfavor the use of the Arabic alphabet by infidels. Since Jewish writers as a rule addressed themselves exclusively to Jewish audiences, they considered it no hardship to use the Hebrew script in their prose writings. Most Jewish philosophers wrote their Arabic works in the Hebrew alphabet. If Saadiah and some copyists of Maimonides' philosophical work departed from this tradition, they merely confirmed the rule. Such a compromise could hardly appeal to poets. Because of rigid metric requirements and the difference between long and short vowels, any transliteration of Arabic poems into Hebrew script necessarily created much confusion in the minds of readers. We need but consider the difficulties of modern scholars in unraveling quotations from Arabic poems in Moses ibn Ezra's Arabic work on Hebrew poetic arts, now extant in a single manuscript written in Hebrew script. Doubtless for this reason Yehudah ibn Tibbon, in his translation of Ibn Gabirol's ethical treatise, preferred to omit altogether quotations from Arab poets (they are restored in the recent Hebrew translation by N. Bar-On), while Abraham ibn Ḥisdai, in his Hebrew translation of an ethical treatise by Al-Ghazzali, replaced Arabic poems by Hebrew verses from the pen of Samuel ibn Nagrela and others.[72]

Such restraint is doubly remarkable, as Jews had actively participated in the creation of Arabic poetry in pre-Islamic Arabia. Not only was Samau'al ibn Adiya a renowned Arabic poet in his own right, but the Jews of the oasis of Teima were generally considered excellent judges of the quality of Arabic poems. According to a contemporary tradition, the leaders of that community were asked to serve as arbiters in a poetic contest between two neighboring Bedouin tribes. On his appearance in Medina, we are told, Mohammed was greeted with derisive poems by K'ab ibn al-Ashraf and a Jewish poetess, Asma, daughter of Merwan. This chain was suddenly broken by the destruction of the Jewish communities on the Peninsula, and it took centuries before the practice was resumed. True, little of the Arabic-Jewish poetry has come down to our day. But there is good evidence that Samuel ibn Nagrela himself wrote some Arabic poems, although the tradition, recorded by Saadiah ibn Danon, that he had once composed a poem in seven languages is most likely apocryphal. The Nagid also encouraged his sons not only to study Arabic poetic writings, but also to exercise their skill in the composition of such works. Moses ibn Ezra, whose Arabic prose was grammatically and stylistically impeccable, though at times a little too ornate, is also recorded as the author of occasional Arabic poems. Among his various linguistic feats Al-Ḥarizi produced a fairly lengthy poem in three languages (Hebrew, Arabic, and Aramaic). His younger contemporary, Abraham ibn Sahl of Seville, actually left behind an entire *Diwan* of Arabic poems, largely written before his conversion to Islam. Perhaps because of its preponderantly erotic content, this

Diwan allegedly sold for ten times the price of a Qur'an. Nor was there any lack of popularizers who, through the composition of didactic poems on certain subjects, wished to impress their teachings on the minds of readers. We find such didactic poems not only on medical subjects, but even on the laws of Jewish ritual slaughtering (by the thirteenth-century poet, Abraham ben Isaac ben Meborakh).[73]

Even stranger in many respects are the occasional Castilian stanzas in Hebrew script appended to some poems by Yehudah Halevi. The great Hebrew poet must have decided to conclude some of his friendship poems addressed to Spanish Jewish grandees with several verses in Castilian, because the latter was the recipient's favorite language. For example, in writing a beautiful Hebrew poem in honor of Joseph ben Ferrizuel, surnamed Cidellus or Cidello, Halevi added four lines which have been reconstructed to read:

Responde[d]; Mio Cidello! venid
Con bona albixar
Como rayo del sol exid
En Guadalajara

Another poem, written on the occasion of Abu'l Hasan Meir ibn Qamaniel's journey from Seville to Marakesh, Morocco (some time before 1130), concluded: "Filiol alienu / Bastaredes mais a meu senu." Although the vocalization of such awkward Hebrew transliterations, which must further have suffered in the course of transmission, is far from certain, Spanish philologists have found in them significant testimony for the early developments of the Castilian dialect.[74]

Compared with both Arabic and Castilian, poetry in the Aramaic language was not viewed as a foreign importation. Even in the first millennium, when Aramaic still was the spoken language of the Near Eastern masses, such Aramaic prayers as the *qaddish* had gained free admission into the liturgy of the synagogue. Especially in the forms incorporated in the two Talmudim, Aramaic had become to all intents and purposes a Jewish idiom, hallowed by the sacred tradition of the leading academies. That is why the liturgical poets of the age, including those of the school of Saadiah, had no compunctions about composing additional *piyyuṭim* in that language. This custom continued long after the disappearance of Aramaic from among the living dialects of the Jewish people. Western Jews, who had never spoken that language, now considered it a part of their religious heritage to cultivate the speech of their talmudic sages. For example, the Worms cantor Meir bar Isaac left behind several significant Aramaic poems, including the widely recited *Aqdamut*. Mystics felt a particular attraction toward that idiom, which was sufficiently Hebraic not to be regarded as an alien growth, and yet unintelligible enough to the masses to allow for the communication of mysteries to initiates only. Even the declaration of R. Johanan concerning the alleged unfamiliarity of the ministering angels with the Aramaic language failed to discourage the composition of Aramaic prayers specifically addressed to angels. Occasionally, however, Aramaic poems were written for other than liturgical purposes. Samuel ibn Nagrela, for example, wrote both a letter and a comforting poem in that language to his friend R. Ḥananel of Kairuwan. Nor did the trilingual "miscellany" by Al-Ḥarizi pursue any religious purpose.[75]

POETIC ARTS

Far more significant than these occasional foreign-language creations were the formal, as well as substantive, influences of the Arabic and, to a lesser extent, the Romance literatures on the Hebrew-writing authors. Although historically uninformed and even lacking in basic historical curiosity, the Spanish Hebrew poets themselves were fully aware of the foreign origin of some of their basic technical devices, particularly their rhythmic forms. In their excessive zeal they were prone to claim absolute priority for the holy language in almost any other field of endeavor, but they could not conceal to themselves and their readers that the new poetry differed fundamentally in many of its methods from the poetry of the Bible. Only in the period of the Italian and Spanish Renaissance, when the memories of the Arabic background grew dimmer while those of the ancient cultures loomed ever brighter, were voices heard saying that the new rhythm had belonged to the forgotten vestiges of a biblical Hebrew, which had once enjoyed greater richness than could be recaptured from its few remnants in the Old Testament. The Spanish poets themselves made no such claims. Some, like Yehudah Halevi, rebelled against this indebtedness and wished to curtail the emulation of Arabic patterns. But even they could not escape the impact of both the environment and an already established tradition, and in practice they employed the new forms in their own works. Others, like Moses ibn Ezra, took it more calmly. In his long poem *Be-shem El* (In the Lord's name), modeled after Ibn Gabirol's "Royal Crown," he actually extolled the combination of the correctness of Hebrew with the vigor of Arabic and the elegance of Greek. In his unbounded admiration for Arabic poetry, he believed that among the Gentile nations it was only to the Arabs that poetry came naturally, whereas all other peoples wrote artificial poems. He even tried to explain this difference by the dry climate and peculiar air of Arabia. In time all opposition was silenced in the domain of secular poetry, where the new techniques now held undisputed sway. Only in sacred poetry did the old forms, aided and abetted by a millennial tradition, persist even in Spain, while most other communities largely maintained their unbroken continuity with the old *piyyuṭ*.[76]

The greatest transformation took place in the Hebrew meter. The biblical meter had always stressed tonality and consisted primarily in the rhythmic scansion of words, rather than syllables. The Arabs, who had long cultivated a syllabic rhythm, developed it further in their contact with the Christian heirs of the Graeco-Roman civilization. In Spain, particularly, their own rhythmic variations increased in number and accentual richness. The purely subsidiary position of vowels in both Arabic and Hebrew, in sharp contrast to their independent quality in the Indo-European languages, stimulated the development of ever new metrical forms. These possibilities were further increased by the frequency of the *sheva mobile* and its *ḥaṭaf* derivatives, which, without quite attaining the status of vowels, were nevertheless distinctly audible and could enter a combination with the subsequent vocalized letter or letters to form a so-called *yated* (peg). Numerous combinations of such "pegs" with syllables, both long and short, lent the new poetry a certain colorful richness and musicality which, at least in the hands of great artists, made possible some of the immortal creations of the "Golden Age." [77]

After many decades of hesitation, modern scholarship has reached a fair degree of unanimity in regarding Dunash ben Labraṭ as the first medieval Hebrew poet who consciously imitated the Arabic meter. His predecessors, including Saadiah, seem purposefully to have avoided the introduction of these strange forms into Hebrew letters. If we are to believe one of Dunash's boasts (the genuineness of that statement is still under debate) a poem written by him in the new meter once elicited the gaon's unbounded admiration. However, Saadiah himself, though generally far from fearful in breaking new ground, never extended his poetic experimentation, both theoretical and practical, into the domain of Arabic meters. Possibly he and his confreres, writing almost exclusively sacred poetry, did not dare to inject such an obviously foreign growth into the synagogue ritual. Dunash, however, who all his life seems to have written secular as well as liturgical verses and very likely had pioneered along these lines even while in his native Fez or in Babylonia, saw no harm in using the new vehicle and even boasted of his "measured poems" (*shirim nishqalim*). Once committed to the new technique, he probably saw no reason for abandoning it in his liturgical poems. Spanish Jewry, doubtless overawed by his linguistic mastery and generally avid to learn from the admired newcomers from eastern lands, seems to have offered no resistance. Even when in the subsequent controversy the disciples of Menaḥem ben Saruq accused Dunash of having "despoiled the holy tongue left to the Remnant by weighing the Hebrew with foreign meters," the Spanish Jewish public paid little heed. In fact, Dunash's pupil, Yehudi, could already point to the universal imitation of Dunash's example by subsequent poets.[78]

Matters were speedily settled when Samuel ibn Nagrela began the extensive use of Arabic meters in his own poetry. His international prestige, as Nagid and juridical expert, practically silenced all opposition. Since most of his poetry was devoted to secular subjects, its formal deviations from the accepted patterns aroused no protests. Samuel even ventured to employ the new meter in some of his Aramaic poems, such as that included in his letter of comfort to R. Ḥananel. According to David Yellin, who made a special study of this subject, Samuel's experimentation with the new medium led him to the employment of more metric forms than any other medieval Hebrew poet—an achievement of which he spoke with considerable pride. Yellin identified no less than fifty-seven distinct meters in Samuel's poems, as against Ibn Gabirol's fifteen, Moses ibn Ezra's eighteen, and Halevi's twenty-three. Eliminating duplications, Samuel's three great successors utilized altogether thirty-one metric forms, of which all but four used by Halevi had already been found in the Nagid's verses. Adding to these another meter apparently first introduced by Abraham ibn Ezra, and two more found in the works of the thirteenth-century poet Todros ben Yehudah Abulafia, Yellin established a total of sixty-four Hebrew meters employed by various medieval Spanish poets. The readers' preference was unequivocal. Even objectors seem to have admitted, to use Samuel Taylor Coleridge's simile, that meter was like yeast "worthless and disagreeable by itself, but giving vivacity and spirit to the liquor with which it is proportionally combined." Of course, some meters were more popular than others, but many remained in vogue until the Italian Renaissance, when the tonal meter began once more to displace the syllabic rhythm of the Arabic poetry. Still later the central European quantitative meter began penetrating European Hebrew poetry as well. But, despite all artificiality, perhaps even the violence it had done to the spirit of the Hebrew language, the Arabic meter helped to discipline generations of Hebrew poets, and it forced them fully to exploit their linguistic resources.[79]

Some poems of the great Spaniards, to be sure, have a rhythm far from pleasing to modern ears. But in these cases the fault usually rests with the reader. It is well known that the rhythm of German poetry does not always appeal to Frenchmen, nor that of French poetry to Germans, unless the verses are recited strictly in accordance with the specific accentuation of these national meters. Similarly, the proper reading of the Syriac poems by St. Ephrem presupposes the attuning of both readers and listeners to the specific scansion of the seven-syllable verses of that liturgical master. Obviously, a special technique, now still in its infancy, is also indicated for the recitation of some of the masterpieces of the Spanish Hebrew poets.[80]

Rhyming, on the other hand, elicited no objections. Whatever one thinks of the biblical antecedents of Hebrew rhymes, they certainly were fully developed by the early medieval *payyeṭanim.* Saadiah, as we recall, began his literary career with a rhyming dictionary, intended to facilitate the composition of new rhymed poems. As in Arabic, the rhyme, sometime extending over an entire lengthy poem, became the most characteristic feature of Hebrew poetry and served as the main instrument of identification. Medieval compilers often arranged their *diwans* (collections) of individual poets in the sequence of rhymes. Even in modern times, many a poem has been identified, and numerous dispersed fragments of the same work reunited, only with the aid of such verse endings rather than the *incipits,* which had often gone astray. Of course, the uniform Hebrew plural forms, *im* and *ot,* and still more the constancy of such suffixes as *ekha* or *ayikh,* made rhyming extraordinarily easy. The greatest of poets at the very height of their achievement readily resorted to this rather simple expedient, which may at times appear tiresome to western readers or listeners. No less a masterpiece than Halevi's famous Zionide poem is all composed with the *ayikh* rhyme. However, a large number of other rhymes in successive, alternating, or other verses likewise came into extensive use.[81]

Apart from rhythm and rhyme, the Spanish poets developed a kaleidoscopic variety of "adornments of poetry," relating to both poetic forms and modes of expression. Here again Arabic examples proved irresistible. Reference has already been made to the pyrotechnics employed by Al-Ḥarizi and others, not only in their poetic works but also in stories and letters written in rhymed prose. We remember Al-Ḥarizi's poems which were so arranged that words could be read backward and forward, in each case yielding a different meaning. This artifice, employed also by such Byzantine writers as Leo the Wise, bore the special Greek designation of "crab poem" (*karkinos*). Among both Arabs and Jews an epistle so written that it conveyed praise or blame for the recipient dependent upon the direction in which it was read, was considered the acme of epistolary skill. We may also add Al-Ḥarizi's exercises in the use of words containing a particular letter. He astounded his readers by presenting them with a two-hundred word epistle in rhymed prose and a ten-verse poem in which every word contained the letter *resh,* and another epistle and poem completely devoid of that letter.[82]

Such linguistic feats aside, however, the Hebrew poets were conscious of using a considerable number of poetic forms of expression which, between them, accounted for the main difference between the poetic and the prose style. Moses ibn Ezra submitted these forms to careful scrutiny, trying to defend them against strong and vocal conservative opposition. Regrettably we have no record of these opposing views, which were evidently silenced by the ultimate popular acceptance of the regnant forms of Spanish Hebrew poetry.

Curiously, in his defense, Ibn Ezra did not hesitate to invoke the testimony of Hebrew Scripture, as well as of the Qur'an and Christian authors. In all he found that the Hebrew poets employed twenty such technical "adornments," in addition to their penchant for parables and riddles. Moses supplemented his theoretical analysis of each of these expedients by illustrative material, quoting with particular frequency poems by such recognized masters as Ibn Gabirol and Samuel ibn Nagrela. For example, the use of metaphors is illustrated not only by quotations from the Bible, but also by Ibn Gabirol's verse describing, "The night clad in an armor of darkness / Which the thunder pierces with the spear of lightning"—similes clearly borrowed from implements of war. Ibn Ezra expressed the hope that

> after the proof I have adduced from our holy Scriptures and the Qur'an I need not fear the strong opposition to the use of metaphors voiced by sages and jurists of our time. Particularly so since I have noticed that the best among the jurists and the greatest thinkers, such as R. Saadiah, R. Hai and others among the thinkers, have solved many problems in the interpretation of difficult prophecies by explaining them as metaphors. In fact, you find the same thing in Christian commentaries. Truly, all those who object to that usage today examine with attentive ears and sharp eyes the small human affairs, but they are struck with blindness when it comes to major concerns.

Of course, not all forms of poetic expression, even license, found vocal objectors. For instance, punning and parallelism, listed by Ibn Ezra as the fourth and sixth poetic "adornments," had been hallowed by so long and universal a usage that they elicited no further debate.[83]

A characteristic technical device, rapidly spreading in Spain in the days of Ibn Ezra, is passed over by him in silence, probably because of its relatively recent origin. Spanish Muslims and Christians, as well as Jews, found great delight in the so-called *muwashshaḥ* poems, despite their very complicated structure. Far simpler were the poems in which each strophe, sometimes each verse, began with the same word on which the preceding verse had ended. Such "chain verses" *(shire ezor,* as they were aptly named by Brody) were not altogether unprecedented in Hebrew poetry. While they cannot yet be fully documented from early *piyyuṭim,* they reflect a general human proclivity toward a word just used. Their preliminaries in the Bible, which seem to have influenced the fifth-century Syriac poet Narses, their occurrence in a few traditional prayers from ancient times, and the aforementioned rudimentary use of them by Ashkenazic liturgists evidently uninfluenced by Spanish prototypes, all make their early antecedents among the Palestinian *payyeṭanim* extremely likely. On the other hand, the biblical origin of the Hebrew strophe seems never to have been forgotten. Although documented in Hebrew letters only at a much later age, the term *bayyit* (house) must have early come to connote the strophic structure of biblical poetry. Borrowed by Byzantine authors, this term (in Greek: *oikos*) came into widespread use, and is still employed in many European languages in the equivalent form of *stanza.*[84]

Debates like these induced Ibn Ezra to compose his treatise on the Hebrew *ars poetica,* the first comprehensive work of its kind. Moses was in a direct line of descent from Aristotle (in his *Poetics*) and a large number of Arab writers, beginning with Ibn al-Mu'tazz in the ninth century. The later Hebrew authors of similar treatises were prompted more by practical considerations and the desire to place in the hands of would-be poets some useful hints. This had, in fact, also been the main reason for Saadiah's *Egron,* both in its early and its later formulations. Moses, however, responded to the more theoretical curiosity of students interested in the nature and historical antecedents of medieval Hebrew versification.

Whether the eight questions addressed to Ibn Ezra by a friend were authentic or a mere literary device, they undoubtedly agitated the minds of many contemporaries. "You fail to understand," the poet replied, "why poetry is natural among the Arabs and artificial among the other nations. You want to know whether the Israelitic people in the days of its monarchy composed poetry in rhyme and rhythm, and when the Jews of the dispersion began to write poems? Why have the Jews of the Spanish dispersion been more successful in writing poetry than their coreligionists in other lands?" The inquirer allegedly also wanted to know the meaning of some poets' assertions that they had composed verses in their dreams, and whether the drinking of wine was conducive to poetic inspiration. Of course, he also wished some guidance as to how best to compose Hebrew poems along the lines of Arabic poetry. Ibn Ezra addressed himself to all these questions in seven chapters, the basic discussion of the Hebrew poetic arts being relegated to the concluding and lengthy eighth section. His fifth chapter has been of particular interest to modern scholars because it contains a brief historic sketch of the author's Spanish Jewish predecessors. This chapter has frequently been cited in our earlier treatment. Of considerable interest also are Ibn Ezra's quotations from medieval poems, including his own, some of which are no longer extant.[85]

More limited in scope and less detached was his friend Halevi's brief treatise on Hebrew meters. Although Ibn Ezra, too, doubtless included a discussion of meters in a section of his book since lost, and the seventeenth-century copyist of Halevi's booklet (of which only eighty-three lines have come down to us) specifically attributes it to Moses ibn Ezra, Halevi's authorship is fairly well established. The views expressed here, apparently during the author's residence in Egypt toward the end of his life, bear striking resemblance to some ideas propagated earlier in his philosophic work. The tenor of the whole essay is to show which rhythmic forms (eleven in all) are aesthetically most acceptable to Hebrew poets, and at the same time to denounce too close an emulation of Arabic patterns because of some basic differences between the two languages. "It is an ugly thing," he declared, "to measure metrically the Hebrew language which was created to unite [vowels], but is made [through adherence to Arabic meters] to separate them. Thus is repeated that which is written, they 'mingled themselves with the nations, and learned their works' [Ps. 106:35]." Everyone agreed, moreover, that adherence to quantitative rhythms often imposed disregard of the accepted ultimate or penultimate word accents and, hence, conflicted with the tonal qualities of Hebrew. Nevertheless Halevi himself, at least during his earlier rich poetic creativity, had never followed such negativistic counsels. Much of the beauty of his poems came from the employment of the manifold Arabic meters, and not only of those eleven forms recommended by him for aesthetic reasons.[86]

Although likewise writing in his old age, in fact adducing his lonesome life in a strange environment "at the end of my days" as one of the reasons for the composition of his book, Moses ibn Ezra probably never learned of his younger friend's change of mind. His views in any case reveal no deviation from his own and his Spanish confreres' unquestioning admiration for the Arabic theory and practice of poetry. Not that Ibn Ezra was innately a rebel against Jewish tradition. In fact, whenever he touched on a problem of theological concern, he made sure that the reader should not suspect him of any radical deviation. For example, when he discussed poetic exaggeration as one of the legitimate "adornments" of versification, he added,

> However, the wonderful predictions included in Scripture with reference to our expected [messianic] reign, may God hasten its coming, were not written in the way of a parable or riddle. All these expected miracles are exactly true and are to be understood literally, for we may learn from the past for the future. But it is not my purpose in this work to explain these matters. He who reads these statements in order to examine them in the light of natural science, or harbors doubts in his heart, is not a believer in the religion of Jews.

For further information Ibn Ezra referred the reader to a collection of all biblical passages relating to miracles performed in behalf of individuals or for the people at large, as well as to the messianic age, which had been prepared not long before by (Abu) Zakariya (Yehudah) ibn Bal'am.[87]

Moreover, the aim of Ibn Ezra's entire work was to show, at the hand of scriptural quotations, that most tenets and methods of Arabic poetry may be detected, at least in rudimentary form, in the Bible itself. The use of biblical and, to a far lesser extent, talmudic phrases was indeed common among all Hebrew poets of the time. Here again Arab influence was decisive, particularly in rhymed prose, for instance in Menaḥem ben Saruq's famous epistle to Ḥisdai ibn Shapruṭ, where citations were unhampered by the exigencies of meter. The more novel a turn was given to a phrase, the more learning and erudition was required on the part of the reader or listener to comprehend the meaning of a biblical allusion, the higher rose the popular esteem for the author. Moses ibn Ezra's poems abound with such biblical ingredients, more than those of Samuel or Ibn Gabirol. But he was overshadowed, in turn, by Abraham ibn Ezra, Al-Ḥarizi, and Todros Abulafia. Certainly only scriptural experts, endowed with considerable ingenuity, could possibly derive any meaning from such a poem as Abraham's *Zekhor-na* (Please Remember), which cited all sorts of biblical names to indicate hidden situations. Not incorrectly, such constant admixture of biblical phrases came to be known as the Musiv style (in Hebrew: *shibbuṣ*), because it resembled a mosaic pattern of old and new word pictures. This style remained a much admired attribute of Hebrew poets throughout the ages, until the excessive addiction to such ready-made borrowings by the writers of the Enlightenment provoked a sharp reaction.[88]

Ashkenazic communities produced no counterpart to Ibn Ezra's and Halevi's analytical discussions. Even Italy brought forth some practical handbooks for aspiring poets, only at a much later date. At best, one could mention in this context the thirteenth-century *Sefer Qerobah,* entirely dedicated to the discussion of sacred poetry. Its author, unfortunately unknown to us, not only assembled a number of earlier liturgical texts, but also submitted them to fairly close scrutiny. As expected, this northern author was less concerned with the methodological, than with the legal aspects of the *qerobot*. Nonetheless, methodology, too, was paid some attention in comments scattered throughout the book.[89]

MUSICAL TRENDS AND THEORIES

Rhythmic poems were often combined with special tunes to which they were supposed to be sung. The nexus between rhythm and music was so obvious that in Halevi's discussion on the preeminence of the Hebrew language, the Khazar king raised the objection as to why, then, "other languages [namely, Arabic] surpass it in songs metrically constructed and arranged for tunes." Halevi's Jewish spokesman replied, "It is obvious that a tune is independent of the meter, or of the lesser or greater number of syllables." Halevi spoke here from rich experience. Musical tunes often had indeed a completely independent existence and, Abraham ibn Ezra's advice to the contrary, were readily borrowed for use in poems of different metrical structure. Such borrowings were quite universal. It appears that the ancient psalmists and, following them, the early medieval Syriac poets or their copyists indicated the tune to which they wished a particular poem to be sung by referring in the heading to a popular song previously recited to that tune. This method soon penetrated Arabic and Hebrew letters as well. Abraham ibn Ezra had this practice in mind when he thus explained the puzzling inscriptions in the book of Psalms. Headings beginning with the Arabic term *laḥn* (tune or melody), followed by the opening words of an Arabic or Hebrew poem, abound in medieval manuscripts. Understandably, those written in Byzantium or the West often substituted for it the Greek or Latin designation of *mousikê* or *musica.*[90]

Such borrowings were particularly widespread among Jews, since their proclivity to compose new and original tunes for other than liturgical poems was seriously hampered by a persistent tradition opposed to secular songs altogether. Almost all the influential molders of Jewish public opinion reiterated the old talmudic objections to rejoicing with wine and song on any but the few religiously hallowed festivities. True, such orthodox spokesmen of Christian and Muslim opinion as Pope Gregory the Great and Al-Ghazzali shared their aversion to secular singing, and the ninth-century author Ad-Dunya al-Qurashi wrote a special treatise, *K. Dhamm al-malāhī* (Disparagement of Musical Instruments), for he believed that "all dissipation begins with music and ends with drunkenness." Yet among Jews this attitude, as we recall, was far more universal. Even such an enlightened and, in all scientific realms, readily secularizing poet as Abraham ibn Ezra drew the following distinction:

> Arabs like singing of love and desires,
> Christians of battlefields and vengeful fires,
> Greeks of wisdom's fruits and speculation,

Hindus of proverbs and divination.
But Israel chants to the Lord of Hosts.[91]

Life, of course, did not allow itself to be entirely regimented under such artificial categories, and there must have existed hosts of young Jews who indulged in gay sociability punctuated by merry songs. The populace, too, then as in later generations, must have created all sorts of folksongs, or at least adapted some tunes and ideas current among its non-Jewish neighbors. Although we have no record of such conscious transformations before the sixteenth century, when the distinguished mystical poet Israel Najara professedly wrote religious poems to many Arabic, Turkish, Greek, and Spanish folksongs current among his coreligionists, such sanctification of profane tunes seems to have proceeded apace in the Middle Ages as well. However, neither the leaders nor the masses consciously encouraged musical creativity. Occasional rebels, who insisted on improvising tunes to their own poems with the accompaniment of such musical instruments as the Arabic *al-'ud* (the English "lute" is its linguistic offshoot), left no permanent imprint on the people. Even late in the thirteenth century, the Provençal Jewish troubadour Isaac Gorni, though feeling confident that his songs had comforted many aggrieved hearts, had every reason bitterly to complain of the ridicule and disdain heaped upon musicians. In fact, as Schirmann pointed out, before long the very name of Gorni was forgotten in Jewish literature, while a commonplace and poetically cumbersome ethical treatise by his contemporary, Yedaiah ha-Penini of Béziers, became one of the "best-sellers" among medieval and early modern Jews, largely because its pious sentiments so greatly appealed to the average reader.[92]

Unfortunately, our information on medieval Hebrew music is extremely limited. Even the few writers concerned with musical theory were discussing poetic rhythm and meter rather than their musical equivalents long after the Arab writers had begun to evince genuine interest in the musical forms as such. Since, moreover, little is known about views held by Jewish leaders before Saadiah—even those expressed by Isaac Israeli and David al-Muqammiṣ earlier in the tenth century are hardly known—we cannot tell whether the Jews were in any way affected by the great debate between the Arab "Classicists" and "Romantics" of the ninth century. All our Jewish sources date from the time when in the Arab environment the innovations of the romantic schools had proved victorious. By that time the influx of Persian and other foreign tunes, and the freedom of the individual composer to deviate from the accepted musical patterns of ancient Arabia, had been fully recognized. It appears, however, that Jewish conservatism was not limited to the view that "melodic modes were of secondary importance to the rhythmic modes"—an attitude partly abandoned by the Arabs late in the tenth century—but extended also to the musical tunes themselves.[93]

Undoubtedly this neglect may be partly explained by the growing nationalist aversion to imitation of foreign melodies. Alfasi's rigid prohibition of applying Arabic tunes to prayers was frequently repeated by later jurists, and, in European countries, it was extended to all music of the Gentiles. German pietists specifically prohibited the singing of Gentile lullabies to Jewish children, as well as the teaching of Jewish tunes to Gentile priests, lest they adapt these melodies to Church use. Whatever interrelations had existed between the music of the ancient Church and that of the Temple in Jerusalem or the ancient synagogue was now completely forgotten, and the emphasis was laid exclusively on the unseemliness of Jewish borrowings from the worship of the hostile religion. Of course, prohibitions of this type often proved futile in the face of the overwhelming power of the environment, especially in the case of anything so subtle and self-insinuating as a popular tune. This is even more true in the case of folksongs, to which no serious objection of "idolatry" could be raised. Here, however, puritans often had a field day in denouncing the "immorality" of the lyrics originally associated with those melodies. Female singers, already repudiated by Sirach and the talmudic sages, offered a particular target, inasmuch as "almost every Arab of substance in those days had his singing-girl, who appears to have been as much in evidence in the household as the pianoforte is with us today." Some rabbis rejected the very idea of even innocuous entertainment as unbecoming to a suffering people in exile. Among the most outspoken objectors was Maimonides:

It is known that music in general and rhythmic music in particular [the great jurist wrote in reply to inquirers evidently disturbed by the widespread singing of Arabic *muwashshaḥat*] is forbidden even

> if it is not joined with words, for the Rabbis say: "The ear listening to song shall be extirpated" [Soṭah 48a]. The Talmud teaches expressly [Giṭṭin 7a] that there is no difference between hearing vocal or instrumental music, and music in general. Such music is forbidden, except when it belongs to prayer which moves the soul either to joy or to sorrow. . . . The listening to any licentious utterance as such is forbidden, even if it is only spoken. If it is accompanied by instrumental music, it would involve three prohibited acts: (1) The listening to licentious and pornographic speech, (2) listening to vocal music, and (3) listening to musical instruments. If it happens in a place where they drink wine there is a fourth prohibition. . . . If the singer is a woman there is a fifth prohibition, . . . the more so if she sings at a banquet.

True, few jurists echoed this radical form of outlawry, and this particular Maimonidean responsum seems rarely to have been copied in the Middle Ages; it remained unpublished until 1873. Nevertheless, it was referred to in Jacob ben Asher's authoritative code, and the underlying antagonism, especially to the borrowings from the popular Arabic erotic songs, was shared by many pious Jews.[94]

Yet music was of much too fundamental and universal human interest to be thus curtly dismissed on moralistic grounds. Maimonides himself and other thoughtful leaders of Jewry under Islam could the less afford to overlook the basic problems of music and its effects on both individuals and society, as great Arab thinkers, including Al-Kindi, Farabi, and the mysic Brethren of Purity had already concerned themselves deeply with musical theory and had utilized to good advantage some of the musicological views of the most admired Greek sages. Nor could Maimonides himself, as we shall see, while acting as a physician, completely disregard the therapeutic value of music.

It is doubly to be regretted, therefore, that we know almost nothing about the musical practitioners among the Jews under Islam. It seems that, for example, Abu'l Fadhl Ḥisdai in Saragossa was both a distinguished musicologist and an able musician, but he may have developed these skills mainly after his apostasy to Islam. A Cordovan Jew, Isaac ibn Sim'an, was said to have composed, like his friend Ibn Bajja, songs in all styles. So preoccupied were the leading Jewish minds with the legalistic aspects of the permissibility of music that they paid no attention to its history.

This conspiracy of silence is the more remarkable as the Arabs had long evinced great interest in the biographies of their own musicians. The famous *Kitab al-Aghani* (Book of Songs) by Al-Isfahani supplied much information on the history of music to the tenth century, while Isfahani's contemporary, Mas'udi, testified to having had at his disposal ample historical and biographical literature pertaining to the history of music and musicians among both the Arabs and the other nations.[95]

Largely for the same reasons the medieval Jewish thinkers, if writing at all on the subject of music, paid least attention to its aesthetic aspects. They all realized, of course, that in order to be accepted by the populace any music had to be pleasing to the ear. Following some Hellenistic and Arab theorists, some of them even looked for connections between the impact of sound on the sense of hearing and those of color on vision, and of odors on the sense of smell. Occasionally they even stressed these physiological and materialistic aspects above all others. Many readers of Al-Ḥarizi's independent rendition of Ḥunayn ibn Isḥaq's philosophic aphorisms were also inclined to agree with the latter's popular saying that music was the best profession, for in it action equaled speech, "as in the case of a lute player, whose melody corresponds to his motions." However, not until the era of the Italian and Spanish Renaissance, with its great emphasis on beauty, did aesthetic considerations play any role in the pertinent Jewish discussions of music by Joseph Albo, Samuel Archevolte, and others.[96]

Almost all Jewish writers of both the earlier and later periods were concerned with the psychological effects of music. Being so deeply interested in concentration on prayer, they realized with Maimonides that music helped prayer to move the soul to either joy or sorrow. The sage of Fusṭaṭ also believed that the power of desire, usually stimulated by music, ought to be restrained, although he admitted that, in the case of exceptional individuals, music might facilitate comprehension of intelligible things and enhance submission to things divine. The connection between music and religious ecstasy had long found champions among the Arab thinkers, particularly Al-Ghazzali, with whose views Maimonides may have been familiar. Even outside the world of Islam the leading German-Jewish pietist advised his readers, "If you cannot add anything [to the prescribed prayers] search for some melody, so that you may pray in a melody which is agreeable and sweet to you. Then you will pray with concentration, and your heart will feel what your lips recite in a prayer of petition. For song makes the heart receptive . . . and gladdens the heart" (*Sefer Ḥasidim,* No. 11).

Saadiah had gone further. He had tried to analyze the correlation between the eight kinds of melody which he enumerated and the singers' physiological and psychological reactions. He believed that the first two moved the humor of blood, and hence stimulated the urge toward domination over others; the third, by stimulating the yellow bile, enhanced courage and audacity; the fourth, affected the phlegm, and was thus conducive to self-abasement and cowardice; the remaining four moved the black bile, and thus produced the contradictory dispositions of gladness and sorrow at diverse times. The gaon shared the view prevalent in certain Arab circles that music might even affect government. He concluded his discussion by saying:

> Kings therefore have the custom of seeking, by means of a suitable intermingling of modes [melodies], to produce within themselves a harmonious balance; so that these melodies may stimulate such dispositions as kings find helpful, causing them to be neither too merciful nor too cruel, neither too aggressive nor too timid, neither too much nor too little given to pleasure.[97]

Music's curative value in cases of mental derangement loomed large in all medieval discussions. Even the fervid opponent of secular music, Maimonides, admitted in another context that a sufferer "from melancholia may rid himself of it by listening to songs and all kinds of instrumental music, by strolling through beautiful gardens and splendid buildings, by associating with beautiful forms [women] and other things that enliven the mind and dissipate gloomy moods." Great healer that he was, he doubtless did not refrain from applying music, both vocal and instrumental, to patients in need of such remedy. His pupil Joseph ibn 'Aqnin embodied these lessons in his system of mental hygiene. In his *Ṭubb an-nufus,* a treatise entirely devoted to the "therapy of souls," he developed a regular educational program in which he encouraged students to devote one each of ten years to the mastery of a significant discipline. In this curriculum he assigned the advanced eighth year to the study of music. Somewhat later, Shem Tob ben Joseph ibn Falaquera in his encyclopedic *Sefer ha-Mebaqqesh* (Book of the Seeker), written in 1264, described the effects of liturgical music which moved worshipers to tears and repentance, other melodies which inspired courage during battle, and still others "invented to be sung in hospitals to bring the sick relief from suffering." In all these views the Jewish physicians merely echoed a medical opinion long regnant among Greeks and Arabs. Ibn 'Aqnin and Falaquera were much indebted particularly to Farabi. Avicenna's classical *Canon* had likewise devoted considerable space to the therapeutic aspects of music, and in both its Arabic original and its later Hebrew translation it greatly influenced Jewish scholarly opinion.[98]

From another physiological aspect of music, namely the connection between the rhythmical musical beat and the human pulse beat, was but a step to a consideration of the basic mathematical aspects of acoustics and, more generally, of the nexus between mathematics and music, which had already been stressed by the ancient Pythagoreans. Great believers in authority, the medieval scholars, Syriac, Arab, and Jewish, readily quoted whatever pertinent scraps of information had reached them from the ancient world and expatiated on the "science" of music almost as if it were but a branch of mathematics. In his *Sefer ha-Mispar* (Book of Numbers) Abraham ibn Ezra bluntly placed musicology as a third science and declared, "It is a very distinguished science, for its measures are composed of both arithmetical and geometrical measures." The great mathematician Abraham bar Ḥiyya (Savasorda) felt induced to translate into Hebrew the brief musicological analysis in Saadiah's philosophic work, evidently because he considered it a necessary part of mathematical knowledge. He also stated his own views on music, apparently at some length, in his *Yesode ha-tebunah* (Principles of Understanding), but regrettably, this section is no longer extant.[99]

These theoretical discussions on music often bore the imprint of abstract speculation, almost wholly divorced from musical realities. If the composers had listened to the musicologists they might even then have developed some abstract music along our own ultra-modern lines. However, many theorists themselves, such as Ibn 'Aqnin or Ibn Falaquera, once again following Farabi's example, drew a sharp line of demarcation between natural and artificial music. According to Ibn Falaquera, the science of theoretical music was concerned "with music in general, abstracted from any instrument or material object." On the other hand, he himself displayed great interest in the practical aspects of music and tried to explain, for example, the special merits of the lute by repeating the then standardized correlation between its four strings and the four "humors" of the human body.[100]

In all these matters Jews largely followed the lead of Arab writers. Their own tradition made them listen with particular attention, however, to theories connecting music with the celestial world. The doctrine of the harmony of the spheres and of the ensuing correspondence between earthly music and celestial melodies had long been developed in ancient Greek philosophy. Despite vehement objections by Farabi and Maimonides, some such correspondence was simply taken for granted by most Jewish authors. It offered too attractive a rationale for the old Jewish concept of the heavenly hosts singing the Lord's praises in unison with Israel to be discarded on mere philosophic grounds. Even the rationalistic Moses ibn Ezra could not deny himself the spiritual elevation of contemplating this harmony between the heavenly and the earthly worshipers. Among his relatively few liturgical poems he included one devoted to the traditional theme of the *qedushah:*

Miraculous *ofanim* [wheels of the Chariot], angels of celestial height,
Stars among heavenly hosts, inquire "Where does God reside?"
Of course, "the heavens are His throne, the earth lies at His feet."
All praise His saintly name wher'er pious congregants meet.

Far more outspoken was the astrologically minded Abraham ibn Ezra. Interpreting the psalmist's description of the Lord's might "above the voices of many waters" (93:4) as clearly indicating "that the spheres have voices," he added bitingly, "These voices are not heard by the deaf, any more than the awesome works of the Lord are seen by the blind." Feeling attuned to this heavenly music, this poet-polyhistor devoted many of his lyrics to astral influences upon the destinies of men.[101]

FREEDOM UNDER AUTHORITY

In poetry, poetic prose, and the accompanying music the Jewish people found a release for its pent-up energies. Instead of appealing to a limited circle of talmudic scholars and, at best, approaching the masses only through the instrumentality of orally delivered homilies, the new generations of writers found a fairly extended group of educated laymen eager to listen to them on a variety of subjects. The ever growing intelligentsia now not only pursued with deep interest the new scientific discoveries, but also wrestled vicariously with the many problems of individual concern so beautifully formulated by contemporary poets. With the broadening of the frontiers of knowledge came also the awakened curiosity about happenings in distant lands and the pearls of wisdom formulated by sages of different ages and faiths. Philological curiosity, combined with widespread familiarity with the more rigid requirements of the new poetic arts, made every new poem by a distinguished author an important literary event. It was considered worthy of extended discussions, showered with vigorous praise or blame, and even provided with ample pecuniary rewards. The quest of perpetuating the memory of one's own achievements through some epic description in poetic form stimulated patronage on the part of the rich and competition among the poets.

All this may have been a mere imitation of ways of life gradually evolving in the new and rich civilization of the Renaissance of Islam. Yet in many respects, rather than representing the assimilation of foreign ways, the new poetry was a deep expression of the revival of national feeling among medieval Jews. At least in their early stages both the Syriac and the Hebrew literatures under Islam affirmatively responded to the challenge of the marvelous expansion of Arab letters. Just as in their linguistic studies Jewish leaders tried to show that Hebrew was no less a pliable language than Arabic, so their poets endeavored to demonstrate to the world that Hebrew poetry could be written with the same ease and mastery of technical detail as the most celebrated works of Arab authors. Occasionally, to be sure, such consistent emulation of Arab methods evoked sharp protests. No less a master of the new techniques than Halevi raised his voice against the unnatural shackles which the Arab meter had imposed upon the differently constructed Hebrew idiom. Nevertheless, the newly acquired discipline in self-expression and the enforced search for the hidden resources of the Hebraic heritage greatly stimulated the spirit of intellectual adventure so characteristic of the Golden Age.

Beyond serving as a nationalistic answer to an external challenge, the new poetry awakened in the souls of the people forces long dormant. However profound was the new sense of style and poetic beauty—only generations endowed with a fine aesthetic taste could have brought forth such immortal works of art—there was little conscious aestheticism in these new quests. We have noticed that even in the theoretical discussion on music there was very little concern for its purely aesthetic functions. In poetry, too, beauty was taken for granted rather than explored. The preoccupation of both poets and critics was mainly concentrated on substantive issues.

Here, too, those of general human or national concern evoked far more frequent and more searching comments than those of a personal nature. Not only in Italy, France, or Germany, but also in Spain, despite its considerable interests in the psychological problems of the individual, there was little room, for example, for simple love poetry. Although following the fashion of the age one might have expected a great many erotic, even bawdy, poems in Hebrew letters, Al-Ḥarizi's (and later Immanuel of Rome's) "naughty" verses, and the popular romances, were rather exceptions confirming the general studied chastity of Hebrew poetry. Some of the greatest poets, such as Samuel ibn Nagrela and Ibn Gabirol, as we recall, wrote very few love poems. Even the most prolific author in this field, Halevi, seems later to have repudiated his preoccupation with love as a youthful indiscretion. Before long even love was spiritualized into that mystic union between the worshiper (or rather the whole Jewish people) and the Creator which had already underlain the rabbinic reinterpretation of the Song of Songs. True, such exclusive preoccupation with religious and national issues must have struck outside observers as a sign of narrowness and spiritual bondage. But Halevi voiced the opinion dominant among his fellow poets when he wrote:

Servants of time are slaves of slaves,
But the Lord's servant is truly free.
Each man prays for his part in life,
But my part, O Master, in Thee I see.[102]

NOTES

ABBREVIATIONS

AJSL	American Journal of Semitic Languages and Literature
'A.Z.	'Abodah Zarah (talmudic tractate)
b.	Babylonian Talmud
BJRL	Bulletin of the John Rylands Library, Manchester
B.Q.	Baba Qamma
BZ	Byzantinische Zeitschrift
CSEL	Corpus Scriptorum ecclesiasticorum latinorum
EI	Encyclopaedia of Islam
Essays Hertz	Essays in honour of J. H. Hertz. London, 1942
Festschrift Harkavy	Festschrift zu Ehren des Dr. A. Harkavy. St. Petersburg, 1908.
Festschrift Steinschneider	Festschrift zum achtzigsten Geburtstag Moritz Steinschneider's. Leipzig, 1896.
Freidus Mem. Vol.	Studies in Jewish Bibliography . . . in Memory of Abraham Solomon Freidus. New York, 1929.
GK	Ginze Kedem
Goldziher Mem. Vol.	Ignace Goldziher Memorial Volume. Vol. 1. Budapest, 1946.
Gulak-Klein Mem. Vol.	Sefer Zikkaron (Studies in Memory of Asher Gulak and Samuel Klein). Jerusalem, 1942.
Hildesheimer Jub. Vol.	Jubelschrift zum siebzigsten Geburtstag Israel Hildesheimers. Berlin, 1890.
HTR	Harvard Theological Review
HUCA	Hebrew Union College Annual
j.	Palestinian Talmud
JA	Journal asiatique
JBL	Journal of Biblical Literature and Exegesis
JJLG	Jahrbuch für jüdische Geschichte und Literatur
JJS	Journal of Jewish Studies
JNES	Journal of Near Eastern Studies (continuation of *AJSL*)
JQR	Jewish Quarterly Review (new series, unless otherwise stated)
JRAS	Journal of the Royal Asiatic Society
JSS	Jewish Social Studies
Kaplan Jub. Vol.	Mordecai M. Kaplan Jubilee Volume. 2 vols. New York, 1953. A volume each of English and Hebrew essays.

Kohut Mem. Vol.	Jewish Studies in Memory of George A. Kohut. New York, 1935.
Krauss Jub. Vol.	Sefer ha-Yobel la-Professor Shemuel (Samuel) Krauss. Jerusalem, 1937.
KS	Kirjath Sepher. Quarterly Bibliographical Review
Löw Mem. Vol.	Semitic Studies in Memory of Immanual Löw. Budapest, 1947.
M.	Mishnah
MGWJ	Monatsschrift für Geschichte und Wissenschaft des Judentums
MJC	Mediaeval Jewish Chronicles, ed. by A. Neubauer
M.T.	Moses ben Maimon's Mishneh Torah (Code)
M.Q.	Mo'ed Qaṭan
O.Ḥ.	Oraḥ Ḥayyim (sections of Jacob ben Asher's *Ṭurim* and Joseph Karo's *Shulḥan Arukh*)
PAAJR	Proceedings of the American Academy for Jewish Research
PG	Patrologiae cursus completus, series Graeca
PL	Patrologiae cursus completus, series Latina
Poznanski Mem. Vol.	Livre d'hommage à la mémoire du Samuel Poznanski. Warsaw, 1927.
r.	Midrash Rabbah (Gen. r. = Bereshit rabbah; Lam. r. = Ekhah rabbati, etc.)
Rashi Anniv. Vol.	American Academy for Jewish Research, Texts and Studies, Vol. I. Rashi Anniversary Volume, New York, 1941.
REJ	Revue des études juives
Resp.	Responsa (*Teshubot* or *She'elot u-teshubot*)
RH	Revue historique
Saadia Anniv. Vol.	American Academy for Jewish Research, Texts and Studies, Vol. II. Saadia Anniversary Volume. New York, 1943.
SB	Sitzungsberichte der Akademie der Wissenschaften (identified by city: e.g., *SB* Berlin, Heidelberg, Vienna)
Schocken Jub. Vol.	'Ale 'Ayyin. In Honor of Salomon Salman Schocken. Jerusalem, 1948–52.
SRIHP	Studies of the Research Institute for Medieval Hebrew Poetry
T.	Tosefta. Ed. by M. S. Zuckermandel
YB	Yivo Bleter
ZAW	Zeitschrift für die alttestamentliche Wissenschaft und die Kunde des nachbiblischen Judentums
ZDMG	Zeitschrift der deutschen morgenländischen Gesellschaft
ZHB	Zeitschrift für hebräische Bibliographie
Zlotnik Jub. Vol.	Minḥah li-Yehudah. Jubilee Volume in Honor of Judah Leb Zlotnik. Jerusalem, 1950.

NOTES

CHAPTER XXX: LINGUISTIC RENASCENCE

1. H. Hirschfeld, "An Unknown Grammatical Work by Abul-Faraj Harun," *JQR,* XIII, 3. This and other passages underscore the interrelation between scriptural exegesis and philology which in essence existed also among the Muslim students of language. Hirschfeld overstates the difference, therefore, in saying that "while for Arab grammarians the minute elaboration of the finesses of their language became an end in itself, Jews brought their linguistic endeavours into the service of the study of the Holy Writ." *Literary History of Hebrew Grammarians and Lexicographers,* p. 7.

2. Ibn Janaḥ's *K. at-Taswiya* (Book of Redress; a grammatical treatise) in his *Opuscules et traités,* ed. by J. and H. Derenbourg, pp. 344 ff.; Baihaqi cited in Mez, *Renaissance of Islam,* p. 239; Hadassi's *Eshkol ha-kofer,* fols. 21cd, 60c ff. The degree of philological sophistication among Jews may be gauged from such complicated intellectual exercises as "Saadya's Piyyut on the Alphabet," reedited on the basis of 19 MSS and early prints by S. Stein in Rosenthal's *Saadya Studies,* pp. 206–26. In this poem the gaon arranged each of the thirty quatrains to begin with a letter of the alphabet. "The words that follow in the first two hemistichs begin with letters whose numerical value corresponds exactly to the number of times the letter in question is to be found in the *Miḳra* [Bible; these range from 1,975 occurrences of the letter *pe* to 76,922 of the letter *vav*]. The other two hemistichs contain each a word from a Biblical verse, in which the number thus indicated happens to occur" *(ibid.,* p. 210). This prodigious stunt naturally imposed severe shackles on the author and challenged the ingenuity of readers. Under the circumstances it is rather surprising that it makes enough sense to enable Stein to present an English translation. On the authenticity of this poem and the gaon's own commentary thereon, see *infra,* Chap. XXXV, n. 13. Saadiah's pupil Dunash ben Labraṭ composed at least ten linguistic riddles included in his *Shirim* (Poems), ed. by N. Allony, pp. 94 ff., 105 ff., 170 ff., 182 f., 190. See also Allony's analysis of "Ten Dunash ben Labraṭ's Riddles," *JQR,* XXXV, 141–46. Much more popular, in fact the source of amusement for countless students, were "The Linguistic Riddles of Abraham ibn Ezra," analyzed in a Hebrew essay by N. H. Torczyner and reprinted in his *Ha-Lashon ve-ha-sefer,* III, 354–65. See also, more generally, B. Klar's suggestive lecture on "The Beginnings of Hebrew Grammar" (Hebrew), reprinted in his *Meḥqarim ve-'iyyunim,* pp. 1–7 (incomplete because of the author's death in ambush). Klar overstated here, however, the difference between the Greek and Indian approaches and, even more, the impact of the transition to the use of codices, instead of rolls, on the development of Masorah. See *supra,* Vol. II, p. 390 n. 35.

3. A. Guillaume's preface to T. Arnold and his edition of *The Legacy of Islam,* p. viii; Mez, *Renaissance,* p. 237. The difference between the official Arabic lan-

guage of the Qur'an and the popular dialects has been closely analyzed ever since 1906, when K. Vollers published his *Volkssprache und Schriftsprache im alten Arabien,* but its impact on the Hebrew philology of the period would merit fuller consideration. See *infra,* nn. 19, 37; and, from another angle, E. Shouby, "The Influence of Arabic Language on the Psychology of the Arabs," *Middle East Journal,* V, 284–302. Its parallel, though in many ways dissimilar, influence on the thinking of Arabic-speaking Jews likewise deserves exploration.

4. Ibn Quraish's *Risala,* Introduction, ed. by Bargès and Goldberg, p. 1 (Hebrew trans. by M. Katz, p. 1; on his date, see *infra,* n. 17); Nissi ben Nuḥ's "Commentary on the Ten Commandments," excerpted in Pinsker's *Lickute kadmoniot,* I, 38. That Nissi was not animated by linguistic xenophobia per se is evident from his assertion, in that very context, that he had consulted for his interpretation Aramaic, Greek, and Latin, as well as Hebrew sources. On the ancient opposition to the vernacular Aramaic, see *supra,* Vol. II, p. 146. The later geonim, on the other hand, tried to uphold its use, as we have seen *supra,* Chap. XXIX, n. 28. One may also mention that even today some isolated Jewish communities in northern Iraq have retained a distinct recollection of old Aramaic proverbs. See J. B. Segal, "Neo-Aramaic Proverbs of the Jews of Zakho," *JNES,* XIV, 251–70 (data collected from Zakho emigrés in Israel).

5. Yehudah ibn Tibbon's introduction to his Hebrew translation of Baḥya's *K. al-Hidāya* (Duties of the Heart), entitled *Ḥobot ha-lebabot,* in A. Zifroni's edition, p. 2. Very similar is his subsequent expostulation in the introduction to his translation of Ibn-Janaḥ's *K. al-Luma'* (*Sefer ha-Riqmah*), ed. by Wilensky, p. 4. Here (pp. 5 f.) the translator also explained his quest for exactitude, so that the translation differ from the original "only with respect to language." See also Ibn Chiquitilla's introduction to his Hebrew rendition of Yehudah Ḥayyuj's *Treatises,* ed. and trans. by J. W. Nutt, pp. 1 (Hebrew), 1 f. (English); and Abraham ibn Ezra's expostulation in the introduction to his *Keli Neḥoshet* (Commentary on Ptolemy's Astrolabe). The Hebrew renditions of Maimonides' *Guide* by Samuel ibn Tibbon and Yehudah al-Ḥarizi, respectively, both prepared shortly after the publication of the original, have long been recognized as standard examples of the dichotomy between exact and elegant translation. See also M. D. Goldmann's dissertation, *Zu den Arabismen bei den hebräischen Übersetzern des Maimonides,* summarized in the *Jahrbuch der Dissertationen der Philosophischen Fakultät . . . Berlin,* 1925–26, pp. 9–11.

Incidentally, this perennial dilemma of translators also deeply colored the adjustment of contemporary Latin renditions, despite the long and venerable traditions of the use of that language in philosophic literature. See the examples cited by M. Hubert in his "Quelques aspects du latin philosophique au XIIe et XIIIe siècles," *Revue des études latines,* XXVII, 211–33. If, on the other hand, Elijah Bashyatchi and others were unable to distinguish between Tobiah ben Moses' original work and a translation by him of a work by Joseph Al-Baṣir (see Z. Ankori's discussion in his "Elijah Bashyachi," *Tarbiz,* XXV, 49 ff.), this uncertainty is understandable because of the combination of bias and lack of philological refinement on the part of the distinguished fifteenth-century Karaite codifier. See *supra,* Chap. XXVI, n. 29.

6. D. H. Baneth, "Maimonides' Translations of His Own Writings as Compared with Those of His Translators" (Hebrew), *Tarbiz,* XXIII, 170–91. See also B. Klar's more general analysis of "Methods of Expanding the Hebrew Language in the Middle Ages" (Hebrew), reprinted in his *Meḥqarim ve-'iyyunim,* pp. 31–41. Klar has shown that even the translators made relatively little use of direct loan words from Arabic. In the more than three thousand philosophic, scientific, and medical terms reviewed in J. Klatzkin's *Oṣar ha-munaḥim ha-pilosofiim* (Thesaurus philosophicus linguae hebraicae) only about eighty, or 2.6 percent, were direct loan words. Most of the adjustments were made by the transmutation of meaning of old Hebrew words or the coining of new Hebrew terms in analogy with the Arabic designations used in the original works.

7. See, e.g., Maimonides' brief autograph responsum, ed. by R. Gottheil in my *Essays on Maimonides,* pp. 123 ff.; B. Chapira's "Textes inédites de Maïmonide," *REJ,* XCIX, 6–33 (publishing an autograph fragment of Maimonides' Arabic commentary on his *Code* and the *Epistle to Yemen* and listing a number of earlier publications); Ibn Janaḥ's *K. al-Luma',* Introduction, p. 13; in the Hebrew *Sefer ha-Riqmah,* ed. by Wilensky, p. 18 (or Metzger's French trans., pp. 15 f.); Samau'al ibn Yaḥya's *Ifḥam,* cited by M. Schreiner in *MGWJ,* XLII, 253. It is less astonishing that such works as Maimonides' commentaries on the Mishnah were written in Hebrew script. A comprehensive autograph of that *Commentary* on two sections of the Mishnah (Mo'ed and Nashim) has in recent years been part of the Sassoon collection. See D. S. Sassoon's catalogue, *Ohel Dawid,* I, 92 f.; and his "Notes on Some Rambam Manuscripts," in I. Epstein's collection of essays on *Moses Maimonides,* pp. 217 f. See also S. D. Sassoon's aforementioned photostatic ed. of that MS of Maimonides' *Commentary;* other literature listed *supra,* Chap. XXVII, n. 65; and, more generally, S. M. Stern's careful analysis of "Autograph Manuscripts of the Commentary on the Mishnah by Maimonides" (Hebrew), *Tarbiz,* XXIII, 72–88 (with 7 facsimiles).

8. See I. Friedlaender, "Die arabische Sprache des Maimonides," in Jakob Guttmann *et al., Moses ben Maimon,* I, 428; and, with fuller lexicographic documentation, his *Der Sprachgebrauch des Maimonides;* and S. L. Skoss's analysis of *The Arabic Commentary of 'Ali ben Suleiman the Karaite on the Book of Genesis,* pp. 64 ff. The study of Judeo-Arabic dialects in their historical evolution still is in its infancy. Even the analysis of dialects now spoken in various communities throughout the Muslim world is limited to a few scholarly works relating to certain aspects of speech in Algiers, Yemen, and Baghdad. See, e.g., L. Brunot and E. Malka's *Textes judéo-arabes de Fès,* supplemented by their *Glossaire judéo-arabe de Fès;* and with reference thereto W. Leslau's "Hebrew Elements in the Judeo-Arabic Dialect of Fez," *JQR,* XXXVI, 61–78 (listing other important publications); his "Judeo-Arabic Dialects" (Yiddish), *YB,* XXVI, 58–78; the three illustrations adduced by D. S. Löwinger in his Hebrew essay, "Observations on the Arabic Language of the Jews" in *Ha-Zofeh,* XII, 105–8; and M. Wald's aforementioned remarks on *Die arabischen Glossen in den Schriften der Geonim.* The present-day dialects will be more fully discussed in their modern context. See also *supra,* n. 5; and, on the environmental influences on medieval Hebrew phonetics, *infra,* n. 40.

9. Al-Jaḥiẓ cited in Goldziher's *Muhammedanische Studien,* I, 162; Baḥya's *K. al-Hidaya 'ila fara'iḍ al-qulub* (Duties of the Heart), ed. by A. S. Yahuda, pp. 22 f. (in Hyamson's ed. and trans. of the Hebrew version, I, 22). The mutual impact of Hebrew and Arabic is well illustrated in the studies by M. H. Gottstein, *Taḥbirah u-millonah shel ha-lashon ha-'ibrit* (Mediaeval Hebrew Syntax and Vocabulary as Influenced by Arabic; Hebrew University dissertation, 1951, typescript); and A. Jeffery, *The Foreign Vocabulary of the Qur'an,* as well as some of the other literature listed *supra,* Chap. XVII, n. 15. The Arab philologists were, of course, familiar with the foreign origin of many Arabic terms, although they did not quite draw therefrom the obvious conclusions for the dignified status of these other languages. See, e.g., the illustrations adduced by A. Siddiqi in his *Ibn Duraid and His Treatment of Loan-Words* (reprinted from *Allahabad University Studies,* VI, Arts section, pp. 669–750).

The "Hebrewisms" in the Western Bible translations have often been treated. To the literature previously mentioned, esp. in Chaps. XXIV and XXIX, add such recent monographs as M. Rehm's fresh analysis of "Die Bedeutung hebräischer Wörter bei Hieronymus," *Biblica,* XXXV, 174–97; and K. Borowicz, "The Hebrew Etymology of the Term 'Missa'" (Polish), *Ruch biblijny i liturgiczny,* V, 445–69. It is small wonder that already in the Middle Ages there was a demand for Hebrew dictionaries. See the brief analysis of the Hebrew-Latin dictionaries of the twelfth century in Avranches and Tours by S. Berger in his still very useful study of medieval Christian Hebraists, *Quam notitiam linguae hebraicae habuerint Christiani medii aevi temporibus in Gallia,* p. 17. More remarkably, some scholars detected Hebrew linguistic influences even in such remote regions as India. See, e.g., the hypothesis of the Hebrew origin of a Sanskrit term advanced by V. S. Agrawala in his "Ancient Contacts between India and the Middle East . . . Hebrew Word Traced," *India and Israel,* IV, No. 4, p. 45.

10. See Goldziher, *Muhammedanische Studien,* I, 194 ff., 203 f.; Steinschneider, *Arabische Literatur,* p. 15; Ibn Quraish, *Risala,* pp. 50, 105 (Hebrew trans., pp. 83 f., 195); J. Mann, *Jews in Egypt,* II, 105 (the text of this Cambridge Genizah fragment is evidently garbled); and *supra,* Chap. XXII, n. 27 (on Sallam). Steinschneider (pp. 35 f.) mentions another leading Arab grammarian of Jewish descent, Harun ibn al-Haik al-Dharir. Descended from some Jews of Ḥira, Harun became one of the luminaries of the school of Kufa, greatly admired by Ta'lab and others.

The implications of Jewish bilingualism and trilingualism are yet to be fully explored. The cultivation of Hebrew, especially, alongside the spoken languages of the respective countries, essentially differed from that of two languages spoken at the same time in the same area. Having long ceased to be the daily medium of communication, largely reserved for the use of the intelligentsia in its higher intellectual pursuits but at the same time appealing to the religious instincts of the masses, Hebrew neither served as a target of antagonistic legislation, as did for instance Gaelic in Ireland, nor did it suffer from the inferiority complexes of languages spoken by many oppressed minorities (including Yiddish). Even the oppressors, whether Muslim or Christian, readily admitted the antiquity and, at times, even sanctity of the Jews' "holy tongue." Within the Jewish community the prestige of Hebrew loomed extremely high throughout the pre-Emancipation era. On the other hand, it lacked the strong moorings of a language spoken by a conservative peasantry or a population residing in inaccessible mountain recesses which rarely could be completely dislodged by the "superior" language of any intellectually and politically dominant group. The dramatic decline of Gaelic in nineteenth-century Ireland and its equally dramatic revival in twentieth-century Eire point up certain factors which, despite their substantial variations, may help elucidate some of the aspects of the speedy Arabicization of the Jewish masses and the simultaneous revival of Hebrew among the intelligentsia so soon after the rise of Islam. See the data assembled in W. H. Rees's dissertation on *Le Bilinguisme des pays celtiques*. These parallels as well as dissimilarities might be the subject of a fascinating monograph.

A reexamination is also needed, with the aid of modern techniques, of the extent to which preoccupation with Hebrew studies in any particular period interfered with the purity of speech and the command of the literary language of the environment by Hebrew-trained children and adults. The educational exploration in this area, still rather sparse and scattered, is largely confined to an examination of the bilingualism of Yiddish-speaking and other "foreign-language" groups in schools. See the literature listed in M. N. H. Hoffman's dissertation on *The Measurement of Bilingual Background*. Methodological studies of this kind, cultivated especially in such multilingual areas as Switzerland, can offer substantial aid also for the examination of the Hebrew problem, provided the investigator will carefully assess the modifications created by the unique position of Hebrew as an unspoken, and yet much alive, literary heritage. See also F. Schneersohn, "The Psychology of Bi-Lingualism in Palestine" (Hebrew), *Hahinnuch*, XII, 1–28; and esp. U. Weinreich, *Research Problems in Bilingualism with Special Reference to Switzerland* (Columbia University dissertation, 1952, microfilm), as well as his briefer study of *Languages in Contact, Findings and Problems.*

11. 'Erubin 53b (with reference to M. v.1, Bekhorot vi.6); B.Q. 3b (with reference to Isa. 21:12, Ob. 6), 6b (with reference to M. i.1); Ibn Janaḥ's *K. al-Luma'*, Introduction, ed. by J. Derenbourg, pp. 5 f. (*Sefer ha-Riqmah,* ed. by Wilensky, I, 14 f., or Metzger's French trans., pp. 5 ff.). In this context Ibn Janaḥ also showed that the talmudic sages never hesitated to illustrate the meaning of a biblical word by a like-sounding word in Greek, Persian, or Arabic. Curiously, some conservatives who objected to linguistic and particularly to comparative studies nevertheless, according to our author, pointed out certain ungrammatical forms in the Mishnah. That these were not Karaite opponents of the Mishnah, as suggested by Wilensky (*ibid.*, p. 19 n. 6), is evident from the context. Nor is it at all likely that the Saragossan grammarian should have felt the need to defend the grammar of the Mishnah against sectarians, whose very presence in his community is yet to be proved, and whom he failed to combat more directly in any other context. Evidently some of the talmudic students themselves tried to discredit philological studies by pointing out that grammatical rules about which philologists were making much ado had been completely disregarded in the Mishnah. Of course, in the Near East, where the sectarian conflicts had reached their apogee in the tenth century, the very disparity in the vocalization and pronunciation of certain biblical words between Babylonians and Palestinians and even between various regions in Babylonia itself, with the ensuing differences in meaning, were grist for the mill of the Karaite assailants of the reliability of the Rabbanite traditions. See the debate on this score between Jacob ben Ephraim the Syrian and Qirqisani, as reported in the latter's *K. al-Anwar,* ii.16–17, ed. by Nemoy, I, 135 ff.; and in B. Klar's some-

what abridged Hebrew trans. in his *Meḥqarim ve-'iyyunim,* pp. 322 ff. Of course, the Hebrew of the Samaritans was far more divergent. See the literature listed *supra,* Chap. XXV, n. 38; and esp. Z. Ben-Hayyim's comprehensive study, *'Ibrit va-aramit nusaḥ Shomeron* (Hebrew and Aramaic of the Samaritan Variety).

12. Abraham Zacuto, *Sefer Yuḥasin ha-shalem* (Lexicon biographicum et historicum), ed. by H. Filipowski, pp. 100b, 206, 217, and elsewhere; Hezekiah ben Samuel's report cited *supra,* Chap. XXVII, n. 28; and S. D. Margoliouth, *Lectures on Arabic Historians,* p. 19. Because of the absence of any direct quotations from Ṣemaḥ's work in the later geonic and medieval letters, L. Ginzberg voiced doubts about the identity of the author and suggested that Zacuto may have used a dictionary prepared by some later author named Ṣemaḥ. See his *Geonica,* I, 159 f. But, apart from the improbability that the informed and extremely careful Zacuto should have committed such an obvious blunder, a good case has been made for the use of Ṣemaḥ's work by Nathan ben Yeḥiel in eleventh-century Rome, or within little more than two centuries after Ṣemaḥ Gaon's death in 890. See the literature cited *supra,* Chap. XXVII, n. 30; and *infra,* n. 31.

13. Harkavy, *Zikhron,* V, 52 ff.; and *supra,* Chap. XXVIII, n. 74. N. Allony has strongly argued for the spelling *Egron* (rather than *Agron*), as it is indeed vocalized in the title of two extant MSS. See his fine Hebrew analysis of this work in Fishman's *Rav Saadya Gaon,* pp. 242 f., reprinted in his *Mi-Torat ha-lashon,* pp. 33–68; and Harkavy's remarks on his edition, p. 29 n. 5. Allony and S. L. Skoss have substantially added to our knowledge of this early Hebrew and Judeo-Arabic philological classic by publishing a number of additional fragments and by their penetrating observations. See Skoss's "Fragments of Unpublished Philological Works of Saadia Gaon," *JQR,* XXIII, 329–36; Allony's Hebrew essays, "A New Fragment of Saadya's Egron," *Tarbiz,* XIX, 89–103 (with additional notes by S. Abramson, *ibid.,* p. 104; XXI, 63); and on the use of "*Telof telef* in Saadiah," *Sinai,* XIV, Nos. 167–68, pp. 144–61. Allony also announces the preparation of a new volume on the *Egron,* which will include a fragment from a Leningrad MS obtained by S. L. Skoss. See his review of Skoss's volume, cited *infra,* n. 40.

14. N. Allony, "From R. Saadiah Gaon's Dictionary on the Mishnah" (Hebrew), *Leshonenu,* XVII, 167–78 (publishing a MS folio from the British Museum; with additional notes by S. Abramson, *ibid.,* Special Issue, 5714 [1954], 49–50).

Among the numerous as yet unsolved questions pertaining to Saadiah's lexicon remains that of the date of the Arabic revision. In his own introduction Saadiah refers vaguely to "some years" having passed since the initial composition. Even if one could be sure that Saadiah's own references to this book in his *Commentary on Sefer Yeṣirah* and the polemical *Sefer ha-Galui* related to the second, and not a third, edition, we would only have a *terminus ad quem* of almost thirty years after the first recension (902). See also E. Ben Ezra's study of the "New Vocabulary Introduced by R. Saadiah Gaon" (Hebrew), *Horeb,* VIII, 135–47; IX, 176–85; X, 295–318. The influence of Arab grammarians, admitted by Saadiah himself (Harkavy, *Zikhron,* pp. 44 f.) is noticeable especially in the gaon's emphasis on the importance of the weak and servile consonants. The debates between the two schools on this score were later summarized by Abu'l-Barakat ibn al-Anbari (1119–81) in his *K. al-Insaf fi masa'il al-ḥilaf* (Die grammatischen Streitfragen der Basrer und Kufer), ed. by G. Weil, pp. 6 ff. (Arabic), 121 f. (German). See also J. Košut's detailed analysis of "Fünf Streitfragen der Basrenser und Kufenser," *SB* Vienna, LXXXVIII, esp. pp. 315 ff.; *supra,* Chap. XXIX, n. 25; and *infra,* n. 37.

15. Saadiah and Mubashshir, quoted in Ibn Ezra's *Commentary* on Jonah 1:3; Harkavy, *Zikhron,* V, 68 ff.; Saadiah's *Commentary* on Gen. 10:4, in his *Oeuvres,* I, 17; Salmon ben Yeruḥim's introduction to his comments on the Ten Commandments in Pinsker's *Lickute kadmoniot,* II, 62 (mentioning Al-Bakhtawi as deceased); Yeshu'a ben Yehudah's *Commentary* on Exod. and Lev., *ibid.,* pp. 73 ff.; and other sources cited by Fürst in his *Geschichte des Karäerthums,* I, 96 f., 170 f. Mubashshir's bias is evident from every page of his critique in his *K. Istidrak,* ed. by Zucker, where, however, our controversy over the meaning of Tarshish is not included. See Zucker's introduction, p. 8. Understandably, Mubashshir aimed his strictures primarily at Saadiah's major works, such as his Bible commentaries and his *Beliefs and Opinions.* The critics' task was greatly facilitated by the gaon's penchant for identifying names simply by the similarity of sound. Nor was he altogether consistent; in his translation of Isa. 23:10, he rendered the "daughter of Tarshish" by "maritime community" (daughter of the sea). See his *Oeuvres,* III, 33; and *supra,* Chap. XXIX, n. 43.

16. Ibn Tamim's *Commentary on Sefer Yeṣirah,* Introduction, ed. by M. Grossberg, p. 17 (or the improved version of the Parma MS cited by Mann in his *Texts and Studies,* I, 74 n. 25; and more fully by G. Vajda in "Le Commentaire kairouanais sur le 'Livre de la création,'" *REJ,* CVII, 126); Rashi's and Ibn Ezra's *Commentaries* on Eccles. 12:5. Cf. Bacher's remarks in *ZDMG,* XLIX, 387; Hirschfeld's *Literary History of Hebrew Grammarians and Lexicographers,* p. 20; and M. Z. (H.) Segal's *Yesode ha-Fonetiqah ha-'ibrit* (Principles of Hebrew Phonetics), pp. 101 ff. Curiously, none of these medieval grammarians refer to Ibn Tamim's alleged temporary conversion to Islam, first mentioned some five centuries after the event by Saadiah ibn Danan of Granada. See his Epistle, published by Z. H. Edelmann in his *Ḥemdah genuzah* (Collection of Manuscript Fragments), p. 16. See also *infra,* Chap. XXXIII.

17. Ibn Quraish's *Risala,* ed. by Bargès and Goldberg, p. 2 (Hebrew version by M. Katz, pp. 3 ff.; here quoted from H. Hirschfeld's English excerpt in his *Literary History,* pp. 17 f.). The date of Ibn Quraish, which largely depends on the time he had met Eldad the Danite (see *supra,* Chap. XVII, n. 52), is still as controversial as ever. After reviewing the pertinent earlier discussions, M. Katz came to the conclusion that Ibn Quraish flourished between 770 and 800, or more than a century before Saadiah. See the intro. to his trans. of the *Risala,* pp. 4 ff. Apart from other difficulties, however, mentioned by Katz's predecessors, it is very unlikely that Ibn Quraish should have moved to Fez soon after its foundation by Idris II in 808 and before the establishment there of a sizeable Jewish community. See also the other arguments (including some inconclusive ones like that stemming from Ibn Quraish's strong anti-anthropomorphism) advanced by G. Vajda in "La Chronologie de Juda ibn Quraysh," *Sefarad,* XIV, 385–87. Vajda favors the original editors' suggestion that Ibn Quraish came to Fez after the destruction of his native city of Tahort in 908, a date which does not necessarily conflict with his possible encounter with Eldad in his younger years.

The third part of Ibn Quraish's work, devoted to comparisons between Hebrew and Arabic words, including such as have undergone the change from an *sh* to an *s* sound and vice versa, seems to have had a separate characteristic title, "Book of Affinity." It is so cited by Ibn Ezra who, however, also mentions it under its *incipit* as the "Book of Father and Mother." On Ibn Quraish's book on the aggadot mentioned by a Karaite polemist in the treatise published by Assaf in *Tarbiz* (IV, 204 f.), and the oft-debated question as to whether he betrayed Karaite sympathies, see Mann's observations in his "Varia," *ibid.,* VI, 66 ff. As elsewhere, this either-or attitude in regard to a scholar's Karaite leanings evidently does violence to the actual historic situation. See Katz's intro. to his trans. of Ibn Quraish, pp. 31 ff.; and *supra,* Chap. XXIX, nn. 15–16. On the other hand, it is almost superfluous to assert that Ibn Quraish, like most other pioneers, did not start absolutely from scratch.

There still is no way of telling whether Ibn Quraish knew any of Saadiah's philological works. It has been noted that even where he had direct occasion to cite the gaon, as in the second section dealing with a comparison of biblical with talmudic terms, he failed to do so. In fact, he mentioned only seventeen of the more than ninety biblical *hapax legomena* which Saadiah tried to explain from rabbinic parallels, and even here he cited as a rule different illustrations from the Mishnah and the Talmud. See D. Yellin's *Toledot hitpathut ha-diqduq ha-'ibri* (Historical Evolution of the Hebrew Grammar), p. 42. However, Ibn Quraish evidently intended to furnish a number of telling illustrations, rather than an exhaustive list of such biblical-rabbinic parallels. See also, more generally, S. Eppenstein's analysis of "Die hebräisch-arabische Sprachvergleichung des Jehuda ibn Koreîsch," *MGWJ,* XLIV, 486–507.

18. David ben Abraham's *K. Jami' al-alfaz,* I, 15, 146, 154, 159, 410; S. L. Skoss's comprehensive introduction thereto, esp. pp. lxxvii f.; and the numerous passages listed in his Index, pp. lxxxiv ff. Skoss has plausibly argued that the author's familiarity with the topography of Palestine and the fact that his dictionary was soon thereafter abridged by Levi ben Jephet in the Holy Land (the introduction to an epitome of this abridgment prepared by 'Ali ben Sulaiman was published by Pinsker in his *Lickute kadmoniot,* I, 183 ff.), indicate that he had left Fez and lived in Palestine. Here apparently he joined the Karaite sect. We possess records of only one Karaite settlement in northwest Africa, namely in the outlying community of Warjalan (Ouargela) in the southern Algerian desert. See Ibn Daud's *Chronicle* in *MJC,* I, 79; Mann's *Texts and Studies,* II, 139 f., 155; and *supra,* Chap. XXVI, n. 74. Both these sources date from the twelfth century, but it seems unlikely that two centuries earlier there had been a Karaite community in the great Jewish center of Fez, birthplace or residence of Dunash ben Labraṭ, Menaḥem ben Saruq, and Isaac Alfasi, without leaving any trace whatsoever. Of course, an individual like David could even there have evinced considerable sympathies with the Karaite point of view while formally still a member of the undivided, and hence Rabbanite, Jewish community. Even later he revealed none of the strong biases characteristic of most Karaite teachers in Jerusalem, and his Karaite orientation is evident only from occasional reference to Karaites as *maskilim* (the enlightened ones) and his preference for some legal interpretations accepted by these sectarians. See Pinsker's *Lickute kadmoniot,* I, 117 ff., 122 ff.; and Skoss's introduction, pp. xlix ff. But did not Mubashshir, Rabbanite though he was,

condemn one of Saadiah's strictures on 'Anan's interpretation by exclaiming, "It was he who blundered, not 'Anan"? See his *K. Istidrak,* pp. 26 (Arabic), 79 (Hebrew). David's extensive use, on the other hand, of the linguistic materials in the Targumim, Mishnah, Talmud, and Midrash (see the numerous passages listed in Skoss's Index, pp. lxxxi ff.) is no proof of his pro-Rabbanite orientation. Such use, practically inescapable (see *supra,* Chap. XXVI, n. 5), became a commonplace among Karaite exegetes. Even Qirqisani, who objected to the Rabbanites' reverence for and reliance on Onkelos in many of their biblical interpretations, did so on purely theological, not linguistic, grounds. See his quotation of several "objectionable" renditions of the Targum in his *K. al-Anwar,* 1.4, 18, ed. by Nemoy, I, 39 f.; and Nemoy's trans., *HUCA,* VII, 361.

19. See *infra,* n. 37. In the Arabic introduction to his second edition, Saadiah argued that "just as the knowledge of the individual is lost from heedlessness, so is that of the multitude forgotten for the same reason," and he blamed on that collective neglect the fact that such important philological treatises as the "Book of Weights" (of Meters?) and that of the "Knowledge of Beginnings" had been lost. See Harkavy's *Zikhron,* V, 45; and Hirschfeld's trans. of this passage in his *Literary History,* pp. 12 f. See also Allony's observations in Fishman's *Rav Saadya Gaon,* pp. 251 ff.; and Brockelmann's *Geschichte,* I, 96, 112 ff., 121 f., 138 f. The story of the interrelations between the Arab and Jewish philology in this crucial era of the development of both still awaits elucidation. See *supra,* nn. 10, 13; and *infra,* n. 28. Thus far even such experts as Bacher (see esp. his *Die hebräische Sprachwissenschaft vom 10. bis zum 16. Jahrhundert*), Hirschfeld, or Yellin have limited themselves to a few generalities.

20. Menaḥem's *Maḥberet* (Set; a dictionary), ed. by H. Filipowski, fols. 11b, 12a, 50b, 54a, 70a, 99ab, 105a. See also the additions and corrections supplied from a Bern MS by D. Kaufmann in "Das Wörterbuch Menachem Ibn Saruk's," *ZDMG,* XL, 367–409. Numerous examples of Menaḥem's explanations of biblical phrases by elliptic or pleonastic usage are adduced by Yellin in his *Toledot hitpatḥut,* pp. 60 ff. The theological bias of Ben Saruq's interpretation of the term *Ehyeh* is doubly evident, as it runs counter to his general effort to connect even rare words with some more familiar ones in the Bible. In this respect his explanation of the genuinely unique term *ṭoṭafot* is far more typical. In fact, on one occasion he listed fully 116 words, "which have none like them in the Torah, but are explained by their context." Unlike Saadiah, however, whose work on the *hapax legomena* he did not mention, he generally refrained from interpreting these words by comparison even with the vocabulary of the Mishnah. Curiously, only fourteen of these words occur in Saadiah's list, and, in the single case where Menaḥem cites a mishnaic parallel, it, too, differs from that of the gaon. See Yellin's remarks, p. 62; and, more generally, Bacher's *Hebräische Sprachwissenschaft,* pp. 23 ff.; and Hirschfeld's *Literary History,* pp. 24 ff. On Menaḥem's likely share in the preparation of Ḥisdai's famous letter to the Khazar king, see *supra,* Chap. XIX, n. 34.

21. Dunash ben Labraṭ's *Teshubot* (Criticae vocum recensiones), ed. by H. Filipowski, p. 75 and *passim.* The biographical data here given, especially the assumptions that Dunash was born in Baghdad rather than in Fez and that his

father's first name was Labraṭ, follow N. Allony's arguments in his edition of Dunash's *Shirim,* pp. 5 ff. Allony's denial (pp. 14 ff.), however, of any connection between Menaḥem's dismissal by Ḥisdai and Dunash's attack is far-fetched. The fact that in the poem addressed to his patron Menaḥem failed to refer to that attack is no more conclusive than Menaḥem's general silence on this score, or the absence of any further reference to his alleged heterodoxy in either his own writings or in the replies by his pupils. See also Allony's additional observations on "Dunash ben Labraṭ's Language" (Hebrew), *Leshonenu,* XV, 161–72; and, mainly with reference to poetic forms and detailed interpretations, A. Mirski's Hebrew review of Allony's ed. of Dunash's *Shirim* in *KS,* XXIV, 16–19. Of course, Menaḥem was not a Karaite sympathizer. He probably did not even know of 'Anan's interpretation, since in Spain Karaism was hardly an issue before the return of Ibn al-Taras from Jerusalem some two generations later. Dunash, on the other hand, coming from the polemically overcharged environment of Saadiah's school, was far more sensitive. Menaḥem's insistence on the literal meaning of the negative *lo,* however, merely upholding the masoretic spelling, antagonized even the great Tosafist, Jacob Tam of Rameru. In his booklet entitled *Hakhra'ot* (Decisions), in which he passed judgment on the merits of the Menaḥem-Dunash controversy, R. Jacob, while generally siding with Menaḥem, pointed out that "even the shallowest of the shallow" could not have so misinterpreted the meaning of Scripture, but that he rather agreed with Dunash and that "both were right." See the text published by Filipowski in parallel columns in his edition of Dunash's *Teshubot,* p. 75; and H. Englander's "Rabbenu Jacob Ben Meir Tam as Grammarian," *HUCA,* XV, 485–95.

22. *Sefer Teshubot* (Liber Responsionum) of Menaḥem's disciples and Yehudi's rejoinder, published by S. G. Stern, Part I, pp. 29, 31 ff., 96 f.; Part II, pp. 18 f. In his notes Stern supplies from the same Parma MS some improved readings of Dunash's strictures as well. Doubtless Menaḥem himself had considered it beneath his dignity to enter the ranks and even failed to refer indirectly to the accusations in his dignified letter to Ḥisdai (published *ibid.,* pp. xxiii ff.), which has long been recognized as a gem of the Spanish-Jewish epistolary style. In his various analyses of the controversial points from the standpoint of the philological knowledge of our day, D. Yellin has shown that the weight of evidence favors most of Dunash's and Yehudi's contentions. See his Hebrew essays on "Dunash ben Labraṭ's Wrangling" in *Gulak-Klein Mem. Vol.,* pp. 105–14; and "Dunash ben Labraṭ's 'Teshubot,'" *Leshonenu,* XI, 202–15. See also his *Toledot hitpatḥut,* pp. 67 ff.

23. Ḥayyuj's *K. an-Nutaf* (Book of Glosses), long known by Ibn Ezra's somewhat misleading reference to his "fourth book" (see *Sefer Mo'znayim,* Intro., fol. 2a), has in part been recovered from a Leningrad MS and published and annotated in P. Kokovtsov's *K'istorii srednevіekovoi evreiskoi filologii* (Contributions to the History of Medieval Hebrew Philology and Judeo-Arabic Literature), II, 1–73 (Russian), 1–58, 191–204 (Arabic). See also S. Poznanski's analysis thereof in his "New Materials to the History of Hebrew and Hebrew-Arabic Philology during the X–XII Centuries," *JQR,* XVI, 258 ff. In this essay (pp. 245 ff.) Poznanski strongly argued also against the long-accepted identification of Ḥayyuj with Menaḥem's disciple involved in the controversy with Dunash. However, his main chronological and geographic arguments are far from conclusive. Ḥayyuj may

well have been born in Fez even before 940 to parents of alleged Christian origin and arrived in Cordova in time to participate in the controversy. In fact, his enmity to Dunash may have dated back to the time they had both resided in Fez. Nor would such Moroccan origin have in any way interfered with his participation in a booklet attacking Dunash, whose superiority complex was clearly eastern rather than Moroccan in nature. Since Ḥayyuj's great contributions are in the field of grammar, rather than lexicography, his theories will be more fully analyzed in the next section. See also N. Allony's "Yehudah ben David and Yehudah Ḥayyuj" (Hebrew), *Zlotnik Jub. Vol.*, pp. 67–82, arguing for their identity, but denying that Ḥayyuj was a *native* of Fez and a *pupil* of Menaḥem.

24. Ibn Janaḥ's *K. al-Mustalḥiq,* in his *Opuscules et traités,* ed. by J. and H. Derenbourg, pp. 140 f.; his *K. Al-Luma',* ed. by J. Derenbourg, Intro. and Chap. xxxi (xxxii), pp. 18, 340 f. (*Sefer ha-Riqmah,* ed. by Wilensky, II, 358, with the editor's notes thereon; Metzger's French trans., pp. 21, 337). Ibn Janaḥ was not only by nature a pugnacious writer, but he was made doubly sensitive by his opponents' frequent imputations of plagiarism on his part. See the data cited by Wilensky in his "On the Biography of R. Jonah ibn Janaḥ" (Hebrew), *Tarbiz,* IV, 100 ff. (Wilensky also makes it plausible here that the grammarian was a native of Lucena, rather than Cordova). Such polemical asides may have detracted somewhat from the author's objectivity, but they doubtless increased the interest of readers in these generally technical and mentally exacting discussions. On Samuel ibn Nagrela's philological works, see *infra,* nn. 27 and 52.

25. Ibn Janaḥ's *K. al-Uṣul* (The Book of Hebrew Roots), ed. by A. Neubauer, cols. 3 f., 431, 579 ff. (*Sefer ha-Shorashim,* in the Hebrew trans. by Yehudah ibn Tibbon, ed. by W. Bacher, pp. 2, 302 f., 407 ff.). On Ibn Janaḥ as a grammarian and his great, if indirect, share in the evolution of biblical exegesis, see *supra,* Chap. XXIX, n. 77; and *infra,* nn. 50–52. Of special interest also are Ibn Janaḥ's contributions to comparative linguistics, in which he went far beyond any of his predecessors. See Bacher's seven decades old, but still very useful, analyses of *Die hebräisch-arabische Sprachvergleichung des Abulwalid* and *Die hebräisch-neuhebräische und hebräisch-aramäische Sprachvergleichung des Abulwalid.* See also the fragment of an otherwise unknown Hebrew dictionary apparently used by Ibn Janaḥ, published by Allony in his *Mi-Sifrut yeme ha-benayim,* pp. 75 ff. The arrangement here is so unsystematic that it, or some other dictionary like it, evoked Ibn Janaḥ's righteous anger. See the latter's *K. al-Uṣul,* col. 12 (*Sefer ha-Shorashim,* p. 7). Some broader aspects are also discussed in M. Madan's brief Hebrew essay on "The Biblical Dictionary of the Spanish-Jewish scholars," *Leshonenu,* XVII, 110–14.

26. On Ibn Parḥon's lexicographical work, see *infra,* n. 29, whereas David Qimḥi's *Sefer ha-Shorashim* (Book of Roots), ed. by J. H. R. Biesenthal and F. Lebrecht (also in many earlier editions), will be more fully considered in connection with the linguistic studies in later medieval Europe. Recent biblical scholarship, prone to abandon some of the excessively critical approaches of the last generation, has increasingly reached the conclusion that, as far as biblical lexicography is concerned, our knowledge has substantially increased beyond that of Ibn Janaḥ and his fellow lexicographers only where the Hebrew vocabulary

could be explained by comparison with other ancient Near Eastern languages. See G. R. Driver's pertinent observations in "L'Interprétation du texte masorétique à la lumière de la lexicographie hébraïque," *Ephemerides theologicae lovanienses,* XXVI, 337–53.

27. Samuel's *K. al-Istighna* (Book of Amplitude) in Kokovtsov's *K'istorii,* II, 74–194 (Russian), 205–24 (Arabic; see also *infra,* n. 52); Abu'l Faraj Harun's *K. al-Mushtamil* in W. Bacher, "Le Grammairien anonyme de Jérusalem et son livre," *REJ,* XXX, 232–56; S. Poznanski's "Aboul Faradj Haroun ben al-Faradj," *ibid.,* XXXIII, 24–39, 197–218, supplemented by his "Nouveaux renseignements," *ibid.,* LVI, 42–69; and the fragment ed. by Hirschfeld in *JQR,* XIII, 1–9; Hai Gaon's *K. al-Ḥawi,* as reconstructed from later quotations by Poznanski in his "Zu Hai Gaon's Kitâb al-Ḥâwi," *ZDMG,* LV, 597–606.

The eighth part of Abu'l Faraj Harun's *Mushtamil* was edited from a British Museum MS under the title "Chapter on Biblical Chaldee," in Hirschfeld's *Arabic Chrestomathy,* pp. 54–60. Its conclusion, mentioning the date 1026, explains the rather unfinished state of this section by the author's illness. It is altogether missing in the voluminous Leningrad MS, the size of which (579 leaves) discouraged P. Kokovtsov from contemplating its full publication. Regrettably, even that Russian orientalist's intention to publish instead Abu'l Faraj's *K. al-Kāfi* (see *infra,* n. 45) has not been realized. See his letter to S. L. Skoss of 1924, communicated in the latter's *Arabic Commentary of 'Ali b. Suleimān,* p. 27 n. 151. See also Ibn Bal'am's *Commentary* on Amos 7:14 and Hab. 2:6, ed. by Poznanski in *JQR,* XV, 32, 45 f. Cf. Hirschfeld's *Literary History,* pp. 53 f., 69 f.

28. Ibn Baron's *K. al-Muwazana* (Concordance between the Hebrew and Arabic Languages) in Kokovtsov's *K'istorii,* I and II, 153–72 (Arabic), with variants and additions, *ibid.,* pp. 216–33 (Russian); Halevi's *K. al-Khazari,* II.68 (in Hirschfeld's English trans., pp. 124 f.). See also S. Eppenstein's detailed analysis of "Ishak ibn Baroun et ses comparaisons de l'hébreu avec l'arabe," *REJ,* XLI, 233–49; XLII, 76–102; and P. Wechter's Dropsie College dissertation on *Ibn Barun's Book of Comparisons Between the Hebrew and the Arabic Languages* (typescript). On the spelling Baron, rather than the more widely accepted Barun, see S. M. Stern, "The Explanation of a Difficult Verse of Yehudah Halevi and the Spanish Etymology of the Name Ibn Baron," *JQR,* XL, 189–91. It may also be noted that Ibn Bal'am, too, though generally very conservative in his theology (see *supra,* Chap. XXIX, nn. 64, 76), did not hesitate to adduce Aramaic and Arabic parallels or even to cite, on occasion, a Christian Bible commentator. See his *Commentary* on Hab. 2:4, ed. by Poznanski in *JQR,* XV, 10, 45 (in n. 10 Poznanski lists other such references by Ibn Bal'am and other medieval exegetes); and his three small grammatical treatises published by Kokovtsov in their Hebrew translation together with some fragments of the Arabic originals in his *K'istorii,* II, 67–152 (Hebrew-Arabic), 201–15 (Russian); and analyzed by Poznanski in his "Hebräisch-arabische Sprachvergleichungen bei Jehūdah ibn Bal'âm," *ZDMG,* LXX, 449–76, LXXI, 270 (here mainly corrections by Goldziher). See also *infra,* n. 57.

29. Ibn Parḥon's *Maḥberet he-'Arukh,* end, ed. by Stern, fol. 75ab. Yehudah ibn Tibbon, writing only a decade after our author, already mistook the latter's intentions. Considering the new dictionary but a translation of Ibn Janaḥ's

work on a par with two other incomplete versions (covering the first twelve letters), Ibn Tibbon censured Solomon for inserting his own observations on the basis of "midrashim and medical books" without clearly marking such interpolations. "This is a great sin and injustice." See his rendition of Ibn Janaḥ's *Sefer ha-Shorashim,* p. 550. Modern scholars have made clear, however, that, deeply indebted as Ibn Parḥon undoubtedly was to his illustrious predecessor, he produced a new book of his own. See esp. W. Bacher's analysis of "Salomon ibn Parchon's hebräisches Wörterbuch," *ZAW,* X, 120–56; XI, 35–99 (offering on pp. 97 ff. some interesting corrections to Stern's edition on the basis of the very Vienna MS used by that editor).

30. C. J. Kasowski, *Oṣar leshon ha-talmud* (Thesaurus Talmudis Concordantia Verborum); and the other concordances listed *supra,* Vol. II, p. 428 n. 6; and Chap. XXIX, n. 33. Investigation of the talmudic idiom has received new impetus in recent years through the publication of such detailed monographs as E. Porath's *Leshon ḥakhamim le-fi mesorot babliyot* (Mishnaic Hebrew as Vocalized in the Early Manuscripts of the Babylonian Jews). See also the interesting comments in their reviews of this work by B. Klar, reprinted in his *Meḥqarim ve-'iyyunim,* pp. 77–81; and P. Kahle in *Orientalistische Literaturzeitung,* XLII, 299–301. Stimulating observations "On the Linguistic Approaches and the Thought of Our Sages" were offered by N. H. Tur-Sinai in a Hebrew essay under this title, reprinted together with several related articles in his *Ha-Lashon ve-ha-sefer,* III, 257 ff. Many important insights into the rabbinic language, particularly as it had been current in ancient Palestine, are scattered in the various publications by S. Lieberman, especially in his *Greek in Jewish Palestine,* his *Hellenism in Jewish Palestine,* and the extensive commentary on his new edition of the *Tosefta,* entitled *Tosefta ki-fshuṭah,* of which thus far Vols. I–II for the order Zera'im have appeared. Of course, the medieval students did not have at their disposal all these paraphernalia of modern scholarship. It is doubly remarkable, therefore, that working empirically with limited materials they achieved a great measure of success.

31. Zacuto's remarks, cited *supra,* n. 12; the analysis thereof in Kohut's introduction to his ed. of the *Aruch completum,* pp. xvii ff., with constant reference to S. J. L. Rapoport's still useful biographic sketch of *Toledoth Rabbenu Nathan ish Romi* (A Biography of R. Nathan of Rome and the Story of His Book). Here Kohut has plausibly shown that Nathan was fully familiar with the work of his predecessor. There is less evidence of Nathan's familiarity with Saadiah's lexicographical work, although the Roman scholar generally made excellent use of the vast materials accumulated in the geonic commentaries on the Talmud and juristic works. See also D. S. Blondheim's "Liste de manuscrits de l'Arouk de Nathan ben Yehiel," *Festschrift Aron Freimann,* pp. 24–30; *supra,* Chap. XXVII, n. 44 and *passim;* and *infra,* n. 32. The dates of Nathan's birth and death are still uncertain. Kohut is entirely noncommittal with respect to both dates, denying even the previously long-accepted year of 1106 for Nathan's demise. Arguing for the latter date as approximately correct, H. Vogelstein suggested *ca.* 1035 as the most likely date of Nathan's birth. See his and Rieger's *Geschichte der Juden in Rom,* I, 357 ff. In his *Mabo le-Sefer Rabiah,* pp. 390 f., V. Aptowitzer advanced the birth date to 1025. Much of that chronology depends on the identification of

Rashi as the inquirer from the community of Rome. See, more generally, *supra,* Chap. XXVII, nn. 134–35. Little progress has been achieved in the whole area of *'Arukh* research during the last half century and more.

32. See the data assembled in Kohut's introduction; and *supra,* Chap. XXVII, n. 32 and *passim.* Kohut seems to go too far, however, in denying Nathan's familiarity with Arabic and, more generally, in underestimating the Roman scholar's considerable independence from his sources and his frequent resort to direct observation. Nathan's use of three different designations for Arabic (*leshon Ṭayit, Ishmael,* and *'Arabit*) is no more proof of ignorance than is his interchangeable use of various designations for the talmudic dialect (*leshon Talmud, Mishnah, gemara, ḥakhamim, rabbanan*). In fact, the greater accuracy of his references to Arabic than to Greek etymologies (in some cases Nathan actually confused Greek with Latin, although the latter differed but little from his own Italian dialect) should have given pause to the editor. Nathan had evidently tried to adhere rather faithfully to the earlier sources, but he had found in them insufficient data to dispense with fresh reasoning and observation. Certainly to declare all reference to Arab, Palestinian, or Babylonian customs as quotations from older sources merely because it is unlikely that "an unworldly man dwelling in the tent of the Torah should have traveled north and south, east and west" (Kohut, p. vi), is a completely anachronistic misreading of the scholars' way of life and pursuit of learning during the Renaissance of Islam. See my remarks in *Saadia Anniv. Vol.,* p. 22.

33. On the much-debated relationships between Rashi and Nathan ben Yeḥiel, see the literature listed in my "Rashi and the Community of Troyes," *Rashi Anniv. Vol.,* p. 54 n. 13; and on Rashi's lexicographic contributions, J. Weinstein and A. Zimroni's unfortunately incomplete compilation of "A Biblical Dictionary According to Rashi" (Hebrew), *Leshonenu,* X, 5–20, 119–34; XI, 29–37 (covers only the first ten letters of the Hebrew alphabet); J. Beniel's lexicographic studies in his "Harvesting in Rashi's Vineyard" (Hebrew), *ibid.,* XI, 3–28; the literature listed *supra,* Chaps. XXVII, n. 58; XXIX, nn. 56–57; and *infra,* n. 48. In his "Rashi as a Lexicographer of the Talmud," *Rashi Anniv. Vol.,* pp. 219–48, B. Cohen not only offered an analysis of the Troyes sage's contributions in this field, but also reported the preparation of a comprehensive dictionary of Rashi's definitions, of which he offered here (pp. 228 ff.) a very instructive sample. A comprehensive review of the linguistic material, both grammatical and stylistic, included in Rashi's commentaries has recently been presented by I. Avinery in his *Heical* [*Hekhal*] *Rashi* (Thesaurus linguae hebraicae auctore Rabbi Shlomo Izhaqi), Vol. III. The French and other foreign words in Rashi's commentaries have been treated *supra,* Chaps. XXVII and XXIX. Their import will be better assessed in the general context of the use of European languages by Jews during the later Middle Ages.

34. See I. Goldziher's *Studien über Tanchûm Jerûschalmi,* pp. 46 ff.; W. Bacher's *Aus dem Wörterbuche Tanchum Jeruschalmi's;* and the brief excerpt from a British Museum MS in Hirschfeld's *Literary History,* pp. 88 f. In his *Texts and Studies,* I, 437 f., J. Mann published the manuscript heading of an elegy by Tanḥum's son Joseph, from which it is evident that Tanḥum died in Cairo on

June 20, 1291. Tanḥum's own linguistic and exegetical contributions will be discussed more fully in a future volume.

35. *Massekhet Soferim* IV.3–4, ed. by Higger, pp. 139 f.; Ibn Janaḥ's *K. al-Luma'*, II, XVIII (XIX), pp. 29, 219 (*Riqmah,* ed. by Wilensky, I, 39; II, 238; Metzger's French trans., pp. 33, 207); Ben Asher's *Diqduqe ha-ṭe'amim,* p. 7. On the great contributions made by the Masorites to the study of Hebrew phonetics and grammar, see W. Bacher, "Die Anfänge der hebräischen Grammatik," *ZDMG,* XLIX, 7 ff., 23 ff.; K. Levy's observations in his *Zur masoretischen Grammatik,* Introduction; Y. F. Gumpertz's more recent "Attempt at a Phonetic-Historical Evaluation of the Reformatory Work of the Vocalizers" (Hebrew), reprinted in his *Mivta'e sefatenu* (Studies in Historical Phonetics of the Hebrew Language), pp. 125–30; and *supra,* Chap. XXIX, nn. 20 ff.

Of course, much depends on our assumptions of what were the prevailing pronunciation and vocabulary of premasoretic Hebrew. This long and often heatedly debated problem is not devoid of actuality, inasmuch as on the answer to that question hinges to a large extent the claim to greater "original purity" of the now prevailing "Sephardic" pronunciation as against that of the other Hebrew dialects. Apart from F. Perez Castro's comprehensive review article, "Problemas de las fuentes de conocimento del hebreo premasoretico," *Sefarad,* VIII, 145–87, and other studies mentioned *supra,* Chap. XXIX, *passim,* see especially several other essays included in Gumpertz's volume; B. Klar's succinct observations "On the History of Hebrew Pronunciation during the Middle Ages" (Hebrew), reprinted in his *Meḥqarim ve-'iyyunim,* pp. 42–46; and various studies in *Leshonenu,* including J. ha-Kohen's "Studies in Grammatical and Masoretic Problems" (Hebrew), *ibid.,* XII, 127–33, 264–67; XIII, 203–10 (largely aimed at Kahle's theories); A. S. Hartom (Artom), "The Hebrew Pronunciation among the Jews of Italy" (Hebrew), *ibid.,* XVI, 52–61; and I. Garbell, "The Pronunciation of Hebrew in Medieval Spain," *Homenaje à Millás Vallicrosa,* I, 647–96. These matters are still very much in flux, however, and probably only the discovery of additional early sources could definitely settle certain highly controversial issues.

36. See Saadiah's *Siddur,* p. 83; and H. Yallon's observations thereon in his Hebrew essays on the "Ten Commandments" *'Inyane lashon,* I, 46–48; and "On the Margin of Saadiah's *Siddur,* II: Linguistic Aspects" in Fishman's *Rav Saadya Gaon,* pp. 561–66. Yallon's illuminating notes are symptomatic of a fairly general reaction in recent years against the previous practice of emending irregular forms found in medieval manuscripts. With the increase of available documentary materials it became manifest that what seemed to be an arbitary deviation from accepted grammatical rules frequently was but a perfectly legitimate usage in a certain period or region. In the case of a linguist like Saadiah, however, the forms used by him reflected not only local deviations from then accepted norms, but also a more or less reasoned acceptance of certain rules which made such deviations not only permissible but well-nigh imperative.

37. Harkavy, *Zikhron,* V, 45, 49 ff. (in the English trans. by Hirschfeld in his *Literary History,* pp. 12 ff.); Saadiah's *Commentary on Yeṣirah,* I.3, ed. by Lambert, pp. 28 f. (Arabic), 49 ff. (French); Dunash ibn Tamim's *Commentary on Yeṣirah,* ed. by Grossberg, p. 16 (cf. Vajda's ed. in *REJ,* CVII, 126 f.); 'Ali ben Yehudah 'Alan cited

by David Qimḥi in his *Mikhlol* (Perfection; a Hebrew grammar), Venice, 1545 ed., fol. 28c; in W. Chomsky's English rendition, p. 25 (on 'Ali's identity, see the authors cited by Chomsky, *ibid.*, p. 44 n. 57). On the importance of the three letters in Arabic philology, see *supra*, n. 14, and M. Bravmann's *Materialien und Untersuchungen zu den phonetischen Lehren der Araber*, pp. 18 f. By adding the *ṭet* to the eleven functional letters enumerated by Saadiah, Ben Asher had counted twelve such letters, "each of which has a judge and lord," that is, depends on the main "radical" letters. See his *Diqduqe*, pp. 3, 5; *supra*, Chap. XXIX, n. 25; Harkavy's excursus, pp. 121 ff. (pointing out the influence of Saadiah's classification of consonants on the subsequent Hebrew grammarians); and Allony's remarks in Fishman's *Rav Saadya Gaon*, pp. 245 f., 251 ff., 270 ff.

Allony shows here Saadiah's indebtedness to Ibn Duraid and reexamines the mnemotechnic symbols employed by the gaon to facilitate remembrance of the auxiliary consonants. Ibn Duraid, however, was but a disciple of a long chain of Baṣran authorities from Sibawaihi to Mubarrad, with whose works Saadiah may have been directly acquainted. Sibawaihi's "Book," ed. by H. Derenbourg (cf. G. Jahn's fully annotated German trans. of his *Buch über die Grammatik*), had long become a classic of Arabic philology, while Mubarrad, who had died not many years before Saadiah's arrival in Baghdad, was vividly remembered by many disciples and opponents as well as by readers of his work. See G. Weil's illuminating introduction to his edition of Ibn al-Anbari's *Grammatische Streitfragen*. In fact, Sibawaihi was to be quoted later by the anonymous Jewish author of the fragment of a grammatical "Book of Definitions," published by H. Hirschfeld in "The Arabic Portion of the Cairo Genizah, XXX," *JQR*, [o.s.] XVIII, 328 f. (Arabic and English); and Ibn Janaḥ (see *infra*, n. 51). On the other hand, Saadiah shows none of Ibn Duraid's penchant for classifying words as of foreign origin merely because of the existence of variant readings and other such superficial criteria. See A. Siddiqi's aforementioned study of *Ibn Duraid and His Treatment of Loan-Words.*

38. In his *K. al-Luma'* (II, XIV [XV], XXI [XXII]) Ibn Janaḥ twice states expressly that Saadiah's comprehensive philological work mentioned in the gaon's *Commentary on Yeṣirah* had not reached Spain, although in another context he quotes a philological treatise "attributed to the gaon," which very likely stemmed from the same collection (pp. 29, 170, 236; *Riqmah*, I, 39, 193, 252; Metzger's French trans., pp. 32, 159, 226). The latter citation, relating to the "swallowing" of the *nun*, seems to have come from the seventh or, more likely, the eighth part, dealing principally with laryngeal letters. Bearing the special title *maqala*, each of these parts constituted a book apart (see Skoss's remarks in "Fragments of Unpublished Philological Works of Saadia Gaon," *JQR*, XXIII, 335 n. 15), and one was apparently known in this form to Ibn Janaḥ.

39. Saadiah's *Kutab al-Lughah* (Books of Language), in the passage ed. and trans. by S. L. Skoss in "A Study of Inflection in Hebrew from Saadia Gaon's Grammatical Work 'Kutub al-Lughah,'" *JQR*, XXXIII, 174 ff. The extant fragments in a Leningrad MS, supplemented by smaller fragments in a Bodleian MS and a Cambridge Genizah MS, are fully reviewed by Skoss in his partly posthumous essays reprinted under the title *Saadia Gaon, the Earliest Hebrew Grammarian.* According to Skoss, we now possess portions of Parts II–VIII, and perhaps

of Part IX. Part I can be partially reconstructed from subsequent references to it by Saadiah himself and by Dunash ben Labraṭ, whereas the very content of the remaining parts still is conjectural. The vast compass of these Saadianic monographs may be gleaned from the subjects dealt with in the first nine parts: "I. A Study of the Alphabet; II. Augmentation and Contraction in Stems; III. Inflection; IV. Dagesh and Rafeh . . . ; V. A Study of Vowels; VI. The Shewa; VII. Vocalization of Affixes when Added to Laryngeals and Non-Laryngeals, and IX. Expletives and Affixes" (Skoss, p. 4). In successive chapters Skoss analyzes all the information now available on the gaon's views. But, thus far, only small segments of the text itself have seen the light of day. See n. 40.

40. Dunash's *Teshubot 'al Rabbi Saadiah Gaon* (Kritik . . . über einzelne Stellen aus Saadia's arabischer Psalmenübersetzung des A.T.), ed. by R. Schröter, p. 40 No. 122. See S. L. Skoss's "Study of Inflection," *JQR,* XXXIII, 174 ff., 192 ff., 212; his "A Study of Hebrew Vowels from Saadia Gaon's Grammatical Work 'Kutub al-Lughah,'" *ibid.,* XLII, 290 ff., 295, 303, 305 ff., 311 ff. (also in an earlier Hebrew article in *Tarbiz,* XXII, 174–84); and his aforementioned monograph on *Saadia Gaon,* together with N. Allony's review thereof in *KS,* XXXII, 55–57. See also Skoss's earlier preliminary study of "Fragments of Unpublished Philological Works of Saadia Gaon," *JQR,* XXIII, 329–36; Z. Ben-Hayyim's "Saadiah Gaon's Theory of Vowels" (Hebrew), *Leshonenu,* XVIII, 89–96; and Bacher's older systematic analysis of Saadiah's grammatical teachings in "Die Anfänge der hebräischen Grammatik," *ZDMG,* XLIX, 38 ff. Although obsolete in many details and, in the absence of documentary material, based on much guesswork, the latter analysis still is eminently informative.

41. Harkavy, *Zikhron,* V, 74 ff., 82 ff.; and Skoss's remarks thereon in *JQR,* XXXIII, 212. Harkavy had hesitantly suggested that anonymous author's indebtedness to Saadiah's *Egron,* whereas Skoss rightly showed the far closer nexus between his as yet undatable treatise and Saadiah's monograph on inflections.

42. Hirschfeld's *Qirqisani Studies,* pp. 31 ff.; and his *Literary History,* pp. 15 ff. Qirqisani's occasional philological observations in his comprehensive *K. al-Anwar* have not yet been subjected to adequate scrutiny. In his own exposition, as well as in his acceptance or rejection of theologically and legally relevant views of others buttressed by peculiar interpretations of biblical verses, Qirqisani often betrays here his own philological biases, which, if thoroughly reviewed, would shed new light on the operation of his grammatical propositions. In his reply to Jacob ben Ephraim, for example, he, though an easterner, argued for the superiority of the Palestinian over the Babylonian and Iranian pronunciation of Hebrew, pointing especially to the former's acceptance in all Christian countries where Jews had lived "since the exile from the Second Commonwealth." See his *K. al-Anwar,* II.17, 5, ed. by Nemoy, I, 139; in Klar's Hebrew trans. in his *Meḥqarim ve-'iyyunim,* pp. 325 f. See also the passages cited *supra,* n. 18; and Chap. XXVI, *passim.*

43. Salmon's *Commentary* on Lam. 1:14, ed. by S. Feuerstein, pp. xl, 8 f., 12 f., 20 f.; his comment on Ps. 102:5, excerpted and translated into Hebrew by Pinsker in his *Lickute kadmoniot,* II, 133 f.; David ben Abraham's *K. Jami' al-alfaẓ,* ed. by

Skoss, I, 14 f. (Arabic), lxxvii f. (English); *supra,* n. 18; and Skoss's earlier essay, "A Chapter on Permutation in Hebrew from David ben Abraham al-Fasi's Dictionary," *JQR,* XXIII, 1–43 (supplemented in the former work, p. xc n. 132).

44. Jephet's appendix to his *Commentary* on Hosea in Hirschfeld's *Literary History,* pp. 103 ff. (Arabic), 32 ff. (English); and P. Birnbaum's introduction to his edition of that *Commentary,* pp. xxxvi f. This supplement, previously published by R. Schröter in the appendix to "Die im Cod. Huntington aufbewahrte arabische Uebersetzung der kleinen Propheten," *Archiv für wissenschaftliche Erforschung des alten Testaments,* ed. by A. Merx, II, 25 ff., is also reproduced in Hebrew letters in Birnbaum's ed., pp. 227 ff. Some other grammatical excursuses scattered through Jephet's exegetical works had been analyzed a century ago by S. Munk in his "Notice sur Abu'l-Walid," *JA,* 4th ser. XV, 312 ff., but a fresh analysis on the basis of the much richer documentary materials now available is clearly indicated.

45. Skoss's *'Ali ben Suleiman,* pp. 10, 20 ff., based in part on the Bacher and Poznanski articles, mentioned *supra,* n. 27. In the aforementioned letter of 1924 (*ibid.*), P. Kokovtsov stated his intention of publishing, in the third volume of his *K'istorii,* Abu'l Faraj's *K. al-Kafi,* which is extant in a Leningrad MS of some four hundred folios, but this plan has not materialized. Here, too, a detailed analysis of Abu'l Faraj's philological views, as expressed in his exegetical works, might effectively supplement and elucidate his grammatical writings. Now with the increased availability of sections of Saadiah's major "Books of Language," an inquiry ought also to be instituted in regard to their influence on Karaite grammarians. For example, Abu'l Faraj's acceptance of the division into two series of eleven letters, rather than of Ben Asher's ten and twelve letter system, very likely stems directly or indirectly from Saadiah. See *supra,* Chap. XXIX, nn. 72, 76.

46. Qirqisani's *K. al-Anwar,* I.3, 4, ed. by Nemoy, I, 15 f. (*HUCA,* VII, 332). One also wonders to what extent Karaite concentration on the *qiyas* (analogy) method in law and, with it, the rejection of extrabiblical sources, whose linguistic materials were at best tolerated, likewise served as a stumbling block. Discussing the role of the *qiyas* in the Baṣran-Kufan controversies, G. Weil noted that "while in [Muslim] canon law the *qiyas* served as a progressive tool, it became in grammar an obstacle to the organic evolution of language, the moment it transcended its purely exegetical function. As such it was inimical to progress." See his introduction to his ed. of Ibn al-Anbari's *Streitfragen,* p. 46. In the Karaite case, we recall, this method, after initial advances, tended to become a force of retrogression even in the domain of law. See also *supra,* Chap. XXVI, nn. 5, 36 ff.; and *infra,* Chap. XXXI, nn. 8 ff.

47. See Dunash's *Teshubot . . . 'al Rabbi Saadiah Gaon,* ed. by Schröter, pp. 12 No. 36, 16 f. No. 51, 31 No. 105, etc.; and his *Teshubot* against *Menaḥem,* ed. by Filipowski, fol. 5b. On his occupation as professional reader, see Allony's ed. of his *Shirim,* pp. 8 ff. Although relatively few poems by Dunash have been preserved, his reputation among his early successors, including Ibn Janaḥ and Ibn Gabirol, rested chiefly upon his poetic attainments. See Allony's Hebrew essay "On the Language of Dunash ben Labraṭ" in *Leshonenu,* XV, 161 f. That he was also a well-trained grammarian may be deduced not only from his ingenious strictures on his opponents, but also from his programmatic introduction to his observations on Menaḥem's

work, which outlined the general problems of Hebrew grammar. It is to be regretted that he did not see fit to follow up his critical theses with a broad positive treatment of some fundamental grammatical problems. See also D. Yellin's analysis in his "Dunash ben Labraṭ's 'Teshubot' " (Hebrew), *Leshonenu,* XI, 205 ff.

48. Ḥayyuj's *K. al-Af'al,* ed. by M. Jastrow under the English title *The Weak and Geminative Verbs in Hebrew,* pp. 1 ff.; and in Moses ibn Chiquitilla's Hebrew translation, ed. and trans. by J. W. Nutt under the title *Two Treatises on Verbs Containing Feeble and Double Letters,* pp. 2 f. (Hebrew), 4 f. (English). See also Nutt's introductory remarks, p. 9. A slightly different translation of the introductory statement here quoted is offered by Hirschfeld in his *Literary History,* pp. 36 f. Ḥayyuj's decision to depart from the Hebrew medium used by Menaḥem enabled him to express his philological laws with greater terminological precision. Although Menaḥem, too, had been deeply convinced of the basic regularity of grammatical forms and with predilection spoke of the "law" (*ḥuqqah* or *mishpaṭ*) of language (see the examples cited by Bacher in "Die Anfänge," *ZDMG,* XLIX, 365), his rather awkward Hebrew style, combined with his avowed aversion to imitation of Arabic patterns, still militated against terminological clarity.

49. Ḥayyuj's *K. at-Tanqit* (Treatise on Punctuation) was ed. together with Abraham ibn Ezra's Hebrew trans. entitled *Sefer ha-Niqqud,* and his own English version, by J. W. Nutt in his *Two Treatises,* while the *K. an-Nutaf* (Book of Glosses) is known mainly in excerpts published by Kokovtsov in his *K'istorii,* II, 1–58, 191–204. See also Poznanski's comments thereon in his "New Material," *JQR,* XVI, 245 ff., esp. pp. 262 f., 266. On the three "mother" letters, see *supra,* n. 43. Ḥayyuj's practical-educational aim comes to the fore also in such rhetorical flourishes as "Know, and may God lead you in the right way," with which he opened his treatise on punctuation. To make his meaning perfectly clear, he avoided here and in his other works the stylistic adornments customary in the Arabic prose of the period. "My only desire has been," he declared, "to make my purpose clear, to express my thoughts in suitable words, which should bring out the full meaning of the author" (Nutt, p. 5).

50. See Halper's remark in his "Jewish Literature in Arabic" (Hebrew), *Hatekufah,* XXIV, 359. Ḥayyuj's influence on the following grammarians is evident already in the writings of Ibn Janaḥ, who not only started his career with a book on Ḥayyuj's work, but also quoted him more frequently than any other author. In Abu'l Walid's *K. al-Luma'* alone Ḥayyuj's name occurs ninety-four times, while his works are cited in ninety-five instances, not always in the same context as the name. See Wilensky's index to *Sefer ha-Riqmah,* II, 490, 492.

51. Ibn Janaḥ's *Opuscules,* pp. 1 ff.; his *K. al-Luma',* Intro., XVIII (XIX), XXIV (XXV), pp. 2 ff., 207, 261 (*Sefer ha-Riqmah,* I, 11 ff., II, 226 f., 277; Metzger's French trans., pp. 3 ff., 195, 232); and *supra,* nn. 11, 24–25. Needless to say, Ibn Janaḥ's explanations indirectly contributed greatly to the understanding of the Bible and significantly influenced the subsequent exegetical literature. See *supra,* Chap. XXIX, n. 77.

52. Most of the data now available for the philological work of Samuel ibn Nagrela are assembled in Kokovtsov's *K'istorii,* II, esp. pp. 205 ff., 235 f. (*see supra,* n. 27). Much can also be reconstructed from the remnants of Ibn Janaḥ's con-

troversial writings, included in the Derenbourgs' ed. of his *Opuscules.* Because the Saragossan proved ultimately victorious, modern scholarship failed to lavish all the care and concentrated attention the Nagid's philological work apparently deserves; if not for its own sake, then at least for that of the numerous older sources which it might have preserved for posterity. Perhaps the example of M. Margulies's successful search for residua of Samuel's *Hilkhata gibrata* (see *supra,* Chap. XXVII, n. 80) and his recovery thereby of many older sources deemed irretrievably lost, may stimulate some specialists to institute a similar inquiry in the world's libraries, private as well as public, for some additional residua of Samuel's twenty-two treatises which a connoisseur like Ibn Ezra called (in his intro. to *Mo'znayim,* fol. 2a), perhaps with an overdose of enthusiasm, "second to none in excellence." In fact, some of the theories espoused by the Nagid have successfully been revived by modern grammarians. For one example, his assumption that the remarkable forms *Yuqqaḥ* (Isa. 49:24) and *Yuttan* (Lev. 11:38) were passives of *qal,* rather than *hif'il,* found quite a few champions among modern Semitists. See David Qimḥi's quotation from the Nagid in his *Mikhlol,* reproduced in English by W. Chomsky, p. 89, with Chomsky's note thereon, p. 103 n. 146.

53. Ibn Parḥon's *Maḥberet he-'arukh,* fol. 54d; the fragment of Abraham the Babylonian's grammatical treatise, published by A. Neubauer in his "Abraham ha-Babli," *JA,* 6th ser., II, 195–216; that of Nathanael of Yemen's treatise on Arabic and Hebrew grammar in Kokovtsov's *K'istorii,* II, 173–89 (Arabic); H. Englander's detailed investigations of "Rashi's Views of the Weak ע״ע and פ״ו Roots," *HUCA,* VII, 399–437; his "Grammatical Elements and Terminology in Rashi's Biblical Commentaries," *ibid.,* XI, 367–89; XII–XIII, 505–21; his "Rabbenu Jacob ben Meir Tam as Grammarian," *ibid.,* XV, 485–95; J. Pereira-Mendoza's study of *Rashi as Philologist;* and M. Ginsburger's aforementioned analysis of the Reuchlin MS in Karlsruhe dated in 1337 in "L'Exegèse biblique des Juifs d'Allemagne au Moyen Age," *HUCA,* VII, 439–56. See also Hirschfeld's *Literary History,* pp. 53 f., 69 f.; and *supra,* n. 33.

54. Dunash ibn Tamim's *Commentary on Yeṣirah,* ed. by Grossberg, p. 18; or the fragment ed. by Vajda in "Le Commentaire kairouanais," *REJ,* CVII, 127 f.; and Menaḥem ben Solomon's *Eben boḥan* (The Touchstone; on Hebrew roots), ed. by L. Dukes in his collectanea entitled *Qobeṣ 'al yad.* See also W. Bacher's analysis of the latter work in "Der Prüfstein des Menachem b. Salomo," *Jubelschrift Graetz,* pp. 94–115.

55. See Ibn Chiquitilla's trans., ed. by J. W. Nutt, pp. 2 (Hebrew), 21 (English). Nutt, whose English version incidentally likewise lacks precision, indicated the additions of the Hebrew translator by square brackets. Poznanski, in his *Ibn Chiquitilla,* pp. 11 f., 71 ff., assumed that the Frenchman Isaac ben Solomon ha-Nasi had commissioned Moses to prepare the Ḥayyuj translations while Moses was visiting in the Provence, perhaps as an itinerant preacher. It appears more likely, however, that Isaac visited Spain and secured there these versions of Ḥayyuj's works. Otherwise it would be difficult to explain why, apparently fairly popular on the Iberian Peninsula, they seem to have remained almost unknown north of the Pyrenees. Joseph Qimḥi and the Tibbonides knew very little about Ibn Chiquitilla's translations and not much more about his Bible commentaries. By 1140 the former were so com-

pletely unknown in Italy that the Roman community induced Abraham ibn Ezra to translate anew these two treatises by Ḥayyuj, and to add to them also a version of the book on punctuation. It should be noted, however, that a thirteenth-century Hebrew-French-German glossary (cited by F. Delitzsch in his "Zur Geschichte der hebräischen Grammatik und Masoretik, I," *Literaturblatt des Orients,* V, 297) did quote an opinion of Ibn Chiquitilla taken from his grammatical work. Ibn Ezra's translation of the treatise on punctuation is likewise available in Nutt's edition, while that of the other two works had previously been published by L. Dukes in his *Grammatische Werke des R. Jehuda Chajjug aus Fez* (H. Ewald and his *Beiträge zur Geschichte der ältesten Auslegung und Spracherklärung des Alten Testamentes,* III). Nutt (pp. x f.) cites from another Bodleian MS an excerpt of still another translation prepared by one Isaac ha-Levi ben Eleazar, but this version seems to have consisted of but random passages included by the author in his own grammatical treatise, *Sefat Yeter* (Overbearing Speech), in which he also quoted other authorities.

56. Moses ibn Chiquitilla's *K. Fi at-tadhkir w'at-t'anit* (Book on Masculine and Feminine Genders) is lost and can be only partially reconstructed from subsequent quotations, particularly in the works of Ibn Ezra. See the fragments assembled by Poznanski in his *Ibn Chiquitilla,* pp. 118 ff., with the comments thereon, pp. 20 ff., 39 ff., 55 ff., 185 ff. Even David Qimḥi, who unlike his father knew Ibn Chiquitilla's translation of Ḥayyuj and occasionally quoted the former's notes thereon, was familiar with the views expressed in Moses' own work only through Ibn Ezra. As usual, however, Ibn Ezra often used Ibn Chiquitilla's findings without citing their author, a procedure so common that, in view of the paucity of extant records, we can never be sure that Ibn Chiquitilla was, indeed, their true originator. See David Qimḥi in W. Chomsky's English rendition, pp. 88, 102 n. 43, 115, 117, 119 f. nn. 181 and 186. We may merely surmise that an original mind like that of Ibn Chiquitilla, who was frequently so independent in his exegetical work (see *supra,* Chap. XXIX, n. 107), was fully capable of reaching new conclusions, particularly since he could utilize to good advantage the vast comparative materials available to him from Arabic philology. Poznanski has rightly stressed our author's good familiarity with the Arabic language and philological literature. As we shall see, Moses was one of the relatively few professing Jews in Spain who even wrote distinguished Arabic poetry. See *infra,* Chap. XXXII.

57. Ibn Ezra's *Sefer Mo'znayim,* ed. by Heidenheim, fol. 13b; Ibn Bal'am's grammatical treatises published by P. Kokovtsov (see *supra,* n. 26); Bacher's data thereon in his "Bemerkungen über die dem Jehuda Ibn Balaam zugeschriebene Schrift zur hebräischen Laut- und Accentlehre," *MGWJ,* XXXIV, 468–80, 497–504; and Ibn Yashush's fragment cited by the Derenbourgs in their ed. of Ibn Janaḥ's *Opuscules,* pp. xix f. n. 1. Needless to say that Ibn Bal'am did not necessarily agree with all of Ibn Chiquitilla's grammatical views. In his *Commentary* on Isa. 28:16, for example, he did not hesitate to attack Moses' interpretation as contrary to both grammar and context. See his *Gloses,* ed. by Derenbourg, pp. 81 f.

58. Ibn Gabirol's *'Anaq,* long a classic of Hebrew poetry as well as of the philological literature (see the long list of editions in I. Davidson's *Thesaurus,* I, 405 No. 8937), is available with a German translation and critical notes in E. Neu-

mark's Würzburg dissertation, entitled *Ibn Gabirol's 'Anak.* See in particular, semistichs 11 ff., 29, 159 ff. The meanings of Gabirol's anagrams are controversial. Their translation here follows a suggestion by D. Kaufmann, based upon Arabic usage. See the bibliographical references, *ibid.,* p. 11. Various other anagrams, very popular among the Spanish grammarians, are cited by David Qimḥi in his *Mikhlol.*

59. Ibn Ezra's introduction to his *Yesod diqduq* (with reference to Isa. 57:19), published by Bacher in the appendix to his comprehensive analysis of *Abraham ibn Esra als Grammatiker,* pp. 148 f., which work, although three quarters of a century old, has not yet been superseded. Bacher had at his disposal only manuscript transcripts by Pinsker. However, other manuscripts of the *Yesod* are now known. See, e.g., H. Hirschfeld, *Descriptive Catalogue of the Hebrew MSS. of the Montefiore Library,* p. 121 No. 404, and N. Allony, "An Unpublished Grammar of Ibn Ezra," *Sefarad,* XI, 91–99 (on the *Yesod diqduq;* based on Pinsker's copy and two additional MSS). Despite its generally elementary character, this work may well deserve publication. Similarly, Ibn Ezra's *Safah berurah* (Pure Language), ed. from a Munich MS by G. H. Lippmann, had to be supplemented by eight pages from the first edition by N. Ben-Menahem in his Hebrew essay "R. Abraham ibn Ezra's *Safah berurah,*" in *Sinai,* IV, No. 7, pp. 43–53. Ibn Ezra's penchant for naturalistic explanations of grammatical phenomena, although in part anticipated by Saadiah and others, was noted already by his early successors. Yedaiah Penini ha-Bedareshi (of Béziers, southern France), reminiscing a century and a half afterwards on the impact of Ibn Ezra's sojourn in his community, observed, "He [Ibn Ezra] also composed grammatical works, in which he explained many principles of grammar, especially the vowels and forms of letters by laws borrowed from the science of man." See his *Iggeret ha-hitnaṣelut* (Letter of Vindication), addressed to R. Solomon ibn Adret and published in the latter's *Responsa,* No. 419, fols. 53b ff., 57bc. See also *infra,* n. 65.

60. Ibn Ezra's *Ṣaḥot,* fol. 18a; his *Sefat Yeter* (Overbearing Speech), fol. 17a, No. 52; and his *Commentary* on Gen. 36:31; Rashi's *Commentary* on Ps. 139:17. In his defense of Saadiah he often sharply repudiated Dunash's view, using such descriptive nouns as "silliness" or "stupidity." At the very outset he declared, "The beginning of his [Dunash's] words is nonsense," because Dunash ventured to use the term *patar* in the meaning "interpret" or "explain" (*Sefat Yeter,* Introduction, fol. 1b). This rejection of a long accepted rabbinic term (see, e.g., I. Heinemann's analysis in his "On the Development of Technical Terms in Bible Exegesis" [Hebrew], *Leshonenu,* XVI, 20 ff.) is typical of Ibn Ezra's uncompromising purism. See also *supra,* Chap. XXIX, n. 59. From the same feeling for linguistic precision came also his great interest in grammatical terminology, upon the exactitude of which he laid constant stress. In fact, his first philological treatise, *Mo'znayim* is devoted mainly to the clarification of fifty-nine grammatical terms. See L. Prijs's comprehensive study of *Die grammatikalische Terminologie des Abraham ibn Esra.* One need but compare the utter terminological helplessness of Rashi and his disciples, which often forced them to use broad circumlocutions to express some fine but basically simple grammatical ideas, to note the significance of this quest for terminological precision.

61. See Joseph Qimḥi's introduction to his *Sefer ha-Galui* (Open Book), ed. by H. J. Matthews, p. 2. On Qimḥi's significant contribution to the understanding of

Hebrew vowels, see his *Sefer Zikkaron* (Book of Remembrance), ed. by W. Bacher, pp. 17 ff. (both these editions contain critical glosses by one of Jacob Tam's disciples, Benjamin); and S. Eppenstein's "Studien über Joseph Kimchi," *MGWJ*, Vols. XL–XLI. Only a short time before Ibn Ezra had devoted the concluding section of his *Yesod diqduq* to an analysis of the seven "kings" (on the term see Ben Asher's *Diqduqe ha-ṭe'amim*, pp. 11 f.), which, with his general penchant for astrological parallels, he compared with the sun, moon, and five planets—a comparison previously drawn by the author of *Yeṣirah* (IV.7) with the seven consonants subject to doubling by a *dagesh* (*BGDKPRT*). See Ibn Ezra's *Ṣaḥot*, fol. 2b, and other references furnished by Bacher in his *Abraham ibn Esra*, pp. 13, 57 ff.

62. Moses Qimḥi's *Mahalakh shebile ha-da'at* (The Course of the Road to Knowledge), first published in Mantua in 1478, was later republished with a Latin translation by Sebastian Münster and a commentary by Elijah Levita in Basel in 1531. David's main works, too, were frequently both reprinted and translated into other languages. Only his *'Eṭ sofer* (The Scribe's Pen), dealing with the technical problems of Masorah, was less popular and had to be edited from a Paris MS by A. Goldberg in 1864. Perhaps because such good analytical work about these two grammarians was done in the nineteenth century, they have been the subject of fewer investigations in recent years. Apart from W. Bacher's general review in *Die hebräische Sprachwissenschaft*, esp. pp. 76 ff., see in particular the older, but still very useful, analysis by J. Tauber, *Standpunkt und Leistung des R. David Kimchi als Grammatiker*, and W. Chomsky's recent introduction and notes in his English rendition of David Qimḥi's *Mikhlol*. Since both brothers lived at the turn from the twelfth to the thirteenth centuries, they mark the beginning of the later medieval era as much as the completion of the work initiated by Saadiah three centuries earlier. Their impact on the later period will have to be discussed, therefore, in a later volume.

63. S. Poznanski's ed. of *Eine hebräische Grammatik aus dem XIII Jahrhundert*, p. 6 (text). From stray references in this booklet, Poznanski argued that the author's name was David, and that he was personally acquainted with the Bohemian grammarian and student of liturgy, Abraham bar 'Azriel, who in 1234 completed his treatise, *'Arugat ha-bosem* (Bed of Spices; reference to Cant. 5:13; commentary on Piyyuṭim). However, because of his occasional references to Karaite views, he probably was a resident of a Balkan rather than of a Central European community, where Karaite teachings were hardly known. See Poznanski's introduction, pp. 6 f. The tenuous nature of this argument is obvious. See also E. E. Urbach's ed. of Abraham bar 'Azriel's *Sefer 'Arugat ha-bosem*. It should be noted that, reciprocally, Karaite scholars like Hadassi did not hesitate to learn from Rabbanite grammarians. Hadassi quotes Ḥayyuj and Ibn Janaḥ and uses particularly his own contemporary, Ibn Ezra, "whose grammatical textbook [Mo'znayim] he wholly appropriates." See his *Eshkol ha-kofer*, fols. 60c ff., 63c, 70b; and W. Bacher's analysis of "Jehuda Hadassi's Hermeneutik und Grammatik," *MGWJ*, XL, 14–32, 68–84, 109–26.

64. Ibn Ezra's *Commentary* on Cant. 8:11; and other sources cited by Bacher in *Abraham ibn Esra*, p. 33 n. 2; his *Commentary* on Gen. 11:1, etc. In the latter passage Ibn Ezra adduces the familiar proof for the antiquity of the Hebrew language from the Hebraic names of Adam, Eve, Cain, and others as explained in the Bible. In this connection he also tries to establish the chronology of the Tower of Babel,

in accordance with the computations of the *Seder 'olam,* "on which we shall rely." Although convinced that Hebrew, Arabic, and Aramaic were originally but one language, he nevertheless tries to prove the priority of the "holy language" by the frequent permutations of *he* and *tav,* also found in the two other languages. He explains this phenomenon by the similarity of the two letters in the Hebrew square characters. See his *Safah berurah,* fol. 23a. These opinions, emphatically restated by Ibn Ezra in many other connections (see Bacher's data in his *Abraham ibn Esra,* pp. 33 ff.), reflected deep-rooted convictions of most Jews of that time. Cf. Ibn Gabirol's and Halevi's views cited *supra,* nn. 28 and 58.

65. Ibn Ezra's *Ṣaḥot,* fol. 11b (going beyond rabbinic opinion in Sanh. 21b–22a); his *Commentary* on Gen. 25:3; and *supra,* n. 18. With his scientific bent he even tried to prove a connection between the anatomic origin of individual sounds and the shape of the corresponding letters in the square script. For example, the *lamed* sign was pointed upwards because the "l" sound can only be uttered by raising the tongue. The designation *lamed* was derived from "study of the highest wisdom, namely that pointing upwards to the cause of all things." He admitted, however, that "because of insufficient knowledge" he could not furnish similar explanations for other letters of the alphabet. See his *Ṣaḥot,* fol. 28ab. At times popular fancy attributed to Ibn Ezra clever, though absolutely fallacious, grammatical epigrams. For example, the distinguished sixteenth-century physician Abraham de Balmes quoted his alleged saying that inanimate objects could interchangeably be used in the masculine and feminine genders (*zokhrehu ve-noqvehu,* a pun on "remember and name it"), merely because Gen. 32:9 betrayed such an inconsistency. See N. Allony's Hebrew essay "Inanimate Objects Are Masculine or Feminine," *Leshonenu,* XVI, 29–33; and, with special reference to Spinoza, M. Wilensky's essay "La Source de la proposition . . . ," *REJ,* XCVIII, 66–71. The abysmal ignorance of the Jewish past of some outstanding grammarians is well illustrated by several passages culled by Bacher from the lexicographical work of Tanḥum Yerushalmi. This philosophically well-informed eastern scholar thought of Herod as of a Greek-pagan monarch, had a garbled recollection of Onias and his Temple, and believed that the various ancient Jewish coins found in different localities all dated from the preexilic period. See Bacher's *Aus dem Wörterbuche Tanchum Jeruschalmi's,* pp. 18 f.

The only comprehensive attempt to describe the historic evolution of the Hebrew language from ancient times to the present was made by M. B. Sznejder in his *Torat ha-lashon be-hitpatḥutah* (The Lore of the Hebrew Language in Its Historic Evolution). Apart from the usual difficulties of pioneering ventures, however, the author was confronted by an almost total lack of *Vorarbeiten* for most periods of Hebrew linguistic creativity. Even the historical grammar of the biblical language has not yet achieved the status of other biblical disciplines. Bedevilled by the endless controversies on the dating of crucial scriptural passages, modern scholars have progressed little beyond H. Bauer and P. Leander's *Historische Grammatik der hebräischen Sprache* which, published in 1922, revealed, apart from other serious shortcomings, the general weaknesses of excessive reliance on the Wellhausenian chronology of biblical letters. On the tannaitic language, on the other hand, there are only occasional asides in M. Z. Segal's systematic, rather than historical, analysis of *A Grammar of Mishnaic Hebrew* (or in the revised Hebrew ed., *Diqduq leshon ha-Mishnah*); and J. N. Epstein's *Mabo le-nusaḥ ha-Mishnah* (An Introduction to the Mishnah Text). See also the auspicious beginning made by Z. Har-Zahav in his *Diqduq ha-lashon ha-'ibrit* (Grammar of the Hebrew Language). Notwithstanding the enormous difficulties inherent in linguistic material transmitted orally over many generations and "processed" by various editors, persistent efforts of specialists over a period of years are likely to shed new and unexpected light on the gradually changing forms of the Hebrew language in the course of ages, as well as on their underlying historical trends.

66. Moses ibn Ezra's *K. al-Muḥadhara* (*Shirat Yisrael*) in Halper's trans., pp. 147 f.; Abraham ibn Ezra's *Commentary* on Eccles. 5:1. See also *supra,* nn. 14, 37; and *infra,* Chap. XXXI, n. 57. The inconsistency of the two Ibn Ezras was pointed out by J. Kanani in his interesting, though incomplete, Hebrew essay on "The Linguistic Influence of the Older *Payyeṭanim* on the Spanish Poets," *Leshonenu,* X, 173–82. This formal rejection of the *payyeṭanim* is put into bolder relief by the general reverence with which the same Spanish writers treated the former's contemporaries of the masoretic schools. See, e.g., the data assembled by Bacher in his *Abraham ibn Esra,* pp. 36 ff.

67. Al-Ḥarizi's *Taḥkemoni,* xxiv, ed. by Lagarde, pp. 108 ff.; ed. by Toporowski, pp. 223 ff. See esp. M. Zulay's succinct observations on "The Language of the Payyeṭanim" (Hebrew), *Melilah,* I, 69–80; and *infra,* Chap. XXXI, nn. 46, 57.

CHAPTER XXXI: WORSHIP: UNITY AMIDST DIVERSITY

1. The psalmist's exclamation, "Seven times a day do I praise Thee" (119:164), which underlay Abu 'Isa's decision, naturally did not escape the attention of the more orthodox members as well. But they explained it away by associating it with the seven benedictions of the Sabbath *'Amidah,* the four benedictions before and after *Shema'* superimposed upon the three biblical paragraphs constituting the *Shema'* itself, and many other liturgical heptads. Incidentally, seven-word benedictions had featured the ancient *'Amidah.* See L. Finkelstein's pertinent observations on "The Development of the Amidah," *JQR,* XVI, 11 ff.; and F. C. Grant's "Modern Study of the Jewish Liturgy," *ZAW,* LXV, 59–77, esp. pp. 63 f. The fullest enumeration of such ceremonial "sevens," combined with the stress on the cosmic importance of that number, is found with special reference to the structure of the *qerobah* (liturgical poem on the silent prayer of Sabbath or holiday) in the so-called *Sefer Qerobah,* apparently written by a thirteenth-century German student of liturgy from the school of Eleazar bar Yehudah (Roqeaḥ) of Worms. See the text, ed. by A. M. Habermann in *SRIHP,* III, 102 f. Ironically, most *qerobot* seem to have consisted of nine rather than seven poems. (On the etymology of *qerobah* and its frequent misspelling see *infra,* n. 55; and Chap. XXXII, n. 89.)

There is no way of ascertaining, however, to what extent such sectarian teachings as those propagated by Abu 'Isa influenced later Jewish liturgical speculations. See also, more generally, *supra,* Chaps. XXV, nn. 36, 38, 54; XXVI, nn. 10, 47; and *infra,* nn. 8, 66. To the studies listed there add N. Wieder, "The Qumran Sectaries and the Karaites," *JQR,* XLVII, 97–113, 269–92. At the same time it appears that these sectarian deviations, however sharp, were less pronounced than in antiquity when they had affected the very Pentateuchal passages used for liturgical purposes. An interesting example is offered by the differing readings and forms found in the Qumran phylacteries as against those detected among the more orthodox followers of Bar Kocheba which were in full consonance with the tannaitic regulations. See K. G. Kuhn's detailed analysis *Phylakterien aus Höhle 4 von Qumran,* contrasting them with those found at Murabba'at.

2. Amram's responsum cited by J. N. Epstein in his "Sur les 'chapitres' de Ben Baboi," *REJ,* LXXV, 184 (also in B. M. Lewin's *Otzar ha-gaonim,* I, Part 1, p. 70); Pirqoi ben Baboi's harangue as reconstructed by Ginzberg in his *Ginze Schechter,* II, 504 ff., 544 ff., 551; Naṭronai's responsum in *Sha'are ṣedeq,* fol. 63b No. 40; a Palestinian responsum in Ginzberg's *Geonica,* II, 52 f. See also other sources cited by A. I. Schechter in his *Studies in Jewish Liturgy,* pp. 22 ff. Schechter goes too far, however, in assuming in another context (*ibid.,* p. 70) that the well-known Aramaic prayer, *Yequm purqan* (May Salvation Be Vouchsafed), in the form preserved in *Seder Ḥibbur berakhot,* apparently compiled by the twelfth-century Italian homilist Menaḥem ben Solomon, was a Palestinian importation from Babylonia. Its democratic undertone, imploring the divine grace to descend on "the holy communities,

who are in the land of Israel, and in the land of Babylonia and in all the lands of *their dispersion,"* with the pointed omission of any reference to the princes of captivity, seems on the contrary an indication of its Palestinian origin. This was suggested by S. J. L. Rapoport in his supplementary Hebrew essay on "The Existence of R. Ḥefeṣ and the Story of His Books" in *Qebuṣat ḥakhamim* (Wissenschaftliche Aufsätze), ed. by W. Warnheim, p. 50. To be sure, its present wording is influenced by the Babylonian usage, especially with reference to the "judges in the gate," which essentially was a Babylonian institution. But the replacement of the single word *di-mata* (of the city) by *di-baba* (of the gate) is more easily explained than the substitution of "the teachers of the order" (*ḥaburata*) by princes of captivity, placed entirely out of their hierarchical seniority after the "heads of the academies" (*kalle;* a title conferred in Babylonia on third-ranking officials in Sura and Pumbedita). One need but note the formula in the Adler MS No. 4053 to realize how a real Babylonian text must have read. See C. (J. K.) Duschinsky, "The Yekum Purkan," *Poznanski Mem. Vol.,* p. 189. See also K. A. Frankel, "The Prayer *Yequm purqan* on the Sabbath" (Hebrew), *Ha-Kerem,* I, 18–24.

3. *Pirqe de-R. Eliezer,* XXVII end, XXXI, XXXV end, ed. by M. Higger in *Horeb,* X, 186 ff. (in Friedlander's trans., pp. 196, 228, 267); the *qerobahs* on the first three benedictions of the silent prayer during the afternoon services of the Day of Atonement (beginning *Etan hikkir,* continued in *Mo'ohab ve-yaḥid,* and *Er'elim be-shem;* see I. Davidson's *Oṣar ha-shirah,* I, 150 No. 3204, 338 No. 7453; III, 70 No. 37) and other services; *Teshubot ha-geonim,* ed. by Harkavy, pp. 132 f. No. 258 (also in Lewin's *Otzar ha-gaonim,* I, Part 1, p. 77). See also *supra,* Vol. II, p. 7. The English translations of the various *incipits* and other passages of the daily prayers are, as a rule, cited here from S. Singer's rendition of *The Authorized Daily Prayer Book.* The patriarchal origin of the first three benedictions may indeed be implied in Sirach's remark concerning *hodu,* as pointed out by W. (Zeeb) Jawitz in his *Meqor ha-berakhot* (Die Liturgie des Siddur and ihre Entwicklung), p. 18 n. 1. However, the genuineness of that entire passage, available only in the Hebrew text following the Greek Sirach 51:12 (see R. Smend's ed., pp. 60 last 3 lines [Hebrew], 93 lines 10–12 [German], and his commentary, pp. 502 f.) is somewhat dubious. Medieval legend ultimately supplied an historical sanction for all other benedictions and ascribed them to biblical heroes from Joseph to Solomon. See Zedekiah Anav degli Mansi, *Shibbole ha-leqeṭ ha-shalem* (Ears of Gleaning; on laws and rituals), ed. by S. Buber, pp. 17 f. See also M. Liber, "Sur les origines de la prière publique dans le judaïsme," *Trait d'Union,* V, 3–12; and the literature listed *supra,* Vol. II, p. 365, n. 41.

4. M. Soṭah VII.1; b. 32b–33a; *Teshubot ha-geonim,* ed. by Harkavy, No. 373 pp. 188 ff.; A. E. Cowley, *Samaritan Liturgy, passim;* S. L. Hurwitz's popular summary of *The Sefer Hakadish* (History of the Kadish); Z. Karl, *Ha-Qaddish* (The Qaddish: From the Creation of That Prayer Until It Received Its Present Form); M. Gaster, "Ein Targum der Amidah," *MGWJ,* XXXIX, 79–90 (with notes thereon by A. Epstein and C. Mendelsohn, *ibid.,* pp. 175–78, 303–5); H. Gollancz, "The Translation of a Targum of the Amidah," *Semitic Studies . . . Kohut,* pp. 186–97; *supra,* Vol. II, pp. 84 f., 145 f., 365 n. 41, 386 n. 24; and *infra,* n. 62. An ancient legend brought the prayer for mourners in connection with a weird story told about R. 'Aqiba's encounter with a hard-working ghost. Ginzberg is doubtless right in

denying this nexus (*Ginze Schechter,* I, 235), but the ancient origin of that prayer remains uncontested. Apart from contributing some curious arguments to the question of the command of Aramaic by the ministering angels, Sherira also mentioned in his responsum liturgical formulas recited at his academy either bilingually (Hebrew and Aramaic), or in Aramaic alone. The less official but undoubtedly popular poems designed to comfort mourners by showing that even the greatest of ancient men had to die, were likewise written in Aramaic. One such *Afṭara* was published with a German translation by M. Zulay in his *Zur Liturgie der babylonischen Juden,* pp. 19 f., 24 f., 37 f., 60 ff. In view of the antiquity of such poems (see Ketubot 8b), it seems likely that Jewish prototypes influenced similar compositions among medieval Christians and Muslims, samples of which are assembled in C. H. Becker's "Ubi sunt qui ante nos in mundo fuere," in his *Vom Werden und Wesen der islamischen Welt Islamstudien,* I, 501–19. Other "Aramaic Poems and Piyyuṭim" were published by J. L. Fishman (Maimon) in his Hebrew essay in *Sinai,* VIII, Nos. 88–91, pp. 30–36 (was to have included Zedekiah Anav's commentary on some such Aramaic *piyyuṭim* for the Festival of Weeks). Most such poems, including those by the Spaniard Isaac ben Yehudah ibn Gayyat and by R. Meir ben Isaac of Worms were but literary exercises in a language long unspoken. On Meir ben Isaac's well-known poem *Aqdamut millin* (Introduction to the Recitation of the Targum) and its influence on West European poetry, see *supra,* Chap. XXV, n. 48; and *infra,* Chap. XXXII, n. 75. See also the literature listed in I. Davidson's *Oṣar,* I, 332 No. 7314. This problem of vernacular prayers was to become the subject of heated controversy during the Reform movement of the nineteenth century, both parties being able to quote ample testimony from ancient and medieval sources.

5. Ginzberg, *Ginze Schechter,* II, 161 ff.; Saadiah's *Siddur,* p. 154, and the introduction thereto, p. 29; the numerous sources cited by C. Z. Taubes in his Hebrew compilation of *Lekutay* (*Liqqute; Collectanea* by R. Isaac ben Judah ibn Gayyat to the tractate Berakhot), pp. 31 ff.; and *infra,* nn. 53 ff. Ginzberg argues here convincingly against A. Büchler's theory (in "Le Mot *Ve-yitqales* dans le Kaddish," *REJ,* LIV, 194–203) that *Ve-yitqales* was an original Palestinian usage taken over by the academy of Sura but not by that of Pumbedita. The tone of the inquiry itself, as summarized here, suggests that those were individual rather than regional variations. See also S. Lieberman's detailed Hebrew analysis of the various shades of meaning of *"Qalles, Qillusin," Schocken Jub. Vol.,* pp. 75–81. It may be noted that, despite Hai's authority, the prevailing practice replaced the ambiguous word *Ve-yitqales,* by the simpler *Ve-yithalel.* Zedekiah Anav degli Mansi, an outstanding Italian student of Jewish liturgy, quoted an older statement of Yehudai Gaon running sharply counter to Hai's view and declared, "It is a simple custom among us not to say it [*Ve-yitqales*]." See his *Shibbole ha-leqeṭ,* ed. by Buber, p. 8; and other sources listed in Saadiah's *Siddur,* p. 36 n. 1. *Ve-yithalel* is, indeed, regularly used in most modern prayer books.

6. To be sure, the element of time saving is but tangentially mentioned in the Talmud in connection with the substitution for the evening *'Amidah* (see Berakhot 29a) and, with special reference to the prayer "Blessed Be the Lord for Evermore, Amen and Amen," also by the thirteenth-century Barcelona rabbi Solomon ibn

Adret. Yet this theory is far more plausible than the other explanations offered, such as (1) its being but a purely Babylonian variation from Palestinian custom (Rashi and Yehudah bar Barzillai); (2) its insertion out of consideration for the great distance and dangers of night travel for villagers attending synagogue services (Moses of Coucy and Asher ben Yeḥiel; this is clearly but another variant of the time-saving rationale); or (3) the unavoidable argument from (unrecorded) persecutions (Asher ben Saul of Narbonne and Abudarham). See the sources cited by Elbogen in *Der jüdische Gottesdienst,* p. 529 n. 8; and the commentaries on *Siddur Oṣar tefillot* (Treasury of Prayers of the Ashkenazic Rite), Vilna, 1928 ed., pp. 545 ff. See also Lewin's *Otzar ha-gaonim,* I, Part 1, pp. 7 f. The length to which the persecution theory sometimes went is illustrated by Asher ben Saul of Narbonne's *Sefer ha-Minhagot* briefly alluded to in David ben Joseph Abudarham's *Ḥibbur Perush ha-berakhot ve-ha-tefillot* (A Commentary on Benedictions, Prayers, and Weekly Lessons), better known as *Sefer Abudarham,* Warsaw, 1877 ed., p. 77a. The Gentile oppressors, we are told, outlawed specifically the evening prayer because, according to different rabbinic legends, this prayer had been first introduced by the patriarch Jacob who was the special protector of the Jews during the present, third exile (Abraham had protected them in Egypt, Isaac during the Babylonian Exile). In other words, this particular prohibition of evening services, recorded in no authoritative source, stemmed from some Gentile legislator's intensive study of the Aggadah!

7. Shabbat 118b; Berakhot 4b; Amram's *Seder,* XII, ed. by Frumkin, I, 168; ed. by D. Hedegard, I, 14 (Hebrew), 33 f. (English); Saadiah's *Siddur,* pp. 10 ff., 13 ff., 32 ff.; the sources cited by Taubes in his comments on Ibn Gayyat's *Lekutay,* pp. 14 f.; and L. J. Liebreich, "An Analysis of *U-ba le-Ṣiyyon* in the Liturgy," *HUCA,* XXI, 176–209. It is known that the ancient prayer beginning *Yehi kebod* (Let the Glory of the Lord) is but a combination of disjointed biblical verses, selected largely from the book of Psalms. The only unifying principle, next to the expression of pious sentiments, seems to be the occurrence in them all of the Ineffable Name. The inclusion by Saadiah (p. 33) of both Psalms 78:38 and 20:10 at the end of that prayer, as it also appears in our prayer books, may be indicative of a ritualistic design to encompass therein nineteen biblical "reminiscences." See Abraham ben Isaac's *Sefer ha-Eshkol,* ed. by S. Albeck, Vol. I, p. 11 n. 12 (pointing out that, while the author counts a total of 28 "reminiscences" corresponding to the 21 verses after *Barukh she-amar* [Blessed be He who said], the kabbalists figured both at 18); and Y. Zimmels's Hebrew studies "On the Margin of R. Saadiah's *Siddur*" in *Rav Saadya Gaon,* ed. by Fishman, p. 539. If so, this may bear some remote resemblance to the nineteen benedictions of the *'Amidah* current in Babylonia and perhaps reflect Babylonian practice. This assumption would further weaken Z. Karl's contention that Saadiah's formulation of the psalmodic selections (*pesuqe de-zimra*) stemmed from Palestinian usage. Certainly Karl's explanation (*Meḥqarim,* p. 45) that the omission of Psalms 146–47 in private, but not in public, services was owing to the psalmist's "Zionist" aspirations (Ps. 146:10, 147:2) and the ensuing fear of denunciation to Roman authorities, is decidedly far-fetched. Apart from the fact that a fragment of an Oriental MS of Saadiah's prayer book, now at Cambridge, includes Psalm 146, as does Amram's *Seder,* XIII (ed. by Frumkin, I, 168 ff.; ed. by Hedegard, I, 14 [Hebrew], 34 [English]) and most later prayer books, neither direct

evidence nor logic favors the assumption that it was more dangerous to recite "subversive" prayers in the privacy of Jewish homes than at public services in synagogues.

8. Qirqisani's *K. al-Anwar,* I.3, pp. 15 f. (English trans. in *HUCA,* VII, 332); VI.17, 1 (Vol. III, pp. 608 ff.); Salmon's *Commentary* on Psalms in the excerpt, ed. from a Firkovitch MS by A. Neubauer in "The Authorship and the Titles of the Psalms according to Early Jewish Authorities," *Studia biblica,* II, 18 ff.; Amram's *Seder,* Preface and Section IX, ed. by Frumkin, I, 49, 138 ff.; ed. by Hedegard, I, 2, 11 ff. (Hebrew), 4, 26 ff. (English). On the Karaite use of Psalms, in their opinion enjoined in Ezra 3:10, see Harkavy, *Zikhron,* VIII, 19 f., 158 No. 11; 'Anan's liturgical regulations in the excerpts published by Mann in his "'Anan's Liturgy," *Journal of Jewish Lore,* I, 349 ff.; and the text published by Ginzberg in his *Ginze Schechter,* II, 439 f. Neither the latter author, nor Qirqisani and Salmon, actually accused their Rabbanite opponents of prohibiting the recitation of psalms, but rather of their lowering the dignity of that biblical work in comparison with the obligatory silent prayer which evidently was a creation of postbiblical rabbis. True to their general attitude, the Karaites, on their part, considered the biblical psalmody the most essential part of their liturgy, while permitting individuals and communities to add freely any number of prayers.

The passage relating to David in the Rabbanite ritual, cited by Qirqisani, need not have been taken from any of the then known prayer books. This Karaite student may have heard it recited in some of the local synagogues in Babylonia or Persia, which even as a Karaite he could have attended. The texts cited by A. Scheiber in "The Rabbanite Prayer-Book Quoted by Qirqisani," *Goldziher Mem. Vol.,* I, Hebrew section, pp. 27–40 (also in *HUCA,* XXII, 307–20); and those published by Assaf in his "From the Order of Prayers in Palestine" (Hebrew), *Dinaburg Jub. Vol.,* pp. 116–31, merely attest the existence of such formulas in the Jewish liturgy of the period, but not that they were quoted by Qirqisani from a regular prayer book. The existence of such a work other than Saadiah's before 937, is yet to be proved. Even Amram's compilation probably long circulated as a responsum, rather than as a regular liturgical handbook. See *infra,* n. 67.

Curiously, even when incorporating some psalms in its liturgy, Rabbanite Jewry introduced them by a prayer revealing the difference between the two sects. While in 'Anan's prayer book (*Journal of Jewish Lore,* I, 333) the emphasis lay on the priests "that make mention of the Lord" (Isa. 62:6), the Rabbanite prayer books invariably stressed that "we [the people] will make mention of Thy name," in reference to Psalm 20:8. See L. J. Liebreich, "The *Pesuke de-zimra* Benedictions," *JQR,* XLI, 195–206; and "The Compilation of the Pesuke de-Zimra," *PAAJR,* XVIII, 255–67. See also J. M. Millás Vallicrosa, "La Tradición del salmo penitencial en la poesia hebráica postbíblica," *Miscellanea Biblica B. Ubach,* pp. 243–78 (includes Spanish translations of several *seliḥot*); and, more generally, L. I. Rabinowitz, "The Psalms in Jewish Liturgy," *Historia Judaica,* VI, 109–22.

9. Amram's *Seder,* LXV, ed. by Frumkin, I, 299 ff.; ed. by Hedegard, I, 53 ff. (Hebrew), 127 ff. (English); Saadiah's *Siddur,* pp. 24 f., 39; Maimonides' *M.T.* Seder tefillot (appendix to the Second Book of "Ahabah"), before the text of the *Qaddish;* Yehudai's, Moses', and Naṭronai's responsa in Lewin's *Otzar ha-gaonim,* I, Part 1, pp. 31, 76 f.; and, more generally, I. Elbogen's *Studien zur Geschichte des jüdischen*

Gottesdienstes, pp. 40 ff. Medieval legend, too, offered various alleged incidents as the reason for the adoption of one or another of these prayers of petition in congregational services—but another illustration of the popular bent for supplying fictitious origins to a puzzling phenomenon. See Karl's *Meḥqarim,* pp. 99 ff.

10. Amram's *Seder,* VIII, ed. by Frumkin, I, 109 f.; ed. by Hedegard, I, 10 f. (Hebrew), 24 f. (English); Ibn Gayyat's *Leckutay,* ed. by Taubes, pp. 19 f. It may also be noted that, despite the unceasing reiteration, the entire liturgical order was intended to replace sacrifices by prayers, the only service referring directly to such substitution and stressing prayers for the restoration of the sacrificial system is the so-called *Musaf* (Additional) service on Sabbaths, new moons, and holidays. The latter includes a special confession of Jewish sins which had led to the destruction of the sanctuary (*U-mipene ḥata'enu;* But On Account of Our Sins). See Elbogen, *Der jüdisches Gottesdienst,* pp. 134 f., 238, 248 f., 263 f. Whether or not this service was finally formulated by Rab (see j. Berakhot IV.6, 8c), it thus clearly betrays its origin after the destruction. See Z. Karl's reconstruction in his *Meḥqarim,* pp. 129 ff.

11. B.Q. 82a; Saadiah's *Siddur,* p. 361; his *Oeuvres,* IX, 162 (J. Müller points out that, though fully concurred in by Maimonides, this view is opposed by R. Jonah Gerondi on purely formalistic grounds); 'Anan's *Book of Commandments* in Harkavy's *Zikhron,* VIII, 38; and J. Mann's comments on " 'Anan's Liturgy," *Journal of Jewish Lore,* I, 330 ff. One may note in this connection the differences of geonic opinion concerning the right of the scholar immersed in study to disregard the required scriptural readings. Perhaps irked by the Karaite insistence on the latter, Palṭoi Gaon answered a pertinent inquiry in the affirmative by referring to a precedent set by R. Sheshet in the third century (Berakhot 8a). Mattathiah Gaon, however, apparently followed by the majority, decided that "deeply as one may yearn for study, one must not sin by failing to complete one's scriptural lessons." See Lewin's *Otzar ha-gaonim,* I, Part 1, pp. 18, 20. Nor does Samuel ibn Nagrela's protestation against the alleged Spanish neglect of the Aramaic Targum, and his denial that this was one of the instances when the law was relaxed "on account of foreign visitors, the pressure on the public, or poor attendance at the academy," ring quite true. See Lewin, *ibid.,* pp. 19 f.; and *supra,* Chap. XXIX, n. 38. On the gradual elimination of the priestly blessing from the daily services (still required in Saadiah's *Siddur,* pp. 39, 94 ff.) in all except Yemenite synagogues, see Elbogen, *Der jüdische Gottesdienst,* p. 523; and *supra,* Vol. II, p. 119. Although nowhere expressly recorded, the element of time saving must have played a certain role in the abandonment of this ancient and revered ritual, the more so as there was a growing popular belief, reflected in contemporary midrashim (e.g., *Pesiqta de-R. Kahana,* ed. by S. Buber, fol. 49a, also cited in Simḥah bar Samuel's *Maḥzor Vitry,* ed. by S. Hurwitz, p. 104), that the divine presence (*shekhinah*) rested between the priests' peculiarly outstretched fingers, directly bestowing its blessing on the assembled worshipers. See also I. Löw's brief remarks in "Die Finger in Literatur und Folklore des Juden," *Gedenkbuch . . . David Kaufmann,* pp. 68 f.

12. *Yosephon,* ed. by D. Günzburg, p. 22; Saadiah's Prayer, published by A. M. Habermann in his "Two Poems of R. Saadya Gaon" (Hebrew), *Tarbiz,* XIII, 54. On the pedagogic use of the sermon, see *supra,* Chap. XXVIII, n. 2.

13. Saadiah's *Beliefs and Opinions,* v.4, 6, pp. 177, 180 (Arabic), 89, 90 (Hebrew), 219, 224 (English); R. Ḥananel's comment on Berakhot 13a in Lewin's *Otzar ha-gaonim,* I, Part 3, p. 13; Baḥya's *Duties of the Heart,* VIII.3; ed. by Yahuda, pp. 308 ff.; in Ibn Tibbon's Hebrew trans., ed. by Zifroni, pp. 211 ff.; Maimonides' *M.T.* Tefillah IV.16; Palṭoi Gaon, cited together with subsequent modifications by Zedekiah Anav in his *Shibbole ha-leqeṭ,* p. 20 No. 20; and the conflicting opinions cited by Ginzberg in his *Ginze Schechter,* II, 100 f., 106 f. From early times (see Berakhot 13b) it became customary to dwell at some length on the pronunciation of the crucial word *eḥad* (one) in the profession of the unity of God. According to some geonim the accent was to be laid on the second and third letters; the time to be apportioned was roughly computed at 1:3:6 units. See Lewin, *Otzar ha-gaonim,* I, Part 2, p. 12. Amram felt the necessity, however, of warning his readers, "One may not prolong it more than is sufficient . . . to declare him [God] king in the heaven, and on the earth, and over the four quarters of the world." See his *Seder,* XXIII, ed. by Frumkin, I, 205 f.; ed. by Hedegard, pp. 25 (Hebrew), 60 (English). Saadiah, too, ruled that one ought to allow only sufficient time for turning one's head "toward heaven, earth, and the four quarters." See the text published by N. Wieder in his "Fourteen New Genizah-Fragments of Saadya's *Siddur*" in Rosenthal's *Saadya Studies,* p. 262. Clearly, the reference here is to the numerical value of the three letters: 1 stands for the unity of God, 8 for the earth and seven heavens, 4 for the four quarters. See also, more generally, H. G. Enelow's "Kawwana: the Struggle for Inwardness in Judaism" in his *Selected Works,* IV, 252–88.

14. Berakhot 13a, 15a, 31a; Amram's *Seder,* XXI, XXIII, ed. by Frumkin, I, 199 ff., 205 ff.; ed. by Hedegard, pp. 21, 25 (Hebrew), 55, 60 (English); Saadiah's *Siddur,* p. 17, and the editors' note thereon; Maimonides' responsum, ed. with a Hebrew trans. by I. Friedlaender in *JQR,* V, 12 ff. (*Resp.,* No. 36); and *supra,* Chap. XXVII, n. 137. Curiously, the very ceremony of prostration described by Maimonides in *M.T.* Tefillah V.13, differed not only among various countries but even between the two Babylonian academies. See *Teshubot ha-geonim,* ed. by Assaf, 1942, p. 89 No. 84, and the editor's n. 1. See also Lewin's *Otzar ha-gaonim,* I, Part 1, pp. 25 ff., 57; Rashi's *Siddur,* pp. 14 f. No. 17; and, more generally, J. Zimmels's "Zur aüsseren Haltung im Gottesdienste," *Nathan Stein Schrift,* pp. 140–54; and *supra,* Vols. I, 350 n. 28; II, 282. We must not believe, however, that the geonim were generally preoccupied with problems of decorum, as the proceedings were quite informal. Although since talmudic times (Berakhot 24b) there was some concern for quiet congregational prayers so that fellow members not be disturbed, Sar Shalom Gaon reported as a matter of course that there often were in the synagogue persons who, evidently because of their late arrival, recited prayers other than those then read by the congregation or its reader. Cf. his responsum in *Sha'are teshubah,* No. 334; and Lewin, *Otzar ha-gaonim,* I, Part 1, p. 57.

15. M. Abot II.18; Berakhot IV.3–4; j. fol. 5ab; b. 29b, 40b; Midrash Tehillim IV.6, ed. by Buber, p. 45; Joseph ibn Abitur's poem cited from an Oxford MS by M. Zulay in his Hebrew essay, "Within the Walls of the Research Institute for Hebrew Poetry," *Schocken Jub. Vol.,* p. 108. The rabbis' discouragement of the use of psalms for the concluding services (see *supra,* n. 9) must also have nurtured the

creative urge of those worshipers who wished to see the congregation linger in the synagogue after the *'Amidah.*

16. Berakhot 17a; j. R.H. I.3, 57a; 'A.Z. I.2, 39c; Saadiah's *Siddur,* pp. 221 f.; and Elbogen's *Der jüdische Gottesdienst,* pp. 80 ff. The fact that in many congregations the word *hamonam* (their multitude) was accompanied by a derogatory expectoration, did not enhance the prayer's popularity in Christian Europe after its denunciation by converted Jews, although the same gesture toward unbelievers is recorded also in the Syriac churches.

Private creativity continued to the modern era. The well-known poem *Lekhah dodi* (Come, My Friend, to Meet the Bride; i.e., the Sabbath), occupying a focal position in the Friday evening services, was composed by the sixteenth-century poet, Solomon Alqabeṣ, evidently first for his own self-edification. This and other instances of the influence of the Safed kabbalistic circle in Jewish liturgy will be discussed more fully in their early modern context.

17. See the old, though undatable, text published by S. Assaf in his "Old Prayers at the Tomb of the Prophet Samuel" (Hebrew), *Jerusalem* (quarterly), I, 71–73; with additional comments by M. Seidel and S. H. Kook, *ibid.,* pp. 135–38; II, 102; M. Zulay, "Prayers Recited at the Tomb of the Prophet Samuel" (Hebrew), *Yerushalayim* (annual), II–V, 42–53; B. M. Lewin, *Otzar ha-gaonim,* I, Part 1, pp. 35 f.; and Ginzberg, *Ginze Schechter,* II, 105, 183. Like their ancient predecessors, medieval Jews were often apprehensive of the basic antagonism to them of even good angels, whom they tried to placate by the recitation of certain magic formulas. A remarkable illustration of such antagonism is attributed to Judah the Patriarch by the medieval compiler of *Midrash Tehillim* (VIII.2, ed. by Buber, p. 73 f.). The apologetic import of "The Discussions of the Angels with God" is ingeniously explained in A. Marmorstein's Hebrew essay in *Melilah,* III–IV, 93–102.

18. Berakhot 16b f.; Fragment from the *Sefer Hekhalot* (Book of Sanctuaries), ed. by A. Jellinek in his *Bet ha-Midrasch,* III, 161 (see also p. xxxiii), or in the slightly improved text quoted from MS by A. M. Habermann in his *Be-Ron yaḥad* (When They Sang Together, with reference to Job 38:2; an Anthology of Old and New Liturgical Poems), p. 2; Ḥagigah 12b; Ginzberg's *Ginze Schechter,* II, 183 f., 186 f.; Amram's *Seder,* LVI, ed. by Frumkin, I, 277 f.; ed. by Hedegard, I, 47 f. (Hebrew), 113 ff. (English).

19. Saadiah's *Siddur,* pp. 20, 38, 121; *Teshubot ha-geonim,* ed. by Harkavy, p. 261 No. 529, with reference to B.B. 25b. The Talmud seems to have used these locations as a mere mnemotechnical expedient. See Rashi *ad loc.* See also Ginzberg's *Geonica,* II, 262; and, on the fairly universal custom of stepping back at the end of the *'Amidah,* Yoma 53b; Lewin's *Otzar ha-gaonim,* VI, 24 (Naḥshon and Hai); and Simḥah bar Samuel's *Maḥzor Vitry,* p. 18. Of course, in its essentials the *Qedushah* had been formulated in ancient times. We recall the rabbinic view that the various *Qedushot* had been introduced by the Men of the Great Synagogue (there are three different ones in the morning services alone, and in a broader sense they also include the blessings recited at the sanctification of the new moon, at betrothals, circumcisions, and the redemption of the first-born; see W. Jawitz's *Meqor ha-berakhot,* p. 44). The fact that no controversy on it is recorded in the

talmudic literature is an indication of that prayer's antiquity and universal acceptance, rather than of its late date. So is its similarity to the Christian *Sanctus,* first mentioned by Tertullian (*De oratione,* III, in *PL,* I, 1257 ff.). See W. O. E. Oesterley's data in *The Jewish Background of the Christian Liturgy,* pp. 68 ff.; and, especially, Eric Werner's remarks in "The Doxology in Synagogue and Church," in *HUCA,* XIX, 292 ff. However, the differences in formulation in the various early prayer books, and the continued divisions on this score among the communities of diverse rites, indicate that the formulas presently in use had undergone considerable change in the early Middle Ages. See also B. Italiener's recent analysis of "The Musaf-Kedushah," *HUCA,* XXVI, 413–24.

The general interrelations of Jewish and Christian liturgies have attracted considerable attention in recent years. Apart from the general reviews by Gavin, Dugmore, and others mentioned *supra,* Vol. II, p. 365 n. 41; and *infra,* n. 30, there appeared a host of monographic studies partially listed in F. Stummer's "Beziehungen der Liturgie zum israelitisch-jüdischen Kult und zum Alten Orient," *Archiv für Liturgiewissenschaft,* IV, 97–126; and K. Hruby's "Autour du plus ancien rituel juif," *Cahiers sioniens,* IX, 303–36 (with reference to Hedegard's edition of Amram's *Seder*). See also P. Fiebig's somewhat older studies, *Das Vaterunser: Ursprung, Sinn und Bedeutung des christlichen Hauptgebetes,* esp. pp. 28 ff.; his "Sinn der Beraka [Benediction]," *Monatsschrift für Gottesdienst,* XXXIV, 201 ff.; F. C. Grant's aforementioned "Modern Study of the Jewish Liturgy," *ZAW,* LXV, 59–77 (with special reference to some newer trends in the "liturgical" interpretation of the Gospels); and such semipopular essays, slanted toward contemporary conditions, as T. W. Currie, "The Prayer Book of Jews and Christians," *Religion in Life,* X, 558–69; and M. R. Bede, "The Blessings of the Jewish Prayer Book," *The Bridge,* II, 224–38. Many comparative data may also be found in such general surveys as H. W. Codrington's *Studies of the Syrian Liturgies;* and T. Klauser's "reflections on recent studies" on *The Western Liturgy and Its History,* English trans. by F. L. Cross.

20. Hai Gaon's resp. in *Teshubot ha-geonim,* Lyck ed., fol. 31 No. 99; Naṭronai in Amram's *Seder,* ed. by Frumkin, II, 344; Sheshna and other geonim in Lewin's *Otzar ha-gaonim,* VI, 62 ff.; and other sources cited by P. Bloch in "Die Mystiker der Gaonenzeit, und ihr Einfluss auf die Liturgie," *MGWJ,* XXXVII, 18–25, 69–74, 257–66, 305–11; and by Ginzberg in his *Ginze Schechter,* II, 120, 123. Complete mystic poems, imbued with the spirit of the *Hekhalot* literature, likewise made their appearance in the geonic age. See, e.g., those published by A. Altmann in his "Qedushah Hymns in the Earliest Hekhalot Literature" (Hebrew), *Melilah,* II, 1–24; and the supplication, partially extant in Cambridge, Oxford, and Sassoon MSS, mentioned by M. Zulay in his "Poetry Fragments from the Genizah in the Sassoon Collection" (Hebrew), *KS,* XXVII, 91, No. 219, 11. On the later age of the *Kol nidre* tune, see *infra,* nn. 86 and 93. The persistence of the tradition concerning Saadiah's approval of *Kol nidre* in both Spain and Yemen (see Assaf's introduction to Saadiah's *Siddur,* pp. 28, 31) makes it likely that he decided in its favor in a special responsum since lost. This may, indeed, be intimated in the formulas that Saadiah had "said" or "written" to this effect. Incidentally, he seems to have used the Hebrew version, *Kol nedarim,* rather than the Aramaic *Kol nidre.* See also Jacob ben Asher's discussion in *Ṭur,* O.Ḥ., 619; Karo's *Bet Yosef, ibid.;* and *supra,* Chap. XXVII, n. 143.

21. These internal struggles and the general prevalence of more or less rationalistic approaches in the Jewish liturgy were overlooked by A. J. Wensinck when, following the fashion of biblical folklorists, he wrote on "Animismus und Dämonenglaube im Untergrunde des jüdischen und islamischen rituellen Gebets," *Der Islam,* IV, 219–35. In fact, only in the Christian Middle Ages did such outright kabbalistic prayers as Samuel the Pious' *Shir ha-yiḥud* (Poem of Unity) become part and parcel of the official liturgy. See A. M. Habermann's ed. of a collection of *Shire ha-yiḥud ve-ha-kabod* (Poems of Unity and Adoration; includes old commentaries thereon). On the other hand, few if any Jewish mystics were concerned about the dichotomy between God's loftiness and His accessibility to prayer, such as disturbed some Muslim mystics. See A. Schimmel, "Some Aspects of Mystical Prayer in Islam," *Die Welt des Islams,* II, 112–25; and, more generally, *supra,* Chap. XXVII, nn. 12 ff.; and *infra,* Chap. XXXIII, n. 11.

22. Tertullian's *Apologogeticus,* xxx.4, in *PL,* I, 504 (*CSEL,* LXIX, 79); *Teshubot ha-geonim,* ed. by Assaf, 1942, pp. 88 f. See also Sherira's responsum in Lewin, *Otzar ha-gaonim,* I, Part 1, p. 58. The phenomenon of villagers congregating in some major district synagogue for High Holiday services became particularly common in the sparsely settled areas of Jewish settlement in medieval Europe. Sherira's objection (echoed by the Spaniard Ibn Gayyat and the Provençal Aaron ben Jacob ha-Kohen, author of the costumal *Oreḥot ḥayyim*) concerned only the reader's recitation of the prayers before the beginning of the services, but was not directed against his familiarizing the uninformed with the sequence and other crucial arrangements of the services (*hasdir*). This term did not lose its original meaning (recorded, for instance, in Megillah 17b) and hence did not necessarily imply complete recitation by the reader, which was often but the simplest form of showing the congregation how to recite its prayers. That is why there is no conflict between the geonic responsa cited in Lewin's *Otzar,* I, Part 1, p. 73; and Maimonides' aforementioned *Resp.,* pp. 34 ff. No. 36. See I. Friedlaender's remarks in "A New Responsum of Maimonides Concerning the Repetition of the Shemoneh Esreh," *JQR,* V, 1 ff.

23. See M. Yoma III.8; j. III.7, 40d; VIII.9, 45c; b. 36b, 87b; Ginzberg, *Ginze Schechter,* I, 198 f. Amram seems still to have included but the original eight sentences. See his *Seder,* ed. by Frumkin, II, 331 (enlarged greatly by copyists *ibid.,* pp. 332 ff., 340 ff.). But an Ashkenazic glossator of the Maimonidean Code already displayed a text of twenty-four sentences, covering the entire alphabet, with two doublets. See *M.T.* Seder Tefillot on *Viddui* with the variants in the Trivulzio MS (14th cent.), cited in J. Hamburger's *Shinnuye nusḥa'ot* (Abweichungen des gedruckten Textes der Jad Hachasaka von einer Handschrift), pp. 15 f.; S. Assaf's comments in the introduction to Saadiah's *Siddur,* p. 37; and the related Cambridge MS published and translated by R. Edelmann in his *Zur Frühgeschichte des Maḥzor,* pp. 7, 32 f., Hebrew section, pp. 11 f. Meantime Saadiah, omitting entirely the paragraph beginning *ashamnu,* proposed four sentences beginning *'al ḥet* and six beginning *'al ḥata'im* (connoting a confession of a "sin" or "sins," both used, however, in their generic sense). See his *Siddur,* pp. 259 f.; and Y. Zimmels's comments thereon in Fishman's *Rav Saadya Gaon,* pp. 555 f. Saadiah added thereto a *piyyuṭ* of his own (*Siddur,* p. 409), expanding the traditional theme. However, this liturgical piece seems not to have been widely recited, and it is extant today

only in a single incomplete fragment in Cambridge. As a result of subsequent accretions the present Ashkenazic ritual includes forty-five *'al ḥet* and nine *'al ḥata'im* sentences. See *Siddur Oṣar ha-tefillot,* pp. 1109 ff. See also Lewin's *Otzar ha-gaonim,* VI, Part 1, pp. 18 ff., 38 ff. (especially the quotation from Yehudah bar Barzillai's *Sefer ha-'Ittim* in No. 105; and Sherira's decision that every member be made to confess on the Day of Atonement in whatever language he understands well; *ibid.,* No. 99); and, more generally, G. Ormann's dissertation, *Das Sündenbekenntnis des Versöhnungstages;* and A. Marmorstein's analysis of the talmudic forms in "The Confession of Sins for the Day of Atonement," *Essays Hertz,* pp. 293–305. Examples of Karaite "confessions," generally shorter and largely consisting of biblical phrases, are found in I. Davidson's ed. of *Ginze Schechter,* III, 174 ff. See M. Zulay, *Zur Liturgie der babylonischen Juden,* p. 68.

24. Mann's edition of a fragment of *Sefer ha-Ma'asim* in *Tarbiz,* I, Part 3, p. 8; Naṭronai's responsum in Lewin's *Otzar ha-gaonim,* I, Part 1, p. 79 (although formally but an antiquarian explanation of tannaitic phraseology, this responsum has a contemporary sound); Amram's *Seder,* LVIII, ed. by Frumkin, I, 280 f.; ed. by Hedegard, I, 48 f. (Hebrew), 117 f. (English). The frequently divergent older sources are discussed in M. Higger's introduction and notes to his ed. of *Massekhet Soferim,* pp. 52, 264 n. 72, 267 n. 81; Lewin's *Otzar,* V, Part 2, pp. 27 f.; Mann's *Texts and Studies,* I, 122, 151 f. In his letter, addressed in 1006 to Kairuwan, Hai Gaon tried to entice his friend and former classmate, Nahum the reader, son of Joseph "the great reader," to return to Baghdad, for "the elders have met and he is now the chief [*muqaddam*] of all the readers in Babylonia." See also S. Spiegel's remarks in A. Diez Macho and his "Fragmentos de Piyyutim de Yannai en vocalización babilonica," *Sefarad,* XV, 316. At times a cantor could abuse the community's trust. If we accept S. M. Stern's reconstruction of two poems published by I. Davidson (in his *Ginze Schechter,* III, 220–23), we have here before us a biting description of the trial of a *ḥazzan* convicted of selling communally owned Scriptures to satisfy extortions by blackmailers. See Stern's note "On Understanding the 'Poem on the Cantor Selling Scripture'" (Hebrew), *Tarbiz,* XIX, 62–63. On the general development of the office of *ḥazzan,* especially in the later Middle Ages, see my *Jewish Community,* II, 100 ff.; III, 135 f.; and other passages listed in the index on p. 428. See also the more recent study by H. H. Harris, *Toledot ha-neginah ve-ha-ḥazzanut be-Yisrael* (Hebrew Liturgical Music); and *supra,* Vol. II, pp. 280 ff., 422 f.

25. Amram's *Seder,* beginning; Lewin's *Otzar ha-gaonim,* I, Part 1, pp. 139 ff.; Maimonides' *M.T.* Tefillah VII.9. Although not specifically stated, Maimonides' opposition is best explained as aimed less at uninformed individuals than at readers wishing to help congregants by anticipating the likely benedictions of the day. This is in line with Maimonides' censure of a custom prevailing "in most eastern countries" for the reader to recite at the beginning of the morning services the benediction over the "washing of hands," although his own hands had been washed long before. See his *Resp.,* p. 22 No. 25.

26. Yehudah al-Ḥarizi's *Taḥkemoni,* XXIV, ed. by Lagarde, p. 108; Lev. r. XXX.1. See also Buber's note on his ed. of the *Pesiqta de-R. Kahana,* fol. 179 n. 23; and S. Lieberman's Hebrew study of "Yannai's *Ḥazzanut*" in *Sinai,* II, Nos. 22–23, pp. 222 ff. On Romanos' *Kontakia,* see N. Kadri's Arabic essay on "The Betrayal of

Judas: a Poem by Romanos the Melodos," *Al-Machriq,* XLII, 413–33; S. Baud-Bowy's related study of "Sur un 'sacrifice d' Abraham' de Romanos et sur l'existence d'un théatre religieux à Byzance," *Byzantion,* XIII, 321–34 (denying such direct influence in opposition to M. Carpenter and others); and E. Mioni's biography of *Romano il Melode.* According to P. Lemerle, one of his pupils, Grosdidier de Maton, was preparing a complete edition and French translation of Romanos' extant works. See his brief communication on "Etudes d'histoire de Byzance," *Annales,* X, 545. See also, more generally, Krumbacher's *Geschichte der byzantinischen Literatur,* pp. 663 ff.; and P. Maas's analysis of "Das Kontakion," *BZ,* XIX, 285–306.

27. Maimonides' *Guide,* 1.59 (this passage is more fully quoted *infra,* n. 55); Samau'al ibn Yaḥya's *Ifḥam,* in the excerpt ed. and trans. by Schreiner in *MGWJ,* XLII, 217 ff. (see *infra,* n. 28); Samuel ibn Nagrela, cited *supra,* Chap. XXIX, n. 38; J. List, *Studien zur Homiletik Germanos* I, p. vii: M. Zulay's text of "An Ancient Poem and the *Prooemia* to *Ekhah Rabbati*" (Hebrew), *Tarbiz,* XVI, 190–95; Ginzberg, *Ginze Schechter,* I, 136 ff., 145 ff., 246 ff., 253 ff.; *Midrash Haggadol* on Gen., ed. by M. Margulies, pp. 17 f., etc. Even if one rejects Ginzberg's arguments in favor of Tobiah ben Eliezer's authorship of that fragment, one must admit the priority of Qalir's *qerobah,* on which see *infra,* n. 47. Similarly, the indebtedness of the later compiler of the introductions to Lam. r. to the author of the *qinah,* rather than the other way around, explains many of the difficulties pointed out by the former's editor, Solomon Buber. Especially the nineteen proems for which Buber was unable to find rabbinic sources or parallels (see "The Character of the Proems in the Midrash Ekhah Rabbati," *Festschrift Steinschneider,* Hebrew section, pp. 27–32) doubtless owed much to our poet or his colleagues. Even when the name of an ancient sage is quoted in the text, if not altogether fictitious, it probably refers only to the kernel of that homily, with much elaboration from later preachers or poets. See W. Bacher, *Die Proömien der alten jüdischen Homilie,* especially p. 107. See *supra,* Chap. XXVIII, nn. 12–13.

28. Yehudah bar Barzillai's *Sefer ha-'Ittim,* p. 252. Ever since S. Z. H. Halberstam, this passage has been associated with Justinian's prohibition of the Jewish *deuterosis.* In *Der jüdische Gottesdienst,* pp. 282 ff., however, I. Elbogen argued against this identification by pointing out that Yehudah's likely source, Samuel ibn Nagrela, had undoubtedly received this information from such a Babylonian author as Samuel ben Ḥofni, and that hence the persecution more probably referred to some unfriendly act by the government of Sassanian Persia. Since, moreover, the convert Samau'al ibn Yaḥya specifically connected some such liturgical changes with Persian persecutions, Elbogen suggested that that great change took place during the darkest period of Jewish life under Persian rule, namely some time between 450 and 589. See Samau'al's *Ifḥam* in Schreiner's trans. in *MGWJ,* XLII, 220; and, on Yehudah's sources, probably similar to those used by Ibn Daud and other chroniclers, A. Epstein's "Sources to the History of the Geonim and the Babylonian Academies," *Festschrift Harkavy,* Hebrew section, pp. 168 f. Elbogen could have been more specific and related the liturgical transformation to the period of Mar Zuṭra III, whose transfer from Babylonia to Tiberias may indeed have stimulated the new liturgical creativity thenceforth centered in northern Palestine. See *supra,* Vol. II, pp. 196, 399 nn. 14–15; and Chaps. XXVIII, n. 61; XXIX, n. 14. Although an ardent Muslim controversialist, Samau'al often reveals good familiarity with

Jewish life, in which he had grown up. He may have been particularly well informed about Hebrew liturgy if, as has often been suggested, he was the son of the well-known Hebrew poet Yehudah ibn 'Abbas (died about 1167 in Fez). See e.g., the Hebrew essays by S. Bernstein, "Unknown Poems by Yehudah ben R. Abbun ('Abbas)" in *Essays Hertz,* Hebrew section, pp. 15–33; and A. Scheiber, "An Unknown Sabbath-Song by Yehudah ben Samuel ibn 'Abbas (from the Kaufmann Genizah)," *Tarbiz,* XXIII, 127–29. However, Samau'al's report is too garbled to allow for any reliable conclusions. Moreover, Persian objections to monotheistic synagogue liturgy could hardly have been met by poems of essentially the same content. Only the Byzantine suppression of Oral Law, coupled with the toleration of Jewish divine services, makes understandable such a shift from Midrash to liturgical poetry. As Benjamin ben Samuel of Constantinople expressed it, "they replaced the Midrash and versified its subject matter." That is also why Palestine, and not Babylonia, became the center of the new liturgy, whereas Babylonian leadership, as we shall see, bitterly resisted the new forms for centuries after the rise of Islam. See also *infra,* nn. 45 and 47.

29. While we have no documentation for such mutual influences in early medieval Christian countries, Alfasi, writing in eleventh-century Spain, taught that a cantor singing Arabic songs ought to be deposed. See his *Resp.,* No. 281. The number of Christian converts to Judaism seems at times to have been quite considerable. In Persia, especially, nothing prevented a Christian, orthodox or sectarian, from joining the Jewish faith. Such conversions may have been particularly numerous in periods of anti-Christian persecutions, and might in part explain the frequent Christian accusations of alleged Jewish instigation. More remarkably, even in the Byzantine Empire, where apostasy from Christianity had been sharply outlawed ever since 357 (see supra, Vol. II, pp. 149 f., 188 f.), at least two of Yannai's poems (in *Piyyuṭe Yannai,* ed. by M. Zulay, pp. 9 f. No. 4, 9; 121 No. 70, 9) seem to refer to a considerable number of proselytes. See Zulay's interpretation in his "Studies in Yannāi" (Hebrew), *SRIHP,* II, 268, as opposed to M. Kober's purely historical explanation in his *Zum Machsor Jannai,* p. 33. Zulay's suggestion, however, that only descendants of Ham, that is Egyptians, were counted here as proselytes, seems to be too literal. The two preceding passages relating to descendants of Japhet, extolling the beauty of their diction and calling them *mamliṣe dat* (paraphrasts of the law in choice language), probably likewise included professing Jews. Unless we assume that those poems were later interpolations reflecting only Palestinian conditions during the Persian occupation of 614–28, when indeed many Christians turned to Judaism as the faith favored by the invaders (see *supra,* Chap. XVI, n. 25), we must not completely gainsay the effectiveness of Jewish proselytism before Mohammed. See also *supra,* Chap. XXIV, n. 40.

30. See E. Peterson's analysis of "Jüdisches und christliches Morgengebet in Syrien," *Zeitschrift für katholische Theologie,* LVIII, 110–13. See also *supra,* n. 19; and Vol. II, pp. 84 f., 188 f., 365 n. 41, 400 f., to which add J. Daniélou, "Une Antique liturgie judéo-chrétienne," *Cahiers sioniens,* IV, 293–302. Needless to say, the differences between the Christian and the Jewish rituals were as significant as the similarities. It suffices to review the practices of the North African churches in the days of Tertullian, as reconstructed in E. Dekkers's *Tertullianus en de geschiedenis der Liturgie,* to realize how far the Church had already traveled

at that time in her deviations from the Palestinian prototypes. Of course, Christian liturgy may have been just as much indebted to sectarian as to orthodox Jewish prototypes. See, e.g., F. Baumgärtel, "Zur Liturgie in der 'Sektenrolle' vom Toten Meere," *ZAW*, LXV, 263–65; and J. A. Jungmann's succinct observations on "Altchristliche Gebetsordnung im Lichte des Regelbuches von 'En Fešcha," *Zeitschrift für katholische Theologie* LXXV, 215–19, with the reservations mentioned *supra,* n. 19. See also the extensive material accumulated in K. Kirchhoff's voluminous study, *Die Ostkirche betet: Hymnen aus den Tagzeiten der byzantinischen Kirche;* R. D. Richardson's "Eastern and Western Liturgies: the Primitive Basis of Their Later Differences," *HTR,* XLII, 125–48; and esp. A. Baumstark's manifold insights into *Liturgie comparée: Principes et méthodes pour l'étude des liturgies chrétiennes,* 3d ed., rev. by B. Botte.

31. For a time the existence of two different poems relating to the same benediction and written by the same author gave rise to doubts about his Palestinian origin. His two poems, it was argued, proved that he lived in the dispersion which observed double holidays. This debate was settled, however, when a third poem turned up; written by the same author for the same holiday service, it could not possibly refer to the observance of a third day. Even more striking is the survival of four different *qerobot* for the Ninth of Ab, written by Qalir. Of course, no one observed even two fast days in succession. See M. Zulay's observations in *SRIHP,* II, 221 n. 1. See also *infra,* nn. 34 and 47.

32. See the numerous editions of *Oḥilah* (ascribed by some scholars to Yose ben Yose), as listed in Davidson's *Oṣar,* I, 78 f. No. 1701; IV, 228; and Saadiah's *Siddur,* p. 188. In this *azharah* for the Festival of Weeks Saadiah, appropriately enough, extolled the Torah, the giving of which to Israel was celebrated on that day. He used the crucial words in the pertinent three verses of Psalms 19:8–10 as a refrain for this alphabetic poem of six four-verse strophes.

33. The use of the simple and multiple alphabetic acrostic dates back to the beginning of the *piyyuṭ,* and was found in some recently discovered poems by Yose ben Yose ha-Kohen. Its antecedents go back not only to the Psalms and other biblical writings, but also to such liturgical functions as those recorded in connection with the first-century *tanna'im* Eliezer ben Hyrcanus and Joshua ben Ḥananiah, who allegedly helped intone so-called *alphabetaria,* that is liturgical songs provided with alphabetic acrostics. See also R. Marcus's data on "Alphabetic Acrostics in the Hellenistic and Roman Periods," *JNES,* VI, 109–15; and A. Dihle's *Studien zur byzantinischen Metrik und Rhytmik.* In time the technique became more complicated and a variety of new modes came into general use, such as the alphabet in reverse order, exemplified in the well-known prayer of the Sabbath *Musaf 'Amidah,* beginning *Tikkanta shabbat* (Thou Didst Institute the Sabbath). Sometimes the first letter was followed by the last, the second by the penultimate letter (known in Hebrew as the *at bash*). There also existed other combinations. Before long the use of the acrostic became so characteristic of the new poetic creativity that a contemporary homilist spoke without much ado about "that *poyyeṭan* who turns out his alphabets." See Eccles. r. 1.13; and, on the spelling, *infra,* n. 35. At times *alphabeta* or, more briefly, *febeta* was used to designate the acrostic poem itself. On the use of crucial catchwords and other far more complicated ex-

pedients, see the numerous examples assembled by Zunz in *Die Ritus des synagogalen Gottesdienstes,* pp. 120 ff.; and *infra,* n. 39 and Chap. XXXII, n. 82. A fuller analysis of these and other technical problems would be greatly facilitated, if M. Zulay's "Plea for a 'Corpus of Geniza Piyyutim'" (*JJS,* I, 111–15; also in Hebrew in *Ha-Kinnus ha-'olami,* I, 261–66) were to be heeded. See *infra,* n. 41.

34. Judges 16:23–24; Isaiah 27:3–5; *Iliad,* II.87–88; IX.236–37. The origins of rhymed poetry are still shrouded in darkness. Long-term efforts to find its nucleus in the Bible have proved unsuccessful. Equally uncertain are the findings concerning the rabbinic letters, such as those quoted by H. Brody in his edition of Immanuel Frances' *Meteq sefatayim* (Hebräische Prosodie), p. 32 n. 10. Somewhat more to the point are K. G. Kuhn's observations of the rhymes in the *'Amidah* (see *supra,* Vol. II, p. 330 n. 5), but these occasional rhymes, too, may have been purely accidental. See also the numerous examples of "the Rhyming Ancients," cited in A. M. Clark's *Studies in Literary Modes,* pp. 142 ff. Yet it is quite possible that such recurrent accidents aroused one of the "messengers" to apply this technique consciously to some of his poems, so as to fortify them against both corruption and total oblivion. However, precisely because the rhymes and acrostics so greatly facilitated memorization, they postponed the day of reckoning when confining the new creations to writing would become an inescapable necessity. That is why so much of that initial evolution must remain in the realm of conjecture. See also M. Wallenstein's brief remarks in his *Some Unpublished Piyyuṭim from the Cairo Genizah,* pp. 7 f.

The above observations were written before the author heard a lecture delivered at the American Academy for Jewish Research by J. Schirmann on "Hebrew Liturgical Poetry and Christian Hymnology," subsequently published in *JQR,* XLIV, 123–61. Some of Schirmann's arguments along astoundingly similar lines have served to confirm his opinion that the Jewish poets of the talmudic and posttalmudic eras were instrumental in introducing the rhyme into Western poetry. Schirmann has not stopped to inquire, however, into the reasons why Jewish poets should have felt the need to invent this technique any more than their Christian or pagan neighbors. This phenomenon becomes understandable, however, in the light of the Jewish concentration on oral transmission. Certainly Christian liturgical authors did not have to resort to mnemotechnic expedients, when they themselves, or some of their assistants, could immediately write down their new poems. Their liturgical improvisations fared no less well than their homiletical outpourings, and, for instance, the twelve secretaries employed by Origen could with equal ease record his liturgical efforts along with his homiletical or exegetical works. Jews, as we recall, had no such assistance. See *supra,* Chap. XXVIII, n. 4. The number of books published by them was generally extremely small, and, even when unhampered by legal objections, ancient and early medieval Jewish poets had little opportunity to spread their works in written form among the masses. In the case of liturgy, we remember, opposition to written prayers was long and sustained. Hence, unlike their Greek or Syriac counterparts, the Jewish poets had to invent some new ways of preserving in the memory of men their ever growing and more complicated liturgical output. This urgent necessity thus became the mother of another significant invention. The story of the Hebrew rhyme and other techniques will be more fully discussed in the next chapter in connection with the various other aspects of the Hebrew *ars poetica.*

35. See the aforementioned fragment of Midrash *Leqaḥ ṭob* published by Ginzberg in his *Ginze Schechter,* I, 256 f., 281, 289, and, for the proof of its authorship, *ibid.,* pp. 246 f. The term *ḥizanah* is used, often with reference to Yannai's work, by Saadiah, Qirqisani, and the unknown author of an old book list. See Harkavy's *Zikhron,* V, 107 f.; Qirqisani's *K. al-Anwar,* I.2, 14; I.4, 11, ed. by Nemoy, I, 13, 35 (*HUCA,* VII, 329, 355); *supra,* Chap. XXVI, n. 79; and the text published by S. Poznanski in *JQR,* [o.s.] XV, 77 line 12. See also Davidson's *Maḥzor Yannai,* pp. xii f., xliii ff.

36. *Sha'are teshubah,* No. 178; M.Q. 25b; M. Zulay's "Contribution to the History of the Liturgical Poetry in Palestine" (Hebrew), *SRIHP,* V, 108 ff. See also Z. Jawitz's significant attempt to link the origins of the *piyyuṭ* with liturgical forms recorded in the Talmud in "The Earliest Liturgical Poems," *Festschrift David Hoffmann,* Hebrew section, pp. 69–82; his *Toledot,* IX, 169 ff.; and S. B. Freehof's demonstration of how private prayers of the ancient sages influenced the later supplications in "The Origin of the Taḥanun," *HUCA,* II, 339–50. Such alterations of ancient prayers, to suit the changing tastes of subsequent generations are also illustrated by A. Mirski in his essay cited *infra,* n. 52. It is noteworthy that these chants had more devotees among the priests than the levites, the chief songsters of the ancient sanctuary. Apparently the priests succeeded in preserving their identity and cohesiveness much better than any other group after the fall of Jerusalem. That they included some spurious claimants appears likely, though this must have happened far less frequently in the Holy Land than in other countries. Even centuries later Hai Gaon would hardly have addressed to the Palestinian priests a letter written in a vein as sarcastic as his alleged epistle to the priests of Ifriqiya, which was published by B. M. Lewin in *GK,* IV, 51–56, 111. See *supra,* Vol. I, 414 n. 30.

37. See Zulay's remarks in *SRIHP,* V, 112, 118 ff.; and his "New Poems of R. Ḥadutha" (Hebrew), *Tarbiz,* XXII, 28–42. The question of the identity of Hadutah with Ḥaduta is still unsolved. The fact that the acrostics in different poems have preserved the distinction between H and Ḥ at the beginning, and H and A at the end, and the other arguments adduced by Zulay in favor of their separation, while fairly strong, have not disspelled all doubts in such a startling coincidence. Each of these names is unique in the annals of Jewish letters. Almost all the Palestinian poets of the period bore long-accepted Hebrew or Aramaic names, for the most part of biblical origin. Among the score of names, including some dubious ones adduced by Zulay himself in his former essay, we find only those of Moses (two poets), Aaron, Joseph (two, including Yose), Joshua, Yeshu'a, Eleazar (two), Yehudah (three, including Yudan), Solomon, Samuel (two), Simon, Johanan, Mishael, Yannai, and Meborakh. To assume, therefore, that two poets bearing the strange names of Hadutah and Ḥaduta should have lived in Palestine in approximately the same period and written the same kind of poetry with no noticeable stylistic or rhythmic variations, rather overtaxes our credulity. However, the specific arguments advanced by J. N. Epstein and others for their identity are even less conclusive. One must also bear in mind that such remembrance of the ancient orders and readiness to resume the priestly services at the Temple was not limited to Palestine. We have the express geonic testimony that Ḥaninah, gaon of Sura and disciple of Yehudai Gaon the protagonist of Babylonian supremacy, was him-

self a priest belonging to a particular priestly family, who used to let his nails grow saying, "The Temple will soon be rebuilt, and they will require a priest qualified for *meliqah*" (the pinching off of a bird's head). See Lewin's *Otzar ha-gaonim,* V, Part 2, p. 30. See also S. Abramson's "Qerobot for the Bridegroom" (Hebrew), *Tarbiz,* XV, 50 ff.

38. See Lewin's *Otzar ha-gaonim,* VI, Part 1, p. 41; and Saadiah's *Siddur,* pp. 264 ff., giving the relatively most authentic texts of *Azkir geburot* and *Attah konanta* (on the numerous other editions see Davidson's *Oṣar,* I, 105 No. 2230, 399 No. 8815; IV, 233, 286). But Saadiah fails to mention Yose's third *'Abodah,* beginning *Asapper gedolot* (I Shall Narrate Great Things about the Maker of Great Things), of which only a few verses are now extant. See Davidson, I, 316 No. 6965; IV, 272. This poem alone is designated in one Oxford MS as intended for use during the afternoon services. See Elbogen's *Studien,* pp. 81, 118. Since Saadiah, Yose's great admirer, knew nothing of this poem, or of any poem to be recited in the afternoon, this annotation by a subsequent copyist suggests at the most that some medieval community had adopted that practice. Yose's *'Abodahs,* it may be noted, had to compete with several others for public attention. A geonic source mentions the titles of three others in use in contemporary synagogues; one of them thus far not otherwise identified. See Lewin's *Otzar,* VI, Part 1, p. 18 (Amram's *Seder,* ed. by Frumkin, II, 352). See also S. Widder, "A List of Piyyuṭim and Poems in the Genizah Collection of the David Kaufmann Library of the Hungarian Academy of Science," *Löw Mem. Vol.,* Hebrew section, pp. 39 No. 26, 69 No. 71, 113. It may also be noted, that Yose ben Yose made good use not only of the Mishnah's description of the services at the Temple, but also of a few telling passages in Sirach, whose work, as we recall, was still known in Palestine during the early Middle Ages. See the plausible arguments presented on this score by C. Roth in his "Ecclesiasticus in the Synagogue Service," *JBL,* LXXI, 171–78.

39. Schechter's *Saadyana,* p. 136; W. Bacher's trans. with comments thereon in his "Aus einer alten Poetik (Schule Saadja's)," *JQR,* [o.s.] XIV, 742 f.; M. Yoma III.8, etc. After Yose it was particularly Yannai who divided his poems by acrostics of the first twelve and the last ten letters. This method is so frequently used that Zulay considers it a typical characteristic of Yannai's *qedushta* (poem on *'Amidah* at which the *trishagion* is recited). See his introduction to *Piyyuṭe Yannai,* p. xiv. See also "The Qedushta of Pinhas for *'Asser te-'asser,*" published by A. Scheiber in *JQR,* XLII, 213–16; and, on the latter recitation, Simḥah bar Samuel's *Maḥzor Vitry,* pp. 445 f. As a parallel one might also cite the ten acrostics at the beginning and end of each verse in the Syriac poet 'Abd Isho ('Ebedjesu) bar Berikha of Sobha's *Paradaisa dh A Edhen* (Paradisus Eden), ed. by G. Cardahi, p. 16. See also F. V. Winnett's introduction to his English translation of the first fourteen homilies entitled *Paradise of Eden,* incidentally stressing that the latter's avowed purpose was "to display the resources and elegances and subtleties" of the Syriac tongue. On this and other technical expedients used by the medieval Hebrew poets, see *infra,* Chap. XXXII, nn. 77 ff.

40. The *Etten tehillah* is conveniently available in H. Brody and M. Wiener's anthology, *Mibḥar ha-shirah ha-'ibrit* (Anthology of Hebrew Poetry), 2d ed., pp. 24 f. See the medieval midrash entitled *Aggadeta de-Shimeon Kaipha* (Legend of

Simon Kaipha) in Jellinek's *Bet ha-Midrasch,* VI, 156 (also in Eisenstein's *Ozar Midrashim,* p. 559); and Zulay's "Studies," *SRIHP,* II, 231. On the other hand, J. Szövérffy, "The Legends of St. Peter in Medieval Latin Hymns," *Traditio,* X, 275–322, does not refer to Peter himself as an author of Hebrew hymns. See also *supra,* Vol. II, pp. 74 f., 361 n. 27.

41. Both these poems by Yose are reprinted in Habermann's *Be-Ron Yaḥad,* pp. 7 ff. Cyrillonas' poem, beginning as a formal *madrasha* but continuing as a simple *memra,* written in poetic prose, was first published by G. Bickell in "Die Gedichte des Cyrillonas nebst einigen anderen syrischen Ineditis," *ZDMG,* XXVII, 583 ff. (with minor corrections, *ibid.,* XXXV, 531 f.) and is also available in his German translation as well as that by P. S. Landersdorfer in the latter's *Ausgewählte Schriften der syrischen Dichter,* pp. 11 ff. The passage here quoted may be found in *ZDMG,* XXVII, 587; Landersdorfer, p. 15.

Zulay's publication in 1940 of Yose's *Erasheh* has deeply altered our outlook on the early *piyyuṭim.* While as late as 1931, Elbogen (in *Der jüdische Gottesdienst,* p. 307) repeated that Yose "had no knowledge of the acrostic [!] and made no use of rhymes," Zulay's discovery has pushed back the record of Hebrew rhymed poetry to the beginning of the *piyyuṭ.* Curiously this fact was long known, but discounted because of an overdose of criticism, from two quotations of Yose's rhymed passages in Ibn Janaḥ's *K. al-Uṣul,* ed. by Neubauer, pp. 436, 595 (*Sefer ha-Shorashim,* ed. by Bacher, pp. 305, 419). The latter quotation is indeed taken from *Erasheh,* and it stands to reason that the other passage (characteristically attached to the introductory prayer of the morning psalmody) was found by the great Spanish grammarian in another authentic poem of Yose, since lost. If J. Marcus's suggestion (without supporting evidence) that the *'Abodah,* published in his *Ginze shirah u-fiyyuṭ* (Liturgical and Secular Poetry of the Foremost Mediaeval Poets), I, 69 ff., was written by Yose should prove correct, we would have here an instance of more complicated and, hence, more advanced rhymes. See also Marcus's ed. of "A New Poem by Yose ben Yose" (Hebrew), *Horeb,* II, 201 ff. (far simpler in its technique); and *infra* Chap. XXXII. Of course, all the authors here mentioned made use of the acrostic.

The answer to many such queries may be given when the Research Institute for Hebrew Poetry in Jerusalem has completed the listing of its 4,000 photostats of MSS containing Hebrew poems from the world's libraries. The dream of many decades may come true, and all medieval poems may be listed not only by their *incipits,* for which Davidson's *Oṣar* still is an excellent guide, but also by their endings and rhymes. Since the beginnings of many medieval poems are lost, such a list alone would enable even a nonspecialist to identify many a fragment as belonging to a poem otherwise known only in part. See Zulay's report in *Schocken Jub. Vol.,* pp. 83 ff.; his essays cited *supra,* n. 33; and esp. I. Davidson's "Rhymes in Hebrew Poetry," *JQR,* XXX, 299–398. In this posthumous essay, edited and introduced by I. Elbogen, Davidson presented a lengthy, though incomplete, list of rhymes occurring in many verses of certain medieval and early modern poets.

42. Rapoport's Hebrew biography of *R. Eleazar ha-Qallir* in his series of *Toledot* (Biographies of Distinguished Rabbis), p. 218 n. 19 (referring to a statement by R. Gershom, the Light of the Exile, that Yannai had "composed *qerobot* for each order of the whole year"); and Zulay's ed. of *Piyyuṭe Yannai.* "Additional Poems

by Yannai" have been published by Zulay in his pertinent Hebrew essay in *Löw Mem. Vol.,* pp. 147–57 (listing also the intervening publications by Mann, Sonne, and S. Widder). See also Zulay's remarks in *Schocken Jub. Vol.,* pp. 83–124; Yannai's poems cited *infra,* n. 53; and M. Kober's earlier study, *Zum Machsor Jannai,* with S. Spiegel's comments "Zum Machsor Jannai," *MGWJ,* LXXIV, 94–104. To be sure, not all the poems definitely ascribed to Yannai by the various editors were necessarily his. Only a few contain the acrostic Yannai, whose Palestinian spelling with three *yods* strengthens its authenticity. Since our author may have been the first Hebrew poet to indicate in this way his proprietary rights, we need not be astonished by his sparing use of this novel device. Most other poems are attributed to him on the basis of the nine criteria developed by Zulay in his "Studies" in *SRIHP,* II, 234 ff. Of course, such criteria are rarely conclusive; especially the distinction between the poet's genuine creations and those of his disciples and imitators will often remain more or less arbitrary. A conscious imitation, for example, of one of Yannai's best known *qerobot,* beginning *One fiṭre raḥamatayim* (The First-Born to Fathers and Mothers), the seventh poem of which (*Az rob nissim;* Then Thou Didst Perform Numerous Miracles) has been recited by untold millions during the Passover celebration (see the entire text in *Piyyuṭe Yannai,* pp. 88 ff.), has a similar beginning (*On kol peṭer reḥem*) and generally follows Yannai's pattern very closely. See the text published by I. Davidson in his *Ginze Schechter,* pp. 24 ff. Were it not that the third poem here has the unmistakable acrostic Shemuel (Samuel), doubtless Samuel the Third of the tenth century, one could never have confidently denied Yannai's authorship on the basis of the few differences in style and method or the fact that the imitation reveals little of the original's anti-Byzantine animus. See also F. Bar's *Liturgische Dichtungen von Jannai und Samuel,* pp. 39 ff. Doubts would have lingered on, particularly, if Yannai's own work had for some reason been lost and the imitation alone had survived. One should also bear in mind that Samuel the Third was a prolific poet in his own right, and that no less than four hundred of his own poems have been identified in some 170 different MSS at the Research Institute in Jerusalem. See Zulay's data in *Schocken Jub. Vol.,* p. 100. Nevertheless Zulay's criteria have already proved extremely helpful in segregating the wheat from the chaff, and especially in reinforcing the genuiness of all those poems attributed to our poet by a more or less persistent tradition. See also *infra,* n. 77; and on more recent publications in this and related fields, H. Schirmann's current bibliographies of "Studies in Hebrew Poetry" (Hebrew), annually published in *KS.*

43. The halakhic content of Yannai's poetry has often attracted attention. Although not devoid of allusions to midrashic teachings (some poems are altogether aggadic in nature), the works of Yannai stand out in the entire history of the *piyyuṭ* by their didactic content with respect to ritualistic requirements. Upon closer examination they have actually served to elucidate certain stages in the post-talmudic legal evolution for which no other sources are extant. See in particular S. Lieberman's aforementioned Hebrew study of "Yannai's *Ḥazzanut*" in *Sinai,* II. On Hai ben David's detection in Yannai's poems of the source of two puzzling decisions by 'Anan, which he had been unable to trace back to any other rabbinic source, see Qirqisani's statement cited *supra,* Chap. XXVI, n. 79. Yannai's expertness in Jewish law underscores, therefore, his radical departure from tradition.

44. Justinian's *Novella* 146, 3, in *Corpus Juris Civilis,* III, ed. by R. Schoell and W. Kroll, p. 717; and in J. Parkes's English trans. in *The Conflict of the Church and the Synagogue,* p. 393 (here slightly altered). Justinian's missionary animus helps explain also the intimate interrelations between Yannai's poetry and the so-called Palestinian Targum. The latter seems to have grown through constant aggadic accretions to several times its original size. Since the government insisted on the reading of a translation, the Jewish leaders seem to have reasoned, they could with its aid communicate to the congregants the desired homiletical teachings by simply inserting into the existing Aramaic version many of those aggadic lessons whose independent exposition was now forbidden by law. In one case, Yannai's poem *Elohe 'olam* (God of the Universe) is the prototype for or a translation of a lengthy excursus in the Palestinian Targum of Gen. 35:9. See the two texts in *Piyyuṭe Yannai,* pp. 48 f. No. 21, 5; and Kahle's *Masoreten des Westens,* I, Hebrew section, pp. 24 f.; II, 12 ff.; and Zulay's comments thereon in his *Zur Liturgie der babylonischen Juden,* pp. 64 f. The connection between Yannai's liturgical poetry and Justinian's *Novella* has also been vigorously stressed by Y. M. Guttmann in his review of Zulay's edition of *Piyyuṭe Yannai* in *Ha-Soqer,* V, 127–31.

45. See Pirqoi's treatise in Ginzberg's *Ginze Schechter,* II, 551 f.; and B. M. Lewin's supplement thereto in *Tarbiz,* II, 397 f. Some such limited Persian interference with Jewish worship is confirmed by the account, otherwise equally confused, in Samau'al ibn Yaḥya's *Ifḥam* in Schreiner's edition and translation in *MGWJ,* XLII, 218 ff. See also *supra,* n. 28.

46. Samau'al's *Ifḥam* in Schreiner's excerpt in *MGWJ,* XLII, 219 f. See also Yehudah al-Ḥarizi's *Taḥkemoni,* XXIV, ed. by Lagarde, pp. 108 ff.; ed. by Toporowski, pp. 223 ff. The substitution of new prayers for the *'Amidah* was not as abrupt a departure from tradition as it might appear. Already in talmudic times occasions arose necessitating such substitution, particularly when the worshiper was in a great hurry. Mar Samuel devised a prayer, beginning *Habinenu* (Make Us Understand), which condensed the thirteen middle benedictions of the weekday prayer into a single blessing. See the slightly varying text given in j. Berakhot IV.3, 8a; and b. 29a; another tripartite text, cited in behalf of Yehudai by Ṣemaḥ Gaon as a very old tradition in Lewin's *Otzar ha-gaonim,* I, Part 1, p. 72; and E. Lewi's comments thereon in his *Yesodot ha-tefillah,* p. 142. There also existed other substitute prayers in ancient and medieval times, even after the opposition to all standardized prayers had long died down. See esp. Elbogen, *Der jüdische Gottesdienst,* pp. 585 f.; and Z. Karl, *Meḥqarim,* pp. 81 f. On the two loud recitations of the *'Amidah* which, in some Byzantine communities, continued down to the days of Maimonides, see *supra,* n. 14.

47. The *Yoṣerot,* apparently introduced with some hesitation into Jewish liturgy by Eleazar Qalir (see, e.g., J. Marcus's *Ginze shirah,* pp. 39 ff.), proliferated greatly soon after. They included, as special subdivisions, poems designated by such names as (1) *ofan,* with reference to the mystical "wheels and the celestial beasts" invoked by the early medieval congregations in connection with the *Qedushah;* and (2) *zulat,* with reference to the declaration "There is no God beside Thee" (*zulatekha*), which follows the recitation of *Shema'*. On these poems, and particularly the very

complicated problem of the *trishagion* and its use in the *Shema'* cycle, see Elbogen's *Der jüdische Gottesdienst,* pp. 61 ff.; Mann's comments on "Changes in the Divine Service of the Synagogue Due to Religious Persecutions," *HUCA,* IV, 261 ff.; and Karl's *Meḥqarim,* pp. 32 f. Ultimately, some poets even composed prayers for week days which, though clearly elective, must have appealed particularly to such an ascetic leisure class as the "Mourners for Zion." See M. Zulay, "*Yoṣerot* for Weekdays" (Hebrew), *Qobeṣ 'al yad,* XIII, Part 1, pp. 9–21; and A. Scheiber, "Everyday Qerobot from the Kaufmann Collection" (Hebrew), *Tarbiz,* XXII, 167–73.

On the basis of Pirqoi's report, R. Edelmann was quick to explain the differences between Yose's early poems intended merely to supplement the existing liturgy and the more complex *piyyuṭim* of Yannai and Qalir, which easily lent themselves for substitution of forbidden prayers. See his "Bestimmung, Heimat und Alter der synagogalen Poesie," *Oriens christianus,* 3d ser. VII, 16–31. Edelmann failed to explain, however, the equally pronounced difference between Yannai's concentration on *qerobot* to the *'Amidah* and the scriptural lessons and Qalir's incipient interest, as was postulated above, in *yoṣerot* connected with the recitation of the blessings before and after *Shema'*. Nor does he offer any reason why any Byzantine administrator should have prohibited the recitation of the latter while permitting Jewish services. In fact, the "Hear, O Israel: the *Lord* our *God,* the *Lord* is one" (Deut. 6:4) often was invoked by Christian theologians as a confirmation of the divine three-in-oneness. See *supra,* Chap. XXIV, n. 49. Both these difficulties are removed if we assume that Qalir was stimulated to offer some substitutes for the *Shema'* services on Sabbaths and holidays during the Persian occupation of Palestine, and that he possibly continued with this creativity after 628 as well. On other liturgical changes introduced in connection with the outlawry of *Shema',* see J. Mann's "Changes in the Divine Service of the Synagogue," *HUCA,* IV, 241–310, where, however, no consideration is given to the basic distinction between Byzantine and Persian persecutions, the latter also affecting Palestine in 614–28. See also the other monographs listed *supra,* Vol. II, p. 399 n. 14.

Regrettably, nothing is known about the life of Eleazar Qalir, by all counts the most prolific and best known *payyeṭan.* His very name—or rather that of his father, Qallir, Qillir, or Qilar—has been given a variety of explanations, although its identification with Cyrill, first suggested by J. Perles (in his "Jüdisch-byzantinische Beziehungen," *BZ,* II, 582 f.) has much to commend it. The fact that some poems are attributed in manuscripts to the son of Qilar, rather than Qalir, and even possess such an acrostic, has induced Zulay to suggest the existence of two poets separated by some two centuries. See his remarks in *SRIHP,* II, 221 f.; his review of J. Marcus's *Ginze shirah* in *KS,* X, 481 ff.; and the more recent comments in his "New Poems by R. Haduta" (Hebrew), *Tarbiz,* XXII, 28 f. After an endless debate initiated in the poet's still noteworthy biography written a century and a quarter ago by S. J. L. Rapoport, scholars have now agreed upon regarding him as a resident of Palestine during the seventh century. Much more fortunate than Yannai, he found permanently responsive audiences in later times, and a great many of his *piyyuṭim* have found their way into Jewish prayer books throughout the world. Yet quite a few new poems have come to light in recent years, especially from the Cairo Genizah. A complete critical edition of his works, in preparation for many years by S. Spiegel, would fill a major lacuna in the history of medieval Hebrew literature and liturgy. For the time being, see the sources listed already by Zunz for more than two hundred of Qalir's poems in his *Literaturgeschichte,* pp.

29 ff.; and such more recent publications as I. Elbogen's "Ḳalir Studies," *HUCA,* III, 215–24; and "Ḳalir Studien," *ibid.,* IV, 405–31; his "Kalirs Geschem-Komposition mit unbekannten Einlagen," *Kohut Mem. Vol.,* pp. 159–77; J. Marcus's "R. Eleazar berabbi Qalir and His New Poems" (Hebrew), *Horeb,* I, 21–31, 151–66; his "Eleazar Ha-Qallir's Poems for New Year's Day and the Day of Atonement" (Hebrew), *ibid.,* II, 6–16; a number of additional poems included in his edition of *Ginze shirah,* I (cf., however, Zulay's reservations in his aforementioned review of this work) and in R. Edelmann's *Zur Frühgeschichte des Maḥzor,* especially the first Cambridge fragment published by him which, he suggests, may be a remnant of a comprehensive *Maḥzor Qalir.* On Qalir's messianic poem, see *supra,* Chap. XXV, n. 14. We must bear in mind, however, that not all poems attributed to Qalir were really his. Especially poems written by his namesake Eleazar, son of Abbun, a poet otherwise little known, were often intermingled with his genuine creations. See S. Spiegel's analysis of "Eleazar berabbi Abbun in the Liturgical Poems of Haqilliri" (Hebrew), *SRIHP,* V, 267–91. On the much-debated Qalirian style, see M. Zulay's succinct characterization in his "R. Saadiah Gaon's Poetic School" (Hebrew), *Orlogin,* VI, 142 ff.

48. The change in Yannai's poem was noted by M. Kober in his *Zum Machsor Jannai,* pp. 17, 37. On the reference to the "pig" in Zion, see Kahle's *Masoreten des Westens,* I, Hebrew section, pp. 17 ff.; and *supra,* Vol. II, p. 152. Other fairly clear-cut allusions are listed by Edelmann in *Oriens christianus,* 3d ser. VII, 27 n. 4. See *Piyyuṭe Yannai,* p. 339 No. 132, 12; 382 No. 23. Some of these allusions are, of course, quite ambiguous. In his beautiful German translation of one of Qalir's poems, M. Sachs allegorized the "foe" as relating to sin, rather than to the imperial enemy. See *Die religiöse Poesie der Juden in Spanien,* pp. 206 ff. He probably would not have suggested this forced interpretation, however, had he dated Qalir's life in the tense period of the outgoing Byzantine regime over Palestine.

One wonders how, under these circumstances, Jews could continue praying for the welfare of the kingdoms under which they lived. Such prayers are very old; they date back to the days of Jeremiah, Cyrus, and the Elephantine soldiers. Even in antiquity they served Jewish apologists well, when these had to prove to a hostile environment that Diaspora Jews were patriotic citizens. See *supra,* Vol. I, pp. 130, 245, 353 n. 37, 404 n. 41. Christians, too, doubtless inherited from the synagogue such prayers as were reformulated already in the first century by Clement of Rome. See his *Epistola I ad Corinthios,* 61:1–2, ed. by F. X. Funk in *Die apostolischen Väter* (rev. ed. by K. Bihlmeyer), I, 68 (missing in *PG,* I, 325 ff.). See also Tertullian's *Apologeticum,* xxx.4 in *PL,* I (*CSEL,* LXIX, 79). Of interest also is Emperor Julian's epistle "To the Community of the Jews," asking "that everywhere during my reign you may have security of mind, and in the enjoyment of peace may offer more fervid prayers for my reign to the Most High God." See *Epistolae* 397C, ed. by Wright, No. 51, III, 178 ff.; and, on its authenticity, *supra,* Vol. II, p. 392 n. 41. For this reason we have no grounds for doubting that the prayer *Ha-Noten teshu'ah* (He Who Gives Salvation unto Kings), found in prayer books of various rites and essentially given in ancient texts (see A. L. Frumkin's comment on his edition of Amram's *Seder,* II, 78), reaches back to remote antiquity. And yet it does not seem likely that the Jews could go much further than pray for both international peace and the cessation of persecutions—the two alternating themes in the ancient Christian liturgy. They need not have mentioned specific hated rulers and their families and confer blessings upon them, any more than did their Christian compatriots. We know that in Constantinople, the very citadel of caesaropapism, the Church dared to delete from its rituals the names of emperors it considered heretical. Similarly, a Byzantine patriarch could admonish his coreligionists in Muslim lands to refrain from mentioning the caliphs in their prayers. See L. Biehl's documentation in *Das liturgische Gebet für Kaiser und Reich,* pp. 33, 38 f. Needless to say, even while contrasting, as they often did, the wicked reign of Edom, Edom-Persia, or Edom-Ishmael, with the downtrodden state of the Jewish people, the Hebrew liturgical poets had none of those political overtones (at least not for the period before the advent of the Messiah) which characterized much of Christian liturgy even before Constantine. See G. Tellenbach's "Römischer und christlicher Reichsgedanke in der Liturgie des frühen Mittelalters," *SB* Heidelberg, 1934–35, I, especially pp. 9 f. Nor must one underestimate the power of patriotic appeals which often overrode many an antagonistic group interest. Did not in recent generations the fervor of countless Russian Jews in praying for the welfare of their Czarist oppressors, including Nicholas I and II, deeply perplex outsiders?

49. This somewhat unwieldy poem which, written in simple and unadorned language, testifies to the author's deep emotional involvement in the revolutionary transformations of that age, was published by Ginzberg in his *Ginze Schechter,* I, 310 ff. While Ginzberg looked to the equally portentous period of the Crusades for an explanation of this apocalyptic clash between the titans of East and West, J. Marcus has shown that a poem beginning *Oto ha-yom asher yabo mashiaḥ* (On the Day of the Redeemer's Advent) is recorded as the last of four poems by Qalir, listed in an Adler MS (*Horeb,* I, 22 ff., 29 f.). His explanation of the contemporary background during the Arab invasion of Palestine is strengthened by the phrase relating to Israel's forcible alienation from its sanctuary, which was particularly poignant under Christian domination, when the Hadrianic prohibition for Jews to visit Jerusalem was often sharply, if not always effectively, enforced. See *supra,* Vol. II, pp. 107 f., 374 n. 23, 377 n. 38. Related to this poem is another piece by Qalir, beginning *'Arba malkhiot* (Four Kingdoms), published by Edelmann in his *Zur Frühgeschichte,* pp. 5 (Hebrew), 20 f. (German). Unfortunately, this fragment is cut off in the middle of the fifth verse, the acrostic indicating that it probably had twenty-two or more verses. With unmistakable reference to Daniel 8:22, the author reviewed the four successive empires which had oppressed the Jews. "While they took counsel," he exclaimed triumphantly, "how to eliminate them [the Jews] from among the peoples [*mi-goy*], they themselves disappeared from the earth [*mi-gay*], and Thou hast increased the people [of Israel]."

Otherwise, the contemporary allusions which can be detected in Qalir's often oblique poems seem to refer to the Byzantine, rather than Muslim, domination. Certainly, his complaint of governmental pressures (*ṭoraḥ*) in his poem *Ansikha malki* (I Shall Offer Libation to My King), usually recited during the *Musaf 'Amidah* of New Year's day, and other allusions in various poems have decidedly anti-Byzantine rather than anti-Muslim connotations, as suggested by Rapoport in his aforementioned *R. Eleazar ha-Qallir* included in his biographical series *Toledot,* pp. 201 f. n. 5. The derogatory epithet *'obede sekhiot* (worshipers of icons) likewise more properly referred to the Christian, than to the imageless Muslim ritual. Even if it were proved, on the other hand, that the poem published by A. Marmorstein in his "Ancienneté de la poésie synagogale," *REJ,* LXXIII, 83 f., was written by Qalir himself, rather than by one of his pupils, this might merely mean that an original composition of about 618 (it specifically mentions that the Temple had been destroyed for 550 years, p. 84 line 24) was revised by the poet, or one of his disciples some two decades later to reflect the new situation when the fate of the Jewish people had been "handed over to Edom and Ishmael" (p. 83, line 4). See Edelmann's comment in *Oriens christianus,* 3d ser. VII, 28 n. 1.

50. The first and the last strophes of Qalir's *Ṭal ten,* a rhymed poem of twenty-four verses written in an inverted alphabetic acrostic are here cited from Israel Zangwill's translation (with a minor variation in the last verse) in J. Davis and N. Adler's *Maḥzor* (Service of the Synagogue), p. 148. This poem is a part of a multipartite *qerobah* to the beginning of the second benediction. As a counterpart thereto Qalir composed also the aforementioned *qerobah* for the prayer for rain during the Feast of Tabernacles. See the text published by Elbogen in *Kohut Mem. Vol.,* pp. 162 ff. Here, too, petitions for a change in weather, such as "Depart in peace, O dew, and arrive in peace, O rain!" alternated with nationalistic prayers for the redemption of the people through the rain of God's grace.

51. Zulay's *Zur Liturgie der babylonischen Juden,* pp. 19 ff.; J. Marcus's ed. of Qalir's poem in *Horeb,* I, 165 f. Most of the poems, related to death and resurrection, published by G. Dawidowicz in his *Liturgische Dichtungen der Juden* (Nos. I–IV, VI, XII), were clearly intended for public recitation in the synagogue, although some also lent themselves to reading during burial services. One (No. III), written in an alphabetic acrostic and provided with a rhyme for every two verses, briefly summarized the laws governing mourning for the dead. It gives the impression of a brief versified manual for the use of mourners. Also intended for private rather than synagogue use were the various *qerobot* recited in connection with blessings after meals. Several such have been published in A. M. Habermann's "Poetic Blessings after Meals" (Hebrew), *SRIHP,* V, 43–105 (includes such blessings at weddings, circumcisions, and houses of mourners). On the other hand, a poem on the circumcision ceremony, such as was published by A. Scheiber (in his Hebrew essay on "Everyday Qerobot from the Kaufmann Collection," *Tarbiz,* XXII, 168), was apparently intended for recitation at the morning services of the synagogue to which the infant's family belonged. See also, more generally, L. Zunz's *Synagogale Poesie des Mittelalters,* 2d ed., pp. 171 ff.

52. Ever since 1892, when Harkavy published the fragment of Saadiah's *Egron* mentioning the names of Pinḥas and Joshua (*Zikhron,* V, 50 f.), scholars have endeavored to find out more about these writers and their works. The quest has thus far proved unrewarding. The few poems bearing the acrostic or a heading containing either of these rather common names may, or may not, have been written by our authors. See, e.g., Davidson's *Ginze Schechter,* III, 307 f.; M. Zulay's data in *Schocken Jub. Vol.,* pp. 84 ff. (the prince Joshua); Habermann, *Be-Ron yaḥad,* pp. 15 f. (a beautiful poem beginning *Arba'ah ra'u* [Four Have Seen] and describing the celestial visions of Moses, Isaiah, Ezekiel, and Daniel; Joshua's authorship is conjectured from the proximity of other poems attributed to him); Marcus's *Ginze shirah,* p. 79 (with the characteristic acrostic, Pinḥas, written with the *mater lectionis, yod*); Dawidowicz's *Liturgische Dichtungen,* No. IV, pp. 4 f. (Hebrew, lines 23–27 have the same acrostic), 19 ff. (German); A. Scheiber's ed. of Pinḥas' *Qedushta*

cited *supra,* n. 39; and especially Zulay's succinct analysis in *SRIHP,* V, 121 ff. (listing 38 known poems by Pinḥas ben Jacob ha-Kohen), 155 ff. (mentioning 9 poems by Joshua ha-Kohen); his "Palestine and Pilgrimages Thereto in R. Pinḥas' Liturgical Poems" (Hebrew), *Jerusalem* (quarterly), IV, 51–81; his "Original and Imitation in the Piyyuṭ" (Hebrew), *Sinai,* XIII, Nos. 147–48, pp. 32–52; and M. Wallenstein's felicitous reconstruction of "A Piyyuṭ by Samuel the Third" (Hebrew), *Melilah,* V, 149–62. Of interest also is "A Piyyut from the Cairo Genizah," analyzed by Wallenstein in the *Journal of the Manchester University,* XXV, 20–24; and *supra,* n. 42.

Of course, there also were later poets named Joshua, and such an acrostic, particularly on a *Yoṣer,* leaves the question of the date wide open. Among the several poets named Solomon are the eleventh-century Palestinian gaon, Solomon ben Yehudah, who combined halakhic learning with extensive poetic creativity, and Sulaiman al-Sanjari whose numerous extant poems were prepared for publication by Zulay. See the latter's observations in *Schocken Jub. Vol.,* pp. 92 ff., 100 f., 116 f. Both of these poets, however, really belong to the later stage of Hebrew poetry to be generally discussed in the next chapter. The fact that original poems of great renown were often used by later poets as a vehicle for the expression of similar sentiments in a closely related form is well illustrated (on the basis of three poems on the theme of *Anshe emunah* [or *Amanah,* Men of Faith] included in Saadiah's *Siddur,* pp. 290, 309, 338 f.) by A. Mirski in his Hebrew essays "On Parallel Poems," *Tarbiz,* XXI, 47–52; and "Parallel Creation in the Old Poetry," *Ha-Kinnus ha-'olami,* I, 267–73. At times even the genre of the poem was changed by the imitator. Two *qerobot* by Yannai were effectively transformed into *yoṣerot* by Solomon-Sulaiman or Yehudah ben Benjamin. See Zulay's analysis in *Löw Mem. Vol.,* pp. 148 f. On the other hand, we must bear in mind that a name found in an acrostic does not necessarily refer to the author. We shall see that such poets as Saadiah and Hai preferred to designate by the acrostic not their own name but that of the person, especially the reader, for whom the poem was written.

53. Saadiah's *Siddur,* p. 251. An interesting example of such Palestinian importation is given by M. Zulay in "Eine Ḥanukka-Qeroba von Pinchas ha-Kohen," *SRIHP,* I, 159 ff. This Palestinian poem, intended for use during the Ḥanukkah services, is extant in a Palestinian MS provided with a few Tiberian vowels and clearly referring to *'Amidah* benedictions in their Palestinian recension. At the same time a Babylonian MS, though supplying some Babylonian vocalization, adheres to that form of the benedictions and thus clearly betrays its indebtedness to the Palestinian prototype. The same holds largely true also for the Babylonian MS used as a basis for the edition of the *Liturgische Dichtungen* by Dawidowicz; and the "Fragmentos de Piyyutim de Yannay en vocalización babilonica," ed. and interpreted by A. Díez Macho and S. Spiegel in *Sefarad,* XV, 287–340. Although Dawidowicz's collection of poems, largely of funereal content, apparently served a special purpose in a Babylonian community (there is no full Palestinian counterpart to it), the poems themselves seem to have been composed for the most part by such Palestinians, as Pinḥas. Dawidowicz may be right that not only the fourth poem, provided with Pinḥas' characteristic acrostic, but also the first poem, not so identified, stemmed from that author, who had apparently lived in the vicinity of Tiberias. See Dawidowicz, pp. 7 ff., 17 ff. (German), 1 ff. (Hebrew). On the other hand, only a few of the extant early poems can definitely be traced back to Babylonian authors. The fact that one or another poem may relate to a weekly lesson according to the annual cycle current

in Babylonia need not be conclusive proof that it was originally composed there. We know that there were congregations of the Babylonian rite in both Palestine and Egypt, and that even those that followed the Palestinian ritual gradually shifted to annual recitation, at least in private worship, while the reader continued to recite the briefer triennial lessons in congregational services. See Lewin's *Otzar ha-gaonim,* I, Part 1, p. 22. The fact, moreover, that most of these poems were found in the Cairo Genizah, and that hence they were at one time brought to or copied in Egypt, adds to the improbability of their purely Babylonian provenance. Only when the pertinent manuscript is also distinguished by the Babylonian punctuation, as in the case of the three *qerobahs* on the weekly lessons beginning with Numbers 25:10, 30:2, and 33:1 published by Zulay in his *Zur Liturgie,* pp. 2 ff., 27 ff., 39 ff., can we claim for it likely Babylonian origin. That even such punctuation is inconclusive may be seen from the Yannai fragments, published and analyzed by A. Díez Macho and S. Spiegel in *Sefarad,* XV, 287 ff.

54. Eleazar of Worms in his unpublished commentary on the prayer book, cited by Joseph Solomon Delmedigo in his *Maṣref le-ḥokhmah* (Refinement of Wisdom, a defense of Kabbalah), Odessa, 1865 ed., pp. 42 f.; R. Naḥshon's, Amram's, and Ṣemaḥ's responsa quoted by J. N. Epstein in "Sur les 'Chapitres' de Ben Baboi," *REJ,* LXXV, 184; also in Lewin's *Otzar ha-gaonim,* I, Part 1, p. 70; Yehudah bar Barzillai's *Sefer ha-'Ittim,* p. 252. In his *Ginze Schechter,* II, 509 f., Ginzberg argues that the sharp geonic responsum could not have been written by Naḥshon, head of the pro-Palestinian academy of Sura which was relatively friendly to the *piyyuṭ,* and suggests either Nehemiah or Nathan of Pumbedita as the real author. Ginzberg's distinction between the two academies is too sharply drawn, however. On the one hand, he himself had published the violent attack on the *piyyuṭ* by Pirqoi ben Baboi, who constantly invoked the testimony of Yehudai Gaon of Sura. On the other hand, next to the "foreigner" Saadiah of that academy, it was the native Babylonian Hai of Pumbedita who composed much liturgical poetry himself. It seems that the attitude at either academy was not fully crystallized, but that considerable leeway was left to personal idiosyncrasies. See also A. A. Wolff's *'Ateret shalom ve-emet. Die Stimmen der ältesten glaubwürdigsten Rabbiner über die Pijutim.* Although a century old and reflective of the then raging controversy over the use of *piyyuṭim,* this vast array of opposing voices shows the intensity of the *piyyuṭ's* early upsurge and the irresistible pressure of its popular backing against the wishes of an influential leadership.

55. Maimonides' *Resp.,* Nos. 32, 360, 370; his *Guide,* I.59, in Friedländer's translation, p. 86; Abraham Maimuni's *Kifayat al-'abadin,* Sections XXIV–XXV, ed. by S. Eppenstein in *Festschrift Israel Lewy,* Hebrew section, p. 49; and his *Resp.,* pp. 132 f. No. 87. Despite D. Z. Baneth's weighty objection, we may assume that Abraham referred here to the beginnings of his official tenure as *nagid* of Egyptian Jewry. See also Maimonides' *Commentary* on M. Abot I.16, ed. by E. Baneth in *Hildesheimer Jub. Vol.,* Hebrew section, pp. 72 ff.; and *infra,* n. 81. Needless to say, so far as the masses were concerned the legal arguments carried greater weight than such philosophical compunctions. Maimonides himself had to admit that at times "the populace did not want to do without" the *piyyuṭim.* He and the later medieval rabbis, moreover, had to contend with what had in the meantime become a hallowed tradition. See the sources cited by Jacob ben Asher in *Ṭur,* O.Ḥ., LXVIII; and

Karo's comments thereon. Incidentally, Karo also records in this connection the medieval misreading *qerobeṣ,* in lieu of *qerobah,* and explains it by its folk etymology as but an abbreviation of Ps. 118:15.

56. Simḥah's *Maḥzor Vitry,* pp. 445 f., and Appendix, pp. 59 No. 101, 84. See also I. Jeiteles, "Die Bedeutung der Pijutim als halachische Quellen," *JJLG,* XIX, 293–306 (listing some forty pertinent halakhic quotations from the *piyyuṭ,* mainly by the Tosafists); S. Lieberman's essay mentioned *supra,* n. 43. Medieval folklore explained the disappearance of Yannai's poems from the accepted liturgy in its own anecdotal way. According to Ephraim of Bonn, the Lombardian communities refused to recite one of Yannai's poems, "because they say that he was jealous of his pupil, Eleazar [Qalir], placed a scorpion in the latter's shoe and killed him. May God forgive all those who spread this rumor if it is untrue." See Rapoport's additions to the biography of Qalir in his *Toledot,* pp. 177 f.

57. Moses ibn Ezra's *K. al-Muḥadharah,* VIII middle (*Shirat Yisrael,* pp. 147 f.; doubtless aimed at the older *payyeṭanim,* as well as at more recent poets); Abraham ibn Ezra's *Commentary* on Eccles. 5:1. In his *Safah berurah* (fol. 14ab), the latter objected especially to the *payyeṭanim*'s use of "difficult words having no biblical origin." To an enlightened Spanish student of Hebrew, exclusively relying on the few monuments of the ancient language accessible to him, the vocabulary of Yannai and Qalir appeared very abstruse, indeed. Many unusual words and forms found in the *piyyuṭim* are listed by Zunz in *Die synagogale Poesie,* pp. 372 ff.; and *Die Ritus,* pp. 234 ff. Another list was culled by I. Davidson from the poems published by him in *Ginze Schechter,* III, 325 ff. See also A. Stutschinsky's dissertation, *Elasar Kalir und die Neubildungen des Verbums in seinen Pijutim* (the appended two lists of Qalir's poems and verbs, still unpublished, can be consulted in typescript in the Zurich Zentralbibliothek). No systematic attempt, however, has thus far been made to analyze in detail the peculiarities of the payyeṭanic idiom and its position within the general evolution of the Hebrew language. An important preliminary step in that direction, namely the publication of a comprehensive dictionary of the *piyyuṭim,* was undertaken several years ago by Isaac Kanaani. But only a brief sample thereof, entitled *Millon qonqordanṣioni li-leshon ha-piyyuṭim* (A Concordance Dictionary to the Language of the Liturgical Poetry), has appeared in print.

Curiously, despite this fairly general contempt of the Spanish for the *piyyuṭ*'s linguistic abuses, the great Spanish poets themselves were deeply indebted to it. See Kanaani's study of "The Linguistic Influence of the Older *Payyeṭanim* on the Spanish Poets" (Hebrew), *Leshonenu,* X, 173–82 (incomplete). See also *supra,* Chap. XXX, nn. 66–67. Older MSS of the *piyyuṭim* can also be used to good advantage for textual criticism of the Bible. In "The Piyyuṭ, with Special Reference to the Textual Study of the Old Testament," *BJRL,* XXXIV, 469–76, M. Wallenstein has furnished several examples in which these liturgical poems differ from the masoretic text and, in part, agree with either the Dead Sea Scrolls or some ancient versions. To be sure, the ambitious parallel undertaking to cull all variants in the scriptural text from the extant medieval rabbinic sources, begun some half a century ago by V. Aptowitzer in *Das Schriftwort in der rabbinischen Literatur,* has never been completed by him, nor by anyone else. The comparatively small use to which Aptowitzer's findings have since been put by biblical scholars is likewise discouraging. In the case of medieval poetry, on the other hand, we must discount the effects of poetic license even in biblical quotations. If rabbinic authors often cited biblical verses from memory, this is doubly true of poets quoting biblical phrases during the cantorial improvisations. Yet, in view of the present availability, at the Research Institute in Jerusalem, of most pertinent manuscript materials from the Western libraries, a concerted effort to analyze the biblical texts quoted therein would contribute significantly to our knowledge of the recorded variants, as well as help elucidate certain phases in the development of the Masorah during the crucial Byzantine and early Muslim eras. Reciprocally, it would shed some new light on the meaning of many an obscure passage in that liturgical poetry.

58. Saadiah's *Siddur,* pp. 110 f., 251, 289; Maimonides' letter to Jonathan ben David ha-Kohen in his *Resp.,* pp. lviii ff.; and his statements mentioned *supra,* n. 55; and *infra,* n. 81; and Chap. XXXII, n. 94. See also his quotation from a poem in his well-known letter to Samuel ibn Tibbon in *Qobeṣ,* ed. by Lichtenberg, II, 27b; and W. Bacher's "Hebräische Verse von Maimuni," *MGWJ,* LIII, 581–88. We must bear in mind, however that only one of the three liturgical poems often ascribed to Maimonides has an acrostic *Moshe berabbi Maimon,* and that even here the spelling Maimon without the usual *vav* raises grave doubts as to its genuineness. See A. I. Schechter's *Lectures,* p. 30. See also H. Schirmann's "Maimonides and Hebrew Poetry" (Hebrew), *Mo'znayim,* III, 433–36 (also quoting additional bibliography). "The Commentary on the Petition for Rain by Eleazar ben Ha-Qalir Attributed to Rashi" was published from a Vatican MS by A. M. Habermann in a Hebrew essay in *Tarbiz,* VII, 186–216. Its provenance from the school of Rashi and especially Eliezer bar Nathan is strongly defended by A. Mirski in "The Commentary on the Geshem Poems Attributed to Rashi" (Hebrew), *KS,* XXIX, 262–69. Sometimes purely aesthetic considerations decided the issue. On one occasion Saadiah apologized for including, contrary to his reiterated intention, a lengthy poem for the *'Abodah* of the Day of Atonement by saying, "Were it not for its extraordinary beauty I should not have reproduced this *piyyuṭ*" (p. 289).

59. David ben Joseph Abudarham, *Sefer Abudarham,* Warsaw, 1877 ed., p. 59a (this passage is quoted with approval two centuries later by Joseph Karo in his *Commentary* on *Ṭur,* O.Ḥ., CXIII end); Saadiah's *Siddur,* pp. 10 f. Abudarham's counting of the words of the *'Amidah* evidently continued the practice of the ancient scribes who thus fortified the reliable transmission of biblical texts. See *supra,* Chap. XXIX, n. 4. The German kabbalists, however, turned such figures to mystic uses. See Jacob ben Asher's report, in his brother Yeḥiel's name, in *Ṭur, loc. cit.;* and, more generally, G. Scholem's *Major Trends in Jewish Mysticism,* pp. 99 ff. See also *infra,* Chap. XXXIII.

60. T. Shabbat XIII.4, p. 128; b. 115b; Zedekiah 'Anav's *Shibbole ha-leqeṭ,* p. 12 No. 12. In his *Commentary* on M. Menaḥot IV.1, Maimonides explained the absence of liturgical hand books by the complete familiarity of both public and "messengers" with all matters relating to prayers. This may be true with respect to the main prayers, which the congregations memorized through daily repetition, but certainly could not apply to the more extensive recitations on holidays. A special preliminary introduction on the part of the congregational leader seems to have been necessary to enlighten the uninformed members even about the texts of the morning blessings preceding the *Shema'*. This was the task of a rather nondescript functionary,

called in the talmudic sources the *pores 'al Shema'*, according to Z. Karl's interpretation of this term in his *Meḥqarim*, p. 41. Cf., however, the different meanings suggested by various medieval and modern scholars and analyzed by L. Finkelstein in "The Meaning of the Word *Paras* in the Expressions *Pores 'al Shema'*," *JQR*, XXXII, 389 ff.

61. Hai's responsum cited by Abraham ben David in his *Temim de'im*, cxix, fol. 13c; Ibn Gayyat's *Sha'are simḥah*, ed. by I. B. (D.) Bamberger, I, 29ab; also cited by Asher ben Yeḥiel in his *Halakhot* (Halakhic Commentary on the Talmud) on R.H. iv.14. In his *Milḥamot Adonai* (Book of the Wars of the Lord; a defense of Alfasi), on R.H. end, Naḥmanides merely denied the universal obligation to recite nine benedictions, although he concluded sharply that "anyone who doubts this negation, undermines the chain of tradition." See also *Sha'are teshubah*, No. 66; and A. I. Schechter's *Studies*, pp. 46 ff. Although not specifically referring to the "house of our teacher in Babylonia," Naḥmanides very likely had in mind Rab's old synagogue which had been rebuilt by R. Ashi according to Sherira's *Iggeret*, ed. by Lewin, p. 90. See A. Marx's "Untersuchungen zum Siddur des Gaon R. Amram," *JJLG*, V, 347 f. The other explanations of that geonic phrase here mentioned have little to commend them. See also *supra*, Chap. XXVII, n. 141; and *infra*, n. 84.

62. T. Berakhot vii.18, p. 16; j. ix.2, 13b; b. 60b; Menaḥot 43b. See the text cited by S. Schechter in "A Version of the Qaddish," *Gedenkbuch Kaufmann*, Hebrew section, p. 53; *supra*, n. 4; and Vols. I, pp. 278 ff., 414 n. 36; II, pp. 242, 272, 282, 286. On the highly probable connection between Paul's exclamation (Gal. 3:28) and the Jewish morning benediction, see D. Kaufmann's suggestive note, "Das Alter der drei Benedictionen von Israel, vom Freien und vom Mann," *MGWJ*, XXXVII, 14–18; and, on the latter's Near Eastern background, J. Darmesteter's *Une Prière judéo-persane* with J. M. Mitchell's comments thereon in "Une Prière judéo-persane," *The Academy*, XLII, 16–17, pointing out similar utterances attributed to Thales and Plato.

63. M. Abot ii.6; Amram's *Seder*, v, ed. by Frumkin, I, 85; ed. by Hedegard, I, 7 (Hebrew), 18 f. (English); Saadiah's *Siddur*, p. 89. See Simḥah bar Samuel's *Maḥzor Vitry*, p. 5. An informant of Abraham Maimonides found an old text of the Talmud which required the recitation of the three morning benedictions only if the worshiper encountered a Gentile, a slave, or a woman. According to this version, these three blessings were to be recited only when an occasion arose, as was the case with most other benedictions. This version allegedly was also reproduced in a MS of Amram's *Seder*. See Moses ben Maimon's *Qobeṣ teshubot*, I, fol. 52bc; and Abraham's *Resp.*, pp. 120 ff. No. 83. None of our texts of Talmud or *Seder*, however, mention this qualification.

64. Menaḥot 43b. Noting the remarkable initiative taken by the Spanish communities—incidentally, western Europe was to remain, as we shall see, the main center of liturgical codification in the subsequent centuries—Marx tried to explain it by the absence of well-rooted liturgical traditions in the younger western communities and the ensuing greater need of an authoritative prayer book (*JJLG*, V, 342). This is less likely, as Spain by that time had had a considerable number of Jewish settlements for at least half a millennium, which, despite Visigothic perse-

cutions, must have maintained a measure of continuity, particularly in their divine services. We have just seen how tenaciously Ibn Gayyat and some of his successors clung to such an old observance with respect to the *Musaf 'Amidah* of the New Year's day. From an interesting, though unfortunately undated, geonic responsum we learn that, some sixty-five years previously, Spanish immigrants had brought with them to Ifriqiya a special prayer for the Day of Atonement. They were allowed to recite it undisturbed in the local synagogue for two generations before some rigid conformists endeavored to stop that practice. The unnamed gaon, probably head of the more tolerant academy of Sura, decided the controversy in favor of the Spaniards. See S. Assaf's ed. of *Teshubot ha-geonim,* 1942, pp. 47, 49 f. On the contrary, it was precisely the persistence of local customs which made so thoroughly bewildering the impact of the talmudic writings and their geonic interpretations when they first began to penetrate in written form the western provinces of the Caliphate. Under the guidance of talmudically trained rabbis, some of them students of the Eastern academies, the talmudic-geonic patterns before long displaced many, but not all, of the local rituals. In the liturgical domain, in particular, the older local customs often reasserted themselves by conscious or unconscious alterations of and interpolations in Eastern liturgical works. See also *supra,* n. 14.

The situation was again different in Khazaria, whose converted group required novel instruction in every phase of Judaism. In his communication to Ḥisdai, Khagan Joseph rightly reported that his ancestor had "brought Jewish sages from all places who explained to him the Torah and arranged [*sidderu*] for him the commandments." A similar emphasis on personnel, rather than literature, is reflected in Yehudah bar Barzillai's narrative in his *Sefer ha-'Ittim.* See both texts in P. Kokovtsov's *Evreisko-khazarskaya perepiska,* pp. 30, 128 (Hebrew), 97, 131 (Russian).

65. Naṭronai's responsum in Ginzberg, *Geonica,* II, 109 f., 115 ff.; and Lewin, *Otzar ha-gaonim,* I, Part 1, pp. 135 ff. Amram opens his prayer book with a slightly different recension of that responsum while still another version is given in Eliezer bar Joel ha-Levi's *Sefer Rabiah,* ed. by V. Aptowitzer, I, 140 f. Aptowitzer has briefly examined all three versions in his detailed comments on Ginzberg's *Geonica,* Vol. II, in *MGWJ,* LV, 638. See also Hedegard's remarks in his notes on Amram's *Seder,* pp. 5 f. The literary antecedents of Naṭronai's liturgical composition are still very obscure. A century before Naṭronai, Yehudai Gaon seems to refer to some recent works resembling prayer books (see Ginzberg's *Geonica,* I, 119 ff.). Kohen Zedek of Pumbedita (*ca.* 843) is said to have "ordered" a prayer in the Passover Haggadah (Ibn Gayyat's *Sha'are Simḥah,* ed. by Bamberger, II, 100b). This may have been done in the form of a responsum to an inquiry, as in the case of Naṭronai's and Amram's later compositions, and hence the difference between *sidder* (ordered) and *shadar* (sent) is not necessarily so serious as is assumed by Marx in *JJLG,* V, 343 f. However, too little is known about these early works to justify their classification as "prayer books" anticipating those by Amram and Saadiah.

66. See the fragments of 'Anan's *Book of Commandment* in Harkavy's *Zikhron,* VIII; Schechter's *Documents,* II; and Mann's essay in the *Journal of Jewish Lore,* I, 348 ff. See also *supra,* nn. 1, 35; and Chap. XXVI, nn. 10, 47. With his main emphasis on as close emulation of the Temple ritual in Jerusalem as possible, and the ensuing stress on recitation of pertinent lessons from Pentateuch and Psalms, 'Anan did not require many additional prayers. He merely had to substitute some benedic

tions for those current among the Rabbanites to have a fairly adequate ritual for his synagogue. That the new blessings betrayed the heresiarch's profound indebtedness to the language and spirit of the traditional Rabbanite prayers is no more surprising than his constant use of the talmudic idiom and technical terms for his legalistic arguments. Before long, however, the rising opposition among the Karaites themselves, led by Daniel al-Qumisi, to the treatment of the synagogue as a direct substitute for the ancient Temple (see *supra*, Chap. XXVI, n. 47), stimulated a new liturgical creativity among the later generations of these sectarians, and ultimately it resulted in the emergence of regular Karaite prayer books. By that time, however, Rabbanite liturgy had been so fully developed, and its main features, both legal and liturgical, so well summarized in handy manuals, that the Karaite authors, rather than setting the pace, clearly showed their indebtedness to these Rabbanite prototypes.

67. See Frumkin's and Hedegard's introductions to their editions; Elbogen, *Der jüdische Gottesdienst*, pp. 353 ff.; and especially Marx's "Untersuchungen" in *JJLG*, V; Ginzberg's observations in *Geonica*, I, 123 ff.; his analysis of "Saadia's Siddur," *JQR*, XXXIII, 315–63 (with constant reference to Amram's earlier compilation; incomplete); J. N. Epstein's careful reexamination of the "Seder R. Amram, Its Redaction and Redactors" (Hebrew), *Ṣiyyunim* (J. N. Simḥoni Mem. Vol.), pp. 122–41; and Y. Zimmels's observations in Fishman's *Rav Saadya Gaon*, pp. 552 ff. The term *seder*, probably used already by Amram's correspondents, harked back to talmudic usage. See S. Krauss's "Zur Literature der Siddurim," *Soncino-Blätter*, II, 1 f. It seems never to have been used by Saadiah who gave his compilation the nontechnical Arabic title *K. Jawami' aṣ-ṣalawat w'at-tasabiḥ* (Collection of Prayers and Hymns) or, according to a later book list, the somewhat more descriptive designation *K. aṣ-Ṣalawat w'ash-sharaya'* (Book of Prayers and Laws). Even the later gaon and his correspondents, who in a responsum published by Ginzberg (*Ginze Schechter*, II, 52, 56) refer to *siddurin*, need not have had Amram's or Saadiah's works in mind. The inquiry speaks, in fact, of a *siddur miṣvot* (order of commandments), a more appropriate designation for a halakhic code or monograph than for a prayer book. Moreover, none of the manuscripts of Amram's Seder contains any discussion relating to the crux of the inquiry, namely, the separation of *ḥallah* from dough (see also Ginzberg's *Geonica*, I, 145 n. 2), while Saadiah discourses briefly on the matter (in his *Siddur*, pp. 101 f.) but has nothing to say on the subject of such separation being principally the obligation of female bakers. This was the burden of the argument which the questioners had "found" in the geonic "order of commandments." In short, there is no evidence that either *seder* or *siddur* had yet become technical liturgical terms in the geonic age.

68. In his essay in *Ṣiyyunim*, pp. 122 ff., J. N. Epstein has made a strong case for attributing the halakhic decisions in the prayer book to Ṣemaḥ, rather than to Amram himself. Only so may we understand why those decisions which happen to be cited in the subsequent literature, are as a rule quoted in Ṣemaḥ's name. Ginzberg's criticisms of this view (in *JQR*, XXXIII, 322 ff.) are on the whole well taken. It would, indeed, be astonishing if, acting at variance with prevalent custom, Amram had specifically mentioned his vice-chairman as co-author of the responsum. His extreme generosity in quoting no less than thirty times his predecessor Naṭronai, whom he had succeeded after a bitter fight (see Sherira's *Iggeret*,

ed. by Lewin, p. 115), is likewise suspect. Ginzberg's own hypothesis is, however, beset with equal difficulties. He assumes that Amram sent to Spain only a compilation of prayers annotated with a few brief quotations from the Babylonian Talmud. Afterward, Ṣemaḥ provided the copy left in the academy archives with extensive halakhic comments, adding some verbatim quotations from geonic (including Naṭronai's) responsa. This assumption presupposes, however, the circulation of two entirely independent versions in the East and the West, for which there is absolutely no evidence. Had Ṣemaḥ's more elaborate work been circulated at the seat of the academy, it certainly would not have escaped Saadiah's, Sherira's, and Hai's attention in the following century (see Epstein's quotations, p. 131; and *infra*, nn. 70, 73). In fact, Ṣemaḥ was quoted by Iberian scholars (the Spanish redactor of *Halakhot gedolot,* Samuel ibn Nagrela, and Isaac ibn Gayyat) much more frequently than he was by those in the East.

We may perhaps come closer to the resolution of these difficulties if we note that practically all such quotations of Ṣemaḥ's views, as well as the direct references in the book to Amram, stem from the second part of Amram's responsum dealing with the holiday rituals (in Frumkin's ed., Vol. II). It has long been noted that this section was subjected to much greater alteration and amplification than the first part dealing with weekday services. See Marx's observations in *JJLG,* V, 351 ff.; and his note on Krauss's article in *Soncino-Blätter,* II, 29. It is not impossible, therefore, that this section indeed owed its origin principally to Ṣemaḥ, rather than to Amram. The former seems to have combined the office of vice-chairman of the academy with that of the "judge of the court" of the exilarch (*dayyana de-baba*). Perhaps for this reason he was singled out for specific mention by Amram at the beginning of his reply (there is complete agreement on this score among all manuscripts), as he was in Amram's responsum to Barcelona, published in *Teshubot ha-geonim,* Lyck ed., No. 56, and confirmed by the Cambridge MS which is cited by J. Mann in "The Responsa of the Babylonian Geonim as a Source of Jewish History," *JQR,* XI, 446 n. 9. An intimation of such authorship may indeed have been given at the beginning of the second section, although it is missing from our late medieval manuscripts, which were more likely to omit here such a legally "irrelevant" personal reference than to insert one at the beginning of the whole work. Later authorities quoting some decisions from this section, therefore, rightly attributed them to Ṣemaḥ. One might even suggest that the Spanish inquiry had been addressed to Sura during the last years of Naṭronai's administration, as a follow-up of the earlier question concerning the one hundred benedictions. In his reply, therefore, Naṭronai's successor, Amram, started with a copy of the former's responsum and mentioned the cooperation of Ṣemaḥ, who was doubtless known to the Spanish correspondents as Naṭronai's intimate collaborator.

69. The morning selections from Numbers 28, M. Zebaḥim v, and the introduction to *Sifra;* Amram's *Seder,* VIII, ed. by Frumkin, I, 109; ed. by Hedegard, I, 10 (Hebrew), I, 24 f. (English); Ginzberg's *Geonica,* I, 124. The insertion, "in Spain," although attested by all manuscripts, evidently was but a local scribe's gratuitous addition or a replacement for Amram's reference to the usage "in Babylonia." The contrast between the relative faithfulness in the transmission of the halakhic comments, with the anarchical diversity of the liturgical texts, likewise militates against Ginzberg's aforementioned theory. Had Amram really

sent to Spain a complete set of liturgical texts fully spelled out, the local scribes would hardly have dared to alter them so completely and at such variance with one another. But if, as we assume, the geonic responsum contained chiefly halakhic observations and, for the most part, alluded to prayers only by some identifying watchwords, the copyists may indeed have felt free to amplify these hints from their own store of knowledge.

70. See Hai's responsum quoted in Ibn Gayyat's *Sha'are simḥah,* I, 65a. See also *Sha'are teshubah,* No. 67. First published by Judah Rosenberg, Saadiah's poem on the 613 commandments is reprinted in his *Siddur,* pp. 157 ff., 179 ff. In his introductory summary, Saadiah observed that such an enumeration of the commandments had become customary during the *Musaf* services of the Festival of Weeks, but that the existing texts were not only verbose and repetitious, but also failed to present the correct number. On closer examination he had come to the conclusion that this total included 200 positive and 277 negative commandments, in addition to 71 prohibitions with a death penalty and 65 precepts applying only to special occasions. Neither this general classification, nor Saadiah's detailed enumeration of individual commandments, ever enjoyed wide acceptance, and the subject continued to be debated for several more centuries. See *supra,* Vol. II, p. 421 n. 51; and Chap. XXVII, n. 105.

71. Saadiah's *Siddur,* p. 11; and *supra,* n. 59. The introduction's entire tenor clearly indicates that Saadiah wrote his work on his own initiative. Consequently, his texts and legal decisions did not have to conform to the practice of any particular congregation. His native Egypt itself hardly possessed a uniform ritual. Although generally under predominantly Palestinian influence, it also embraced communities of the Babylonian rite and undoubtedly cherished certain peculiar observances of its own. None of the customs mentioned in Saadiah's work, whether sharply rejected by him (pp. 21 f., 100) or tolerated with a nod (pp. 34 f., 40, 109 ff.), can be clearly documented as being of Egyptian provenance. Some are evidently of Palestinian origin; others grew up in Babylonia. Cf. also I. Elbogen's brief observations in his "Saadia's Siddur," *Saadia Anniv. Vol.,* pp. 256 f.; S. Bernstein's equally succinct analysis of "Saadia's Siddur" (Hebrew), *Bitzaron,* III, No. 34, pp. 845–56; and M. Zulay's essay cited *infra,* n. 77. The argument frequently adduced from certain similarities between Saadiah's and Maimonides' liturgical regulations, which are allegedly best explained by their common derivation from the Egyptian ritual (see A. I. Schechter's *Lectures,* pp. 25 f.), overlook (1) the literary influence of Saadiah's work on the sage of Fusṭaṭ; (2) the equally serious differences between them; and, most significantly, (3) the fact that the Maimonidean Code itself hardly reflected Egyptian realities. See also S. Assaf's remarks in his introduction to Saadiah's *Siddur,* pp. 24 ff.

72. In his comments on Saadiah's text (pp. 1 f.), S. Assaf suggested a reconstruction of the missing reasons. Of course, without support of documentary evidence, all such restorations must needs remain conjectural. Nor must one overlook the difference in tone and quality between the three reasons found in our manuscript, all of which have a more or less direct connection with the silent prayer, and some of the other reasons which, though attested from outside sources, have only a superficial and mechanical similarity with the "eighteen" benedictions.

73. Compare Amram's *Seder*, LXX ff., ed. by Frumkin, I, 341 ff.; ed. by Hedegard, I, 59 ff. (Hebrew), 139 ff. (English), with Saadiah's *Siddur*, pp. 102 ff. There is no way of telling whether the two prayers of petition, included in the only extant manuscript of the *Siddur* (pp. 47 ff.), were part and parcel of the gaon's original composition. Nor do we know when the two other similar compositions published by Habermann (in his "Two Poems by R. Saadiah Gaon," *Tarbiz*, XIII) were written, and whether they were intended for inclusion in the prayer book. A tone of great despondency permeating the entire second prayer (*Siddur*, pp. 64 ff.), and the fact that Saadiah himself translated it, and apparently it alone, into Arabic, might suggest that it was the product of the years of Saadiah's exile after his deposition by David ben Zakkai. See my remarks in *Saadia Anniv. Vol.*, pp. 69 f. Of equally uncertain date are the "Twelve *Seliḥot* [Penitential Prayers] Attributed to Saadiah" published by M. Zulay in his Hebrew essay in *Tarbiz*, XXIII, 112–19. Most other parts of the *Siddur*, on the other hand, seem to have been prepared some time before his appointment to the geonic office in 928. Since we know, however, that Saadiah was in the habit of constantly revising his earlier writings, the present work may indeed be a composite of liturgical pieces and legal observations produced at different times and subsequently inserted into the original text.

74. See the text recovered by N. Wieder and published in his "Fourteen New Genizah-Fragments of Saadya's *Siddur*" in Rosenthal's *Saadya Studies*, p. 254; and the manuscripts of Amram's *Seder*, quoted in the notes of Hedegard's edition, I, 19. See also Saadiah's similar objections to brief insertions in the *'Amidah* in his *Siddur*, pp. 21 f. The scribal notes in Amram's *Seder* indicate that the "new light" blessing was deleted from the earlier prayer book only out of deference for Saadiah's categorical prohibition. See Ginzberg's *Geonica*, I, 127 f. The fact that this formula is also absent from many medieval rituals, as pointed out by A. I. Schechter (in his *Studies*, pp. 55 ff.), merely proves that Saadiah's objections, directly or indirectly, also affected the authors of these later prayer books. Schechter himself noticed that the twelfth-century Italian homilist, Menaḥem ben Solomon, the probable author of the ritualistic *Seder ḥibbur berakhot*, was familiar with Saadiah's objection and tried to meet it by inserting the additional phrase "And we shall all soon be privileged to enjoy His light." There certainly is no reason for assuming that Amram failed to quote the original formula, since we have Sherira's testimony that "although R. Saadiah, blessed be his memory, had been head of the academy of Sura, they had not accepted his view, and never discontinued reciting 'And the new light' and are still reciting it today" (Lewin's *Otzar ha-gaonim*, I, Part 1, pp. 32 ff.). Evidently, Saadiah was here more Babylonian than the Babylonians themselves. See my remarks in *Saadia Anniv. Vol.*, pp. 47 n. 84, 69; and *supra*, Chaps. XXIII, n. 35; and XXVII, n. 144.

75. See Lewin's *Otzar ha-gaonim*, I, Part 1, p. 33; III, Part 2, pp. 7 f., 127 f.; VIII Part 1, pp. 26 f.; Saadiah's *Siddur*, p. 37. If it be true that Hai compiled his prayer book (occasionally mentioned by Zedekiah Anav) for the benefit of some foreign congregations (see Ginzberg's *Geonica*, I, 175), one might see here another instance of the impact of the new talmudic revolution on the long-established rituals in Byzantium or the Crimea. See *supra*, n. 64. Assaf (Intro. to Saadiah's *Siddur*, pp. 33 ff.) and Ginzberg (*JQR*, XXXIII, 334 ff.) have assembled considerable data on

the influence of Saadiah's prayer book on the subsequent writers. Although neither list claims completeness, it is evident that, unlike Amram's work, Saadiah's compilation was known in Western lands chiefly from quotations in later works. Such a great admirer of the gaon as Abraham ibn Ezra evidently knew Saadiah's prayers not from the *Siddur* but from some independent anthology. Isaac Alfasi, well-informed student of geonic letters, often betrayed complete unfamiliarity with the great gaon's liturgical work. Later jurists like R. Jacob Tam knew of the existence of Saadiah's *Siddur,* but extolled only the merits of Amram's compilation. Tam considered only the latter on a par with the tractate Soferim, the major midrashim, or Simon Qayyara's Code as a final authority concerning rituals not mentioned in the Talmud. "We observe many customs," he concluded, "because of their dicta." See his *Sefer ha-Yashar* (Responsa), ed. by F. Rosenthal, pp. 81 f.; and Assaf's comment in Saadiah's *Siddur,* Intro., p. 37.

76. Among these liturgical works, only that of Solomon ben Nathan of Segelmessa has been known to scholars for some time. It is extant in an Oxford manuscript written in 1202 and briefly mentioned by M. Steinschneider in his Hebrew "Letter to the Editor Senior Sachs" in *Kerem Chemed,* IX, 37 ff. Solomon was familiar with Saadiah's prayer book and quoted it expressly eight times. See Assaf's intro. to the latter, pp. 37 f. But, with respect to the earlier North African authorities, Assaf was able to adduce only one express and one oblique testimony by Ibn al-Jasus (*ibid.,* pp. 35 f.). In his numerous exchanges Ibn al-Jasus must occasionally have discussed Saadiah's work with his master, Nissim, but we find no direct reference to it in the latter's own published works. See also Assaf's ed. of a "Fragment from a Work by Ibn al-Jasus (or Gasum) on Liturgy" (Hebrew), *KS,* XXVIII, 101–9. As to the prayer books allegedly written by R. Nissim himself and other contemporary North Africans, see the dubious sources quoted by Krauss in *Soncino-Blätter,* II, 4 f., 26. For example, the prayer book, attributed to R. Ḥananel ever since Rapoport, turned out to be a mere misreading of an abbreviation in Mordecai bar Hillel's compendium (R. Ḥ. in lieu of R. T., that is, R. Tam). See S. Poznanski's remarks in his essay on "The Men of Kairuwan," *Festschrift Harkavy,* Hebrew section, p. 196.

77. In some respects Saadiah was more successful as a liturgical poet than as the compiler of a prayer book. Not only were many of his prayers recited in various communities, but he created a style of his own which found ready imitators, for example, in Samuel the Third. See esp. the illustrations assembled by M. Zulay in his "R. Saadiah Gaon's Poetic School" (Hebrew), *Orlogin,* VI, 142–52; VIII, 197–209; X, 17–29, although this essay is largely devoted to an analysis of Saadiah's own works. Since we know very little about most authors of these poems, we may assume that their association with Saadiah's "school" consisted largely in spiritual and technical emulation, rather than in physical membership of any kind. Such influence could extend over many generations of poets to Yehudah Halevi and beyond. See the interesting examples adduced by Zulay also in his Hebrew essay on "Source and Imitation in Liturgical Poetry," *Sinai,* XIII, Nos. 147–48, pp. 37 ff. As in his biblical work, Saadiah's liturgical creativity left its greatest imprint among Yemenite Jews, whose numerous liturgical poems of later years show unmistakable traces of the gaon's influence. See the publications listed by Y. Ratzaby in his "Yemenite Liturgical Poetry: a Bibliography" (Hebrew), *KS,* XXII, 247–61; XXVII, 378–81.

78. See J. Schor's and S. Albeck's introductions to their respective editions of Yehudah bar Barzillai's *Sefer ha-'Ittim,* and Abraham ben Isaac's *Sefer ha-Eshkol;* Albeck's Hebrew essay on the *Sefer ha-'Ittim,* picturesquely entitled "The Lawgivers of Judah" in *Festschrift Israel Lewy,* Hebrew section, pp. 104–31; and D. Simonsen's brief remarks "Ueber die Vorlage des *Sefer ha-Eshkol," Freidus Mem. Vol.,* pp. 291–92. On Ibn al-Jasus' (al-Gasum's) prayer book, see Maimonides' *Resp.,* p. 80 No. 81, which assumes its availability in twelfth-century Baghdad; and *supra,* n. 76.

79. In "Der Ritus im Mischne Thora," in Jakob Guttmann *et al., Moses ben Maimon,* I, 319–31, I. Elbogen correctly pointed out that despite its brevity the Maimonidean summary corresponds fully to neither the Spanish, nor the Babylonian, nor the Palestinian ritual, but that it took over certain parts of each. This conclusion has been borne out by more recent evidence. In fact, even Elbogen's assumption that the Fusṭaṭ jurist-philosopher closely followed in Saadiah's footsteps has proved to be an overstatement. Certainly, whatever Maimonides remembered of the customs and literature of his Spanish homeland, and whatever he had learned from such teachers as Ibn Megas and, indirectly, Alfasi, was not very propitious for his ready submission to the gaon's influence. See *supra,* n. 75.

80. Maimonides' amazing success and the ensuing growth of liturgical uniformity in the synagogues of the entire Arabic-speaking world has been pointed out by L. Zunz in *Die Ritus,* pp. 26 f. While the evidence uncovered during the last hundred years has shown that greater local variations had persisted after 1200 C.E. than were known to this founder of the historic investigation of Jewish liturgy, it has basically confirmed his well-considered judgment. Bartenora's observations are included in his oft-quoted *Epistle,* reprinted in A. Yaari's *Iggerot Ereṣ Yisrael,* pp. 115 f., 119; and in the English translation by E. N. Adler in *Jewish Travellers,* pp. 222 ff.

81. Maimonides' *M.T.* Qeri'at shema' I.7; Tefillah VII.9; his *Resp.,* pp. 28 f. Nos. 31–32; Abraham Maimuni's *Resp.,* pp. 62 ff. No. 62, 120 ff. No. 83 and the editor's notes thereon. See also, more generally, A. I. Schechter's *Lectures,* pp. 23 ff.; M. S. Geshuri's "Music and Poetry in Maimonides' Works and His Time" (Hebrew) in *Rabbenu Mosheh ben Maimon,* ed. by J. L. Fishman, pp. 288–302; *supra,* n. 58; and *infra,* Chap. XXXII, n. 94. Even Moses Maimuni was forced to allow considerable leeway for local and personal variants, in so far as they did not affect the regular sequence of basic prayers. He admitted, for instance, that "everything is according to custom" in regard to the daily recitation of the Song of the Red Sea (Exod. 15), or *Ha'azinu* (Give Ear; Deut. 32), or both *(M.T.* Tefillah VII.13). Nor did he seem to object to deviations in the generally accepted benedictions which did not run counter to his dogmatic preconceptions or the overt intentions of the Talmud. That is probably why he refrained from spelling out every inconsequential detail in the brief liturgy which he appended to the second book of his *Code.* He not only left out numerous "voluntary" prayers, but also failed to supply the full texts of the required recitations, except in so far as they were needed for closer identification or in order to avoid some dogmatic or legalistic pitfalls. For this reason, it appears, the widely held opinion that the present abridgment of the prayers cited in the Maimonidean *Code* is the work of careless or

paper-saving copyists has no justification in fact. Nor is it borne out by the manuscript tradition. All the manuscripts of the Maimonidean *Code,* some going back to autograph versions partially extant today, are in fair agreement as to the basic readings, although they vary in numerous minor details. Certainly copyists abbreviating a given text would hardly have hit on precisely the same abridged forms. See also *supra,* n. 69; and Chap. XXVII, nn. 114 ff.

Of considerable interest also is Maimonides' decision with respect to Karaite worshipers in Rabbanite synagogues or homes. While objecting to the inclusion of such sectarians in the required quorum of ten or three, "because they do not recognize that requirement," he did not object to their participation in Jewish services as such. See his *Resp.,* pp. 14 f. No. 14. Both the inquiry and the tone of the reply indicate that this was not a purely academic question in twelfth-century Egypt. See also *supra,* Chap. XXIX, n. 16.

82. See S. Buber's extensive introductions to his editions of Rashi's *Sefer ha-Orah* and (with revisions by J. Freimann) *Siddur;* S. Hurwitz's intro. to his ed. of Simḥah of Vitry's *Maḥzor Vitry;* and *supra,* Chap. XXVII, n. 84. On the other hand, Rashi's *Sefer ha-Pardes,* perhaps the relatively most authentic record of the master's views, has never been issued in a modern scholarly edition. That by H. L. Ehrenreich is merely a reprint of the first edition (Constantinople, 1707). While better than the intervening Warsaw edition (1870), which, entirely derived from the latter, was distinguished only by many errors and some arbitrary reshuffling of the chapters according to a preconceived scheme, the accuracy of the new edition leaves even more to be desired than does that of the other works. Ehrenreich's introductory comments, too, though rather useful, are far less exhaustive. That is why one may doubly welcome I. S. Elfenbein's plan to edit from a Munich MS, or rather a copy thereof, Rashi's *Sefer ha-Sedarim* (Book of [Liturgical] Orders). See the first installment published in *Horeb,* XI, 123–56. While adding little to our substantive knowledge of Rashi's liturgical decisions, this work, together with Elfenbein's extensive notes, adds certain data to the documentation of Rashi's views and modifies them in some details. The same holds true of Rashi's *Teshubot* (Responsa) which, though covering the entire range of halakhic interests, shed considerable light on liturgical problems as well. Here, too, Elfenbein's extensive introduction and notes, together with some additional notes by L. Ginzberg, help clarify and decide many detailed problems left open in the other works. Rashi's *Sefer Issur ve-hetter* (Book of Forbidden and Permitted Matters) is analyzed from a Merzbacher MS and compared with MSS of the *Sefer ha-Orah* and *Maḥzor Vitry* by S. Buber in his introduction to Rashi's *Sefer ha-Orah,* pp. 35 ff., 40 ff. See also the more general literature on Rashi and his school's legal and exegetical work mentioned *supra,* Chaps. XXVII, nn. 54 ff.; XXIX, nn. 56–57.

83. See Rashi's *Siddur,* ed. by Buber and Freimann, pp. 86 ff., 274 ff., 295 f.; and the *Liqquṭe ha-Pardes* (Ritualistic Collectanea), first published in Venice, 1519, and frequently reprinted since. In its present form the latter work seems to be an early thirteenth-century compilation by one Samuel of Bamberg. But Samuel evidently used earlier manuscripts current in his country of the original work from Rashi's school. See I. A. Benjacob's note in his *Ozar ha-sepharim* (Thesaurus librorum hebraicorum), pp. 265 f.; and Buber's introduction to Rashi's *Sefer ha-Orah,* pp. 94, 141 ff.

84. Jacob Tam's *Sefer ha-Yashar,* ed. by F. Rosenthal, p. 82. This grandson of Rashi here expressly names R. Simḥah as the *Maḥzor's* author. There is no question, however, that in its present form the work contains a great many additions from later hands, including materials taken from authorities living long after R. Simḥah. The author seems also to have been greatly influenced by R. Shemayah, Rashi's close relative and confidant, although the evidence hitherto adduced does not suffice to attribute to Shemayah any direct part in the composition of the *Maḥzor.* See the theories summarized in V. Aptowitzer's *Mabo,* pp. 414 f. (suggesting that there were two works by the same title written by Shemayah and Simḥah). The title, as well as the author's interchangeable use of the designation Amram's *Maḥzor* and *Seder* (see *Maḥzor Vitry,* pp. 444 f. and other passages listed in Hurwitz's introduction, pp. 74 f., 79 f.), are likewise noteworthy. Clearly, the later distinction between *Siddur,* principally devoted to weekday and Sabbath prayers, and *Maḥzor,* supplying liturgical material for holidays alone, does not apply to our compilation, most of which deals with daily and Sabbath problems, and includes a large commentary on the "Sayings of the Fathers" (pp. 461 ff.). These chapters in the Mishnah used to be recited on Saturday afternoons in Rab's ancient synagogue in Sura, according to Shalom Gaon's testimony. See *Sha'are teshubah,* No. 220; and Saadiah's *Siddur,* pp. 122 f. This custom, widely adopted and subjected to manifold regional variations, doubtless inspired our author to his exegetical effort. All this goes far in confirming the impression, gained from other sources, that even at the beginning of the twelfth century prayer books were not yet clearly distinguished as a group from other halakhic works.

85. Ginzberg's *Geonica,* I, 119 f.; Saadiah's *Siddur,* I, 152 f.; Rashi's responsum cited in Simḥah's *Maḥzor,* p. 358, and in Rashi's *Teshubot,* ed. by Elfenbein, p. 76 No. 65; and Abudarham, *Sefer Abudarham,* Prague, 1784 ed., fol. 73bc (on *mi-pene ḥata'enu* in the holiday *Musaf*). See also my brief remarks in *Rashi Anniv. Vol.,* p. 51. Ginzberg's objections to this interpretation, and his own explanation that the sole reason for the continued recitation of the *'Amidah* by heart sprang from the worshiper's apprehension lest he drop his prayer book and thus lose his concentration (*JQR,* XXXIII, 316 ff.), are too mechanistic. Certainly the medieval Jews could have introduced lecterns or some other supports for the prayer book, as did their successors after the invention of printing. On the use of ordinary codices even for the reading of required scriptural lessons, see Rashi's *Teshubot,* pp. 312 f. No. 276.

86. Mordecai ben Abraham Jaffe (Yafeh), *Sefer ha-Lebushim* (Vestments; on Jewish law and ethics), *Lebush ha-tekhelet,* Prague, 1711 ed., fols. 297 f. No. 619; T. Megillah IV.21, p. 227; *Massekhet Soferim* XIV.9, ed. by Higger, p. 263; Nathan the Babylonian's Report in *MJC,* II, 83; and A. Z. Idelsohn, "The Kol Nidre Tune," *HUCA,* VIII–IX, 493–509. Nathan's emphasis on *baḥurim* (young men) seems to indicate the presence of boys' choirs in some larger synagogues of the tenth century. Such choirs, customary in the later communities, cannot otherwise be documented from early medieval sources. See also *supra,* Chap. XXVII, n. 143.

87. *Testamentum Domini,* cited by J. Mearns in his careful analysis of *The Canticles of the Christian Church,* pp. 7 f.; Pirqoi's diatribe in Ginzberg's *Ginze Schechter,* II, 552; Samau'al's *Ifḥam,* in the excerpt ed. and trans. by Schreiner in

MGWJ, XLII, 218 f. See *supra,* n. 28. Unfortunately, the available sources enable us to reconstruct neither the origin of the *ṭe'amim,* nor the precise musical sounds which they were to denote. Even the general beginnings of the so-called ekphonetic notation, and the question of Jewish or Syro-Byzantine priority in its discovery, are shrouded in almost total darkness. Since the cantillation itself undoubtedly antedated the rise of Christianity, and since such informed medieval authors as Isidore of Seville readily admitted that the "laudation, that is the singing of *halleluyah,* is a Hebrew chant" (*De ecclesiasticis officiis,* 1.13, 1 in *PL,* LXXXIII, 750), there is no reason to deny some sort of initiative also to the early Jewish Masorites in the invention of symbols to guide students and readers. See *supra,* Chap. XXIX, n. 8. How such early ekphonetic symbols could later be transcribed into the younger Byzantine notation was well illustrated at the hand of a tenth or eleventh-century MS (Sinaiticus 8) by C. Høeg in *La Notation ekphonétique.* See also H. J. W. Tillyard's twin essays, "The Stages of the Early Byzantine Musical Notation," *BZ,* XLV, 29–42; and "The Byzantine Modes in the Twelfth Century," *Annual* of the British School at Athens, XLVIII, 182–90; and, more generally, the older literature reviewed by R. Aigrain in his "Musicologie byzantine," *Revue des études grecques,* LIV, 81–121. On the other hand, some two centuries later, the Hebrew copyist of a poem for the Festival of the Rejoicing in the Torah provided his text with neumes developed by the Roman Church. See E. Werner, "The Oldest Sources of Synagogue Chant," *PAAJR,* XVI, 225–32. Another century passed, and the copyist of a beautifully illuminated Catalan Bible reproduced the contemporary cantillation in Western notation. See B. Szabolcsi's brief analysis of "A Jewish Musical Document of the Middle Ages," *Löw Mem. Vol.,* pp. 131–33 (with reference to the fuller description of "Eine spanisch-jüdische Bilderbibel von 1400," by Z. Ameisenowa in *MGWJ,* LXXXI, 193–209). However, even with the aid of these late medieval records it is next to impossible to reconstruct the original sounds which corresponded to the masoretic accents. Only by working backward from modern ritualistic practices in various communities could A. Z. Idelsohn argue plausibly that the extraordinary resemblance in the sounds uttered by Torah readers from Persia and Bukhara to Morocco and the western Sephardic, as well as Ashkenazic, synagogues presupposes a single ancient or early medieval prototype. See the very interesting "comparative table of accent motives for the intoning of the Pentateuch" in his *Jewish Music in Its Historical Development,* pp. 44 ff. A systematic attempt to come to grips with the historical evolution of Jewish Bible cantillation, pursued for many years by S. Rosowsky, who used the present-day recitation in synagogues of the Ashkenazic rite (particularly in Lithuania) as a point of departure, has finally resulted in the publication of his volume *The Cantillation of the Bible: the First Books of Moses.* See also his earlier study, "The Music of the Pentateuch: Analytical Theory of Biblical Cantillations," *Proceedings of the Musical Associations,* LX, 38–66.

88. See Ben Asher's *Diqduqe ha-ṭe'amim,* fols. 15 ff. No. 15; Petaḥiah of Ratisbon, quoted *infra,* n. 91; *Manuel de lecteur,* ed. by J. Derenbourg, p. 75; Aaron ben Jacob of Lunel's *Oreḥot ḥayyim* (The Ways of Life; a custumal), I, fol. 6b No. 26; Abraham ben Nathan of Lunel's *Sefer ha-Manhig* (Guide; on customs and rituals), ed. by J. M. Goldberg, fol. 33b. The latter author gives the recitation of Psalm 91 (called "the song of evil spirits" in Shebuot 15b) on Saturday nights a lugubrious meaning, namely that such prolonged chanting extends the period of grace for the

souls of the damned who do not have to return to hell until after the completion of these post-Sabbath services. Jacob ben Asher, on the other hand, following the lead of *Midrash Tehillim* (on 91:1, ed. by Buber, p. 396), considered this very psalm as a song of blessing, and hence an appropriate initiation for the coming week. See *Ṭur*, O.Ḥ., 295. See also Amram's *Seder*, XCVI, ed. by Frumkin, I, 393; ed. by Hedegard, I, 75 f. (Hebrew), 171 (English). Despite numerous questionable and now often obsolete views, W. Wiekes's *Treatise on the Accentuation of the Three So-Called Poetical Books of the Old Testament* (includes the Arabic text of Ibn Bal'am's essay on this subject) and *Treatise on the Accentuation of the Twenty-One So-Called Prose Books of the Old Testament* still offer the most comprehensive data on the origin and meaning of these symbols relating to both pronunciation and intonation. Cf., however, the serious reservations suggested, especially on the basis of manuscripts containing the Babylonian and old Palestinian accents, in P. Kahle's *Masoreten des Ostens*, pp. 171 ff.; his *Masoreten des Westens*, I, 24 f., 32 ff.; A. Spanier's more tangential, and rather overcritical, observations on the musical aspects of *Die masoretischen Akzente;* and the musicological comments thereon in Høeg's *Notation*, pp. 139 ff. Kahle has shown that especially the so-called *mesharetim*, or subsidiary accents, were introduced at a later stage. However, they had been fully developed in the early Middle Ages.

While rightly emphasizing that the primary purpose of the masoretic accentuation was elocutionary rather than musical, H. M. Lazarus pointed out that several early rabbis insisted on the musical rendering not only of the Bible, but also of talmudic lessons. This evidently was but a reaction to the Graeco-Roman schools of rhetoric, which had deprecated the oriental forms of speaking in singsong (Cicero, Quintillian, and others). See Lazarus, "The Rationale of the Tiberian Graphic Accentuation (XXI Books)," *Essays Hertz*, pp. 271–91. See also, for other angles, B. Heller's "Von *tropos* und *troparion* zum Tropp," *MGWJ*, LXXX, 125–27; E. Werner's "Preliminary Notes for a Comparative Study of Catholic and Jewish Musical Punctuation," *HUCA*, XV, 335–66; and the large older literature listed in A. Sendrey's *Bibliography of Jewish Music*, pp. 82 ff. See also E. Werner's forthcoming volume, *The Sacred Bridge*. The comparative neglect in the intonation of psalms is the more remarkable as the *vox psallentium* coming from a neighboring synagogue had so greatly disturbed Pope Gregory the Great. See *supra*, Vol. II, p. 282. However, when we study carefully the description of psalmody in early seventh-century churches given by the Pope's contemporary, Isidore of Seville and especially the statement that in the primitive church the singer "made his voice resound by so moderate an inflection, that he was closer to declamation than singing" (*De ecclesiasticis officiis*, 1.5,2, *PL* LXXXIII, 742 ff.), we may find a clue for the early, more declamatory recitation of the psalms in the ancient synagogues as well. It may be noted, however, that Abraham ibn Ezra was so certain that individual psalms were sung to different tunes that he explained the meaning of the numerous headings as referring to particular melodies. See his *Commentary* on Ps. 7:1, 22:1, and other passages, and, more generally, A. Neubauer's data in *Studia biblica*, II, 35 f., and *passim*. But Ibn Ezra's observation, although historically correct, reflected the practice of medieval poets, rather than the traditional synagogue ritual. See also L. Levi, "Sul rapporto tra il canto sinagogale in Italia e le origini del canto liturgico cristiano," *Scritti in memoria di Sally Mayer*, pp. 139–93; and, for comparative purposes, E. Wellesz's *Eastern Elements in Western Chant;* and the literature listed *supra*, Vols. I, pp. 362 f. n. 22; II, pp. 330 n. 5, 389 n. 34, to which add H. Hucke, "Die Entwicklung des christlichen Kultgesangs zum Gregorianischen Gesang," *Römische Quartalschrift,* XLVIII, 147–87; W. Apel's general review of the *Gregorian Chant;* and U. Bomm's bibliographical survey of "Gregorianischer Gesang," *Archiv für Liturgiewissenschaft,* IV, 184–222, esp. pp. 195 ff. Also of considerable importance, of course, is the literature relating to the development of secular music in the Jewish community as well as in the outside world and the theoretical works on music written by Muslim authors, on which consult the general works listed *infra,* n. 93; and the numerous monographs discussed *infra,* Chap. XXXII, nn. 96 ff.

89. Rashi on Berakhot 62a; and Idelsohn's *Jewish Music,* pp. 67 f. The Yemenite precentors seem long to have cultivated the memory of some special signs accompanying the respective tunes. According to the *Manuel de lecteur,* ed. by J. Derenbourg, grammarians attributed to the biblical accents both special intonations and a variety of gestures with one or more fingers (p. 108). See also Idelsohn's *Toledot ha-neginah ha-'ibrit* (History of Jewish Music), I, 95 ff.; and, on Saadiah's use of accents in his pamphlets, *supra,* Chap. XXIII, n. 21.

90. Hai Gaon, cited by both Ibn Gayyat and Abraham ben Nathan of Lunel, in Lewin's *Otzar ha-gaonim,* VI, Part 2, p. 58 No. 144 (relating to a "messenger" who recited an uncalled-for blessing). One wishes that we had a detailed description of the ancient and early medieval Jewish responsoria. In his brief reference to the Church responses, Isidore of Seville ascribes them to ancient Italian origins (*De ecclesiasticis officiis,* I.9, *PL,* LXXXIII, 744), but he undoubtedly had in mind only the particular exchange between a choir and one, two, or three singers singing in unison. The description of the parts sung by the cantor and the choir's responses during the installation ceremonies of a new exilarch in Nathan the Babylonian's Report (*MJC,* II, 83) gives no indication of the sections recited or sung by the congregation at large. See E. Werner's "Notes on the Attitude of the Early Church Fathers towards Hebrew Psalmody," *Review of Religion,* VII, 339–52. In "The Origin of the Eight Modes of Music (Octoechos)," *HUCA,* XXI, 211–55, Werner points out that Saadiah interpreted Psalm 6:1 to mean that Levites used these eight modes in their Temple chants. A medieval *payyeṭan* and Petaḥiah likewise referred to those modes which underlie several known synagogue chants. However, Werner admits that the material at hand does not allow for a reconstruction of the original *octoechos* of the synagogue. See also Werner's other studies listed *supra,* Vol. II, pp. 330 n. 5, 389 n. 34; and B. J. Cohon's brief general characterization of "The Structure of the Synagogue Prayer-Chant," *Journal of the American Musicological Society,* III, 17–32 (analyzing various modes in four basic scales). On the refrains in the *piyyuṭim,* see, for example, the aforementioned Qalirian prayer for dew, *supra,* n. 50.

91. F. Altheim and R. Stiel, "Eine Bekehrungsschrift aus der Synagoge von Dura-Europos," *Zeitschrift für Religions- und Geistesgeschichte,* VII, 193–224; Petaḥiah's *Sibbub,* XVIII, ed. by L. Grünhut, pp. 24 (Hebrew), 32 f. (German), or in the English translation by A. Benisch, p. 47; Soṭah 48a; Berakhot 24a; Ta'anit 16ab; Maimonides' *M.T.* Tefillah VIII.11; Yehudai Gaon in Lewin's *Otzar ha-gaonim,* V, Part 2, p. 27. In his German note, p. 33 n. 111, Grünhut suggested, in opposition to L. Löw, that even in Baghdad instrumental music was allowed only on the half holidays of the

Feast of Tabernacles, in memory of the ancient water procession, but not on Passover. However, by his failure to stress this distinction Petaḥiah would have suppressed the most important part of his story. Among the ten extraordinary feats of piety attributed to Rab and recorded by Hai Gaon was also his habit of using his beautiful voice by frequently descending to the pulpit and also by serving as an interpreter for his teacher or for anyone else who needed his services. See *Sha'are teshubah,* No. 178. Maimonides (*loc. cit.*) and other rabbis agreed, however, with Amram's aforementioned decision that, where no better "messenger" was available, any boy of thirteen was eligible to conduct services. See *supra,* n. 24. On the medieval rabbis' general antagonism to instrumental music even for liturgical purposes, and the theories of music expounded by some of them, see *infra,* Chap. XXXII, nn. 94 ff.

92. *Pesiqta r.,* xxv, ed. by Friedmann, fol. 127a; Immanuel ben Solomon of Rome's *Maḥbarot* (Maqamas), xv, xxvi.16, xxviii, ed. by A. M. Habermann, pp. 419 f., 752 ff., 810 f.; Alfasi's *Resp.,* No. 281. See also *Midrash Tehillim,* xvii.5, ed. by Buber, pp. 128 ff. Gullible cantors sometimes contributed mightily to the spread of superstitious customs. Sharing an old conviction that the public recitation of the *Qiddush* on a Sabbath eve had beneficial medicinal effects, some cantors began pouring the ceremonial wine on the hands of congregants, who then rubbed it into their eyes. Hai Gaon, however, protested sharply against such magic use, and the practice seems not to have spread. See the data cited in Lewin's *Otzar ha-gaonim,* I, Part 1, p. 97 Nos. 170–71.

93. See Abraham ben Nathan's *Sefer ha-Manhig,* pp. 23 f.; Simḥah bar Samuel's *Maḥzor Vitry,* p. 388 (giving a purely psychological explanation); Lewin's *Otzar ha-gaonim,* I, Part 1, pp. 12 ff., 70; Part 3, pp. 3 f.; Saadiah, quoted in Yehudah bar Barzillai's *Commentary on Yeṣirah,* pp. 34 f.; *Sefer Ḥasidim* (Book of the Pious), ed. by Wistinetzki, No. 11, pp. 8 f.; and the data assembled by A. Z. Idelsohn in "The Kol Nidre Tune," *HUCA,* VIII–IX, 493 ff. The constant lengthening of the services often led to the exhaustion of the precentors, especially since old men were preferred. That is why Hai, for example, relaxed his requirement that the "messenger" also lead the priestly blessing. If a cantor was too tired, the gaon decided, he could be replaced by someone else for this part of the service. See *Sha'are teshubah,* No. 177. It also became customary to entrust to two different precentors the morning and the *Musaf* services, the men in charge of the latter service usually being the more highly esteemed officials. In large congregations they subdivided the services further, but this was often done not in order to spare the precentor's efforts, but rather to accommodate a larger number of willing candidates. See also, in general, Zunz, *Synagogale Poesie,* pp. 113 ff.; Idelsohn, *Jewish Music;* P. Gradenwitz, *The Music in Israel: Its Rise and Growth through 5,000 Years;* A. M. Rothmüller, *The Music of the Jews: an Historical Appreciation;* and H. Harris, *Toledot ha-neginah, passim.* Although containing little directly Jewish material, such general handbooks as G. Reese's *Music in the Middle Ages: With an Introduction on the Music of Ancient Times* (includes an extensive bibliography, pp. 425 ff.); and J. Combarieu, *Histoire de la musique des origines au début du XXe siècle,* Vol. I (to the end of the sixteenth century), are also to be consulted with profit.

CHAPTER XXXII: POETRY AND BELLES-LETTRES

1. Sukkah 26a; A. Baumstark, *Geschichte der syrischen Literatur,* pp. 35, 103, 105. The Greek and Latin authors of the Byzantine Empire, including such close neighbors of the Palestinian rabbis as Eusebius and Jerome, were no less prolific. See also *supra,* Chap. XXIX, n. 54.

2. L. Finkelstein, *Jewish Self-Government in the Middle Ages,* pp. 48, 178, 188, 195, 201; and *supra,* Chap. XXII, n. 21. In his *Be-Ohole Ya'aqob,* pp. 1 ff., S. Assaf has assembled a number of interesting data on the relations between " 'The People of the Book' and the Book," but his sources are chiefly European, of medieval and early modern vintage. See also J. L. Maimon, "The People of the Book and Its Book Treasures" (Hebrew), *Sinai,* XVII, Nos. 201–3, pp. 47–66; *supra,* Vol. II, 390 n. 35; and *infra,* n. 5. A comprehensive and detailed study of ancient and medieval Jewish books and libraries clearly is much to be desired.

3. Maimonides, *M.T.,* "Annual order of Prayers," appended to Book II (Ahabah). See *supra,* Chaps. XXVII, n. 21; XXIX, n. 16; and A. I. Schechter's analysis of "The Prayer Book of Maimonides" in his *Lectures on Jewish Liturgy,* pp. 23 ff.

4. Hai Gaon's *Shire Musar haskel* (Poems of Wise Conduct), verse 172 (on Hai's authorship of this work, see *infra,* n. 42); Ibn Daud's "Chronicle," in *MJC,* I, 72 f.; Samuel ibn Nagrela's *Ben Mishle* (Son of Proverbs) as edited by S. Abramson in *Kol Shire* (Collected Poems), ed. by A. M. Habermann and S. Abramson, IV, 9 No. 25, 159 No. 555; Yehudah ibn Tibbon's "Will" in I. Abrahams's *Hebrew Ethical Wills,* pp. 57 f., 64. Ironically, Samuel ibn Nagrela's own grammatical treatises circulated only in few copies and speedily disappeared from the market. Even his fine Introduction to the Talmud was salvaged from total oblivion only by its brief Hebrew synopsis. See *supra,* Chaps. XXVII, n. 35; and XXX, n. 52. Because of the stringent requirements governing the use of parchment in scrolls of Law, even entire communities, particularly in the younger, sparsely populated Jewish settlements, were unable to procure scrolls for their services. True, there were many regional variations, and few rabbis were prepared to subscribe to Pirqoi ben Baboi's extremist denunciation of the Palestinian scrolls because they had been written on parchment manufactured at variance with the Babylonian practice, but all agreed that the materials used must meet certain exacting conditions. See the sources cited by L. Ginzberg in his *Ginze Schechter,* II, 527 ff. Combined with the even stricter requirements for scribal exactitude, which disqualified for liturgical use any scroll containing minute scribal errors, the production of scrolls often became very costly. Many a small and struggling congregation, unable to acquire an adequate scroll, had to recite the weekly lesson from an ordinary codex. Although urging all communities to purchase scrolls "satisfactory in every point of law," Maimonides not only recognized the existence of such emergency situations, but also declared that the use of parchment scrolls was required only

"for the honor of the public." He decided, therefore, that at public recitations from ordinary copies the worshipers be allowed to recite the usual blessings. Something of a novelty in the populous Near Eastern communities, he contended that such practice had long been known among Western scholars, including his teacher, Joseph ibn Megas, and Isaac Alfasi. See his *Resp.*, pp. 42 ff. No. 43. West European communities even more frequently had to resort to this unwelcome expedient. See Rashi's *Teshubot,* pp. 312 f. No. 276; and *supra,* Chap. XXXI, n. 85.

5. P. K. Hitti, *History of the Arabs,* 6th ed., pp. 413 f. See also other data assembled by J. Pedersen in his article "Masdjid," *EI,* III, 361; R. S. Mackensen in her "Four Great Libraries of Medieval Bagdad," *Library Quarterly,* II, 279–99; and her monographs in *AJSL,* Vols. LI–LIV, LVI; and, more generally, F. Milkau and G. Leyh, *Handbuch der Bibliothekswissenschaft,* Vol. III: *Geschichte der Bibliotheken,* which includes chapters on Byzantine, Muslim, and medieval libraries, pp. 146–498. A good sample of what books were available in a typical thirteenth-century Arab library is given in P. Sbath's *Choix des livres qui se trouvaient dans les bibliothèques d'Alep.*

6. Abraham ben Isaac's responsum, in *Sifran shel rishonim* (Book of Medieval Rabbis), ed. by S. Assaf, pp. 32 f. Nos. 30, 32; Immanuel of Rome's *Maḥbarot* (Maqamas; a poetic miscellany), VIII, ed. by Habermann, pp. 250 ff. Among the extant book lists from the Genizah that recording the collection of the Egyptian scholar Abraham ben Hillel is of particular interest. In 1223, less than a year after the owner's death, his library was disposed of, apparently by public auction in two sessions, at the Palestinian synagogue of Fusṭaṭ. See the texts published by E. J. Worman in his "Two Book-Lists from the Cambridge Genizah Fragments," *JQR,* [o.s.] XX, 460 ff.; S. Poznanski in his "Jüdisch-arabische Bücherlisten aus der Geniza in Cambridge," *ZHB,* XII, 112 ff.; and Mann in his *Jews in Egypt,* II, 327 f. None of these lists contained more than some two hundred codices, some of which, of course, contained more than one title. See, e.g., the extensive, and yet incomplete, lists published by Mann in his *Texts and Studies,* I, 651 ff., and by S. Assaf in his "Ancient Book Lists" (Hebrew), *KS,* XVIII, 272–81 (includes one long and three shorter lists of the twelfth and thirteenth centuries). Mann (p. 643) and Assaf mention also the book lists previously published. Of more recent vintage is M. Zulay, "A Book-List in Which an Unknown Work of Saadiah Gaon is Mentioned" (Hebrew), *KS,* XXV, 203–5; and S. Abramson's aforementioned Hebrew study of "R. Joseph Rosh ha-Seder" in *KS,* XXVI, 72–95. Even if we should add the number of books left behind by R. Joseph in Baghdad, the total collection of this bibliographically well-informed scholar hardly exceeded a few hundred volumes.

7. I. Abrahams, *Hebrew Ethical Wills,* pp. 63, 80 ff. Because of the difficulty of reconciling the social need of extensive book-lending with the private owner's discretion over his property, the attitude of various rabbis differed in accordance with changing conditions or their varying personal temperaments. While Ibn Tibbon hedged the advice to his son to lend books freely to all "who can be trusted to return the volumes" (*ibid.,* pp. 81 f.), a fourteenth-century Spanish judge fined a reluctant lender 10 guilders for each day he withheld his books from general circulation. Asher ben Yeḥiel approved of this action, merely suggesting that the borrower supply security for whatever damage might accrue to the owner, accord-

ing to the estimate of three appraisers. See his *Resp.*, XCIII.3. Since most of our pertinent sources come from the later medieval communities, this subject will be more fully discussed in a later volume.

8. See J. Weiss's suggestive observations in his brief preliminary essay on *Tarbut ḥaṣranit ve-shirah ḥaṣranit* (Court Culture and Court Poetry). The fuller treatment of Spanish Hebrew poetry from this angle promised by the author has thus far failed to appear. See *infra*, n. 19; and for comparable illustrations among medieval Spanish Arab poets, M. M. Antuña, "La Corte literaria de Alhaquem II en Cordoba," *Religion y Cultura*, 1929. See also, more generally, H. Schirmann's comprehensive anthology, with its very informative introductions on the various poets, entitled *Ha-Shirah ha-'ibrit bi-Sefarad u-be-Provence* (Hebrew Poetry in Spain and the Provence).

9. Saadiah's *Siddur*, pp. 45 ff., 64 ff.; Abraham ibn Ezra's *Commentary* on Eccles. 5:1; Maimonides' *Resp.*, pp. 39 f. No. 41 (the reply ignores the part of the question relating to standing during the recitation). Explaining the need for an Arabic translation of the first prayer of petition, Ṣemaḥ ben Joshua stated, "Many students have learned both these prayers by heart because of their profit in this world and their good reward in the world to come. Some of these students, however, have lost the understanding of a few expressions of this laudation intended for joyous days and yet wish to comprehend them" (*Siddur*, p. 46). The fact that no Arabic translations of the two other prayers of petition by Saadiah (published by Habermann in his "Two Poems by R. Saadiah Gaon," *Tarbiz*, XIII, 52–59) are recorded anywhere, reinforces the editor's view of their independent composition (against Zunz's *Literaturgeschichte*, pp. 95 ff.).

10. See M. Zulay, "Saadiah Gaon as Payyeṭan under Pseudonym" (Hebrew), *Melilah*, III–IV, 166–84. Aided by some headings in medieval fragments, but relying largely on linguistic criteria, Zulay believes he has identified twenty such poems by Saadiah giving the name of Solomon. Some of the gaon's other poems were apparently written for another cantor, David. See *Siddur*, pp. 21 n. 16, 395 ff., 430.

11. See Saadiah's *Siddur*, pp. 385 f.; Suidas' admiring comment on the poems of John and Cosmas cited by Krumbacher in his *Geschichte*, p. 675; and R. A. Nicholson, *A Literary History of the Arabs*, p. 325.

12. See B. M. Lewin's new edition of the various extant fragments of *Essa meshali* in Fishman's *Rav Saadya Gaon*, esp. pp. 518 ff.; and, on its very complicated technique, Lewin's intro., pp. 501 ff.; and I. Davidson's comments in his "Further Fragments of Saadiah Gaon's *Essa meshali*," *Kohut Mem. Vol.*, Hebrew section, pp. 10 ff. See also *supra*, Chaps. XXIII, n. 21; XXIX, nn. 15, 88; XXX, n. 13. Apart from Saadiah's learned allusions, the extraordinary richness of his language and style, combined with his sovereign disregard of the accepted interpretations and rules, must have made his poems extremely arduous reading even for well-informed contemporaries. In fact, many expressions were derived from some of Saadiah's peculiar explanations of biblical words twisted into a new and wholly unprecedented poetic form. Handicapped by the loss of most of Saadiah's biblical

commentaries, modern students are often unable to extract any meaning from these intellectual acrobatics. But even contemporaries and early successors, to whom Saadiah's works were still fully accessible, required some such aids as the gaon's or his disciples' Arabic paraphrases. See S. Abramson's analysis of "Saadiah's Language in *Essa meshali*" (Hebrew) in Fishman's *Rav Saadya Gaon,* pp. 677–85; B. Chapira's comments on the style of the fragment of the prose pamphlet, *Sefer ha-Galui,* published by him in *REJ,* LXVIII, 3; and Zulay's observations in *Melilah,* III–IV, 167 ff. No wonder Saadiah's linguistic innovations readily lent themselves to misinterpretation and repudiation, as in Mubashshir's and Dunash ben Labraṭ's aforementioned attacks. See *supra,* Chap. XXX, n. 15.

13. This wedding song, first published by S. A. Wertheimer, was republished with an English trans. by S. Solis-Cohen in Malter's *Saadia Gaon,* pp. 337 f. Even Saadiah's outright liturgical poems cannot be entirely divorced from his personal experiences and battles. Particularly his sufferings and exposure to constant danger during his conflict with the exilarch inspired him to compose some of his most moving prayers. A passage such as: "Suffering and oppression have afflicted me, and Thou hast saved me. Strangers have risen against me, and Thou hast rescued me from their hands. Many times have I reached the gates of death, and Thou hast revived me" (*Siddur,* p. 69) included in the second prayer of petition, has a decidedly contemporary ring. Similarly, his lamentation beginning *Ata ha-yom* (The Day I Feared Has Arrived; *ibid.,* pp. 412 f.) includes the melancholy admission that his inborn love of controversy had brought him to the brink of ruin (verses 12 ff.). Despite the use of biblical clichés, such outcries came from a heart wounded by the struggles of the day, and now tired and resigned. See my remarks in *Saadia Anniv. Vol.,* pp. 70 n. 133, 74 n. 142.

14. Al-Nahrawani's poems, ed. by M. Zulay in *Haaretz,* September 25, 1946. See *supra,* Chap. XXIII, n. 21; and, on the contemporary objections to the employment of blind "messengers," see Lewin's *Otzar ha-gaonim,* V, Part 1, pp. 43 f. Nos. 157 ff. Curiously, although Saadiah seems to have written exclusively Hebrew poetry, only one of his extant liturgical pieces (a *yoṣer* beginning *Az bi-beṭoah,* or Then In Reliance on Hollow Support, in his *Siddur,* pp. 382 f.) concludes with the Hebrew acrostic Saadiah or Saadiahu. In all others his authorship, if indicated at all, is given by an acrostic forming the name Sa'id ben Joseph, often amplified by his academic title *alluf.* Sometimes, as in the case of Saadiah's *Azharot* (exhortations on the theme of the 613 commandments) the author is obliquely indicated by the opening line having a total numerical value of 469, the *gemaṭria* of that name and title. As pointed out by Rapoport, Saadiah imitated here Qalir's methods of self-identification. See his *Siddur,* p. 185; and Malter's *Saadia,* pp. 150, 152 n. 336, 331.

15. See Joseph al-Baradani's poem identified in S. Bernstein's "Who Is the Poet 'R. Joseph' in the *Maḥzor 'Ḥizzunim'?*" (Hebrew), *Tarbiz,* XIII, 150–64, and the literature listed there (on that rare *Maḥzor,* see *infra,* n. 30); and in Mann's *Texts and Studies,* I, 151 f.; A. M. Habermann's ed. of Simon bar Isaac's *Piyyuṭim* (Liturgical Poems; includes also those by Moses bar Kalonymos); and Meir bar Isaac's poems analyzed in Zunz's *Literaturgeschichte,* pp. 145 ff., 248 ff., 610 (Note 13).

See also *supra,* Chaps. XXV, n. 48; XXXI, n. 24. Fuller light on Sulaiman and his position in the community may be expected only from the publication of his numerous extant poems, once promised by Zulay.

16. See Habermann's introduction to his edition of Simon bar Isaac's *Piyyuṭim,* p. 21; Brody's list in his appendix to *Maḥzor Vitry.* Without further evidence, the existence of a synagogue of Ashkenazi rite in medieval Cairo will remain very dubious. It is far safer to assume either borrowings of Western poems by an Eastern congregation, as suggested in the text, or the chance survival of a manuscript left behind by an Ashkenazi visitor in Egypt.

17. H. Brody, "Religious and Laudatory Poems by R. Hai Gaon" (Hebrew), *SRIHP,* III, 20 l. 20, 24 l. 14, 45, 46 ll. 14–15. In the remarkable lamentation on the theme *Et mi zanakhta* (Whom Didst Thou Forsake?; on its authorship see *infra,* n. 18), included in the Avignon prayer book, the author went so far as to claim, "On whom didst Thou inflict exile without redemption / So that it became our [unending] second exile" (Brody, p. 12 line 3). The poet seems to express here more than is imputed to him by S. D. Luzzatto, namely that the Babylonian Exile did not turn into full redemption, because it was so speedily followed by the second, the Roman exile. Hai may rather have wished to complain here of the historic fact that the first, the Egyptian exile, was followed by the second and unending exile, which, begun in Babylonia, was never really interrupted by full-scale redemption. Clearly, the Second Jewish Commonwealth through most of its history remained but a dependency of some larger empire. Although only five of the twenty-one poems edited by Brody are clearly identified by an acrostic *Hayy,* the others are expressly attributed to this gaon in various extant headings. Senior Sachs's attempt to explain away some of these headings as originating from a mistaken reading of the abbreviation *le-R.H.* (interpreted as "By R. Hai" instead of "For *Rosh ha-shanah,*" indicating the poem's postulated recitation on New Year's day), has been controverted by several Genizah fragments. In addition to those quoted by Brody, see also the heading cited in S. Widder's "List" in *Löw Mem. Vol.,* p. 23 No. 8/2; and A. M. Habermann's "Supplementary Material on Certain Poems" (Hebrew), *Tarbiz,* XIX, 185. On Hai's *Musar haskel,* see *infra,* n. 42. It should also be noted that the *Sha'are dine memonot* (Books of Civil Law and Books of Oaths), written in metric form probably by a thirteenth-century European author, were long incorrectly attributed to Hai. See Steinschneider, *Arabische Literatur,* pp. 99 f. See also Brody's analytical Hebrew essay, "R. Hai Gaon as *Payyeṭan* and Poet" in *Sinai,* I, Nos. 12–13, pp. 517–21.

18. See Davidson's *Oṣar,* I, 387 No. 8560 (ascribing the poem *Et mi zanakhta* to Joseph ibn Abitur rather than Hai); III, 488 No. 1738; J. Marcus's edition of the "Penitential Prayers by R. David the Exilarch" (Hebrew), *Horeb,* VI, 27–40; VII, 92–102; VIII, 49–59; A. Scheiber's edition of "A *Yoṣer* by an Exilarch" (Hebrew), *Sinai,* XVI, No. 198, pp. 238–43 (attributing it to David ben Zakkai); Solomon ben Yehudah's four poems, ed. by A. Scheiber in his "Everyday *Qerobot* from Kaufmann's Collection" (Hebrew), *Tarbiz,* XXII, 171 ff. (see also the literature listed there); and A. M. Habermann's ed. of Gershom bar Yehudah's *Seliḥot u-pizmonim* (Penitential Prayers and Odes). None of these poems are included in R. Simḥah's *Maḥzor Vitry,* although, for instance, R. Gershom's responsum

concerning the liturgical status of a priestly convert to another faith who had reconverted to Judaism is quoted there in extenso (pp. 96 f.).

19. Moses ibn Ezra's *K. al-Muḥadhara* (*Shirat Yisrael,* pp. 64 f.); N. Allony's introduction to his edition of Dunash's poems, pp. 7 ff., and the text, *ibid.,* p. 70 verses 33, 37. See also *supra,* Chap. XXX, nn. 21 ff.; and, more generally, the data collected by B. Klar in his Hebrew essay on "Poetry and Life: the Role of Poetry in the Cultural Life of Spanish Jewry" (1943), reprinted in his *Meqorot ve-'iyyunim,* pp. 85–106; and by J. Schirmann in "The Function of the Hebrew Poet in Medieval Spain," *JSS,* XVI, 235–52. Of course, this flattery of powerful individuals was not limited to Spain. We recall the Hebrew panegyrics in honor of an exilarch and another Baghdad grandee published by A. Scheiber. But in Spain the very importance generally attached to poetry, combined with the peculiar Jewish sociopolitical situation, promoted the growth of court poetry in an unprecedented degree. See *supra,* n. 8; and Chap. XXIII, n. 7. See also K. B. Starkova, "The Panegyric in Medieval Hebrew Poetry" (Russian), *Sovetskoe Vostokovedenie,* IV, 135–56, in which the author somewhat overstresses the contrast between the Eastern emphasis on valor and the Spanish glorification of Jewish learning and righteousness. Much pertinent material is also scattered throughout H. Schirmann's and other anthologies listed *infra,* n. 47.

20. Todros ben Joseph Abulafia's *Gan ha-meshalim ve-ha-ḥiddot* (Garden of Parables and Riddles: a Diwan), ed. by D. Yellin, pp. 126 ff. No. 396; Moses ibn Ezra's *K. al-Muḥadhara* (*Shirat Yisrael*); Pérès, *La Poésie andalouse,* p. 76.

21. See Samuel's large collection of aphorisms, *Ben Mishle,* named after the biblical book of Proverbs, Nos. 11, 310, 727, in D. S. Sassoon's ed. of the *Diwan of Shemuel Hannaghid,* pp. 154, 205; in S. Abramson's edition, pp. 106 No. 378, 229 No. 797, 309 No. 1083; and the parallels listed by Abramson, esp. *ibid.,* pp. 380 f., 445. On the social position of the contemporary Spanish-Arab poets, see Pérès, *La Poésie andalouse,* pp. 23 ff. See also *supra,* Chap. XVIII, nn. 41–42; and Y. Ratzaby's recent trans. and analysis of "A New Spanish-Arabic Source for R. Samuel Ha-Nagid and His Son" (Hebrew), *Orlogin,* XIII, 270–75 (includes translations of several of Muntafil's poems).

22. Menaḥem's letter to Ḥisdai in S. G. Stern's ed. of the *Teshubot* of Menaḥem's disciples to Dunash, pp. xxxiii ff.; Baḥya's *Duties of the Heart,* vi.9, ed. by Yahuda, pp. 277 f. (in Ibn Tibbon's Hebrew trans., ed. by Zifroni, p. 189); Maimonides' *Commentary* on M. Abot 1.16. See *supra,* Chap. XXXI, nn. 55 and 58. Moses ibn Ezra, who ruefully reminisced about his own youthful indiscretions in writing satirical poems, later agreed that "their worst feature is to insult important persons, the supreme insult being one which remains for generations." See his *K. al-Muḥadhara,* vi (*Shirat Israel,* p. 92).

23. Ibn Daud's "Chronicle," in *MJC,* I, 71 f.; Samuel's *Ben Mishle,* ed. by Abramson, pp. 271 f. Nos. 953–54, 340 No. 1196; ed. by Sassoon, pp. 224 Nos. 883–84, 254 No. 1123; Eliasaf's recollection in his introduction to Samuel's *Diwan, ibid.,* p. 2 (in Abramson's ed., pp. ii f.); Joseph's poetic efforts referred to by Samuel in *Ben Tehillim, ibid.,* p. 62 No. 90 (ed. by Habermann, I, 69 ff.). From the very battle-

field Samuel sent Joseph a selection of Arabic poems for careful study, accompanied by a hortatory Hebrew poem of his own. *Ibid.*, pp. 67 f. Nos. 96–97 (in A. M. Habermann's *loc. cit.*). Early training of children in poetic arts spread also to the Orient. In his comprehensive educational program, outlined as a part of his views on mental hygiene, Joseph ibn 'Aqnin recommended such instruction. He emphasized, however, that laudatory, satirical, and love poems be omitted from elementary school curricula, since their subject matter might prove injurious to the children's morals. See his *Ṭubb an-nufus* (Recreation of Souls; in Hebrew, *Refuat ha-nefesh*), in M. Güdemann, *Das jüdische Unterrichtswesen während der spanisch arabischen Periode,* pp. 58 f. (German), 10 (Arabic).

24. Al-Ḥarizi's *Taḥkemoni.* See J. Schirmann, "Isaac Gorni, poète hébreux de Provence," *Lettres romanes,* III, 175–200 (appeared also in Hebrew in *Orlogin,* III, 91–101). See also the texts of Gorni's poems and those by his opponents published in Appendixes IV and V of H. Gross's "Zur Geschichte der Juden in Arles, Nachträge," *MGWJ,* XXXI, 509 f.; Pérès, *La Poésie andalouse,* pp. 70 ff.; and *supra,* Chap. XXX, n. 51. Such dependence on both patrons and public opinion helps to explain also the extraordinary length to which the Spanish poets, Jewish and non-Jewish, went in their self-praise and self-advertising. Blowing one's own horn was considered as legitimate as the praise of wares displayed by merchants in the bazaars. This fashion, taken over from Arabic poetry, became so irresistible that even the financially wholly independent Nagid Samuel time and again extolled his own merits. His *Ben Tehillim* especially, or rather that part of it which may be reconstructed from his *Diwan,* is full of such self-laudatory poems. In verses addressed to R. Nissim of Kairuwan, for one example, he assured the distinguished jurist that his poems would be living long after his grandsons had died at a ripe old age (vv. 17–18, ed. by Sassoon, pp. 3f. No. 6; ed. by Habermann, II, No. 5, p. 12).

25. Sassoon's edition of the *Diwan* is, like the unique MS from which it is taken, unvocalized and far from complete. Both deficiencies are remedied as far as possible in the edition by Habermann and Abramson. All three editors have refrained, however, from furnishing more than the bare outlines of Samuel's life and creativity. Although somewhat less up-to-date than the latter editors' concise data, J. Schirmann's Hebrew sketch of "Samuel ha-Nagid as Poet," *Keneset,* II, 393–416, still offers the most authoritative summary. See also the same author's Hebrew bibliographical sketch in *KS,* XIII, 373–82; his "Samuel Hanaggid, the Man, the Soldier, the Politician," *JSS,* XIII, 99–126; D. Yellin's *Ketabim nibḥarim* (Selected Writings), II, 222 ff.; and J. Lewin's "R. Samuel ha-Nagid" (Hebrew), *Orlogin,* IX, 132–51; XI, 225–50. See also *infra,* nn. 31 and 40.

26. Ibn Gabirol's *Lu hayetah nafshi* (If My Soul Had Asked for Little), vv. 5–6 in his *Shire* (Poems), ed. by H. N. Bialik and J. H. Rawnitzky, 2d ed., I, 25 f.; Joseph Solomon Delmedigo's *Maṣref le-ḥokhmah* (Refinement of Wisdom), Odessa, 1865 ed., p. 19; Yehudah al-Ḥarizi's *Taḥkemoni,* XVIII, ed. by Lagarde, p. 89 (ed. by J. Toporowski, p. 185). On the *'Anaq,* see *supra,* Chap. XXX, n. 58.

27. Ibn Gabirol's *Shire,* Nos. 41 vv. 21–22, 112 vv. 47–52; his poem *Ezkerah shimkha* cited from a Schocken MS by A. Parnes in his "Dicta concerning the Lord in the Poetry of Solomon ibn Gabirol" (Hebrew), *Keneset,* VII, 293; Moses ibn

Ezra's *K. al-Muḥadhara,* v (*Shirat Yisrael,* p. 71). Ibn Gabirol's bitterness toward his Saragossan enemies is explained by H. N. Bialik as a continuation, a generation later, of the conflict between the disciples of Menaḥem and Dunash. See Bialik's interpretation of "A Stray Stanza of Ibn Gabirol" (Hebrew), *Tarbiz,* II, 503–6. On the other hand, his glorification of Yequtiel must have conjured up in any learned Jewish reader's mind the association of that name with Moses in the ancient legend. See Megillah 13a; and *infra,* n. 34.

Despite numerous weaknesses pointed out by critics, the collection of Ibn Gabirol's poems by Bialik and Rawnitzky has hitherto remained unsurpassed. It includes a total of more than four hundred authentic poems. Among more recent publications see esp. R. Edelmann's "Unbekannte Pijutim von Salomo ibn Gabirol," *MGWJ,* LXXVII, 437–47; and the poems published by S. Bernstein in his "Two Unknown Poems by Solomon ibn Gabirol" (Hebrew), *Hadoar,* XXVIII, 537–39; and his "Four New Poems by R. Solomon ibn Gabirol" (Hebrew), *ibid.,* XXX, 476–78. Some improved readings on the basis of manuscripts are offered in J. Schirmann's textbook edition of Ibn Gabirol's *Shirim nibḥarim* (Selected Poems), while I. Davidson's edition of our poet's *Selected Religious Poems* has been provided with English translations by Israel Zangwill, whose pertinent remarks "On Translating Gabirol" (*ibid.,* pp. xlv–liv) point up the difficulties of reproducing the flavor of medieval Hebrew poetry in a Western language. See also A. Mandelbaum's more recent English translation of "Seven Secular Poems—Solomon ibn Gabirol," *Commentary,* XI, 181–83; and H. Abt's succinct review of "English Translations of the Machzor," *Jewish Affairs,* IX, No. 9, pp. 21–24. Even long-known and apparently complete poems have been shown by better manuscripts to have been defectively reproduced by careless or arbitrary copyists. See the three poems by Ibn Gabirol, as well as one each by Moses ibn Ezra and Halevi, more fully restored by A. M. Habermann in his "Supplementary Material on Certain Poems" (Hebrew), *Tarbiz,* XIX, 187 ff. A new comprehensive and critical edition of Ibn Gabirol's poems is, therefore, definitely indicated, as is also a detailed biography, reexamining the scattered bits of evidence in the light of the present state of our knowledge. For the time being, see the comprehensive Hebrew study by J. N. Simhoni (Simchowitsch), "R. Solomon ibn Gabirol" in *Hatekufah,* X, 143–223; XII, 149–88; XVII, 248–94; H. Schirmann's "On the Study of the Life of Solomon ibn Gabirol" (Hebrew), *Keneset,* X, 244–57; and the biographical sketches by Davidson in the introduction to his edition; by J. M. Millás Vallicrosa in his *Šelomó ibn Gabirol como poeta y filósofo;* and by E. Bertola in his *Salomon ibn Gabirol* (*Avicebron*), the latter emphasizing Ibn Gabirol's philosophy.

28. Moses ibn Ezra's *K. al-Muḥadhara,* v (*Shirat Yisrael,* p. 70); his *Be-rishpe ha-bekhi* (Sparks of Wail) in his *Shire ha-ḥol* (Secular Poems), ed. by H. Brody, I, 175 No. 176 v. 7; and Al-Ḥarizi's *Taḥkemoni,* XVIII, ed. by Lagarde, p. 91 (ed. by Toporowski, pp. 189 f., 442). See also *supra,* n. 22; and *infra,* n. 37. Although Moses ibn Ezra lived in the full light of history, and his own as well as his confreres' writings abound with biographical references, many phases of his life are still obscure. Even the romantic legend of his unhappy love for his niece and his ensuing life as a broken-hearted lover has been exploded only in recent years. See esp. H. Brody's "Moses ibn Ezra—Incidents in His Life," *JQR,* XXIV, 309 ff.; and the introduction to his ed. of *Selected Poems* by Moses ibn Ezra (with an English trans. by S. Solis-Cohen), pp. xxvi f., 180 ff. Nor does there exist so far

a complete collection of Ibn Ezra's poems. True, the secular poems have found two successive editors in Bialik and Rawnitzky, and, with greater attention to critical detail, in H. Brody. The latter compilation is distinguished also by its arrangement of the poems in the alphabetical order of their rhymes—a system widely practiced in medieval Arabic and Hebrew editions of poetry but long since abandoned in Jewish letters. See I. Elbogen's critique in his "Zur hebräischen Poesie des Mittelalters," *MGWJ*, LXXXII, 306 ff. Ibn Ezra's prolific output of religious poems, too, has been recently assembled in S. Bernstein's ed. of the poet's *Shire ha-Qodesh* (Sacred Poems). Yet, much of it still awaits critical evaluation. See *infra*, n. 51.

The poet's early popularity contributed to the uncertainties of his authorship of certain poems. For example, a well-known liturgical composition, *El nora 'alilah* (God of Awe-Inspiring Deeds), so deeply impressed a later poet, Joseph bar Isaac, that he prefaced it by a poem twice its length which he identified by an acrostic of his own. This introductory poem misled later scholars into attributing the whole *piyyuṭ* to the younger author. See Bernstein, "Who Composed the *Piyyuṭ El Nora 'Alilah?*" (Hebrew), *Hadoar*, XXXI, 754–55. See also R. Castillo, "Poesias de Moisés ibn Ezra," *Arbor*, XVIII, 525–29; D. Yellin, *Ketabim*, II, 331 ff.; A. J. Borisov, "Observations on the Poetry of Moses ibn Ezra" (Russian), *Izvestiya* (Bulletin) of the Academy of Science of the USSR, 7th ser., 99–117; D. Gonzalo Maeso, "Semblanza literaria de Mosé ibn Ezra," *Miscellanea de Estudios árabes y hebraicos* of the University of Granada, IV, 241–55; and *infra*, n. 51.

29. Halevi's *Diwan*, ed. by Brody, I, 18 No. 14 vv. 53–54; 154 f. No. 101 vv. 1–4, 13–16; in his *Kol Shire* (Collected Poems), ed. by I. Zemorah, I, Part 3, pp. 22 No. 8, 173 No. 2, or in his *Selected Poems*, ed. by H. Brody, p. 78 No. 41 (Nina Salaman's trans. is based on a different interpretation). The poet's alleged vow in old age to quit versifying, related by his purported disciple, Solomon ibn Parḥon (*Maḥberet he-'arukh*, ed. by S. G. Stern, p. xxii and fol. 5ab), if authentic, may have been but a disconsolate outburst reflecting a temporary mood. Halevi's great erudition came to the fore also in his poetic works. Not only were they filled, even more than those of his confreres, with allusions to biblical and rabbinic letters understandable only to well-informed readers, but he also was a learned student of earlier poetic writings. In his Hebrew essay, "Source and Imitation in Poetry," *Sinai*, XIII, Nos. 147–48, pp. 36–52, M. Zulay has pointed out how greatly Halevi was influenced by poetic patterns first developed by Saadiah. The poet also quoted with great reverence such outstanding rabbinic authorities as Alfasi and Ibn Megas. See *supra*, Chap. XXVII, n. 94 and the concluding paragraphs of that Chapter. Similarly, Halevi's "Riddle of Birds" (*Diwan* I, 107 No. 74; ed. by Zemorah, I, Part 3, pp. 239 f.) can only be understood in the light of some Spanish-Arabic correspondence, described by S. M. Stern in his "Two Medieval Hebrew Poems Explained from the Arabic," *Sefarad*, X, 325–38. See also the Hebrew essays by I. Ratzaby, "Collectanea and Addenda to the Poetry of Yehudah Halevi," *Tarbiz*, XXIII, 16–25; and A. Mirski, "Notes on the Text of Yehudah Halevi's Poems," *Sinai*, XIV, Nos. 171–74, pp. 43–57, 173–90. It is small wonder, then, that the personality and work of the great poet-philosopher has fascinated generations of scholars. An interesting selection of comments on Halevi by representative writers of several generations was published by I. Zemorah under the title *R. Yehudah Halevi: Qobeṣ meḥqarim ve-ha'arakhot* (A Collection of Studies and Evaluations). See H. Schirmann's comprehensive study of "The Life of Yehudah

Halevi" (Hebrew), *Tarbiz,* IX, 35–54, 219–40, 284–305; X, 237–39; XI, 125; J. M. Millás Vallicrosa's *Yehudah ha-Levi como poeta y apologista;* the anniversary volume published on the occasion of the octocentennial of the poet's death by the American Academy for Jewish Research; and *Rabbi Yehudah Halevi: Qobeṣ torani-madda'i,* ed. by J. L. Fishman. See also the collection of essays in the special issue of *Hadoar,* XX, No. 10, pp. 145–66; *infra,* n. 46; Chap. XXXIV, n. 12; and, on the impact of the crusading age, my "Yehudah Halevi: an Answer to an Historic Challenge," *JSS,* III, 243–72. More recently, S. D. Goitein has published interesting new letters, evidently stemming from the archives of a wealthy Egyptian merchant, Ḥalfon ben Nethanel, who made the poet's acquaintance on a visit to Spain. These shed much light on Halevi's last years. See "The Last Phase of R. Yehudah Halevi's Life in the Light of the Genizah Papers" (Hebrew), *Tarbiz,* XXIV, 21–47, 139–49, 468. At the same time we must bear in mind that the name Yehudah Halevi was not unique. An earlier poet by that name was unearthed by M. Zulay, who published a number of liturgical poems by that Palestinian author in his Hebrew essay "R. Yehudah Halevi Who Is Not Yehudah Halevi," *Eretz Israel,* IV, 138–44.

30. Most of the works of these poets have become more fully known only during the last several decades. In addition to N. Allony's aforementioned edition of Dunash ben Labraṭ's *Shirim,* see especially S. Bernstein's Hebrew essays: "The First Poet of the 'Golden Age': R. Joseph ibn Abitur and His Liturgical Poetry," *Sefer ha-Shanah li-Yehude Amerika,* 5701, pp. 171–85 (also reprint); "Poems of the Priestly Orders by R. Joseph ibn Abitur," *Sinai,* XV, Nos. 187–88, pp. 284–309; XVI, Nos. 189–90, p. 128 (with comments thereon by A. Mirski, *ibid.,* XV, Nos. 187–88, p. 310); "Unknown 'Penitential Poems' by Joseph ibn Abitur," *Sura,* I, 26–47; and "Who Is the Poet 'R. Joseph'?" *Tarbiz,* XIII, 150–64, denying Ibn Abitur's authorship of a poem (see *supra,* n. 15). Sometimes, on the other hand, Ibn Abitur's authorship of his genuine poems was forgotten. M. Zulay succeeded, by ingenious argument, to recover for him a number of liturgical compositions from among anonymous fragments. See his "From the *Yoṣerot* by R. Joseph ibn Abitur on the Pentateuchal Lessons" (Hebrew), *KS,* XXX, 243–53.

On Isaac ibn Gayyat, whom he considers influenced by Ibn Abitur, see Bernstein, "New Spanish Poems from the Golden Age" (Hebrew), *Alim,* II, 57–78; "New Poems from Spain and France," *Tarbiz,* X, 1–29 (includes on p. 3 a bibliographical summary of Ibn Gayyat's published poems); "New Poems by R. Isaac ibn Gayyat," *ibid.,* XI, 295–325 (includes fourteen new poems); "Poetic Remnants from the 'Golden Age,'" *HUCA,* XVI, Hebrew section, pp. 99–159 (esp. pp. 112 ff.; from the aforementioned *Maḥzor Ḥizzunim,* published in Venice about 1580–85, and now extremely rare; it is more fully described by I. Davidson in his bibliographical sketch, "Ḥizzunim," in *Poznanski Mem. Vol.,* Hebrew section, pp. 59–77; and by S. Bernstein in "The 'Unknown Mahzor' in the Library of the Jewish Theological Seminary of America," *Journal of Jewish Bibliography,* III, 1–11, furnishing also an alphabetical list of the 135 poems included in that volume); "New Piyyuṭim by Isaac ibn Gayyat from MSS" (Hebrew), *Talpioth,* V, 493–532; and I. Mendelsohn, "Poems by R. Isaac ben Yehudah ibn Gayyat and R. Israel ben Moses Najara" (Hebrew), *Horeb,* IX, 50–58. The work of other early poets is described by H. Schirmann in his "Isaac ben Saul, the Poet of Lucena" (Hebrew), *Sefer Assaf,* pp. 496–514; and by S. Abramson in his "In the Paths of Hebrew Poetry in Spain" (Hebrew), *Sinai,* XVIII, No. 219, pp. 538–45.

In many ways different is the poetry of the Bible exegetes Ibn Chiquitilla and

Ibn Ezra. See S. Poznanski, "Moses ibn Chiquitilla as Poet," *HUCA,* I, 599–601 (with I. Davidson's "Note" thereon, *ibid.,* p. 601); and H. Brody's ed. of "Poems by Moses ha-Kohen ibn Chiquitilla" (Hebrew), *SRIHP,* III, 65–90 (ten poems including such doubtful ones as No. 10, which more likely stemmed from Moses ibn Ezra's pen). Abraham ibn Ezra's poetic creativity, long known from his *Diwan,* ed. by J. Egers and supplemented by D. Rosen's *Reime und Gedichte des Abraham Ibn Esra* (also from D. Kahana's Hebrew compilation), has been enriched in recent years by many new publications. See esp. S. Bernstein's and J. Marcus's editions of new liturgical poems listed *infra,* n. 52; H. Brody's "Hitherto Unpublished Poems by Abraham ibn Ezra, First Collection" (Hebrew), *SRIHP,* VI, 1–45 (includes 39 liturgical and 2 secular poems; the continuation failed to appear because of the editor's death); and N. Ben Menahem's ed. of "Abraham ibn Ezra's Liturgical Poems from the Genizah" (Hebrew), *Sinai,* XIII, Nos. 153–54, pp. 69–74. See also *supra,* Chaps. XXI, n. 54; XXIX, n. 59.

Of the literature concerning later poets we need but mention that Al-Ḥarizi's popular *Taḥkemoni* has been supplemented by S. Bernstein's ed. of his "New 'Maqamas'" (Hebrew), *Horeb,* I, 179–87 (also *infra,* nn. 54–55). See also A. M. Habermann's comments on "The Poems by Ḥarizi" (Hebrew), *Mizraḥ u-ma'arab,* IV, 18–21; and K. Albrecht's older but still useful survey of *Die im Taḥkemoni vorkommenden Angaben über Ḥarizis Leben, Studien und Reisen.* Isaac ibn Ezra's *Shirim* (Poems), ed. by N. Ben-Menahem (with A. Mirski's extensive review thereof in *KS,* XXVII, 300–308) are likewise supplemented by J. L. Fleischer's biographical study "On the Life Story of Isaac Ibn Ezra" (Hebrew), *Sinai,* XI, Nos. 126–27, pp. 263–76. See also S. Bernstein, "Unknown Poems by R. Yehudah ben R. Abun [ibn Abbas]" *Essays Hertz,* Hebrew section, pp. 15–33; and A. Scheiber, "An Unknown Sabbath-Song by Yehudah ben Samuel ibn Abbas" (Hebrew), *Tarbiz,* XXIII, 127–29 (from a Kaufmann MS, referring also to earlier publications, especially by H. [J.] Schirmann); and H. Brody, "Poems and Letters by R. Meir ha-Levi Abulafia" (Hebrew), *SRIHP,* II, 1–90.

31. Samuel ibn Nagrela's *Diwan,* ed. by Sassoon, pp. 8 f. No. 10 vv. 52 ff.; ed. by Habermann, I, No. 1, pp. 7 f. The inscription on this poem, doubtless placed there by the original editor, Samuel's son Joseph, indicates that the poem described the battle of Friday, Elul 1, 4798 (August 4, 1037). On the historical background of the Nagid's battle poems assembled by Habermann in the first volume of his edition, see especially the careful analysis by H. Schirmann in "The Wars of Samuel ha-Nagid" (Hebrew), *Zion,* I, 261–83, 357–76; and his aforementioned survey, "Le Divan de Šemuel Hannagid considéré comme source pour l'histoire espagnole," *Hespéris,* XXXV, 163–88. Among the few other contemporary descriptions of military clashes one may note particularly Solomon ben Joseph ha-Kohen's poetic description of the Turkmen defeat in Egypt in 1077 (see *infra,* n. 44); and Al-Ḥarizi's imaginary prose narrative and poems in his *Taḥkemoni,* VII, ed. by Lagarde, pp. 40 ff. (ed. by Toporowski, pp. 83 ff.).

32. Halevi's *Diwan,* ed. by Brody, II, 12 No. 7 (ed. by Zemorah, I, Part 2, p. 28, No. 11; see N. Salaman's trans., p. 51); Samuel ibn Nagrela's *Diwan,* ed. by Sassoon, p. 92 No. 132 (ed. by Habermann, III, 58, No. 18). Halevi's love poems, occupying in Zemorah's edition an entire book (Vol. I, Part 2), are testimony to the ardent desires of his youth. At times quite outspoken, especially in the twenty-one poems

addressed to the *ya'alat ḥen* (gracious gazelle), they never transcended the bounds of propriety. They nevertheless must have shocked some of his own puritanical contemporaries, and they allegedly were cause for regret to the poet himself in his declining years.

33. Ibn Gabirol's *Shire,* I, 145 No. 74. Of course, not all Arabic love poems of the period addressed themselves to carnal desires. Many authors, even in Spain, sang the praises of Platonic love, even the mystical love of God. See A. González Palencia's observations in "El amor platónico en la corte de los Califas," *Boletín* of the Royal Academy of Sciences in Cordova, VIII, 1–25. The erotic poems addressed by Halevi and other poets to male friends were, however, clearly the reflection of a poetic fashion taken over from the Arab environment, for there is no evidence that Jewish society ever countenanced any kind of homosexual love, even in its more spiritualized forms. In fact, in a single reconstructed case, a poet-cantor's homosexual attachment seems to have led to blackmail and ultimately to his public disgrace, if we accept S. M. Stern's interpretation of two difficult poems of unknown authorship (published in I. Davidson's *Ginze Schechter,* III, 220–23) in his Hebrew essay "On the Understanding of 'The Maqama' of the Precentor Selling Sacred Books" in *Tarbiz,* XIX, 62–63. On Jacob ben Eleazar's love stories written in poetic prose, see *infra,* n. 70.

34. Ibn Gabirol's *Shire,* ed. by Bialik and Rawnitzky, I, 41 ff., especially p. 50 No. 21, and 64 No. 27; Moses ibn Ezra's, *K. al-Muḥadhara,* v (*Shirat Yisrael,* p. 71). On Yequtiel, see *supra,* n. 27. Of course, not all of Ibn Gabirol's satire was biting and bitter. Some of it, as his famous song on the substitution of wine by water, *Kikhlot yeyni* (When I Finished My Wine, My Eyes Poured Forth Streams of Water; *Shire,* I, 156 No. 83) was delightfully humorous.

35. Samuel ibn Nagrela's *Diwan,* ed. by Sassoon, p. 28 No. 34 (ed. by Habermann II, 98 f. Nos. 2–3, both relating to Isaac's death in the early morning hours of Thursday, Iyyar 25, 4801 = April 30, 1041); Abraham ibn Ezra's *Diwan,* ed. by Egers, pp. 93 f. No. 205, 166 ff.; Isaac ibn Ezra's *Shirim,* ed. by N. Ben Menahem, pp. 37 ff. Since Isaac's conversion apparently occurred not long after 1143 (see *ibid.,* p. 44), our poem was probably written soon thereafter, many years before Abraham's death. However, Ben Menahem's arguments for Isaac's relatively early death, despite his complaints of old age creeping up on him (*ibid.,* pp. 7, 24, 45), are unconvincing. J. L. Fleischer made a far better case for dating the poet's demise in 1164, but three years before that of his famous father. See his "On the Life Story of Isaac ibn Ezra" (Hebrew), *Sinai,* XI, Nos. 126–27, pp. 263–76. See also A. Mirski's Hebrew review of Ben Menahem's edition in *KS,* XXVII, 300–308; and H. Schirmann's observations in *Ha-Shirah ha-'ibrit,* I, 624 ff.

36. Halevi's friendship poems occupy a large part of his *Diwan,* ed. by Brody, and are assigned a substantial special book (Vol. I, Part 3) in Zemorah's edition. See especially *ibid.,* p. 11 No. 3; and *supra,* n. 29. Muslim Andalusia was often called the "West" in contrast to "Eastern," that is Christian, Spain. See J. M. Millás Vallicrosa's *Yehudá Ha-Levi como poeta y apologista,* pp. 13 f. The friends to whom these poems were addressed have been subjected to careful scrutiny by modern scholars. See especially Schirmann's detailed biography of Halevi in *Tarbiz,*

IX; and the data assembled in his "Poets, Contemporaries of Moses ibn Ezra and Yehudah Halevi" (Hebrew), *SRIHP,* II, 117–212; IV, 247–96; VI, 249–347.

37. See Ibn Ezra's renowned poems, *Eyne sela'im* (Rocks' Eyes Have Shed Tears Over Me), and *'Ad 'an be-galut* (How Long Yet Must My Feet . . . the Path of Exile Tread?) in his *Shire ha-ḥol,* ed. by Brody, I, 66 No. 67, 164 No. 164 (the latter also in Solis-Cohen's translation, pp. 2 ff.); Halevi's *Ekh akhrekha* in his *Diwan,* ed. by Brody, II, 328 ff. (ed. by Zemorah, I, Part 3, p. 11 No. 3); and Moses ibn Chiquitilla's poem, reedited by Brody in *SRIHP,* III, 67. See also A. Moar's analysis of "Moses ibn Ezra's Family Poems" (Hebrew), *Mabbua,* I, 404–9.

38. See *supra,* Chap. XXX, n. 58; Abraham ibn Ezra's *Diwan,* ed. by Egers, pp. 17 ff. (in D. Rosin's translation, I, 167 ff.); Dunash's *Shire,* pp. 94 ff. (with Allony's comments, *ibid.,* pp. 170 ff.; and in his "Ten Dunash ben Labraṭ's Riddles," *JQR,* XXXVI, 141 ff.); and Halevi's *Keli mekhil* in his *Diwan,* II, 195 (ed. by Zemorah, II, Part 6, p. 355 No. 5). See N. H. Tur-Sinai's Hebrew analyses of "The Linguistic Riddles of Abraham ibn Ezra" and "The Linguistic Pointedness in the Poems of Eleazar ben Simon ha-Babli," reprinted in his *Ha-Lashon ve-ha-sefer,* III, 354–65, 366–80; Y. Ratzaby's "Juristic Riddles in Yemenite Poetry," *Sinai,* XI, Nos. 128–30, pp. 36–44 (he believes that this type was first cultivated in Yemen); and N. Ben-Menahem's recent interpretation of a poem by Moses ibn Ezra in his "A Banquet in Spanish Granada: the Solution of a Riddle" (Hebrew), *Sinai,* XXI, No. 245, pp. 18–36.

39. Ibn Gabirol's *Shire,* I, 60 No. 24; Meir ha-Levi Abulafia's "Poems and Letters," ed. by H. Brody in his Hebrew essay in *SRIHP,* II, 82 No. 35. See also the examples cited in Yellin's *Ketabim,* II, 282 f.; and A. Moar's "Nature in the Poetry of Yehudah Halevi" (Hebrew), *Bitzaron,* XIII, No. 146, pp. 104–16. A detailed monograph on the descriptions of natural phenomena in medieval Hebrew poetry would doubtless yield some valuable insights.

40. Samuel ibn Nagrela's *Diwan,* ed. by Sassoon, pp. 117 ff., 136 No. 162, etc.; his *Ben Mishle* (Offshoots of Proverbs), ed. by S. Abramson, p. 45 No. 161. See M. Seidel's "Notes and Comments on R. Samuel ha-Nagid's *Ben Mishle*" (Hebrew), *Sinai,* XVI, No. 194, pp. 354–74. In his introductory survey of the contents of these epigrams Abramson shows that more than threescore refer to kings and their service (pp. 19 ff.). Many bear a clearly personal imprint, although they, too, may reflect in part the accumulated wisdom of Arab courtiers, who in turn had learned much from their Persian predecessors. Other Jewish authors of aphorisms paid much less attention to rulers and their behavior. See A. S. Halkin's brief comments in his "Classical and Arabic Material in Ibn 'Aḳnīn's 'Hygiene of the Soul,'" *PAAJR,* XIV, 28 n. 4. That Samuel borrowed heavily not only from current Near Eastern folklore, but also from Arabic prose and poetic letters, of which he was an avid reader (see *supra,* n. 23; and *infra,* n. 73), has long been recognized. In his *K. al-Muḥadhara,* v (*Shirat Yisrael,* p. 66) Moses ibn Ezra asserted that Samuel had "introduced in this book [*Ben Mishle*] many Arabic and Persian proverbs, philosophic wisdom, and gems of peoples long vanished, as well as sayings by our own ancient men of piety." See the specific examples of such indebtedness to Ibn Qutaiba and others in N. Bar-On's brief essay, "On the Study of the Sources of *Ben Mishle*

by Samuel ha-Nagid" (Hebrew) in *Ha-Kinnus ha-'olami,* I, 279–84. Such erudition in Arabic poetry did not interfere, of course, with the Nagid's even more learned allusions to rabbinic concepts and phrases, which presupposed much talmudic expertness on the part of readers. See the telling illustrations cited by S. Abramson in his "Words of the Sages in the Nagid's Poetry" (Hebrew), *ibid.,* pp. 274–78. At the same time, their purely secular objectives may help us understand some statements which seem out of line with Samuel's general orthodoxy. He who in his legal work was a rather rigid halakhist, and even in a poem once expostulated that he did not wish to impute an error to a gaon, allowed himself here some satirical comments on synagogues and academies; he advised his readers not to spend their days in pious works, but rather to "give Him [God] half a day and give the other half to your own pursuits." See his *Diwan,* pp. 50 f. No. 73, 110 No. 171 (ed. by Habermann, III, 19 No. 6, 88 No. 26).

Samuel's failure to indicate his sources required no apology to his contemporaries, even if his rendition from other languages had not sufficed to make the borrowed sections appear as parts of a new work. Generally standards of literary property throughout the medieval world, Muslim, Christian, and Jewish, were far less rigorous than today. Since adherence to traditions and bookish learning were generally more highly appreciated than personal originality, the authors themselves did not necessarily intend to display their own ingenuity in substantive matters. They and their readers were often satisfied with a purely formal, even technical innovation. See also G. E. von Grunebaum's analysis of "The Concept of Plagiarism in Arabic Theory," *JNES,* III, 235–53; and *supra,* Chap. XXIV, n. 4.

41. Moses ibn Ezra's *K. al-Muḥadhara,* v (*Shirat Yisrael,* pp. 67 f.). Among the critics of Samuel's philological concepts was, as we recall, no less an authority than Ibn Janaḥ. See *supra,* Chap. XXX, n. 52.

42. Hai Gaon's *Shire Musar haskel,* with an English trans. by H. Gollancz (the earlier editions included one annotated by M. E. Vogel, as well as Latin translations by J. Mercier and Jacob Ebert; the latter first appeared in T. Ebert's *Poetica hebraica,* and was subsequently republished in B. Ugolini's well-known *Thesaurus antiquitatum sacrarum,* XXXI, pp. ciii ff.). Cf. Z. Karob's affirmative answer to his query, "Did R. Hai Gaon Write the Poems *Musar Haskel?*" (Hebrew), *Mizraḥ u-ma'arab,* IV, 347–51; and *supra,* n. 17.

43. Ibn Gabirol's *Sefer Mibḥar ha-peninim* (Choice of Pearls), ed. with an English trans. by B. H. Asher (Latin extracts therefrom had appeared in J. Drusius's *Apophtegmata Ebraeorum ac Arabum,* 2d. ed., pp. 58 ff.). The numerous other editions of, as well as studies on, this work are listed in A. M. Habermann's Hebrew bibliographical survey in *Sinai,* XIII, Nos. 147–48, pp. 53–63. See also N. Bar-On's "Studies in Gabirol's *Mibḥar ha-peninim*" (Hebrew), *Tarbiz,* XXIII, 192–97. Despite all these intensive efforts some of the main critical problems, including the very authorship of this work by Ibn Gabirol, still are far from solved. The great similarity of Joseph Qimḥi's *Sheqel ha-qodesh* (Sacred Shekel) to this work has been definitely proved, however, especially by the two lengthy tables of comparison in H. Gollancz's critical edition of the *Sheqel,* pp. 127 ff. See also A. Marx's careful analysis of "Gabirol's Authorship of the Choice of Pearls and the Two Versions of Joseph Ḳimḥi's *'Sheḳel Haḳodesh,'*" *HUCA,* IV, 443–48; and *supra,* n. 4.

44. See Moses ibn Chiquitilla's "Poems," ed. by H. Brody, in *SRIHP,* III, 85 No. 9 lines 9–11; Mann's *Jews in Egypt,* I, 30 ff., 155 ff.; II, 30 ff., 176 ff.; and M. Zulay's "Liturgical Poems on Various Historical Events" (Hebrew), *SRIHP,* III, 151–83. Of greater interest is Solomon ben Joseph ha-Kohen's poem describing *The Turkoman Defeat at Cairo* in 1077, which spared the Jewish community, too, much suffering. See J. Greenstone's edition; and Mann's comments thereon in his *Jews in Egypt,* I, 207 f. See also *supra,* n. 29; *infra,* n. 62; and, on the general problem of history-mindedness among medieval Jewry, *supra,* Chap. XXVIII, *passim.*

45. Ibn Gabirol's *Zulat,* first published by R. Edelmann in *MGWJ,* LXXVII, 438 f., 444 ff.; Halevi's *Ototenu* in I. Ratzaby's fuller edition in his "Collectanea and Addenda to the Poetry of Yehudah Halevi" (Hebrew), *Tarbiz,* XXIII, 21 ff. (see N. Salaman's trans., pp. 136 f.). The Leningrad MS of Ibn Gabirol's poem is unfortunately in very poor condition, and Edelmann's efforts to restore the text and give it an adequate interpretation have not proved altogether successful.

46. Halevi's *Diwan,* ed. by Brody, II, 155 f. (ed. by Zemorah, I, Part 1, pp. 5, 53 ff.). Miss Salaman's rendition of *Libbi be-mizraḥ* (My Heart Is in the East) differs from ours, while she herself offers two different versions of *Ṣiyyon ha-lo tish'ali* (Zion Dost Thou Not Ask?). See her trans., pp. 2 ff., 151 ff. But no less than eight English translations of this extremely popular poem, alongside seventeen German, six Yiddish, five French, four Russian, and many other renditions, were listed some twenty years ago by H. Schirmann in his bibliographical study of "Translations of Yehudah Halevi's *Ṣiyyon ha-lo tish'ali*" (Hebrew), *KS,* XV, 360–67. On the numerous Hebrew editions of that poem and its even more numerous imitations, see I. Davidson's *Oṣar,* III, 321 ff. See also "Yehudah Halevi's Letter to Ḥabib al-Makhdevi," reedited with a Russian trans. and comments by K. B. Starkova in *Sovetskoe Vostokovedenie,* VI, 423–37; and "R. Yehudah Halevi's Letter on His Emigration to the Land of Israel" (Hebrew), ed. by S. Abramson in *KS,* XXIX, 133–44. The nationalist and "Zionist" emphases permeating Halevi's poetry have frequently been emphasized; they form a major part of every biographical and literary analysis. In addition to works already mentioned, esp. *supra,* n. 29, see also J. L. Fishman's study of "The Roots of R. Yehudah Halevi's Nationalism," in the collective Hebrew volume *Rabbi Yehudah Halevi,* ed. by Fishman, pp. 67–77; M. Ish-Shalom's "National-Sacred Poetry (On the Religious-National Poetry of R. Yehudah Halevi)," *ibid.,* pp. 77–95; and I. Efros's more popular survey, *Judah Halevi as Poet and Thinker.*

47. Ibn Gabirol's *Shire,* III, 3 f. No. 2, 105 No. 81; IV, 3, 56 (the first also in Zangwill's trans., p. 67 No. 39). See A. Parnes, "Ecstasy in the Life of Ibn Gabirol" (Hebrew), *Mo'znayim,* IV, 265–78, 386–98. On the linguistic deviations of his liturgical poetry see the examples analyzed by D. Yellin in his *Ketabim,* II, 303 ff.; and, more generally, the latter's Hebrew essay on "Solomon ibn Gabirol, the Man and the Poet," in *Sefer Klausner,* pp. 243–66; and Millás Vallicrosa's *Šelomo ibn Gabirol,* pp. 90 ff. Writing religious poetry, Ibn Gabirol and the other authors took for granted the readers' verbal recollection of Scripture; they often employed biblical phrases in an abbreviated fashion comprehensible only to readers filling in the rest from memory. See the data assembled by Yellin in his Hebrew essay on "Shortcuts in Spanish Poetry," *Keneset,* IV, 339–44. But they merely followed

therein the example of ancient homilists who briefly cited beginnings of scriptural verses when they sought support for their particular ideas in the unspoken continuation. Evidently both preacher and poet had the right to rely on the biblical erudition of their audiences, just as a modern speaker will usually intimate, rather than spell out, a familiar proverb.

Among the numerous writings on the sacred poetry of the Spanish school, the old volume by M. Sachs, *Die religiöse Poesie der Juden in Spanien,* has retained much of its charm and the value of its fine insights. Subsequently, good semi-popular reviews were offered in German by A. Sulzbach in J. Winter and A. Wünsche's *Jüdische Literatur,* III, 3–216, 904; and in Spanish by J. M. Millás Villacrosa in *La Poesia sagrada hebraico-española.* Cf. H. Schirmann's very instructive Hebrew review of the latter volume in *KS,* XXII, 123–29. For the last half century H. Brody, together with K. Albrecht and later with M. Wiener, has supplied the Hebrew-reading public with excellent anthologies of medieval Hebrew poetry. His and Wiener's *Mibḥar ha-shirah ha-'ibrit* (Anthology of Hebrew Poetry) was more recently reissued in a revised, though greatly abridged, form by A. M. Habermann, who has, moreover, added several more specialized selections, referred to in our previous and forthcoming notes. The Brody-Wiener anthology has, in part, been reproduced in a French translation by C. de Mouilleron in his *Poèmes hébreux anciens, traduits et annotés.* These publications have been overshadowed, but even in Hebrew not completely superseded, by H. Schirmann's basic anthology, *Ha-Shirah ha-'ibrit,* of which the first volume, covering the period from 950 to 1150, is particularly relevant to our treatment. Among the various critical evaluations of that volume, see esp. A. Mirski, "The Best of Spanish Hebrew Poetry Known to Our Generation" (Hebrew), *Beḥinnot,* VIII, 63–73. Important additional material has recently been published from the precious Lisbon MS by S. Bernstein in his aforementioned *'Al neharot Sefarad* (Spanish Litanies on the Fall of Jerusalem and Persecutions to 1391).

48. Samuel ibn Nagrela's *Diwan,* edited by A. M. Habermann, III, 153 No. 24; Ibn Abitur's *qedushahs* ("Holy, Holy, Holy"). Evidently but parts of his reputed full cycle of liturgical poems for the Day of Atonement, the latter are readily available in Hebrew with a German trans. and analysis in M. Sachs's *Religiöse Poesie,* pp. 40 ff., 248 ff., Hebrew section, pp. 9 ff. See also *supra,* n. 30; and Chap. XXIII, n. 65. Akin to Ibn Abitur's work is that of Isaac ibn Chiquitilla, one of Menaḥem ben Saruq's three pupils who took up the cudgels in the teacher's defense. Ibn Chiquitilla's *Azharot,* especially, bear the imprint of the school of Saadiah. See their partial reconstruction and analysis by M. Zulay in his "Azharot of R. Isaac ibn Chiquitilla" (Hebrew), *Tarbiz,* XX, 161–76. Since Isaac flourished only a short time after Ibn Abitur's departure from Spain, the latter's poetic creativity cannot be due mainly to his sojourn in the East. Both poets rather illustrate the early penetration of the Eastern *piyyuṭ,* along with the Babylonian approaches to talmudic learning, into the Iberian Peninsula. Both poetic themes, moreover, are found in more fully developed form in Ibn Gabirol's liturgical *Ofanim* and *Azharot,* respectively. See *infra,* nn. 50 and 82.

49. Al-Ḥarizi's *Taḥkemoni,* III, ed. by Lagarde, p. 22 (ed. by Toporowski, p. 41); Moses ibn Ezra's *K. al-Muḥadhara,* v (*Shirat Yisrael,* p. 72). A number of Ibn Gayyat's poems and studies thereon were listed in 1939 by S. Bernstein in his

"New Poems from Spain" (Hebrew), *Tarbiz,* X, 3 n. 11. Since that time considerable new material was published by Bernstein and others. See *supra,* n. 30.

50. Ibn Gabirol's *Shire,* III, 56 f. No. 58, 62 ff. No. 62, 135 ff. No. 99; IV, 30 ff., 34 ff., 72 ff.; VI, 50 ff. No. 58. See also Zangwill's trans. of the "Royal Crown," pp. 82 ff. No. 50; with I. Davidson's introduction thereto, pp. xxix ff.; Millás Vallicrosa's Spanish trans. and introductory remarks in his *Šelmo ibn Gabirol,* pp. 152 ff.; and especially the detailed Hebrew commentary by J. A. Seidman in his new edition of Ibn Gabirol's *Keter malkhut;* and A. Chouraqui's annotated French trans. and brief analysis of "Salomon ibn Gabirol La Couronne du Royaume," *Revue thomiste,* LII, 403–40. Of considerable interest is also F. P. Bargebuhr's analytical study, "Ibn Gabirol's Poem Beginning 'Ahavtikha' [I Have Loved Thee]," *Review of Religion,* XV, 5–18; and, with minor variations, "Die Bedeutung des Weltalls für Gott nach Ibn Gabirols philosophischem Gedichte," *Zeitschrift für Religions- und Geistesgeschichte,* VI, 18–36. Our poet's apparent unfamiliarity with Saadiah's enumeration of the six hundred and thirteen commandments (in the latter's *Siddur,* pp. 157 ff.; see *supra,* Chap. XXXI, n. 70) is the more remarkable, as Isaac ibn Chiquitilla's *Azharot* had clearly betrayed the gaon's influence alongside that of the *Halakhot gedolot* (see *supra,* n. 48). However, Isaac may have learned Saadiah's views indirectly, rather than from his prayer book, which seems to have become popular in Spain only at a somewhat later date. Even such an ardent collector as Samuel ibn Nagrela, who maintained close contact with the Babylonian academies, seems not to have possessed a copy. The only possible quotation from the *Siddur,* transmitted in the Nagid's name by Abraham ben Isaac of Narbonne (in his *Eshkol,* ed. by Albeck, I, 185), may have stemmed either from somebody else's earlier citation or from a similar statement in one of Saadiah's juristic or exegetical writings. The first Spaniard to make full use of Saadiah's liturgical *magnum opus* appears to have been Isaac ibn Gayyat. See Assaf's introduction to Saadiah's *Siddur,* pp. 34, 36.

51. Moses ibn Ezra's *Shire ha-ḥol,* ed. by Brody, I, 237 ff. No. 234 vv. 4–5 (unfortunately Brody's comments on this poem have remained unpublished); his *Selected Poems,* trans. by S. Solis-Cohen, pp. 105 ff. No. 44; and Meir Abulafia's poem *Yeḥidah de'i ṣurekh* (My Soul, Know Thy Creator), ed. by Brody in *SRIHP,* II, 79 ff. No. 34. Brody's fine edition of Moses ibn Ezra's secular poems includes such philosophic odes as the *Be-shem El* (In the Lord's Name), quoted here. This poem, the longest of all of our author's extant lyrics, borders on sacred poetry, having been deeply influenced by Ibn Gabirol's "Royal Crown." Remarkably, among the highest human attainments Ibn Ezra noted here the combination of correct Hebrew and Arabic speech and Greek learning. Of the more recently published poems, see especially the ten *piyyuṭim* ed. by S. Bernstein in his "Two New Liturgical Poems by R. Moses ibn Ezra" (Hebrew), *Hadoar,* XV, 259–61; and in his aforementioned "Poetic Remnants" (Hebrew), *HUCA,* XVI, 130 ff., beginning with a didactic poem on Ḥanukkah, and S. Abramson's detailed review of Brody's edition of *Shire ha-ḥol,* II, Part 1, in *Tarbiz,* XIII, 250–58. See also *supra,* n. 28. On the other hand, more recent investigations have shown that several poems previously ascribed to Moses ibn Ezra were really written by Moses ibn Chiquitilla, the distinguished Bible exegete of approximately the same period. See H. Brody's introduction to his edition of the latter's poems in *SRIHP,* III, 67 ff. Brody admits,

however, that one of these poems (No. 10, pp. 86 ff.) is more probably of Ibn Ezra's authorship. If this hypothesis should prove correct, we would have before us one of the relatively few love poems by Ibn Ezra. The paucity of such writings by Ibn Ezra and Ibn Gabirol doubtless stimulated popular imagination to weave the aforementioned amorous legends around both masters. See *supra,* nn. 26–28.

52. The sacred poetry of Abraham ibn Ezra still awaits a definitive edition. Despite the meritorious efforts of Egers, Rosin, and Kahana several decades ago (see *supra,* n. 30), so many new poems from the pen of this distinguished polyhistor have since come to light that a new critical edition is clearly indicated. See esp. J. Marcus's publication from an Adler MS of "New Liturgical Poems by R. Abraham ibn Ezra" (Hebrew), *Mizraḥ u-ma'arab,* V, 273–88; S. Bernstein's edition of "Liturgical Poems from an Unknown *Diwan* by R. Abraham ibn Ezra" (Hebrew), *Tarbiz,* V, 61–74; of one additional poem, in his "New Poems," *ibid.,* X, 3, 8 f.; and of eight more in his "Poetic Remnants," *HUCA,* XVI, 140 ff.

53. Halevi's *Yah, ana emṣa'akha* and *Yah, shimkha aromimkha* in his *Diwan,* ed. by Brody, III, 150 No. 82 (in the English trans. by S. Solis-Cohen in his essay on "Judah Halevi" reprinted in his *Judaism and Science,* pp. 174 ff.), 230 No. 128; or in his *Kol Shire,* ed. by Zemorah, III, Part 7, pp. 121 f.; Part 10, pp. 641 f. N. Salaman offers different translations (pp. 94 ff. No. 46, 127 ff. No. 70, 134 ff. No. 73, 168 f.). See Halevi's *K. al-Khazari,* v.21 end ed. by H. Hirschfeld, pp. 356 f. (in his English trans., p. 292, with David Cassel's comments on Ibn Tibbon's Hebrew trans. in his ed., p. 429 n. 3); and, more generally, I. Heinemann's careful analysis of "The Philosopher-Poet: a Selection of Poems by R. Yehudah Halevi" (Hebrew), *Keneset,* IX, 163–200. See also *supra,* n. 29; and Chaps. XXV, n. 17; XXVIII, n. 97.

54. Baḥya's poems reprinted in Yahuda's and Zifroni's editions of his "Duties of the Heart" (see *infra,* Chap. XXXIV, n. 11); Joseph ibn Ṣaddiq's *Yeminenu be-ḥeq qoṣer 'aṣurah* (Our Right Hand Is Detained) in *Sha'ar ha-shir. The New Hebrew School of Poets of the Spanish-Arabian Epoch,* ed. by H. Brody and K. Albrecht, p. 127; Halevi's reply in his *Diwan,* ed. by Brody, I, 118 f. No. 83 (ed. by Zemorah, I, Part 3, p. 155); H. Brody's "R. Meshullam da Piera against Maimonides: Two Poems" (Hebrew), *Sefer Klausner,* pp. 267–73 (listing also other anti-Maimonidean poems, in part aimed at the translators); and his "Limericks on Maimonides and His Books" (Hebrew), *Mo'znayim,* III, 402–13. The latter include, of course, also pro-Maimonidean poems. On Ibn Ṣaddiq's poetry, see esp. H. Schirmann's comprehensive Hebrew study of "Poets Contemporary with Moses ibn Ezra," *SRIHP,* II, 163 ff. The poem *Yigdal* has, ever since Luzzatto's discovery of a pertinent reference in a late medieval Italian MS, been attributed to Daniel ben Yehudah (*ca.* 1300). The contrary view, emphatically reiterated by H. Hirschfeld, who ascribed the poem to Immanuel of Rome (see "The Author of the Yigdal Hymn," *JQR,* XI, 86–88), has little to commend itself. On Maimonides' attitude to poetry see *supra,* Chap. XXXI, nn. 55 and 58.

55. S. J. L. Rapoport's Hebrew introduction to his Purim drama, *She'erit Yehudah* (the Remnant of Judah) in *Bikkure ha-'ittim,* 5588, p. 184; Amittai's poem, *Adon maggid* (The Master Foretells), reprinted in the collection of early Italian Hebrew poems in the appendix to B. Klar's ed. of Aḥimaaz' *Chronicle,* pp. 72 ff. See also

infra, n. 61. The same themes pervade also the few surviving poems of Amittai's father, Shefaṭiah, and of the first known Italian-Hebrew poet, the unfortunate Silano. See *supra,* Chap. XXIII, n. 65. We must bear in mind that these poets lived in southern Italy under its oppressive Byzantine domination. The transformation under the Norman and Hohenstaufen regimes is well illustrated by the data supplied by S. M. Stern in "A Twelfth-Century Circle of Hebrew Poets in Sicily," *JJS,* V, 60–79, 110–13. See also J. Schirmann's *Anthologie der hebräischen Dichtung in Italien,* which is mainly concerned with the later periods, however. An analysis of that later poetry, including Immanuel's, must be relegated here to a later volume.

56. Isaac bar Moses' *Sefer Or zaru'a* (R. Gershom had acted "out of an excess of mourning"); *Ma'aseh Buch* (Story Book), compiled by an unknown German author, probably between 1580 and 1602 (the date of the first Amsterdam edition) and translated into English by M. Gaster, No. 188 (II, 410 ff.); the collection of *Ma'asiyot* (Stories), ed. by A. Jellinek in his *Bet ha-Midrasch,* V, 148–52; VI, 137–39; and his introductory comments, *ibid.,* V. pp. xxxvii f.; VI, xxx ff. (both texts are reprinted in Eisenstein's *Ozar Midrashim,* pp. 329 ff. Nos. 12–13). See also J. Meitlis's careful analysis of *Das Ma'assehbuch.* The historical background of Amittai's poem, *Ahabtikha* (in Klar's ed. of the Aḥimaaz chronicle, pp. 95 ff.), has been plausibly reconstructed by I. Sonne in his "Note sur une Keroba d'Amitai publiée par Davidson," *REJ,* XCVIII, 81–84. See also J. Starr's *Jews in the Byzantine Empire,* pp. 5 f., 127 No. 62.

Conversions of scions of distinguished Jewish families were not altogether rare, even under the domination of Islam. In their diverse ways Isaac ben Abraham ibn Ezra and Samuel (Samau'al) ibn 'Abbas al-Maghribi left behind significant literary works shedding considerable light both on the psychological vicissitudes of their authors and the social position of their Jewish contemporaries. On the other hand, a son of the poet Abu 'Amr ibn Ḥisdai, friend of Samuel ibn Nagrela and author of the famous *shirah yetomah* (Orphan Poem, reedited together with Samuel's reply in the latter's *Diwan,* ed. by Sassoon, pp. 70 ff.), turned to politics and, after his conversion to Islam, assumed the name of Abu'l Fadhl ibn Ḥisdai. As a Muslim he became an Arab polyhistor and influential statesman at the court of three Muslim kings of Saragossa (end of the 11th cent.). See Millás's *Poesia sagrada,* pp. 44, 83; and *infra,* n. 95. However, such conversions in the north, especially among the leading families, made a more lasting impression in so far as the communities themselves were far smaller and more closely knit. While in Spain and in the Near East such tragedies could still be shrugged off as individual whims and misfortunes, they loomed as major communal calamities in the weak and struggling Ashkenazic communities. Incidentally, the legend of the Jewish pope Elḥanan and his father's successful mission to Rome doubtless arose from a curious combination of Jacob ben Yekutiel's intervention in 1007–10 and the election of the "Jewish" Pope Anacletus II in 1130. See *supra,* Chap. XX, nn. 8 and 74. It could not have originated, therefore, until several generations after Simon's death.

57. Simon bar Isaac's *El El ḥai arannen* (I Shall Sing to the Living God) verse 8; and his *Eleh ba-rekheb* (They Glory in Chariots) in his *Piyyuṭe,* ed. by Habermann, pp. 40, 159 ff. (see also B. Klar's review of that edition reprinted in his

Meḥqarim ve-'iyyunim, pp. 145–49); Amittai's *Ezkerah Elohim* (I Remember the Lord) in Klar's ed. of Aḥimaaz' *Chronicle,* pp. 108 f.; and "Some Religious Poems by R. Solomon the Babylonian" (Hebrew), ed. by D. Goldschmidt in *Tarbiz,* XXIII, 198–204. Very effective also is Gershom's *Elekha niqra* (We Cry Out to Thee), describing in unminced language the terrific conversionist pressures and the stout resistance of the Jewish communities. Habermann's ed. of Gershom's *Seliḥot u-pizmonim,* pp. 12 ff.; *supra,* Chap. XXI, n. 3; and, in the context of his other works, S. Eidelberg's aforementioned biographical sketch of "R. Gershom" in *Sinai,* XVIII, No. 214, pp. 57 ff. Christian censorship, which might have interfered with the circulation of such outspoken declarations, was not to become effective until the age of printing presses.

58. Amittai's *En lanu Elohim* (We Have No other God but Thee), vv. 21–22, in Klar's ed. of Aḥimaaz' *Chronicle,* p. 97; Gershom's *Ayyeh kol nifleotekha* (Where Are All Thy Miracles?), vv. 29–30, in his *Seliḥot,* p. 8. Needless to say, the messianic problem was not absent from the Muslim-Jewish controversies. However, it obviously could not play quite the same role there as it did in the Judeo-Christian debate as to whether the Messiah had already come. That is why the anonymous "Polemical Poem on the Messianic Idea," beginning *She'aluni doreshai* (My Inquirers Asked Me), and published by I. Davidson in a pertinent Hebrew essay in *Sefer Klausner,* pp. 274–76, very likely stems from a Christian, rather than a Muslim, environment. That the end of the poem is indicated by an Arabic term merely betrays the Arabic speech of the copyist. The poem's utter simplicity and the absence of a rhyme or a self-identifying acrostic might even point to an early Byzantine milieu. See also the messianic poems discussed *supra,* Chap. XXV, nn. 13 ff.

59. The poem *Titnem le-ḥerpah* (Put Them to Shame), published on the basis of three MSS by A. H. Freimann in his Hebrew essay under this title in *Tarbiz,* XII, 70–74 (attributes it to Rashi; see below); Baruch bar Samuel's "Liturgical Poems," ed. by A. M. Habermann in *SRIHP,* VI, 47–160 including (on pp. 133 ff. No. 25) the penitential prayer *Esh okhloah esh* (Fire Devouring Fire) on the martyrs of Blois. See also S. Spiegel's aforementioned stimulating essay, *"In Monte Dominus Videbitur:* the Martyrs of Blois and the Early Accusation of Ritual Murder," *Kaplan Jub. Vol.,* Hebrew section, pp. 267–87. Ephraim bar Jacob of Bonn's *Sefer Zekhirah* (Book of Remembrance), has frequently been cited above from the Neubauer and Stern edition, as well as from A. M. Habermann's anthology, *Sefer Gezerot Ashkenaz ve-Ṣarefat* (Persecutions in Germany and France), pp. 115 ff. Reprinting here also *Titnem le-ḥerpah* (pp. 105 f.), Habermann points out (p. 254) its similarity with the poem *Aniah ve-ta'aniah* (Lament and Wailing) by Joseph ben Isaac (probably Ibn Abitur), published by I. Davidson in his *Ginze Schechter,* III, 320. But the differences, both formal and substantive, are greater than the similarities. That is why the possibility of Rashi's authorship of that vindictive poem is not entirely disproved by the argument adduced by Habermann in his critical edition of *Piyyuṭe Rashi* (Rashi's Liturgical Poems), p. 34. Although more sharply formulated, the sentiments here expressed do not differ materially from those in the poem *Torah ha-temimah* (The Integral Torah), vv. 41 ff., 49 f., the latter obviously aimed at the conquering Crusaders in Palestine. See *ibid.,* p. 23. In any case, both poems emanated from the school of Rashi not long after the tragic events of 1096. See also R. F. Aronstein's Hebrew review of

Habermann's *Sefer Gezerot* in *Orlogin,* IV, 265; S. Bernstein's earlier succinct observations on "Rashi as a Poet" (Hebrew), *Hadoar,* XX, 205–7; and *supra,* Chap. XXI, nn. 60 and 65.

60. Gershom's *Gadol 'avoni* (My Transgression Is Great) in his *Seliḥot,* pp. 24 ff. See *supra,* Chap. XXXI, n. 34. On the antecedents and manifold variations of the chain verse technique see *infra,* n. 84.

61. Amittai's *Attah hu* (It Is Thou Whose Years Are Never Ended) in Klar's edition, p. 101. See *supra,* n. 55, and, on the apologetic aspects of medieval sexual ethics, *supra,* Chap. XXIV, n. 67. Ashkenazic poetry is, indeed, filled with passages like the following. "Into my transgressions before Thee I pry, / My people's failings, too, I sadly decry. / Lord! have mercy on penitents gone awry." See Gershom's *Eshpokh siḥi lefanekha* (I Pour Out My Prayer before Thee), vv. 4–6, in his *Seliḥot,* p. 17. In fact, even before the era of the great massacres, northern letters were filled with self-recrimination, testifying to the overpowering sense of guilt permeating these Jewish communities. This guilt complex evidently was but the counterpart to, and rationale of, the Jewish sufferings.

62. Moses bar Kalonymos' poems, in part newly published in the appendix to Habermann's ed. of Simon bar Isaac's *Piyyuṭe,* pp. 191 ff.; the latter's Passover *qerobot, ibid.,* pp. 62 ff.; and numerous poems included in Habermann's *Sefer Gezerot, passim.* Among these northern poets, it was Gershom bar Yehudah who seems to have been endowed with a particularly keen historical sense. Of his ten extant poems two (*Attah mi-qedem* [From of Old Thou Hast Been Our God and Master] and *Zekhor berit Abraham* [Remember the Covenant of Abraham] in his *Seliḥot,* pp. 21 ff., 30 ff.) are wholly based on brief historical surveys demonstrating the divine guidance of history. Several others contain at least some historical allusions. In contrast thereto one feels far less immediate urgency even in the beautiful and learned poem, *Elohim mi-qedem* (God, Thou Hast Reigned from of Old) by Yehudah Halevi, which ends in the triumphant finale of Exodus. See the text recently recovered by Ratzaby in *Tarbiz,* XXIII, 16 ff.

63. Amittai's *Er'elim u-mal'akhim* (Divine Spirits and Angels) and in his *El 'ir gibborim* (To the City of the Mighty; that is, Heaven, according to the aggadic interpretation of Prov. 21:22), in Klar's collection, pp. 75 ff., 91 ff., both with reference to *Pesiqta rabbati,* xx, ed. by M. Friedmann, fols. 86 ff.; and "The *Shema'* Hagadah" (Hebrew), ed. by A. Jellinek in his *Bet ha-Midrasch,* V, 165–69 (with his comments, *ibid.,* pp. xl f., 54–56); Simon bar Isaac's *Ve-'attah banim* (And Now, My Sons) in his *Piyyuṭe,* pp. 44 f. In his Hebrew "Studies in Yannai," *SRIHP,* II, 235, M. Zulay has rightly discerned strong traces of both Yannai's and Qalir's poetry in Amittai's liturgical compositions. Of course, Jewish mysticism, in its newer kabbalistic forms, soon penetrated also the Iberian Peninsula. Yet one need but compare these Italo-German poems with Ibn Gabirol's "Royal Crown," Abraham ibn Ezra's astrological poems, or even those more closely related by the twelfth-century author Oheb ben Meir ha-Nasi (e.g., his *Er'elim ve-ḥashmalim* [Divine Spirits and Glittering Angels] in Habermann's anthology *Be-Ron yaḥad,* p. 66) and the still later distinguished kabbalistic exegete, Naḥmanides (e.g., his *Mitnaseh 'al kisse* [He Who Sits Erect upon the Throne], *ibid.,* p. 79), to note

the differences in tone and degree of sophistication. Neither does Naḥmanides' famous liturgical poem on the peregrinations of the human soul from heaven to earth and back again, recited as a memento on New Year's day, have a counterpart in the earlier Ashkenazic liturgy. See the text and translation in M. Sachs's *Religiöse Poesie,* pp. 135 ff., 328 ff., and Hebrew section, pp. 50 f.; as well as G. Scholem's German translation of the "Hymnus vom Schicksal der Seele" in *Schocken Almanach,* 5696, pp. 86–89. See also Scholem's "Tradition und Neuschöpfung im Ritus der Kabbalisten," *Eranos-Jahrbuch,* XIX, 121–80 (also more briefly in French in *Evidences,* VI, 34–39) which, although dealing with later periods, also sheds light on the liturgical approaches of earlier mystics. These differences will become somewhat clearer *infra,* Chaps. XXXIII and XXXIV.

64. A collection of these poems was assembled and critically edited by A. M. Habermann in his volume *Shire ha-yiḥud ve-ha-kabod* (Poems of Unity and Adoration). See esp. pp. 11 ff. (including the introductory statement to R. Tabyomi's commentary), 46 ff., 99 ff.

65. See Habermann's intro., *ibid.,* p. 11. On the text of *An'im zemirot,* see also D. Simonsen's "Unechte Verse im *Schir ha-kabod,*" *MGWJ,* XXXVII, 463–67.

66. Hariri of Boṣra's *Maqamas,* first published under the title *Les Séances* by Sylvestre de Sacy in 1822, has since been the subject of numerous scholarly investigations; its first part appeared in the English translation by Thomas Chenery. Al-Ḥarizi's translation, too, under the name *Maḥberot Ithiel,* was edited by Chenery, and more recently reedited, on the basis of the same unsatisfactory but so far unique Bodleian manuscript, by I. Perez. Perez also furnished a brief bio- and bibliographical sketch of Al-Ḥarizi's life and his work as translator of Hariri. See esp. Perez's edition, pp. 48, 221 ff.; and J. Schirmann's careful analysis of *Die hebräische Uebersetzung der Maqamen des Hariri.* Schirmann points out that while many other Hebrew authors did not hesitate to reproduce entire verses from the Qur'an in Hebrew translation, Al-Ḥarizi, with minor exceptions, either omitted such citations entirely or replaced them by appropriate biblical passages. If Hariri, for example, praised highly the effects on the readers of the first *sura,* the Hebrew translator recommended instead the recitation of the ninety-first psalm (*Maqama,* XII; ed. by Perez, p. 99). On this literary genre and its Arabic and Hebrew terminology, see also S. D. Goitein's Hebrew essay on "The *Maqama* and the *Maḥberet*" in *Maḥberot le-sifrut,* V, 26–40; and B. Klar's "Titles of Four Books," reprinted in his *Meḥqarim ve-'iyyunim,* pp. 343 ff.

67. Al-Ḥarizi's *Taḥkemoni* (Maqamas; a poetic miscellany), XVIII, L, ed. by Lagarde, pp. 88 ff., 184 ff. (ed. by Toporowski, pp. 173 ff., 187 ff., 384 ff., 441 f.; the latter poems are not reproduced in Lagarde's ed.). The shortcomings of the existing editions of this Hebrew classic, whose extraordinary versatility, "unknown to the ancients," was so greatly extolled by Immanuel of Rome, Al-Ḥarizi's worthy successor, are analyzed by A. M. Habermann in "The Book *Taḥkemoni* by R. Yehudah al-Ḥarizi" (Hebrew), *Sinai,* XV, Nos. 183–84, pp. 112–27. See also Habermann's earlier comments on "Al-Ḥarizi's Poems" (Hebrew), *Mizraḥ u-ma'arab,* IV, 18–21. In his "On the Sources of Al-Ḥarizi's *Taḥkemoni*" (Hebrew), *Tarbiz,* XXIII, 205–9, H. Schirmann rightly points out that, the author's professions of

originality to the contrary, his miscellanies included a great many passages which can still be traced back to some of his sources, particularly Hamadani's famous work. Among poems in the latter section of Al-Ḥarizi's book, quite a few have a decidedly homosexual coloring. This is particularly true of those he indirectly exculpates as poems of his youth. There is no way of ascertaining whether this was a genuine reflection of their author's personal sentiments or the result of his conscious or unconscious imitation of the accepted literary fashions (on the pertinent passages in his trans. of Hariri, see the examples cited by Schirmann in his *Hebräische Uebersetzung,* p. 22). See also, from another angle, S. Bernstein's observations in his "New 'Maqamas,'" *Horeb,* I, 179 ff.; and S. M. Stern's analysis of "The Arabic Source of the 'Maqama of the Cock' [x] by Al-Ḥarizi" (Hebrew), *Tarbiz,* XVII, 87–100.

As has frequently been noted, the technique of many *maqamas,* a dialogue between the narrator and the hero of the tale, has the earmarks of dramatic presentation. And yet there was no link between this poetic genre and either the Renaissance Hebrew drama or what is known of its ancient biblical and Hellenistic antecedents. In fact, there was nothing resembling a drama in medieval Hebrew literature. Undoubtedly, the connection between pagan as well as Christian worship and the existing public presentations discouraged emulation. Not even the Muslims, despite certain rites cultivated by the Shi'ites and other sectarians, ever developed a religious drama of their own, and hence they also lacked all the stimuli necessary to the rise of secular dramatic arts as well. See the interesting discussion on W. Hoenerbach's query "How may the complete absence of an Arab drama be explained?" summarized in G. E. von Grunebaum's *Studies in Islamic Cultural History,* pp. 20 ff.; and B. Hunningher's correct emphasis on the liturgical background of the Western theatrical arts in *The Origin of the Theater.* This problem will be more fully analyzed in connection with the rise of the Hebrew literary drama, if not yet the Hebrew theater, in the early modern period.

68. Al-Ḥarizi's *Taḥkemoni,* XII, in a Leningrad manuscript (not in the published editions); Joseph ben Meir ibn Zabara's *Sefer Sha'shu'im* (Book of Delight), VII.88–89, VIII.160–61, ed. by I. Davidson, 2d ed., pp. 66 n. 4 (Intro.), 76 (citing in n. 6 interesting parallels from Hebrew letters, both original and translated), 90. In his English version of *The Book of Delight,* pp. 109, 117, M. Hadas offers a somewhat different translation. Davidson seems to go too far in denying Ibn Zabara's authorship of almost all the poems inserted in the *Book of Delight,* merely because one, beginning *Er'eh demut odem* (I See the Image of Red over Sapphire), can definitely be proved to be part of a poem included in Halevi's *Diwan* (ed. by Brody, II, 7 ff. No. 4; *Mah lakh ṣeviyah,* or Why, O Gazelle; also in Zemorah's ed., I, Part 2, pp. 18 ff.). See Davidson's ed. of *Sefer Sha'shu'im,* p. 134 n. 3. Just because plagiarism in literature was then generally viewed with far greater condescension than today (see *supra,* n. 40, and Chap. XXIV, n. 4), we ought not to assume that, once a plagiarist, a man was always a plagiarist. Moreover, it is well known that the later compilers of Halevi's poetic works often sinned by an excess of zeal, and occasionally included poems of other authors. After all, we have to rely on a single manuscript for Ibn Zabara's work. Other manuscripts may well have contained the full verse, the present fragment of which, as Davidson himself admits, reads better than that given in Halevi's *Diwan.* Be that as

it may, Ibn Zabara's general independence in retelling, and in many ways reshaping, even the more common tales which had migrated from one civilization to another over many centuries, is attested by the analytical comments of both Davidson and M. Sherwood in the respective introductions to the edition and translation. Much more comparative work, however, is still needed before the tangled strains in Ibn Zabara's and his confreres' folkloristic borrowings will be fully unravelled. See also M. Hadas's "Joseph Zabara and Diogenes Laertius," *JQR,* XXVII, 151–54; and, more generally, I. Berger's "On the Sources and Influence of the Book of Delight by R. Joseph ben Meir ibn Zabara" (Hebrew), *Ha-Zofeh,* XII, 227–41; and L. de Malkiel's Spanish essay on "Yosef ben Meir ibn Zabara," *Davar* (Buenos Aires), XXXVI, pp. 5–17.

69. Yehudah ben Isaac Shabbetai's *Minḥat Yehudah Soneh nashim* (Yehudah's Offering: The Misogynist) is available only in a far from satisfactory collection of manuscript fragments, *Ṭa'am zekenim* (A Taste of the Ancients), ed. by E. Aschkenazi, fols. 1–12; and in a German trans. based thereon by L. Stein, which appeared in installments in *Der Freitagabend,* 1851, Nos. 41–49. Excerpts from the latter are more readily available in A. Sulzbach's aforementioned essay in J. Winter and A. Wünsche, *Jüdische Literatur,* III, 150 ff. A new critical edition is clearly indicated. Solomon ibn Ṣiqbal's *Ne'um Asher ben Yehudah* (Thus Spake Asher ben Yehudah) was republished with introductory comments by J. Schirmann in *SRIHP,* II, 152–62, 193. See Al-Ḥarizi's *Taḥkemoni,* III, XX, ed. by Lagarde, pp. 23, 97 ff. (ed. by Toporowski, pp. 45, 202 ff.), and Schirmann's comments in *Tarbiz,* XXIII, 201 n. 10. Yedaiah ha-Penini's *Oheb nashim* was edited by A. Neubauer in *Jubelschrift L. Zunz,* pp. 138–40, Hebrew section, pp. 1–19. See also J. Chotzner's "Yedaya Bedaresi," *JQR,* [o.s.] VIII, 414–25; and I. Davidson's *Parody in Jewish Literature,* pp. 8 f. Of course, antifeminism had long animated the authors of popular sayings among many peoples; e.g., the sayings attributed to Socrates by Joseph ibn 'Aqnin in his *Ṭubb an-nufus.* See his collection of aphorisms in Arabic and English, ed. and trans. by A. S. Halkin in "Classical and Arabic Material in Ibn 'Aḳnin's 'Hygiene of the Soul,'" *PAAJR,* XIV, 128 ff.

70. Abraham ben Samuel ibn Ḥisdai's *Ben ha-melekh ve-ha-nazir* (Prince and Dervish), first published in Constantinople, 1518, has been reissued several times, most recently by A. M. Habermann (includes a Hebrew trans. of a brief Arabic fragment of the underlying story of Barlaam and Joasaph and a bibliography). Considerable excerpts in German translation were included in the poetic anthology *Manna,* by the then youthful M. Steinschneider, pp. 1 ff., 41 ff., 72 ff., and partly reprinted in Winter and Wünsche, *Jüdische Literatur,* III, 172 ff. According to I. Zinberg, however, a Firkovitch MS in Leningrad offers many better readings than the printed editions. See his *Geshichte fun der Literatur ba Yidn,* I, 172 n. 2. Jacob ibn Eleazar (Abenalazar), on the other hand, was far less fortunate. His very name was regularly given in the Hebrew sources as Ben Eleazar, which could mean a patronymic rather than a family name. Only a part of his translation of *Kalilah ve-Dimnah,* preserved in a Paris MS, was published with a fragment from another Hebrew rendition by J. Derenbourg in his *Deux versions hébraïques du livre Kalîlâh et Dimnâh,* pp. 311 ff. Although extant in three complete manuscripts, Ibn Eleazar's *Sefer Pardes rimmone ha-ḥokhmah* (Orchard of Pomegranates of Wisdom) was only partially (Chaps. XIII–XXIII) edited by I. David-

son in "A Fragment from a Philosophic Work by an Unknown Author," *Ha-Zofeh,* X, 94–105; XI, 96. His *Sefer ha-Meshalim* (Book of Parables) is likewise available only in a partial edition (maqamas v–vii, ix) by H. Schirmann, from a thirteenth-century French manuscript now in Munich, in his Hebrew essay on "The Love Stories of Jacob ben Eleazar" in *SRIHP,* V, 209–66, where the few available data on the life and work of our author are likewise briefly analyzed.

71. Isaac ben Solomon ibn Sahula's *Meshal ha-qadmoni* (Ancient Parable), ed. by I. Zemorah; Berakhiah ben Naṭronai's *Mishle shu'alim* (Fox Parables), first published in Mantua, 1557–59, were often reprinted. A fine new printing, based on the first edition and adorned by woodcuts by Leo Michelson, was published by L. Goldschmidt in 1921 (with a brief, mainly bibliographical introduction in German), while the latest edition by A. M. Habermann is based on four manuscripts and adds a few parables to a total of 119. It contains nineteen Gustave Doré illustrations borrowed from a La Fontaine edition. The book's enormous popularity is also attested by the appearance of a Judeo-German rhymed version by Jakob Koppelmann in Freiburg, 1588, and of a Latin version by Melchior Hanel (of the Society of Jesus) in Prague, 1661. On Ibn Sahula and his circle, see S. M. Stern's "Rationalists and Kabbalists in Medieval Allegory," *JJS,* VI, 75–86. A fuller consideration of the work of this poet and of his contemporary Berekhiah must be relegated to the period after 1200.

The *Mishle Sindbad* (Parables of Sinbad), available in several editions including a fairly recent one by A. M. Habermann, and its interrelations with similar tales in both East and West have long intrigued scholars. None of the existing texts and hypotheses are wholly satisfactory, however. For this reason M. Epstein has reexamined the existing manuscripts and reviewed much of the secondary literature in the preparation of a fine critical edition of the text, which he entitled *Mishle Sendebar.* In this unpublished New York University dissertation, provided also with a good English translation, Epstein argues for the Hebrew origin of this collection of tales and dates it back to between the fourth and the second pre-Christian centuries. This is highly improbable. The editor's main argument, from the similarities in thought and style of some of these tales with the book of Esther, could be readily duplicated from many later tales, since medieval story tellers, and not only those writing in Hebrew, were greatly impressed by this biblical narrative. We have seen that even such Muslim writers as Mas'udi and Firdausi were deeply impressed by the biblical stories and the biblical reconstruction of history. This is of course doubly true in the case of Christians, to whom the Old Testament was a constant source of inspiration. See *supra,* Chap. XXVIII, esp. n. 96. On the other hand, *Sendebar* reveals few similarities with the Hellenistic romances, the ancient story of *Aḥiqar,* or the narratives preserved in the Jewish Apocryphal literature.

We shall probably have to resign ourselves to the profession of inability to date all such folk tales which had traveled from country to country in oral form for many generations before they ever found any literary expression. Such chance literary records are, therefore, even if themselves impeccably datable (which is rare), of little assistance in tracing back the true origins of each particular tale or even of parts of any particular collection. The same holds true for such other folkloristic tales as are represented by the *Ma'ase Yerushalmi* (The Story of the

Jerusalemite) attributed to R. Abraham ben Maimon (not the well-known Abraham Maimonides), which its recent editor, J. L. Zlotnik, ascribes to the geonic age. This date is, of course, conjectural, but at least the form and content of the narrative seem to be truly Hebraic. Certainly the motif of a congregation of demons in a far-off land observing the Sabbath and other Jewish laws has all the earmarks of genuine Jewish origins. These demons sufficiently appreciated Jewish learning to give in marriage their own beautiful princess, daughter of their King Ashmodai, to a shipwrecked Jewish scholar, who had miraculously found his way to them. See also M. Gaster, "An Ancient Fairy Tale Translated from the Hebrew," *Folk-Lore,* XLII, 156–78; and his older "Fairy Tales from Inedited Hebrew MSS. of the Ninth and Twelfth Centuries" (1896), reprinted in his *Studies and Texts,* II, 908–42.

In general, it is not easy to distinguish between these anonymous folkloristic tales, akin to those assembled by Nissim ibn Shahin and the other homilists discussed *supra,* Chap. XXVIII, and the more artistic romances of the Spanish Golden Age. Neither branch of literature has yet been subjected to that comprehensive analytical treatment which it so amply deserves. Apart from the aforementioned general histories of Jewish literature by Winter and Wünsche, Zinberg, and Waxman, one need but refer here to the brief surveys by Y. A. Klausner, *Ha-Novelah ba-sifrut ha-'ibrit* (The Novel in Hebrew Literature from Its Inception to the End of the Haskalah Period); and by A. Díez Macho, *La Novelistica hebraica medieval* (a lecture).

72. Compare Ibn Tibbon's Hebrew version of Ibn Gabirol's *Tikkun middot ha-nefesh,* ed. by E. L. Silber with the Arabic original *K. Islaḥ al-akhlaq,* ed. by S. S. Wise under the title of *The Improvement of the Moral Qualities,* and N. Bar-On's recent Hebrew trans., esp. pp. 41 f. (also his Intro., p. 3 n. 2). Abraham ibn Ḥisdai's Hebrew version of Al-Ghazzali's *K. Misan al-amal,* entitled *Mo'zne ṣedeq* (Righteous Scales), was first published in 1839. See J. Goldenthal's introduction to his ed.: M. Steinschneider's *Arabische Literatur,* p. 127; and, more generally, his "Introduction to the Arabic Literature of the Jews," *JQR,* [o.s.] XII, 608 ff. See also A. S. Halkin's ed. of Abraham ibn Ḥisdai's Hebrew version of Maimonides' *Iggeret Teman* (Epistle to Yemen), esp. p. 36; *supra,* Chap. XXV, nn. 62 ff.; and *infra,* Chap. XXXIV, n. 17.

73. T. Nöldeke's *Beiträge zur Kenntnis der Poesie der alten Araber,* pp. 52 ff.; Saadiah ben Maimon ibn Danan's *Seder ha-dorot* (Chronicle) in Z. H. Edelmann's *Ḥemdah genuzah,* p. 29; the heading of Samuel ibn Nagrela's poem, *Yehosef qaḥ lekha* (Joseph Take the Book), in his *Diwan,* ed. by Sassoon, p. 67 No. 96 (ed. by Habermann, I, 69); Moses ibn Ezra's *Shire ha-ḥol,* ed. by Brody, I, 299. On Abraham ibn Sahl's *Diwan,* and Abraham Isaac ben Meborakh's *Kasida* on slaughtering, see Steinschneider's *Arabische Literatur,* pp. 160 f., 240 f. See also *supra,* Chaps. XVI, n. 87; XVII, nn. 6–7 and 15. Remarkably, the memory of even Samau'al ibn Adiya was very slight among later Jewish poets; Moses ibn Ezra was among the very few to mention his name. See his *K. al-Muḥadhara,* III (*Shirat Yisrael,* p. 49). Yet some Jews, including women, continued to write Arabic poems. See esp. E. Mainz, "Quelques poésies judéo-arabes du manuscrit 411 de la Bibliothèque du Vatican," *JA,* CCXXXVII, 51–83 (in vocalized Hebrew Characters; the first

seven poems perhaps by Solomon Aaron ben Pinḥas); and W. Bacher, "Eine jüdische Dichterin in arabischer Sprache," *MGWJ,* XX, 186–87 (of indeterminate date). Jewish familiarity with Arabic poetry came to the fore also in the numerous overt or tacit translations of Arabic poems into Hebrew. Failure to mention the original authors was owing not so much to the reluctance to admit a poem's foreign origin, as to the peculiar notions of literary ownership characteristic of the Middle Ages. See *supra,* n. 40. Certainly, when Todros Abulafia rendered into Hebrew a poem by Ibn Quzman or any other Arab author he was not conscious of any act of plagiarism, since the new product was so much altered in the process of translation. See S. M. Stern's "Imitations of Arabic *Muwashshaḥat* in Spanish-Hebrew Poetry" (Hebrew), *Tarbiz,* XVIII, 186 (tracing the common origin of poems by Ibn Quzman and Abulafia). Of special interest is the early Hebrew rendition of a poem by Hallaj, the famous martyr of Islamic mysticism. See the text published by Hirschfeld in his "Arabic Portion," *JQR,* [o.s.] XV, 177, 181.

74. Halevi's *Rashe 'am* (When the Heads of the People Foregather) and *Pannu derakhenu* (Clear Our Way) in his *Diwan,* ed. by Brody, I, 157 f. No. 102, 176 f. No. 108 (ed. by Zemorah, I, Part 3, pp. 109 f., 324 f.) and the reconstruction of the Castilian texts by Millás Vallicrosa in his *Yehudah Ha-Levi,* pp. 53 ff. See also his "Sobre los más antiguos versos en la lengua castellana," *Sefarad,* VI, 362–71. This reconstruction is based upon the final interpretation of "The Political Situation of the Spanish Jews in the Age of Yehudah Halevi" in a Hebrew essay by Y. Baer in *Zion,* I, 6–23. See also *supra,* Chap. XX, n. 46. A new reconstruction of both these endings is offered by S. M. Stern in his comprehensive studies: "Les Vers finaux en espagnol dans la muwaššaḥas hispano-hébraïques," *Al-Andalus,* XIII, 311 ff., 317 f., 335 ff., supplemented by "Some Textual Notes on the Romance jarŷas," *ibid.,* XVIII, 133–40, and *Les Chansons mozarabes.* Further discussions on this significant problem have been conducted by F. Cantera in his "Versos españoles en las muwaššaḥas hispano-hebreas," *Sefarad,* IX, 197–234; by E. García Gomez in his "Más sobre las 'jarŷas' romances en 'muwaššaḥas' hebreas," *Al-Andalus,* XIV, 409–17 (summarizing the twenty texts under review); his "Nuevas observaciones sobre las 'jaryâs' romances en muwaššaḥas hebreas," *ibid.,* XV, 157–77; his "Dos nuevas jarŷas romances (XXV y XXVI) en muwaššaḥas arabes," *ibid.,* XIX, 369–91; and by J. Schirmann in "Un Nouveau poème hébreux avec vers finaux en espagnol et en arabe," *Homenaje a Millás-Vallicrosa,* II, 347–53 (possibly by Yehudah ibn Gayyat, with additional bibliography). See also E. Lévi-Provençal's "Arabica-Occidentalia II: Quelques observations à propos du déchiffrement des ḫarǧas 'mozarabes,'" *Arabica,* I, 201–8; and, more generally, F. de la Granja's brief review article, "Los Estudios sobre poesía arábigoandeluza," *Al-Andalus,* XVIII, 224–29; and *infra,* n. 84. The general familiarity of the Spanish and other Western Jews with the Romance languages of their environment will be more fully discussed in its later medieval context.

75. Samuel ibn Nagrela's letter and poem *Ma'im,* in his *Kol Shire,* ed. by Habermann, III, 161 ff. (see *ibid.,* pp. 177 ff., and the older literature listed by Sassoon in his edition of the *Diwan,* p. xix); Al-Ḥarizi's *Taḥkemoni,* XI, ed. by Lagarde, p. 57 (ed. by Toporowski, pp. 116 ff.). See *supra,* n. 15; Chap. XXIX, n. 38; and Vol. II, 145 f. Incidentally, Meir bar Isaac's *Aqdamut* made history. Its key phrase,

"If All the Sky Were Parchment," penetrated also many Western poems, as is shown by I. Linn in a comparative study under this title in the *Publications of the Modern Language Association,* LIII, 951–70.

76. N. Allony's *Torat ha-mishqalim* (The Scansion of Medieval Hebrew Poetry: Dunash, Yehudah Halevi, and Abraham ibn Ezra), pp. 9 ff. (offering a good survey of the history of studies of the Hebrew rhythm); Moses ibn Ezra's *Shire ha-ḥol,* ed. by Brody, I, 243, No. 234 vv. 131–33; his *K. al-Muḥadhara,* III (*Shirat Yisrael,* pp. 47 ff.). See also D. Yellin's *Torat ha-shirah ha-sefaradit* (Introduction to the Hebrew Poetry of the Spanish Period); and the critique thereof in Allony's *Mi-torat ha-lashon,* pp. 17–32. Even in Spain before the expulsion, Moses ibn Ḥabib, shown in Murviedro the aforementioned ancient funeral inscription supposedly recording the death of an emissary of King Amaziah of Judah, saw therein clear proof that "this method of poetic scansion had existed since the time when our forefathers lived on their soil." See his *Darkhe no'am* (Pleasant Paths; on Hebrew Prosody), VI.2, cited *supra,* Chap. XVI, n. 41. This spurious inscription, as well as the underlying acceptance of the antiquity of the Hebrew syllabic meter, found wide currency in contemporary Hebrew letters. See the sources cited by Allony in his *Torat ha-mishqalim,* pp. 16 f.

77. One of the main objections, voiced by Halevi against the adoption of the Arabic meter in Hebrew poetry (see below), was that the laws governing the use of the two *shevas* so greatly differed in the two languages. See his *K. al-Khazari,* II.78; ed. by Hirschfeld, pp. 128 ff. (in his English trans., pp. 127 f.; see also *ibid.,* p. 302 n. 46); and the sources mentioned *infra,* n. 86. On the importance of the *sheva* in the whole structure of the Hebrew language, see *supra,* Chap. XXIX, n. 20.

78. Dunash ben Labraṭ's *Teshubot* on Saadiah, ed. by Schröter, p. 31; *Teshubot talmide Menaḥem,* p. 7 line 44; and Yehudi's rejoinder, *ibid.,* p. 4 line 18. If Saadiah indeed approved of rhythmic poetry along Arabic lines, Dunash's innovation antedated Saadiah's death in 942. In any case, it definitely appears in Dunash's poems written after his arrival in Spain and dated not later than 958. See H. Brody's Hebrew essay "On the Arabic Meter in Hebrew Poetry," *Krauss Jub. Vol.,* pp. 117–26; Allony's *Torat,* pp. 9 ff.; and his edition of Dunash's *Shirim,* pp. 32 ff.

79. Samuel ibn Nagrela's poem, cited *supra,* n. 75 (see also Habermann's ed., pp. 173 f.); D. Yellin's *Ketabim,* II, 190 ff., 205 ff.; S. T. Coleridge, *Biographia literaria,* XVIII, in "Everyman's Library" ed., p. 198. In his comprehensive *Torat ha-shirah ha-sefaradit,* Yellin has also pointed out that whatever the merits of the controversy over the appropriateness of the use of Arabic meters in Hebrew poetry may have been, we ought to be grateful for this widespread imitation not only because it so greatly enhanced the richness of Hebrew metric forms, but also because it helped stem excessive quotations from the Bible. When one compares the prose writings of the period, studded with biblical citations not always appropriate or relevant to the theme, one will indeed appreciate the inability of poets to incorporate entire passages from the poetic sections of the Old Testament, written in an entirely different rhythm. We shall see that even this obstacle did not completely overcome the penchant of medieval poets to detect ever new meanings in the biblical text, and to employ scriptural phrases in some such

novel meanings in their poems. See also M. Hak's "Sproutings of Tonal Rhythm in Hebrew Poetry" (Hebrew), *Tarbiz,* XI, 91–109 (mainly relating to the later Middle Ages).

80. See H. Schirmann's advice as to "How Is One to Recite the Metric Poems of Our Spanish Writers?" (Hebrew), *Ha-Kinnus,* I, 296–301; and, with minor variations, in "La Métrique quantitative dans la poésie hébraïque du Moyen Age," *Sefarad,* VIII, 323–32. On the reading of Syriac poetry, see M. Sprengling's pertinent remarks in his dissertation on "Antonius Rhetor on Versification," *AJSL,* XXXII, 162 ff. Here the detailed researches on the problem of Syriac meter are carefully reviewed. It is truly astonishing how little work has been done even in the last four decades concerning the interrelations between the Syriac and the Hebrew or Arabic meters.

81. Halevi's *Ṣiyyon ha-lo tish'ali,* cited *supra,* n. 46. The *ayikh* rhyme courses through the entire poem; it appears in all even-numbered verses of the total of sixty-eight. With its accent for the most part on final syllables, Hebrew offered great temptation to rhyme words ending on the same sound. Purists insisted, however, that a proper rhyme must include at least two syllables, and Abraham ibn Ezra, punning on Deut. 22:10, counseled a would-be poet: *Lo taḥaroz be-shor u-ba-ḥamor* (Thou shalt not *rhyme* with an ox and an ass). See the comparison with Arabic poetry in Yellin's *Torat ha-shirah,* pp. 11 ff.

In his *Studies in Literary Modes* (pp. 144 f.), A. M. Clark stresses the differences between the Greek and the Latin or English consonantal structures. Greek is a highly vocalic language, the average ratio of vowels to consonants being 54.4:45.6. In Latin the opposite is true. Here the ratio is 45.7:54.3. In English the preponderance of consonants is even greater, the average ratio of vowels declining further to 42.4:57.6. "Thus Greek scansion," Clark explains, "came to be based on the comparative duration of syllables, classified into long and short," while the larger number of consonants made both Latin and English far more susceptible to the adoption of rhymes. This is evidently doubly true in the case of Hebrew, where the vowel has a decidedly secondary importance. Although no detailed study of its relative frequency seems to have been published, there is little doubt that it plays an even lesser role than in English. There is, moreover, that intermediary sound, the *sheva mobile,* which Ben Asher had already described as "serving to indicate about half a tone" (*Diqduqe ha-ṭe'amin,* p. 15), because its audibility depends entirely on the following syllable.

To secure a random but fairly representative sample, we have reviewed the first nine verses of the book of Isaiah and the first chapter of Psalms, disregarding entirely the *matres lectionis.* The resulting figures were for Isaiah 400 consonants, 242 vowels and 46 mobile *shevas* (including *ḥaṭafs),* or a ratio of about 58:35:7. The count in the first psalm was quite similar: 204 consonants, 129 vowels and 25 *shevas,* yielding a ratio of almost 57:36:7. Substantially similar results were also obtained in a letter count of two short poems by Ibn Gabirol and Halevi, except that here, owing to the exigencies of the Arabic meter and the use of "pegs," the number of vowels and *shevas* per verse was fairly constant. In Ibn Gabirol's wedding poem *Shilḥah le-bat nadib* (Send to the Patron's Daughter), the consonants included in each verse ranged from 14 to 18, but there were invariably only 10 vowels and 2 *shevas,* except for the somewhat garbled sixth verse. No such irregularity occurs in Halevi's similar poem, *Se'u shalom* (Carry

Ye Greetings to the Choicest of Bridegrooms), each verse of which includes 8 vowels, 3 *shevas,* and 13–16 consonants. See Ibn Gabirol's *Shire,* ed. by Bialik and Rawnitzky, II, 34 No. 28 (*Selected Poems,* ed. by Davidson, p. 18); and Halevi's *Diwan,* ed. by Brody, II, 13 f. No. 9 (ed. by Zemorah, I, Part 2, p. 115; and in N. Salaman's trans., p. 52). Even these self-imposed shackles, however, did not seriously alter the basic ratios. They are 58:36:6 in Ibn Gabirol's poem, and 57:31:12 in that of Halevi. This obvious vocalic inferiority doubtless greatly facilitated the introduction of rhymes into Hebrew poetry, when for other reasons this expedient was found intellectually and socially desirable. See *supra,* Chap. XXXI, n. 34.

Nor did the Hebrew poets, unlike their Byzantine and Latin confreres, have to combat a hostile tradition. Although the biblical rhymes were undoubtedly accidental, they could be invoked, if needed, against any likely opposition. The dichotomy, on the other hand, between the educated quantitative rhythm and the plebeian rhymed doggerel, which had proved such an obstacle to the general adoption of rhymed poetry in the classical literatures (see Clark's *Studies,* pp. 146 ff.), had no counterpart in Hebrew letters, which no longer reflected popular speech habits. See also O. Dingeldein's older study of *Der Reim bei den Griechen und Römern;* and F. Dölger's more recent analysis of *Die byzantinische Literatur in der Reinsprache.* Among modern editions arranged according to rhymes, one may mention especially H. Brody's ed. of Moses ibn Ezra's *Shire ha-ḥol.* I. Davidson was right, therefore, in trying to compile a comprehensive list of "Rhymes in Hebrew Poetry." However, his preparatory work was still incomplete at the time of his demise, and I. Elbogen could publish for him posthumously but an incomplete index to selected authors, ranging from Samuel ibn Nagrela to Moses ibn Zur (18th cent.), in *JQR,* XXX, 299–398.

82. Al-Ḥarizi's *Taḥkemoni,* XI, ed. by Lagarde, pp. 56 ff. (ed. by Toporowski, pp. 115 ff.), and *supra,* n. 66. Far simpler and more usual was the figure of speech called by Moses ibn Ezra, the "mixture of doubt with certainty and of a positive with a negative assertion." Though quoting, as he always does, a few biblical examples, Ibn Ezra admitted that such mixtures, which he illustrates from both Hebrew and Arabic poems, were rare in Scripture but became frequent in medieval letters because of emulation of Arabic patterns. See his *K. al-Muḥadhara,* VIII.20 (*Shirat Yisrael,* pp. 195 ff.). See also further illustrations in Yellin's *Torat ha-shirah ha-sefaradit,* pp. 270 ff.; and the detailed analyses of several of these "adornments," found in Ibn Ezra's *Poetics,* against their biblical background by A. Díez Macho in his "Algunas figures retóricas," *Sefarad,* IV, 255–74; "La Metáfora y la alusión bíblica," *ibid.,* V, 49–81; "Estudio de la hăzara," *ibid.,* VII, 3–29, 209–30; "La Homonimia o paronomasia," *ibid.,* VIII, 293–321. Of interest also is A. Mirski's dissertation, *Ṣurot noy* (Rhetorical Forms and Poetic Elements in the Midrashim as Prototypes for the Palestinian Piyyuṭim; multigraphed) which were inherited by the later secular poets as well. Of course, here, too, the question of the priority of homilist or liturgical poet remains open. It would certainly appear that the poetic imagination of the creative precentor must have injected also some of these aesthetic adornments into their presentations, and influenced also the delivery of many sermons. See *supra,* Chap. XXXI.

83. Ibn Ezra's *K. al-Muḥadhara,* VIII.1, 4, 6 (*Shirat Yisrael,* pp. 160 ff., 169 ff., 172 f.), citing Ibn Gabirol's poem, *Ani ha-ish* (I Am the Man Who Has Donned

His Girdle), vv. 37–38, ed. by Bialik and Rawnitzky, I, 6 f. Ibn Ezra failed to indicate that the opposition undoubtedly objected less to metaphors as such than to the excessive quest for strange and unexpected similes which characterized much of the contemporary Arabic and Jewish letters. A. Mez has rightly pointed out, however, that this "striving after uncommon metaphors . . . powerfully stimulated the tendency to penetrate into the most hidden secrets of things and to see the oddest peculiarities in them." See his *Renaissance of Islam,* p. 259. We must bear in mind that, long before the spread of Arab poetry, homilies and poems by oriental authors such as Ephrem Syrus were "filled with metaphors, daring figures of speech, allegories, hyperboles and flights of imagination unknown to Greeks and Romans" (Chabot in his *Littérature syriaque,* p. 27).

84. The influence of the Arabic *muwashshaḥ* on Spanish-Hebrew poetry has been carefully examined only in recent years, although occasional references thereto are also found in such earlier monographic studies as B. Halper's still meritorious analysis of "The Scansion of Medieval Hebrew Poetry," *JQR,* IV, 153–224. A brief description of the *muwashshaḥ* technique is offered by S. M. Stern in his "Studies on Ibn Quzman," *Al-Andalus,* XVI, 381. See also the numerous recent publications in this field by him, E. García Gomez, and other authors, listed *supra,* n. 74; and, more generally, the older but still useful study by M. Hartmann, *Das arabische Strophengedicht, I: Das Muwaššaḥ;* and A. R. Nykl's *Hispano-Arabic Poetry and Its Relations with the Old Provençal Troubadours,* especially pp. 266 ff. (on Ibn Quzman). On the biblical antecedents of the medieval Hebrew stanzas, see especially C. F. Kraft's dissertation, *The Strophic Structure of Hebrew Poetry as Illustrated in the First Book of the Psalter* (includes a survey of the older literature); and J. A. Montgomery's "Stanza Formation in Hebrew Poetry," *JBL,* LXIV, 379–84 (directed against C. C. Torrey's *Second Isaiah).* On the techniques used by the *payyeṭanim,* see also the literature cited *supra,* Chap. XXXI.

85. Ibn Ezra's *K. al-Muḥadhara,* Intro., and Chaps. v and VIII (*Shirat Yisrael,* pp. 33, 62 ff., 109 ff.). On Saadiah's *Egron,* see *supra,* Chap. XXX, n. 14. The Arabic original of Ibn Ezra's work still awaits publication. A fairly full description of the only extant (Bodleian) manuscript was submitted by M. Schreiner as far back as 1890–91. See "Le Kitâb al-Mouhâdara wa-l-moudhâkara de Moise b. Ezra et ses sources," *REJ,* XXI, 98–117; XXII, 62–81, 236–49. For the last three decades scholars have, therefore, been limited to B. Z. Halper's Hebrew translation, which also lists the few Arabic excerpts previously published (pp. 24 f.). Although prepared by a competent student of both the Arabic language and medieval Hebrew letters, this translation is frequently too free to reproduce precisely the author's ideas. See, e.g., the criticisms voiced in J. N. Simhoni's otherwise sympathetic review in *Hatekufah,* XXIII, 491–500. See also J. M. Millás Vallicrosa's Spanish trans. of Chap. v in "Un Capítulo del 'Libro de Poética' de Mosé Abenezra," *Boletín de la R. Academia Española,* XVII, 423–47. N. Bar-On's (Braun's) intention, therefore, to publish both a critical edition of the Arabic text and a new Hebrew translation is to be highly welcomed.

Not even all the important Arabic works on poetic arts have thus far been published. See the more recent discussions by I. Krachkovsky (or Krachkovskii) in "Die arabische Poetik im IX. Jahrhundert," *Monde orientale,* XXIII, 23–39 (mainly on Al-Mu'tazz, Jaḥiẓ, and Qudama); and by G. E. von Grunebaum in his annotated translation of Al-Baqillani's section on poetry in *A Tenth-Century Document of Arabic Literary Theory and Criticism.* The significance of the query concerning the inspirational quality of wine can only be understood in the light of the great importance ascribed to drinking in contemporary Arabic letters. Perhaps because of their sense of guilt over the violation of a religious prohibition, the Muslim writers devoted disproportionate space to the pros and cons of imbibing wine. The Kairuwan historian Abu Isḥaq ibn ar-Raqiq an-Nadim (d. 1026) compiled a comprehensive anthology of Arabic poems discussing its merits and demerits. See W. M. de Slane's comment on his translation of Ibn Khaldun's *Histoire des Berbères,* I, 292 n. 3. Jews followed suit, although some of their poems extolling the Bacchian qualities of that mildly intoxicating liquor bear the clear imprint of contemporary fashion. Only some of the youthful wine songs of Halevi carry real conviction.

86. The brief fragment of Halevi's treatise, which even in its complete form apparently did not exceed the size of a large broadside, was first published in 1930 by H. Brody under the title *Jehuda Ha Levi, Die schönen Versmasse.* Brief textual "Notes on the Text of Yehudah Halevi's Article on Poetic Meters" (Hebrew) were supplied by S. M. Stern in *Tarbiz,* XXI, 62, while Allony, in his *Torat ha-mishqalim,* pp. 119 ff. subjected the entire treatise and parallel statements in *K. al-Khazari* to close scholarly scrutiny. Allony analyzed here (pp. 161 ff.) in considerable detail Abraham ibn Ezra's *Sefer Ṣaḥot* which, unlike the works of his namesake Moses or Halevi, was written in Hebrew, and thus helped popularize the metric theories of the Spanish schools among the Jews of Christian Europe. A later Hebrew work on meters, aptly entitled *Sheqel ha-qodesh* (Sacred Shekel, or Measure, to be distinguished from the aforementioned moralistic work by Joseph Qimḥi) is attributed to David ibn Yaḥya (1440–1524) by Allony in his pertinent Hebrew essay in *KS,* XVIII, 192–98. See also J. Llamas's "Tres capítulos de métrica rabínica de R. David ben Šelomo ibn Yaḥya," *Sefarad,* VIII, 277–91 (from Escorial MSS).

87. Moses ibn Ezra's *K. al-Muḥadhara,* Intro. and viii.16 (*Shirat Yisrael,* pp. 34, 185 ff.). On Ibn Bal'am's work, no fragment of which seems to be extant, see the literature listed *supra,* Chaps. XXIX, n. 76. Of course, all the great Spanish poets included at least some messianic poems in their *diwans.* See *supra,* Chap. XXV. The problem of the frequently exaggerating language of the Bible, however, evidently disturbed many pious contemporaries and was grist for the mill of the numerous skeptics. That is why Maimonides felt it necessary to devote an entire lengthy chapter in his *Guide* (ii.29) to demonstrating that such figures of speech, especially in Isaiah, were never intended to be taken literally. The public, however, was generally prepared to accept the metaphoric meaning of poetic descriptions and often repeated the old adage that "the best part of the poem is its lie." See L. Dukes's *Naḥal qedumim* (Ancient Brook; essays on medieval Hebrew poetry), pp. 54 ff.; and I. Davidson's comments in the intro. to his ed. of "The First Chapter of the Book *Bate ha-nefesh ve-ha-leḥashim* by Levi ben Abraham ben Ḥayyim" (Hebrew), *SRIHP,* V, 9.

88. Menaḥem ben Saruq's epistle in *Teshubot talmide Menaḥem,* ed. by Stern, pp. xxiii ff.; Abraham ibn Ezra's *Zekhor-na* (Please Remember), ed. with a com-

mentary in S. Pinsker's *Lickute kadmoniot,* II, 136 (cf. Davidson's *Oṣar,* II, 213 No. 130). That the author was Abraham (and not Moses) ibn Ezra, two manuscript annotations to the contrary, has been proved by S. Abramson in his "Notes on Medieval Hebrew Poetry" (Hebrew), *KS,* XVII, 243 f. On the *shibbuṣ* in general, see Moses ibn Ezra's *K. al-Muḥadhara,* VIII.20 (*Shirat Yisrael,* pp. 205 f.); and the more detailed illustrations assembled by L. Dukes in his still useful monograph, *Zur Kenntnis der neuhebräischen religiösen Poesie,* pp. 112 ff.; and Yellin's *Torat ha-shirah,* pp. 118 ff. At times the metaphors became so complicated that few readers were able to divine the poet's intention. This gave rise to commentaries, such as the very learned modern commentary, *Gibe'at Sha'ul* by Saul Joseph on the poems of Yehudah Halevi, or Joseph ibn Waqar's lengthy exposition on his own poem. See *supra,* n. 64. Obviously, when such learned treatises began taking the place of the living communication between author and reader, this was an unmistakable sign of poetry's incipient decay.

89. The *Sefer Qerobah* has long been known to scholars; it was frequently quoted by Zunz. But it was first published in full, from an Oxford MS, by Habermann in *SRIHP,* III, 91–132. This booklet has preserved a number of older traditions unrecorded elsewhere. Even the spurious reports have considerable value for the understanding of the successive generations' changing appreciation of the early *piyyuṭim.* Our author not only equated, for example, Eleazar Qalir with the Tanna Eleazar ben Simon, but also attributed the introduction of liturgical poems to the need of communicating the rabbinic teachings to the unlearned masses who never came to the academy. In this context the term *qerobah* is explained (apparently for the first time) as derived from *qerab,* "come near Me, that is engage Satan in combat" (with reference to j. Berakhot IV.4, 8b). See *SRIHP,* III, 101; and *supra,* Chap. XXXI.

90. Halevi's *K. al-Khazari,* II.69–70, in Hirschfeld's ed., pp. 126 f., and his trans., p. 125; Abraham ibn Ezra's *Sefer Ṣaḥot,* ed. by Lippmann, fol. 11b; and his *Commentary* on Ps. 8:1. On the use of the various metric-musical terms, see the comprehensive list included in E. Werner and I. Sonne's detailed analysis of "The Philosophy and Theory of Music in Judaeo-Arabic Literature," *HUCA,* XVI, 305 ff.; and in H. Löwenstein's related Hebrew essay on "Musical Terminology in Medieval Hebrew Literature," *Leshonenu,* XIII, 140–49; and "Musicology in Jewish Sources from the Tenth to the Seventeenth Centuries," *ibid.,* XXI, 187–92.

91. Ibn abi Ad-Dunya al-Qurashi's *K. Dhamm al-malāhī* (Disparagement of Musical Instruments), ed. with an English trans. by J. Robson in his *Tracts on Listening to Music, passim;* Abraham ibn Ezra's poem, *Ha-Yishme'elim* (The Ishmaelites) in D. Rosin's ed. of his *Reime und Gedichte,* pp. 222. As late as 1302 a Moroccan author felt it incumbent upon himself to write in the defense of secular singing to a moderate extent. See J. Robeson's English trans. of an excerpt from "A Maghribi MS on Listening to Music," *IC,* XXVI, 113–31. By the twelfth century Persian poetry and music had evidently so thoroughly been absorbed in the mainstream of Arabic arts, that even this world traveler did not find it necessary to allude to its particular range of interests. The more provincial Moses ibn Ezra had mentioned in his aforecited poem only Arabs, Greeks, as well as Jews, although he was of course familiar with some of the literary output of the Spanish Christians,

and with the Indian proverbs and tales which had achieved ever growing circulation among his own coreligionists. That our poet was not consciously parochial, however, is evident in the same poem, when he tried to explain nature's great diversities by the influence of the seven climates and the seventeen thousand cities. See his *Shire ha-ḥol,* ed. by Brody, I, 240 No. 234 v. 67.

92. Israel ben Moses Najara's *Zemirot Yisrael* (Songs of Israel), Venice, 1599 ed., Intro.; Isaac Gorni's *Diwan,* cited from a Munich manuscript by J. Schirmann in *Orlogin,* III, 93, 95 (in French trans. in *Lettres Romanes,* III, 180, 184; Improving upon H. Gross's edition in his "Zur Geschichte der Juden in Arles; Nachträge," *MGWJ,* XXXI, 513 f.). On the relations between Gorni and the Bedershis, father and son (Abraham and Yedaiah), see Gross, *ibid.,* pp. 507 ff.; and Schirmann, pp. 95 ff. (*Lettres romanes,* III, 176 ff., 185 f.). See also *supra,* n. 69.

93. See esp. H. G. Farmer's comprehensive work *A History of Arabian Music to the XIII Century,* pp. 145 ff.; supplemented by "The Religious Music of Islam," *JRAS,* 1952–53, pp. 60–65 (showing that, because of music's ancient connection with paganism, there never developed any regular "Mosque music," similar to Church music); his essay on "The Jewish Debt to Arabic Writers on Music," *IC,* XV, 59–63; and other studies listed in the next notes.

94. Alfasi's *Resp.,* No. 281; *Sefer Ḥasidim,* ed. by Wistinetzki, Nos. 347–48; H. G. Farmer's "Music" in the *Legacy of Islam,* ed. by Arnold and Guillaume, p. 358; Maimonides' *Resp.,* pp. 338 f. No. 370; Jacob ben Asher's *Ṭur* O.Ḥ., MLX end (Joseph Karo in his comments thereon betrays his unfamiliarity with the text of Maimonides' reply). The Maimonidean responsum, first published in the Arabic original with a German trans. by I. Goldziher in *MGWJ,* XXII, 174–80, is available in a revised Arabic text with the Hebrew and an English version in H. G. Farmer's *Maimonides on Listening to Music.* Our version largely follows that of Werner and Sonne in *HUCA,* XVI, 341. Farmer raises, but does not answer, the question as to the possible indebtedness of Maimonides' enumeration of the five stages of forbidden music to Al-Ghazzali's classification of five kinds of music which are prohibited to Muslims. However, the differences are even greater than the similarities, and mere coincidence in number is far more likely. See also Maimonides' *Guide* III.8; B. Cohen's analysis of *The Responsum of Maimonides concerning Music* (also referring to two pertinent responsa by Hai Gaon, ed. by B. M. Lewin in *GK,* V, 33–35 and 58–59 No. 59); *supra,* n. 54; and Chap. XXXI, n. 31. In his *Code,* Maimonides briefly restated his opinion that the rabbis had long prohibited singing as well as all instrumental music; even mere joyful listening to music was outlawed "because of the destruction" of the Temple. He admitted, however, that one could sing religious songs even over wine. See *M.T.* Ta'aniyot v.14. It is doubly remarkable, therefore, that his aversion to instrumental music did not dampen his exegetical ardor as Mishnah commentator. In explaining the various instruments recorded in M. 'Arakhin II.3, he tried to identify each instrument by its structure and its Arabic equivalents, "as they were explained to us." Incidentally, Rashi, too, as elsewhere, evinced considerable interest in these ancient *realia,* and on that occasion identified the biblical-talmudic *ḥalil* with the contemporary French *chalumeau.* See his *Commentary* on b. 'Arakhin 10a. Historically inaccurate though this rendition may be, it reveals the great exegete's genuine

effort to approximate for his readers the shape of the ancient flute which the Babylonian Talmud itself had difficulty in identifying. On purely logical grounds, it equated this instrument with the *abbub* likewise mentioned in the Mishnah. See A. Darmesteter and D. S. Blondheim, *Les Gloses françaises dans les commentaires talmudiques de Raschi,* I, 23 No. 182, 82 No. 592; and C. Sachs, *The History of Musical Instruments,* pp. 118 ff.

95. Ibn Abi 'Usaibiya's *'Uyun al-Anba'* (Choicest News on the Classes of Physicians), ed. by A. Müller, II, 50; J. Ribera y Tarragó's *Music in Ancient Arabia and Spain, Being La Música de las Cantigas,* English trans., p. 72; Mas'udi's *K. at-Tanbiḥ,* in De Goeje's *Bibliotheca,* VIII, 103. Other Arabic writings containing much biographical and historical material on musicians and music are listed in Farmer's *History,* p. 153. On Abu'l Fadhl Ḥisdai, see *supra,* n. 56.

96. Ḥunayn ibn Iṣhaq's *K. Ādāb al-falāsifa* (Die Sinnsprüche der Philosophen), I.19 end, in Al-Ḥarizi's Hebrew trans. entitled *Musere ha-pilosophim,* ed. by A. Löwenthal, p. 16; and in the English rendition by Werner and Sonne in *HUCA,* XVII, 530 (on its sources, see *ibid.,* pp. 558 ff.); Joseph Albo's *Sefer ha-'Iqqarim* (Book of Principles), XXIII. 8, ed. and trans. by I. Husik, IV, 211 (essentially, however, echoing the statement of the German pietist, cited below); and Samuel Archevolte's *'Arugat ha-bosem* (Bed of Spices; on grammar and rhythm), XXI, Amsterdam, 1730 ed., fols. 100 f. See also K. Merkle's dissertation, *Die Sinnsprüche der Philosophen "Kitâb Âdab al-Falâsifa" von Ḥonain ibn Ishâq in der Ueberarbeitung des Muhammad ibn 'Ali Al-Anṣari.* In his detailed analysis of the various Arabic and Hebrew texts of the musicological passage in Saadiah's *Beliefs and Opinions,* X.18, ed. by Landauer, p. 317 (in Ibn Tibbon's Hebrew trans., p. 160; in Rosenblatt's English trans., pp. 402 ff.), H. G. Farmer points out that, although not clearly stating his pertinent views, Saadiah, like Al-Kindi, implied his belief in the nexus between colors, perfumes, and melodies which was then being more fully developed by the Brethren of Purity. See his *Sa'adya Gaon on the Influence of Music,* pp. 8 f.; and E. Gerson-Kiwi's review thereof in *KS,* XX, 206–9.

97. Saadiah's *Beliefs, loc. cit.,* in Werner and Sonne's trans. in *HUCA,* XVII, 535 f. (the concluding paragraph is not reproduced in the extracts cited by Farmer in his study of Saadiah). Evidently because of this psychological connection, the gaon also insisted that the psalms had to be recited by the levites at the Temple in precisely those tunes which were indicated in the headings. See his *Commentary* on Ps. 5:1, 76:1, ed. respectively by S. H. Margulies, pp. 5 (Arabic), 13, 22 (German), and by S. Galliner, pp. viii, 23; Werner and Sonne's remarks in *HUCA,* XVI, 295 f.

98. Maimonides' *Commentary* on M. Abot, Introduction known as the *Shemonah Peraqim* (Eight Chapters), ed. with an English trans. by J. I. Gorfinkle, pp. 31 (text), 70 (trans.; our deviation from Gorfinkle's version commends itself by both the Arabic text and the Ibn Tibbon version); Joseph ibn 'Aqnin's *Ṭubb an-nufus,* XXVII, in M. Güdemann's edition in *Das jüdische Unterrichtswesen,* pp. 94 ff. (German), 32 f. (Arabic; also in S. Assaf's *Meqorot le-toledot ha-ḥinukh,* II, 38); Shem Tob ben Joseph ibn Falaquera's *Sefer ha-Mebaqqesh* (Book of the Seeker), ed. by Mordecai Tamal, fols. 39b f. (also in the excerpts and trans. by Werner and Sonne in *HUCA,* XVII, 545 ff.). Ibn 'Aqnin's passage, essentially but

a quotation from Farabi, is also reproduced in facsimile from the unique Oxford MS by Farmer as the frontispiece of *Al-Farabi's Arabic-Latin Writings on Music.* The use of music in hospitals is also mentioned by the Brethren of Purity, and H. G. Farmer saw "a Hebrew manuscript with a minature depicting the lutenist in the anteroom of a physician awaiting, presumably, to effect a cure or allay a distemper by means of his art" (*Sa'adyah Gaon,* p. 8).

99. Abraham ibn Ezra's *Sefer ha-Mispar* (Book of Numbers), ed. by Silberberg, p. 46; Abraham bar Ḥiyya's version of the excerpts from Saadiah's *Beliefs,* x, in Farmer's *Sa'adyah Gaon,* pp. 49 ff. (offering both a revised text and a detailed commentary); his general introduction to mathematical science entitled *Yesode ha-tebunah* (Principles of Understanding). See *infra,* Chap. XXXV. It had indeed long been customary among Arab students, for instance Avicenna, to include a section on music in their discussion of mathematical science (*'ulum riyadhiyya*). See Farmer's *History of Arabian Music,* p. 219. Avicenna's chapter is likewise lost, and hence there is no way of ascertaining the extent to which the Spanish Jewish scientist was indebted to his Persian Muslim predecessor.

100. Ibn 'Aqnin in Güdemann, *Das jüdische Unterrichtswesen, loc. cit.;* Ibn Falaquera's *Sefer ha-Mebaqqesh, loc. cit.* See also the latter's introductory textbook, *Reshit ḥokhmah* (Beginnings of Wisdom), ed. by M. David, pp. 46 f. (reproduced with an English trans. by Werner and Sonne in *HUCA,* XVII, 542 ff.), discussing the distinction between practical and theoretical music and subdividing the musical theory into five categories. One wonders whether Ibn Falaquera referred to a lute of four strings merely because he uncritically copied the physiological doctrine of Farabi, or whether he really saw such lutes in the Provence, although one of five strings seems to have become much more common in the West. See C. Sachs, *The History of Musical Instruments,* pp. 273 f.

101. Moses ibn Ezra's poem *Yah, shekhinatkha* (Lord, Thy Presence is Among Men) in his *Selected Poems,* ed. by Brody, pp. 97 f.; Abraham ibn Ezra's *Commentary* on Ps. 93:4. The opposition of Farabi (in his *K. al-Musiqi al-Kabir* [Grand traité de la musique], French trans. by R. d'Erlanger in *La Musique arabe,* I, 28) and Maimonides (*Guide,* II.8, in Friedländer's English trans., p. 163) is discussed, together with the more numerous affirmative views, by Werner and Sonne in *HUCA,* XVI, 288 ff. The latter also point out that, like the Vulgate, some Jewish interpreters understood the *nible shamayim* (Job 38:37) not as "bottles of heaven," but rather as heavenly violins. See, e.g., Abraham ben David's *Commentary* on *Yeṣirah,* I.1 end, Mantua ed., fol. 27c. See also *supra,* n. 63.

102. Halevi's poem, *'Abde zeman* (Servants of Time), in his *Diwan,* ed. by Brody, II, 300 (ed. by Zemorah, II, Part 5, p. 209 No. 11). See *supra,* n. 52.

ROBERT LOUIS STEVENSON
in the South Seas

Portrait of Robert Louis Stevenson

R.L.S.

IN THE SOUTH SEAS

AN INTIMATE PHOTOGRAPHIC RECORD

With an introduction and edited by

ALANNA KNIGHT

c. 1

Paragon House
New York

First U.S Edition published by
PARAGON HOUSE PUBLISHERS
2 Hammarskjöld Plaza
New York, New York 10017

First published by Mainstream Publishing
Company, Edinburgh, Scotland in 1986

Library of Congress Cataloging-in-Publication Data

Robert Louis Stevenson in the South Seas.

Rev. ed. of: R.L.S. in the South Seas.
1. Stevenson, Robert Louis, 1850-1894—Journeys—Oceania—Pictorial works. 2. Oceania—Description and travel—Views. 3. Authors, Scottish—19th century—Biography—Pictorial works. I. Knight, Alanna.
II. R.L.S. in the South Seas.
PR5495.R63 1986 828′.803 [B] 86-25171
ISBN 0-913729-32-9

DEDICATION

For
Konrad Hopkins
and
David Jensen

Acknowledgements

Photographs (unless otherwise stated) are reproduced by courtesy of the Edinburgh City Libraries, whose invaluable assistance and many kindnesses during the production of this volume are gratefully acknowledged.

Photographs on pages 47-50, 81 and 123 by kind permission of University of Oklahoma.

Literary excerpts:

THE WORKS OF ROBERT LOUIS STEVENSON, Tusitala Edition (Heinemann, London 1924): *In the South Seas*, (Vol. 20); *Vailima Papers* — A Footnote to History; Father Damien, (Vol. 21); *Letters, Volume III* (Vol. 33).

AN INTIMATE PORTRAIT OF R.L.S. by Lloyd Osbourne (Scribner's Magazine, New York, 1924).

THE CRUISE OF THE 'JANET NICOLL' AMONG THE SOUTH SEA ISLANDS by Mrs R. L. Stevenson (Chatto & Windus, London 1915).

FROM SARANAC TO THE MARQUESAS & BEYOND by Mrs Margaret Isabella Balfour Stevenson (Methuen, London, 1903).

Recommended Reading

Day, A. Grove: TRAVELS IN HAWAII (University Press of Hawaii, Honolulu, 1973).

Ferguson, De Lancey & Waingrow, Marshall: ROBERT LOUIS STEVENSON'S LETTERS TO CHARLES BAXTER (Oxford University Press, 1956).

Field, Isobel (Belle Strong): THIS LIFE I'VE LOVED (Michael Joseph, London, 1937).

Fletcher, C. Brundson: STEVENSON'S GERMANY: THE CASE AGAINST GERMANY IN THE PACIFIC (Heinemann, London, 1920).

Furnas, J. C: VOYAGE TO WINDWARD (Faber & Faber, London 1952).

Knight, Alanna: ROBERT LOUIS STEVENSON TREASURY (Shepheard-Walwyn, London, 1985).

McGaw, Sister Martha Mary: STEVENSON IN HAWAII (University of Hawaii Press, Honolulu 1950).

Mackay, Margaret: THE VIOLENT FRIEND: THE STORY OF MRS ROBERT LOUIS STEVENSON (Doubleday, New York 1968: Dent, London 1969).

Menikoff, Barry: R.L.S. & THE BEACH OF FALESA (Edinburgh University Press 1984).

Mrantz, Maxine: R. L. STEVENSON: POET IN PARADISE (Aloha Graphics, Honolulu, 1977).

Stevenson, Fanny Van der Grift & Robert Louis: OUR SAMOAN ADVENTURE, Weidenfeld & Nicholson, London 1956.

Author's Note

The original text (Tusitala Edition 1924) has been used for Stevenson's letters. There are some irregularities in spelling; also 'Taiti' becomes the conventional 'Tahiti' in later letters. Fanny used 'Nichol' instead of 'Nicoll' (correct) in her Diary of the cruise. The elipses in letters most frequently indicate a repetition in other letters or in Margaret Stevenson's letters to her sister, where the same event was being described by both writers, or when Stevenson's letters were dealing with business or writing projects at some length.

Regarding Stevenson's main correspondents: Charles Baxter (1848-1919) was an Edinburgh Lawyer, a friend since student days and in charge of his affairs while abroad. Sir Sidney Colvin (1845-1927) had been introduced to Stevenson by Fanny Sitwell (later to become Lady Colvin) during the time of Stevenson's infatuation for this 'older woman' in 1873. The friendship with novelist Henry James (1843-1916) dates from Bournemouth days (1885); also with Adelaide Boodle, a neighbour at 'Skerryvore' who became a devoted friend.

Fanny, Belle Strong, Louis and Mrs Margaret Stevenson

Contents

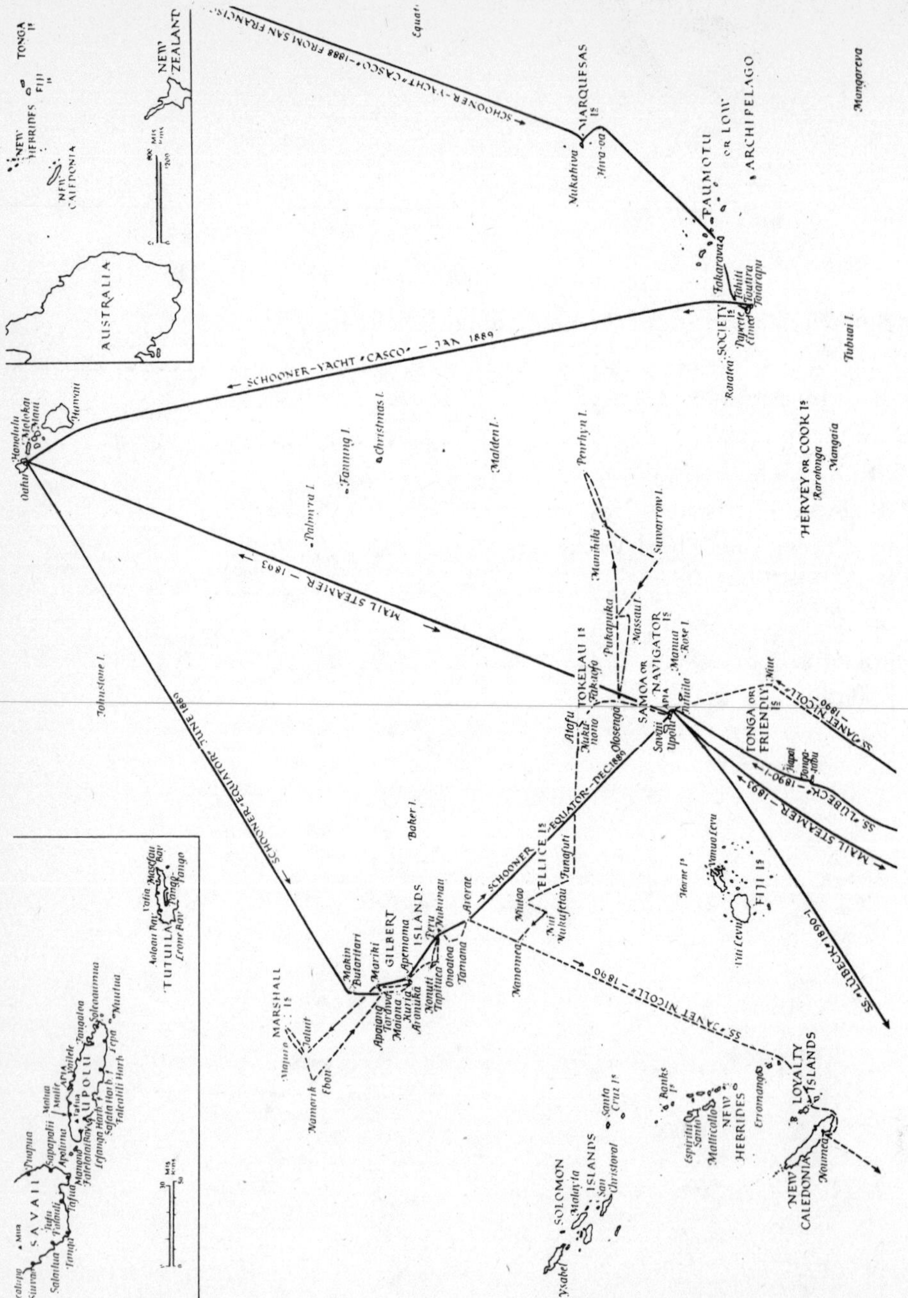

Map of Stevenson's 3 Cruises

List of Illustrations

INTRODUCTION

In 1879 Robert Louis Stevenson first visited America, his main purpose to marry Fanny Osbourne. At that time he was twenty-nine years old and a relatively unknown Scottish writer. Eight years later, in 1887, New York gave a hero's welcome to 'R.L.S.', the famous author of *Dr Jekyll and Mr Hyde* and *Kidnapped*, who was then a chronic invalid returning to America in search of health.

During a winter of appalling severity in Saranac, New York State, Stevenson supported his family by writing articles for the New York *World*. Its editor, Sam McClure, suggested chartering a yacht to voyage in the South Seas, to be financed by a syndicated weekly column, with payment guaranteed beforehand. Stevenson responded with enthusiasm. Long before his success with *Treasure Island* (1882), a New Zealand visitor to his Edinburgh home had told him:

> . . . all about the South Sea Islands till I was sick with desire to go there; beautiful places, green for ever; perfect climate, perfect shapes of men and women with red flowers in their hair; and nothing to do but study oratory and etiquette, sit in the sun and pick up the fruits as they fall. Navigator's Island is the place; absolute balm for the weary.

A chance remark to Fanny, who was visiting her family in California, led to her chartering the schooner-yacht *Casco*, a ninety-five-feet schooner, seventy-two tons register, the property of a wealthy doctor. The *Casco*, with a crew of eleven, set sail under the command of Captain A. H. Otis. The captain was unimpressed by his distinguished passenger, having read *Treasure Island* and having dismissed it as an example of poor seamanship.

Stevenson wrote few letters after the first voyage. His mother, Margaret Stevenson, writing to her sister, Jane Whyte Balfour in Edinburgh, in a letter reproduced in *From Saranac to the Marquesas* (1903), provides a vivid account of everyday life on an ocean-going yacht. There was a reason:

> By the way, Louis would like you to keep all the letters I write on the voyage for his benefit, as he may want to refer to them if ever he brings out a book. . . .

The health-seeking cruise of a few months' duration now held the exciting prospect of a definitive illustrated history of the South Seas and for this more ambitious project their luggage included a typewriter, cameras, photographic equipment and a magic lantern.

Photography at this time was a novel but very haphazard hobby for amateurs. The photographic camera had developed from the camera obscura, familiar to artists and scientists since the seventeenth century as a portable drawing instrument, complete with lens and focusing mechanism. Had the science of chemistry been as far advanced as optics, then photography would have been in use much earlier.

In 1816, a Frenchman, Joseph Nicéphore Niépce, had substituted paper, light-sensitised with silver salts, for ground glass but was unable to print positive impressions from his negatives. Niépce's introduction of bellows and iris diaphragm was a great step forward, and in 1830 another Frenchman, J. M. Daguerre, used similar camera obscuras fitted with an achromatic meniscus lens. This become known as the daguerreotype process. The first commercially available camera was made by his brother-in-law, Alphonse Giroux, for Daguerre in 1839, but like Niépce's model it was bulky and consisted of two wooden boxes of similar size to produce wholeplate pictures, with a lens cap to act as shutter.

William Henry Fox-Talbot had also experimented in 1834-35 with the camera obscura, but for large objects and buildings this process took hours to gather enough darkening to form an image. By accident, he discovered the process of development which, with the action of gallic acid, multiplied the silver grains.

Further progress was made in 1851 by Frederick Scott Archer's discovery of coating glass plates with collodion. Wet collodion photographs opened up a new dimension but the main drawback was that photographers had to carry a portable darkroom to operate the process. For outdoor work such cumbersome equipment was inconvenient, even though ambitious projects such as Roger Fenton's Crimean War photographs were made possible. Before wet collodion, it had been practically impossible to capture movement, and sitters had to be 'clamped' in place; however, this process reduced exposure times from minutes to seconds or tenths of seconds. It opened up a new era of photography. Scott Archer did not apply for a patent and, as no licence was required, anyone able to afford the equipment could set himself up in business. At the same time, public interest in photography was increasing: family groups were greatly in demand, and even Queen Victoria had her own darkroom specially equipped in Windsor Castle.

In 1875 the first book of photo journalism, *Street Life in London*, was published. Tripods and camera with collapsible bellows became available and, in 1881, Kodak introduced their first camera. George Eastmann replaced glass with flexible celluloid and in 1885 a simple box camera containing a 100-exposure roll film followed. Ten years later, in 1895 (the year after Stevenson's death in Samoa), the first 'pocket Kodak' was on the market.

The period of Stevenson's voyages — 1888-1890 — therefore, covers the rapid development of portable photography. There is no indication in the letters from the voyages of the models used, but we can presume from Margaret Stevenson's references to 'field' camera, plate films and the exhausting carrying of heavy equipment and tripod that roll films were either still too novel or too expensive to

Lloyd Osbourne, Fanny and Louis Stevenson at Saranac

be in general use. Writing to Charles Baxter from Tahiti, Stevenson apologises for 'bad proofs' because 'the paper was so bad'.

While his stepson, Lloyd Osbourne, is often referred to as 'taking pictures', one Stevenson letter suggests that using the camera was an entire family activity: 'We are all pretty gay on board, and have been photographing and draught-playing and skylarking like anything.' We know also that Stevenson, travelling alone to the leper settlement, took his camera.

There are almost ninety photographs in this book. There should have been twice that number. Fanny Stevenson's diary, *The Cruise of the 'Janet Nicol' Among the South Sea Islands*, records that ninety were lost in a disastrous shipboard fire in April 1890, doubtless including those Stevenson intended sending to Burlingame, his editor, at Scribner's:

> . . . a portrait of Tembinoka, a view of the palace or of some of the 'matted men' at their singing, also T's flag, which my wife designed for him, and a few photographs of the war, which will do for illustrations [for the projected travel book].

In a letter from Anaho Bay, 29 July 1889, Margaret Stevenson also recounts other disasters, in particular:

> Today a great misfortune has befallen us; Lloyd's camera has fallen overboard. It had been left overnight onshore, and was brought out this morning; and while being handed up from the boat, slipped out of its strap and went straight to the bottom. Lloyd has taken a few pictures, but it is a serious loss coming so early in our trip. . . .

Then from Hiva-Oa, on 25 August:

> We got one piece of good news, young Keane has a camera and has used up all his plates, so was quite willing to sell it to Lloyd, who thinks he can cut his plates to fit it.

At sea or on land Stevenson's main preoccupation was the daily exercise of his writing craft. He had no excuse for dallying; he was a good sailor, his health was excellent, and his mother declared his appetite splendid, considering him fitter than at any time in the past ten years. In Tahiti during October 1888 he worked on *The Master of Ballantrae*, to be published in twelve monthly instalments in *Scribner's Magazine* (November 1888-October 1889). To Colvin he wrote: 'it [*The Master of Ballantrae*] contains more human work than anything of mine but *Kidnapped*.'

On arrival at Papeete in Tahiti, Stevenson fell victim to the 'new' island epidemic, influenza. He was welcomed into the household of the chief, Ori a Ori, at Tautira, where he was nursed by Princess Moe. Soon all three were great friends, 'exchanging names'. His enforced stay produced two South Seas ballads: *Feast of Famine*, a Marquesas story, *Song of Rahero* and, for 'Songs of Travels', the nostalgic 'Home no more home to me, whither must I wander?'. It was not until they reached Honolulu, from where the *Casco* was sent back to its owner in San Francisco, that Stevenson wrote Burlingame in January 1889:

> As soon as I am through with *The Master*, I shall finish *The Game of Bluff* — now rechristened *The Wrong Box* [written in collaboration with his stepson Lloyd Osbourne]. This I wish to sell, cash down. It is of course copyright in the States; and I offer it to you for five thousand dollars. Please reply on this by return. Also please tell the typewriter who was so good as to be amused by our follies that I am filled with admiration for his piece of work. I may also be

Stevenson in 1893

> deceived as to the numbers of *The Master* now going, or already gone; but to me they seem First Chop, sir, First Chop. I hope I shall pull off that damned ending; but it still depresses me; this is your doing, Mr Burlingame; you would have it there and then, and I fear it — I fear that ending.

He finished the book in March and in April wrote again:

> I am quite worked out, and this cursed end of *The Master* hangs over me like the arm of the gallows; but it is always darkest before dawn and no doubt the clouds will soon rise; but it is a difficult thing to write, above all in Mackellarese [the narrator], and I cannot yet see my way clear. If I pull this off, *The Master* will be a pretty good novel or I am the more deceived; and even if I don't pull it off, it'll still have some stuff in it.'

To Will Low, on 20 May:

> I have at length finished *The Master*; it has been a sore cross to me; but now he is buried, his body's under hatches — his soul, if there is any hell to go to, gone to hell; and I forgive him; it is harder to forgive Burlingame for having induced me to begin the publication, or myself for suffering the induction.

By October he and Lloyd were at work on *The Wrecker*. To Colvin, he wrote:

> . . . strange ways of life, I think, they set forth: things I can scarce touch upon, or even not at all, in my travel book; and the yarns are good, I do believe. *The Pearl Fisher* [later retitled *The Ebb Tide*] is for the *New York Ledger*; the yarn is a kind of Monte Cristo one. *The Wrecker* is the least good as a story, I think; but the characters seem to me good. *The Beachcombers* is more sentimental. [This book was never written.]

The main task of gathering material for his illustrated history continued and as early as November 1888 he was optimistically dedicating this work to fellow-writer John Addington Symonds. In Honolulu the Stevensons made friends with King Kalakaua, who had a penchant for apeing the manners and methods of European monarchies, and six months later, in June 1889, they boarded the *Equator*, a small copra-trading schooner with a crew of sixteen and a Scottish captain named Reid, bound for the Gilbert Islands. The Stevensons were to be dropped at Samoa to take ship to Sydney and, as Stevenson wrote to his mother (who had returned to Edinburgh to nurse her sister Jane): 'We shall turn up in England by May or June.' And to Colvin, on 2 December 1889:

> 'I am minded not to stay very long in Samoa and confine my studies there (as far as anyone can forecast) to the history of the late war.'

Samoa was first visited by a Dutchman, Jacob Roggeveen, in 1722. The island's strategic position in the early 1800s combined with its wealth in copra, the oil-yielding kernel of the coconut, made it an attractive acquisition to Great Britain, Germany and the United States. In 1878 the three powers signed treaties with the result that their interests were soon in conflict. The rival factions of Catholic and Protestant missionaries were also at loggerheads, and the bewildered Samoans were ruthlessly exploited by the white man, of whom Trader Wiltshire in *The Beach of Falesá* is a typical example.

In *A Footnote to History*, Stevenson wrote:

> The handful of whites have everything; the natives walk in a foreign town. . . . Within the memory of man the white people of Apia lay in the worst squalor of degradation. They are now unspeakably improved, both men and women. Today they must be called a more than

'King' Mataafa of Samoa

> fairly respectable population, and a much more than fairly intelligent. The trouble (for Samoa) is that they are all here after a livelihood. Some are sharp practitioners, some are famous (justly or unjustly) for foul play in business . . . commerce, like politics shows its ugly side, and becomes as personal as fisticuffs. Close at their elbows, in all this contention, stands the native looking on. Like a child, his true analogue, he observes, apprehends, misapprehends, and is usually silent. . . .

But not all South Sea Islanders were cannibals, nor were all white men corrupt. Harry J. Moors, an American trader and local politician, provides interesting descriptions of Stevenson in *With Stevenson in Samoa:*

> A young-looking man came forward to meet me. He appeared to be about thirty years of age, although really nine years older, of fair and somewhat sallow complexion, and about five feet ten inches in height. He wore a slight, scraggy moustache, and his hair hung down about his neck after the fashion of artists. This was Stevenson — R.L.S., 'the best beloved initials in recent literature' — and I knew it even before he spoke. He was not a handsome man, and yet there was something irresistibly attractive about him. The genius that was in him seemed to shine out of his face. I was struck at once by his keen, inquiring eyes, brown in colour they were strangely bright, and seemed to penetrate you like the eyes of a mesmerist. . . . I needed not to be told that he was in indifferent health, for it was stamped on his face. He appeared to be intensely nervous, highly strung, easily excited. When I first brought him ashore he was looking somewhat weak, but hardly had he got into the street when he began to walk up and down it in a most lively, not to say eccentric, manner. He could not stand still. When I took him to my house, he walked about the room, plying me with questions, one after another, darting up and down, talking on all sorts of subjects, with no continuity whatever in his conversation. His wife was just as fidgety as himself, Lloyd Osbourne not much better. The long lonesome trip on the schooner had quite unnerved them, and they were delighted to be on shore again.
>
> Stevenson was very much addicted to the 'bare feet' habit, but before long I became aware of other eccentricities . . . in a rage he was a study. Once excite him, and you had another Stevenson. I have seen him sitting on my table, dangling his bony legs in the air, chatting away in the calmest possible manner; and I have seen him, becoming suddenly agitated, jump from the table and stalk to and fro across the floor like some wild forest animal, to which he has, indeed, been already compared. His face would glow and his eyes would flash, hypnotising you with their brilliance and burning fires within. In calm they were eyes of strange beauty, with an expression that is almost beyond the power of pen to describe. Eyes half alert, half sorrowful, a strange mixture of what seemed to be at once the sorrow and the joy of life, and there appeared to be a haunting sadness in their very brightness.

The Rev. W. E. Clarke, of the London Missionary Society, was less impressed and, at first glimpse, presumed that he was witnessing the arrival of a band of down-at-heel entertainers eager to make a few dollars, while Henry Adams, the American humorist and friend of Henry James, described Stevenson as:

> A man so thin and emaciated that he looked like a bundle of sticks in a bag, with dirty striped pyjamas, the baggy legs tucked into coarse woollen stockings, one of which was bright brown in colour, the other a purplish dark tone. . . . He appeared first, looking like an insane stock, very warm and restless.

As for Fanny Stevenson:

> A woman in the usual missionary nightgown which was no cleaner than her husband's shirt

Mataafa's rival, Tamasese

> and drawers, but she omitted the stockings . . . her complexion and eyes were dark and strong, like a half-breed Mexican. . . .

Moors' account continues:

> One day Stevenson told me he would like to make his home in Samoa permanently. 'I like this place better than any I have seen in the Pacific,' he said. Tahiti and the Marquesas pleased him, but of all places he liked Samoa best. 'Honolulu's good — very good,' he added, 'but this seems more savage!' He asked me to look out for a nice piece of property that would suit him. Money matters seemed to trouble him, however — not so much the first cost of the land, but the cost of the improvements that would necessarily have to follow. 'Elbow room! Let's have elbow room!' said Stevenson.
>
> Finally, after several fine properties had been submitted to him for inspection, he decided that the Vailima land was the most attractive. At his request, I negotiated the purchase. There were four hundred acres, and I paid $4000. . . .

During this first sojourn in Samoa, Stevenson completed *The Bottle Imp* before embarking on the third voyage, from Sydney by the steamer *Janet Nicoll*:

> . . . near 500 tons, a mighty fine affair for the likes of us; or would be, if she could be induced to stop rolling and wallowing like a drunken tub

wrote Stevenson to his mother, enclosing a plan of accommodation.

> The main cabin is 15 feet long, with 7 feet headroom. Above the cabin is a spar deck and above that again the bridge; abaft the cabins are the galley and the engines. It is very pleasant to have the engines behind; but there is no use in trying to blink the fact that the *Janet* is a pig. I never saw such a roller. Again, last night since I began to write, I was nearly thrown out of my bunk, and eating is a toil and trial.

Not surprisingly he was to write later of 'a cruel rough passage to Auckland'. His writing suffered too: *The Wrecker* was in the doldrums.

In August, back in Sydney, he wrote to Marcel Schwob, a Frenchman who wished to translate *The Black Arrow*:

> I am just now overloaded with work. I have two huge novels on hand — *The Wrecker* and *The Pearl Fisher* [*The Ebb Tide*] in collaboration with my stepson; the latter, *The Pearl Fisher*, I think highly of, for a black, ugly, trampling, violent story, full of strange scenes and striking characters. And then I am about waist-deep in my big book on the South Seas, *the* big book on the South Seas it ought to be, and shall. And besides, I have some verses in the press, which, however, I hesitate to publish. For I am no judge of my own verse; self-deception is there so facile. All this and cares of an impending settlement in Samoa keep me very busy, and a cold (as usual) keeps me in bed.

Once settled in Samoa, Stevenson's determination to meddle in island politics upset the authorities and caused his friends at home both embarrassment and anxiety. To Sidney Colvin, Stevenson wrote on 9 May 1892:

> You are to understand: if I take all this bother, it is not only from a sense of duty, or a love of meddling — damn the phrase, take your choice — but from a great affection for Mataafa. He is a beautiful, sweet old fellow, and he and I grew quite fulsome on Saturday night about our sentiments.

But for the intervention of the British Foreign Secretary, Lord Rosebery, who admired his books, he might well have been deported on the visiting man-of-war lurking in the harbour. Typically, Stevenson immediately made friends with the

Mataafa's natural daughter

crew. Unrepentant, he continued to support the 'rebel' king while his family bore gifts for the lesser chiefs who were imprisoned in Apia. When warriors in war paint, known to take heads, male and female, stared in the windows and the war drums interrupted family prayers, Stevenson would console his terrified womenfolk with a shrug: 'Why worry, we have friends on both sides.' Peace returned to Samoa in 1893 and the chiefs expressed their gratitude by building a link road to Vailima, aptly named 'the Road of Loving Hearts'.

According to Lloyd Osbourne in *An Intimate Portrait:*

> Stevenson made a very large income, and spent it all on Vailima. His letters often show much anxiety about money, and some of his intimate correspondents lectured him severely on his extravagance. Often in moments of depression he called Vailima his Abbotsford, and said he was ruining himself like Scott.

To Colvin on 8 March 1892, Stevenson wrote:

> 'Is this not Babylon the Great I have builded? Call it Subpriorsford.'

Lloyd, Fanny and Louis Stevenson in the Great Hall, Vailima

Dictating to step-daughter Belle in his study

Like Scott, he died of a cerebral haemorrhage from overwork, on 3 December 1894. His life was spartan: sometimes he rose at four a.m. and he wrote at all times and all hours. He described his working day to Colvin (June 1891):

> . . . knee-deep in books, nearly all the shelves are filled, alas. It is a place to make a pig recoil, yet here are my interminable labours begun daily by lamplight and sometimes not yet done when the lamp has once more to be lighted.

Moors quotes his reaction to life in Samoa:

> I love the land; and I have chosen it to be my home while I live, and my grave after I am dead. And I love the people and have chosen them to be my people to live and die with.

And to Colvin, in August 1893, Stevenson wrote:

> I would like you to see Vailima, for it's beautiful and my home and tomb that is to be; though it's a wrench not to be planted in Scotland — that I can never deny —if I could be buried in the hills, under the heather and a table tombstone like the martyrs, where the whaups and plovers are crying. . . . Singular that I should fulfil the Scots destiny throughout, and live a voluntary exile, and have my head filled with the blessed beastly place all the time.

And so it was reflected in his writing in those last years. *Treasure Island* had been written in 1881 during a bleak summer in Scotland, when Stevenson's

On the verandah at Vailima

passion for islands held no hint of the destiny that awaited him. Once settled in Samoa, the short story, *The Beach of Falesá*, was his last work on the South Seas and he proceeded to write out his nostalgia for Scotland with *Catriona, St Ives, Weir of Hermiston*. In place of the 'the *big* book', Stevenson's projected Illustrated History, for which these unique photographs were intended, he completed only *A Footnote to History* and a collection of essays, *In the South Seas*. In conjunction with his *Letters* (from Vol. 3) and extracts from the books above-mentioned, they bring vividly to life Stevenson the writer and champion of lost causes, aboard ship, and at home among the Cannibal Islanders.

Alanna Knight
Aberdeen
April 1986

PART ONE

FIRST VOYAGE

June 1888-January 1889

In the yacht *Casco* for seven months from San Francisco to the Marquesas, the Paumotus, Tahiti, and thence northwards to Hawaii.

Mrs Margaret Stevenson wearing lei

In the South Seas: The Marquesas

An Island Landfall

For nearly ten years my health had been declining; and for some while before I set forth upon my voyage I believed I was come to the afterpiece of life, and had only the nurse and undertaker to expect. It was suggested that I should try the South Seas; and I was not unwilling to visit like a ghost, be carried like a bale, among scenes that had attracted me in youth and health. I chartered accordingly Dr Merrit's schooner, the *Casco*, seventy-four tons register; sailed from San Francisco towards the end of June 1888, visited the eastern islands, and was left early the next year at Honolulu. Hence, lacking courage to return to my old life of the house and sick-room, I set forth to leeward in a trading schooner, the *Equator*, of a little over seventy tons, spent four months among the atolls (low coral islands)

On board the Casco

of the Gilbert group, reached Samoa towards the close of '89. By that time gratitude and habit were beginning to attach me to the islands; I had gained a competency of strength; I had made friends; I had learned new interests; the time of my voyages had passed like days in fairyland; and I decided to remain. I began to prepare these pages at sea, on a third cruise, in the trading steamer *Janet Nicoll*. If more days are granted me, they shall be passed where I have found life most pleasant and man most interesting; the axes of my black boys are already clearing the foundations of my future house; and I must learn to address readers from the uttermost parts of the sea.

Letter from Mrs Margaret Stevenson to Jane Whyte Balfour
Yacht Casco, *Sunday, July 1 1888*

This is our fourth day at sea and all goes well I am thankful to say. Everybody was at lunch today except Fanny; she and Lloyd and Valentine spent most of their time during the first three days in bed, and even the captain did not appear at meals for two days, so that Louis and I had them all by ourselves. I missed only the first breakfast and that was because I had been on deck for two hours and was not able to face red herrings and mutton chops after that.

We were towed out by the *Pelican*. There was a heavy swell outside and we were amused to watch the little steamer first lifted high above us, and then, as the wave passed, she, and even the mountains of the coast, were shut out entirely. Our vessel seemed very small among those enormous waves, and I felt nervous when I saw how she heeled over; however, I was told it was all right, and I am already getting accustomed to it. The swell, too, is beginning to go down.

I must try to describe the vessel that is to be our home for so long. From the deck you step down into the cockpit, which is our open-air drawing-room. It has seats all round, nicely cushioned, and we sit or lie there most of the day. The compass is there, and the wheel, so the man at the wheel always keeps us company. Here, also, is the companion, and at the bottom of the stair on the right-hand side is the captain's room. Straight ahead is the main or after cabin, a nice bright place with a skylight and four portholes. There are four sofas that can be turned into beds if need be, and there are lockers under them in which our clothes are stored away. Above and behind each sofa is a berth concealed by white lace curtains on brass rods, and in these berths we three women are laid away as on shelves each night to sleep. There is a table fastened to the floor in the centre of the cabin, covered with crimson Utrecht velvet. The sofas are upholstered to match, and the carpet is crimson Brussels. There is one large, heavy swivel chair, and opposite the entrance is a mirror let into the wall, with two small shelves under it. On each side of this mirror is a door. The one to the right leads through a small dressing-room with a fixed basin to Lloyd's cabin, and beyond that again is the forward cabin, or dining-room. The door to the left opens into another small dressing-room, and beyond this is Louis's sleeping-room. It is very roomy, with both a bed and a sofa in it, so that he will be very comfortable; and at night, when we are all in bed, all the portholes and skylights and doors are left open for the sake of air.

The dining-room has a long table and chairs, two mirrors at the end, and between the doors a very ugly picture of fruits and cake. Louis would fain cover it up if we could spare a flag with which to do it. Two doors at the further end lead to the pantry and galley, and beyond these are the men's quarters, which I have not yet explored.

Tuesday, July 3

Sunday was cloudy and squally, but Louis was able to read a short service in the cockpit at 4 p.m., which was the time that suited best for the men. . . . We are nearing the tropics and beginning to feel it. We saw one whale the day we sailed, and four pilot-birds have followed us all the way. It is delightful to see them alighting on the waves and walking along for a few steps, leaving little white footprints behind them on the water. Louis says that they follow the vessel for 'grease', and that they suppose the yacht is an immense bird, and that we are the fleas upon its back! . . .

Thursday, July 5

Yesterday we had a new sensation — a calm. The sails flapped idly, and we only made about two knots an hour; the sun was very hot, but we could generally find shade behind one or other of the sails. The sea was beautifully smooth, and we had the rare pleasure of a distant horizon. Usually we seem to be shut in by the waves.

We all had a very active fit. Fanny, Valentine and I took to making pyjamas and jackets for Louis of thin flannel, to be ready for the hot weather. . . . During the day I had a good long walk outside of the cockpit, which was quite a treat. Louis won't let me attempt it unless the sea is very smooth, because the passage is narrow and the bulwarks not very high. He and Fanny think me much too adventurous, and declare I will fall over. Fanny said to the captain one day, 'What would you do if Mrs Stevenson were to fall overboard?' and the captain, who loves a joke, solemnly replied, 'Put it in the log!'. This morning Valentine tossed Fanny's cushion up the companion stairs and very nearly sent it overboard. Louis asked, 'Would you have put that in the log if it had gone over?' 'Yes, if you thought it worth while to send Valentine after it. . . .'
[*Valentine Roch, the Stevensons' Swiss maid*]

July 15

. . . We have had some very hot weather since I last wrote. The thermometer has been up to eighty-nine degrees in the cabin, but is more often about seventy-four degrees, and of course it is hotter on deck. Fanny and Valentine have taken to *mumus* and *holakus* but I am putting off as long as I can. So far I have been content to discard all woollen garments and stiff or fitted bodices, and I often wear boots

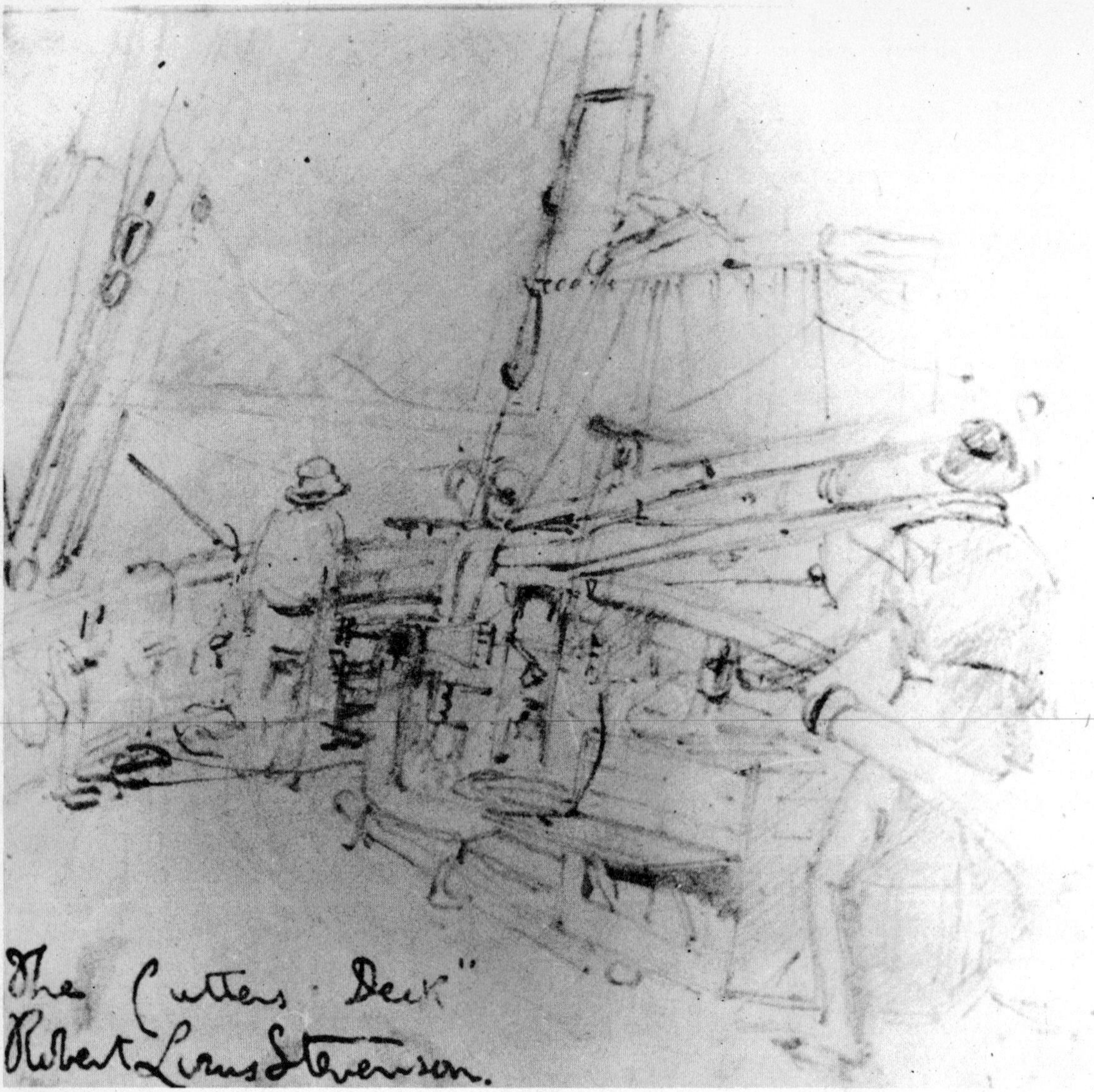

Sketch by R. L. Stevenson

without stockings. Louis goes about in shirt and trousers, and with bare feet; he and Lloyd got their faces and arms so tanned at the beginning that they must now be surely sun-proof. He is up the first in the morning, and is generally the last to go to bed. What do you think of that? . . .

I have seen many flying-fish now, and love to watch them. They look so happy flitting about in the water that one longs to join them in their play. As to our occupations, I have finished a pair of socks for Louis. We are reading Gibbon's *Decline and Fall* and are now in the second volume. Most of it I've to read aloud, as reading in the open air was too much for Louis. We cannot stay on deck in the heat of the day, but it is much cooler below; though once or twice I have been glad to take a siesta. Louis has given up his stateroom because it was too airless, and now sleeps in the fourth berth in the main cabin; so we have turned his room into a dressing-room, and its size permits us to start our indiarubber bath and to have a salt-water 'tub' every morning.

The sailors all have coffee at 6 a.m., as well as any of us who wish for it. Breakfast is at eight. I am generally up at seven and sometimes earlier; once I was even out at five to see the sunrise. After breakfast we all go on deck till Valentine has done up the cabin and made it into a drawing-room once more. After that we 'decline and fall' off, or write and work. At twelve is lunch, and at five dinner. After dinner we go on deck for the sunset, which is the great spectacle of the day. We have had some magnificent ones, but they are about as variable in the tropics as elsewhere and do not always 'come off'. Then we play two rubbers at whist —the captain and I are now eight rubbers ahead; and afterwards we put out the lamps and go on deck to let the cabin cool before going to bed. The evenings are generally delicious, the stars bright, and the air heavenly. We saw the new moon first on Thursday, when it was three days old, but looked very large; though, as Valentine said, when I remarked upon its size, 'Perhaps it was born large'. It may be the way in the tropics! On Friday we had our first peep at the Southern Cross, but unfortunately it was just ahead of the vessel, and partly hidden by the sails, so we cannot be said to have seen it properly yet.

Our little vessel sails splendidly. It is wonderful how she picks her way among the heavy seas and ships so few; but we do get a fair sprinkling of spray now and then. Last Sunday Lou got a regular shower-bath in the cockpit; and I had two lesser ones, one through the skylight in the cabin, and another in the cockpit, one day when it was very stormy. Once, also, when I was sitting in the captain's chair, I was sent spinning across the cabin and struck my head upon the sofa. But see the advantage of a hard Scottish head! I was not hurt in the least, though Louis insisted on banishing the chair, lest another time it might be more serious.

Friday, July 20

In port at last! I cannot tell you how thrilling it was to hear Louis's call of 'Land!' at five o'clock this morning. We fairly tumbled into our dressing-gowns, and rushed on deck. . . .

Yacht Casco, *Anaho Bay, Nuka-hiva, July 22*

This, at last, is my *beau-ideal*! The climate is simply perfect, much more delightful than I could have believed possible so near the Equator. The sun is certainly hot, but there is always a delightful breeze, and it is never in the least sultry or airless. I fancy we have arrived at a fortunate time, as the rainy season is just over and everything is looking new-made and beautiful — *how* beautiful it is hard to make you realise. We all feel as if we wanted to 'draw in our chairs' and stay here a considerable time; even the captain, who was inclined to think the whole expedition quixotic, is charmed. We have an awning over the deck which shades us from the sun, and we spend our whole time when not on shore in the cockpit. At last I have open-air life enough to satisfy even me!

Now I must go back to Friday . . . a large canoe with six or seven natives arrived, bringing cocoanuts, oranges, and bananas for sale. We went on deck to see them, and it was a strange and, to us, rather alarming sight. They were in every stage of undress: two most respectable looking old gentlemen wore nothing but small red and yellow loincloths and *very* cutty sarks on top. There was even some who wore less! The display of legs was something we were not accustomed to; but as they were all tattooed in most wonderful patterns, it really looked quite as if they were wearing open-work silk tights. There was a good deal of bargaining about the price of the fruits, and the wag of the party, who did most of the talking, said it was certainly a very fine vessel, but there seemed to be very little money on board!

Louis took them all over the yacht. . . . They followed him in Indian file, making strange sounds of satisfaction and pleasure all the time. Most of them were distinctly good-looking, but there was one with a very strange, unpleasant face, and an immense mouth that at once suggested cannibalism to us all.

When the chief went on shore, Captain Otis and Lloyd went with him . . . almost as soon as they left us, there arrived two other canoes, and we had presently fourteen natives swarming over the deck. We women were a little frightened, but we made signs that we had no money to buy anything and they soon went away, quite satisfied and apparently not at all surprised. We are told that their own women hold a very inferior position, and are permitted to share very few of the privileges enjoyed by the men. Only very lately has the last *tabu* been removed that forbade the women to walk on roads which men had made, or to use a bridge which men had built; they were compelled, if they desired to cross over, to do so only by wading a creek. Even now they are not allowed to ride in a saddle belonging to a native, though they may use a foreigner's; and as there is only one person in the island who possesses a side-saddle, you may imagine it is in constant request. In some of the other islands, moreover, a woman is not allowed to eat meat; the men form themselves into 'clubs' or parties, where all the pork and other meat is consumed. Would you not think they had taken a hint from civilised society? . . .

Yesterday we had a delightful day. Lloyd, Valentine and I went ashore at 11 a.m., taking bathing-suits and luncheon with us. We found a grove of palm trees for a dressing-room and had a delicious bathe, which reminded me that it was twenty-six years since I had ventured on such a pleasure; but here the water is

Anaho Bay, Nuka-hiva

delightfully warm, and we can stay in as long as we like without risk of chill. After bathing, we lunched on sardines, biscuits and beer, and a native brought us some cocoanuts and oranges, which are a green kind, very juicy and delicious. . . . We saw many of the women while we were on shore, and some of them are very pretty. . . . They wore light-coloured *holakuas* with long trains, a very pretty garment, in which they looked most graceful; their feet were bare but tattooed in such beautiful patterns that they had the appearance of wearing open-work silk stockings. They tattoo their legs all over, and Fanny and I feel naked with our plain white legs when we are bathing. . . .

This morning we had a visit from a much more important chief than ours . . . Kooamua is very intelligent and went all round the yacht, looking at things with a really critical appreciation: everything was carefully and thoughtfully examined. He was greatly pleased with the captain's rifle, did not care much for Lloyd's fiddle; but the thing that charmed him most was the typewriter. He went off at last, very happy, with a *Casco* ribbon for his hat, a piece of plug tobacco in his pocket, and his name and that of every member of his family printed by himself with the typewriter. He looked such a mild and benevolent old gentleman that it is difficult to believe he was till quite recently a cannibal. He is now a wealthy and important man with a large European house in which he entertains the governor; and the French do nothing that concerns the native without consulting him.

The typewritten 'family tree' proved to be so popular that the very same evening our own chief sent us a list of his family to be written out in the same way. Kooamua, however, remained the only one to try the machine for himself. What children they are, happy and contented, with no wants that nature cannot supply. I wonder if we are wise or kind to rouse them to all the cares and anxieties of civilised life. My dear husband used always to say that dogs had much happier lives than ours, and these Kanakas seem as free from every conscious care and responsibility as ever a dog could be. Their conduct to each other and to strangers, so far as kindliness and courtesy are concerned, is much more Christ-like than that of many professing Christians; but I am told that although the Roman Catholic missionaries have been teaching them for a number of years, they have produced very little real effect, save that the islanders have ceased to worship idols. Fanny has secured the last that remained in this bay, a very uncouth attempt at a human figure carved in wood, and in rather a decayed state.

In the South Seas: The Marquesas
An Island Landfall

Few men who come to the islands leave them; they grow grey where they alighted; the palm shades and the trade-wind fans them till they die, perhaps cherishing to the last the fancy of a visit home, which is rarely made, more rarely enjoyed, and yet more rarely repeated. No part of the world exerts the same attractive power upon the visitor, and the task before me is to communicate to fireside travellers some sense of its seduction, and to describe the life, at sea and ashore, of many hundred thousand persons, some of our own blood and language, all our contemporaries, and yet as remote in thought and habit as Rob Roy or Barbarossa, the Apostles or the Caesars.

The first experience can never be repeated. The first love, the first sunrise, the first South Sea island, are memories apart and touched a virginity of sense. On the 28th of July 1888, the moon was an hour down by four in the morning. In the east a radiating centre of brightness told of the day; and beneath, on the skyline, the morning bank was already building, black as ink. We have all read of the swiftness of the day's coming and departure in low latitudes; it is a point on which the scientific and sentimental tourist are at one, and has inspired some tasteful poetry. The period certainly varies with the season; but here is one case exactly noted. Although the dawn was thus preparing by four, the sun was not up till six; and it was half-past five before we could distinguish our expected islands from the

The Needles of Ua-pu, Nuka-hiva

clouds on the horizon. Eight degrees south, and the day two hours a-coming. The interval was passed on deck in the silence of expectation, the customary thrill of landfall heightened by the strangeness of the shores that we were then approaching. Slowly they took shape in the attenuating darkness. Ua-huna, piling up to a truncated summit, appeared the first upon the starboard bow; almost abeam arose our destination, Nuka-hiva, whelmed in cloud; and betwixt and to the southward, the first rays of the sun displayed the needles of Ua-pu. These pricked about the line of the horizon; like the pinnacles of some ornate and monstrous church they stood there, in the sparkling brightness of the morning, the fit signboard of a world of wonders.

Not one soul aboard the *Casco* had set foot upon the islands, or knew, except by accident, one word of any of the island tongues; and it was with something perhaps of the same anxious pleasure as thrilled the bosom of discoverers that we drew near these problematic shores. The land heaved up in peaks and rising vales; it fell in cliffs and buttresses; its colour ran through fifty modulations in a scale of pearl and rose and olive; and it was crowned above by opalescent clouds. The suffusion of vague hues deceived the eye; the shadows of clouds were confounded with the articulations of the mountain; and the isle and its unsubstantial canopy rose and shimmered before us like a single mass. There was no beacon, no smoke of towns to be expected, no plying pilot. Somewhere, in that pale phantasmagoria of cliff and cloud, our haven lay concealed; and somewhere to the east of it — the only seamark given — a certain headland, known indifferently as Cape Adam and Eve, or Cape Jack and Jane, and distinguished by two colossal figures, the gross statuary of nature. These we were to find; for these we craned and stared, focussed glasses, and wrangled over charts; and the sun was overhead and the land close ahead before we found them. To a ship approaching, like the *Casco*, from the north, they proved indeed the least conspicuous features of a striking coast; the surf flying high above its base; strange, austere, and feathered mountains rising behind; and Jack and Jane, or Adam and Eve, impending like a pair of warts above the breakers. . . .

Thence we were borne away along shore. On our port beam we might hear the explosions of the surf; a few birds flew fishing under the prow; here was no other sound or mark of life, whether of man or beast, in all that quarter of island. Winged by her own impetus and the dying breeze, the *Casco* skimmed under cliffs, opened out a cove, showed us a beach and some green trees, and flitted by again, bowing to the swell. The trees, from our distance, might have been hazel; the beach might have been in Europe; the mountain forms behind modelled in little from the Alps, and the forests which clustered on their ramparts a growth no more considerable than our Scottish heath. . . .

Under the eastern shore, our schooner, now bereft of any breeze, continued to creep in. From close aboard arose the bleating of young lambs; a bird sang on the hillside; the scent of the land and of a hundred fruits or flowers flowed forth to meet us; and, presently, a house or two appeared, standing high upon the ankles of the hills, and one of these surrounded with what seemed a garden. These conspicuous habitations, that patch of culture, had we but known it, were a mark of the passage of whites; and we might have approached a hundred islands and not found their parallel. It was longer ere we spied the native village, standing (in the universal fashion) close upon a curve of beach, close under a grove of palms; the sea in front growling and whitening on a concave arc of reef. For the cocoa-tree and the island man are both lovers and neighbours of the surf. 'The coral waxes, the palm grows, but man departs' says the sad Tahitian proverb; but they are all three, so long as they endure, co-haunters of the beach. The mark of anchorage was a blow-hole in the rocks, near the south-easterly corner of the bay. Punctually to our use, the blow-hole spouted; the schooner turned upon her heel. . . .

Before yet the anchor plunged a canoe was already paddling from the hamlet. It contained two men; one white, one brown and tattooed across the face with bands of blue, both in immaculate white European clothes; the resident trader, Mr Regler, and the native chief, Taipi-Kikino. 'Captain, is it permitted to come on board?' were the first words we heard among the islands. Canoe followed canoe till the ship swarmed with stalwart six-foot men in every stage of undress; some in a shirt, some in a loincloth, one in a handkerchief imperfectly adjusted; some, and these the more considerable, tattooed from head to foot in awful patterns; some

'The gross statuary of nature': Omoo Valley

barbarous and knived; one, who sticks in my memory as something bestial, squatting on his hams in a canoe, sucking an orange and spitting it out again to alternate sides with ape-like vivacity — all talking, and we could not understand one word; all trying to trade with us who had no thought of trading, or offering us island curios at prices palpably absurd. There was no word of welcome; no show of civility; no hand extended save that of the chief and Mr Regler. As we still continued to refuse the proferred articles, complaint ran high and rude; and one, the jester of the party, railed upon our meanness amid jeering laughter. Amongst other angry pleasantries — 'Here is a mighty fine ship,' said he, 'to have no money on board!' I own I was inspired with sensible repugnance; even with alarm. The ship was manifestly in their power; we had women on board; I knew nothing of my guests beyond the fact that they were cannibals; the Directory [Findlay's Directories of the World] (my only guide) was full of timid cautions; and as for the trader whose presence might else have reassured me, were not whites in the Pacific the usual instigators and accomplices of native outrage? When he reads this confession, our kind friend, Mr Regler, can afford to smile.

Later in the day, as I sat writing up my journal, the cabin was filled from end to end with Marquesans; three brown-skinned generations, squatted cross-legged upon the floor, and regarding me in silence with embarrassing eyes. The eyes of all Polynesians are large, luminous, and melting; they are like the eyes of animals and some Italians. A kind of despair came over me, to sit there helpless under all these staring orbs, and be thus blocked in a corner of my cabin by this speechless crowd; and a kind of rage to think they were beyond the reach of articulate communication, like furred animals, or folk born deaf, or the dwellers of some alien planet. . . .

Visitors to Casco

Methought, in my travels, all human relation was to be excluded; and when I returned home (for in those days I still projected my return) I should have but dipped into a picture-book without a text. Nay, and I even questioned if my travels should be much prolonged; perhaps they were destined to a speedy end; perhaps my subsequent friend, Kauanui, whom I remarked there, sitting silent with the rest, for a man of some authority, might leap from his hams and with an ear-splitting signal, the ship be carried at a rush, and the ship's company butchered for the table.

There could be nothing more natural than these apprehensions, nor anything more groundless. In my experience of the islands, I had never again so menacing a reception; were I to meet with such today, I should be more alarmed and tenfold more surprised. The majority of Polynesians are easy folk to get in touch with, frank, fond of notice, greedy of the least affection, like amiable, fawning dogs; and even with the Marquesans, so recently and so imperfectly redeemed from a blood-boltered barbarism [cannibalism], all were to become our intimates, and one, at least, was to mourn sincerely our departure.

Letter to Sidney Colvin, Yacht Casco, *Anaho Bay,*
Nuka-hiva, Marquesas Islands, July 1888

My dear Colvin, — From this somewhat (ahem) out of the way place, I write to say how d'ye do. It is all a swindle: I chose these isles as having the most beastly population, and they are far better, and far more civilised than we. I know one old chief, Ko-o-amua, a great cannibal in his day, who ate his enemies even as he walked home from killing 'em, and he is a perfect gentleman and exceedingly amiable and simple-minded: no fool, though.

The climate is delightful; and the harbour where we lie one of the loveliest spots imaginable. Yesterday evening we had near a score of natives on board; lovely parties. We have a native god; very rare now. Very rare and equally absurd to view.

This sort of work is not favourable to correspondence: it takes me all the little strength I have to go about and see, and then come home and note, the strangeness around us. I shouldn't wonder if there came trouble here some day, all the same. I could name a nation that is not beloved in certain islands — and it does not know it! Strange: like ourselves, perhaps, in India! Love to all and much to yourself.

R.L.S.

Letter from Margaret Stevenson to Jane Whyte Balfour
July 28

. . . Yesterday a native dance was got up for our benefit. None of the dancing-women appeared, but five men, nicely dressed in shirts and trousers, danced together with great spirit and grace. The music was provided by a drum made out of an old tin box. Many of the steps reminded me of a Highland reel, but were curiously mixed up with calisthenic, and even gymnastic, exercises: the hands in particular were used very gracefully, and they often took off their hats and waved them to and fro. But they also climbed on each other's shoulders, and did other strange things. After dancing for some time, they sang songs to us in a curious, low, weird kind of crooning. Altogether it was a strange sort of afternoon party!

When we came away . . . we were accompanied by some of the women, who had expressed a wish to visit the yacht; the chief's wife and five others. . . . The mirrors were the things that delighted them most; and this little trait of sex greatly delighted Louis, as none of the men had taken any notice of them at all. One of the ladies had her feet and legs tattooed in really the most wonderful patterns; she was quite pleased when we admired them, and gave us a *most liberal* view of them! At the same time, I must in justice add that they were all perfectly well-behaved and lady-like, though some of the books of travel say that their manners are such that it is impossible for a lady even to land on the island. . . .

In the South Seas: The Marquesas:
Making Friends

I was the showman of the *Casco*. She, her fine lines, tall spars, and snowy decks, the crimson fittings of the saloon, and the white, the gilt, and the repeating mirrors of the tiny cabin, brought us a hundred visitors. The men fathomed out her dimensions with their arms, as their fathers fathomed out the ships of Cook; the women declared the cabins more lovely than a church; bouncing Junos were never weary of sitting in the chairs and contemplating in the glass their own bland images; and I have seen one lady strip up her dress and, with cries of wonder and delight, rub herself bare-breeched upon the velvet cushions. Biscuits, jam and syrup was the entertainment; and as in European parlours, the photograph album went the round. This sober gallery, their everyday costumes and physiognomies, had become transformed, in three weeks' sailing, into things wonderful and rich and foreign; alien faces, barbaric dresses, they were now beheld and fingered, in the swerving cabin, with innocent excitement and surprise. Her Majesty was often recognised, and I have seen French subjects kiss her photograph. . . .

'The Maroon'

On the beauties of Anaho books might be written. I remember waking about three to find the air temperate and scented. The long swell brimmed into the bay and seemed to fill it full and then subside. Gently, deeply and silently the *Casco* rolled; only at times a block piped like a bird. Oceanward, the heaven was bright with stars and the sea with their reflections. . . .

And then I turned shoreward, and high squalls were overheard; the mountains

'I was the showman of the Casco'

loomed black, and I could have fancied I had slipped ten thousand miles away and was anchored in a Highland loch; that when the day came it would show pine, and heather, and green fern, and roofs of turf sending up the smoke of peats; and the alien speech that should next greet my ears must be Gaelic, not Kanaka.

And day, when it came, brought other sights and thoughts. I have watched the morning break in many quarters of the world; it has been certainly one of the chief joys of my existence, and the dawn that I saw with most emotion shone upon the bay of Anaho. The mountains abruptly overhang the port with every variety of surface and of inclination, lawn, and cliff, and forest. Not one of these but wore its proper tint of saffron, of sulphur, of the clove, and of the rose. The lustre was like that of satin; on the lighter hues there seemed to float an efflorescence; a solemn bloom appeared on the more dark. The light itself was the ordinary light of morning, colourless and clean; and on this ground of jewels, pencilled out the least detail of drawing. Meanwhile, around the hamlet, under the palms, where the blue shadow lingered, the red coals of cocoa husk and the light trails of smoke betrayed the awakening business of the day; along the beach men and women, lads and lasses, were returning from the bath in bright raiment, red and blue and green, such as we delighted to see in the coloured little pictures of our childhood; and presently the sun had cleared the eastern hill, and the glow of the day was over all.

The glow continued and increased, the business, from the main part, ceased before it had begun. Twice in the day there was a certain stir of shepherding along the seaward hills. At times a canoe went out to fish. At times a woman or two languidly filled a basket in the cotton patch. At times a pipe would sound out of the shadow of a house, ringing the changes on its three notes, with an effect like *Que le jour me dure* repeated endlessly. Or at times, across a corner of the bay, two natives might communicate in the Marquesan manner with conventional whistlings. All else was sleep and silence. The surf broke and shone around the shores; a species of black crane fished in the broken water; the black pigs were continually galloping by on some affair; but the people might never have awaked, or they might all be dead.

My favourite haunt was opposite the hamlet where was a landing in a cove under a lianaed cliff. The beach was lined with palms and a tree called the purao, something between the fig and mulberry in growth, and bearing a flower like a great yellow poppy with a maroon heart. In places rocks encroached upon the sand; the beach would be all submerged; and the surf would bubble warmly as high as to my knees, and play with cocoa-nut husks as our homely ocean plays with wreck and wrack and bottles. As the reflux drew down, marvel of colour and design streamed between my feet; which I would grasp at, miss, or seize: now to find them what they promised, shells to grace a cabinet or be set in gold upon a lady's finger; now to catch only *maya* of coloured sand, pounded fragments and pebbles, that, as soon as they were dry, became as dull and homely as the flints

Marquesas Islands cannibal chief

upon a garden path. I have toiled at this childish pleasure for hours in the strong sun, conscious of my incurable ignorance; but too keenly pleased to be ashamed. . . .

Letter from Margaret Stevenson to Jane Whyte Balfour
Anaho Bay, July 29

. . . Fanny and I took the letters to the village, and then went to our usual bathing place, to hunt for shells, bathe, and amuse ourselves generally. About 4.30 the boat came to take us off. As we were returning to the *Casco*, we remarked with some surprise that she had changed her position . . . by the time we had got them all into the boat we were getting very uneasy about the yacht. We could see that she was moving out seawards, and worse than that, seemed to be drifting towards the most rocky and dangerous part of the shore. There appeared to be no one on deck and nothing was being done. We were in a great fright, and got up sail and hurried after her as fast we could; and as soon as we were within hearing, one of our men shouted out, 'You're drifting ashore!' We were all quickly bundled on deck and found the captain, with a very white face, giving orders all round. We took the visitors down to the cabin and kept them occupied there — and I am not sure that it was not the most agonising task; we could hear the bustle on deck, and could follow all that was being done. Another anchor was dropped, a sail hoisted, and a rope attached to the yacht, and some of the sailors getting into the boat, hauled her out from the cliff. . . . The chief and his three brothers-in-law and Lloyd were called up to lend a hand at the windlass, to get up the first anchor, which had fouled, and so was the cause of all the trouble. Fortunately the water is deep close to the cliffs at that point and their efforts were in time; no damage resulted and in about two hours we were comfortably settled in a new and better anchorage, in the centre of the bay just opposite the mouth of it.

At first it had seemed a terrible encumbrance to have so many visitors at such a time, but we were soon very thankful for their help, and indeed should have been very badly off without them. We gave them each a glass of wine, some hard biscuits, half a dollar, and a piece of tobacco to carry away with them, and they were more than content. It appeared that the captain was at supper below, the two sailors at supper on deck. Louis also was on deck, and I think this was the strangest thing of all, for he was admiring the view of a peculiar rocky peak among the mountains, and it struck him that he had not seen it since the day that we entered the bay. Yet he never took fright! It was most providential that we happened to come off just at the time, and in time to warn them.

The strange chief was greatly taken up with my gloves, which he called 'British tattooing'. He smelt them, and made me put them off and on more than once. He was especially delighted with the buttons, and took it much to heart that one had come off. He also admired my sateen dress, and thinks 'shaped' dresses much prettier than *holakus*.

Beach at Anaho

Letter from Margaret Stevenson to Alison Cunningham
Anaho Bay, Nuka-hiva, August 2

My dear Cummy, — . . . Fanny and I are dressed like the natives, in two garments, one being a sort of long chemise with a flounce round the edge, and an upper garment something like a child's pinafore, made with a yoke, but fastening in front [*mumus* and *holakus*]. As we have to wade to and from the boat in landing and coming back, we discard stockings, and on the sands we usually go barefoot entirely. Louis wears only a shirt and trousers with the legs and arms rolled up as far as they will go, and he is always bare-footed. You will not therefore be surprised to hear that we are all as red as lobsters. It is a strange, irresponsible, half-savage life, and I sometimes wonder if we shall ever be able to return to civilised habits again. . . .

Louis is looking so well and has even got a little fatter since we have been staying in this lovely, quiet spot. He sends you his love and bids me tell you that he is just living over all the books you used to read to him. For instance, this morning, when the juice of a cocoa-nut effervesced like ginger-beer, he called out delightedly, 'Oh, I remember Cummy telling me of that long ago, and I thought it so wonderful. And only fancy that poor little sick chap she nursed ever seeing it actually and truly for himself!'

In the South Seas: The Marquesas
Death

. . . When a native habitation is deserted, the superstructure — pandanus thatch, wattle, unstable tropical timber — speedily rots, and is speedily scattered by the wind. Only the stones of the terrace endure; nor can any ruin, cairn, or standing stone, or vitrified fort present a more stern appearance of antiquity. . . . Such ruins are tapu in the strictest sense; no native must approach them; they have become outposts of the kingdom of the grave. It might appear a natural and pious custom in the hundreds who are left, the rearguard of perished thousands, that their feet should leave untrod these hearthstones of their fathers. I believe, in fact, the custom rests on different and more grim conceptions. But the house, the grave, and even the body of the dead, have been always particularly honoured by Marquesans. Until recently the corpse was sometimes kept in the family and daily oiled and sunned, until, by gradual and revolting stage, it dried into a kind of mummy. . . .

Hatiheu

. . . It was what is called a good passage, and a feather in the *Casco*'s cap; but among the most miserable forty hours that any one of us has ever passed. We were swung and tossed together all the time like shot in a stage thunderbox. The mate was thrown down and his head cut open; the captain was sick on deck; the cook sick in the galley. Of all our party only two sat down to dinner. I was one. I own that I felt wretchedly; and I can only say of the other, who professed to feel quite well, that she fled at an early moment from the table. . . .

The port of entry

The port — the mart, the civil and religious capital of these rude islands — is called Tai-o-hae, and lies strung along the beach of a precipitous green bay in Nuka-hiva.

It was midwinter when we came thither, and the weather was sultry, boisterous, and inconstant. Now the wind blew squally from the land down the gaps of splintered precipice; now, between the sentinel islets of the entry, it came in gusts from seaward. Heavy and dark clouds impended on the summits; the rain roared and ceased; the scuppers of the mountain gushed; and the next day we would see the sides of the amphitheatre bearded with white falls. Along the beach the town shows a thin file of houses, mostly white and all ensconced in the foliage of an avenue of green puraos; a pier gives access from the sea across the belt of breakers; to the eastward there stands, on a projecting bushy hill, the old fort which is now the calaboose, or prison; eastward still, alone in a garden, the Residency flies the colours of France. Just off Calaboose Hill, the tiny Government schooner rides almost permanently at anchor, marks eight bells in the morning (there or thereabouts) with the unfurling of her flag, and salutes the setting sun with the report of a musket.

Long-Pig — A cannibal high place

Nothing more strongly arouses our disgust than cannibalism, nothing so surely unmortars a society; nothing, we might plausibly argue, will so harden and degrade the minds of those that practise it. And yet we ourselves make much the same appearance in the eyes of the Buddhist and the vegetarian. We consume the carcases of creatures of like appetites, passions and organs with ourselves; we feed on babes, though not our own; and the slaughterhouse resounds daily with screams of pain and fear. We distinguish indeed; but the unwillingness of many nations to eat the dog, an animal with whom we live on terms of the next intimacy, shows how precariously the distinction is grounded. The pig is the main element of animal food among the islands. . . . Many islanders live with their pigs as we do with our dogs, both crowd around the hearth with equal freedom.

The Marquesans intertwined man-eating with the whole texture of their lives; 'long-pig' was in a sense their currency and sacrament; it formed the hire of the artist, illustrated public events, and was the occasion and attraction of a feast. Today they are paying the penalty of this bloody commixture. The civil power, in its crusade against man-eating, has had to examine one after another all Marquesan arts and pleasures, has found them one after another tainted with a cannibal element, and one after another has placed them on the proscript list. The art of tattooing stood by itself, the execution exquisite, the designs most beautiful and intricate; nothing more handsomely sets off a handsome man; it may coast some pain in the beginning, but I doubt if it be near so painful in the long run, and I am sure it is far more becoming than the ignoble European practice of tight-lacing among women. And now it has been found needful to forbid the art. Their

Place of Sacrifice, Hiva-Oa

songs and dances were numerous (and the law has had to abolish them by the dozen). They now face empty-handed the tedium of their uneventful days; and who shall pity them? The least rigorous will say that they were justly served.

Death alone could not satisfy Marquesan vengeance, the flesh must be eaten . . . they did not dare to hold a public festival. The body was accordingly divided; and every man retired to his own house to consummate the rite in secret, carrying his proportion of the dreadful meat in a Swedish match-box. The barbarous substance of the drama and the European properties employed offer a seizing contrast to the imagination.

House of Temoana

. . Vaekehu lives at the other end of the town from the Residency, beyond the buildings of the mission. Her house is on the European plan; a table in the midst of the chief room; photographs and religious pictures on the wall. . . . Here in the strong through-draught, Her Majesty received us in a simple gown of print, and with no mark of royalty but the exquisite finish of her tattooed mittens, the elaboration of her manners, and the gentle falsetto in which all the highly refined among Marquesan ladies (and Vaekehu above all others) delight to sing their language. An adopted daughter interpreted . . . Vaekehu is very deaf, 'merci' is her only word of French; upon that first occasion, we were conscious of a sense of district-visiting on our part, and reduced evangelical gentility on the part of our hostess. The other impression followed after she was more at ease, and came with Stanislao and his little girl to dine on board the *Casco*. She had dressed for the occasion; wore white, which very well became her strong brown face; and sat among us, eating or smoking her cigarette, quite cut off from all society, or only now and then included through the intermediary of her son. It was a position that might have been ridiculous, and she made it ornamental; making believe to hear and be entertained; her face, whenever she met our eyes, lighting with the smile of good society; her contributions to the talk, when she made any, and that was seldom, always complimentary and pleasing. No attention was paid to the child, for instance, but what she remarked and thanked us for. Her parting with each, when she came to leave, was gracious and pretty, as had been every step of her behaviour. When Mrs Stevenson held out her hand to say goodbye, Vaekehu took it, and then, as upon a kindly afterthought, and with a sort of warmth of condescension, held out both hands and kissed my wife on both cheeks. Given the same relation of years and rank, the thing would have been so done on the boards of the Comédie Francaise. . . . The next moment she had taken Stanislao's arm, and they moved off along the pier in the moonlight, leaving me bewildered.

This was a queen of cannibals; she was tattooed from hand to foot, and perhaps the greatest masterpiece of that art now extant, so that a while ago, before she was grown prim, her leg was one of the sights of Tai-o-hae; she had been passed from chief to chief; she had been fought for and taken in war; perhaps, being so great a lady, she had sat on the high place, and throned it there, alone of her sex, while the drums were going twenty strong and the priests carried up the bloodstained baskets of long-pig. And now behold her, out of that past of violence and sickening feasts, step forth, in her age, a quiet, smooth, elaborate old lady, such as you might find at home (mittened also, but not often so well-mannered) in a score of country houses. Only Vaekehu's mittens were of dye, not of silk; and they had been paid for, not in money, but the cooked flesh of men. It came tc my mind with a clap, what she could think of it herself, and whether at heart, perhaps, she might not regret and aspire after the barbarous and stirring past. But when I asked Stanislao — 'Ah,' said he, 'she is content; she is religious, she passes all her days with the sisters.'

Letter from Margaret Stevenson to Jane Whyte Balfour
Yacht Casco *Tai-o-hae, Nuka-hiva, August 17*

. . . Louis, Fanny and I went ashore to call on Queen Vaekehu. She is a most dignified old lady, with quantities of beautiful grey hair brushed back from her forehead. Being slightly deaf, we found it difficult to hold much conversation with her. I am told she was the first person converted to Christianity by Bishop Dordillon. She lives in a pretty wooden house of three rooms a little above the bay, and received us seated in the centre of the middle room. The wooden floors were all spotlessly clean, the walls painted a very pretty turquoise blue. For furniture there were two tables with handsome covers, many chairs, and a few very bad pictures. Through the open door in front had a lovely view of the bay, and the one to the back looked out upon the mountains. . . . An adopted daughter sat beside Vaekehu and acted as interpreter, and brought us also seven coconuts to drink. . . .

On Wednesday, as it was a *fête*-day, there was an early service. . . . The church is quite small, whitewashed inside, and has the usual display of gilding, paper flowers and wax candles. There were nearly a hundred of the girls (from the school), all nicely dressed in white *holakus* and broad-brimmed straw hats trimmed with black ribbon. They looked very neat and were very well-behaved, acting as the choir and singing the service in the crooning, humming native fashion. I can compare the sound to nothing but a gigantic lime-tree full of bees, and I found it so soporific that I very nearly went to sleep . . . a long sermon in Kanaka, in which, by the way, nearly all the service was conducted; and at the close of the Mass about a dozen people took Communion, the queen among them. We were seated beside her majesty and I spoke to her when the service was at an end. She wore a very pretty white *holaku* with three embroidered flounces, a 'cardinal's cape' of black grenadine trimmed with lace, and a leghorn hat trimmed with black ribbon. . . .

In the afternoon (Thursday) Louis, Fanny and I called on Stanislas, [Stanislao] who is the son of the late king and step- and adopted son of Queen Vaekehu. He lives in a wooden house, smaller than her majesty's and it is by no means so nicely kept, neither so spotlessly clean nor so orderly. He is about forty years old, and handsome, in spite of being heavily pockmarked, having had smallpox when it decimated the islands some twenty years ago. His father was one of the many who were carried off by it. Stanislas has been well educated and speaks excellent French, and is evidently both intelligent and sensible. His wife is pretty, but hopelessly untidy. I fancy that our visit had been expected, for no sooner had we arrived than presents were brought out: a piece of *tapa* [native cloth made from tree-bark] for each of us and an old man's beard for Louis. These beards are very highly thought of here, and are difficult to obtain. They are worn by men as ornaments and are fastened on the forehead by a wreath made of porpoise teeth. We were given also green coconuts to drink, which we always enjoy.

Today (Friday) was another busy day. . . . At five we expected Stanislas with

Queen Vaekehu and her adopted daughter

his wife and little grand-daughter, but as his wife was ill and could not come, he brought Queen Vaekehu in her place. This was a great compliment to us, for she had previously told us that she could not manage it, as the rheumatism in her knees made it difficult for her to climb into the yacht; and indeed we could see it was painful for her. She is a delightful old lady, with gentle, caressing manners, very dignified and serene. She wore a thinner white *holaku* than she had worn at church, a white china crepe shawl, and a leghorn hat. She was very kind and courteous to us all, and we liked her very much. . . . They all conducted themselves perfectly at table, and Stanislas talked in a most interesting way and showed us a charming old-time French gallantry —declaring, for instance, that I did not look more than forty! The queen's hands are covered with the finest tattooing I have yet seen, all over the back, like exquisite lace mittens; but I noticed that only the first finger was done, the others being untouched. I asked her son the reason of this, and he shrugged his shoulders and said, 'It is too painful'. When we went on deck, Stanislas said, 'The Kanaka ladies smoke.' Louis went to get a pipe for her majesty, but it occurred to Fanny she might like a cigarette in the Mexican fashion, so she showed her how to roll one. The queen seemed to be delighted with the idea, and copied every movement most deftly. Fanny took a cigarette also to keep her company, and we all sat and smiled and patted each other, in the absence of any mutual language. Meanwhile, Stanislas was going the round of the yacht with Louis and was greatly pleased and interested in everything. I forgot to say the queen brought us presents, a piece of *tapa* for each of us, a finely carved cocoa-nut cup, and another 'old man's beard'.

Monday, August 20

. . . Stanislas invited us to go an excursion today up one of the valleys to see a rocking-stone. He was to provide horses and refreshments; but you may imagine how terribly disappointed we were when the morning turned out hopelessly wet. Saturday also was a rather bad day, the worst since our arrival; but this promised to be much worse. . . .

We intended to leave Tai-o-hae tomorrow, but we may be detained a day or two longer, for our Japanese cook went ashore without leave on Saturday evening, got drunk, and stayed away all night. Yesterday morning, it appears, he was taken up and put in the calaboose till this morning, when he was brought on board and was most insolent to the captain. He may have to be turned off, and it is possible the four sailors may elect to go with him; but we find that we can get others without difficulty and at lower wages. We have already engaged a mate for we found we were 'short-handed' in a storm. . . . If the new sailors are Kanakas, Lou will be delighted as he will be able to get so much information out of them.

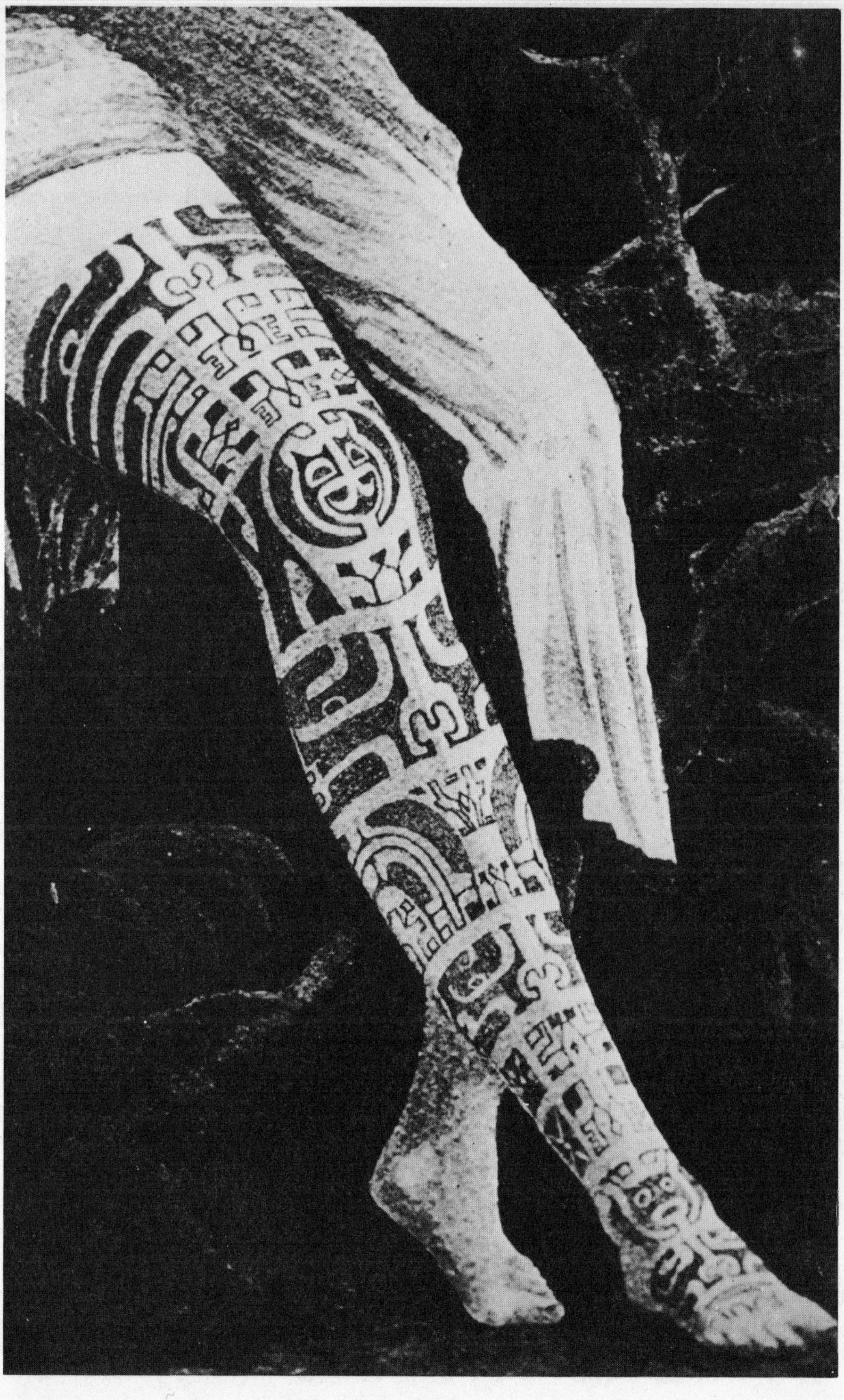

'Her leg was one of the sights of Tai-o-hae'

From a letter written on Casco, *August 25*

. . . After closing your letter on Tuesday, I went ashore to pay farewell visits alone, as Fanny had a headache and could not accompany me. . . . In the evening Louis and Fanny went ashore to present their photographs to the queen and Stanislas, and to say goodbye. At parting Louis kissed the queen's hand, which evidently delighted her. . . .

In the South Seas: The Marquesas
Two Chiefs of Atuona

. . . The photographer became aware of a sensation in the crowd and, looking around, beheld a very noble figure of a man appear upon the margin of a thicket and stroll nonchalantly near. The nonchalance was visibly affected; it was plain he came there to arouse attention and his success was instant. He was introduced; he was civil, he was obliging; he was always ineffably superior and certain of himself; a well-graced actor. It was presently suggested that he should appear in his war costume; he gracefully consented; and returned in that strange, inappropriate, and ill-omened array (which very well became his handsome person) to strut in a circle of admirers and be thenceforth the centre of photography. Thus had Moipu effected his introduction, as by accident, to the white strangers, made it a favour to display his finery, and reduced his rival Paaaeua to a secondary *rôle* on the theatre of the disputed village. . . .

Moipu formally proposed to 'make brothers' with Mata-Galahi — Glass-Eyes — the not very euphorious name under which Mr Lloyd Osbourne passed in the Marquesas. The feat of brotherhood took place on board the *Casco*. . . . Moipu, as if to mark every point to the opposition, came with a certain feudal pomp, attended by retainers bearing gifts of all descriptions, from plumes of old men's beards to little, pious Catholic engravings.

I had met the man before this in the village, and detested him on sight; there was something indescribably raffish in his looks and ways that raised my gorge; and when man-eating was referred to, and he laughed a low, cruel laugh, part boastful, part bashful, like one reminded of some dashing peccadillo, my repugnance was mingled with nausea. . . . In his appreciation of jams and pickles, in his delight in the reverberating mirrors of the dining cabin, and consequent endless repetition of Moipus and Mata-Galahis, he showed himself engagingly a child. And yet I am not sure; and what seemed childishness may have been rather courtly art. His manners struck me as beyond the mark; they were refined and caressing to the point of grossness, and when I think of the serene absent-mindedness with which he first strolled in upon our party, and then recall his running on hands and knees along the cabin sofas, pawing the velvet, dipping into the beds, and bleating commendary '*mitais*' with exaggerated emphasis like some enormous over-mannered ape. And I sometimes wonder next, if Moipu were quite alone in this polite duplicity, and ask myself whether the *Casco* were quite so much admired in the Marquesas as our visitors desired us to suppose.

I will complete the sketch of an incurable cannibal grandee with two incongruous traits. His favourite morsel was the human hand, of which he speaks today with an ill-favoured lustfulness. And when he said goodbye to Mrs Stevenson, holding her hand, viewing her with tearful eyes, and chanting his farewell improvisation in the falsetto of Marquesan high society, he wrote upon her mind a sentimental impression which I try in vain to share.

Letter from Margaret Stevenson to Jane Whyte Balfour
Yacht Casco, *Taahaku, Hiva-oa, August 25*

. . . We sailed at 8 a.m. on Wednesday morning and reached our anchorage here at 3 p.m. on Thursday. We had a headwind, and a very high sea; and, as usual, everyone was more or less sick except myself. The captain was very bad indeed, and so was Louis; and our new cook, Au Fou, being also ill, we had to take what food we could get. We passed the island of U-apu during the night and on Thursday morning we were in sight of this island Hiva-oa, which, I am told, means 'Yonder far'. . . . While we were going through the canal, *Frère* Michel pointed out to us two nice large houses that belonged to a 'chieftess', as they say here who adopted him. . . . Fanny and I then said that above everything else we would like to be adopted by a chief; and he declared that nothing was easier, and that when he landed he would arrange for us to be adopted at once.

These islands are much like the others that we have seen, with high mountains sloping up from the beach curiously serrated in outline, and rising here and there to fine abrupt peaks. There are numbers of wooded valleys, and most of the bays have curious detached rocks guarding the entrance which are called 'sentinels'. . . .

On Friday morning Louis got up with a bad headache and looked so wretched that he said he must rest all day. However, he went ashore with us to see if he felt the better of being on land. Fanny, Lloyd and I intended to go to the village, which is at some little distance, to hunt for eggs. . . . We went first to the Keanes who were most kind and hospitable and lent us a horse for Fanny. . . . Lloyd and I walked beside her to the village of Atuona, two miles away, in the next bay. . . . The whole village, it appeared, was *en fête* and charmed with the honour that we were doing them.

Atuona is beautifully situated at the foot of a high and steep mountain, and has more houses gathered together than we have seen in any native village. . . .

Our house (I mean the one belonging to our new parents) is quite magnificent, with no less than three doors and six glazed windows. It is built on a high *pae-pae*, as they call the large stone platforms that support the houses, with a verandah all round, and the windows and doors, as usual, standing wide open. The house is entirely lined with twisted reeds, and the floor covered with matting, and everything was exquisitely clean and fresh. Our new 'papa' was ready to receive us, dressed in a blue coat and white trousers; his name is *Pa-a-a-e-u-a*, and he is a very good-looking man, but more depressed than is general with natives. His wife is quiet and very pleasant, but not good-looking. They have a little adopted child, who was at once introduced to us; he is the son of an Austrian sailor who escaped from a burning ship some fourteen years ago, and who refused ever to go to sea again. He settled down here and married the chief's sister, and this is his son.

While the feast was being made ready, we went to see the pretty little church, where a kind old *père* showed us everything with great pride, and then we visited the mission and the *soeurs*. After this we returned to our house, where we found the tablecloth spread on the floor. It was made of three large banana-leaves, each about four feet long and one and a half wide. On the thick green leaves were laid two dishes of *ka-ku*, a roast chicken, small green onions, water in beer bottles, salt on a small leaf, baked bread-fruit, and cocoa-nut bowls as finger-glasses. Fanny, Lloyd and I sat on the floor, and covered our feet with a corner of the mat, as we had been taught to do at Anaho. Our new father and mother and 'little brother Joseph' seated themselves near us. The roast pig was on the floor behind, and near by, on a round table, was fruit, beer and cocoa-nuts. An elegantly-dressed native stood behind to wait on us, the old *père* beamed most benignantly on us from his chair, and *Frère* Michel, as master of ceremonies, stood beside him. Windows and doors were blocked by interested natives, eagerly watching all the proceedings; and when we could get a peep between them, we caught sight of gaily-dressed women and girls sitting on the spreading roots of a large bread-fruit tree. And the bright sunshine made everything resplendent.

We were offered spoons, but declined, as we wished to show we could be true Kanakas; and, plunging our two forefingers into the bowl, we ate greedily of the *ka-ku*. I asked *Frère* Michel why he did not join us, but he said, 'No, that would not be *convenable*, as I do not belong to your family.' It was, you see, a sort of ceremonial feast, a rite of adoption . . . all that remained to do was for us to give presents to our new relatives. This perplexed us at first, as we had of course come unprepared; but Lloyd took the *Casco* ribbon off his hat, and I gave it to our new 'papa', and Fanny made our 'mamma' happy with a pen-knife. As long as we live we have now a right to come here and share all things with our new family, so you people at home must make yourselves very agreeable if you want to keep us with you! . . .

Frère Michel told us that he was very sorry we could not understand the language and hear the remarks made by the natives. He said they were so gratified by our keeping to the native customs that our popularity was increasing every minute; and the strange thing was that, although we were the observed of all the observers, we all confessed to not having felt in the least awkward or embarrassed. . . . We came back to the yacht, very full of all we had seen and done. Poor Lou was terribly disappointed, however. He said that if we had sent back the horse for him he would have come to the feast even at the risk of having to suffer for it; but this had never occurred to us, as we thought he was feeling too ill to think of such a thing.

August 27

On Saturday our new relatives came to visit us, and we had great discussions as to what presents we should give them. *Frère* Michel told us that they would like a black coat better than anything else in the world, and Lloyd thought he had one that he could spare; but it turned out, unfortunately, that it had been left behind at San Francisco. The captain good-naturedly came to the rescue, and offered us a grey one, with tails. He rather crowed over us, when he saw our difficulties, and declared he was glad that he had not happened to accompany us, and so had no Kanaka parents. After much discussion, however, we ended by giving the 'mamma' a whole piece of print printed calico (forty yards), and a bottle of perfume; and to 'papa' a very nice clasp-knife with a spring to it that Lloyd had bought in San Francisco, a whole box of cigars, and another bottle of scent. Also to 'little brother Joseph' a silk handkerchief, which had been a present to Lloyd. Fanny afterwards added a photograph of herself, and a fan, for the 'mamma'. They all seemed greatly pleased with their presents. . . .

Yesterday afternoon I climbed to the top of a steep hill higher than Arthur's Seat, and had a magnificent view over many lovely valleys and the sea lying

Government House, Nuka-hiva

beyond. This island is more beautiful than Nuka-hiva; but on account of the greater moisture, the climate is perceptibly more trying. We often have regular Scottish mists about the mountains here, and there is such a heavy dew at night we cannot stay late on deck. . . .

Our house at Farakava, Paumotos Islands, September 12, 1888

Louis found the cabin so close on Sunday night that he thought it would be a good plan to take a house by the week, so that he might sleep on shore; and here we are in a dear little wooden erection of three rooms, with a verandah front and back. It is one of the best houses on the island after the Residency. The sitting-room is quite large and airy, with two doors opening on to the verandahs, two windows to the front, one to the back and one at the far end; the two bedrooms open off the other end, and all are painted white, with the doors and windows panelled in blue. In the sitting-room there are two rocking chairs, four round-backed chairs, and a table, and no less than three sewing-machines! (What a pity you are not here!) There are also two brackets on the wall, three framed pictures, a small mirror and a gun. There are wooden bedsteads in the bedroom, small wardrobes, basin-stands, and so on, and actually a copy of David Wilkie's 'Village School' framed and hanging up in one. We were rather afraid of the wooden beds, so we brought ashore our mattresses from the *Casco*, keep them in the bedrooms through the day and at night bring them out and spread them where we please. Usually Louis and Fanny take the front verandah, Lloyd the back, and Valentine and I retire to different corners of the sitting-room, leaving both doors wide open so that there is plenty of air. The only drawback is mosquitoes, but one can't expect absolute perfection in this world. Our house stands beside the little church, but the priest is away just now and there is only a native catechist left in charge. I would fain go to the service, but twenty minutes to six a.m. (when the bell rings) is rather much of a good thing in the way of early rising for me. As it is, the sun wakes us soon after six, and we make breakfast with the help of a paraffin cooking-stove; we have coffee, soup, bread and butter, and marmalade. For lunch and dinner we return to the *Casco*. . . .

The people here are much darker and smaller and not nearly so handsome as the Marquesans; but it is only fair to add that they seem to be better behaved. For instance, the Seventh Commandment is really understood and respected amongst them, and few among them will drink rum to excess, even when they have the chance. In the Marquesas the men cared for nothing else, and the gendarme had to warn us that we must never give them more than *one* glass, however much they might beg for it. . . .

Church at Farakava

Thursday, September 13

Louis was not feeling very well yesterday and wished to get a thorough rest, so Lloyd and I returned on board the yacht and left him and Fanny alone in peace and quiet. . . .

September 16

. . . One disadvantage of a yacht is that everything must be kept so spick and span about her that whenever we are at anchor we live in a chronic state of house-cleaning. All the time we were at Anaho it was going on, and here again we are being repainted, and today two natives have been sitting on a rope in the water cleaning the copper. Then the deck must be holystoned again, and after that has been done we have to wipe our boots with our pocket-handkerchief before we venture on board! We sometimes threaten to go our next trip in a trading schooner or a canal barge in order to escape such trying tidiness. I don't mean to state that we are actually ordered to wipe our boots, but one cannot help entering into the spirit of the thing!

Monday, September 17

Yesterday we attended service in the native church and were very much interested. It was 9 a.m. — there were eight men and seventeen women present, including two babies who never made a sound. The catechist was dressed in a black gown with a small cape trimmed with lace; he looked very ministerial, I thought. The service was entirely in the native language, and the people joined in most of it with great interest; a woman acted as clerk and led the singing, which was not bad, but had a considerable nasal twang which reminded me of Gaelic congregations in Arran many years ago. . . .

Tuesday morning

A schooner has just come into the bay, and will take three letters, so I shall finish this and send it off.

Louis was better yesterday, and would have come on board again, but Valentine has a bad cold, and he is afraid of infection; so Lloyd will stay on shore as man-of-all-work to look after the household. Louis is trying to hire a small cutter which belongs to a trader here, to go and see two of the neighbouring islands that have not good enough anchorage for the *Casco*; unfortunately Captain Smith, the owner, is ill, and can't go himself, and he has not yet made up his mind as to whether he can trust his cutter to another person. If we do not arrange this, we shall start very soon for Tahiti, where God grant I may get good news of you all. I do so long for letters after these three months of silence!

Letter to Sidney Colvin
Farakava, Low Archipelago, September 21st, 1888

My dear Colvin, — Only a word. Get out your big atlas, and imagine a straight line from San Francisco to Anaho, the NE corner of Nuka-hiva, one of the Marquesas Islands; imagine three weeks there; imagine a day's sail on August 12th round the eastern end of the island to Tai-o-hae, the capital; imagine us there till August 22nd; imagine us skirt the east side of Ua-pu — perhaps Rona-poa on your atlas — and through the Bondelais Straits to Taakauku in Hiva-oa, where we arrive on the 23rd; imagine us there until September 4th, when we sailed for Farakava, which we reached on the 9th, after a very difficult and dangerous passage among these isles. Tuesday, we shall leave for Taiti, where I shall knock off and do some necessary work ashore. It looks pretty bald in the atlas; not in fact; nor I trust in the 130-odd pages of diary which I have just been looking up for these dates: the interest, indeed, has been *incredible*: I did not dream there were such places or such races. My health has stood me splendidly; I am in for hours wading over the knees for shells; I have been five hours on horseback; I have been up pretty near all night waiting to see where the *Casco* would go ashore, and with my diary all ready — simply the most entertaining night of my life. Withal I still have colds; I have one now, and feel pretty sick too; but not as at home: instead of being in bed, for instance, I am at this moment sitting snuffling and writing in an undershirt and trousers; and as for colour, hands, arms, feet, legs, and face, I am browner than the berry: only my trunk and the aristocratic spot on which I sit retain the vile whiteness of the north.

Please give my news and kind love to Henley, Henry James, and any whom you see of wellwishers. Accept from me the very best of my affection: and believe me ever yours.

THE OLD MAN VIRULENT

Island belles

Market Place, Papeete

Papeete, Taiti, October 7, 1888

Never having found a chance to send this off, I may add more of my news. My cold took a very bad turn, and I am pretty much out of sorts at this particular, living in a little bare one-twentieth-furnished house, surrounded by mangoes, etc. All the rest are well, and I mean to be soon. But these Taiti colds are very severe and, to children, often fatal; so they were not the thing for me. Yesterday the brigantine came in from San Francisco, so we can get our letters off soon. There are in Papeete at this moment, in a little wooden house with grated verandahs, two people who love you very much, and one of them is

ROBERT LOUIS STEVENSON

Letter from Margaret Stevenson to Jane Whyte Balfour

September 26. At sea, on our way to Tahiti.

On Monday we said goodbye to all our good friends at Farakava, and gave them a few farewell gifts. When the captain and I went ashore, we found Taniera [the catechist] sitting with Louis in his working clothes — he is a boat-builder by trade — which consist of blue cotton trousers, and an apron with a bib, leaving an ample stretch of brown satin skin exposed to view. What wonderful skins they all have, by the way! Lloyd introduced him to the captain, saying, 'This is the clergyman of the district; you must shake hands with him'; and I must say the designation and the attire *did* make a very ludicrous combination. When we took leave of Taniera, Lloyd wanted to give him a good present, and the only thing left that we could reasonably do without was a little carriage-clock that I had bought in New York; it had a leather case, and kept excellent time, and was really a wonder for its price. It had originally been intended for giving away; but as all our watches have learnt Kanaka habits and have refused to work in the tropics, we have found the little clock too useful for us to be parted with. However, after an internal struggle which I own was severe, my respect for the church carried the day, and Taniera became its happy possessor.

Government House, Papeete

Tahiti, September 30, 1888

This morning I set off for church, hoping for an English service; but alas! the minister was ill and the church was closed, which was a great disappointment. It appears that there has been an epidemic of influenza here lately; it was brought from Chile, and was of a very severe type; and we are inclined to believe that Louis was somehow infected with it at Farakava. His cough was so bad yesterday that we sent for the doctor, who prescribed some medicine for him that certainly gave him a quiet and fairly comfortable night. It is terribly vexing to us all, when we remember how well he was before this, but I trust he will soon throw it off.

I don't much like Tahiti. It seems to me a sort of halfway house between savage life and civilisation, with the drawbacks of both and the advantages of neither. Also a disagreeable feature of the place is the prevalence of land-crabs. The ground is literally riddled with the large holes made by them. . . . Louis's illness, of course, depresses us all, and keeps us from seeing much or having any desire to do so. . . . Lloyd has attended to those duties that could not well be put off. . . . Two of them [officers of the French man-o-war lying in the bay] have since returned the call and were very polite, but they were amazed when I assured them that I enjoyed being at sea, and seemed to think it most unnatural; no Frenchwoman has ever been heard of who could endure it!

Louis and Fanny moved to the small house I spoke of. . . . You would be surprised to see how comfortable they are, under the circumstances. But the cold is still troublesome, and I grieve to say that the last two days there have been slight threatenings of haemorrhage — nothing to be called serious, but still it is always alarming and distressing. Of course we can make no plans until he is better, and when we may reach Honolulu and get the letters that must be there awaiting us, who can tell? . . .

Letter to Charles Baxter

Taiti, as ever was, 6th October 1888

My dear Charles, — . . . You will receive a lot of mostly very bad proofs of photographs; the paper was so bad. Please keep them very private, as they are for the book. We send them, having learned so [to] dread a fear of the sea, that we wish to put our eggs in different baskets. We have been thrice within an ace of being ashore: we were lost(!) for about twelve hours in the Low Archipelago, but by God's blessing had quiet weather all the time; and once, in a squall, we cam' so near gaun heels ower hurdies, that I really dinna ken why we didnae a'thegither. Hence, as I say, a great desire to put our eggs in different baskets, particularly on the Pacific (haw-haw-haw) Pacific Ocean.

You can have no idea what a mean time we have had, owing to incidental beastliness, nor what a glorious, owing to the intrinsic interest of these isles. I hope the book will be a good one; nor do I really very much doubt that — the stuff is so curious; what I wonder is, if the public will rise to it. A copy of my journal, or as much of it as is made, shall go to you also; it is, of course, quite imperfect, much being needed to be added and corrected; but O, for the eggs in the different baskets.

All the rest are well enough, and all have enjoyed the cruise so far, in spite of its drawbacks. We have had an awfae time in some ways, Mr Baxter; and if I wasnae sic a verra patient man (when I ken that I *have* to be) there wad hae been a braw row, and ance if I hadnae happened to be on deck about three in the marnin', I *think* there would have been *murder* done. The American Mairchant Marine is a kent service; ye'll have heard its praise, I'm thinkin': and if ye never did, ye can get *Twa Years Before the Mast*, by Dana, whaur forbye a great deal o' pleisure, ye'll get a' the needcessary information. Love to your father and all the family. — Ever your affectionate friend.

ROBERT LOUIS STEVENSON

Letter to Sidney Colvin
Taiti, October 16, 1888

. . . We leave here soon, bound for Uahiva, Raiatea, Bora-bora, and the Sandwiches.

O, how my spirit lánguishes
To step ashore on the Sanguishes;
For there my letters wait,
There shall I know my fate.
O, how my spirit languidges
To step ashore on the Sanguidges.

18th — I think we shall leave here if all is well on Monday. I am quite recovered, astonishingly recovered. It must be owned these climates and this voyage have given me more strength than I could have thought possible. And yet the sea is a terrible place, stupefying to the mind and poisonous to the temper, the sea, the motion, the lack of space, the cruel publicity, the villainous tinned foods, the sailors, the captain, the passengers — but you are amply repaid when you sight an island, and drop anchor in a new world. Much trouble has attended this trip, but I must confess more pleasure. Nor should I ever complain, as in the last few weeks, with the curing of my illness indeed, as if that were the bursting of an abscess, the cloud has risen from my spirits and to some degree from my temper. Do you know what they called the *Casco* at Farakava? *The Silver Ship*. Is that not pretty? . . . I think of calling the book by that name: *The Cruise of the Silver Ship* — so there will be one poetic page at least — the title. At the Sandwiches we shall say farewell to the S.S. with mingled feelings. She is a lovely creature: the most beautiful thing at this moment in Taiti.

Well, I will take another sheet, though I know I have nothing to say. You would think I was bursting; but the voyage is all stored up for the book, which is to pay for it, we fondly hope; and the troubles of the time are not worth telling; and our news is little.

Here I conclude (Oct. 24th, I think), for we are now stored, and the Blue Peter metaphorically flies.

R.L.S.

Letter from Margaret Stevenson to Jane Whyte Balfour
Yacht Casco, *Papeete Bay, Tahiti, October 13, 1888*

. . . The island is very beautiful, with strangely shaped mountains that remind me of the Giant's Causeway, but still none of us would allow that it came up to the Marquesas; we are faithful still, and I think I always shall be, to our first love in the South Seas. The little steamer that carried us there and back was filthily dirty, and we were all glad to get 'home' to our own clean, bright *Casco* once more, and told the captain we should never again grumble at any amount of wet paint and varnish!

October 19

I am glad to tell you that Louis keeps much better. He has been to lunch at the hotel several times, and for dinner twice although he and Fanny usually have their meals sent in to them. He has also called on the governor, and yesterday he even took a short drive. We had thought of taking a drive right round the island; this, however, we gave up for we did not like to be away four days from Louis, and it would have been out of the question for him. So we decided on some short drives instead, but there is not much variety, as there are only two driving roads.

October 20

. . . We first went to see the tamarind tree planted by Captain Cook; it has been dead for a long time and has been taken possession of by the proprietors of a sort of public-house nearby called *'a l'arbre de Cook'*. We carried off a little piece of the tree, which is fast going to decay, and which is quite unprotected and exposed. . . .

Tautira, Tahiti. November 5, 1888

We left Taravao on Friday morning; and after a rough and rather unpleasant voyage round the peninsula, where everyone on board was more or less ill but myself, we cast anchor inside the reef here at 8 a.m. on Saturday . . . Lloyd brought us tolerable accounts of Louis. He is delighted with his surroundings here, and that is a great matter. He is in the very midst of the large village, and the life of it goes on all around him; the little girls even play special games of hopscotch — or should I call it hop-Tahiti? — before his window to amuse him. The chief, who lives just opposite, has been most kind, and Princess Moe has been really devoted

Native craft, Tahiti

in her attentions. She sometimes cooks dishes herself specially for his dinner, and the chief carries them across with an apron on! One night, when Louis was not at all well, she could not sleep, she was so much distressed about him, and in the morning she insisted upon his moving into her own house, which she has put at his service for as long as he likes. . . . The princess is a delightful creature, and speaks English very well indeed. . . .

November 6

We had a deluge of rain yesterday, which came through the skylight, stopped my writing, and drove me into a corner for shelter. . . . Louis is fairly well again, and is able to go out for a little walk from time to time; but he is terribly thin and white, and has lost all the fine, healthy-looking sunburn that we were so proud of, which disappoints us very much. Still we are very thankful to see him so far better, and we feel that the simple, cheerful life here has helped him very much. . . . This is a very lovely place. High and beautifully-formed mountains sweep close down to the beach, and they are densely wooded to the very top; from the *Casco*'s deck we

Stevenson playing flageolet

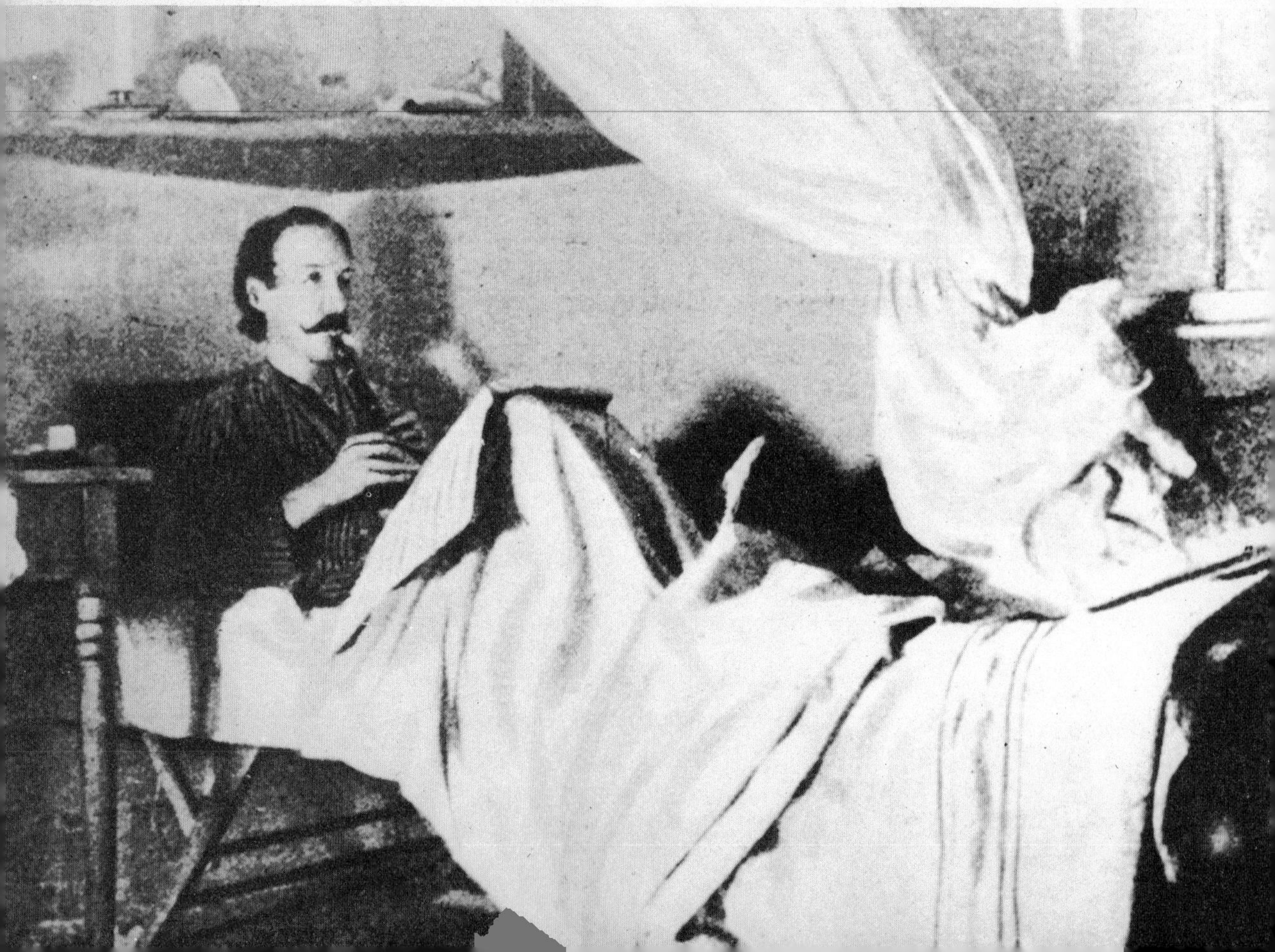

look up a beautiful, winding valley with a cataract tumbling down it, which I long to visit, but alas! there are no roads save the one to Taravao. We are quite at the world's end here, in every way; there is not a shop of even the most primitive kind, which seems strange in so large and populous a village. The people get what they need from small schooners that come into the bay to trade, and about once a week, if he has time, the Chinaman from Taravao drives over with bread and other things for sale. . . .

Fanny is quite *une femme Tahitienne* in her *holaku* and bare feet. She lies on a pillow in the chief's smoking-room (which is open all round and has a roof of cocoanut bark), and can even take a whiff of a native cigarette and pass it on to the other members of the company in the approved way. They pass much of the day there, the ladies generally engaged in plaiting hats of various kinds; I want to get a lesson in the work, which is pretty and useful, but I have not managed it yet. . . .

On shore at Tautira, Tahiti, 15th November 1888

I little thought when I sent off my letter to you last week that I should write another from this place. But just after it started the captain discovered there was something wrong with the main mast of the *Casco*, and after minute examination it turned out that there was dry rot in it; that it must have been going on for years, and that it was an actual miracle it did not give way in the gale we encountered between Papeete and Taravao. The captain is very indignant that the yacht should have been allowed to start on such a cruise and blames the last captain, who assured Dr Merrit that the vessel was in perfect order. We feel very thankful that it was found out before anything more serious happened; and I declare that it was in answer to the prayers of my kind old ladies that it was discovered before we went to sea, and indeed on the evening of the very day of my party. . . . It turned out that no mast large enough for the yacht was to be found in Papeete, so the old one is to be patched up. The captain declares that it can be made quite safe by the help of iron rings and bolts. He expects to have everything ready and in order by the end of next week, when he will return here to pick us up, and we shall start at once for Honolulu; but this business will make us at least a fortnight later in getting our longed-for letters. It is fortunate, however, that we are in a place that we like so much, and where the people are so kind to us, where, in spite of so much that is strange about us, we still have learnt to feel at home. . . .

I have now sailed all round Tahiti, and driven round half of it. It is certainly a very beautiful island; the scenery is so varied, and near Papeete is quite park-like in character, with large and splendid trees, many of them covered with bloom. The scarlet-flowered acacia was in full beauty and profusion, and was perhaps the loveliest of all. . . .

Louis's birthday party was a great success. Two small pigs had been presented to him, and we had them both roasted in a native oven. This way of cooking certainly preserves all the flavour of the meat and is delicious . . . with an excellent sauce made of grated cocoa-nut, lime juice, and sea water, Irish potatoes and roast *fei*; after that canned peaches and cake. We also had two bottles of champagne. . . .

Letter to Charles Baxter
Tautira (The Garden of the World) otherwise called
Hans-Christian-Andersen-ville, November 1888

My dear Charles, — Whether I have a penny left in the wide world, I know not nor shall know, till I get to Honolulu, where I anticipate a devil of an awakening. It will be from a mighty pleasant dream at least: Tautira being mere heaven. But suppose, for the sake of argument, any money to be left in the hands of my painful doer, what is to be done with it? Save us from exile would be the wise man's choice, I suppose; for the exile threatens to be eternal. But yet I am of opinion —in case there should be some dibbs in the hand of the P.D. i.e. painful doer; because if there be none, I shall take to my flageolet on the high-road, and work home the best way I can, having previously made away with my family — I am of opinion that if —— [word deleted] and his are in customary state, and you are thinking of an offering, and there should be still some funds over, you would be a real good P.D. to put some in with yours and tak' the credit o't, like a wee man! I know it's a beastly thing to ask; but it, after all, does no earthly harm, only that much good. And besides, like enough there's nothing in the till, and there is an end. Yet I live here in the full lustre of millions; it is thought I am the richest son of man that has yet been to Tautira: I! — and I am secretly eaten with the fear of lying in pawn, perhaps for the remainder of my days, in San Francisco. As usual, my colds have much hashed my finances.

Do tell Henley I write this just after having dismissed Ori the sub-chief, in whose house I live, Mrs Ori, and Pairai, their adopted child, from an evening hour of music; during which I Publickly (with a k) Blow on the flageolet. These are words of truth. Yesterday I told Ori about W.E.H., counterfeited his playing on the piano and the pipe, and succeeded in sending the six foot four there is of that sub-chief somewhat sadly to his bed; feeling that his was not the genuine article after all. Ori is exactly like a colonel in the Guards. — I am, dear Charles, ever yours affectionately.

R.L.S.

Tautira, 10 November 1888

My dear Charles, — Our mainmast is dry-rotten, and we are all to the devil; I shall lie in a debtor's jail. Never mind, Tautira is first chop. I am so besotted that I shall put on the back of this my attempt at words to Wandering Willie; if you can conceive at all the difficulty, you will also conceive the vanity with which I regard any kind of result; and whatever mine is like, it has some sense, and Burns's has none.

Ori a Ori: 'a Roman Emperor in bronze'

Home no more home to me, whither must I wander?
    Hunger my driver, I go where I must.
Cold blows the winter wind over hill and heather;
    Thick drives the rain, and my roof is in the dust.
Loved of wise men was the shade of my roof-tree;
    The true word of welcome was spoken in the door —
Dear days of old, with the faces in the firelight,
    Kind folk of old, you come again no more.

Home was home then, my dear, full of kindly faces,
    Home was home then, my dear, happy for the child.
Fire and the windows bright glittered on the moorland;
    Song, tuneful song, built a palace in the wild.
Now, when day dawns on the brow of the moorland,
    Lone stands the house, and the chimney-stone is cold.
Lone let it stand, now the friends are all departed,
    The kind hearts, the true hearts, that loved the place of old.

R.L.S.

Letter to John Addington Symonds

Dear Symonds, — I send you this (November 11th), the morning of its completion. If I ever write an account of this voyage, may I place this letter at the beginning? It represents — I need not tell you, for you too are an artist — a most genuine feeling, which kept me long awake last night; and though perhaps a little elaborate, I think it a good piece of writing. We are *in heaven here*. Do not forget.

R.L.S.

Please keep this: I have no perfect copy.

Tautira, on the peninsula of Taiti

One November night, in the village of Tautira, we sat at the high table in the hall of assembly, hearing the natives sing. It was dark in the hall, and very warm; though at times the land wind blew a little shrewdly through the chinks, and at times, through the larger openings, we could see the moonlight on the lawn. As the songs arose in the rattling Tahitian chorus, the chief translated here and there a verse. Farther on in the volume you shall read the songs themselves; and I am in hopes that not only you, but all who can find a savour in the ancient poetry of places, will read them with some pleasure. You are to conceive us, therefore, in strange circumstances and very pleasing; in a strange land and climate, the most beautiful on earth; surrounded by a foreign race that all travellers have agreed to be the most engaging; and taking a double interest in two foreign arts.

We came forth again at last, in a cloudy moonlight, on the forest lawn which is the street of Tautira. The Pacific roared outside upon the reef. Here and there one of the scattered palm-built lodges shone out under the shadow of the wood, the lamplight bursting through the crannies of the wall. We went homeward slowly, Ori a Ori carrying behind us the lantern and the chairs, properties with which we had just been enacting our part of the distinguished visitor. It was one of those moments in which minds not altogether churlish recall the names and deplore the absence of congenial friends; and it was your name that first rose upon our lips. 'How Symonds would have enjoyed this evening!' said one, and then another. The word caught in my mind; I went to bed and it was still there. The glittering, frosty solitudes in which your days are cast arose before me: I seemed to see you walking there in the late night, under the pine-trees and the stars; and I received the image with something like remorse.

There is a modern attitude towards Fortune; in this place I will not use a graver name. Staunchly to withstand her buffets and to enjoy with equanimity her favours was the code of the virtuous of old. Our fathers, it should seem, wondered and doubted how they had merited their misfortunes; we, rather how we have deserved our happiness. And we stand often abashed, and sometimes revolted, at those partialities of fate by which we profit most. It was so with me on that November night: I felt our positions should be changed. It was you, dear Symonds, who should have gone upon that voyage and written this account. With your rich stores of knowledge, you could have remarked and understood a thousand things of interest and beauty that escaped my ignorance; and the brilliant colours of your style would have carried into a thousand sick-rooms the sea air and the strong sun of tropic islands. It was otherwise decreed. But suffer me at least to connect you, if only in name and only in the fondness of imagination, with the voyage of the *Silver Ship*.

ROBERT LOUIS STEVENSON

[Stevenson met the English poet and critic at the Swiss consumptive clinic in Davos in 1880. Despite a wife and four daughters, Symonds was homosexual and wrote of 'the beautiful companionship of the Shelley-like man, the eager gifted wife and the boy (Lloyd), for whom they both thought in all their ways and hours'. Stevenson described this friendship as 'an adventure in a thornbush, but his mind is interesting'.]

Letter from Margaret Stevenson to Jane Whyte Balfour
Tautira, November 17

. . . Bathing is very fashionable here; but the people all bathe in the river, not in the sea — I can't make out why. The boys and girls climb into the high trees and throw themselves into the water like ripe fruit dropping; they swim like very fishes, and the brown creatures look very pretty as they tumble about. Men and women, boys and girls, all bathe together, but they are all decently clothed in *pareus*; indeed, the people here are very modest and particular in such matters, and no one is allowed to bathe without a *pareu* even in the most secluded spot. The other day I went off by myself to find a quiet place where I might bathe without spectators, but I had not gone far when six children joined in my train. When I had found a nice place with a grove of pandanus trees for a dressing-room, I told the children to go away; they retreated about a couple of yards and then drew themselves up in a line to watch my every movement. It was rather trying, but I used the trees as a screen as best I could; and when the dip was over, they again assisted at my dressing with the greatest interest, and were especially charmed when I took a buttonhook from my pocket and buttoned my boots with it. At present I have a little crowd of boys round about me watching my writing with great eagerness and interest! . . .

Tautira, Thursday, November 23

The Princess Moe arrived on Tuesday. I wanted to give up my room to her, but Ori would not hear of that, and insisted on turning out of the one room he had hitherto kept for their own use; so she is practically living in our house, and we see a great deal of her and like her very much. She has taught us several new plaits for hat-making, and Fanny and she have 'exchanged names' in the native fashion, which is looked on here as a real bond of relationship. She has given Fanny her mother's name, *Terii-Tauma-Terai*, part of which word means 'heaven', I believe, and part is connected with some land in this neighbourhood, and gives Fanny the right to claim it if she has a mind to. In return Fanny gave Moe her own mother's name, which is Hester. Louis and Ori have also 'made brothers' and exchanged names; the name 'Louis' is Rui in the native pronunciation, so that Ori only alters his name very slightly. He has given Louis his own Christian name of *Teriitera*. In making brothers, they have to eat together, but it is not nearly so formal a ceremony here as at Atuona, when we were adopted by the chief, and the feast was only and solely for us and our new family. The princess has also given Lloyd and me complimentary names, but I am not sure of them yet, and will tell you them later.

Letter from Fanny Stevenson to Sidney Colvin
Tautira, Tahiti, December 4th, 1888

Dear, long neglected, though never forgotten Custodian, I write you from fairyland, where we are living in a fairy story, the guests of a beautiful brown princess. We came to stay a week, five weeks have passed and we are still indefinite as to our time of leaving. It was chance brought us here, for no one in Papeete could tell us a word about this part of the island except that it was very

Woman preparing poi-poi

fine to look at, and inhabited by wild people — 'almost as wild as the people of Anaho!'. That touch about the people of Anaho inclined our hearts this way, so we finally concluded to take a look at the other side of Tahiti. The place of our landing was windy, uninhabited except by mosquitoes, and Louis was ill. The first day Lloyd and the Captain made an exploration, but came back disgusted. They had found a Chinaman, a long way off, who seemed to have some horses but no desire to hire them to strangers, and they had found nothing else whatever. The next morning I took Valentine and went on a prospecting tour of my own. I found the Chinaman, persuaded him to let me have two horses and a wagon, and went back for the rest of my family. When asked where I wished to go, I could only say to the largest native village and the most wild. Ill as Louis was, I brought him the next day, and shall never cease to be thankful for my courage, for he has gained health and strength every day. He takes sea baths and swims, and lives almost entirely in the open air as nearly without clothes as possible, a simple pyjama suit of striped light flannel his only dress. As to shoes and stockings we all have scorned them for months except Mrs Stevenson, who often goes barefoot and never, I believe, wears stockings. Lloyd's costume, in which he looks remarkably well, consists of a striped flannel shirt and a *pareu*. The *pareu* is no more or less than a large figured blue and white cotton window curtain twisted about the waist, and hanging a little below the bare knees. Both Louis and Lloyd wear wreaths of artificial flowers, made of the dried pandanus leaf, on their hats.

Moe has gone to Papeete by the command of the king, whose letter was addressed 'To the great Princess at Tautira, P.V.'. P.V. stands for Pomare 5th. Every evening, before she went, we played Van John lying in a circle on pillows in the middle of the floor with our heads together; and hardly an evening passed but it struck us afresh how very much you would like Moe, and we told her of you again. The house (really here a palace) in which we live, belongs to the sub-chief, Ori, a subject and relation of the Princess. He and his whole family, consisting of his wife, his two little adopted sons, his daughter and her two young babies, turned out to live in a little bird-cage hut of one room. Ori is the very finest specimen of a native we have seen yet; he is several inches over six feet, of perfect though almost gigantic proportions, and looks more like a Roman Emperor in bronze than words can express. One day, when Moe gave a feast, it being the correct thing to do, we all wore wreaths of yellow leaves on our heads; when Ori walked in and sat down at the table, as with one voice we all cried out in admiration. His manners and I might say his habit of thought are English. In some ways he is so like a Colonel of the Guards that we often call him Colonel. It was either the day before or the morning of our public feast, that Louis asked the Princess if she thought Ori would accept his name. She was sure of it, and much pleased at the idea. I wish you could have seen Louis, blushing like a schoolgirl, when Ori came in, and the brotherhood was offered. . . .

Let me tell you of our village feast. The chief, who was our guide in the matter, found four large fat hogs which Louis bought; and four cases of ship's

'God's sweetest works — Polynesians'

biscuits were sent over from the *Casco*, which is lying at Papeete for repairs. Our feast cost in all about eighty dollars. Every Sunday all things of public interest are announced in the Farehau (an enormous public bird cage) and the news of the week read aloud from the Papeete journal, if it happens to turn up. Our feast was given on a Wednesday and was announced by the chief the Sunday before, who referred to Louis as 'the rich one'. Our hogs were killed in the morning, washed in the sea, and roasted whole in a pit with hot stones. When done they were laid on their stomachs in neat open coffins of green basket work, each hog with his case of biscuits beside him. Early in the morning the entire population began bathing, a bath being the preliminary to everything. At about three o'clock — four was the hour set — there was a general movement towards our premises, so that I had to hurry Louis into his clothes, all white, even to his shoes. Lloyd was also in white, but barefoot. I was not prepared, so had to appear in a red and white muslin gown, also barefoot. As Mrs Stevenson had had a feast of her own, conducted on religious principles, she kept a little in the background so that her dress did not matter so much. The chief, who speaks French very well, stood beside Louis to interpret for him. By the time we had taken our respective places on the verandah in front of our door, an immense crowd had assembled. . . . All were dressed in their gayest *pareus*, and many had wreaths of leaves or flowers on their heads. The prettiest sight of all was the children, who came marching two and two abreast, the bamboo poles lying lengthwise across their shoulders.

When all the offerings had been piled in five great heaps upon the ground, Louis made his oration to the accompaniment of the squealing of pigs, the cackling of hens, and the roar of the surf which beats man-high upon the reef. . . . Each speaker finished by coming forward with one of the smaller things in his hand, which he offered personally to Louis, and then shook hands with us all and retired. Among these smaller presents were many fish-hooks for large fishing, laboriously carved from mother-of-pearl shell. One man came with one egg in each hand saying, 'Carry these to Scotland with you, let them hatch into cocks, and their song shall remind you of Tautira'. The schoolmaster, with a leaf-basket of rose apples, made his speech in French. Somehow the whole effect of the scene was like a story out of the Bible, and I am not ashamed that Louis and I both shed tears when we saw the enchanting procession of schoolchildren. The Catholic priest, Father Bruno, a great friend of ours, said that for the next fifty years the time of the feast of the rich one will be talked of: which reminds me of our friend Donat, of Farakava, who was temporary resident at the time we were there. 'I am so glad,' he said, 'that the *Casco* came in just now, otherwise I should be forgotten: but now the people will always say this or that happened so long before — or so long after — the coming of the *Silver Ship*, when Donat represented the government.'

In front of our house is a broad stretch of grass, dotted with cocoanuts, breadfruits, mangoes, and the strange pandanus tree. I wish you could have seen them, their lower branches glowing with the rich colours of the fruits hung upon

Supplies Day

them by Ori and his men, and great heaps lying piled against their roots, on the evening of our feast. . . . But there was a day of reckoning at hand. Time after time we ran down to the beach to look for the *Casco*, until we were in despair. For over a month we had lived in Ori's house, causing him infinite trouble and annoyance, and not even his, at that. Areia (the chief — means the Prince) went to Papeete and came back with a letter to say that more work had to be done upon the *Casco*, and it might be any time before she could get to Tautira. We had used up all our stores, and had only a few dollars of money left in Tautira, and not very much in Papeete. Could we stand the journey to Papeete, we could not live upon the yacht in the midst of the workmen, and we had not money enough left to live at an hotel. We were playing cards on the floor, as usual, when this message came, and you can imagine its effect. I knew perfectly well that Rui would force us to stay on with him, but what depressed me the most of all, was the fact of Louis having made brothers with him just before that took place. Had there been a shadow of doubt on our dear Rui's face, I should have fled from before him. Sitting there on the floor waiting for him was too much for my nerves and I burst into tears, upon which the princess wept bitterly. In the meantime the priest dropped in, so that we had him and Moe, and Areia, as witnesses to our humiliating position. First came Madame Rui, who heard the story, and sat down on the floor in silence, which was very damping for a beginning, and then Ori of Ori, the magnificent, who listened to the tale of the shipwrecked mariners with serious dignity, asking one or two questions and then spoke to this effect. 'You are my brother; all that I have is yours. I know that your food is done, but I can give you plenty of fish and taro. We like you, and wish to have you here. Stay where you are till the *Casco* comes. Be happy — *et ne pleurez pas*.' Louis dropped his head into his hands and wept, and then we all went up to Rui and shook hands with him and accepted his offer. . . . Reduced as we were, we still had a few bottles of champagne left. Champagne being an especial weakness of our gigantic friend, it occurred to someone that this was a proper occasion to open a couple of bottles. Louis, the Princess and I were quite, as the Scotch so well say, 'begrutten', Areia's immense eyes were fairly melting out of his head with emotion, the priest was wiping his eyes and blowing his nose; and then for no apparent cause we suddenly fell to drinking and clinking glasses quite merrily: the bewildered attendant clinked and drank too, and then sat down and waited in case there should be any repetition of the drinking part of the performance. And sure enough there was, for in the midst of an animated discussion as to ways and means, Mrs Stevenson announced that it was St Andrew's Day, so again the attendant clinked and drank with Ori's mad foreigners.

It is quite true that we live almost entirely upon native food, our luncheon today consisted of raw fish with sauce made of cocoanut milk mixed with sea water and lime juice, taro *poi-poi*, and bananas roasted in hot stones in a little pit in the ground with cocoanut cream to eat with them. Still we like coffee in the evening, a little wine at dinner, and a few other products of civilisation. It would be possible, the chief said, to send a boat, but that would cost sixty dollars. A final arrangement, which we were forced to accept, was that Rui should go in his own boat, and the chief would appoint a substitute for some public work that he was then engaged upon. Early the next morning, amidst a raging sea and a storming wind, Rui departed with three men to help him. It is forty miles to Papeete and Rui, starting in the early morning, arrived there at nine o'clock; but alas the wind was against him, and it was altogether six days before he got back. . . .

Louis has done a great deal of work on his new story, *The Master of Ballantrae*, almost finished it, in fact, while Mrs Stevenson and I are deep in the mysteries of hat-making, which is a ladies' accomplishment taking the place of water-colour drawing in England. It is a small compliment to present a hat to an acquaintance. Altogether we have about thirteen. Next door to us is Areia's out-of-door house, where he and the ladies of his family sleep and eat; it has a thatched roof of palm branches, and a floor of boards, the sides and ends being open to the world. On the floor are spread mats plaited of pandanus leaves, and pillows stuffed with silk cotton from the cotton tree. We make little calls upon the ladies, lie upon the mats, and smoke cigarettes made of tobacco leaves rolled in a bit of dried pandanus, and admire their work or get a lesson; or they call upon us and lie upon our mats. One day there was an election in the Farehau. . . . In the beginning, the

French deposed the born chiefs and told the people to elect men for themselves. The choice of Tautira fell upon Rui, who declined the honour, saying that Areia was his natural chief and he could not take a position that should belong to his superior; upon which the people elected Areia chief and Rui sub-chief and head councillor. . . . The Farehau is an immense bird-cage of bamboos tied together with pandanus fibre and thatched with palms. In front of the dais the ground is deeply covered with dried leaves. The costume of the dignitaries was rather odd. Areia wore a white shirt and blue flannel coat, which was well enough; but on his plump legs were a pair of the most incredible trousers; light blue calico with a small red pattern, such as servant girls wear for gowns in England: on his feet were neat little shoes and stockings. Rui was a fine sight, and we were very proud of him; he sat, exactly like an English gentleman, holding himself well in hand, alert as a fox and keen as a greyhound; several men spoke from the farther end of the hall, making objections of some sort, we could see. Rui listened with a half satirical, half kindly smile in his eyes, and then dropped a quiet answer without rising from his seat, which had the effect of raising a shout of laughter and quite demolishing his opponent. Voters came up to the table and dropped their bits of paper into a slit in a box. . . . Both Lloyd and I grew very sleepy and as we did not like to leave till the election was decided, we just threw ourselves down and took a nap at the feet of the councillors: nor did we wake till the chief called out to us in English: 'It is finished.' I never thought I should be able to calmly sleep at a public meeting on a platform in the face of several hundred people: but it is wonderful how quickly one takes up the ways of a people when you live with them as intimately as we do.

I hear dinner coming on the table, so with much love from us all to you and other dear ones, including our dear friend Henry James, believe me, affectionately yours.

FANNY V. de G. STEVENSON

Letter from Margaret Stevenson to Jane Whyte Balfour

Tautira, Tahiti. December 4, 1888

On Sunday afternoon, there was an extra long discussion after church service, when several evidently amusing remarks were made and much applauded. In the evening I asked Moe many questions about it all; it appears that on these occasions all the three sermons they have heard in the day are discussed and criticised, and the minister asks questions to see if they have listened and understood the meaning. It seems to me an excellent plan for keeping their attention and interest, and I should like to see it introduced into some country places at home. I asked also what the jokes had been. She told me that one of the sermons was about Nebuchadnezzar, and apparently his being made to eat grass like the beast, as a punishment for pride, had provoked most of the laughter. Louis here broke in rather flippantly, and asked the princess, 'Where was Moses when the candle went out?' . . . Our deacon put several questions, which we managed to answer with some credit; and then he asked what was the reason of the 'shaved heads' of the Roman Catholic priests, and started Louis on the ancient history of the tonsure. . . .

December 5

The high wind still continues, and there is no saying when Ori may get back. We only hope he is safe at Papeete, where there are said to be six boats from Tautira and six from Taravao, all waiting at Point Venus for a change of wind, and unable to get home till it comes. We are more than vexed that Ori should go through all this on our account; everyone made sure of a change in the weather on Monday, with the new moon; but we were disappointed in our hopes. Meanwhile we are all perforce teetotallers, having nothing left of a spiritous character save a bottle of very new rum that Ori gave us; the taste of which, to the unaccustomed palate, is so very unpleasant that nothing short of the direst necessity will induce us to touch it.

I think what we suffer most from, however, is the want of books. I have only one with me, and Lloyd had none at all, so he has shared mine, and I am sure has read it two or three times entirely through. I said to him one day that I thought he could pass an examination in it now, and he replied, 'Yes, if I just crammed up a few dates and some of the pieces of poetry, I could go in for a first class with honours.' It is the *Life of Sir Henry Lawrence*, and very interesting, but I have no doubt you have read it.

December 8

Ori came back in safety on Thursday evening, bringing our stores, so we are relieved about him and no longer feel like shipwrecked mariners. He was greatly delighted with his visit to the *Casco*; he had lived on board from Saturday till Monday and declared that it was 'just like having a father at Papeete'. . . .

December 16

. . . This has been another Communion Sunday here. . . . I little thought that I should have another opportunity of 'keeping the feast' with my good friends, but so it has been, and much shaking of hands we had when all was over. How often I shall remember it when I am far away!

Fanny has turned this house into a veritable picture-gallery. First she did a silhouette of Ori by taking the shadow of his head on the wall, with the help of a lamp, drawing the outline and then filling it in with Indian ink. This was for us to carry away with us; but it turned out so good that Ori demanded to have all *our* likenesses in return, and she has been hard at work to satisfy him, Lou doing the

'R.L.S.'

outline of her own head for her. All are really good but I think mine is the greatest success of the lot and I wished my dear T. could have seen it. He was never quite satisfied with what he called 'ordinary' photographs of me! Louis has printed under them all our names, both in English and native. On his own he has put 'Teriitera, Robert Louis Stevenson, and party, came ashore from yacht *Casco*, November 1888; and were two months the guests of Ori, to whom, having little else, they gratefully bequeathed their shadows in memoriam'. Under Fanny's various names is added, 'Made these shadows for the house of Ori the tall, December 1888'.

On board the Casco, *at sea, December 27*

. . . After church a number of the congregation came to say goodbye, sitting round the room and on the verandah, as sad and solemn as if they were at a funeral. We only managed to slip out for a few minutes to snatch a farewell visit to *Père* Bruno and the chief. At 11.30 the captain came with the boat to take us off, our final adieus had to be said, and we tore ourselves sorrowfully away from the kind friends and the lovely place where we had spent two happy months. Heavy rain came on after we got on board; but in spite of that, Ori and many of the people, both young and old, gathered under the trees, at the place whence they could watch our departure. It was about 2.30 before all was ready and the wind favourable; we then weighed anchor, and as we passed out through the reef the captain fired thirteen shots from his rifle and the flag was thrice dipped in a farewell salute. Seven shots were fired from the shore in answer, and we replied with another three: while we all stood on deck frantically waving our handkerchiefs to the friends whom we could still see watching us. We could not tear ourselves away till they were quite out of sight. The rain was over by this time, and the sun shone on our departure; but it was a very sad Christmas Day, and we do not wish to make so long a stay at any other place — it makes the parting too trying. We did our best to cheer up at dinner, and had a game of whist in the evening, but it was half-hearted work.

I must tell you, while I think of it, a *bon mot* of Ori's. Louis was telling him about his father and the 'Northern Lights'; when Ori, with a wave of his hand towards the portraits, immediately said, '*He* made lights, and *she* (Fanny) makes shadows.' . . . One evening he asked Louis how much he made by his books, and when he was told what *Kidnapped* brought in the first year, he could not believe that there was not some mistake, and though it was 10 p.m. went off to bring the chief as interpreter, and make *sure*. As they scarcely read themselves, it must be strange and almost incredible to them that book-making should be a paying occupation! . . .

The other thing is that this same *Père* Bruno is going to take Louis as the text of the sermon! I think this should delight Cummy's heart when she hears of it, and I wonder how often Lou is to appear in the pulpit, either in person, or through his books. This time he is to be held up to the people of Tautira because he was so cheerful and uncomplaining during his stay there, 'though he had to put up with many things that must have been hardships to him'; and then his style of dress is to be held up as an example: 'he only wore what was useful and necessary, and never went in for anything ornamental or extravagant'!! Louis is delighted that he has *at last* found someone who appreciates his taste in dress, and wishes he could have a copy of the sermon to send to some of his scoffing friends. *I* may here

Stevenson with guest

privately mention that I think his dress should rather have been held up as a beacon to warn than an example to imitate, seeing that he seldom wore anything but a pyjama suit intended only for sleeping in, very badly shaped, and *dreadfully* unbecoming!

Well, we spent nine weeks in all at Tautira, and so far as Lou's health is concerned, the long detention has proved a blessing. The change in him is something marvellous; all the first week he was in bed with constant cough, high fever, and all the worst symptoms, and now he is better than I have known him since 1879, is able for a good long walk, and has been for some time bathing in the sea almost every day. His appetite, too, has been splendid — he has been able to write a good deal and has nearly finished *The Master*, and we think and hope that he is a little fatter even than when he was in the Marquesas, which was the highest level he had hitherto reached. All this makes us start our journey northward — and the long-run homeward — in a very thankful frame of mind.

January 1, 1889

Another lovely night after a hot summer day. It is hard to believe that this is New Year's Day, and harder to realise what this day was last year at Saranac, when we shivered amidst the surrounding snows. How like a dream that part of our trip seems now!

We had a very quiet day, and the only notable event was that we had stewed duck for lunch, the last of our fresh meat. Louis dined with us — he generally takes his meals in the after cabin for the sake of greater coolness — and our dinner consisted of salt beef, salt pork, a stew of tinned mutton, vegetables, duff, and champagne, in which you may be sure we drank to you all at home. In the evening, as a mild excitement, we played 'what is my thought like' in the starlight. I am sorry to say, however, that they promise us a change of weather with the new moon.

January 6

That promised change came, with a vengeance. Since Tuesday night the weather has been very unpleasant, squalls of wind, rain pouring as it only can in the tropics, thunder and lightning, hail and gloom. For two whole days we were shut up in the cabin, and got through the time as best we could with the help of Gibbon, hat-plaiting and cards. I am also reading Lawrence's life and enjoying it very much. . . . We ought to be nearing Honolulu (and our letters!) by this time. . . . I wonder how our stores, at any rate of luxuries, will hold out. When we left Tautira, Ori gave us a boatload of fruit and vegetables, which have been a great boon, but unfortunately the rain has spoiled the bananas and the mangoes too are on their last legs. The vegetables are almost finished, but we still have cocoanut cream for our coffee.

Letter to Sidney Colvin
Yacht Casco, *at sea, 14th January 1889*

My dear Colvin, — Twenty days out from Papeete. Yes, sir, all that, and only (for a guess) in 4 degrees north or at the best 4 degrees 30′, though already the wind seems to smell a little of the north Pole. My handwriting you must take as you get, for we are speeding along through a nasty swell, and I can only keep my place at the table by means of a foot against the divan, the unoccupied hand meanwhile gripping the inkbottle. As we begin (so very slowly) to draw near to seven months of correspondence, we are all in some fear; and I want to have letters written before I shall be plunged into that boiling pot of disagreeables which I constantly expect at Honolulu. What is needed can be added there.

We were kept two months at Tautira in the house of my dear old friend, Ori a Ori, till both the masts of this invaluable yacht had been repaired. It was all for the best; Tautira being the most beautiful spot, and its people the most amiable I have ever found. Besides which, the climate suited me to the ground; I actually went sea-bathing almost every day, and in our feasts (we are all huge eaters in Taiarapu) have been known to apply four times for pig. And then again I got wonderful materials for my book, collected songs and legends on the spot; songs still sung in chorus by perhaps a hundred persons, not two of whom can agree on their translation; legends, on which I have seen half a dozen seniors sitting in conclave and debating what came next. Once I went a day's journey to the other side of the island to Tati, the high chief of the Tevas — *my* chief, that is, for I am now a Teva and Teriitera, at your service — to collect more and correct what I had already. In the meanwhile I got on with my work, almost finished *The Master of Ballantrae*, which contains more human work than anything of mine but *Kidnapped*, and wrote the half of another ballad, the *Song of Rahero*, on a Taiarapu legend of my own clan, sir — not so much fire as the *Feast of Famine*, but promising to be more even and correct. But the best fortune of our stay at Tautira was my knowledge of Ori himself, one of the finest creatures extant. The day of our parting was a sad one. We deduced from it a rule for travellers: not to stay two months in one place — which is to cultivate regrets.

At last our contemptible ship was ready; to sea we went, bound for Honolulu and the letter-bag, on Christmas Day; and from then to now have experienced every sort of minor misfortune, squalls, calms, contrary winds and seas, pertinacious rains, declining stores. Here is a page of complaint, when a verse of thanksgiving had perhaps been more in place. For all this time we must have been skirting past dangerous weather, in the tail and circumference of hurricanes, and getting only annoyance where we should have had peril, and ill-humour instead of fear.

I wonder if I have managed to give you any news this time, or whether the usual damn hangs over my letter? 'The midwife whispered, be thou dull!' or at least inexplicit. Anyway I have tried my best, am exhausted with the effort, and fall back into the land of generalities. I cannot tell you how often we have planned our arrival at the Monument:* two nights ago, the 12th January, we had it all planned out, arrived in the lights and whirl of Waterloo, hailed a hansom, span up Waterloo Road, over the bridge, etc. etc. and hailed the Monument gate in triumph and with indescribable delight. My dear Custodian, I always think we are too sparing of assurances: Cordelia is only to be excused by Regan and Goneril in the same nursery; I wish to tell you that the longer I live, the more dear do you become to me; nor does my heart own any stronger sentiment. If the bloody schooner didn't send me flying in every sort of direction at the same time, I would say better what I feel so much; but really, if you were here, you would not be writing letters, I believe; and even I, though of a more marine constitution, am much perturbed by this bobbery and wish — O ye gods, how I wish! — that it was done, and we had arrived, and I had Pandora's Box (my mailbag) in hand, and was in lively hope of something eatable for dinner instead of salt horse, tinned mutton, duff without any plums, and pie fruit which now make up our whole repertory. O Pandora's Box! I wonder what you will contain. As like as not you will contain but little money: if that be so, we shall have to retire to 'Frisco on the *Casco* and thence by sea *via* Panama to Southampton, where we should arrive in April. I would like fine to see you on the tug: ten years older both of us than the last time you came to welcome Fanny and me to England. If we have money, however, we shall do a little differently: send the *Casco* away from Honolulu empty of its high-born lessees, for that voyage to 'Frisco is one long dead beat in foul and at least in cold weather; stay a while behind, follow by steamer, cross the States by train, stay a while in New York on business, and arrive probably by the German Line in Southampton. But all this is a question of money. We shall have to lie very dark a while to recruit our finances: what comes from the book of the cruise, I do not want to touch until the capital is repaid.

R.L.S.

[**Colvin's house near the British Museum.*]

Letter from Margaret Stevenson to Jane Whyte Balfour
January 20

On Thursday we got fairly into the Trades, and have been flying along at a great rate ever since, making 170 miles in the first twenty-four hours, and 230 in the twenty-four ending today. But I cannot call it 'pleasure sailing', as it has been a 'beam sea' all the time, and we are tired out with the constant holding-on and

Diamond Head, Honolulu

effort required to keep oneself fairly steady. Such a knocking-about is very fatiguing after a time, and there is no rest night or day. The spray comes over so much that it is almost impossible to sit in the cockpit; and last night, though only a small bit of the lee side of the cabin skylight was open, a bucket of water poured itself straight on my head at 3.30 this morning, and I awoke, screaming and soaked. I took refuge on the floor, and presently saw the same thing exactly happen to Lloyd. Fanny suffers a good deal from seasickness, and declares that when only she reaches Honolulu she is going *ashore* and never means to leave it again. The captain has bad earache in both ears, so we shall not be sorry when the voyage comes to an end, which we hope it may do by Tuesday. And then for six months' supply of letters and papers! . . . One thing we have all realised lately, and that is the loneliness of this great ocean; we have been four weeks out and have only seen a single sail. It gives one some idea of the hopelessness of expecting help should anything go wrong, and makes one more than ever thankful for our safety hitherto.

Tuesday, January 22

Yesterday morning at 10.30 we sighted Hawaii, a lofty mountain with white clouds wreathed about it, above which its head was lifted. We were spinning along at such a rate that the captain quite thought we should reach Honolulu by the evening, and we were pleasantly excited. But alas, when we got under the lee of the land the wind fell; and this morning we are becalmed and only a little further north than the bay where Captain Cook was murdered. This side of Hawaii is very bleak and treeless, with high cliffs, and it is hard to be stopped when we are so near port, but I am thankful to say our food supplies have held out. That is to say, we have still salt beef and macaroni and tinned tomatoes, and pickles and jam; and we have a *very* little flour and coffee and sugar. But the captain is suffering much from earache, and both Louis and Valentine are threatened with the same, so you may imagine how we long to 'get in'.

Wednesday, 1 p.m. We are slowly drawing nearer to Honolulu. We have now three small islands on our right, Maui, Lanai, and that sad tomb of the living, Molokai; and far ahead we can see the very striking outline of Oahu. We hope to land in time for dinner, and are longing for some fresh food and our letters. God grant this long-awaited news of you all may be good news and happy.

The Stevensons' arrival at Royal Hawaiian Hotel

Royal Hawaiian Hotel

Honolulu, Friday 25

After all it was 3 p.m. on Thursday 24th before the calms allowed us to cast anchor in the harbour of Honolulu. Our luncheon that last day consisted of salt beef and biscuits, for all else had given out; so you see we narrowly escaped 'starvation diet', and I must confess our dinner that night at the hotel seemed to be the very finest banquet of which I had ever partaken. But, oh dear me, this place is so civilised! And to come back from Tautira to telephones and electric light is at first very bewildering and unpleasant. I grant the conveniences, but we realise that our happy cruise in the South Seas has come to an end. Thank God, the end is a happy one, and we are met by good news of all we love. But it is the end, nevertheless.

Letter to E. L. Burlingame
(Editor of Scribner's Magazine, New York)
Honolulu, January 1889

My dear Burlingame, — Here at last I have arrived. We could not get away from Tahiti till Christmas Day and then had thirty days of calms and squalls, a deplorable passage. This has thrown me all out of gear in every way. I plunge into business. . . . Tomorrow the mail comes in, and I hope it will bring me money either from you or home, but I will add a word on that point.

My address will be Honolulu — no longer yacht *Casco*, which I am packing off — till probably April.

Henry the Trader has not yet turned up: I hope he may tomorrow, when we expect a mail. Not one word of business have I received either from the States or England, nor anything in the shape of coin; which leaves me in a fine uncertainty and quite penniless on these islands. H.M. [King Kalakaua] (who is a gentleman of a courtly order and much tinctured with letters) is very polite; I may possibly ask for the position of palace doorkeeper. My voyage has been a singular mixture of good and ill-fortune. As far as regards interest and material, the fortune has been admirable; as far as regards time, money, and impediments of all kinds, from

Joe Strong, Stevenson and King Kalakaua

With King Kalakaua

His Hawaiian Majesty

squalls and calms to rotten masts and sprung spars, simply detestable. I hope you will be interested to hear of two volumes on the wing. The cruise itself, you are to know, will make a big volume with appendices; some of it will first appear as (what they call) letters in some of M'Clure's papers. I believe the book when ready will have a fair measure of serious interest: I have had great fortune in finding old songs and ballads and stories, for instance, and have many singular instances of life in the last few years among these islands. . . . To resume my desultory song, I desire you would carry the same fire (hereinbefore suggested) in your decision on *The Wrong Box*; for in my present state of benighted ignorance as to my affairs for the last seven months — I know not even whether my house or my mother's house have been let — I desire to see something definite in front of me — outside the lot of palace doorkeeper. I believe the said *Wrong Box* is a real lark; in which, of course, I may be grievously deceived; but the typewriter is with me. . . .

R.L.S.

[To King Kalalaua from R.L.S.: presented to the King during the Waikiki laua on February 3, 1889 together with the gift of a mounted gold pearl from the Tuamoto Islands. The Silver Ship is the yacht *Casco.*]

From 'Ballads and Other Poems'

The Silver Ship, my King — that was her name
In the bright islands whence your fathers came —
The Silver Ship, at rest from winds and tides,
Below your palace in your harbour rides:
And the seafarers, sitting safe on shore,
Like eager merchants count their treasures o'er.

One gift they find, one strange and lovely thing,
Now doubly precious since it pleased a king.
The right, my liege, is ancient as the lyre
For bards to give to kings what kings admire.
'Tis mine to offer for Apollo's sake;
And since the gift is fitting, yours to take.
To golden hands the golden pearl I bring:
The ocean jewel to the island king.

Letter to Charles Baxter
Honolulu, February 8th, 1889

My dear Charles, — Here we are at Honolulu, and have dismissed the yacht, and lie here till April anyway, in a fine state of haze, which I am yet in hopes some letter of yours (still on the way) may dissipate. No money, and not one word as to money! However, I have got the yacht paid off in triumph, I think; and though we stay here impignorate, it should not be for long, even if you bring us no extra help from home. The cruise has been a great success, both as to matter, fun and health; and yet, Lord, man! we're pleased to be ashore! Yon was a very fine voyage from Tahiti up here, but — the dry land's a fine place too, and we don't squalls any longer, and eh, man, that's a great thing. Blow, blow, thou wintry wind, thou hast done me no appreciable harm beyond a few grey hairs! Altogether, this foolhardy venture is achieved; and if I have but nine months of life and any kind of health, I shall have both eaten my cake and got it back again with usury. But, man, there have been days when I felt guilty, and thought I was in no position for the head of a house.

Your letter and accounts are doubtless at S.F. and will reach me in course. My wife is no great shakes; she is the one who has suffered most. My mother had had a Huge Old Time; Lloyd is first chop; I so well that I do not know myself — sea-bathing, if you please, and it is far more dangerous, entertaining and being entertained by His Majesty here, who is a very fine intelligent fellow, but O, Charles, what a crop for the drink. He carries it, too, like a mountain with a sparrow on its shoulders. We calculated five bottles of champagne in three hours and a half (afternoon) and the sovereign quite presentable, although perceptibly more dignified at the end. . . .

The extraordinary health I enjoy and variety of interests I find among these islands would tempt me to remain here; only for Lloyd, who is not well placed in such countries for a permanency; and a little for Colvin, to whom I feel I owe a sort of filial duty. And these two considerations will no doubt bring me back — to go to bed again — in England. Yours ever affectionately,

R.L.S.

Letter to his cousin, R. A. M Stevenson
Honolulu, February 1889

My dear Bob, — My extremely foolhardy venture is practically over. How foolhardy it was I don't think I realised. We had a very small schooner and, like most yachts, over-rigged and over-sparred, and like many American yachts on a very dangerous sail plan. The waters we sailed in are, of course, entirely unlighted, and very badly charted; in the Dangerous Archipelago, through which we were fools enough to go, we were perfectly in ignorance of where we were for a whole night and half the next day, and this in the midst of invisible islands and rapid and variable currents; and we were lucky when we found our whereabouts at last. We have twice had all we wanted in the way of squalls; once, as I came on deck, I found the green sea over the cockpit coamings and running down the companion like a brook to meet me; at the same moment the foresail sheet jammed and the captain had no knife; this was the only occasion on the cruise that ever I set hand to a rope, but I worked like a Trojan, judging the possibility of haemorrhage better than the certainty of drowning. Another time I saw a rather singular thing: our whole ship's company as pale as paper from the captain to the

Princess Lilioukalani (sister of Kalakaua)

cook; we had a black squall astern on the port side and a white squall ahead to starboard; the complication passed off innocuous, the black squall only fetching us with its tail, and the white one slewing off somewhere else. Twice we were a long while (days) in the close vicinity of hurricane weather, but again luck prevailed, and we saw none of it. These are dangers incident to these seas and small craft. What was an amazement, and at the same time a powerful stroke of luck, both our masts were rotten, and we found out — I was going to say in time, but it was stranger and luckier than that. The head of the mainmast hung over so that hands were afraid to go to the helm; and less than three weeks before — I am not sure it was more than a fortnight — we had been nearly twelve hours beating off the lee shore of Eimeo (or Moorea, next island to Tahiti) in half a gale of wind with a violent head sea: she would neither tack nor wear once, and had to be boxed off with the mainsail — you can imagine what an ungodly show of kites we carried — yet the mast stood. The very day after that, in the southern bight of Tahiti, we had a near squeak, the wind suddenly coming calm; the reefs were close in with, my eye! what a surf! The pilot thought we were gone, and the captain had a boat cleared, when a lucky squall came to our rescue. My wife, hearing the order given about the boats, remarked to my mother: 'Isn't that nice? We shall soon be ashore.' Thus does the female mind unconsciously skirt along the verge of eternity. Our voyage up here was most disastrous . . . we were in the midst of the hurricane season, when even the hopeful builder and owner of the yacht had pronounced these seas unfit for her . . . we were quite given up for lost in Honolulu: people had ceased to speak to Belle [Stevenson's stepdaughter] about the *Casco*, as a deadly subject.

But the perils of the deep were part of the programme and though I am very glad to be done with them for a while and comfortably ashore, where a squall does not matter a snuff to anyone, I feel pretty sure I shall want to go to sea again ere long. The dreadful risk I took was financial and double-headed. First, I had to sink a lot of money in the cruise, and if I didn't get health, how was I to get it back? I have got health to a wonderful extent; and as I have the most interesting matter for my book, bar accidents, I ought to get all I have laid out and a profit. But, second (what I own I never considered till too late), there was the danger of collisions, of damages and heavy repairs, of disablement, towing, and salvage; indeed, the cruise might have turned round and cost me double. Nor will this danger be quite over till I hear the yacht is in San Francisco; for though I have shaken the dust of her deck from my feet, I fear (as a point of law) she is still mine till she gets there.

From my point of view, up to now the cruise has been a wonderful success. I never knew the world was so amusing. On the last voyage we had grown so used to sea-life that no one wearied, though it lasted a full month, except Fanny, who is always ill. All the time our visits to the islands have been more like dreams than realities: the people, the life, the beachcombers, the old stories and songs I have

Lloyd, Fanny, Louis and Margaret Stevenson entertain King Kalakaua aboard Casco

picked up, so interesting; the climate, the scenery, and (in some places) the women, so beautiful. The women are handsomest in Tahiti, the men in the Marquesas, both as fine types as can be imagined. Lloyd reminds me, I have not told you one characteristic incident of the cruise from a semi-naval point of view. One night we were going ashore in Anaho Bay; the most awful noise on deck; the breakers distinctly audible in the cabin; and there I had to sit below, entertaining in my best style a negroid native chieftain, much the worse for rum! You can imagine the evening's pleasure.

This naval report on cruising in the South Seas would be incomplete without one other trait. On our voyage up here I came one day into the dining-room, the hatch in the floor was open, the ship's boy was below with a baler, and two of the hands were carrying buckets as for a fire; this meant that the pumps had ceased working.

One stirring day was that in which we sighted Hawaii. . . . The swell the heaviest I have ever been out in — I tried in vain to estimate the height, *at least* fifteen feet — came tearing after us about a point and a half off the wind. We had the best hand — old Louis — at the wheel; and really, he did nobly, and had noble luck, for it never caught us once. At times it seemed we must have it; old Louis would look over his shoulder with the queerest look and dive down his neck into his shoulders; and then it missed us somehow, and only sprays came over our quarter. . . . I never remember anything more delightful and exciting. Pretty soon after we were lying absolutely becalmed under the lee of Hawaii, of which we had been warned: and the captain never confessed he had done it on purpose, but when accused, he smiled. Really, I supposed he did quite right, for we stood committed to a dangerous race, and to bring her to the wind would have been rather a heart-sickening manoeuvre.

R.L.S.

Letter to Charles Baxter
Honolulu, 8th March 1889

My dear Charles, — At last I have the accounts; the Doer has done excellently . . . I have the retrospective horrors on me when I think of the liabilities I incurred; but, thank God, I think I'm in port again, and I have found one climate in which I can enjoy life. Even Honolulu is too cold for me; but the south isles were a heaven upon earth to a puir, catarrhal party like Johns'one. We think, as Tahiti is too complete a banishment, to try Madeira. It's only a week from England, good communications, and I suspect in climate and scenery not unlike our dear islands; in people, alas! there can be no comparison. But friends could go, and I could come in summer, so I should not be quite cut off.

Lloyd and I have finished a story, *The Wrong Box*. If it is not funny, I am sure I do not know what is. I have split over writing it. Since I have been here, I have been toiling like a galley slave. . . . This spasm of activity has been chequered with champagne parties: Happy and Glorious, Hawaii Ponoi paua; kuo moi — (Native Hawaiians, dote upon your monarch) Hawaiian God save the King. (In addition to my other labours, I am learning the language with a native moonshee.) Kalakaua is a terrible companion; a bottle of fizz is like a glass of sherry to him; he thinks nothing of five or six in an afternoon as a whet for dinner. You should see a photograph of our party after an afternoon with H.H.M.: my! what a crew! —Yours ever affectionately.

ROBERT LOUIS STEVENSON

Letter to Sidney Colvin
Honolulu, March 1889

My dear Colvin, — Still no word from you! I am utterly cast down; but I will try to return good for evil and for once give you news. We are here in the suburb of Honolulu in a rambling house or set of houses in a great garden. . . . The town is some three miles away, but the house is connected by telephone with the chief shops, and the tramway runs to within a quarter of a mile of us. I find Honolulu a beastly climate after Tahiti and have been in bed a little; but my colds *took on no catarrhal symptom*, which is staggeringly delightful. . . . Fanny is, I think, a good deal better on the whole, having profited like me by the tropics; my mother and Lloyd are first-rate. I do not think I have heard from you since last May; and this really frightens me. Do write, even now. Scribners Sons it should be; we shall probably be out of this some time in April, home some time in June. But the world whirls to me perceptibly, a mass of times and seasons and places and engagements, and seas to cross, and continents to traverse, so that I scarce know where I am. Well, I have had a brave time. . . . Is it possible I have wounded you in some way? I scarce like to dream that it is possible; and yet I know too well it may be so. If so, don't write, and you can pitch into me when we meet. I am, admittedly, as mild as London Stout now; and the Old Man Virulent much a creature of the past. My dear Colvin, I owe to you and Fleeming Jenkin, the two older men who took the trouble, and knew how to make a friend of me, everything I have or am: if I have behaved ill, just hold on and give me a chance, you shall have the slanging of me and I bet I shall prefer it to this silence. — Ever, my dear Colvin, your most affectionate

R.L.S.

Feast for the King and Princess of Hawaii

The Bush, Hawaii

Letter from Fanny Stevenson to Fanny Sitwell
Honolulu, towards the end of March 1889

My dear Friend, — Louis has improved so wonderfully in the delicious islands of the South Seas, that we think of trying yet one more voyage. We are a little uncertain as to how we shall go, whether in a missionary ship, or by hiring schooners from point to point, but the 'unregenerate' islands we must see. I suppose we shall be off some time in June, which will fetch us back to England in another year's time. You could hardly believe it if you could see Louis now. He looks as well as he ever did in his life, and has had no sign of cough or haemorrhage (begging pardon of Nemesis) for many months. It seems a pity to return to England until his health is firmly re-established, and also a pity not to see all that we can see quite easily starting from this place; and which will be our only opportunity in life. Of course there is the usual risk from hostile natives, and the horrible sea, but a positive risk is so much more wholesome than a negative one, and it is all such joy to Louis and Lloyd. As for me, I hate the sea, and am afraid of it (though no one will believe that because in time of danger I do not make an outcry — nevertheless I *am* afraid of it, and it is not kind to me), but I love the tropic weather, and the wild people, and to see my two boys so happy. Mrs Stevenson is going back to Scotland in May, as she does not like to be longer away from her old sister, who has been very ill. And besides, we do not feel justified in taking her to the sort of places we intend to visit. As for me, I can get comfort out of very rough surroundings for my people, I can work hard and enjoy it. I can even shoot pretty well, and though I 'don't want to fight, by jingo if I must', why I can. I don't suppose there will be any occasion for that sort of thing — only in case.

I am not quite sure of the names, but I *think* our new cruise includes the Gilberts, the Fijis, and the Solomons. Louis will write the particulars. As for myself, I have more cares than I was really fit for. To keep house on a yacht is no easy thing. When Louis and I broke loose from the ship and lived alone amongst the natives, I got on very well. It was when I was deathly sick, and the question was put to me by the cook, 'What shall we have for the cabin dinner, what for tomorrow's breakfast, what for lunch? and what about the sailors' food? Please come and look at the biscuits, for the weevils have got into them, and show me how to make yeast that will rise of itself, and smell the pork which seems pretty high, and give me directions about making a pudding with molasses — and what is to be done about the bugs?' — etc., etc. In the midst of heavy dangerous weather, when I was lying on the floor clutching a basin, down comes the mate with a cracked head, and I must needs cut off the hair matted with blood, wash and dress the wound and administer restoratives. I do not like being 'the lady of the yacht', but ashore! O, then I felt I was repaid for all. I wonder did any of my letters from beautiful Tautira ever come to hand, with the descriptions of our life with Louis's adopted brother Ori a Ori? Ori wrote to us, if no one else did, and I mean to give you a translation of his letter. . . .

I find my head swimming so that I cannot write any more. I wish some rich Catholic would send a parlour organ to Pere Bruno of Tautira. I am going to try and save money to do it myself, but he may die before I have enough. I feel ashamed to be sitting here when I think of that old man who cannot draw because of scrivener's paralysis, who has no one year in and year out to speak to but natives (our Rui is a Protestant, not bigoted like the rest of them — but still a Protestant) and the only pastime he has is playing on an old broken parlour organ whose keys are mostly dumb. I know no more pathetic figure. Have you no rich Catholic friends who would send him an organ that he could play upon? Of course, I am talking nonsense, and yet I know somewhere that person exists if only I knew the place.

Our dearest love to you all. FANNY

Letter to Henry James
Honolulu, March 1889

My dear James, — Yes — I own up — I am untrue to friendship and (what is less, but still considerable) to civilisation. I am not coming home for another year. There it is, cold and bald, and now you won't believe in me at all, and serve me right (says you) and the devil take me. But look here, and judge me tenderly. I have had more fun and pleasure in my life these past months than ever before, and more health than in any time in ten long years. And even here in Honolulu I have withered in the cold; and this precious deep is filled with islands, which we may still visit; and though the sea is a deathful place, I like to be there, and like squalls (when they are over); and to draw near to a new island, I cannot say how much I like. In short, I take another year of this sort of life, and mean to try to work down among the poisoned arrows, and mean (if it may be) to come back again when the thing is through, and converse with Henry James as heretofore. . . . My wife has just sent to Mrs Sitwell a translation of a letter I have had from my chief friend in this part of the world; go and see her, and get a hearing of it; it will do you good; it is a better method of correspondence than even Henry James's. I jest, but seriously it is a strange thing for a tough, sick, middle-aged scrivener like R.L.S. to receive a letter so conceived from a man fifty years old, a leading politician, a crack orator, and the great wit of his village; boldly say 'the highly popular M.P. of Tautira'. My nineteenth century strikes here, and lies alongside of something beautiful and ancient. I would rather have received it than written *Redgauntlet* or

Iolani Palace, Honolulu

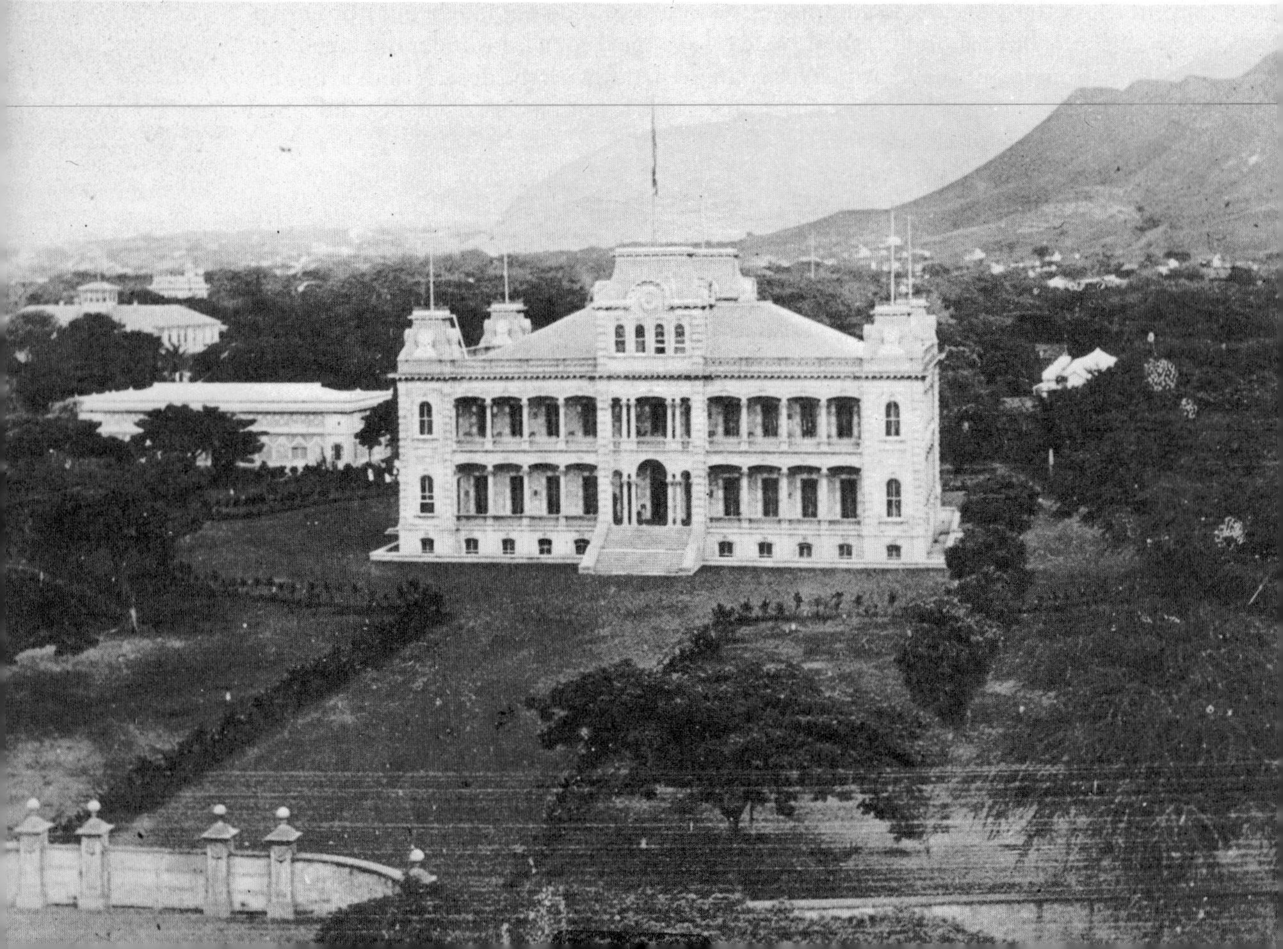

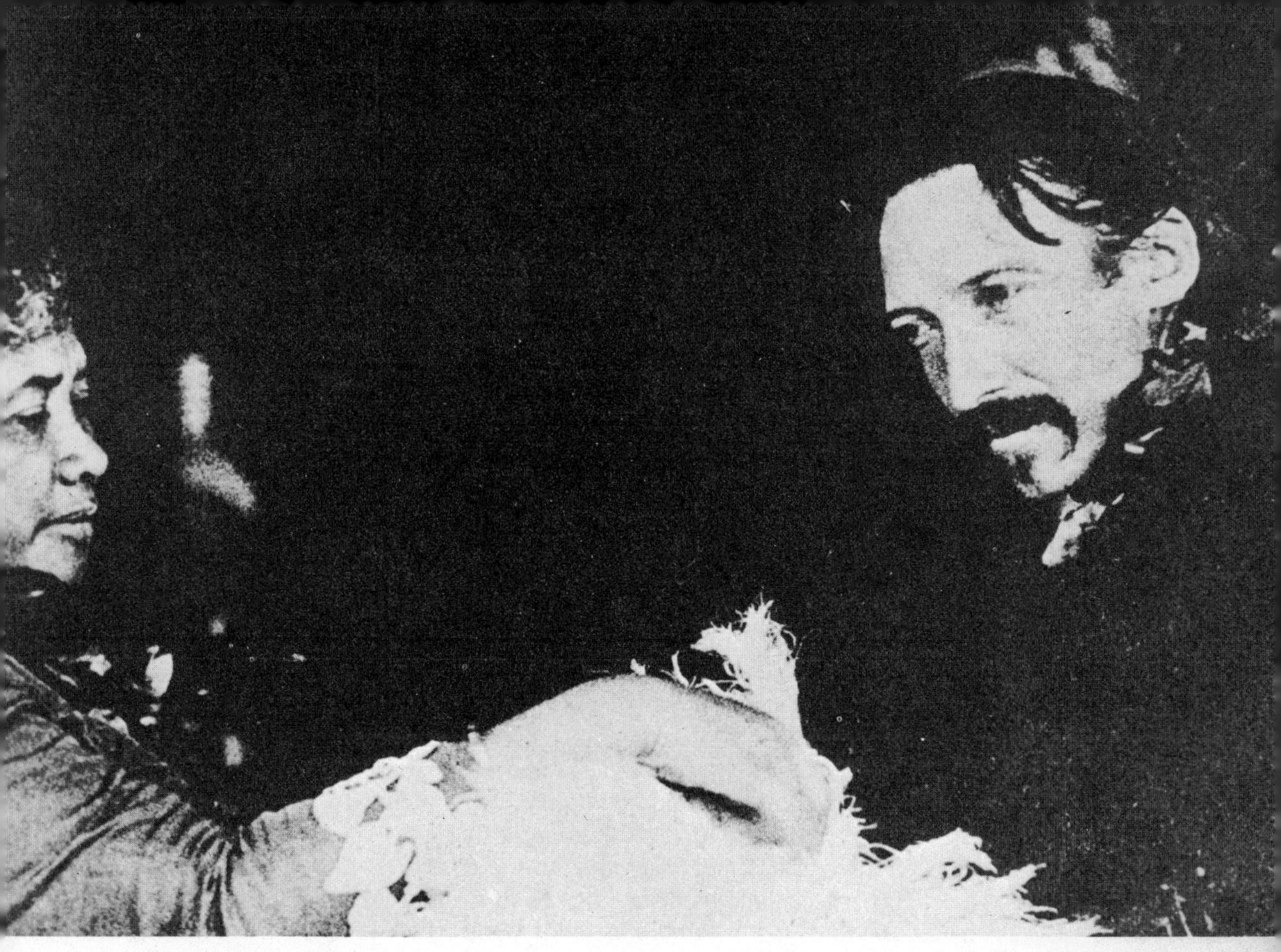

Stevenson with Princess Lilioukalani

the sixth *Aeneia*. All told, if my books have enabled or helped me to make this voyage, to know Rui, and to have received such a letter, they have (in the old prefatorial expression) not been writ in vain. It would seem from this that I have been not so much humbled as puffed up; but, I assure you, I have in fact been both. A little of what the letter says is my own earning; not all, but yet a little; and the little makes me proud, and all the rest ashamed; and in the contrast, how much more beautiful altogether is the ancient man than him of today!

Well, well, Henry James is pretty good, though he is of the nineteenth century, and that glaringly. And to curry favour with him, I wish I could be more explicit. . . . All are fairly well — the wife, your countrywoman, least of all; troubles are not entirely wanting; but on the whole we prosper, and we are all affectionately yours,

ROBERT LOUIS STEVENSON.

Letter to Sidney Colvin
Honolulu, April 2nd, 1889

My dear Colvin, — I am beginning to be ashamed of writing on to you without the least acknowledgement, like a tramp; but I do not care — I am hardened; and whatever be the cause of your silence, I mean to write till all is blue. I am outright ashamed of my news, which is that we are not coming home for another year. I cannot but hope it may continue the vast improvement of my health; I think it is good for Fanny and Lloyd; and we have all a taste for this wandering and dangerous life. My mother I send home, to my relief, as this part of our cruise will be (if we can carry it out) rather difficult in places . . . but if we can pull it off in safety, gives me a fine book of travel, and Lloyd a fine lecture and diorama, which should vastly better our finances.

I feel as if I were untrue to friendship; believe me, Colvin, when I look forward to this absence of another year, my conscience sinks at thought of the Monument; but I think you will pardon me if you consider how much this tropical weather mends my health. Remember me as I was at home, and think of me sea-bathing and walking about, as jolly as a sandboy: you will own the temptation is strong; and as the scheme, bar fatal accidents, is bound to pay into the bargain, sooner or later, it seems it would be madness to come home now, with an imperfect book, no illustrations to speak of, no diorama, and perhaps fall sick again by autumn. I do not think I delude myself when I say the tendency to catarrh has visibly diminished.

It is a singular thing that as I was packing up old papers ere I left Skerryvore, I came on the prophecies of a drunken Highland sibyl, when I was seventeen. She said I was to be very happy, to visit America, and *to be much upon the sea*. It seems as if it were coming true with a vengeance. Also, do you remember my strong, old, rooted belief that I shall die by drowning? I don't want that to come true, though it is an easy death; but it occurs to me oddly, with these long chances in front. I cannot say why I like the sea; no man is more cynically and constantly alive to its perils; I regard it as the highest form of gambling; and yet I love the sea as much as I hate gambling. Fine, clean emotions; a world all and always beautiful; air better than wine; interest unflagging; there is upon the whole no better life. — Yours ever,

R.L.S.

Letter to Miss Adelaide Boodle
Honolulu, April 6th, 1889

My dear Miss Boodle, — . . . The Sandwich Isles do not interest us very much; we live here, oppressed with civilisation, and look for good things in the future. But it would surprise you if you came out tonight from Honolulu (all shining with electric lights, and all in a bustle from the arrival of the mail, which is to carry you these lines) and crossed the long wooden causeway along the beach, and came out on the road through Kapiolani park, and seeing a gate in the palings, with a tub of goldfish by the wayside, entered casually in. The buildings stand in three groups by the edge of the beach, where an angry little spitfire sea continually spirts and thrashes with impotent irascibility, the big seas breaking further out on the reef.

The first is a small house, with a very large summer parlour, or *lanai*, as they call it here, roofed, but practically open. There you will find the lamps burning and the family sitting about the table, dinner just done; my mother, my wife, Lloyd, Belle, my wife's daughter, Austin her child, and tonight (by way of rarity) a guest. All about the walls our South Seas curiosities, war clubs, idols, pearl shells, stone axes, etc.; and the walls are only a small part of a *lanai*, the rest being glazed or latticed windows, or mere open space. You will see there no sign of the Squire, however. . . . The next group of buildings is ramshackle, and quite dark, and here is another door — all these places open from the outside — and you go in, and find photography, tubs of water, negatives steeping, a tap, and a chair and an ink-bottle, where my wife is supposed to write; round a little further, a third door, entering which you find a picture upon the easel and a table sticky with paints; . . . no sign of the Squire in all this. But right opposite the studio door you have observed a third little house . . . it is a grim little wooden shanty;

The Stevensons 'at home': Waikiki lanai *(cottage)*

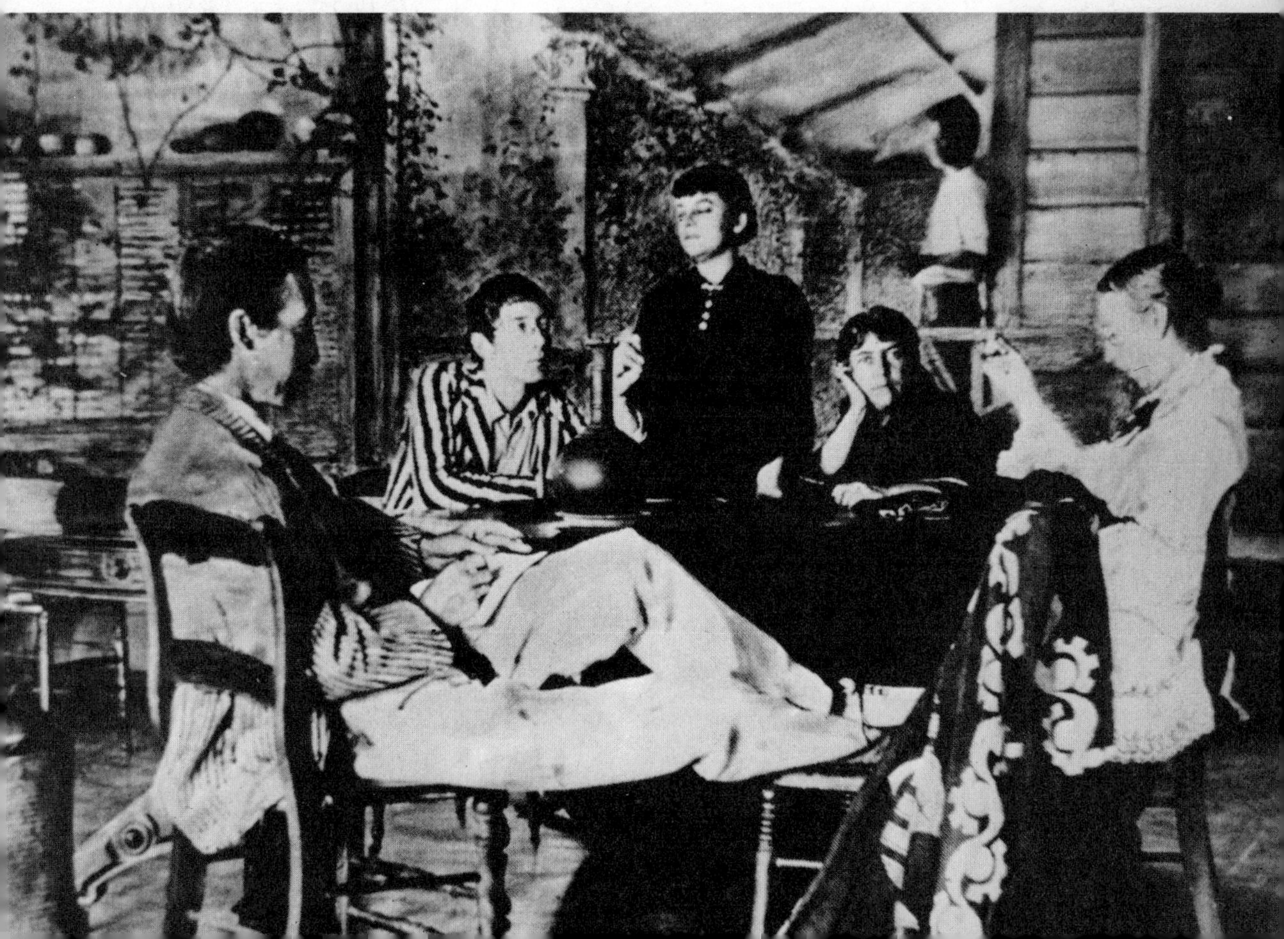

cobwebs bedeck it; friendly mice inhabit its recesses; the mailed cockroach walks upon the wall; so also, I regret to say, the scorpion. Herein are two pallet beds, two mosquito curtains, two tables laden with books and manuscripts, three chairs, and, in one of the beds, the Squire busy writing to yourself, as it chances, and just at this moment somewhat bitten by mosquitos. He has just set fire to the insect powder, and will be all right in no time; but just how he contemplates large white blisters, and would like to scratch them, but knows better. The house is not bare, walls pasted over with pages from the *Graphic*, *Harper's Weekly*, etc. The floor is matted, and I am bound to say the matting is filthy. There are two windows and two doors, one of which is condemned; on the panels of that last a sheet of paper is pinned up, and covered with writing. I cull a few plums: "A duck hammock for each person. A patent organ like the commandant's at Taillo hae. Cheap and bad cigars for presents. Revolvers. Permangate of potass. Liniment for the head and sulphur. Fine tooth-comb."

What do you think this is? Simply life in the South Seas foreshortened. These are a few of our desiderata for the next trip, which we jot down as they occur. . . . Tomorrow — think of it — I must be off by a quarter to eight to drive in to the palace and breakfast with his Hawaiian Majesty at 8.30: I shall be dead indeed. . . . To you we send all kinds of things, and I am the absentee Squire,

ROBERT LOUIS STEVENSON.

Stevenson at 39.

From An Intimate Portrait of RLS *by Lloyd Osbourne*

The seven months' cruise had had a marvellous effect on RLS. He had become almost well; could ride, take long walks, dine out, and in general lead the life of a man in ordinary health. Such climates were supposed to be harmful for tubercular patients, whom the local doctors sent away at once — but Stevenson throve. His fine complexion had regained its ruddy tint; his hair, now cut short, was no longer lank, but glossy and of a lighter brown; his eyes, always his most salient feature and always brilliant, had no longer that strange fire of disease: he walked with a firm, light step, and though to others he must have appeared thin and fragile, to us the transformation in him was astounding. In his soft white shirt, blue serge coat, white flannel trousers, white shoes and white yachting cap (such caps were his favourites till his death) he looked to perfection the famous author who had arrived in a yacht and who 'dressed the role' as the actors say, in a manner worthy of his dashing schooner.

It was typical of Stevenson that instead of choosing the best room in the house for his own, he should seek out a dilapidated, cobwebby little shack. . . . King Kalakaua would occasionally drop in on him for a long and confidential talk, while the horses of the royal equipage flicked their tails under a neighbouring tree, and the imposing coachman and footman dozed on their box. . . .

Sketch of R.L.S. 'famous author'

Stevenson and he became great friends, finding their strongest bond in Polynesian lore and antiquities. The king was a mine of information on these subjects. It was his hobby of hobbies to record the fast-fading history of his race and to pierce the mist in which so much of it was enveloped. Together they projected an excavation of the ancient royal tombs on Diamond Head, but at the last moment had to abandon it lest the king should play into the hands of his enemies and be accused of ransacking these graves for his personal profit . . . (Kalakaua) was always urging Stevenson to 'stay and make your home with us. Hawaii needs you'.

This home, wherever it was going to be, was causing Stevenson a good deal of concern. At first he anticipated returning to England; in fact for a while this was as good as settled; 'Skerryvore' (in Bournemouth) was still there temporarily rented, and absence, perhaps, was endowing it with a certain glamour. But most compelling of all, I think, was R.L.S.'s desire to stroll into the Savile Club and electrify his old friends as the returned seafarer from the South Sea Islands. At least he was constantly dwelling on this phase of his return, and choosing the exact hour when he could make the most dramatic entrance. But as the conviction grew that he never could be so well as in the Pacific, and with the vague and romantic idea of finding an island of his own, he began to talk of another cruise and look for the means.

The means, alas, were strictly limited to one ship, the missionary vessel, *Morning Star*, which in a few months' time was due to start on her annual tour of mission stations. Her itinerary was extraordinarily attractive; she went to many of the wildest and least-known islands of the Western Pacific; but her drawbacks were frightful — no smoking, not a drink, no profanity, church, nightly prayer meetings and an enforced intimacy with the most uncongenial of people. American missionaries often are excessively narrow, intolerant and puritanical; the prospect of four months in their society was calculated to make the stoutest hearts quail. . .   Our plans all seemed concentrated on the *Morning Star*, which was not due to sail for a long while; and it was with no sense of hurry or indecision that we remained on in Waikiki, one pleasant day merging into another in unbroken peace. But suddenly, out of a clear sky, we were thrown into a tremendous turmoil. One noonday R.L.S. came driving in from Honolulu, his horses in a lather, and it needed but a single look at his face to see that he was wildly excited.

'Have chartered a schooner!' he shouted out before he even jumped down; and as we all crowded about him, he breathlessly continued: 'Arranged the details and signed the charter-party as she was casting off — tug tooting, and people pulling at the owner's coat-tails, and the sweat running off our faces in a tin office! The *Equator*, sixty-eight tons, and due back from San Francisco in a month to pick us up for the Gilbert Islands. Finest little craft you ever saw in your life, and I have the right to take her anywhere at so much a day!'

The Pali, Hawaii

A hectic luncheon followed; champagne was opened in honour of the occasion, and we drank to the *Equator* in foaming bumpers; everybody talked at once amid an unimaginable hilarity, for were we not to sail away in a vessel of our own, and freed from the nightmare of the *Morning Star*?

'And we can smoke on that blessed ship!' cried Stevenson, with uplifted glass.

'And drink!' cried I. 'Hurrah for the *Equator*.'

'And swear!' exclaimed my mother delightedly — she who had never said 'damn' in her life.

. . . We looked out on one of the most inspiriting sights I have ever seen in my life — the *Equator* herself, under a towering spread of canvas, and as close in as her captain dared to put her, parting the blue water in flashes of spray on the way to San Francisco.

We were still watching when she broke out her ensign, and dipped it to us in farewell.

Our ship!

Letter to Charles Baxter
Honolulu, 10th May 1889

My dear Charles, — . . . This new cruise of ours is somewhat venturesome; and I think it needful to warn you not to be in a hurry to suppose us dead. In these ill-charted seas, it is quite on the cards we might be cast on some unvisited, or very rarely visited, island; that there we might lie for a long time, even years, unheard of; and yet turn up smiling at the hinder end. So do not let me be 'rowpit' till you get some certainty we have gone to Davie Jones in a squall, or graced the feast of some barbarian in the character of Long Pig.

I have just been a week away alone on the lee coast of Hawaii, the only white creature in many miles, riding five and a half hours one day, living with a native, seeing four lepers shipped off to Molokai, hearing native causes, and giving my opinion as *amicus curiae* as to the interpretation of a statue in English; a lovely week among God's best — at least God's sweetest works — Polynesians. It has bettered me greatly. If I could only stay there the time that remains, I could get my work done and be happy; but the care of my family keeps me in vile Honolulu, where I am always out of sorts, amidst heat and cold and cesspools and beastly *haoles*. What is a haole? You are one; and so, I am sorry to say, am I. [The Hawaiian name for white men.] After so long a dose of whites, it was a blessing to get among Polynesians again even for a week.

Well, Charles, there are waur haoles than yoursel', I'll say that for ye; and trust before I sail I shall get another letter with more about yourself. Ever your affectionate friend,

R.L.S.

Princess Kaiulani

Letter from R.L.S. to W. H. Low
Honolulu, (about) 20 May 1889

My dear Low, — . . . If you want to cease to be a republican, see my Kaiulani as she goes through —but she is gone already. You will die a red. I wear the colours of that little royal maiden, *Nous allons chanter à la ronde, si vous voulez*. Only she is not a blonde by several chalks, though she is but a half-blood and the wrong half Edinburgh Scots like mysel'. But, O, Low, I love the Polynesian: this civilisation of ours is a dingy, ungentlemanly business; it drops out too much of man, and too much of that the very beauty of the poor beast; who has his beauties in spite of Zola and Co. . . . But if you could live, the only white folk, in a Polynesian village; and drink that warm light *vin du pays* of human affection and enjoy that simple dignity of all about you — I will not gush, for I am now in my fortieth year, which seems highly unjust, but there it is, Mr Low, and the Lord enlighten your affectionate

R.L.S.

[Princess Kaiulani was born in Honolulu in 1875, daughter of Archibald S. Cleghorn from Edinburgh, who had married the sister of King Kalakaua, Princess Miriam Likelike. Kaiulani was the only child and heiress to the throne. Her mother died when she was twelve and she became a close friend of visitor R.L.S. whom her father had welcomed to his home in Honolulu. He called her his critic and said: 'If you like what I write, I know it is good.' In 1889, she was sent to boarding school in Britain to prepare her for her royal inheritance.]

To Princess Kaiulani (from *Ballads and Other Poems*)

Forth from her land to mine she goes,
The island maid, the island rose,
Light of heart and bright of face:
The daughter of a double race.
Her islands here, in Southern Sun,
Shall mourn their Ka'iulani gone,
And I, in her dear banyan shade,
Look vainly for my little maid.

But our Scots islands far away
Shall glitter with unwonted day,
And cast for once their tempests by
To smile in Ka'iulani's eye.

Written in April to Ka'iulani in the April of her age; and at Waikiki, within easy walk of Ka'iulani's banyan. When she comes to my land and her father's, and the

Princess Kaiulani, her father, A. G. Cleghorn and friend

rain beats upon the window (as I fear it will), let her look at this page; it will be like a weed gathered and pressed at home; and she will remember her own islands, and the shadow of the mighty tree; and she will hear the peacocks screaming in the dusk and the wind blowing in the palms; and she will think of her father sitting there alone. — R.L.S.

[Kaiulani returned to Hawaii in November 1897 her health shattered by Britain's climate. Stevenson was dead and she survived him by less than five years, dying in March 1899, aged 24. She lay in state dressed in white, on a purple velvet pall covered by the royal cloak of yellow feathers. Two crowns, one of white carnations, the other of the royal flower, yellow ilima, and the fragrant vine vaile, lay at her head.]

Letter from Fanny Stevenson to Sidney Colvin
Honolulu, May 21st, 1889

Best of Friends, — It was a joy inexpressible to get a word from you at last. . . . I wish you could have seen us both throwing over the immense package of letters searching for your handwriting. Now that we know you have been ill, please do let someone send us a line at our next address telling us how you are. What that next address may be we do not yet know, as our final movements are a little uncertain. To begin with, a trading schooner, the *Equator*, will come along some time in the first part of June, lie outside the harbour and signal to us. Within forty-eight hours we shall pack up our possessions, our barrel of sauer kraut, our barrel of salt onions, our bag of cocoanuts, our native garments, our tobacco, fish hooks, red combs and Turkey red calicoes (all the latter for trading purposes), our hand organ, photograph and painting materials, and finally our magic lantern — all these upon a large whaleboat. . . . Lloyd, also, takes a fiddle, a guitar, a native instrument, something like a banjo, called a taro-patch fiddle, and a lot of songbooks. We shall be carried first to one of the Gilberts, landing at Butaritari. The *Equator* is going about amongst the Gilbert group, and we have the right to keep her over when we like within reasonable limits. Finally she will leave us, and we shall have to take the chances of what happens next. We hope to see the Marshalls, the Carolines, the Fijis, Tonga and Samoa (also other islands that I do not remember), perhaps staying a little while in Sydney, and stopping on our way home to see our friends in Tahiti and the Marquesas.

I am very much exercised by one thing. Louis has the most enchanting material that anyone ever had in the whole world for his book, and I am afraid he is going to spoil it all. He has taken into his Scotch Stevenson head that a stern duty lies before him, and that his book must be a sort of scientific and historic impersonal thing, comparing the different languages (of which he knows nothing really) and the different peoples, the object being to settle the question as to

Princess Kaiulani with friends

whether they are of common Malay origin or not. Also to compare the Protestant and Catholic missions, etc., and the whole thing to be impersonal, leaving out all he knows of the people themselves. And I believe there is no one living who has got so near to them, or who understands them as he does. Think of a small treatise on the Polynesian races being offered to people who are dying to hear about Ori a Ori, the making of brothers with cannibals, the strange stories they told, and of the extraordinary adventures that befell us: suppose Herman Melville had given us his theories as to the Polynesian language and the probable good or evil results of the missionary influence instead of *Omoo* and *Typee*. . . . Louis says it is a stern sense of duty that is at the bottom of it, which is more alarming than anything else. I am so sure that you will agree with me that I am going to ask you to throw the weight of your influence as heavily as possible in the scales with me. Please refer to the matter in the letters we shall receive at our first stopping place, otherwise Louis will spend a great deal of time in Sydney actually reading other people's books on the islands. What a thing it is to have a 'man of genius' to deal with. It is like managing an overbred horse. Why with my own feeble hand I could write a book that the whole world would jump at. Please keep any letters of mine that contain any incidents of our wanderings. They are very exact as to facts, and Louis may, in this conscientious state of mind (indeed I am afraid he has), put nothing in his diary but statistics. Even if I thought it a desirable thing to write what he proposes, I should still think it impossible unless after we had lived and studied here some twenty years or more.

Now I am done with my complaining, and shall turn to the pleasanter paths. Louis went to one of the other islands a couple of weeks ago, quite alone, got drenched with rain and surf, rode over mountain paths — five and a half hours one day — and came back none the worse for it. Today he goes to Molokai, the leper island. He never has a sign of haemorrhage, the air cushion is a thing of the past, and altogether he is a new man. How he will do in the English climate again I do not know, but in these latitudes he is very nearly a well man, nothing seems to do him harm but overwork. That, of course, is sometimes difficult to prevent. Now, however, *The Master* is done, we have enough money to go upon and there is no need to work at all. I must stop. My dear love to you all.

FANNY V. DE G. STEVENSON

Letter to Fanny Stevenson

Kalawao, Molokai, May 1889

Dear Fanny, — I had a lovely sail up. Captain Cameron and Mr Gilfillan, both born in the States, yet the first still with a strong Highland, and the second still with a strong Lowland accent, were good company; the night was warm, the victuals plain but good. Mr Gilfillan gave me his berth, and I slept well, though I heard the sisters sick in the next stateroom, poor souls. Heavy rolling woke me in the morning; I turned in all standing, so went right on the upper deck. The day was on the peep out of a low morning bank, and we were wallowing along under stupendous cliffs. As the lights brightened, we could see certain abutments and buttresses on their front where wood clustered and grass grew brightly. But the whole brow seemed quite impassable, and my heart sank at the sight. Two thousand feet of rock making 19 degrees (the Captain guesses) seemed quite beyond my powers. However, I had come so far; and, to tell you the truth, I was so cowed with fear and disgust that I dared not go back on the adventure in the interests of my own self-respect. Presently we came up with the leper promontory, low-land, quite bare and bleak and harsh, a little town of wooden houses, two churches, a landing-stair, all unsightly, sour, northerly, lying athwart the sunrise, with the great wall of the pali cutting the world out on the south. Our lepers were sent on the first boat, about a dozen, one poor child very horrid, one white man, leaving a large grown family behind him in Honolulu, and then into the second boat stepped the sisters and myself. I do not know how it would have been with me had the sisters not been there. My horror of the horrible is about my weakest point; but the moral loveliness at my elbow blotted all else out; and when I found that one of them was crying, poor soul, quietly under her veil, I cried a little myself; then I felt as right as a trivet, only a little crushed to be there so uselessly. I thought it was a sin and a shame she should feel unhappy; I turned round to her, and said something like this: 'Ladies, God Himself is here to give you welcome. I'm sure it is good for me to be beside you; I hope it will be blessed to me; I thank you for myself and the good you do me.' It seemed to cheer her up; but indeed I had scarce said it when we were at the landing-stairs, and there was a great crowd, hundreds of (God save us) pantomime masks in poor human flesh, waiting to receive the sisters and the new patients.

Every hand was offered: I had gloves, but I had made up my mind on the boat's voyage *not* to give my hand; that seemed less offensive than the gloves. So the sisters and I went up among that crew, and presently I got aside (for I felt I had no business there) and set off on foot across the promontory, carrying my wrap and the camera. All horror was quite gone from me; to see these dread creatures smile and look happy was beautiful. On my way through Kalaupapa I was exchanging cheerful *alohas* with the patients coming galloping over on their horses; I was stopping to gossip at house-doors; I was happy, only ashamed of myself that I was here for no good. One woman was pretty, and spoke good English, and was infinitely engaging and (in the old phrase) towardly; she thought I was the new white patient; and when she found I was only a visitor, a curious change came into her face and voice — the only sad thing, morally, sad, I mean — that I met that morning. But for all that, they tell me none want to leave. Beyond Kalaupapa the houses become rare; drystone dykes, grassy, stony land, one sick pandanus; a dreary country, from overhead in the little clinging wood shogs of the pali chirruping of birds fell; the low sun was right in my face; the trade blew pure and cool and delicious; I felt as right as ninepence, and stopped and chatted with the patients whom I still met on their horses, with not the least disgust. About halfway over, I met the superintendent (a leper) with a horse for me, and O, wasn't I glad! But the horse was one of those curious, dogged cranky brutes that always dully want to go somewhere else, and my traffic with him completed my crushing fatigue. I got to the guest-house, an empty house with several rooms, kitchen, bath, etc. There was no one there, and I let the horse go loose in the garden, lay down on the bed and fell asleep.

Dr Swift woke me and gave me breakfast, then I came back and slept again while he was at the dispensary, and he woke me for dinner; and I came back and slept again, and he woke me about six for supper; and then in about an hour I felt tired again, and came up to my solitary guest-house, played the flageolet, and am now writing to you. As yet, you see, I have seen nothing of the settlement, and my crushing fatigue (though I believe that was moral and a measure of my cowardice) and the doctor's opinion make me think the pali hopeless. 'You don't look a strong man,' said the doctor; 'but are you sound?' I told him the truth; then he said it was out of the question, and if I were to get up at all, I must be carried up. But, as it seems, men as well as horses continually fall on this ascent: the doctor goes up with a change of clothes — it is plain that to be carried would in itself be very fatiguing to both mind and body; and I should then be at the beginning of thirteen miles of mountain road to be ridden against time. How should I come through? I hope you will think me right in my decision: I mean to stay, and shall not be back in Honolulu till Saturday, June first.

Dr Swift has a wife and infant son, beginning to toddle and run, and they live here as composed as brick and mortar — at least the wife does, a Kentucky German, a fine enough creature, I believe, who was quite amazed at the sisters shedding tears! How strange is mankind! Gilfillan too, a good fellow I think, and far from stupid, kept up his hard Lowland Scottish talk in the boat while the sister was covering her face; but I believe he knew, and did it (partly) in embarrassment and part perhaps in mistaken kindness. And that was one reason, too, why I made my speech to them. Partly, too, I did it because I was ashamed to do so, and remembered one of my golden rules, 'When you are shamed to speak, speak up at once'. But, mind you, that rule is only golden with strangers; with your own folk, there are other considerations. This is a strange place to be in. A bell has sounded at intervals while I wrote, now all is still but a musical humming of the sea, not unlike the sound of the telegraph wires; the night is quite cool and pitch dark, with a small fine rain; one light over in the leper settlement, one cricket whistling in the garden, my lamp here by my bedside, and my pen cheeping between my inky fingers.

Next day, lovely morning, slept all night, 80 degrees in the shade, strong, sweet Anaho trade-wind.

LOUIS

The Stevensons at cards

Letter to Sidney Colvin
Honolulu, June 1889

My dear Colvin, — I am just home after twelve days' journey to Molokai, seven of them at the leper settlement, where I can only say that the sight of so much courage, cheerfulness, and devotion stung me too high to mind the infinite pity and horror of the sights. I used to ride over from Kalawao to Kalaupapa (about three miles across the promontory, the cliff-wall, ivied with forest and yet inaccessible from steepness, on my left), go to the Sisters' home, which is a miracle of neatness, play a game of croquet with seven leper girls (90 degrees in the shade), get an old-maid meal served me by the sisters, and ride home again, tired enough, but not too tired. The girls all have dolls, and love dressing them. You who know so many dressmakers, please make it known it would be an acceptable gift to send scraps for doll dressmaking to the Reverend Sister Maryanne. . . .

I have seen sights that cannot be told, and heard stories that cannot be repeated: yet I never admired my poor race so much, nor (strange as it may seem) loved life more than in the settlement. A horror of moral beauty broods over the place: that's like bad Victor Hugo, but it is the only way I can express the sense that lived with me all these days. And this even though it was in great part Catholic, and my sympathies flew never with so much difficulty as towards Catholic virtues. The passbook kept with heaven stirs me to anger and laughter. One of the sisters calls the place 'the ticket office to heaven'. Well, what is the odds? They do their darg, and do it with kindness and efficiency incredible; and we must take folk's virtues as we find them, and love the better part. Of old Damien, whose weaknesses and worse perhaps I heard fully, I think only the more. It was a European peasant: dirty, bigoted, untruthful, unwise, tricky, but superb with generosity, residual candour and fundamental good-humour: convince him he had done wrong (it might take hours of insult) and he would undo what he had done and like his corrector better. A man, with all the grime and patriness of mankind, but a saint and hero all the more for that.

The place as regards scenery is grand, gloomy and bleak . . . the low, bare, stony promontory edged in between the cliff and the ocean, two little towns (Kalawao and Kalaupapa) seated on either side of it, as bare almost as bathing machines upon a beach; and the population — gorgons and chimaeras dire. All this tear of the nerves I bore admirably; and the day after I got away, rode twenty miles along the opposite coast and up into the mountains; . . . and I was riding the day after, so I need say no more about health. Honolulu does not agree with me at all: I am always out of sorts there, with slight headache, blood to the head, etc. I had a good deal of work to do and did it with miserable difficulty; and yet all the time I have been gaining strength, as you see, which is highly encouraging. By the time I am done with this cruise I shall have the material for a very singular book of travels: names of strange stories and characters; so generous a farrago. I am going down now to get the story of a shipwrecked family who were fifteen months on an island with a murderer: there is a specimen. The Pacific is a strange place; the nineteenth century only exists there in spots; all round, it is a no-mans land of the ages, a stir-about of epochs and races, barbarisms and civilisations, virtues and crimes.

It is good of you to let me stay longer, but if I had known how ill you were, I should be now on my way home. I had chartered my schooner and made all arrangements before (at last) we got definite news. I feel highly guilty; I should be back to insult and worry you a little. . . . Yours ever,

R.L.S.

The leper settlement, Molokai

In the South Seas — The Eight Islands: The Kona Coast

. . . It was on a Saturday afternoon that the steamer conveyed me to Hookena. She was charged with tourists on their way to the volcano; and I found it hard to justify my choice of a week in an unheard-of hamlet, rather than a visit to one of the admitted marvels of the world. . . . On other islands I had been the centre of attention; here none observed my presence. One hundred and ten years before, the ancestors of these indifferents had looked in the faces of Cook and his seamen with admiration and alarm, called them gods, called them volcanoes; took their clothes for a loose skin, confounded their hats and their heads, and described their pockets as a 'treasure door, through which they plunge their hands into their bodies and bring forth cutlery and necklaces and cloth and nails', and today the coming of the most attractive stranger failed (it would appear) to divert them from Miss Porter's *Scottish Chiefs*: for that was the novel of the day. . . .

Letter to James Payn
[Met in his days of writing for Cornhill Magazine]
Honolulu, H.I., June 13th, 1889

My dear James Payn, — I get sad news of you here at my offsetting for further voyages: I wish I could say what I feel. Sure there was never any man less deserved this calamity; for I have heard you speak time and again, and I remember nothing that was unkind, nothing that was untrue, nothing that was not helpful from your lips. It is the ill-talkers that should hear no more. God knows, I know no word of consolation; but I do feel your trouble. You are the more open to letters now; let me talk to you for two pages. I have nothing but happiness to tell; and you may bless God you are a man so sound-hearted that (even in the freshness of your calamity) I can come to you with my own good fortune unashamed and secure of sympathy. It is a good thing to be a good man, whether deaf or whether dumb; and all of our fellow-craftsmen (whom yet they count a jealous race), I never knew one but gave you the name of honesty and kindness: come to think of it gravely, this is better than the finest hearing. We are all on the march to deafness, blindness, and all conceivable and fatal disabilities; we shall not all get there with

Father Damien with leper children

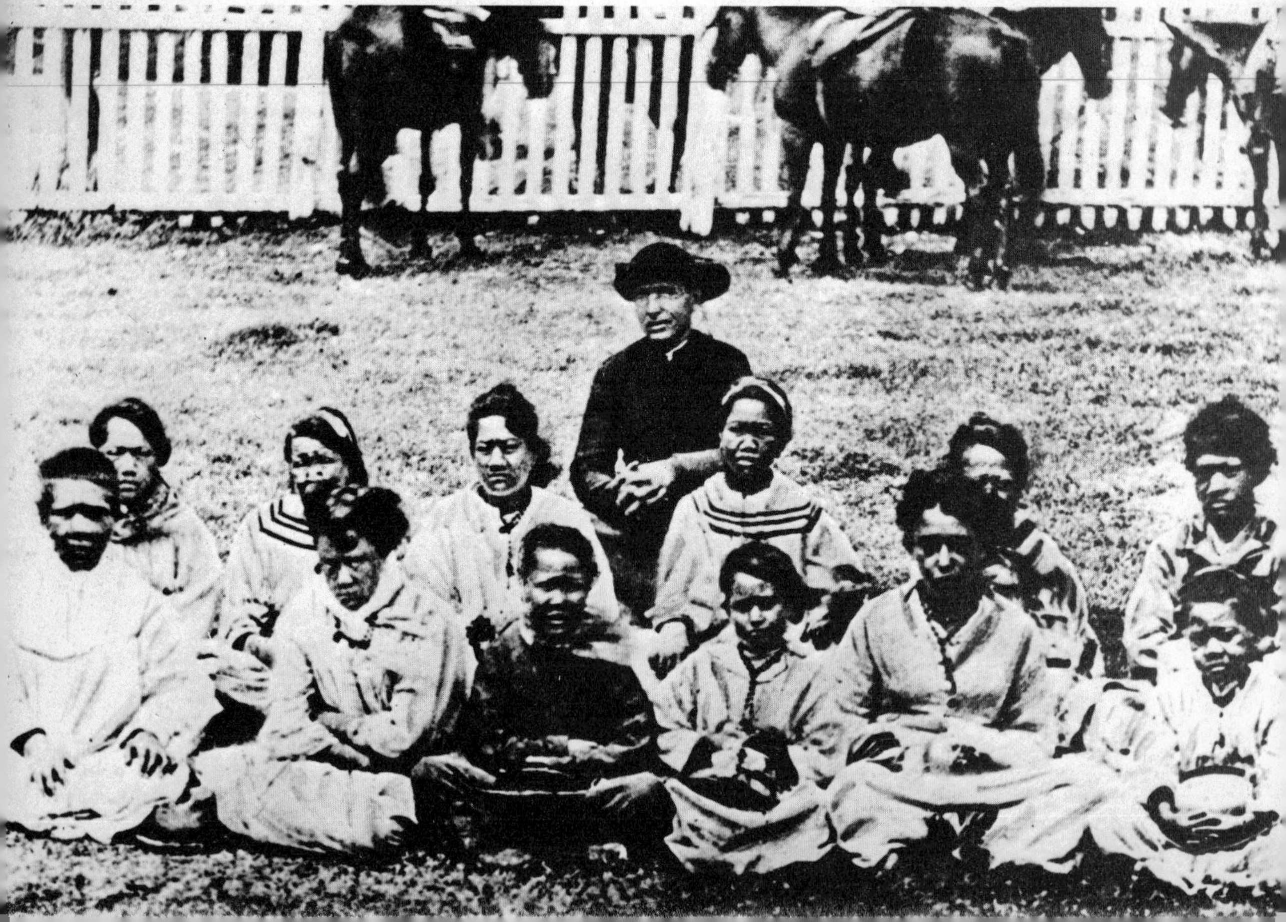

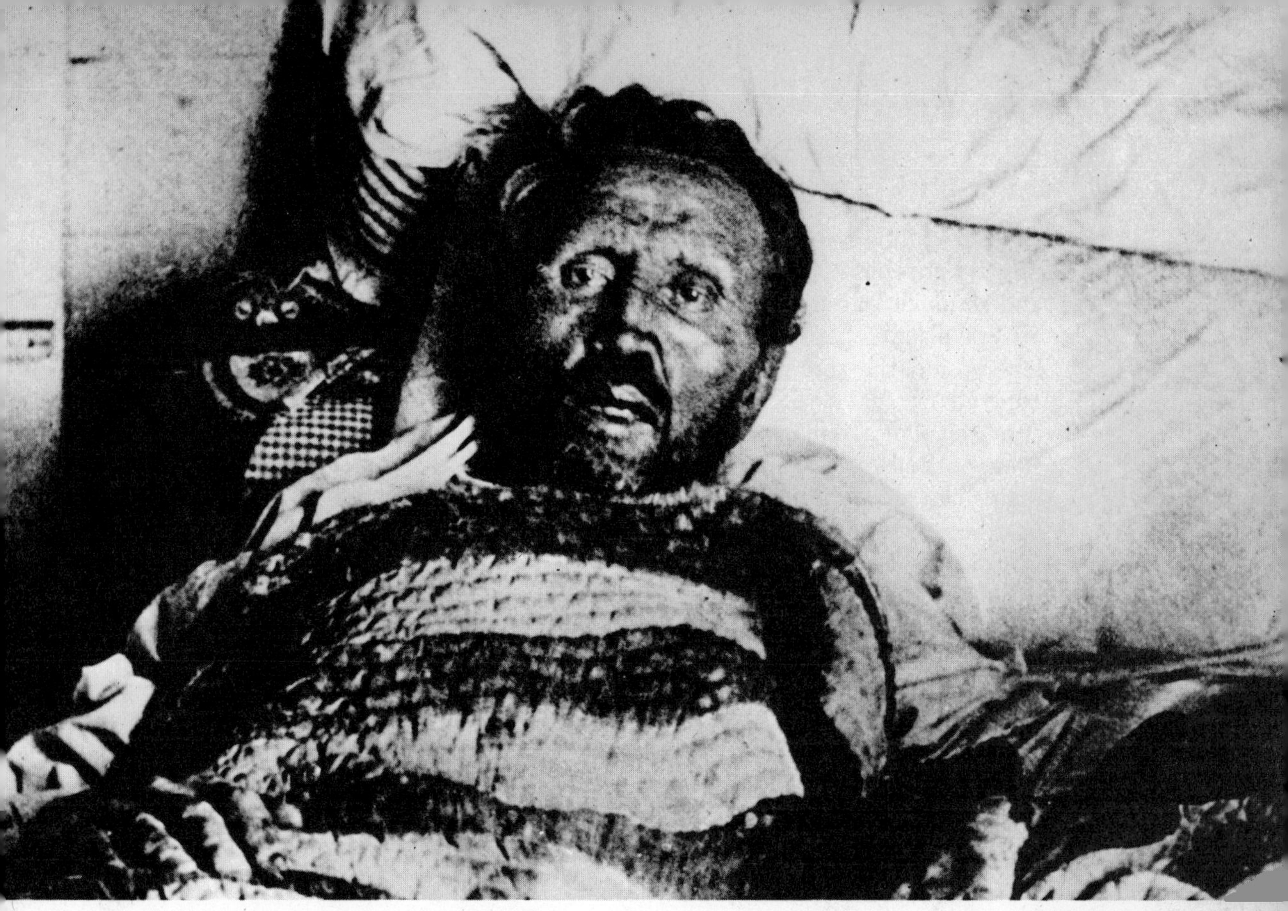

Damien on deathbed

a report so good. My good news is a health astonishingly reinstated. This climate; these voyagings; these landfalls at dawn; new islands peaking from the morning bank; new forested harbours; new passing alarms of squalls and surf; new interests of gentle natives — the whole tale of my life is better to me than any poem.

I am fresh just now from the leper settlement of Molokai, playing croquet with seven leper girls, sitting and yarning with old, blind, leper beachcombers in the hospital, sickened with the spectacle of abhorrent suffering and deformation amongst the patients, touched to the heart by the sight of lovely and effective virtues in their helpers, no stranger time have I ever had, nor any so moving. I do not think it a little thing to be deaf, God knows, and God defend me from the same! — but to be a leper, or one of the self-condemned, how much more awful! and yet there's a way there also. 'There are Molokais everywhere,' said Mr Dutton, Father Damien's dresser; you are but new landed in yours; and my dear and kind adviser, I wish you, with all my soul, that patience and courage which you will require. . . .

Yours affectionately (although so near a stranger),

ROBERT LOUIS STEVENSON

Letter to Mrs Thomas Stevenson
Honolulu, June 1889

My dear Mother, — . . . I was a week in the leper settlement, hag-ridden by horrid sights but really inspired with the sight of so much goodness in the helpless and so much courage and unconsciousness in the sick. The Bishop Home (the Sisters' place) is perfect; I went there most days to play croquet with seven little lepers, and the thermometer sometimes ninety in the shade. . . . The girls enjoyed the game a good deal, and the honour and glory of a clean Laole gentleman for playmate yet more. They were none of them badly disfigured, but some of the bystanders were dreadful; but indeed I have seen sights to turn any man's hair white. The croquet helped me a bit, as I felt I was not quite doing nothing; Sister Maryanne wanted me to sit down the second day, and only tell the girls; I said, 'They would not enjoy that' — 'Ah,' said she, with a smiling eye, 'you say that, but the truth is you enjoy playing yourself!' And so I did. When I came on board the *Mokolii* (little 40-ton steamer) to leave, I had no proper pass and was refused entrance. I saw some very remarkable fireworks, I can tell you, for I had had enough and to spare of the distressful country. But it was all made right; the captain took me ashore the same evening at the north end of the island, gave me a mount, introduced me to an innumerable Irish family where I had supper and a bed, and gave me a horse and a mounted guide next day, with whom I rode twenty miles to Mr Meyer's house. The next day I had another ride, a mighty rough drive over a kind of road to the landing place; caught the *Mokolii* again, and was in Honolulu the morning after about nine, very sunburnt and rudely well. How is that for activity and rustic strength?

Grace is not invariable but (I may say) frequent; and when not forgotten is (ahem!) very well said. Joe, Lloyd and I are getting up music; guitar, taropatch, flageolet and voice for the show. Le bon Damien is to give us a choice of his comic slides; he has given us already a complete set of the life of Christ; we have a fine magic lantern. . . . Ah Foo is death on Damien, but indeed we all exceedingly like him; he reminds us of Colvin in many ways, which you know is a big word for us. . . .

Was at a school examination yesterday (girls' school); it is a plain-looking race; more pretty girls in the little box at Tautira than in all this big hall; but they sang, and recited, and played the piano, like any European school and for the singing (and the recitation too) far away better. Must dry up. Much love. — Ever afft. son,

R.L.S.

PART TWO

SECOND VOYAGE

June to December 1889

In the trading schoon *Equator*, from Honolulu, the Hawaiian capital, where Stevenson had stayed in the interval, to the Gilberts and thence to Samoa.

Schooner Equator

Passengers and crew on Equator

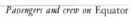

News item from *Honolulu Pacific Advertiser*
24 June 1889

Robert Louis Stevenson and party leave today by the schooner *Equator* for the Gilbert Islands. . . . It is to be hoped that Mr Stevenson will not fall victim to native spears; but in his present state of bodily health, perhaps the temptation to kill him may not be very strong.

In the South Seas: The Gilberts — Butaritari

At Honolulu we said farewell to the *Casco* and to Captain Otis, and our next adventure was made in changed conditions. Passage was taken for myself, my wife, Mr Osbourne, and my China boy, Ah Fu, on a pigmy trading schooner, the *Equator*, Captain Dennis Reid; and on a certain bright June day in 1889, adorned in the Hawaiian fashion with the garlands of departure, we drew out of port and bore with a fair wind for Micronesia.

The whole extent of the South Seas is a desert of ships; more especially that part where we were now to sail. No post runs in these islands; communication is by accident; where you may have designed to go is one thing, where you shall be able to arrive, another. It was my hope, for instance, to have reached the Carolines, and returned to the light of day by way of Manila and the China ports; and it was in Samoa that we destined to reappear and be once more refreshed with the sight of mountains. Since the sunset faded from the peaks of Oahu six months had intervened, and we had seen no spot of earth so high as an ordinary cottage. Our path had been still on the flat sea, our dwellings upon unerected coral, our diet from the pickle-tub or out of tins; I had learned to welcome shark's flesh for a variety; and a mountain, an onion, an Irish potato or a beefsteak, had been long lost to sense and dear to aspiration.

The two chief places of our stay, Butaritari and Apemama, lie near the line; the latter within thirty miles. Both enjoy a superb ocean climate, days of blinding sun and bracing wind, nights of a heavenly brightness . . . they show the customary features of an atoll; the low horizon, the expanse of the lagoon, the sedge-like rim of palm-tops, the sameness and smallness of the land, the hugely superior size and interest of sea and sky. Life on such islands is in many points like life on shipboard. The atoll, like the ship, is soon taken for granted; and the islanders, like the ship's crew, become soon the centre of attention. The isles are populous, independent, seats of kinglets, recently civilised, little visited. In the last decade many changes have crept in; women no longer go unclothed till marriage; the widow no longer sleeps at night and goes abroad by day with the skull of her dead husband; and, firearms being introduced, the spear and the shark-tooth sword are sold for curiosities. Ten years ago all these things and practises were to be seen in use; yet ten years more, and the old society will have entirely vanished. We came in a happy moment to see its institutions still erect and (in Apemama) scare decayed. . . .

Populous and independent — warrens of men, ruled over with some rustic pomp — such was the first and still the recurring impression of these tiny lands. As we stood across the lagoon for the town of Butaritari, a stretch of the low shore was seen to be crowded with the brown roofs of houses; those of the palace and the king's summer parlour (which was of corrugated iron) glittered near one end conspicuously bright; the royal colours flew hard by on a tall flagstaff; in front, on an artificial islet, the gaol played the part of a martello. Even upon this first and distant view, the place had scarce the air of what it truly was, a village; rather of that which it was also, a pretty metropolis, a city rustic and yet royal. . . .

We may thus be said to have taken Butaritari by surprise. A few inhabitants were still abroad in the north end, at which we landed. As we advanced, we were soon done with encounter, and seemed to explore a city of the dead. Only, between the posts of open houses, we could see the townsfolk stretched in the siesta, sometimes a family together veiled in a mosquito net, sometimes a single sleeper on a platform like a corpse on a bier. . . .

It was now some while since we had met any but slumberers; and when we had wandered down the pier and stumbled at last into this bright shed, we were surprised to find it occupied by a society of wakeful people, some twenty souls in all, the court and guardsmen of Butaritari. The court ladies were busy making mats; the guardsmen yawned and sprawled. Half a dozen rifles lay on a rock and a cutlass was leaned against a pillar; the armoury of these drowsy musketeers. At the far end, a little closed house of wood displayed some tinsel curtains, and proved, upon examination, to be a privy on the European model. In front of this, upon some mats, lolled Tebureimoa, the king; beside him, on the panels of the house, two crossed rifles represented fasces. He wore pyjamas which sorrowfully misbecame his bulk; his nose was hooked and cruel, his body overcome with sodden corpulence, his eye timorous and dull; he seemed at once oppressed with drowsiness and held awake by apprehension; a pepper rajah muddled with opium, and listening for the march of a Dutch army, looks perhaps not otherwise. We were to grow better acquainted, and first and last I had the same impression; he seemed always drowsy, yet always to hearken and start; and, whether from remorse or fear, there is no doubt he seeks a refuge in the abuse of drugs.

The rajah displayed no sign of interest in our coming. But the queen, who sat beside him in a purple sacque, was more accessible; and there was present an interpreter so willing that his volubility became at last the cause of our departure. He greeted us upon our entrance:

'That is the honourable King, and I am his interpreter,' he had said, with more stateliness than truth. For he held no appointment in the court, seemed extremely ill-acquainted with the island language, and was present, like ourselves, upon a visit of civility. Mr Williams was his name; an American darkey, runaway ship's cook, and barkeeper at *The Land We Live In* tavern, Butaritari. I never knew a man who had more words in his command or less truth to communicate; neither the gloom of the monarch, nor my own efforts to be distant,

Maniap of Tembinok's harem

could in the least abash him; and when the scene closed, the darkey ws left talking.

The town still slumbered, or had but just begun to turn and stretch itself; it was still plunged in heat and silence. So much the more vivid was the impression that we carried away of the house upon the islet, the Micronesian Saul wakeful amid his guards, and his unmelodious David, Mr Williams, chattering through the drowsy hours.

The Four Brothers

On the death of King Tetimararoa, Tebureimoa's father, Nakaeia, the eldest son, succeeded. He was a fellow of huge physical strength, masterful, violent, with a certain barbaric thrust and some intelligence of men and business. Alone in his islands, it was he who dealt and profited; he was the planter and the merchant; and his subjects toiled for his behoof in servitude. When they wrought long and well their taskmaster declared a holiday, and supplied and shared a general debauch. The scale of his providing was at times magnificent; six hundred dollars' worth of gin and brandy was set forth at once; the narrow land resounded with the noise of revelry; and it was a common thing to see the subjects (staggering themselves) parade their drunken sovereign on the forehatch of a wrecked vessel, king and commons howling and singing as they went. At a word from Nakaeia's mouth the revel ended; Makin became once more an isle of slaves and of teetotallers; and on the morrow all the population must be on the roads or in the taro-patches toiling under his bloodshot eye.

The fear of Nakaeia filled the land. No regularity of justice was affected; there was no trial, there were no officers of the law; it seems there was but one penalty, the capital; and daylight assault and midnight murder were the forms of process. The king himself would play the executioner; and his blows were dealt by stealth, and with the help and countenance of none but his own wives. These were his oarswomen; one that caught a crab, he slew incontinently with the tiller; thus disciplined, they pulled him by night to the scene of his vengeance, which he would then execute alone and return well pleased with his connubial crew. The inmates of the harem held a station hard for us to conceive. Beasts of draught, and driven by the fear of death, they were yet implicitly trusted with their sovereign's life; they were still wives and queens, and it was supposed that no man should behold their faces. They killed by the sight like basilisks; a chance view of one of those boatwomen was a crime to be wiped out with blood.

In the days of Nakaeia the palace was beset with some tall cocoa-palms which commanded the enclosure. It chanced one evening, while Nakaeia sat below at supper with his wives, that the owner of the grove was in a treetop drawing palm-tree wine; it chanced that he looked down, and the king at the same moment looking up, their eyes encountered. Instant flight preserved the involuntary criminal. But during the remainder of that reign he must lurk and be hid by friends in remote parts of the isle; Nakaeia hunted him without remission, although still in vain; and the palms, accessories to the fact, were ruthlessly cut down. Such was the ideal of wifely purity in an isle where nubile virgins went naked as in paradise. And yet scandal found its way into Nakaeia's well-guarded harem. He was at that time the owner of a schooner, which he used for a pleasure-house, lodging on board as she lay anchored; and thither one day he summoned a new wife. She was one that had been sealed to him; that is to say (I presume), that he was married to her sister, for the husband of an elder sister has the call of the cadets. She was to be arrayed for the occasion; she would come scented, garlanded, decked with fine mats and family jewels, for marriage, as her friends supposed; for death, as she well knew. 'Tell me the man's name, and I will spare you,' said Nakaeia. But the girl was staunch; she held her peace, saved her lover; and the queens strangled her between the mats.

Nakaeia was feared; it does not appear that he was hated. Deeds that smell to us of murder wore to his subjects the reverent face of justice; his orgies made him popular; natives to this day recall with respect the firmness of his government; and even the whites, whom he long opposed and kept at arm's length, give him the name (in the canonical South Sea phrase) of 'a perfect gentleman when sober'.

When he came to lie, without issue, on the bed of death, he summoned his next brother, Nanteitei, made him a discourse on royal policy, and warned him he was too weak to reign. The warning was taken to heart, and for some while the government moved on the model of Nakaeia's. Nanteitei dispensed with guards and walked abroad alone with a revolver in a leather mailbag. To conceal his weakness he affected a rude silence; you might talk to him all day; advice, reproof, appeal, and menace alike remained unanswered. The number of his wives was seventeen, many of them heiresses; for the royal house is poor, and marriage was in these days a chief means of buttressing the throne. Nakaeia kept his harem busy for himself; Nanteitei hired it out to others. In his days, for instance, Messrs. Wightman built a pier with a verandah at the north end of the town. The masonry was the work of the seventeen queens, who toiled and waded there like fisher lasses; but the man who was to do the roofing durst not begin till they had finished, lest by chance he should look down and see them.

It was perhaps the last appearance of the harem gang. For some time already Hawaiian missionaries had been seated at Butaritari — Maka and Kanoa, two brave childlike men. Nakaeia would have none of their doctrine; he was perhaps jealous of their presence; being human, he had some affection for the persons. In the house, before the eyes of Kanoa, he slew with his own hand three sailors of Oahu, crouching on their backs to knife them, and menacing the missionary if he interfered; yet he not only spared him at the moment, but recalled him afterwards (when he had fled) with some expressions of respect. Nanteitei, the weaker man, fell more completely under the spell. Maka, a lighthearted, lovable, yet in his own trade very rigorous man — gained and improved an influence on the king which

Fanny and Louis Stevenson with Nan Tok' and Nei Takauti

Island Speak House: Interior and Exterior

soon grew paramount. Nanteitei, with the royal house, was publicly converted; and, with a severity which liberal missionaries disavow, the harem was at once reduced. It was a compendium act. The throne was thus impoverished, its influence shaken, the queens' relatives mortified, and sixteen chief women (some of them great possessions) cast in a body on the market. I have been shipmates with a Hawaiian sailor who was successively married to two of these *impromptu* widows, and successively divorced by both for misconduct. That two great and rich ladies (for both of these were rich) should have married 'a man from another island' marks the dissolution of society. The laws besides were wholly remodelled, not always for the better. I love Maka as a man; as a legislator he has two defects: weak in the punishment of crime, stern to repress innocent pleasures.

War and revolution are the common successors of reform; yet Nanteitei died (of an overdose of chloroform) in quiet possession of the throne, and it was in the reign of the third brother, Nabakatokai, a man brave in body and feeble of character, that the storm burst. About this period, in almost every part of the group, the kings were murdered . . . Nabakatokai was more fortunate, his life and the royal style were spared him, but he was stripped of power. . . . He died some months before my arrival in the islands and no one regretted him; rather all looked hopefully to his successor. This was by repute the hero of the family. Alone of the four brothers, he had issue, a grown son, Natiata, and a daughter three years old. Natemat', *Mr Corpse*, was his appalling nickname, and he had earned it well. Again and again, at the command of Nakaeia, he had surrounded houses in the dead of night, cut down the mosquito bars and butchered families . . . he was installed, he proved a puppet and a trembler, the unwieldy shuttlecock of orators; and the reader has seen the remains of him in his summer parlour under the name of Tebureimoa.

The change in the man's character was much commented on in the island, and variously explained by opium and Christianity. To my eyes, there seemed no change at all, rather an extreme consistency. Mr Corpse was afraid of his brother; King Tebureimoa is afraid of the Old Men. Terror of the first nerved him for deeds of desperation; fear of the second disables him for the least act of government. He played his part of bravo in the past, following the line of least resistance, butchering others in his own defence: today, grown elderly and heavy, a convert, a reader of the Bible, perhaps a penitent, conscious at least of accumulated hatreds, and his memory charged with images of violence and blood, he capitulates to the Old Men, fuddles himself with opium, and sits among his guards in dreadful expectation. The same cowardice that put into his hand the knife of the assassin deprives him of the sceptre of a king. . . .

The justice of facts is strange, and strangely just; Nakaeia, the author of these deeds, died at peace discoursing on the craft of kings; his tool suffers daily death for his enforced complicity. Not the nature, but the congruity of men's deeds and circumstances damn and save them; and Tebureimoa from the first has been incongruously placed. At home, in a quiet by-street of a village, the man had been a worthy carpenter, and, even bedevilled as he is, he shows some private virtues. He has no lands, only the use of such as are impignorate for fines, he cannot enrich himself in the old way by marriages; thrift is the chief pillar of his future, and he knows and uses it. Eleven foreign traders pay him a patent of a hundred dollars, some two thousand subjects pay capitation at the rate of a dollar for a man, half a dollar for a woman, and a shilling for a child: allowing for the exchange, perhaps a total of three hundred pounds a year. He had been some nine months on the throne: had bought his wife a silk dress and hat, figure unknown, and himself a uniform at three hundred dollars; had sent his brother's photograph to be enlarged in San Francisco at two hundred and fifty dollars; had greatly reduced that brother's legacy of debt; and had still sovereigns in his pocket. An affectionate brother, a good economist; he was besides a handy carpenter, and cobbled occasionally on the woodwork of the palace. It is not wonderful that Mr Corpse has virtues; that Tebureimoa should have a diversion filled me with surprise.

Around our house

The men are of a marked Arabian cast of features, often bearded and mustached, often gaily dressed, some with bracelets and anklets all stalking hidalgo-like, and accepting salutations with a haughty lip. The hair (with the dandies of either sex) is worn turban-wise in a frizzled bush; and like the daggers of the Japanese, a pointed stock (used for a comb) is thrust gallantly among the curls. The women from this bush of hair look forth enticingly: the race cannot be compared with the Tahitian for female beauty; I doubt if the average be high; but some of the prettiest girls, and one of the handsomest women I ever saw, were Gilbertines. Butaritari, being the commercial centre of the group, is Europeanised; the coloured sacque or the white shift are common wear, the latter for the evening; the trade hat, loaded with flowers, fruit and ribbons, is unfortunately not unknown; and the characteristic female dress of the Gilberts no longer universal. The *ridi* is its name: a cutty petticoat or fringe of the smoked fibre of cocoa-nut leaf, not unlike tarry string; the lower edge not reaching the mid-thigh, the upper adjusted so low upon the haunches that it seems to cling by accident. A sneeze, you think, and the lady must surely be left destitute. 'The perilous, hairbreadth *ridi*'. . . . Yet if a pretty Gilbertiner would look her best, that must be her costume. In that, and naked otherwise, she moved with an incomparable liberty and grace and life, that marks the poetry of Micronesia. Bundle her in a gown, the charm is fled, and she wriggles like an English woman.

A tale of a tapu

On the morrow of our arrival (Sunday, 14th July 1889) our photographers were early stirring. . . . A few children followed us, mostly nude, all silent; in the clear, weedy waters of the canal some silent damsels waded, baring their brown thighs; .

Gilbert Islands dancers

. . and to one of the maniap's before the palace gate we were attracted by a low but stirring hum of speech.

The oval shed was full of men sitting cross-legged. The king was there in striped pyjamas, his rear protected by four guards with Winchesters, his air and bearing marked by unwonted spirit and decision; tumblers and black bottles went the round. . . . But the hour appeared unsuitable for a carouse; drink was besides forbidden equally by the law of the land and the canons of the church. . . . We had come, thinking to photograph him surrounded by his guard, and at the first word of the design his piety revolted. We were reminded of the day — the Sabbath — in which thou shalt take no photographs — and returned with a flea in our ear, bearing the rejected camera.

At church, a little later, I was struck to find the throne unoccupied. So nice a Sabbatarian might have found the means to be present. . . . Tom, bar-keeper at the *Sans Souci*, was in conversation with two emissaries from the court. The king, they said, wanted gin, failing which, brandy. No gin, was Tom's reply, and no brandy, but beer, if they pleased. It seems they had no use for beer, and departed sorrowing.

'Is the island on the spree?' I asked.

Such was the fact. On the 4th of July a feast had been made, and the king, at the suggestion of the whites, had raised the tapu against liquor. There is a proverb

Missionary and converts

about horses; it scarce applies to the superior animal of whom it may be rather said, that any one can start him drinking, not any twenty can prevail upon him to stop. The tapu was not yet reimposed; for ten days the town had been passing the bottle or lying in hoggish sleep; and the king, moved by the Old Men and his own appetites, continued to maintain the liberty, to squander his savings on liquor, and to join in and lead the debauch. The whites were the authors of the crisis . . . in the interests of trade, they were doubtless pleased it should continue. . . .

The conduct of drunkards even at home is always matter for anxiety; and at home our populations are not armed from the highest to the lowest with revolvers and repeating rifles, neither do we go on a debauch by the whole townful —kings, magistrates, police, and army joining in one common scene of drunkenness . . . we were here in barbarous islands, rarely visited, lately and partly civilised. First and last, a really considerable number of whites have perished in the Gilberts, chiefly through their own misconduct . . . this was the chief consideration against the sudden closing of the bars; the bar-keepers stood in the immediate breach and dealt direct with madmen; too surly a refusal might at any moment precipitate a blow, and the blow might prove the signal for massacre.

Monday, 15th — At the same hour we returned to the same maniap'. Kummel (of all drinks) was served in tumblers; in the midst sat the crown prince, a fatted youth, surrounded by fresh bottles and busily plying the corkscrew; and king, chief, and commons showed the loose mouth, the uncertain joints, and the blurred and animated eye of the early drinker. It was plain we were impatiently expected; the king retired with alacrity to dress, the guards were despatched after their uniforms; as we were left to await the issue of these preparations with a shedful of tipsy natives. The orgie had proceeded further than on Sunday. The day promised to be of great heat; it was already sultry, the courtiers were already fuddled; and still the kummel continued to go round, and the crown prince to play butler . . . and a funny dog, a handsome fellow, gaily dressed, and with a full turban of frizzed hair, delighted the company with a humorous courtship of a lady in a manner not to be described. It was our diversion, in this time of waiting, to observe the gathering of the guards. They have European arms, European uniforms, and (to their sorrow) European shoes. We saw one warrior (like Mars) in the article of being armed; two men and a stalwart woman were scarce enough to boot him; and after a single appearance on parade the army is crippled for a week.

At last, the gates under the king's house opened; the army issued, one behind another, with guns and epaulettes; the colours stooped under the gateway; majesty followed in his uniform bedizened with gold lace; majesty's wife came next in a hat and feathers, and an ample trained silk gown; the royal imps succeeded; there stood the pageantry of Makin marshalled on its chosen theatre. Dickens might have told how serious they were; how tipsy; how the king melted and streamed under his cocked hat; how he took station by the larger of his two cannons — austere, majestic, but not truly vertical; how the troops huddled, and were straightened out, and clubbed again; how they and their firelocks raked at various inclinations like the masts of ships; and how an amateur photographer reviewed, arrayed, and adjusted them, to see his dispositions change before he reached the camera . . . and we had one more sight of Gilbert Island violence. In the church where we had wandered photographing, we were startled by a sudden piercing outcry. The scene, looking forth from the doors of that great hall of shadow, was unforgettable. The palms, the quaint and scattered houses, the flag of the island streaming from its tall staff, glowed with intolerable sunshine. It the midst two women rolled fighting on the grass. The combatants were the more easy to be distinguished, because the one was stripped to the *ridi* and the other wore a *holoku* of some lively colour. The first was uppermost, her teeth locked in her adversary's face, shaking her like a dog; the other impotently fought and scratched. For a moment we saw them wallow and grapple there like vermin; then the mob closed and shut them in.

It was a serious question that night if we should sleep ashore. But we were travellers, folk that had come far in quest of the adventurous; on the first sign of an adventure it would have been a singular inconsistency to have withdrawn; and we sent on board instead for our revolvers. Mindful of Taahauku, Mr Rick, Mr Osbourne and Mrs Stevenson held an assault of arms on the public highway and fired at bottles to the admiration of the natives. Captain Reid stayed on shore with us to be at hand in case of trouble, and we retired to bed at the accustomed hour, agreeably excited by the day's events. The night was exquisite, the silence enchanting; yet as I lay in my hammock looking on the strong moonshine and the quiescent palms, one ugly picture haunted me of the two women, the naked and the clad, locked in that hostile embrace. The harm done was probably not much, yet I could have looked on death and massacre with less revolt. The return to these primeval weapons, the vision of man's beastliness, of his ferality, shocked in me a deeper sense than that with which we count the cost of battles. There are elements in our state and history which it is a pleasure to forget, which it is perhaps the better wisdom not to dwell on. Crime, pestilence, and death are in the day's work; the imagination readily accepts them. It instinctively rejects, on the contrary, whatever shall call up the image of our race upon its lowest terms, as the partner of beasts, beastly itself, dwelling pell-mell and hugger-mugger, hairy man with hairy woman, in the caves of old. And yet to be just to barbarous islanders we must not forget the slums and dens of our cities: I must not forget that I have passed dinnerward through Soho, and seen that which cured me of my dinner.

Tuesday, July 16. — It rained in the night, sudden and loud, in Gilbert Island fashion. . . . Through the desert streets, and past the sleeping houses, a deputation took its way at an early hour to the palace . . . . Mrs Rick (the only white woman on the island) being a sufficient mistress of that difficult tongue, was spokeswoman; she explained to the sick monarch that I was an intimate personal friend of Queen Victoria's; that immediately on my return I should make her a report upon Butaritari; and that if my house should have been again invaded by natives, a man-of-war would be despatched to make reprisals. It was scarce the fact — rather a just and necessary parable of the fact, corrected for latitude; and it certainly told upon the king. He was much affected . . . and the missionary house was tapu'd under a fine of fifty dollars. . . . The protection gained was welcome. It had been the most annoying and not the least alarming feature of the day before, that our house was periodically filled with tipsy natives, twenty or thirty at a time, begging drink, fingering our goods, hard to be dislodged, awkward to quarrel with. Queen Victoria's friend (who was soon promoted to be her son) was free from these intrusions . . . even on our walks abroad we were guarded and prepared for; and, like great persons visiting a hospital, saw only the fair side. . . .

Hula Dancers

Wednesday, July 24. — . . . Whether the Old Men recoiled from an interview with Queen Victoria's son, or whether the step flowed naturally from the fears of the king, the tapu was early that morning re-enforced; not a day too soon, from the manner the boats began to arrive thickly, and the town was filled with the big rowdy vassals of Karaiti. The effect lingered for some time on the minds of the traders; it was with the approval of all present that I helped to draw up a petition to the United States, praying for a law against the liquor trade in the Gilberts; and it was at this request that I added, under my own name, a brief testimony of what had passed — useless pains, since the whole reposes, probably unread and possibly unopened, in a pigeon-hole at Washington.

The Five Days Festival

Thursday, Juy 25. — Of all so-called dancing in the South Seas, that which I saw in Butaritari stand easily the first. The *bula*, as it may be viewed by the speedy globetrotter in Honolulu, is surely the most dull of man's inventions, and the spectator yawns under its length as at a college lecturer or a parliamentary debate. But the Gilbert Island dance leads on the mind; it thrills, rouses, subjugates; it has the essence of all art . . . here is a page from my wife's diary, which proves that I was not alone in being moved. . . . 'The conductor gave the cue, and all the dancers, waving their arms, swaying their bodies, and clapping their breasts in perfect time, opened with an introductory. The performers remained seated, except two, and once three, a twice and twice a single soloist. These stood in a group making a slight movement with the feet and rhythmical quiver of the body as they sang. . . . The leading man, in an impassioned ecstasy which possessed him from head to foot, seemed transfigured; once it was as though a strong wind swept over the stage — their arms, their feathered fingers thrilling with an emotion that shook my nerves as well: heads and bodies followed like a field of grain before a gust. My blood came hot and cold, tears prickled my eyes, my head whirled, I felt an almost irresistible impulse to join the dancers. . . .'

Saturday, July 27. — We had announced a performance of the magic lantern tonight in church; and this brought the king to visit us. In honour of the Black Douglas (I suppose) his usual two guardsmen were now increased to four; and the squad made an outlandish figure as they straggled after him, in straw hats, kilts and jackets. Three carried their arms reversed, the butts over their shoulders, the muzzles menacing the king's plump back; the fourth passed his weapon behind his back, and held it there with arms extended like a backboard. The visit was extraordinary long. The king, no longer galvanised with gin, said and did nothing. He sat collapsed in a chair and let a cigar go out. It was hot, it was sleepy, it was cruel dull; there was no resource but to spy in the countenance of Tebureimoa for some remainder trait of *Mr. Corpse* the butcher. His hawk nose, crudely depressed and flattened at the point, did not truly seem to us to smell of midnight murder. . . .

While the magic lantern was showing, I skulked without in the dark. The

Missionaries Maka, Marymaka, Kanoa and Mrs Kanoa

voice of Maka (the missionary) excitedly explaining the Scripture slides, seemed to fill not the church only, but the neighbourhood . . . . a distant sound of singing arose and approached; a procession drew along the road, the hot clean smell of the men and women striking in my face delightfully. At the corner, arrested by the voice of Maka and the lightening and darkening of the church, they paused. They had no mind to go nearer, that was plain . . . staunch heathens, contemners of the missionary and his works. Of a sudden, however, a man broke from their company, took to his heels, and fled into the church; next moment three had followed him; the next it was a covey of near upon a score, all pelting for their lives. So the little band of the heathen paused irresolute at the corner, and melted before the attractions of a magic lantern, like a glacier in spring. The more staunch vainly taunted the deserters; three fled in a guilty silence, but still fled; and when at length the leader found the wit or the authority to get his troop in motion and revive the singing, it was with much diminished forces that they passed musically on up the dark road.

Meanwhile inside the luminous pictures brightened and faded. I stood for some while unobserved in the rear of the spectators when I could hear just in front of me a pair of lovers following the show with interest, the male playing the part of interpreter and (like Adam) mingling caresses with his lecture. The wild animals, a tiger in particular, and that old school-treat favourite, the sleeper and the mouse, were hailed with joy; but the chief marvel and delight was in the gospel series. Maka, in the opinion of his aggrieved wife, did not properly rise to the occasion. 'What is the matter with the man? Why can't he talk?' she cried. The matter with the man, I think, was the greatness of the opportunity; he reeled under his good fortune, and whether he did ill or well, the exposure of these pious 'phantoms' did as a matter of fact silence in all that part of the island the voice of the scoffer. 'Why then,' the word went round, 'why then, the Bible is true!' And on our return afterwards we were told the impression was yet lively, and those who had seen might be heard telling those who had not, 'O yes, it is all true; these things all happened, we have seen the pictures.' The argument is not so childish as it seems; for I doubt if these islanders are acquainted with any other mode of representation but photography; so that the picture of an event (on the old melodrama principle that 'the camera cannot lie, Joseph,') would appear strong proof of its occurrence. The fact amused us the more because our slides were some of them ludicrously silly, and one (Christ before Pilate) was received with shouts of merriment, in which even Maka was constrained to join. . . .

Sunday, July 28 (From *A Tale of Tapu*). — This day we had the afterpiece of the debauch. The king and queen, in European clothes, and followed by armed guards, attended church for the first time, and sat perched aloft in a precarious dignity under the barrel-hoops. Before the sermon His Majesty clambered from the dais, stood lopsidedly upon the gravel floor, and in a few words abjured drinking. The queen followed suit with a yet briefer allocution. All the men in church were next addressed in turn; each held up his right hand, and the affair was over — throne and church were reconciled.

Monday, July 29 (From *The Five Days' Festival*). — . . . The last stage and glory of this auspicious day was of our own providing — the second and positively the last appearance of the 'phantoms' — this was the accepted word — All round the church, groups sat outside, in the night, where they could see nothing; perhaps ashamed to enter, certainly finding some shadowy pleasure in the mere proximity. Within, about one-half of the great shed was densely packed with people. In the midst, on the royal dais, the lantern luminously smoked; . . . the pictures shone and vanished on the screen; and as each appeared there would run a hush, a whisper, a strong shuddering rustle, and a chorus of small cries among the crowd. There sat by me the mate of a wrecked schooner. 'They would think this a strange sight in Europe or the States,' said he, 'going on in a building like this, all tied with bits of string.'

Letter to Sidney Colvin
Schooner 'Equator', Apaiang lagoon, August 22nd, 1889

My dear Colvin, — . . . I am glad to say I shall be home by June next for the summer, or we shall know the reason why. For God's sake be well and jolly for the meeting. I shall be, I believe, a different character from what you have seen this long while. This cruise is up to now a huge success, being interesting, pleasant and profitable. The beachcomber is perhaps the most interesting character here; the natives are very different, on the whole, from Polynesians: they are moral, stand-offish (for good reasons), and protected by a dark tongue. It is delightful to meet the few Hawaiians (mostly missionaries) that are dotted about, with their Italian *brio* and their ready friendliness. The whites are a strange lot, many of them good, kind, pleasant fellows; others quite the lowest I have ever seen in the slums of cities. I wish I had time to narrate to you the doings and character of three white murderers (more or less proven) I have met. One, the only undoubted assassin of the lot, quite gained my affection in his big home out of a wreck, with his New Hebrides wife in her savage turban of hair and yet a perfect lady, and his three adorable little girls in Rob Roy Macgregor dresses, dancing to the hand organ, performing circus on the floor with startling effects of nudity, and curling up together on a mat to sleep, three sizes, three attitudes, three Rob Roy dresses, and six little clenched fists: the murderer meanwhile brooding and gloating over his chicks, till your whole heart went out to him; and yet his crime on the face of it was dark; disembowelling, in his own house, an old man of seventy, and him drunk. It is lunchtime, I see, and I must close with warmest love to you. I wish you were here to sit upon me when required. I will never leave the sea, I think; it is only there that a Briton lives: my poor grandfather, it is from him I inherit the taste, I fancy, and he was round many islands in his day: would you be surprised to learn that I contemplate becoming a ship-owner? I do, but it is a secret. Life is far

King Tembinok and party leaving Equator

better fun than people dream who fall asleep among the chimney stacks and telegraph wires.

Love to Henry James and others near. Ever yours, my dear fellow,

ROBERT LOUIS STEVENSON.

Husband and wife

The trader accustomed to the manners of Eastern Polynesia has a lesson to learn among the Gilberts. The *ridi* is but a spare attire; as late as thirty years back the women went naked until marriage; within ten years the custom lingered; and these facts, above all when heard in description, conveyed a very false idea of the manners of the group. A very intelligent missionary described it as a 'Paradise of naked women' for the resident whites. It was at least a platonic Paradise, where Lothario ventured at his peril. Since 1860, fourteen whites have perished on a single island, all for the same cause, all found where they had no business, and speared by some indignant father of a family; the figure was given me by one of their contemporaries who had been more prudent and survived. The strange persistence of these fourteen martyrs might seem to point to monomania or a series of romantic passions; gin is the more likely key. The poor buzzards sat alone in their houses by an open case; they drank; their brain was fired; they stumbled towards the nearest houses on chance; and the dart went through their liver. In place of a Paradise the trader found an archipelago of fierce husbands and of virtuous women. 'Of course if you wish to make love to them, it's the same as anywhere else,' observed a trader innocently; but he and his companion rarely so choose.

The trader must be credited with a virtue: he often makes a kind and loyal husband. Some of the worst beachcombers in the Pacific, some of the last of the old school, have fallen in my path, and some of them were admirable to their native wives, and one made a despairing widower. . . . All these women were legitimately married. It is true that the certificate of one, when she proudly showed it, proved to run thus, that she was 'married for one night', and her gracious partner was at liberty to 'send her to hell' the next morning; but she was none the wiser or the worse for the dastardly trick.* Another, I heard, was married on a work of mine in a pirated edition; it answered the purpose as well as a Hall Bible. . . . Ten or twenty years ago it was a capital offence to raise a woman's *ridi*; to this day it is still punished with a heavy fine; and the garment itself is symbolically sacred. Suppose a piece of land to be disputed in Butaritari, the claimant who shall first hang a *ridi* on the tapu-post has gained his cause, since no one can remove or touch it but himself. The *ridi* was the badge not of the woman but the wife, the mark not of her sex but of her station. It was the collar on the slave's neck, the brand on merchandise.

Polygamy, the particular sacredness of wives, their semi-servile state, their seclusion in kings' harems, even their privilege of biting, all would seem to indicate a Mohammedan society and the opinion of the soullessness of woman. And not so in the least. It is mere appearance. After you have studied these extremes in one house, you may go to the next and find all reversed, the woman the mistress, the man only the first of her thalls. . . . There is but the one source of power and the one ground of dignity — rank. The king married a chief-woman; she became his menial and must work with her hands on Messrs. Wightmans pier. The king divorced her; she regained at once her former state and power. She married the Hawaiian sailor, and behold the man is her flunkey and can be shown the door at pleasure. Nay, and such low-born lords are even corrected physically, and, like grown but dutiful children, must endure the discipline.

We were intimate in one such household, that of Nei Takauti and Nan Tok'; I put the lady first of necessity. Nan Tok', the husband, was young, extremely handsome, of the most approved good humour, and suffering in his precarious station from suppressed high spirits. Nei Takauti, the wife, was getting old; her grown-up son by a former marriage had just hanged himself before his mother's eyes in despair at a well-merited rebuke. Perhaps she had never been beautiful, but her face was full of character, her eyes of sombre fire. She was a high chief-woman, but by a strange exception for a person of her rank, was small, spare, and

*[Theme of *The Beach of Falesa*]

sinewy, with lean small hands and corded neck. Her full dress of an evening was invariably a white chemise — and for adornment, green leaves (or sometimes white blossoms) stuck in her hair and thrust through her huge earring-holes. The husband on the contrary changed to view like a kaleidoscope. Whatever pretty thing my wife might have given to Nei Takauti — a string of beads, a ribbon, a piece of bright fabric — appeared the next evening on the person of Nan Tok'. It was plain he was a clothes-horse; that he wore livery; that, in a word, he was his wife's wife. They reversed the parts indeed, down to the last particular; it was the husband who showed himself the ministering angel in the hour of pain, while the wife displayed the apathy and heartlessness of the proverbial man.

When Nei Takauti had a headache Nan Tok' was full of attention and concern. When the husband had a cold and a racking toothache the wife heeded not, except to jeer. It was always the woman's part to fill and light the pipe; Nei Takauti handed hers in silence to the wedded page; but she carried it herself, as though the page were not entirely trusted. Thus she kept the money, but it was he who ran the errands, anxiously sedulous. A cloud on her face dimmed instantly his beaming looks; on an early visit to their maniap' my wife saw he had cause to be wary. Nan Tok' had a friend with him, a giddy young thing, of his own age and sex; and they had worked themselves into that stage of jocularity when consequences are too often disregarded. Nei Takauti mentioned her own name. Instantly Nan Tok' held up two fingers, his friend did likewise, both in an ecstasy of slyness. It was plain the lady had two names; and from the nature of their merriment and the wrath that gathered on her brow, there must be something

Nan Tok' and Nei Takauti 'at home'

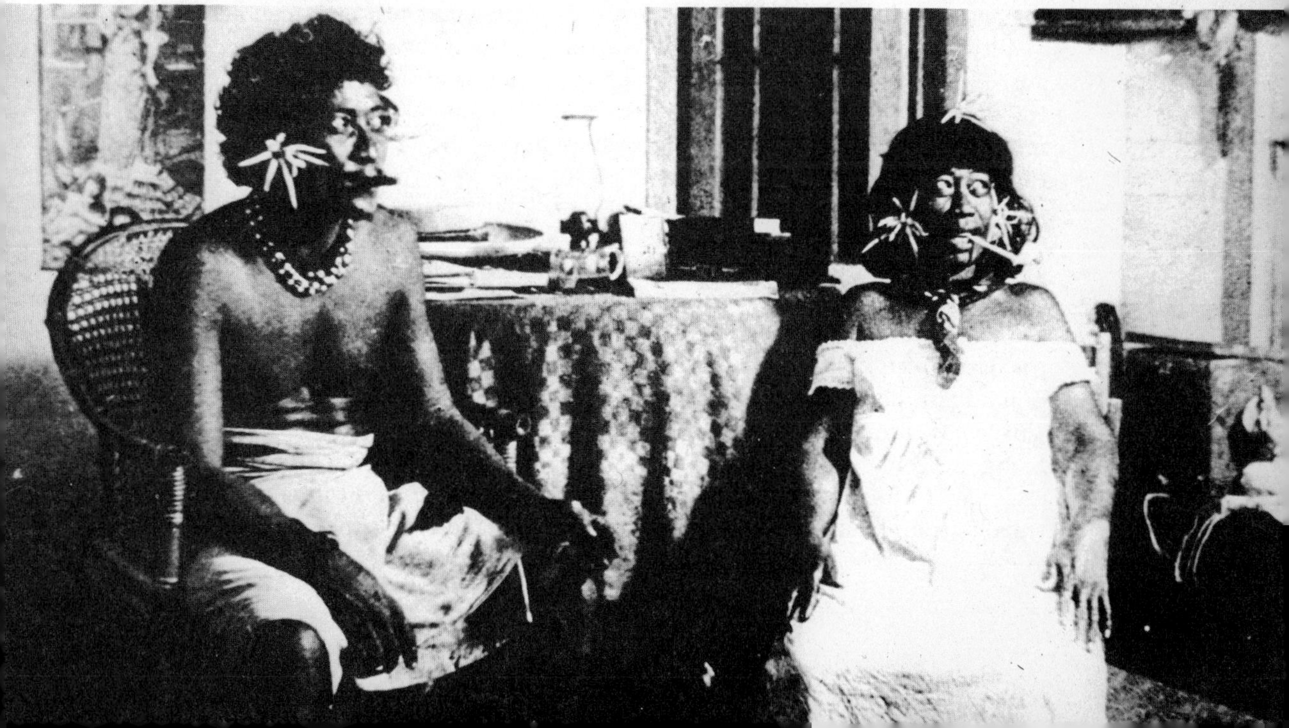

ticklish in the second. The husband pronounced it; a well-directed cocoa-nut from the hand of his wife caught him on the side of the head, and the voices and the mirth of these indiscreet young gentlemen ceased for the day. . . . We had once supplied them during a visit with a pipe and tobacco; and when they had smoked and were about to leave, they found themselves confronted with a problem: should they take or leave what remained of the tobacco. The piece of plug was taken up, it was laid down again, it was handed back and forth, and argued over, till the wife began to look haggard and the husband elderly. They ended by taking it, and I wager were not clear of the compound before they were sure they had decided wrong. Another time they had been given each a liberal cup of coffee, and Nan Tok' with difficulty and disaffection made an end of his. Nei Takauti had taken some, she had no mind for more, plainly conceived it would be a breach of manners to set down the cup unfinished, and ordered her wedded retainer to dispose of what was left. 'I have swallowed all I can, I cannot swallow more, it is a physical impossibility,' he seemed to say; and his stern officer reiterated her commands with secret imperative signals. Luckless dog! but in mere humanity we came to the rescue and removed the cup.

I cannot but smile over this funny household; yet I remember the good souls with affection and respect. Their attention to ourselves was surprising. The garlands are much esteemed, the blossoms must be sought far and wide; and though they had many retainers to call to their aid, we often saw themselves passing afield after the blossoms, and the wife engaged with her own hands in putting them together. It was no want of heart, only that disregard so incident to husbands, that made Nei Takauti despise the sufferings of Nan Tok'. When my wife was unwell she proved a diligent and kindly nurse; and the pair, to the extreme embarrassment of the sufferer, became fixtures in the sick-room. This rugged, capable, imperious old dame, with the wild eyes, had deep and tender qualities. Her pride in her young husband it seemed that she dissembled, fearing possibly to spoil him; and when she spoke of her dead son there came something tragic in her face. But I seemed to trace in the Gilbertines a virility of sense and sentiment which distinguishes them (like their harsh and uncouth language) from their brother islanders in the east.

The King of Apemama

There is only one great personage in the Gilberts: Tembinok' of Apemama; solely conspicuous, the hero of song, the butt of gossip. Through the rest of the group the kings are slain or fallen in tutelage: Tembinok' alone remains, the last tyrant, the last erect vestige of a dead society. The white man is everywhere else, building his houses, drinking his gin, getting in and out of trouble with the weak native governments. There is only one white on Apemama, and he on sufferance, living far from court, and hearkening and watching his conduct like a mouse in a cat's ear. Through all the other islands a stream of native visitors comes and goes, travelling by families, spending years on the grand tour. Apemama alone is left

Fanny and Louis Stevenson on bridge of Equator

upon the side, the tourist dreading to risk himself within the clutch of Tembinok'.

. . . We were scarce yet moored, however, before distant and busy figures appeared upon the beach, a boat was launched and a crew pulled out to us bringing the king's ladder. Tembinok' had once an accident; has feared ever since to intrust his person to the rotten chandlery of South Seas traders; and devised in consequence a frame of wood, which is brought on board a ship as soon as she appears, and remains lashed to her side until she leaves. . . . Not long ago he was overgrown with fat, obscured to view, and a burthen to himself. Captains visiting the island advised him to walk; and though it broke the habits of a life and the traditions of his rank, he practised the remedy with benefit. His corpulence is now portable; you would call him lusty rather than fat; but his gait is still dull, stumbling and elephantine. He neither stops nor hastens, but goes about his business with an implacable deliberation. We could never see him and not be struck with his extraordinary natural means for the theatre: a beaked profile like Dante's in the mask, a mane of long black hair, the eye brilliant, imperious and inquiring: for certain parts, and to one who could have used it, the face was a fortune. His voice matched it well, being shrill, powerful, and uncanny, with a note like a seabird's. Where there were no fashions, none to set them, few to follow them if they were set, and none to criticise, he dressed — as Sir Charles Grandison lived — 'to his own heart'. Now he wears a woman's frock, now a naval uniform; now (and more usually) figures in a masquerade costume of his own design; trousers and a singular jacket with shirt-tails, the cut and fit wonderful for island workmanship, the material always handsome, sometimes green velvet, sometimes cardinal red silk. This masquerade becomes him admirably. In the woman's frock he looks ominous and weird beyond belief. I see him now come pacing towards me in the cruel sun, solitary, a figure out of Hoffman.

A visit on board ship, such as that at which we were now assisted, makes a chief part and by far the chief diversion of the life of Tembinok'. He is not only the sole ruler, he is the sole merchant of his triple kingdom. . . . If he be pleased with his welcome and the fare he may pass days on board, and every day, and sometimes every hour, will be of profit to the ship. He oscillates between the cabin, where he is entertained with strange meats, and the trade-room, where he enjoys the pleasures of shopping on a scale to match his person. A few obsequious attendants squat by the house door, awaiting his least signal. In the boat, which has been suffered to drop astern, one or two of his wives lie covered from the sun under mats, tossed by the short sea of the lagoon, and enduring agonies of heat and tedium. This severity is now and then relaxed and the wives allowed on board. Three or four were thus favoured on the day of our arrival; substantial ladies airily attired in *ridis*. Each had a share of copra, her *peculium*, to dispose of for herself. The display in the trade-room — hats, ribbons, dresses, scents, tins of salmon — the pride of the eye and the lust of the flesh — tempted them in vain. They had but one idea — tobacco, the island currency, tantamount to minted gold; returned to shore with it, burthened but rejoicing; and late into the night, on the royal terrace, were to be seen counting the sticks by lamplight in the open air.

The king is no such economist. He is greedy of things new and foreign. House after house, chest after chest, in the palace precinct, is already crammed with clocks, musical boxes, blue spectacles, umbrellas, knitted waistcoats, bolts of stuff, tools, rifles, fowling-pieces, medicines, European foods, sewing-machines, and, what is more extraordinary, stoves: all that ever caught his eye, tickled his appetite, pleased him for its use, or puzzled him with its apparent inutility. And still his lust is unabated. He is possessed by the seven devils of the collector. He hears a thing spoken of, and a shadow comes on his face. 'I think I no got him,' he will say; and the treasures he has seem worthless in comparison. If a ship be bound for Apemama, the merchant racks his brain to hit upon some novelty. This he leaves carelessly in the main cabin or partly conceals in his own berth, so that the king shall spy it for himself. 'How much you want?' inquires Tembinok', passing and pointing. 'No, king; that too dear,' returns the trader. 'I think I like him,' says the king. This was a bowl of goldfish. On another occasion it was scented soap. 'No, king; that cost too much,' said the trader; 'too good for a Kanaka.' 'How much you got? I take him all,' replied his majesty, and became the lord of seventeen boxes at two dollars a cake. Or again, the merchant feigns the article is not for sale, is private property, an heirloom or a gift; and the trick infallibly succeeds. Thwart the king and you hold him. His autocratic nature rears at the affront of opposition. He accepts it for a challenge; sets his teeth like a hunter going at a fence; and with no mark of emotion, scarce even of interest, stolidly piles up the price. Thus, for our sins, he took a fancy to my wife's dressing-bag, a thing entirely useless to the man, and sadly battered by years of service. Early one forenoon, he came to our house, sat down, and abruptly offered to purchase it. I told him I sold nothing, and the bag at any rate was a present from a friend; but he was acquainted with these pretexts from of old, and knew what they were worth and how to meet them. He drew out a bag of English gold, sovereigns and half-sovereigns, and began to lay them one by one in silence on the table; at each fresh piece reading our faces with a look. In vain I continued to protest I was no trader; he deigned not to reply. There must have been twenty pounds on the table, he was still going on, and irritation had begun to mingle with our embarrassment, when a happy idea came to our delivery. Since his majesty thought so much of the bag, we said, we must beg him to accept it as a present. It was the most surprising turn in Tembinok's experience. He perceived too late that his persistence was unmannerly, hung his head a while in silence: then, lifting up a sheepish countenance, 'I 'shamed,' said the tyrant. It was the first and last time we heard him own to a flaw in his behaviour. Half an hour after he sent us a camphor-wood chest, worth only a few dollars — but then heaven knows what Tembinok' had paid for it. . . .

* * * *

The palace, or rather the ground which it includes, is several acres in extent. . . . There is no parade of guards, soldiers, or weapons; the armoury is under lock and key; and the only sentinels are certain inconspicuous old women lurking day and night before the gates. By day, these crones were often engaged in boiling syrup or the like household occupation; by night, they lay ambushed in the shadow or crouched along the palisade, filling the office of eunuchs to this harem, sole guards upon a tyrant life.

Female wardens made a fit outpost for this palace of many women. Of the number of the king's wives I have no guess; and but a loose idea of their function. He himself displayed embarrassment when they were referred to as his wives, called them himself 'my pamily' and explained they were his 'cutcheons'—cousins. We distinguished four of the crowd: the king's mother; his sister, a grave, trenchant woman, with much of her brother's intelligence; the queen proper, to whom (and to whom alone) my wife was formally presented; and the favourite of the hour, a pretty graceful girl, who sat with the king daily, and once (when he shed tears) consoled him with caresses. In the background figured a multitude of ladies, the lean, the plump, and the elephantine, some in sacque frocks, some in the hairbreadth *ridi*; high born and low, slave and mistress; from the queen to the scullion, from the favourite to the scraggy sentries at the palisade. . . . They were key-bearers, treasurers, wardens of the armoury, the napery, and the stores. Each knew and did her part to admiration. Should anything be required — a particular gun perhaps, or a particular bolt of stuff — the right queen was summoned; she came bringing the right chest, opened it in the king's presence, and displayed her charge in perfect preservation — the gun cleaned and oiled, the goods duly folded. Without delay or haste, and with the minimum of speech, the whole great establishment turned on wheels like a machine. Nowhere have I seen order more complete and pervasive. . . . Should one out of many prove faithless, should the armoury be secretly unlocked, should the crones have dozed by the palisade and the weapons find their way unseen into the village, revolution would be nearly certain, death the most probable result. Yet those whom he so trusts are all women, and all rivals.

I conceived they made rather a hero of the man. A popular master in a girls' school might, perhaps, offer a figure of his prepondering station. But then the master does not eat, sleep, live, and wash his dirty linen in the midst of his admirers; he escapes, he has a room of his own, he leads a private life; if he has nothing else, he has the holidays, and the more unhappy Tembinok' is always on the stage and on the stretch. . . .

He would come strolling over, always alone, a little before a meal-time, take a chair, and talk and eat with us like an old family friend. Gilbertine etiquette appears defective on the point of leave-taking; and there was something childish and disconcerting in Tembinok's abrupt 'I want to go home now', accompanied by a kind of ducking rise, and followed by an unadorned retreat. It was the only blot upon his manners, which were otherwise plain, decent, sensible and

Tutuila

dignified. He never stayed long nor drank much, and copied our behaviour where he perceived it to differ from his own. Very early in the day, for instance, he ceased eating with his knife. It was plain he was determined in all things to wring profit from our visit, and chiefly upon etiquette. The quality of his white visitors puzzled and concerned him; he would bring up name after name, and ask if its bearer were a 'big chiep', or even a 'chiep' at all. His vocabulary is apt and ample to an extraordinary degree. God knows where he collected it, but by some instinct or some accident he has avoided all profane or gross expressions. . . . It was my part not only to supply new information, but to correct the old. We were showing the magic lantern; a slide of Windsor Castle was put in, the 'outch (house)'of Victoreea. 'How many pathom (fathom) he high?' he asked, and I was dumb before him. It was the builder, the indefatigable architect of palaces, that spoke; collector though he was, he did not collect useless information; and all his questions had a purpose. . . . 'My patha (father) he tell me', or 'White man he tell me', would be his constant beginning. 'You think he lie?' Sometimes I thought he did. A schooner captain had told him of Captain Cook; the king was much interested in the story; and turned for more information — not to Mr Stephen's Dictionary, nor to the *Britannica*, but to the Bible in the Gilbert Island version (which consists chiefly of the New Testament and the Psalms). Here he sought long and earnestly; Paul he found, and Festus, and Alexander the coppersmith: no word of Cook. The inference was obvious: the explorer was a myth. So hard it is, even for a man of great natural parts like Tembinok', to grasp the ideas of a new society and culture. . . .

As the time approached for our departure Tembinok' became greatly changed; a softer, a more melancholy, and in particular, a more confidential man appeared in his stead. . . . We showed fireworks one evening on the terrace. It was a heavy business; the sense of separation was in all our minds and the talk languished. The king was specially affected, sat disconsolate on his mat, and often sighed. Presently after we said goodnight and withdrew Tembinok' detained Mr Osbourne, patting the mat beside him saying: 'Sit down. I feel bad, I like talk . . . I very sorry you go. Miss Stlevens (Fanny), he good man, woman he good man, boy he good man; all good man. Woman he smart all the same man. My woman' (glancing towards his wives) 'he good man, no very smart. I think Miss Stlevens he big chief all the same cap'n man-o-wa'. I think Miss Stlevens he rich all the same me. All go schoona. I very sorry. My father he go, my uncle he go, my cousins, he go, Miss Stlevens he go: all go. You no see king cry before. King all the same man: feel bad, he cry. I very sorry.' . . .

In the morning it was the common topic in the village that the king had wept. To me he said: 'Last night I no can 'peak: too much here,' laying his hand upon his bosom. 'Now you go away all the same my family. My brothers, my uncle go away. All the same.'

Letter to Sidney Colvin
Equator Town, Apemama, October 1889

. . . The king is a great character — a thorough tyrant, very much of a gentleman, a poet, a musician, a historian, or perhaps rather more of a genealogist — it is strange to see him lying in his house among a lot of his wives (nominal wives) writing the History of Apemama in an account-book; his description of one of his own songs, which he sang to me himself, as 'about sweethearts, and trees, and the sea — and no true all-the-same lie', seems about as compendious a definition of lyric poetry as a man could ask. Tembinok' is here the great attraction: all the rest is heat and tedium and villainous dazzle, and yet more villainous mosquitoes. We are like to be here, however, many a long week before we get away, and then whither? A strange trade this voyaging: so vague, so bound-down, so helpless. Fanny has been planting some vegetables, and we have actually onions and radishes coming up: ah, onion-despiser, were you but a while in a low island, how your heart would leap at sight of a coster's barrow! I think I could shed tears over a dish of turnips. No doubt we shall all be glad to say farewell to low islands — I had near said forever. They are very tame; and I begin to read up the directory and pine for an island with a profile, a running brook, or were it only a well among the rocks. The thought of a mango came to me early this morning and set my greed on edge; but you would not know what a mango is, so —

Samoan belles

I have been thinking a great deal of you and the Monument of late, and even tried to get my thoughts into a poem, hitherto without success. God knows how you are: I begin to weary dreadfully to see you — well, in nine months, I hope; but that seems a long time. I wonder what has befallen me too, that flimsy part of me that lives (or dwindles) in the public mind; and what has befallen *The Master*, and what kind of a Box the Merry Box has been found. It is odd to know nothing of all this. We had an old woman to do devil-work for you about a month ago, in a Chinaman's house on Apaiang (August 23rd or 24th). You should have seen the crone with a noble masculine face, like that of an old crone [sic], a body like a man's (naked all but the feathery female girdle), knotting cocoanut leaves and muttering spells: Fanny and I, and the good captain of the *Equator*, and the Chinaman and his native wife and sister-in-law, all squatting on the floor about the sibyl; and a crowd of dark faces watching from behind her shoulder (she sat right in the doorway) and tittering aloud with strange, appalled, embarrassed laughter at each fresh adjuration. She informed us you were in England, not travelling and now no longer sick; she promised us a fair wind next day, and we had it, so I cherish the hope she was as right about Sidney Colvin. The ship-owning has rather petered out since I last wrote, and a good many other plans beside.

Health? Fanny very so-so; I pretty right upon the whole, and getting through plenty work: I know not quite how, but it seems to me not bad and in places funny . . . a hot-bed of strange characters and incidents: Lord, how different from Europe and the Pallid States! Farewell. Heaven knows when this will get to you. I burn to be in Sydney and have news.

R.L.S.

Letter to Mrs Margaret Stevenson
Schooner Equator, *at sea 240 miles from Samoa*
Sunday, December 1st, 1889

My dear Mother, — We are drawing (we fondly hope) to the close of another voyage like that from Tahiti to Hawaii; we sailed from Butaritari on the 4th November, and since then have lain becalmed under cataracts of rain, or kicked about in purposeless squalls. We were sixteen souls in this small schooner, eleven in the cabin; our confinement and overcrowding in the wet weather was excessive; we lost our foretopmast in a squall; the sails were continually being patched (we had but the one suit) and with all attention we lost the jigtopsail almost entirely and the staysail and mainsail are far through. To complete the discomfort, we have carried a very mild weatherglass. . . . I wonder are you already so far out of key with the South Seas, that 79 degrees at noon will seem warm to you? You should have seen the great coats out! I myself wore two wool undershirts, a knitted waistcoat — the gift of the King of Apemama — and a flannel blazer; and I was seriously thinking of a flannel shirt, when the cold let up. My birthday was a great event; Mr Rich, the agent of the firm at Butaritari, who make on this trip one of the eleven being in the cabin, had his on the twelfth; so we had two days' festivity — champagne, music, the capture of sharks, dolphins and skipjack — mighty welcome additions to our table. . . .

We had a fine alert once; a reef ahead — three positions indicated, our own disputed — a very heavy sea running — the boats cleared and supplied with bread and water, our little packets made (medicines, papers and woollen clothes) and the poor passenger for Waikiki trying rather ruefully to insure his little all which was on board. It was rather fine going to bed that night; though had we struck the reef the boat voyage of four or five hundred miles would have been no joke.

Fanny has stood the hardships of this rough cruise wonderfully; but I do not think I could enforce her to another of the same. I've been first rate, though I am now done for lack of green food. Joe [Strong] is, I fear, really ill; and Lloyd has bad sores in his leg. We shall send Joe on to Sydney by the first steamer; and Lloyd, Fanny and I shall stay on awhile (time quite vague) in Samoa. Write to Sydney. We shall turn up in England by May or June. Ever your afft. son.

R.L.S.

Letter to Sidney Colvin
Schooner Equator, *at sea 190 miles off Samoa*
Monday, December 2, 1889

My dear Colvin, — We are just nearing the end of our long cruise. Rain, calms, squalls, bang — there's the foreto mast gone; rain, calm, squalls, away with the stay-sail; more rain, more calm, more squalls; a prodigious heavy sea all the time, and the *Equator* staggering and hovering like a swallow in a storm; and the cabin, a great square, crowded with wet human beings, and the rain avalanching the deck, and the leaks dripping everywhere: Fanny in the midst of fifteen males, bearing up wonderfully. But such voyages are at the best a trial.

. . . I am minded not to stay very long in Samoa and confine my studies there (as far as anyone can forecast) to the history of the late war. My book is now practically modelled: if I can execute what is designed, there are few better books now extant on this globe, bar the epics, and the big tragedies, and histories, and the choice lyric poetics and a novel or so — none. But it is not executed yet; and let not him that putteth on his armour, vaunt himself. At least, nobody has had such stuff, such wild stories, such beautiful scenes, such singular intimacies, such manners and traditions, so incredible a mixture of the beautiful and horrible, the savage and civilised. I will give you some idea of the table of contents, which ought to make your mouth water. I propose to call the book *The South Seas*; it is rather a large title, but not many people have seen more of them than I, perhaps no one — certainly no one capable of using the material. . . .

Even so sketched it makes sixty chapters, not less than 300 Cornhill pages; and

I suspect not much under 500. Samoa has yet to be accounted for: I think it will be all history, and I shall work in observations on Samoan manners, under the similar heads in other Polynesian islands. It is possible, though unlikely, that I may add a passing visit to Fiji or Tonga, or even both; but I am growing impatient to see yourself, and I do not want to be later than June of coming to England. Anyway, you see it will be a large work, and as it will be copiously illustrated, the Lord knows what it will cost. We shall return, God willing, by Sydney, Ceylon, Suez, and, I guess, Marseilles the many-masted (copyright epithet). I shall likely pause a day or two in Paris, but all that is too far ahead — although now it begins to look near — so near, and I can hear the rattle of the hansom up Endell Street and see the gates swing back, and feel myself jump out upon the Monument steps — Hosanna! — home again. My dear fellow, now that my father is done with his troubles, and 17 Heriot Row no more than a mere shell, you and that gaunt old Monument in Bloomsbury are all that I have in view when I use the word home; some passing thoughts there may be of the rooms at Skerryvore, and the blackbirds in the chine on a May morning; but the essence is S.C. and the Museum. Suppose, by some damned accident, you were no more; well, I should return just the same, because of my mother and Lloyd, whom I now think to send to Cambridge; but all the spring would have gone out of me, and ninety per cent. of the attraction lost. I will copy for you here a copy of verses made in Apemama.

I heard the pulse of the besieging sea
Throb far away all night. I heard the wind
Fly crying, and convulse tumultuous palms.
I rose and strolled. The isle was all bright sand,
And flailing fans and shadows of the palms:
The heaven all moon, and wind, and the blind vault —
The keenest planet slain, for Venus slept.
The King, my neighbour, with his host of wives,
Slept in the precinct of the palisade:
Where single, in the wind, under the moon,
Among the slumbering cabins, blazed a fire,
Sole street-lamp and the only sentinel.
    To other lands and nights my fancy turned,
To London first, and chiefly to your house,
The many-pillared and the well-beloved.
There yearning fancy lighted; there again
In the upper room I lay and heard far off
The unsleeping city murmur like a shell;
The muffled tramp of the Museum guard
Once more went by me; I beheld again
Lamps vainly brighten the dispeopled street;

View of Apia harbour, Samoa

Again I longed for the returning morn,
The awaking traffic, the bestirring birds,
The consentaneous trill of tiny song
That weaves round monumental cornices
A passion charm of beauty: most of all,
For your right foot I wearied, and your knock
That was the glad reveille of my day.
Lo, now, when to your task in the great house
At morning through the portico you pass,
One moment glance where, by the pillared wall,
Far-voyaging island gods, begrimed with smoke,
Sit now unworshipped, the rude monument
Of faiths forgot and races undivined;
Sit now disconsolate, remembering well
The priest, the victim, and the songful crowd,
The blaze of the blue noon, and that huge voice
Incessant, of the breakers on the shore.
As far as these from their ancestral shrine,
So far, so foreign, your divided friends
Wander, estranged in body, not in mind.

R.L.S.

Letter to Charles Baxter
Samoa, December 1889

My dear Baxter, — . . . I cannot return until I have seen either Tonga or Fiji or both: and I must not leave here till I have finished my collections on the war — a very interesting bit of history, the truth often very hard to come at, and the search (for me) much complicated by the German tongue, from the use of which I have desisted (I suppose) these fifteen years. The last two days I have been mugging with a dictionary from five to six hours a day; besides this, I have to call upon, keep sweet, and judiciously interview all sorts of persons — English, American, German and Samoan. It makes a hard life; above all, as after every interview I have to come and get my notes straight on the nail. . . .

Samoa, Apia at least, is far less beautiful than the Marquesas or Tahiti: a more gentle scene, gentler acclivities, a tamer face of nature; and this much aided for the wanderer, by the great German plantations with their countless regular avenues of palms. The island has beautiful rivers, with pleasant pools and waterfalls and overhanging verdure, and often a great volume of sound, so that once I thought I was passing near a mill, and it was only the voice of the river. I am not specially attracted by the people; but they are courteous; the women very attractive, and dress lovely; the men purposeful, well set up, tall, lean and dignified. . . .

R. L. STEVENSON

PART THREE

THIRD VOYAGE

April to September 1890

In the trading steamer *Janet Nicoll*, which set out from Sydney and followed a very devious course, extending as far as Penrhyn in the Eastern to the Marshall Islands in the Western Pacific.

R.L.S.

Letter to Charles Baxter
Februar den zen 1890
Dampfer Lubeck zwischen Apia und Sydney

My dear Charles, — I have got one delightful letter from you, and heard from my mother of your kindness in going to see her. Thank you for that: you can in no way more touch and serve me. . . . Ay, ay, it is sad to sell 17 [Heriot Row]; sad and fine were the old days: when I was away in Apemama, I wrote two copies of verse about Edinburgh and the past, so ink black, so golden bright. I will send them, if I can find them for they will say something to you, and indeed one is more than half addressed to you. This is it —

TO MY OLD COMRADES

Do you remember — can we e'er forget?
How, in the coiled perplexities of youth,
In our wild climate, in our scowling town,
We gloomed and shivered, sorrowed, sobbed, and feared?
The belching winter wind, the missile rain,
The rare and welcome silence of the snows,
The laggard morn, the haggard day, the night,
The grimy spell of the nocturnal town,
Do you remember? — Ah, could one forget!
As when the fevered sick that all night long
Listed the wind intone, and hear at last
The ever-welcome voice of the chanticleer
Sing in the bitter hour before the dawn —
With sudden ardour, these desire the day:
(Here a squall sends all flying.)
So sang in the gloom of youth the bird of hope;
So we, exulting, hearkened and desired.
For lo! in the palace porch of life
We huddled with chimeras from within —
How sweet to hear! — the music swelled and fell
And through the breach of the revolving doors
What dreams of splendour blinded us and fled!
I have since then contended and rejoiced;
Amid the glories of the house of life
Profoundly entered, and the shrine beheld;
Yet when the lamp from my expiring eyes
Shall dwindle and recede, the voice of love
Fall insignificant on my closing ears,
What sound shall come but the old cry of the wind

In our inclement city? what returns
But the image of the emptiness of youth,
Filled with the sound of footsteps and that voice
Of discontent and rapture and despair?
So, as in darkness, from the magic lamp,
The momentary pictures gleam and fade
And perish, and the night resurges — these
Shall I remember, and then all forget.

They're pretty second-rate, but felt. I can't be bothered to copy the other.

I have bought 314½ acres of beautiful land in the bush behind Apia; when we get the house built, the garden laid, and cattle in the place, it will be something to fall back on for shelter and food; and if the island could stumble into political quiet, it is conceivable it might even bring a little income. . . . We range from 600 to 1500 feet, have five streams, waterfalls, precipices, profound ravines, rich tablelands, fifty head of cattle on the ground (if anyone could catch them), a great view of forest, sea, mountains, the warships in the haven: really a noble place. Some day you are to take a long holiday and come and see it; it has been all planned.

With all these irons in the fire, and cloudy prospects, you may be sure I was pleased to hear a good account of business. I believed *The Master* was a sure card: I wonder why Henley thinks it grimy; grim it is, God knows, but sure not grimy, else I am the more deceived. I am sorry he did not care for it; I place it on the line with *Kidnapped* myself. We'll see as time goes on whether it goes above or falls below.

R.L.S.

Vailima Papers: Excerpt from An Open Letter to the Reverend Dr Hyde of Honolulu

[in defence of Father Damien who ministered to the lepers of Molokai until he died of the disease in 1889]

Sydney, February 25, 1890

. . . Damien is dead and already somewhat ungratefully remembered in the field of his labours and sufferings. 'He was a good man, but very officious,' says one. Another tells me he had fallen (as other priests so easily do) into something of the ways and habits of thought of a Kanaka; but he had the wit to recognise the fact, and the good sense to laugh at it. A plain man it seems he was; I cannot find he was a popular. . . .

Of Damien I begin to have an idea. He seems to have been a man of the peasant class, certainly of the peasant type; shrewd, ignorant and bigoted, yet with an open mind, and capable of receiving and digesting a reproof if it were bluntly

Auckland harbour

administered; superbly generous in the least thing as well as in the greatest, and as ready to give his last shirt (although not without human grumbling) as he had been to sacrifice his life; essentially indiscreet and officious, which made him a troublesome colleague; domineering in all his ways, which made him incurably unpopular with the Kanakas, but yet destitute of real authority, so that his boys laughed at him and he must carry out his wishes by the means of bribes. He learned to have a mania for doctoring; and set up the Kanakas against the remedies of his regular rivals: perhaps if anything matter at all in the treatment of such a disease? the worst thing that he did, and certainly the easiest.

The best and worst of the man appear very plainly in his dealings with Mr Chapman's money; he had originally laid it out entirely for the benefit of Catholics, and even so not wisely; but after a long, plain talk, he admitted his error fully and revised the list. The sad state of the boys' home is in part the result of his lack of control; in part, of his own slovenly ways and false ideas of hygiene. Brother officials used to call it 'Damien's Chinatown'. 'Well,' they would say, 'your Chinatown keeps growing.' And he would laugh with perfect good nature, and adhere to his errors with perfect obstinacy. So much I have gathered of truth about this plain, noble human brother and father of ours; his imperfections are the traits of his face, by which we know him for our fellow; his martyrdom and his example nothing can lessen or annul; and only a person here on the spot can properly appreciate their greatness.

Letter to Mrs Margaret Stevenson
Union Club, Sydney, March 5, 1890

My dear Mother, — I understand the family keeps you somewhat informed. For myself I am in such a whirl of work and society, I can ill spare a moment. My health is excellent and has been here tried by abominable wet weather, and (what's waur?) dinners and lunches. As this is likely to be our metropolis, I have tried to lay myself out to be sociable with an eye to yoursel'. Several niceish people have turned up: Fanny has an evening, but she is about at the end of the virtuous effort, and shrinks from the approach of any fellow creature.

Have you seen Hyde's (Dr not Mr) letter about Damien? This has been one of my concerns; I have an answer in the press . . . to come out as a pamphlet; of which I make of course a present to the publisher. I am not a cannibal, I would not eat the flesh of Dr Hyde — and it is conceivable it will make a noise in Honolulu. I have struck as hard as I knew how; nor do I think my answer can fail to do away (in the minds of all who see it) with the effect of Hyde's incredible and really villainous production. What a mercy I wasn't this man's *guest* in the *Morning Star*! I think it would have broke my heart.

Time for me to go! I remain, with love,

R.L.S.

Letter to Charles Baxter
Union Club, Sydney, March 7th, 1890

My dear Charles, — I did not send off the enclosed before from laziness; having gone quite sick, and being a blooming prisoner here in the club, and indeed in my bedroom. I was in receipt of your letters and your ornamental photo, and was delighted to see how well you looked, and how reasonably well I stood. . . . I am sure I shall never come back home except to die; I may do it, but shall always think of the move as suicidal, unless a great change comes over me, of which as yet I see no symptom. This visit to Sydney has smashed me handsomely; and yet I made myself a prisoner here in the club upon my first arrival. This is not encouraging for further ventures; Sydney winter — or, I might almost say, Sydney spring, for I came when the worst was over — is so small an affair, comparable to our June depression at home in Scotland. . . . The pipe is right again; it was the springs that had rusted, and ought to have been oiled. Its voice is now that of an angel; but,

Lord! here in the club I dare not wake it! Conceive my impatience to be in my own backwoods and raise the sound of minstrelsy. What pleasures are to be compared with those of the Unvirtuous Vituoso. Yours ever affectionately, the Unvirtuous Virtuoso,

ROBERT LOUIS STEVENSON

Letter to Sidney Colvin
S.S. Janet Nicoll, *off Upolu, Spring 1890*

My dearest Colvin, — I was sharply ill at Sydney, cut off, right out of bed, in this steamer on a fresh island cruise, and have already reaped the benefit. . . . The truth is, I fear, this life is the only one that suits me; so long as I cruise in the South Seas, I shall be well and happy — alas, no, I do not mean that, and *absit omen*! — I mean that, so soon as I cease from cruising, the nerves are strained, the decline commences, and I steer slowly but surely back to bedward. We left Sydney, had a cruel, rough passage to Auckland, for the *Janet* is the worst roller I was ever aboard

Oxford Hotel, Sydney

Sydney Harbour

of. I was confined to my cabin, ports closed, self shied out of the berth, stomach (pampered till the day I left on a diet of perpetual egg-nog) revolted at ship's food and ship eating, in a frowsy bunk, clinging with one hand to the plate, with the other to the glass, and using the knife and fork (except at intervals) with the eyelid. No matter: I picked up hand over hand. After a day in Auckland, we set sail again; were blown up in the main cabin with calcium fires as we left the bay. Let no man say I am unscientific: when I ran, on the alert, out of my stateroom, and found the main cabin incarnadined with the glow of the last scene of a pantomime, I stopped dead: 'What is this?' said I. 'This ship is on fire, I see that; but why a pantomime?' And I stood and reasoned the point, until my head was so muddled with the fumes that I could not find the companion. A few seconds later, the captain had to enter crawling on his belly, and took days to recover (if he has recovered) from the fumes. By singular good fortune, we got the hose down in time and saved the ship, but Lloyd lost most of his clothes and a great part of our photographs was destroyed! Fanny saw the native sailors tossing overboard a blazing trunk; she stopped them in time, and behold it contained my manuscripts. Thereafter we had three (or two) days fine weather: then got into a gale of wind, with rain and a vexatious sea. As we drew into our anchorage a man ashore told me afterwards the sight of the *Janet Nicoll* made him sick; and indeed it was rough play, though nothing to the night before. All through this gale I worked four to six hours per diem, spearing the ink-bottle like a flying fish, and holding my papers together as I might. For, of all things, what I was at was history — the Samoan business — and I had to turn from one to another of these piles of manuscript notes, and from one page to another in each. . . . All the same, this history is a godsend for a voyage; I can put in time, getting events co-ordinated and the narrative distributed, when my much-heaving numskull would be incapable of finish or fine style. . . . We met the missionary barque *John Williams*. I tell you it was a great day for Savage Island; the path up the cliffs was crowded with gay islandresses (I like that feminine plural) who wrapped me in their embraces, and picked my pockets of all my tobacco, with a manner which a touch

Map of Cruise of Janet Nicoll

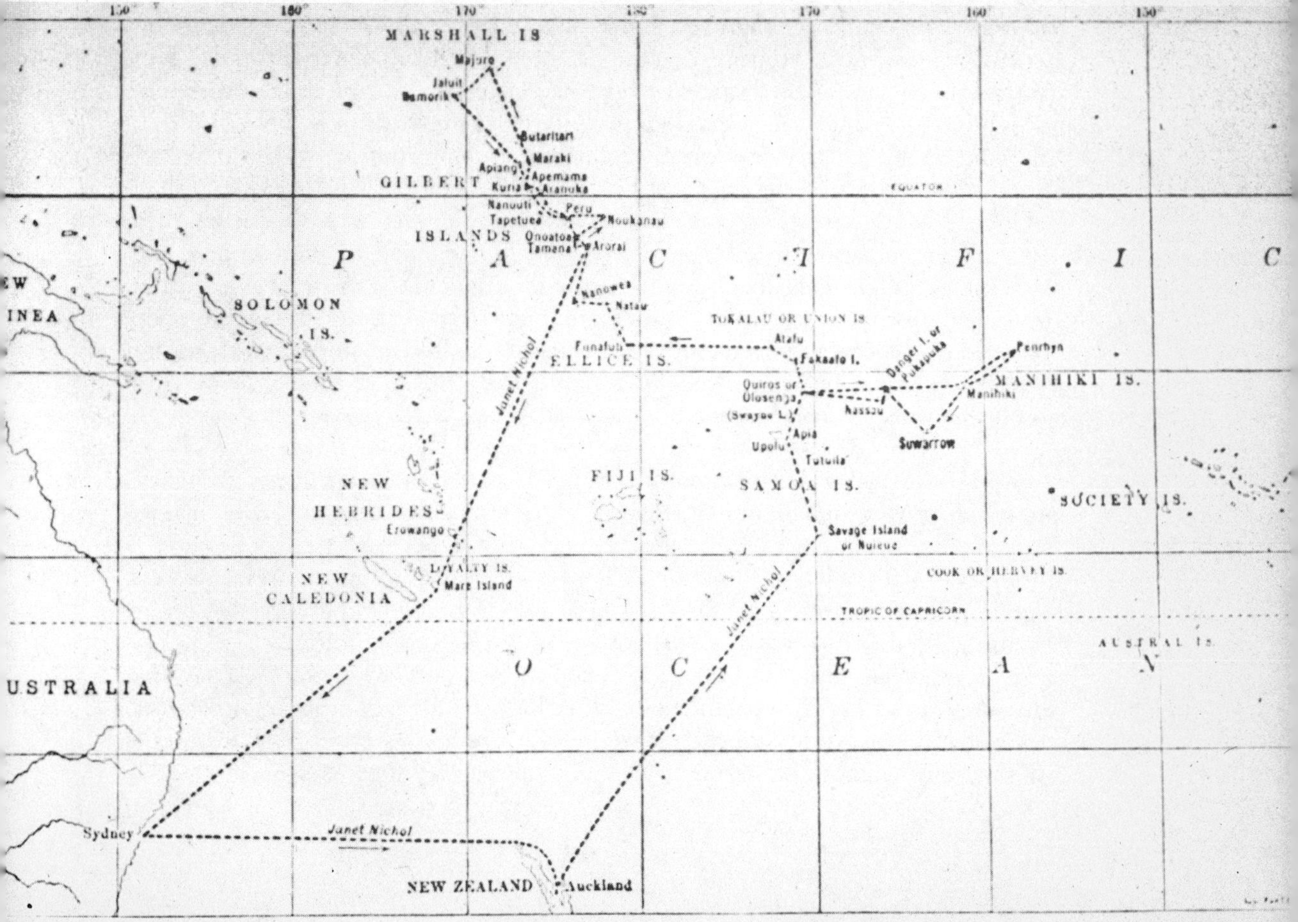

would have made revolting, but as it was, was simply charming, like the Golden Age. One pretty, little, stalwart minx, with a red flower behind her ear, had searched me with extraordinary zeal; and when, soon after, I missed my matches, I accused her (she still following us) of being the thief. After some delay, and with a subtle smile, she produced the box, gave me *one match*, and put the rest away again. Too tired to add more. Your most affectionate

R.L.S.

From the cruise of the Janet Nicoll *among the South Sea Islands*
(a diary by Mrs Robert Louis Stevenson, 1890)
[*Off Friendly Is.*]

18th April. — . . . Coloured fire and thick white vapour belching from our ports must have given us a very strange and alarming aspect. Lloyd looked over the opposite side of our ship and saw the ports there, also, vomiting vapour like a factory. To our surprise the cartridge-boxes were only slightly scorched. Our personal loss, however, has been very severe. About ninety photographs were destroyed and all of Lloyd's clothes except those on his back. Neither he nor I have even a toothbrush left. The annoying thing is that Tin Jack [a fellow passenger] lost nothing whatever. Lloyd is very bitter about the discrimination shown in the matter of trousers by the fire. I stopped a couple of black boys just in time to prevent them throwing overboard a blazing valise containing four large boxes of Louis's papers. A black bag, its contents at present unknown, is burned, and innumerable small necessaries that conduce to comfort on shipboard are lost. I have ever since been in a tremor lest Louis have a haemorrhage. If he does, I shall feel inclined to do something very desperate to the chemist, who, for the sake of a few shillings, put us all in such deadly peril. A horrid smell still hangs about the place and everyone feels ill. Though I hardly breathed in the room, I have a heavy oppression on my chest, and my throat and lungs burn as though I were inhaling pepper. From the time we left Auckland, the water as been as smooth as glass, and there has been no jarring or knocking about; the stuff must have gone off by a simple spontaneous combustion.

21st April. — Still drying the remains of Lloyd's clothes, burned and wet in the fire and discovering more and more losses. . . . Both our cameras escaped as by magic.

26th April. — The desire to own an island is still burning in my breast. In this neighbourhood, nearer Samoa, is just the island I want, owned, unfortunately, by a man in Tahiti. It is called Nassau and is said to be uninhabited.

Last night an immense rat ran over me in bed, and Mr Henderson had the same unpleasant experience. In the hold of the *Janet* are a number of pure white rats with red eyes, which appeared of themselves quite mysteriously. The captain will not allow them to be harmed, which I think is very nice and sentimental of

'A pretty, little, stalwart minx'

Marshall island canoe

him. It was amusing to see our dog's perplexity when we came to anchor, and put his head out of a porthole to have a look at Auckland. His tail expressed alarmed surprise. . . .

Mr Henderson has just told us as a secret that our next island will be Upolu, Samoa, and we are now as wildly excited as the second steward (who took his 'billet' under the head steward from a romantic hope of seeing Samoa, of which he had once read a description in a newspaper). On Wednesday afternoon, at four o'clock, we shall arrive at Apia, and the next morning, at break of day, off we fly to Vailima. As we were discussing the subject, the captain called out that there was a white rat in his cabin and he wished to catch and tame it, so I ran to help him. It was under his bed, he said, and the loveliest rat in the world. As he was dilating on its beauty, out it flashed, jumping on him and rebounding against my breast like a fluff of white cotton wool. The captain laughed and screamed with shrill, hysterical cries, in which I joined, while the loveliest rat in the world scurried away.

27th April. — The weather really abominable, so cold that I have had to put on a flannel bodice. . . . After I had closed my diary last night Mr Henderson got out the chart and showed us his own islands and the supposed location of Victoria Island which he is looking for. I offered to toss him for the latter, to which he agreed. Louis threw up a piece of money and I won. I have yet, however, to find Victoria.

Nuieue has not yet recovered from the effects of last year's hurricane, and we shall not get many delicacies here. There are no ripe cocoanuts, few bananas, and no breadfruit. Someone said that I could get spring onions. 'How do they grow them?' I asked; meaning did they sow seeds or plant sets. 'On the graves,' was the rather startling answer.

Last night Mr Henderson pulled off a rat's tail. He thought to pull the rat from a hole from which the tail protruded, but the tail came off, and the rat ran away. The captain tells me that there is generally a plague of flies in Nuieue. It is too cold for them now, but usually when the natives come out in their canoes, their backs especially, are black with flies. Someone has sent me a basket of bananas almost too sweet and rich, also some excellent oranges. I have mended the bellows of our camera, where it has been eaten by cockroaches, with sticking-plaster.

28th. — Steamed round to the other side of the island to the missionary station . . . we watched the *John Williams* (the missionary ship on her way to Samoa) plunging to and fro, now close under the cliffs, now skirting the *Janet*, now fetching our hearts in our mouths as she stayed, and forereached in staying, till you would have thought she had leaves on her jib-boom. We actually got up the camera to take a photograph of the expected shipwreck. We were told afterward that it was only Captain Turpie showing off his seamanship. . . .

Mr Henderson and Louis came back with some return labour boys for Danger Island. One who had signed to serve for five years had been waiting another three for a vessel to take him home. He was once disappointed, and nearly died of it. I am thankful he had this opportunity. (The 'labour boys' do, sometimes, die of homesickness. A black boy called Arriki whom we hired did so die after we left Samoa. The man to whom he was assigned by the German firm told me that both Arriki and a friend of his began to droop and become sullen, and then went quite mad; soon after they died at about the same time from no apparent disease, but he said he knew the symptoms — 'just plain homesickness for a cannibal island'. Arriki, in a moment of confidence, once described to me his life in his own land. It seemed to consist of flight from one unsafe spot to another, with death hunting on every hand. Both his father and mother had been killed and eaten, with the most of his friends; and yet Arriki died of homesickness.)

4th May. — Ran through a light squall in the night and sighted Danger Island at four in the morning. . . . We could see the natives gathering on the beach in great force. They seemed thunderstruck at the sight of a vessel with furled sails moving so rapidly against a strong headwind, the *Janet* being the first steamer that had touched at Pukapuka. As soon as our passengers were recognised, a joyful shout ran up and down the beach, and canoes were launched and paddled out to meet us. When they were just abreast of us Captain Henry blew the steam-whistle. The natives were appalled; every paddle stopped short, and the crowds on the beach seemed stricken to stone . . . it was some time before they took heart and resumed their paddling. The king, a shabbily clad man of rather mean appearance, was among them.

The meeting between the long-parted friends was very pretty and touching. I like their mode of showing affection better than ours. They took hands and pressed their faces together lightly with a delicate sniff, as I have often seen a white mother caress her baby. . . . The sheep, which the strangers saw for the first time, were studied with much interest. A group of middle-aged respectable men stood off at some distance and whistled to the sheep as though they were dogs; getting no response, they ventured a little nearer, when one of the sheep happened to move. The crowd fell back in dire confusion, and one man who had been in the van, but now occupied a rear position, asked in a trembling voice if the bite of those animals was very dangerous. . . . When a ship comes in, the natives, men, women and children, often smoke the strong trade tobacco until they fall down insensible, sometimes becoming convulsed as in epilepsy.

The trader, a half-caste, had already boarded the *Janet* in a boat of his own, but his wife, a stout, good-natured, sensible-looking woman, was waiting on the beach to receive us. She at once took possession of me as her right, and I was triumphantly swept off to her house, the crowd at our heels; here we were regaled on cocoanuts, while all the population who could crowd into the room gazed on us unwinking. The windows, also, were filled, which cut off the air and made the place rather suffocating. The children were made to sit down in the front row so that the older people could see over their heads. One old woman made me feel quite uncomfortable. Her eyes remained fixed, her jaw dropped, and nothing for a single moment diverted her attention from what she evidently regarded as a shocking and wonderful spectacle. Natives have said that the first sight of white people is dreadful, as they look like corpses walking. I have myself been startled by the sight of a crowd of whites after having seen only brown-skinned people for a long time. Louis has a theory that we whites were originally albinos. Certainly we are not a nice colour. I remember as a child the words 'flesh colour' were sickening to me, and I could not bear to see them in my paint-box. . . .

. . . Mr Hird recalls the following grisly incident that occurred when he was stopping on Penrhyn. A man who was paralysed on one side had a convulsion which caused spasmodic contractions on the other side. One of the sick man's family began at once to make a coffin. 'But the man's not dead,' said Mr Hird. 'Oh yes,' was the reply; 'he's dead enough; it's the third time he has done this, so we are going to bury him.' Mr Hird went to the native missionary, but his remonstrances had no effect; he kept on protesting until the last moment. 'Why look,' he said, 'the man's limbs are quivering.' 'Oh that's only live flesh,' was the reply, and someone fell to pommelling the poor wretch to quiet the 'live flesh'. The belief was that the man's spirit had departed long before and a devil who wished to use the body for his own convenience had been keeping the flesh alive. Mr Hird thinks that the man was insensible when buried and must soon have died.

At another time some natives had been 'waking' a corpse; tired out, they all fell asleep except a single man who acted as 'watcher'. By and by he, too, dropped off. The party were awakened by a great noise. The watcher explained that he had been napping and suddenly opened his eyes to behold the dead man sitting up. 'A corpse sitting up just like this!' he exclaimed indignantly; 'but I was equal to him; I ran at him and knocked him down, and now he's decently quiet again.' And so he was, dead as a door-nail from the blow he had received.

7th June. — Have been lying at Nanomea, the last of the Ellices we shall visit, for three days, unable to get the cargo on board till today owing to the fearful surf. A good many canoes are broken to pieces, and our own boats have had many escapes. . . . It is always a great pleasure to the natives to help raise the ship's boats to the davits for the night. They know that white sailors make a sort of cry or 'chanty' when hauling on a rope, so they, too, try to do the correct thing. The result is a noise very like a mob of schoolgirls letting loose a confusion of soprano screams. No one would suspect the sounds to come from the throats of men. Our own black sailors are the same; we hear them screaming and laughing in the forecastle exactly like girls. We are so used to island life that it has but just struck us as odd and picturesque that our almost naked sailors (they wear only a short *lava-lava* round their loins) should be working in wreaths like queens of the May.

It is only today that any women have been able to get on board. . . . They began pulling off their rings to put on my hands; I did not like taking their rings, but I need have had no scruples, for one of them with prompt energy removed a gold ring from my finger to her own. These exchanges made, they fell to examining my clothes, which filled them with admiration. The next thing, they were trying to take my clothes off; finding this stoutly resisted, they turned up my sleeves to the shoulders. Their taste differed from mine, for, while I was thinking what a cold, ugly colour a white arm looked beside their warm, brown ones, they were crying out in admiration. One woman kissed my feet (the island kiss) and sniffed softly up and down my arms. She was plainly saying to the others, 'She's just like a pickaninny; I would like to have her for a pet,' holding out her arms as she spoke and going through the motions of tossing and caressing a baby. My hands and feet were measured by theirs and found to be much smaller (they were large women made on a more generous scale than I). 'Pickaninny hands and feet,' they said. The discovery of vaccination marks caused great excitement. In a moment all their husbands' heads appeared at the doors and windows. My sleeves, in spite of my struggles, were dragged to my shoulders and, to my dismay, my petticoats were whipped up to my knees. At that I began to cry, when the men instantly disappeared, and except for an occasional sniffing the women behaved with more decorum. One woman was most anxious that I should stop on the island with her. I really think she had some hope that she might keep me as a sort of pet monkey. At last they were warned that the ship would be off soon, so they fled to their canoes. . . .

In the afternoon Louis was dictating to Lloyd who used his typewriter. All the air and most of the room was cut off from them by heads at the portholes. I watched the faces and saw one intelligent old man explaining to the others that Lloyd was playing an accompaniment to Louis singing; the old man several times tried to follow the tune but found it impossible. He did not appear to think it a good song, and once, with difficulty, restrained his laughter.

13th. — Tom Day is — must be — 'the flower of the Pacific'. Tom is fifty years of age with a strong, alert figure and the mobile face of an actor; his eyes are blue-grey in deep orbits, blazing with energy and drink and high spirits. 'Tom Day' is not his real name, he says, and Tom Drunk would do quite as well; he had found it necessary to go to the expense of a shilling to have it changed, as he had three times deserted from men-of-war. 'I've been in prison for it,' he said cheerfully, 'and I got the cat for it, and if you like you can see the stars and stripes on my back yet.' He took pleasure in representing himself as the most desperate of ruffians. * Tin Jack asked him to go back to Sydney with him. 'I couldn't leave my old woman behind,' said he, 'and besides, you see, I got into trouble there. The fact is, I've got another wife there, and I think I'd do better to keep away.'

(*Tin Jack came to a bad end. He possessed a certain fixed income which, however, was not large enough for Jack's liking, so he spent most of the year as a South Seas trader, using the whole of his year's income in one wild burst of dissipation in the town of Sydney. One of his favourite amusements was to hire a hansom cab for the day, put the driver inside, and drive the vehicle himself, calling upon various passers-by to join him at the nearest public house. Some years ago, when Jack was at his station, he received word that his trustee, who was in charge of his property, had levanted with it all. Whereupon poor Jack put a pistol to his head and blew out what brains he possessed. He was a beautiful creature, terribly annoying at times, but with something childlike and appealing — I think he was close to what the Scotch call a natural — that made one forgive pranks in him that would be unforgivable in others. He was very proud of being the original of 'Tommy Hadden' in *The Wrecker* and carried the book wherever he went.)

Tom Day

Letter to E. L. Burlingame
S.S. Janet Nicoll, *off Peru Island, Kingsmills Group*
July 13, 1890

. . . I shall probably return to Samoa direct, having given up all idea of returning to civilisation in the meanwhile. There, on my ancestral acres which I purchased six months ago from a blind Scots blacksmith, you will please address me until further notice. The name of the ancestral acres is going to be Vailima; . . . (they) run to upwards of three hundred; they enjoy the ministrations of five streams, hence the name. They are all at the present moment under a trackless covering of magnificent forest, which would be worth a great deal if it grew beside a railway terminus. To me, as it stands, it represents a handsome deficit. Obliging natives from the cannibal islands are now cutting it down at my expense. You would be able to run your magazine to much greater advantage if the terms of the authors were on the same scale with those of my cannibals. We also have a house about the size of a manufacturer's lodge. 'Tis but the egg of the future palace, over the details of which on paper Mrs Stevenson and I have already shed real tears; what it will be when it comes to paying for it, I leave to you to imagine. . . .

R.L.S.

The Vailima Household: L. to R: Joe Strong, Margaret Stevenson, Lloyd Osbourne, Louis and in front of Fanny, Belle Strong and son Austin

With Vailima servants

Letter to Charles Baxter
Hotel Sebastopol, Noumea, August 1890

My dear Charles, — I have stayed here a week while Lloyd and my wife continue to voyage in the *Janet Nicoll*; this I did partly to see the convict system, partly to shorten my stay in the extreme cold — hear me with my extreme! *moi qui suis originaire d'Edinbourg* — of Sydney at this season. I am feeling very seedy, utterly fatigued, and overborne with sleep. I have a fine old gentleman of a doctor, who attends and cheers and entertains, if he does not cure me; but even with his ministrations I am almost incapable of the exertion sufficient for this letter; and I am really, as I write, falling down with sleep. What is necessary to say, I must try to say shortly. Lloyd goes to clear out our establishments: pray keep him in funds, if I have any; if I have not, pray try to raise them. . . . Here is the idea: to install ourselves, at the risk of bankruptcy, in Samoa. It is not the least likely it will pay (although it may); but it is almost certain it will support life, with very few external expenses. If I die, it will be an endowment for the survivors, at least for my wife and Lloyd; and my mother, who might prefer to go home, has her own. Hence I believe I shall do well to hurry my installation. The letters are already in

Visiting warship at Vailima

part done; in part done is a novel for Scribner; in the course of the next twelve months I should receive a considerable amount of money. . . . Better to build the house and have a roof and farm of my own; and thereafter, with a livelihood assured, save and prepay. There is my livelihood, all but books and wine, ready in a nutshell; and it ought to be more easy to save and repay afterwards. Excellent, say you, but will you save and will you repay? I do not know, said the Bell of Old Bow. . . . The deuce of the affair is that I do not know when I shall see you and Colvin. I guess you will have to come and see me: many a time already we have arranged the details of your visit in the yet unbuilt house on the mountain. I shall be able to get a decent wine from Noumea. We shall be able to give you a decent welcome, and talk of old days. . . .

The morrow. — I feel better, but still dim and groggy. Tonight I go to the governor's; such a lark — no dress clothes — twenty-four hours' notice — able-bodied Polish tailor — suit made for a man with the figure of a puncheon — same hastily altered for self with the figure of a bodkin — sight inconceivable. Never mind; dress clothes, 'which nobody can deny'; and the officials have been all so civil that I liked neither to refuse nor to appear in mufti. Bad dress clothes only prove you are a grisly ass; no dress clothes, even when explained, indicate a want of respect. . . .

View of Noumea harbour

Penal Settlement, Noumea

I hope you never forget to remember me to your father, who has always a place in my heart, as I hope I have a little in his. His kindness helped me infinitely when you and I were young; I recall it with gratitude and affection in this town of convicts at the world's end. There are very few things, my dear Charles, worth mention: on a retrospect of life, the day's flash and colour, one day with another, flames, dazzles, and puts to sleep; and when the days are gone, like a fast-flying thaumatrope, they make but a single pattern. Only a few things stand out; and among these — most plainly to me — Rutland Square. — Ever, my dear Charles, your affectionate friend,

R.L.S.

P.S. — Just returned from trying on the dress clothes. Lord, you should see the coat! It stands out at the waist like a bustle, the flaps across in front, the sleeves are like bags.

Letter to Henry James
Union Club, Sydney, August 1890

. . . I must tell you plainly — I can't tell Colvin — I do not think I shall come to England more than once, and then it'll be to die. Health I enjoy in the tropics; even here, which they call sub- or semi-tropics, I come only to catch cold. I have not been out since my arrival; live here in a nice bedroom by the fireside, and read books and letters from Henry James. . . . But I can't go out. The thermometer was nearly down to 50 degrees the other day — no temperature for me, Mr James: how should I do in England? I fear not at all. Am I very sorry? I am sorry about seven or eight people in England, and one or two in the States. And outside of that, I simply prefer Samoa. These are the words of honesty and soberness. (I am fasting from all but sin, coughing . . . a couple of eggs and a cup of tea.) I was never fond of towns, houses, society or (it seems) civilisation. Nor yet it seems was I ever fond of (what is technically called) God's green earth. The sea, islands, the islanders, the island life and climate, make and keep me truly happier. These last two years I have been much at sea, and I have never wearied; sometimes I have indeed grown impatient for some destination; more often I was sorry that the voyage drew so early to an end; and never once did I lose my fidelity to blue water and a ship. It is plain, then, that for me my exile to the place of schooners and islands can be in no sense regarded as a calamity. Goodbye just now . . . I must take a turn at my proofs.

R.L.S.

Main Street, Noumea

The last photograph, Vailima 1894

Letter to Mrs Charles Fairchild
Union Club, Sydney, September 1890

My dear Mrs Fairchild, — . . . It is always harshness that one regrets . . . I regret also my letter to Dr Hyde. Yes, I do; . . . it was virtuous to defend Damien; but it was harsh to strike so hard at Dr Hyde. When I wrote the letter, I believed he would bring an action, in which case I knew I could be beggared. And as yet there has come no action; the injured Doctor has contented himself up to now with the (truly innocuous) vengeance of calling me a 'Bohemian Crank', and I have deeply wounded one of his colleagues whom I esteemed and liked.

Well, such is life. You are quite right; our civilisation is a hollow fraud — all the fun of life is lost by it; all it gains is that a larger number of persons can continue to be contemporaneously unhappy on the surface of the globe. . . . When, observe that word, which I will write again and larger — WHEN you come to see us in Samoa, you will see for yourself a healthy and happy people.

You see, you are one of the very few of our friends rich enough to come and see us; and when my house is built, and the road is made, and we have enough fruit planted and poultry and pigs raised, it is undeniable that you must come — must is the word; that is the way in which I speak to ladies. You and Fairchild — we'll arrange details in good time. It will be the salvation of your soul, and make you willing to die.

Let me tell you this: in '74 or 5 there came to stay with my father and mother a certain Mr Seed, a prime minister or something of New Zealand [he was Servant to the Customs and Marine Department]. He spotted what my complaint was; told me that I had no business to stay in Europe; that I should find all I cared for, and all that was good for me, in the Navigator Islands; sat up till four in the morning persuading me, demolishing my scruples. And I resisted: I refused to go so far from my father and mother. O, it was virtuous, and O, wasn't it silly! But my father, who was always my dearest, got to his grave without that pang; and now in 1890, I (or what is left of me) go at last to the Navigator Islands. God go with us! It is but a Pisgah sight when all is said; I go there only to grow old and die; but when you come, you will see it is a fair place for the purpose.

ROBERT LOUIS STEVENSON

The empty hall at Vailima

APPENDIX 1:

This excerpt from the marriage certificate of Robert Louis Stevenson and Fanny Osbourne is interesting for its curious mis-spellings and also the fact that Fanny described herself not as 'divorced' but as 'widowed'. The minister was Rev. Dr William A. Scott, of St John's Presbyterian Church in San Francisco, and president of the local St Andrew's Society. The couple exchanged silver rings since Stevenson could not afford the more traditional gold wedding rings and Rev. Scott received for his services ten dollars and a copy of *Christianity Confirmed by Jewish and Heathen Testimony* by Thomas Stevenson.

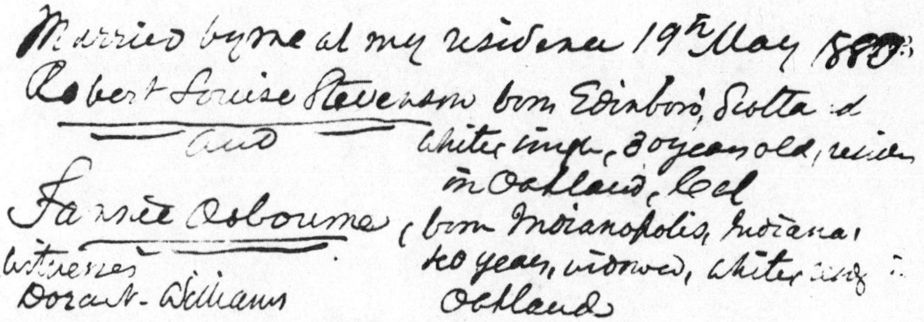
Married by me at my residence 19th May 1880
Robert Louise Stevenson born Edinboro, Scotland
and White single, 30 years old, resides in Oakland, Cal
Fannie Osbourne (born Indianopolis, Indiana, 40 years, widowed, White resid Oakland
Witnesses
Dora N. Williams

APPENDIX 2:

This map of *Treasure Island*, frontispiece of the first edition published by Cassell & Co in 1883, is not, sadly, the original drawn by Lloyd Osbourne in Braemar which inspired the book's creation as *The Sea Cook*, a serial for *Young Folk's Magazine.*

'The proofs came' (from Cassell) wrote Stevenson, 'they were corrected, but I heard nothing of the map. I wrote and asked: was told it had never been received, and sat aghast. It is one thing to draw a map at random and write up a story to the measurements. It is quite another to have to design a map to suit the data. I did it, and the map was drawn again in my father's office, with embellishments of blowing whales and sailing ships. But somehow it was never *Treasure Island* to me'.

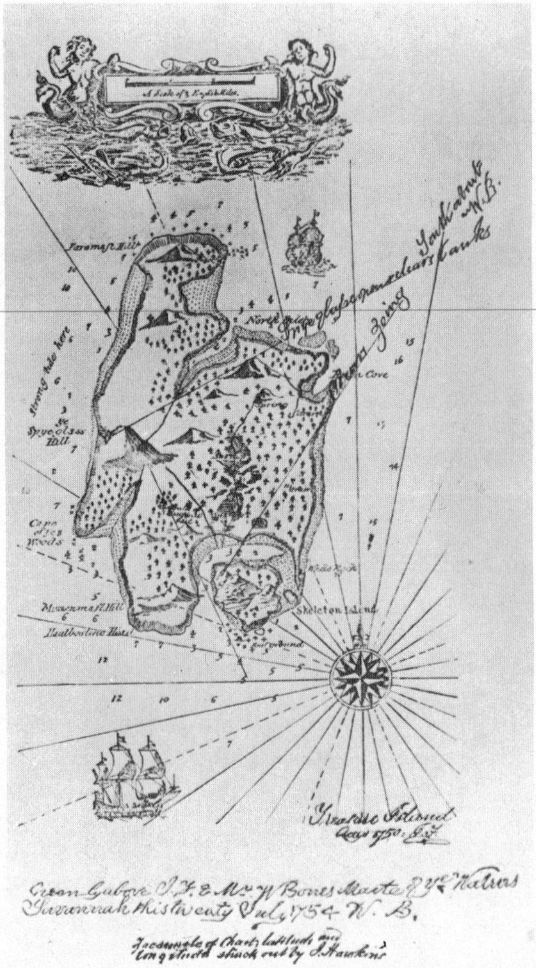

APPENDIX 3:

A sea- and travel-stained page from Stevenson's journal relating to his travels around the Kona coast of the Island of Hawaii, for Saturday, 27 April 1889.

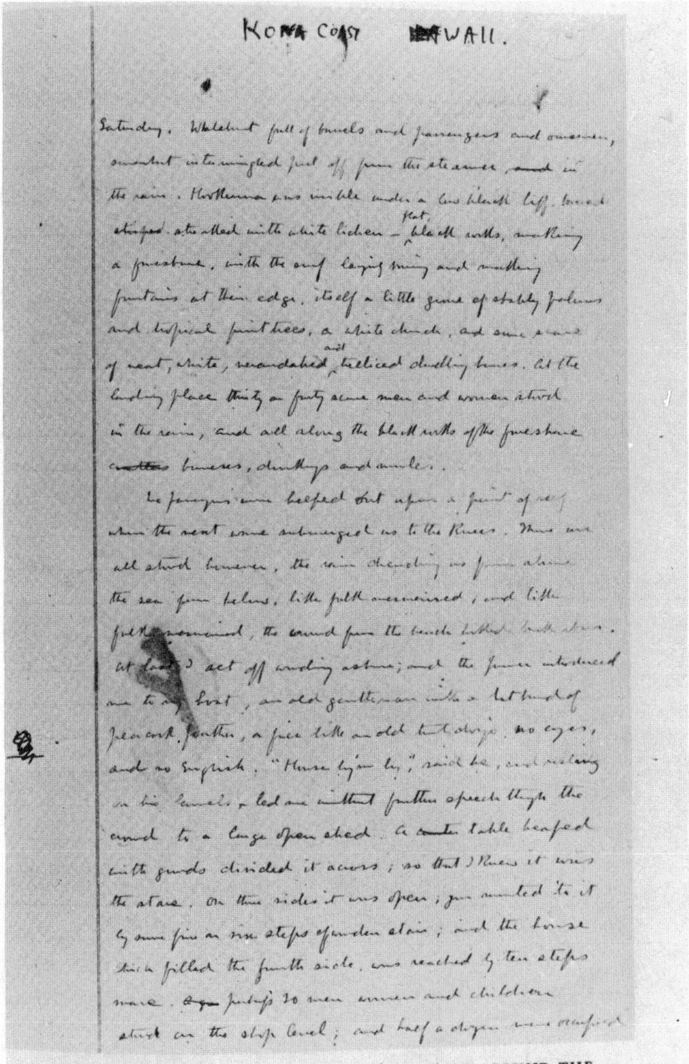

KONA COAST HAWAII.

Saturday. Whaleboat full of bundles and passengers and women, [illegible] intermingled put off from the steamer, and in the rain. Hookena was visible under a low black cliff, [illegible] striped [illegible] with white lichen – flat black rocks, making a foreshore, with the surf leaping [illegible] and making fountains at their edge. itself a little grove of stately palms and tropical fruit trees, a white church, and some scores of neat, white, verandahed and trelliced dwelling houses. At the landing place thirty or forty [illegible] men and women stood in the rain, and all along the black rocks of the foreshore [illegible] horses, donkeys and mules.

The passengers were helped out upon a point of reef where the next [illegible] submerged us to the knees. There we all stood however, the rain drenching us from above the sea from below, little folk unreceived, and little folk received, the sound from the beach [illegible]. At last I set off wading ashore; and the purser introduced me to my host, an old gentleman with a hat band of peacock feathers, a face like an old bulldog, no eyes, and no English. "House by'm by," said he, and relaxing on his [illegible], led me without further speech through the crowd to a large open shed. A counter table heaped with goods divided it across; so that I knew it was the store. On three sides it was open; you mounted to it by some five or six steps of wooden stair; and the house which filled the fourth side, was reached by ten steps more. [illegible] perhaps 30 men women and children stood on the shop level; and half a dozen were [illegible]

The stained journal of Stevenson's travels around the Kona coast of the island of Hawaii begins on Saturday, April 27, 1889.

APPENDIX 4

Page from the manuscript of *Weir of Hermiston*. Stevenson was at work on this novel on the morning of his death at Vailima, 3 December 1894.

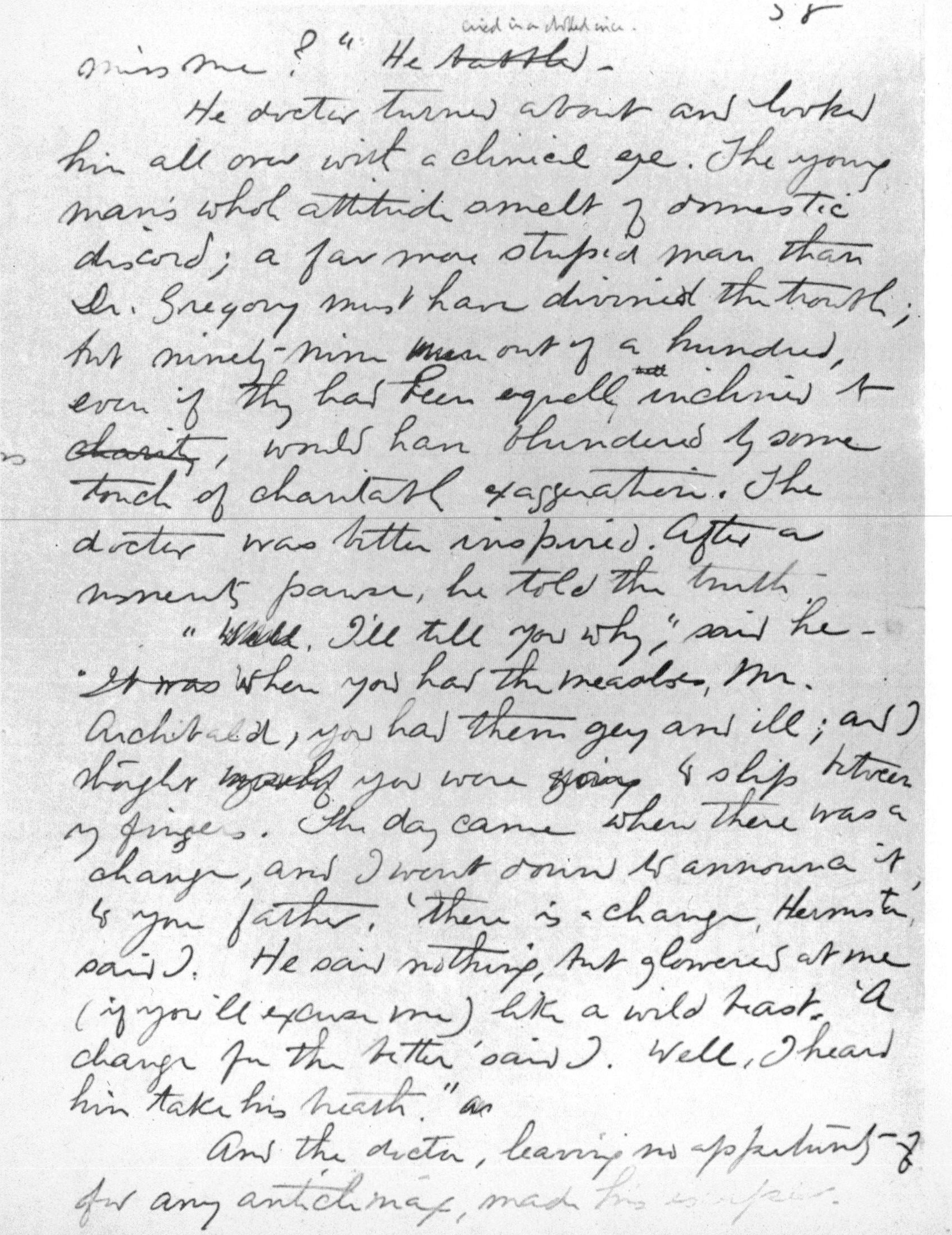

38

miss me?" He ~~rattled~~ cried in a choked voice.

The doctor turned about and looked him all over with a clinical eye. The young man's whole attitude smelt of domestic discord; a far more stupid man than Dr. Gregory must have divined the trouble; but ninety-nine ~~men~~ out of a hundred, even if they had been equally inclined to ~~charity~~, would have blundered by some touch of charitable exaggeration. The doctor was better inspired. After a moment's pause, he told the truth.

"~~Well~~. I'll tell you why," said he. "~~It was~~ When you had the measles, Mr. Archibald, you had them gey and ill; and I thought ~~myself~~ you were ~~going~~ to slip between my fingers. The day came when there was a change, and I went down to announce it to your father. 'There is a change, Hermiston,' said I. He said nothing, but glowered at me (if you'll excuse me) like a wild beast. 'A change for the better,' said I. Well, I heard him take his breath."

And the doctor, leaving no opportunity for any anticlimax, made his escape.